Sport and Exercise Psychology

A CANADIAN PERSPECTIVE SECOND EDITION

EDITED BY **PETER R.E. CROCKER**

UNIVERSITY OF BRITISH COLUMBIA

Pearson Canada

Toronto

Library and Archives Canada Cataloguing in Publication
Sport and Exercise Psychology: A Canadian Perspective / Peter R. E. Crocker, editor.—2nd ed.

Includes index.
First ed. published under title: Sport Psychology.
ISBN 978-0-13-608534-8

1. Sports—Psychological aspects—Textbooks. 2. Exercise—Psychological aspects—Textbooks. I. Crocker, Peter R. E. (Peter Ronald Earl) II. Title: Sports psychology

GV706.4.S67 2011 796.01 C2009-904247-9

ISBN: 978-0-13-608534-8

Vice-President, Editorial Director: Gary Bennett
Acquisitions Editor: Michelle Sartor
Marketing Manager: Colleen Gauthier
Developmental Editor: Catherine Belshaw
Production Editor: Lila Campbell
Copy Editor: Kelly Davis
Proofreader: Jordan Rudow
Production Coordinator: Lynn O'Rourke
Compositor: Glyph International
Permissions Editor/Photo Researcher: Terri Rothman, M.L.S.
Art Director: Julia Hall
Cover and Interior Designer: Quinn Banting
Cover Image: Chris Cole/Iconica/Getty Images

1 2 3 4 5 14 13 12 11 10

Printed and bound in United States of America

For permission to reproduce copyrighted material, the publisher gratefully acknowledges the copyright holders listed in the sources throughout the text, which are considered an extension of this copyright page. Chapter-opening photos: Chapter 1, © Polka Dot Images/Jupiter Images; Chapter 2, © Jim Parkin/Shutterstock; Chapters 3, © Sport/Jupiter Images; Chapter 4, © Corbis RF/Jupiter Images; Chapter 5, © Photodisc/Getty Images; Chapter 6, © Pixland/Jupiter Images; Chapter 7, Tony Zhang/Alamy/Getstock.com; Chapter 8, © Score/Jupiter Images; Chapter 9, © Creatas/Jupiter Images; Chapter 10, © Workbook Stock/Jupiter Images; Chapter 11, © Comstock/Jupiter Images; Chapter 12, © BrandX/Jupiter Images; Chapter 13, © Photodisc/Getty Images; Chapter 14, © Thinkstock/Jupiter Images.

I would like to dedicate this book to my life love, Linda; to my children Doug and Julisa; to my mother Dorothy; and to the memory of my father, Ellard.

P.R.E.C.

About the Editor

Peter R.E. Crocker

Dr. Peter Crocker is a professor in the School of Human Kinetics at the University of British Columbia and is an associate member in the Department of Psychology. His research focuses on stress and adaptation, with a particular interest in understanding sport, exercise, and health-related behaviour. Ongoing research includes investigating stress and coping in adolescent athletes, physical self-perceptions and health behaviour, the role of self-conscious emotions in motivation in physical activity settings, coping with social physique anxiety, and stress processes in breast cancer survivors.

Dr. Crocker is a two-time president of the Canadian Society of Psychomotor Learning and Sport Psychology (SCAPPS) and a section head for sport and exercise psychology in the Canadian Psychological Association (2008–2010). In 2004, he was recognized as a Fellow of the Association for Applied Sport Psychology. Actively involved as a reviewer for several scholarly journals and granting agencies, he is a former editor of *The Sport Psychologist* (1996–1999) and is currently an associate editor for the *Journal of Sport and Exercise Psychology,* as well as an editorial board member of the *Journal of Applied Sport Psychology*. Dr. Crocker has served as a consultant for athletes in gymnastics, volleyball, basketball, and baseball. He was also a soccer coach for several university and provincial-select soccer teams.

Dr. Crocker completed an undergraduate degree in psychology and a master's degree in Kinesiology from Simon Fraser University. His PhD, under the supervision of Dr. Rikk Alderman at the University of Alberta, focused on sport psychology and skill learning. He has taught previously at Lakehead University (1986–1990) and the University of Saskatchewan (1990–1999). In his leisure time he struggles with golf and word games on the Internet. He lives in Vancouver, British Columbia with his wife Linda and has two children, Julisa and Douglas.

About the Contributors

Dr. Joseph Baker is an associate professor in the School of Kinesiology and Health Science at York University. His research examines the development and maintenance of expert performance across the lifespan and the psychosocial factors influencing involvement in physical activity in older adults. Joe has also been the president of the Canadian Society for Psychomotor Learning and Sport Psychology (SCAPPS). In his leisure time, Joe is an avid runner and cyclist.

Dr. Enrique Garcia Bengoechea is an assistant professor in the Department of Kinesiology and Physical Education at McGill University. His research interests include the educational and psychosocial dimensions of young people's experiences in physical activity and sport and interventions to promote physical activity across the lifespan.

Dr. Gordon A. Bloom is an associate professor in the Department of Kinesiology and Physical Education at McGill University. He teaches courses in sport psychology, coaching psychology, and pedagogy. His research interests lie in coaching, team building, hockey aggression, and concussions. When not competing in sports himself, he can often be found coaching his children in ice hockey, soccer, or baseball.

Dr. Jean Côté is a professor and director of the School of Kinesiology and Health Studies at Queen's University. His research interests are in the areas of children in sport, athlete development, and coaching. Dr. Côté is co-editor of the *International Journal of Sport and Exercise Psychology*. He holds a cross appointment as a visiting professor in the School of Human Movement Studies at the University of Queensland in Australia.

Dr. Kimberley A. Dawson is a professor in the Kinesiology and Physical Education Department at Wilfrid Laurier University, specializing in psychological factors associated with participation in physical activity. She teaches courses in research design, sport psychology, behaviour modification, and children and sport. She is the mental skills consultant for the National Endurance Centre runners in Guelph, Ontario. Her research interests focus on exercise adherence, sport performance, injury rehabilitation factors, and using physical activity as a coping mechanism for dealing with chronic disease.

Dr. Kim D. Dorsch is an associate professor in the Faculty of Kinesiology and Health Studies at the University of Regina. Her current research interests include examining the influence of body checking upon many psychosocial concepts (including perceptions of aggression and motivation) in minor league hockey. She is also intrigued by collective efficacy expectations and their relationship to other group factors like cohesion, performance, and performance outcome. Another line of research that she pursues is sources of stress and practical applications of coping among officials.

Dr. Guy Faulkner is currently an associate professor in the Faculty of Physical Education and Health at the University of Toronto. His research has focused on two interrelated themes: the effectiveness of physical activity promotion interventions and physical activity and psychological well-being. He is the founding co-editor of the new Elsevier journal *Mental Health and Physical Activity* and co-editor of the book *Exercise, Health and Mental Health* published by Routledge in 2005.

Dr. Jessica Fraser-Thomas is an assistant professor in the School of Kinesiology and Health Science at York University. Her research focuses on positive youth development through sport in the areas of life skill development, psychosocial influences, and prolonged engagement in sport. In her leisure time she enjoys competing in triathlons, coaching and consulting athletes, and spending time with her family.

Dr. Kimberley L. Gammage is an associate professor at Brock University. Her research focuses on social-psychological factors related to exercise and health behaviours, with a particular focus on self-presentational concerns and body image. She is especially interested in how these factors may operate in group exercise settings. In addition, she is currently involved in research examining osteoporosis knowledge and beliefs and bone health in young adults. Finally, she is also interested in the effects of exercise on psychological and balance outcomes in older adults.

Dr. Patrick Gaudreau is an associate professor in the School of Psychology at the University of Ottawa. His research interests are in the self-regulation of achievement-related behaviours with research projects on coping, goal management, and motivation in sport, education, and exercise. The overarching goal of his research program is to uncover the role of self-regulatory processes in goal attainment and psychological adjustment of individuals in performance-related activities. In his spare time, he enjoys spending time with Melanie and Olivier. He can also be found in the bushes searching for his golf ball!

Dr. Melanie Gregg is an assistant professor in the department of Kinesiology and Applied Health at the University of Winnipeg. Her research interests focus on athletes' motivational imagery ability and examining the effectiveness of psychological skill use by athletes with intellectual disability. Dr. Gregg also does applied work with athletes from a variety of sports and enjoys coaching track and field.

Dr. Craig Hall is a professor in the School of Kinesiology at the University of Western Ontario. He has been conducting research in sport and exercise psychology for over 30 years. His research has focused on imagery use in sport, exercise, and athletic injury rehabilitation. He has also investigated other topics including self-efficacy, self-talk, motivation, and observational learning. He has conducted mental training programs with athletes of all competitive levels.

Dr. Sharleen Hoar is an assistant professor in the Department of Kinesiology and Physical Education at the University of Lethbridge. A former competitive figure skater, her research focuses on stress and coping, and positive emotional development of children and adolescents through participation in sport and physical activity.

Dr. Sean Horton is an assistant professor at the University of Windsor. His research focus is on skill acquisition and expert performance throughout the lifespan, as well as how stereotypes of aging affect seniors' participation in exercise. In his spare time, Sean can usually be found on the squash court or on the golf course.

Dr. Gretchen Kerr is a professor in the Faculty of Physical Education and Health at the University of Toronto. In her research, she addresses the psychosocial development of young people in and through sport, including experiences of stress and issues of child protection. Dr. Kerr is a member of the research committee of the Coaching Association of Canada and serves as the harassment officer for Gymnastics Ontario and Gymnastics Canada.

Dr. Kent C. Kowalski is an associate professor of Kinesiology at the University of Saskatchewan. His general area of interest includes coping with stress and emotion in sport and physical activity. He is also currently an assistant coach with the University of Saskatchewan Huskie Men's soccer program.

Dr. Larry M. Leith is a professor in the Faculty of Physical Education and Health at the University of Toronto. His current research interests include the relationship between exercise and mental health, as well as aggression in sport. He teaches undergraduate courses in sport psychology and administrative theory/organizational behaviour, and a graduate course in exercise psychology. Larry's favourite recreational activities include jogging, walking, golf, and tennis.

Dr. Todd M. Loughead is an associate professor in the Department of Kinesiology at the University of Windsor. His current research interests include group dynamics in sport and exercise and aggression in hockey. Specifically, his interests are cohesion in sport, and the influence of athlete leadership in sport and its impact on team functioning. Dr. Loughead is also investigating the psychosocial variables that influence aggression in hockey and the effect of aggression on enjoyment and participation. He teaches courses in group dynamics, mental training, and exercise psychology.

Dr. Diane E. Mack is an associate professor in the Department of Physical Education and Kinesiology at Brock University. Research interests include the role of health-enhancing physical activity as a mechanism to promote well-being and the cognitive and behavioural manifestations of self-presentation on health behaviours.

Dr. Kathleen A. Martin Ginis is a professor in the Department of Kinesiology at McMaster University. Her research focuses on psychosocial antecedents and consequences of physical activity participation. She has a particular interest in studying physical activity among people with spinal cord injury and is a co-author of *The Psychology of Exercise: Integrating Theory and Practice*.

Dr. Meghan McDonough is an assistant professor in the Department of Health and Kinesiology at Purdue University. Her research focuses on social relationships, motivation, and emotion in sport and physical activity. She has conducted research with breast cancer survivors, low-income youth, overweight women, Special Olympians, and adults and youth involved in sport. In her spare time she enjoys marathon canoeing, kayaking, mountain biking, skiing, running, and yoga.

Dr. Krista Munroe-Chandler is an associate professor in the Kinesiology Department at the University of Windsor. Her research interests include imagery use in sport and exercise as well as youth-sport development and body image issues. She works with able-bodied athletes as well as athletes with a disability of all ages, levels, and sports, helping them achieve their personal performance goals.

Dr. David Paskevich is an associate professor in the Faculty of Kinesiology at the University of Calgary. His research examines collective efficacy in sport; disordered eating in sport and exercise; obesity, Type II diabetes, and physical activity; cardiac rehab and social psychological variables; and volunteer activity in sport and culture.

Dr. Ryan E. Rhodes is an associate professor in the School of Exercise Science, Health and Physical Education at the University of Victoria, British Columbia and director of the UVic Behavioral Medicine Laboratory. He has research expertise in physical activity and social cognition theories, personality theory, psychometric measurement, analysis and design, with an applied focus on physical activity and early family development.

Dr. Jennifer Robertson-Wilson is an assistant professor in the Department of Kinesiology and Physical Education at Wilfrid Laurier University. Her primary research interests include understanding the implementation of school-based physical activity policy and the influence of school policy and environment factors on youth physical activity. A second line of research inquiry examines the impact of the built environment on physical activity and obesity.

Dr. Catherine Sabiston is an assistant professor of exercise and health psychology in the Department of Kinesiology and Physical Education at McGill University. Her research examines the interrelations among physical self-perceptions and emotions, social influences, and physical activity motivation in diverse populations who tend to be at risk for low levels of physical activity, including breast cancer survivors, overweight and obese individuals, and adolescents.

Dr. David Scott is an associate professor of sport psychology in the Faculty of Kinesiology at the University of New Brunswick in Fredericton. He teaches and researches in the area of sport and exercise psychology, focusing primarily on performance enhancement and physical activity and mental health. He has been a psychological consultant with a number of national teams in addition to working with teams in the National Hockey League.

Dr. Whitney A. Sedgwick is a registered psychologist and clinical coordinator at the University of British Columbia's Counselling Services. She has taught undergraduate and graduate sport psychology courses at three Canadian universities and has co-authored a mental training book for triathletes. Dr. Sedgwick has also been consulting with athletes at all levels for the past 13 years, including a year in Paris, France, where she worked with national team and Olympic athletes.

Dr. Kevin S. Spink is a professor in the College of Kinesiology at the University of Saskatchewan, specializing in group dynamics, specifically cohesion. He teaches courses involving the application of social psychology to exercise and sport behaviour. One focus of his research is the study of group dynamics and the application of group interventions to promote exercise and adherence behaviour. His other main interest is in examining the relationship between various social-psychological correlates/determinants and adherence to physical activity across the lifespan.

Dr. Philip M. Wilson is an associate professor of Physical Education and Kinesiology in the Faculty of Applied Health Sciences at Brock University. His research interests focus on the interplay between measurement and theory for understanding motivational processes responsible for health behaviours. In his spare time, Dr. Wilson can be found enjoying active living with Diane, Wembley, and Shankley while finding time to follow his two favourite football teams (Liverpool F.C. and England).

Brief Contents

Chapter 1 Introducing Sport and Exercise Psychology
Peter R. E. Crocker, David Scott, and Melanie Gregg 1

Chapter 2 Research Perspectives in Sport and Exercise Psychology
Philip M. Wilson and Enrique García Bengoechea 26

Chapter 3 Personality in Sport and Exercise
Whitney A. Sedgwick, Peter R. E. Crocker, and Ryan E. Rhodes 53

Chapter 4 Motivation and Behavioural Change
Diane E. Mack, Catherine M. Sabiston, Meghan H. McDonough, Philip M. Wilson, and David M. Paskevich 79

Chapter 5 Anxiety in Sport and Exercise
Sharleen D. Hoar and Kimberley L. Gammage 111

Chapter 6 Stress and Coping in Sport and Exercise
Kent C. Kowalski and Patrick Gaudreau 138

Chapter 7 Group Cohesion in Sport and Exercise
Kevin S. Spink 166

Chapter 8 Aggression and Moral Behaviour in Sport
Todd M. Loughead and Kim D. Dorsch 196

Chapter 9 Youth Involvement and Positive Development in Sport
Jean Côté and Jessica Fraser-Thomas 226

Chapter 10 Aging and Involvement in Sport and Physical Activity
Joseph Baker and Sean Horton 256

Chapter 11 Coaching Psychology
Gordon A. Bloom 278

Chapter 12 Exercise and Mental Health
Larry M. Leith, Gretchen A. Kerr, and Guy E. Faulkner 306

Chapter 13 Physical Activity Interventions
Kimberley A. Dawson, Jennifer Robertson-Wilson, and Kathleen Martin-Ginis 337

Chapter 14 Sport Psychology Interventions
Krista Munroe-Chandler and Craig Hall 363

Contents

Preface xv
Acknowledgments xxi

1 Introducing Sport and Exercise Psychology 1

Common Myths about Sport and Exercise Psychology 3
Introduction 3
The Nature of Sport and Exercise Psychology 4
Sport and Exercise Psychology: A Multidimensional Perspective 4
Positive Psychology in Sport and Exercise 5
Careers in Sport and Exercise Psychology 6
Teaching 6
Research 7
Consulting 8
Training to Be a Sport and Exercise Psychology Specialist 9
Sport Science Education 9
Clinical and Counselling Sport and Exercise Psychology 10
Courses and Programs for Undergraduate Students 10
Licensing of Sport and Exercise Psychologists 11
Standards of Conduct and Practitioner Competencies in Sport and Exercise Psychology 12
Sport and Exercise Psychology in Canada and the United States 14
Sport and Exercise Psychology around the World 18
Key Historical World Events in Sport and Exercise Psychology 19
Predicted Trends and Issues in Canada 19
Increased Specialization and Diversification 19
Increased Research and Teaching Opportunities 20
Increased Demands for Training in Clinical and Counselling Psychology 20
Interdepartmental Collaboration in Teaching, Research, and Practice 20
Ethics and Competencies 21
Working in Performance Enhancement Teams 21
Online Consulting and Service Provision 21
Consulting with Athletes and Exercisers with Disabilities 21
Knowledge Translation 22

Chapter Summary 22
Common Myths about Sport and Exercise Psychology Revisited 23
Review Questions 23
Suggested Reading 24
References 24

2 Research Perspectives in Sport and Exercise Psychology 26

Common Myths about Research in Sport and Exercise Psychology 28
Introduction 28
Science and Scientific Research 29
Basic Research Terminology 31
Ethical Approval for Sport and Exercise Psychology Research 34
Measurement in the Research Process 37
Levels of Measurement 37
Basic Measurement Concepts 38
Sampling in Sport and Exercise Psychology Research 40
Research Design: A Blueprint for Action 41
Randomized Experimental Designs 42
Quasi-experimental Designs 43
Non-experimental Designs 43
Qualitative Research in Sport and Exercise Psychology 44
Characteristics of Qualitative Inquiry 44
Common Approaches to Doing Qualitative Research 46
Judging the Merit of Qualitative Research 48

Chapter Summary 48
Common Myths about Research in Sport and Exercise Psychology Revisited 49
Review Questions 50
Suggested Reading 50
References 50

3 **Personality in Sport and Exercise 53**
Some Common Myths about Personality in Sport and Exercise 55
Introduction 55
What Is Personality? 55
Personality Traits 56
How Does Personality Develop? 58
Psychodynamics 58
Humanistic Psychology 58
Cognitive-Behavioural Approach 59
Interactionist Approach: Dealing with the Person–Situation Debate 61
The Measurement of Personality 62
Sport-Specific Measures 62
Ethical Considerations of Personality Measurement 64
Personality Research in Sport and Exercise 65
Risk Taking and Sensation Seeking 66
Competitiveness 67
Perfectionism 68
Mental Toughness 70
Personality Traits and Exercise: Is There an Exercise Personality? 72
Targeting Exercise Programs Based on Personality 72

Chapter Summary 73
Common Myths about Personality in Sport and Exercise Revisited 74
Review Questions 74
Suggested Reading 75
References 75

4 **Motivation and Behavioural Change 79**
Common Myths about Motivation and Behavioural Change 80
Introduction 80
Approaches to Understanding Motivation for Behavioural Change 81
Behavioural Approaches 81
Cognitive Approaches 82
Cognitive-behavioural Approaches 82
Models of Motivation and Behavioural Change 83
Transtheoretical Model 83
Theory of Planned Behaviour 85
Social Cognitive Theory 88
Self-determination Theory 91
Achievement Goal Theory 96
Theory of Competence Motivation 98
Sport Commitment Model 101
Moving Beyond Individual Approaches to Social Approaches to Motivation 103
Research Linking Social Influences to Motivational Outcomes and Behaviour 103
Social Influence in Practice 104

Chapter Summary 104
Common Myths about Motivation and Behavioural Change Revisited 105
Review Questions 105
Suggested Reading 106
References 106

5 **Anxiety in Sport and Exercise 111**
Common Myths about Anxiety in Sport and Exercise 113
Introduction 113
Definitions and Basic Concepts of Anxiety 113
Anxiety Is Not Arousal 114
Anxiety Is an Emotion and Is Multidimensional in Nature 114
Anxiety Is Context Specific 115
Anxiety Has Both Trait and State Components 116
Dimensions of the Anxiety Response 116
Sources of Anxiety 117
Personal Sources of Anxiety 117
Environment-based Sources of Anxiety 121
Anxiety Influences on Exercise Behaviour and Sport Performance 124
The Influence of Anxiety on Exercise Behaviours 125
Anxiety–Sport Performance Relationship Models 126
Underlying Mechanisms of the Anxiety–Performance Relationship 129

Chapter Summary 131
Common Myths about Anxiety in Sport and Exercise Revisited 132
Review Questions 132
Suggested Reading 133
References 133

6 **Stress and Coping in Sport and Exercise 138**
Common Myths about Stress and Coping in Sport and Exercise 140
Introduction 140
The Concept of Stress 141
Stress and Emotion 143
Sources of Stress in Sport 143
Types of Stressors 145

Self-Presentation and Exercise 147
The Concept of Coping 148
Micro- and Macro-analytic Levels of Coping 149
Coping Style 150
Distinguishing between Coping and Outcomes of Coping 151
Coping Effectiveness 152
A Closer Look at Coping in Sport 153
Sociodemographic Factors 155
Individual Factors 156
Coping Interventions 158

Chapter Summary 159
Common Myths about Stress and Coping in Sport and Exercise Revisited 160
Review Questions 161
Suggested Reading 161
References 162

7 Group Cohesion in Sport and Exercise 166

Common Myths about Group Cohesion in Sport and Exercise 167
Introduction 168
The Nature of Group Cohesion 170
Measuring Group Cohesion 171
Conceptual Model of Group Cohesion 171
Correlates of Group Cohesion 172
Environmental Correlates of Group Cohesion 173
Leadership Correlates of Group Cohesion 175
Personal Correlates of Group Cohesion 180
Team Correlates of Group Cohesion 184
Group Cohesion as a Mediator 187

Chapter Summary 189
Common Myths about Group Cohesion in Sport and Exercise Revisited 189
Review Questions 190
Suggested Reading 191
References 191

8 Aggression and Moral Behaviour in Sport 196

Common Myths about Aggression and Moral Behaviour in Sport 198
Introduction 198
Development of Moral Character 198
Structural-developmental Perspective 198
Social Learning Perspective 199
Factors Influencing Moral Behaviour 199
Sport Environment 199
Motivational Climate 200
Team Norms 200
Goal Orientation 201
Aggression 201
Theories of Aggression 205
Psychodynamics 205
Frustration-Aggression Theory 205
Physiological Explanations 206
Social Learning Theory 206
Moral Disengagement 207
Summary of Theories of Aggression 208
Factors Influencing Aggression 209
Personal Factors Influencing Aggression 209
Situational Factors Influencing Aggression 213
Group Factors Influencing Aggression 214
Consequences of Aggressive Behaviour 215
Fan Violence 216
Reducing Aggression in Sport 217
Punishment and Encouragement 218
Educational Interventions 218
Behavioural Modification Practices 219
Changes to the Sporting Environment 219
Aggressive Behaviour in the Media 219

Chapter Summary 220
Common Myths about Aggression and Moral Behaviour in Sport Revisited 220
Review Questions 221
Suggested Reading 221
References 222

9 Youth Involvement and Positive Development in Sport 226

Common Myths about Youth Involvement in Sport 228
Introduction 228
Objectives of Youth Sport 229
Outcomes Associated with Youth-Sport Participation 230
Principles of Positive Youth Development 231
Developmental Assets 231
Desirable Youth-Sport Program Settings 233
Fostering Initiative through Constructive Activities 234
Five C's of Positive Youth Development 235
Considerations for Youth-Sport Programs 235
Youth-sport Program Activities 236
Role of Coaches 239
Role of Parents 241

Models of Sport Motivation 243
Mediational Model of Global Self-worth 243
Achievement Goal Theory 244
Self-determination Theory 244
The Developmental Model of Sport Participation 245
Trajectory 1: Recreational Participation through Sampling 245
Trajectory 2: Elite Performance through Sampling 247
Trajectory 3: Elite Performance through Early Specialization 248
Other Trajectories 248
Youth-Sport Programs: Best Practices 248

Chapter Summary 249
Common Myths about Youth Involvement in Sport Revisited 250
Review Questions 251
Suggested Reading 251
References 251

10 Aging and Involvement in Sport and Physical Activity 256
Common Myths about Aging and Involvement in Sport and Physical Activity 257
Introduction 257
Cognitive and Physical Decline with Advancing Age 259
The Compensation Model of Skill Maintenance 260
The Selective Maintenance Model of Skill Maintenance 261
Maintenance of Athletic Performance 262
Barriers to Exercise for Older Adults 263
Negative Stereotypes: A Unique Barrier for Older Adults 263
Determinants of Physical Activity and Sport Involvement in Older Adults 266
Demographic and Biological Factors 266
Behavioural Attributes 267
Social and Cultural Factors 267
Physical Environment Factors 267
Psychological, Cognitive, and Emotional Factors 268
Self-Efficacy and Older Adults 268
Successful Aging 270
The Master Athlete: A Model of Successful Aging? 270
Participant Motives in Master Sport 271
Master-level Competitors versus Non-competitor Older Athletes 271
Early Sport Involvement 272
Mood and Personality 272
General Recommendations for Working with Master Athletes 272

Chapter Summary 273
Common Myths about Aging and Involvement in Sport and Physical Activity Revisited 273
Review Questions 273
Suggested Reading 274
References 274

11 Coaching Psychology 278
Common Myths about Coaching Psychology 280
Introduction 280
Coach Education 280
Coach Development 284
Youth-Sport Coaching 286
Characteristics of Youth Coaches 286
Ideal Behaviours of Youth Coaches 287
Coaching Knowledge 289
Sport Leadership 289
Coaching Efficacy 291
Coaching Model 293

Chapter Summary 301
Common Myths about Coaching Psychology Revisited 302
Review Questions 302
Suggested Reading 302
References 303

12 Exercise and Mental Health 306
Common Myths about Exercise and Mental Health 308
Introduction 308
Depression 309
Exercise and Depression 309
Anxiety 312
Anxiety and Exercise 313
Mood 315
Exercise and Mood 315
Stress 318
Exercise and Stress 318
Self-Concept and Self-Esteem 321
Exercise and Self-esteem 321
The Exercise and Mental Health Relationship: Suggested Mechanisms of Change 325
The Endorphin Hypothesis 325
The Monoamine Hypothesis 325

The Thermogenic Hypothesis 327
The Distraction Hypothesis 327
Other Possible Psychological Explanations 328
Exercise and the Prevention of Mental Health Problems 328

Chapter Summary 330
Common Myths about Exercise and Mental Health Revisited 331
Review Questions 332
Suggested Reading 332
References 332

13 Physical Activity Interventions 337
Common Myths about Physical Activity Interventions 338
Introduction 339
The Importance of Maintaining a Physically Active Lifestyle 339
Determinant and Intervention Research 340
Intervention Research Involving Physical Activity 342
Physical Activity as an Outcome in Intervention Research 343
Theory-based Physical Activity Intervention Research 343
Non-theory-based Intervention Research 348
Conclusions about Interventions Used to Increase Physical Activity 352
Physical Activity as a Treatment in Intervention Research 354
Cancer 354
Spinal Cord Injury 355
Parkinson's Disease 356
Conclusions about Interventions Used as Treatment 357

Chapter Summary 357
Common Myths about Physical Activity Interventions Revisited 358
Review Questions 358
Suggested Reading 359
References 359

14 Sport Psychology Interventions 363
Common Myths about Sport Psychology Interventions 364
Introduction 364
Goal Setting 365
Types of Goals 365
Effectiveness of Goal Setting 366
Assessing Goals 366
Recommendations for Goal Setting 367
Common Goal-setting Problems 368
Conclusions about Goal Setting 369
Imagery 369
The Nature of Imagery 370
Analytic Model of Imagery 370
Imagery Assessment Tools 373
Recommendations for Using Imagery 374
Conclusions about Imagery 375
Self-Talk 375
Functions of Self-talk 375
Assessment of Self-talk 376
Recommendations for Using Self-talk 377
Conclusions about Self-talk 379
Arousal Regulation 379
Techniques to Reduce Arousal 380
Techniques to Increase Arousal 382
Measurement of Arousal Levels 383
Conclusions about Arousal Levels 383
Attention Control 384
Assessing Attention as a Limited Resource 384
Assessing Selective Attention 385
Using Attention-control Strategies 386
Conclusions about Attention Control 387

Chapter Summary 388
Common Myths about Sport Psychology Interventions Revisited 388
Review Questions 388
Suggested Reading 389
References 389

Glossary 393
Index 402

Preface

Sport and exercise psychology has come to play an increasingly prominent role in sport and exercise science. Most people are aware of the term *sport psychology* from watching popular media. Announcers frequently refer to elite athletes who work with sport psychologists to enhance performance. However, this is only a small part of sport and exercise psychology. Research and practice cover all areas of physical activity and age groups and have had a significant impact on the lives of exercisers, athletes, coaches, health professionals, and scholars in the field. Today, many Canadian scholars are recognized as world leaders in this research and practice. Their important work has influenced the lives of the many Canadians involved in sport and physical activity. This book celebrates their contributions.

In this edition, we have provided more information on the growing area of exercise psychology, in response to the requests of many instructors across Canada. Thus, we have made several important changes in the second edition. To start, the first several chapters cover both sport and exercise psychology research and practice related to research methods, personality, motivation and behavioural change, anxiety, stress and coping, group cohesion, and older adult participants. In addition, we have added two new chapters that focus on exercise psychology. These chapters on exercise and mental health (Chapter 12) and physical activity interventions (Chapter 13) provide the student with more critical theoretical and practical information about these important topics. At the same time, we have updated specific chapters that focus on sport psychology related to youth sport, coaching, psychological interventions, and aggression and moral behaviour. Based on reviewer feedback, we have integrated gender issues throughout the book, where relevant. All the chapters have been updated with the latest developments in research and practice appropriate for an undergraduate textbook.

In this edition we have also retained many of the positive features from the first edition. We cover key concepts that are supported in the sport and exercise psychology literature, and we provide Canadian examples of them. Three key unique features characterize this book. First, the chapters are written by Canadian scholars who are actively teaching undergraduate courses in sport and exercise psychology, as well as being actively engaged in research. Second, the book provides many Canadian examples to illustrate important concepts. Third, the book highlights research by Canadian scholars while recognizing the contribution of other scholars around the world.

The increased focus on exercise psychology has resulted in many changes in the content of specific chapters. For example, the chapter on motivation and behavioural change now includes theories that have been popular in the exercise psychology literature. We have dropped theories and models that have witnessed waning popularity over the last decade. Other major changes are also apparent in the chapters on stress and coping and on anxiety. Other chapters have undergone smaller changes. In all chapters, authors have updated references, captured emerging issues, provided contemporary examples, and used case studies to highlight important topics.

This book is written specifically for a Canadian introductory undergraduate course in sport and exercise psychology. The book presents an overview of sport and exercise psychology and provides a solid foundation in core concepts required for upper-level undergraduate courses. The organization of the book allows instructors to focus on specific areas of sport and exercise psychology to meet specific academic course requirements.

ORGANIZATION

The 14 chapters of this book present the key topics covered in a typical introductory course. The chapters may be viewed in four groups. In Chapters 1–5, we introduce the basic domains of sport and exercise psychology. Here, we provide an overview of the field and discuss research perspectives, personality, motivation, and anxiety. In Chapters 6–8, we proceed to the more general themes of stress and coping, group cohesion, and aggression and moral behaviour in sport. In Chapters 9–12, we relate the basic domains and general themes to the more global topics of youth involvement in sport, aging and involvement in sport and physical activity, coaching psychology, and exercise and mental health. The last section, Chapters 13 and 14, focuses on intervention strategies in exercise and sport populations.

Chapter 1 provides an overview of the field. Topics include the diverse nature of sport and exercise psychology, differences in career orientations and educational training opportunities, a brief history of sport and exercise psychology in Canada and the world, ethics in sport and exercise psychology, and predicted trends. The contributions of Canadians and Canadian organizations are highlighted.

Chapter 2 focuses on research perspectives in sport and exercise psychology. This chapter covers a number of basic research concepts, such as applied versus theoretical research, the role of theories and models in sport and exercise psychology, qualitative versus quantitative methods, different types of research designs, psychological testing, and the ethics of using test scores. We believe this chapter is crucial for many students because it helps them understand the strengths and limitations of sport psychology research. Relevant examples are used throughout the chapter. However, some instructors may not use this chapter as students may have already taken a research methods course.

Chapter 3 deals with personality perspectives in sport and exercise. It covers personality measurement, ethics related to measuring personality, recent findings in sport and exercise psychology personality research, and the limitations of personality in explaining athletic behaviour and performance as well as exercise behaviour.

Chapter 4 has been significantly revised and focuses on models and principles of motivation and behavioural change in sport and exercise. It provides students with a brief review of behavioural, cognitive, and cognitive-behavioural principles. It includes various theories and models of motivation applied to sport, such as the transtheoretical model, theory of planned behaviour, competence motivation theory, social cognitive theory, achievement goal theory, self-determination theory, and sport commitment. The chapter also discusses social approaches to motivation.

Chapter 5 deals with anxiety in sport and exercise. It defines types and dimensions of anxiety, personal sources of anxiety in sport and exercise settings, the specificity of anxiety to competitive and exercise settings, and how anxiety affects exercise and sport behaviour. It also explains how anxiety affects sport performance using three different theories, including multidimensional anxiety theory, zones of optimal functioning, and cusp catastrophe theory.

Chapter 6 focuses on stress and coping. We cover this area in more detail than most undergraduate textbooks because it is a key component of sport and exercise psychology. Students are very interested in stress. The chapter emphasizes types of cognitive evaluations, types of coping, and the relationship between appraisal, stress, and diverse emotions such as anger, happiness, anxiety, and fear. This chapter also integrates information from the previous chapters on personality, motivation and behavioural change, and anxiety.

Chapter 7 provides a comprehensive review of group cohesion in sport and exercise. Students will learn about group dynamics, group cohesion and its measurement, how and why cohesion affects behaviour in both sport and exercise settings, a conceptual model of cohesion, team-building concepts, and important correlates of cohesion. The chapter also covers social loafing, self-handicapping, role clarity and acceptance, and leader behaviour.

Chapter 8 focuses on aggression and moral behaviour in sport. An important addition to this chapter is a review of factors related to moral development. It integrates key information from previous chapters on motivation and personality. It reviews various perspectives on how youth learn moral behaviour in sport, and the role of the environmental and personality factors, such as motivational climate, team and sport norms, and motivational orientation. The chapter also discusses key theories useful for understanding why athletes (and spectators) behave aggressively. As well, it explores how personal, situational, and group factors influence aggressive behaviour and examines ways to reduce aggressive behaviour in sport.

Chapter 9 focuses on the health and developmental benefits of youth-sport participation. The chapter describes the outcomes that can result from youth-sport participation, principles of positive youth development, how youth-sport programs and types of activities lead to positive sport experiences, and the role of parents and coaches in this process. It also reviews key models of youth-sport motivation and sport development.

Chapter 10 covers the psychological factors related to sport and exercise in the older person. One of the main reasons we have included this chapter is to acknowledge that many "older" Canadians are, and should be, involved in physical activity. The chapter covers a wide range of issues, including the factors influencing sport and exercise involvement in this group, the impact of societal perceptions of aging on physical and cognitive performance, and strategies for increasing sport and physical activity involvement in older adult populations.

Chapter 11 describes the complexity of coaching psychology. It discusses the emerging structure and process of coaching education in Canada, the steps to becoming an elite coach, and the common characteristics and coaching principles of youth-sport coaches. The chapter also explains a coaching model, discusses effective coaching, and considers the psychological factors involved in coaching.

Chapter 12 is a new chapter that focuses on the relationship between exercise and mental health. It provides an overview of the prevalence of specific mental health disorders in Canada; reviews the evidence for the positive impact of exercise on depression, stress, anxiety, mood, and self-concept; and covers how exercise may prevent mental health problems. It also covers the different mechanisms that could explain the relationship between exercise and mental health and provides guidelines for using exercise to improve mental health in both non-clinical and clinical settings.

Chapter 13 on physical activity interventions is a new chapter that builds on concepts from previous chapters and highlights means of increasing physical activity in all populations. It describes how specific theories can be used to understand and enhance physical activity, non-theoretical approaches to exercise intervention, the key components to increase the success rate of exercise interventions, and how exercise can enhance the lives of clinical populations such as cancer survivors, individuals with spinal cord injuries, and individuals with Parkinson's disease. The chapter includes many case studies and examples to highlight concepts and research findings.

Chapter 14 focuses on how sport psychology interventions can enhance performance and well-being in sporting populations. It addresses specific intervention techniques for arousal control, discusses emotion management, and describes psychological and coping skills training. Specific topics include relaxation procedures, psyching up strategies, attention-control, self-talk, imagery, and goal setting. The chapter features many applied examples and exercises.

Instructors may wish to vary the sequence in which the chapters are studied. The first five chapters serve as the foundation for the remaining chapters. These foundation chapters should be covered in the order presented, although Chapter 2 (Research Perspectives in Sport and Exercise Psychology) may be redundant for students who have already completed a research methods course. Depending on the academic needs of specific courses, some instructors may wish to cover Chapter 14 (Sport Psychology Interventions) before covering Chapter 12 (Exercise and Mental Health) and Chapter 13 (Physical Activity Interventions). Many of the chapters after Chapter 6 can be sequenced according to instructors' preferences.

PEDAGOGICAL FEATURES

We have made a special effort with the second edition to continue to use the pedagogical features that instructors have found helpful in facilitating learning and enhancing understanding.

- **Chapter Objectives** A set of four to eight learning objectives at the beginning of each chapter provides a road map to help students read the material more effectively. The learning objectives also form the basis of the review questions found at the end of the chapter.
- **Vignette** Each chapter begins with a scenario, many of which are real, that raises issues and topics to be addressed in the chapter.
- **Common Myths** Each chapter includes three to five common myths about the subject of the chapter. A change in the second edition is that we clarify and dispel each myth by presenting clear evidence to the contrary near the end of the chapter.
- **Key Terms** Key terms are boldfaced where they are introduced in the text, and they are listed in the Glossary at the end of the book.
- **Case Studies** Case studies are included in most chapters to clarify key ideas and concepts.
- **Reflections Boxes** Each chapter contains several reflections boxes that require students to integrate key concepts and ideas into their personal knowledge and experiences.
- **Canadian Examples** Numerous Canadian examples are used to help clarify and highlight concepts.
- **Canadian Profile Boxes** Profiles are included in select chapters that describe the important contributions of Canadian researchers, athletes, and coaches to sport and exercise psychology.

- **Figures and Tables** Diagrams, graphs, and tables are provided in the chapters to illustrate and clarify important points.
- **Photos** Numerous photos throughout the book serve to emphasize Canadian athletes and participants in physical activity.
- **Weblinks** References to useful websites are interspersed in the chapters where appropriate. They include links to sport and exercise psychology sites, professional organizations, and scholarly journals.
- **Chapter Summary** A summary of the main points is provided near the end of each chapter.
- **Review Questions** A set of review questions requiring short answers will help instructors and students determine whether the learning objectives have been mastered.
- **Suggested Reading** Each chapter closes with a list of several selected advanced readings for the interested student.
- **References** All references cited in the text are listed at the end of each chapter.
- **Glossary** All the key terms are provided chapter-by-chapter with their definitions in a Glossary at the back of the book.

SUPPLEMENTS

To aid instructors in presenting lectures, fostering class discussion, and administering examinations, we have carefully prepared an Instructor's Resource CD-ROM that contains the following three instructor supplements:

- **Instructor's Manual** The Instructor's Manual is designed to enhance the organization and presentation of course materials. Each chapter includes:
  - Chapter Overview
  - Learning Objectives
  - Key Terms
  - Lecture Outline
  - Projects and Assignments
  - Case Studies for Class Discussion
  - Answers to Review Questions
  - Discussion Questions
  - Additional Teaching Resources
- **PowerPoint Slides** PowerPoint slides are available for each chapter and can be used in electronic form to present materials in class or in printed form to guide the preparation of new lecture notes. Over 250 slides are available in total.
- **Computerized Testbank (Pearson TestGen)** The Pearson Education Canada TestGen enables instructors to view and edit questions, generate tests, and print the tests in a variety of formats. Powerful search and sort functions make it easy to locate questions and arrange them in any order. TestGen also enables instructors to administer tests on a local area network, have the tests graded electronically, and have the results prepared in electronic or printed reports. Pearson TestGen is compatible with Windows or Macintosh systems.

We have put considerable effort into updating and improving the TestGen for this edition, and contributors for each chapter have provided new questions. For each question, the following information is provided:

- The correct answer
- The question's difficulty level (easy, moderate, or challenging)
- The question's skill type (recall or applied)
- The relevant section reference from the text

Most of these instructor supplements are available for download from a password-protected section of Pearson Education Canada's online catalogue (vig.pearsoned.ca). Navigate to your book's catalogue page to view a list of the supplements that are available. See your local sales representative for details and access.

- **CourseSmart** This text is also available as a CourseSmart eTextbook.CourseSmart is a new way for instructors and students to access textbooks online anytime from anywhere. With thousands of titles across hundreds of courses, CourseSmart helps instructors choose the best textbook for their class and give their students a new option for buying the assigned textbook as a lower-cost eTextbook. For more information, visit www.coursesmart.com.

Acknowledgments

We would like to acknowledge all the contributors to this textbook. These individuals represent the future of sport and exercise psychology in Canada, and they have all made a special contribution.

We would also like to recognize those instructors who provided us with formal reviews of parts of the manuscript. Their observations, ideas, and comments greatly improved the quality of all chapters:

- Gary Bonczak, Sir Sandford Fleming College
- Michelle Dionne, Ryerson University
- Isaac Engel, Ryerson University
- Roger Friesen, University of the Fraser Valley
- Nicolas L. Holt, University of Alberta
- Basil Kavanagh, Memorial University of Newfoundland
- John Meldrum, University of Victoria
- Kelly Purdy, Vanier College
- Carolyn Savoy, Dalhousie University
- Philip Sullivan, Brock University
- Jill Tracey, Wilfrid Laurier University
- Gary L. Worrell, University of New Brunswick

Finally, I greatly appreciate all the staff at Pearson Education Canada: Michelle Sartor (Acquisitions Editor); Colleen Gauthier (Marketing Manager); Catherine Belshaw (Developmental Editor); Lila Campbell (Production Editor); Lynn O'Rourke (Production Coordinator); Quinn Banting (Designer); Terri Rothman (Permissions Editor/Photo Researcher); Kelly Davis (Copy Editor); and Jordan Rudow (Proofreader). Their talent, support, and patience were so critical in completing this book.

Chapter 1

Introducing Sport and Exercise Psychology

Peter R. E. Crocker
David Scott
Melanie Gregg

Chapter Objectives

After reading this chapter, you should be able to do the following:

1. Explain what sport and exercise psychology is and what sport and exercise psychology specialists do.
2. Explain the differences between educational and clinical/counselling orientations in sport and exercise psychology.
3. List the diverse educational training opportunities in sport and exercise psychology.
4. Identify the basic standards of conduct and service in sport and exercise psychology.
5. Identify key moments in the history of sport and exercise psychology in Canada.
6. Outline developments in sport and exercise psychology around the world.
7. List key sport and exercise psychology journals and scholarly organizations.
8. Describe future trends in sport and exercise psychology.

Nicole is a 17-year-old soccer player. She has been playing soccer for several years and has had her share of successes and failures. At soccer practice, she works hard and is always enthusiastic and positive. Recently, she finds herself thinking more about other activities like dancing and swimming.

Although she loves soccer, Nicole recently has found that she is not enjoying the intensely competitive games. She reports that prior to competitive games she feels anxious, does not look forward to playing, gets extremely nervous, and sometimes feels physically ill. As the anxiety about upcoming performances starts to mount, her confidence decreases. This is compounded by her belief that she is letting down herself, her teammates, her coaches, her family, and her friends. As a consequence, Nicole's on-field performance is often at a level far below expectations. Not surprisingly, she reports that she is enjoying soccer less and less.

Nicole also finds herself worrying more about her mother's low physical activity levels. Nicole knows that her mother has a healthy body weight and no obvious health problems, but she has learned in school about the importance of physical activity and health, especially as people age. Nicole and her mother often talk about the challenges that they both face in sport and exercise.

Nicole and her mother decide that they could benefit from professional help. Through a registry established by the provincial Sport Medicine Council, Nicole's parents are able to contact Dr. Holowalchuk, who is a professor of sport and exercise psychology at the local university. Dr. Holowalchuk is well known for her research on stress and coping in youth athletes. Dr. Holowalchuk also involves the services of Dr. Lee, a well-known expert in exercise psychology and older adults. What can Dr. Holowalchuk and Dr. Lee do to help?

The above vignette illustrates a common situation that involves the services of qualified sport and exercise psychology consultants. To help Nicole and her mother, a sport and exercise psychology consultant must have expertise in a number of areas. These areas include knowledge of how psychological factors may influence performance and motivation; knowledge about exercise adoption and adherence in older adults; knowledge of the technical, physical, and psychological demands of soccer; assessment knowledge to determine the psychological skills of the athlete; knowledge related to motivational factors in exercise; and intervention skills to design and implement an effective intervention for either Nicole or her mother. For example, if we just focus on Nicole, a consultant may suspect that anxiety is the "villain of the piece." The consultant will be familiar with various theories on the link between anxiety and performance and will have knowledge of the relationship between different types of anxiety and self-confidence. A proper assessment protocol would be necessary. If anxiety is a central problem, it is important that the consultant have an understanding of various strategies for managing feelings of anxiety and promoting self-confidence. Once the consultant has identified the source of the problem, devised strategies for dealing with it, and explained them to Nicole, there then follows a period of application. During this stage, the consultant has moved from a theorist position to one of practitioner. The consultant must now have the ability to teach Nicole mental skills that will help her enjoy and perform better in competitive games. In contrast, helping Nicole's mother might require a different, but related, set of skills associated with exercise motivation in older adults.

Are interventions related to performance enhancement or exercise adoption the only roles of sport and exercise psychology specialists in Canada? How does one become a sport and exercise psychology specialist? In this chapter, we will discuss the various roles and training in sport and exercise psychology. As you will discover, sport and exercise psychology specialists work in a variety of settings, have a multiplicity of educational training opportunities, and possess varying competencies. There are also ethical issues that govern the application of sport and exercise psychology principles. Many of the practices and controversies in sport and exercise psychology, especially in applied sport psychology, were shaped by its history, a history unlike that of other fields in psychology. In this chapter, we will address many of these issues related to sport and exercise psychology, but before we go any further, it is important to identify a few common myths about sport and exercise psychology. We will address these myths at the end of the chapter.

Common Myths about Sport and Exercise Psychology

MYTH: Only athletes or exercisers with serious mental problems need a sport or exercise psychologist.

MYTH: All sport psychology specialists work with elite athletes to enhance their performance.

INTRODUCTION

Sport and exercise are important elements of Canadian life. Physical activity experiences might involve running a 10K Vancouver Sun Run, playing hockey on an outdoor rink in the Prairies, canoeing the waterways of the Yukon or Quebec, working out in an exercise class in Winnipeg, engaging in a specialized activity session for people with spinal cord injuries in Hamilton, or competing in a golf tournament on the Highlands Links on Cape Breton Island.

Sport and exercise are complex and involve many subdisciplines in the sport sciences, including sport and exercise psychology. Reflect on your own experiences of participating in and watching sports or exercise. How do we make sense of athletes who are unable to concentrate or control anxiety in crucial situations, of acts of aggression by athletes and fans, of athletes' feelings of joy or shame after events, and of individual differences in the interpretation of and reactions to sporting situations? What are the characteristics and behaviours of effective coaches? Why do some people seem to find it easy to be physically active whereas others cannot even get started, despite their best intentions? How do we answer even the seemingly simple question of why people choose to participate in a specific physical activity? It is little wonder that people are interested in sport and exercise psychology.

Sport and exercise psychology has made major advances throughout the world as a legitimate scientific and applied discipline (Lidor, Morris, Bardaxoglou, & Becker, 2001; Weiss, 2008) and is an important component of the sport sciences in Canada. National accreditation standards identify sport and exercise psychology as a core discipline in undergraduate kinesiology and physical education programs (www.ccupeka.ca). Yet there remain many misconceptions and limitations in understanding what sport and exercise psychology is all about. We will provide you with a clearer understanding about sport and exercise psychology, especially in Canada.

THE NATURE OF SPORT AND EXERCISE PSYCHOLOGY

The term sport and exercise psychology means different things to various people in an array of situations. If you entered "definition of sport and exercise psychology" into an Internet search engine, the results would reveal numerous definitions. Some definitions would emphasize sport science, some would emphasize performance enhancement, and still others would address psychological principles applied to physical activity settings. The only consistency would be some reference to psychology and sport/exercise/physical activity (see Feltz & Kontos, 2002; Vealey, 2006).

As we will see in a later section, sport and exercise psychology in Canada and the United States has its parentage primarily in the sport sciences. In Canada, students can take sport and exercise psychology courses in most sport science programs (kinesiology, physical education, human kinetics). Most university professors in sport and exercise psychology also work in sport science programs. Thus, Gill (2000, p. 7) suggested, "Sport psychology is the branch of sport science that involves the scientific study of human behavior in sport and in the practical application of that knowledge in sport." Vealey (2006) argued that sport and exercise psychology should be viewed as an umbrella term that might be best described as a subdiscipline of sport science.

However, some professionals may see sport and exercise psychology more as a subdiscipline of psychology, much like health psychology or abnormal psychology. In this sense, sport and exercise psychology is "a science in which the principles of psychology are applied in a sport or exercise setting" (Cox, 1998, p. 4). One reason for this lack of agreement is that sport and exercise psychology has been shaped by theoretical and methodological influences of both kinesiology and psychology (Feltz & Kontos, 2002; Vealey, 2006). However, as you will see throughout this book, much of the research and practice in sport and exercise psychology are heavily dominated by theoretical perspectives that were developed in the general field of psychology.

The academic home of sport and exercise psychology has become increasingly complex since it is recognized within both the Canadian Psychological Association (CPA) and the American Psychological Association (APA) Division 47. An increasing number of psychology programs are offering sport and exercise psychology courses at the undergraduate level.

Does it matter whether one views sport and exercise psychology as a subdiscipline of sport sciences or of psychology? We believe that such perspectives are limiting and will hamper the scientific growth of the field. Sport and exercise psychology is an interdisciplinary scientific and applied field that embraces the integration of sport science and psychological knowledge. As the following sections reveal, sport and exercise psychology is dynamic and constantly evolving (Weiss, 2008).

Sport and Exercise Psychology: A Multidimensional Perspective

Students might ask what makes sport and exercise psychology unique as a field of study and practice from other areas of psychology. Not only does it integrate both sport science and psychological knowledge, but it integrates many areas of psychology (Anshel, 2003). There are many traditional and emerging disciplines within psychology that continue to have an impact on sport and exercise psychology. These include, but are not restricted to, cognitive psychology, clinical and counselling psychology, physiological psychology, social psychology, developmental psychology, and health psychology. You will recognize the impact of many areas of psychology on sport and exercise psychology throughout the chapters in this book.

It should be recognized that all areas of psychology are influenced by developments in other academic disciplines, including computer science, sociology, medicine, education, family studies, and women's studies, to name a few. The search for knowledge regarding human challenges goes beyond arbitrary, human-defined, academic boundaries. Think about a person trying to recover physical and social functioning following a stroke. Recovering, rediscovering, and redefining oneself will require integrating knowledge from many disciplines, including neurophysiology, exercise physiology and rehabilitation, exercise motivation, stress and emotion, social psychology, and counselling. Canadian researchers and practitioners are cognizant of the fact that many human health and wellness challenges require a transdisciplinary approach. As you will see throughout this book, sport and exercise psychology specialists are well positioned to make a positive contribution to Canadian society.

Positive Psychology in Sport and Exercise

There is a common belief that sport and exercise psychology focuses on abnormal or problematic behaviour. That is, that the field is driven by a medical model to reduce or eliminate pathological mental behaviours. Indeed, much has been made of how sport and exercise can be employed as an effective intervention with respect to certain psychological problems and their possible solutions. There can be little doubt that this has had important and positive consequences with regard to the growth of sport and exercise as a vehicle for bringing about improvements in quality of life. However, the question of what makes life worth living remains more elusive. What role does sport and exercise play with regard to general satisfaction and happiness with life? For example, does supporting a particular team or playing a specific sport allow people to thrive? Can sport and exercise contribute to an individual's self-acceptance, personal growth, purpose in life, and positive social relationships? What kinds of sporting and/or physical activities do people who are contented, satisfied, and fulfilled with everyday life participate in?

In recent years there has been renewed interest in the field of **positive psychology**, an area of psychology concerned primarily with understanding what makes normal life more fulfilling. Seligman (2002) criticized psychology (and much of his own earlier work) for focusing too much on mental illness and repair and not enough on the human side of strength and personal growth. This is not to say that studying such phenomena like anxiety or fear is not worthwhile; however, much can be learned from the positive aspects of life. Seligman and Csikszentmihalyi (2000) have suggested that positive psychology can be thought of as an examination of the subjective experience: well-being, satisfaction, fulfillment, pleasure, and happiness.

So how does positive psychology relate to sport and exercise? First, much of the research in sport and exercise psychology is directed toward enhancing performance, social and physical well-being, and positive emotion. Sport psychologists often work with athletes to improve performance and life satisfaction (see Chapter 14, Sport Psychology Interventions). Peak performance in athletics and exercise is all about psychological, physical, and emotional strength. Furthermore, there have been many studies in sport and exercise psychology research devoted to such key factors as optimistic disposition, flow states, enjoyment, satisfaction, psychological growth, and challenge (Jackson, 1992; Sabiston, McDonough, & Crocker, 2007). Even when exercise psychologists work with clinical conditions such as spinal cord injuries, cancer, and cardiac rehabilitation, a major focus is related to enhancing well-being by increasing positive qualities like confidence, independence, social and physical functioning, and life satisfaction (Baldwin & Courneya, 1997; Latimer, Martin Ginis, Hicks, & McCartney, 2004). You will see many examples of positive psychology throughout the book.

CAREERS IN SPORT AND EXERCISE PSYCHOLOGY

Specialists in sport and exercise psychology are involved in a number of career options that typically require graduate-level degrees. These options can be classified into three major areas: teaching, research, and consulting. We will briefly discuss each of these roles below.

Teaching

Most sport and exercise psychology specialists are employed in universities and colleges and have a primary responsibility for teaching undergraduate and graduate courses. Courses may range from introductory sport and exercise psychology to more specialized courses such as applied sport psychology, mental training, motivational counselling, developmental and lifespan sport and exercise psychology, and behavioural medicine. Some sport and exercise psychologists also provide educational services to community and sport organizations (Anshel, 2003). These teaching situations may involve increasing the awareness of sport and exercise psychology, teaching basic principles of sport and exercise psychology, helping athletes to develop and use psychological skills to enhance performance, or working with clients to enhance exercise behaviour and well-being (Cox, 1998).

Teaching is an important role for many sport and exercise psychology specialists.
Photograph by John MacLeod.

Research

A primary responsibility of sport and exercise psychology specialists working in universities is to advance knowledge. Through specialized training, researchers are able to design, conduct, and evaluate many research questions. There are several areas of research that will be described in this textbook, including personality, motivation, anxiety, stress and coping, group cohesion, aggression and moral behaviour, youth sport, aging and physical activity, leadership and coaching, exercise and mental health, physical activity interventions, and sport psychology interventions. Researchers in these areas seek to describe, predict, explain, and sometimes change cognition, emotion, and

Table 1.1 Selected Sport and Exercise Psychology Professional Organizations

Organization	Website
Canadian Society for Psychomotor Learning and Sport Psychology/Société Canadienne D'Apprentissage Psychomoteur et de Psychologie du Sport (SCAPPS)	www.scapps.org
Canadian Sport Psychology Association (CSPA)	www.en.cspa-acps.ca
International Society of Sport Psychology (ISSP)	www.issponline.org
European Federation of Sport Psychology/Fédération Européenne de Psychologie des Sports et des Activités Corporelles (FEPSAC)	www.fepsac.org
Association for Applied Sport Psychology (AASP)	www.appliedsportpsych.org
American Psychological Association Division 47: Exercise and Sport Psychology	www.apa47.org
North American Society for the Psychology of Sport and Physical Activity (NASPSPA)	www.naspspa.org
Australian Psychological Society: College of Sport Psychologists	www.psychology.org.au/units/colleges/sport

Table 1.2 Representative Sport and Exercise Psychology Journals

Journal	Website
Journal of Sport & Exercise Psychology	www.humankinetics.com/JSEP/journalAbout.cfm
Journal of Applied Sport Psychology	www.tandf.co.uk/journals/tf/10413200.html
The Sport Psychologist	www.humankinetics.com/TSP/journalAbout.cfm
International Journal of Sport and Exercise Psychology	www.fitinfotech.com/IJSEP/IJSEP.tpl
International Journal of Sport Psychology	www.ijsp-online.com
Psychology of Sport and Exercise	www.sciencedirect.com/science/journal/14690292
Athletic Insight: The Online Journal of Sport Psychology	www.athleticinsight.com

behaviour in physical activity settings. There are many different types of research methodologies, which are described in more detail in Chapter 2, but all research is conducted under strict ethical guidelines. Sport and exercise psychology researchers not only conduct research but also present their findings at conferences and in refereed journals and books (see Tables 1.1 and 1.2 for a listing of professional organizations and journals, respectively). These presentations and publications allow scholars to engage in discussions and debates about the strengths and limitations of various theories, methods, and paradigms. (The research process is described in greater detail in Chapter 2.)

Consulting

A third major role of the sport and exercise psychology specialist is to help individuals, teams, and organizations improve performance, change physical activity behaviour, manage sport and life demands, and enhance personal well-being. These specialists providing consulting services might be licensed sport psychologists. Other specialists providing services might be individuals who have a strong knowledge of educational and psychological skills but who are not formally licensed. The issues concerning who can provide sport and exercise psychology services and who can call themselves sport and exercise psychologists are discussed later in this chapter.

In Canada, many professional sport teams and national sport organizations employ sport psychology consultants. In the United States, many major universities have full-time consultants (Weinberg & Gould, 2003), but this is not the case in Canada. However, an increasing number of Canadian universities do use sport psychology consultants on a

An increasing role of sport psychology specialists is as a consultant to athletes. Dr. Whitney Sedgwick and former University of British Columbia basketball player Pasha Bains discuss psychological strategies to enhance performance.
Photograph by John MacLeod.

limited basis. There are also consultants working in the fitness industry, in rehabilitation settings, and progressively more in the business community (Anshel, 2003). In Canada, there are very few individuals who make their living as full-time sport and exercise psychology consultants. Most sport and exercise psychology specialists combine sport consulting with university or college careers or psychological consulting in other areas.

Sport and exercise psychology consultants tend to play three general roles. Educational consultants typically teach people psychological skills to facilitate performance, increase exercise, and enhance well-being. Counselling consultants help people with developmental concerns, adjustment, and challenges (Petitpas, 1996). Clinical psychology consultants can assist clients in educational and counselling areas, but they also have special training in psychopathology. Of course, both counselling and clinical psychologists might also provide educational services in physical activity settings. We will discuss the specialized training required in the next section.

TRAINING TO BE A SPORT AND EXERCISE PSYCHOLOGY SPECIALIST

Since sport and exercise psychology is an interdisciplinary field, there are multiple career pathways. The training required to be a sport and exercise psychology specialist, however, is contentious and a source of constant debate. Silva (2002) noted that there was little controversy in the 1960s and 1970s since most sport and exercise psychology specialists were academically oriented. Now an increasing number of students and academics are interested in applied sport and exercise psychology. However, working in applied settings requires a different set of competencies than that required in academic settings.

So what kind of training is required? Unfortunately, there is no easy answer! To a large extent, educational training depends on what career path a person chooses. There are multiple career tracks that combine teaching, research, performance enhancement, and the provision of clinical/counselling services. The APA provides some guidance on graduate training and career possibilities in exercise and sport psychology (www.apa47.org/pracGrad.php).For simplicity, we will briefly describe two general training orientations: (1) sport science education and (2) clinical and counselling sport and exercise psychology.

Sport Science Education

In Canada, most sport and exercise psychology specialists work in university and college settings and thus require strong teaching and research skills. Typically, they are extensively trained in the sport sciences and in research methods and take additional courses in psychology and/or counselling (see Table 1.3). Nevertheless, there are trends toward more interdisciplinary training that combines the sport sciences and psychology. Currently, a wide range of academic programs that provide varied learning experiences are available to students. Interested students can find relevant information in a directory of graduate programs in Canada, the United States, Australia, and Great Britain that is published for the Association for Applied Sport Psychology (AASP).

Table 1.3 Examples of Graduate Courses in Sport and Exercise Psychology

Sport Science Orientation	Clinical and Counselling Orientation
Sport psychology	Psychological assessment
Exercise psychology	Psychotherapy
Skill acquisition	Psychopathology
Motor development	Cognitive behavioural therapy
Adapted physical activity	Counselling theory
Psychological intervention in sport	Health psychology
Research methods	Social psychology
Advanced statistics	Professional ethics
Professional ethics	Research methods
Sport psychology internship	Advanced statistics
Behavioural medicine	Internship

Clinical and Counselling Sport and Exercise Psychology

Clinical psychology and counselling psychology are closely associated fields. Clinical psychology training typically focuses on the assessment and rehabilitation of serious psychological dysfunctions. Counselling training tends to focus more on helping people with adjustment or development problems. However, there is significant overlap in the training of clinical and counselling psychologists (see Petitpas, 1996).

The training of clinical and counselling psychologists is well grounded in psychological theory, assessment, intervention, research methods, and ethics and often requires a supervised internship (see Table 1.3). Clinical and counselling psychologists who work as sport psychologists usually have completed graduate courses or supplementary training in the sport sciences. The specific training for clinical psychologists is linked to the registration (licensing) standards of individual provincial and territorial regulatory bodies. Students interested in the specific requirements and accredited academic programs can visit the CPA website (www.cpa.ca) for appropriate links.

Courses and Programs for Undergraduate Students

Entry into either a sport science or a psychology graduate program often requires very different undergraduate coursework. So what should a student do to prepare for a career in sport and exercise psychology? Ideally, the student should take a double major in sport sciences and psychology. This background would allow the greatest flexibility in pursuing graduate work. If this is not possible, then the student should combine a major and a minor in an undergraduate degree. However, the exact program and courses will be determined by the career path and the entrance requirements of various sport science or psychology (clinical and counselling) programs. It is hoped that, in the near future, more universities will create opportunities that will allow students greater flexibility to pursue academic programs in both the sport sciences and psychology.

LICENSING OF SPORT AND EXERCISE PSYCHOLOGISTS

Many individuals providing performance enhancement services to athletes are called sport psychologists by the media. However, is this appropriate? In Canada, provincial and territorial laws regulate the use of the term *psychologist*. These laws were enacted to protect people from being exploited, possibly by untrained individuals. In most cases, psychologists must complete specific types of educational training and pass examinations set by psychological licensing boards. The specific rules for the use of the title *psychologist* vary across provinces and territories. Some provinces and territories allow certain exemptions to the use of the term *psychologist*. For example, in British Columbia, a person who has an appointment in an academic program as a psychologist may call themselves a psychologist. The types of exemptions are covered by various health profession, university, and education acts that are far too involved to cover in any detail in this chapter.

There are a number of professionals who are well trained in sport sciences, exercise motivation counselling, psychology, and performance enhancement techniques, but they are not licensed sport psychologists. Unless they meet the exemption criteria, they should not call themselves sport or exercise psychologists. Within universities and colleges, such titles as *instructor* or *professor of sport and exercise psychology* might be appropriate if they describe the individual's teaching or research responsibilities. In applied settings, people have used such designations as *mental* trainer, *sport and exercise psychology consultant*, and *sport science consultant*. Regardless of the title that practitioners adopt, they are responsible for meeting standards of conduct when providing sport and exercise psychology services. The CPA, the Canadian Sport Psychology Association (CSPA), and the AASP have been proactive in identifying the necessary standards and competencies required for providing sport and exercise psychology services to athletes (see Table 1.4). The next section discusses these standards and competencies.

Table 1.4 Membership Criteria for the Canadian Sport Psychology Association

The Canadian Sport Psychology Association lists consultants who fulfill the following basic criteria:

- A master's degree in sport psychology or a related field
- Successful completion of a variety of courses relevant to sport psychology consultation and foundational disciplines, such as human kinetics or kinesiology, psychology, and counselling
- Extensive sport psychology consulting experience
- Hands-on experience in sport
- Favourable supervisor and client evaluations

Case Study 1.1

Sport and Exercise Psychology Competencies and Referral

Rick has been working as a consultant with the university rowing team for the past year as part of a supervised internship for his doctoral degree. Rick's role mostly involves meeting with the team and educating them on various psychological skills such as goal setting and building team dynamics. He also meets with some athletes one-on-one when either the athlete or the coach makes a request. Rick meets with his internship supervisor, a professor of sport and exercise psychology, once every two weeks. At these meetings, Rick and his supervisor discuss what he is doing with the team, the next steps, and any issues that arise. At his initial meeting with the team, Rick described his own role and outlined the role of his supervisor.

Recently, the team's head coach approached Rick and voiced her concerns about one of the athletes on the team. The athlete was losing weight, stopped eating at team outings, and seemed to be "down in the dumps" lately. The coach asked Rick to help the athlete and report back on the athlete's progress. Rick was uncertain what his role should be and told the coach that he would consider the situation and discuss it with his supervisor. After meeting with his supervisor and considering the CPA code of ethics, Rick decided that he did not have the level of competence or adequate supervision to help the athlete since neither he nor his supervisor were registered (licensed) psychologists (see Table 1.5, Principle 2). Rick decided to meet with the athlete and refer her to the university counselling services, where she could get help with a clinical concern such as an eating disorder. Although she did not seek consultation from Rick, he determined that the athlete's health may be at risk if the intervention did not occur (Principle 1). Finally, Rick met with the coach and explained that he could not disclose any information to her about the athlete without the athlete's permission (Principle 1). The referral process was a success because Rick (1) was aware of his limitations, (2) followed the CPA's ethical code, and (3) had adequate supervision for making decisions. From this experience, Rick learned that when consulting with a team or individual he should make his competencies clear from the start and discuss concerns about privacy, confidentiality, and freedom to consent.

STANDARDS OF CONDUCT AND PRACTITIONER COMPETENCIES IN SPORT AND EXERCISE PSYCHOLOGY

An increasing role for sport and exercise psychology specialists is that of consultant for athletes, teams, and coaches. However, who should provide specific types of sport and exercise psychology services? How do consultants deal with conflicts of interest, demands from coaches for athletes' private information, challenges that exceed their professional competencies, or potential romantic interest in clients? The style in which each individual consultant works with an athlete or a team will probably differ considerably from one consultant to another. Nevertheless, a number of basic standards of conduct and service always apply when a sport and exercise psychology consultant interacts with clients.

Ethics is concerned with matters of right and wrong as they relate to human behaviour. With regard to the duties and responsibilities of a sport and exercise psychology consultant, ethics also refers to the nature, terms, and parameters of the relationship between the consultant and the client. Consultants provide a service, but they must be mindful that this service can be both beneficial and harmful to clients. Consultants have an ethical responsibility (at best) to assist athletes and (at worst) to do no harm. However, consultants often find themselves faced with situations in which the right course of action is far from clear (Moore, 2003). This is where ethical codes become invaluable because they provide guidelines for what to do, when to do it, and how to do it (see Case Study 1.1).

A number of professional organizations have drawn up codes of ethics, or guidelines, that govern the relationship between a practitioner and a client. Three of these codes of ethics are particularly relevant to the sport and exercise psychology consultant working in Canada:

1. Ethics Code: AASP Ethical Principles and Standards (http://appliedsportpsych.org/about/ethics/code)
2. CSPA Code of Ethics (www.en.cspa-acps.ca/publications/publications.html)
3. CPA Canadian Code of Ethics for Psychologists (www.cpa.ca/cpasite/userfiles/Documents/Canadian%20Code%20of%20Ethics%20for%20Psycho.pdf)

Professional ethics are normally covered in more detail in advanced sport and exercise psychology courses. We provide a brief overview of the CPA guidelines in Table 1.5. However, you should be aware that ethical standards are complex and are constantly being modified and refined (see Moore, 2003; Whelan, Meyers, & Elkin, 2002).

Table 1.5 CPA Canadian Code of Ethics for Psychologists

The code is comprised of four general principles, listed below in order of priority:

Principle 1: Respect for the Dignity of Persons

This principle reinforces the moral rights of all people regardless of individual differences, including culture, religion, gender, marital status, sexual orientation, etc. Respect extends to upholding the individual's privacy, confidentiality, and freedom to consent for consulting services and as a research participant. These rights must be upheld at all times, particularly for vulnerable persons (e.g., children), except in circumstances when the physical safety of an individual is threatened if intervention does not occur.

Principle 2: Responsible Caring

This principle requires sport and exercise psychology consultants to weigh the costs and benefits of various methods and select those that will minimize harm and maximize benefits. The consultant must take responsibility and corrective action for any harmful effects that may have occurred as a result of their research, teaching, or practice. To avoid causing harm, sport and exercise psychologists work within their range of competence or engage in activities for which they have adequate supervision.

Principle 3: Integrity in Relationships

This principle is upheld through self-knowledge and critical analysis. Sport and exercise psychologists are expected to be accurate and honest, to be straightforward and open, to be as objective and unbiased as possible, and to avoid conflicts of interest.

Principle 4: Responsibility to Society

Sport and exercise psychologists benefit society through the development of knowledge and by practising freedom of inquiry and debate. However, respect and responsible caring for the athlete must be the first priority and must not be violated by attempts to benefit society.

Source: Canadian Psychological Association, *Canadian Code of Ethics for Psychologists*, Third Edition, © 2000

REFLECTIONS 1.1

A practitioner in Ontario is providing exercise psychology services to women enrolled in a fitness facility. The specialist is teaching a number of psychological strategies, such as goal setting, increasing confidence, and relaxation training. There were, however, some questions about the specialist's knowledge and practices. Although the person is a former elite athlete, there was no indication that the specialist had formal training in the theory and use of psychology strategies in exercise settings. What principles might the specialist have violated, based on the CPA standards of conduct?

SPORT AND EXERCISE PSYCHOLOGY IN CANADA AND THE UNITED STATES

The previous sections have highlighted how sport and exercise psychology is a multidisciplinary field that involves both psychology and the sport sciences, but how did it evolve into its present condition in Canada and the United States? The development of sport and exercise psychology in both countries has been closely intertwined. A brief history will allow the student to more clearly understand the present day issues, challenges, and status of sport and exercise psychology in Canada.

In the early 20th century, Canadian universities were few and enrolment was low. In sport and exercise psychology, there was little evidence of systematic research or teaching. However, south of the border, Dr. Coleman Griffith developed a sport psychology laboratory at the University of Illinois in 1925. His research focused on understanding psychological and social factors that influenced skill performance (Gould & Pick, 1995), and he was a consultant for the Chicago Cubs baseball team. Griffith penned two of the first sport psychology texts: *The Psychology of Coaching* (1926) and *Psychology and Athletics* (1928). Despite Griffith's early work, sport psychology witnessed little development during the 1930s and 1940s.

The post–World War II expansion of universities in the United States had an important impact on sport and exercise psychology. Several universities established laboratories in motor learning and behaviour, seeking to determine how people learned motor skills and how practice and feedback influenced learning. Dr. Franklin Henry, a faculty member at the University of California, Berkeley, became a strong advocate of a scholarly and scientific approach to physical education studies. Notably, two graduates of Dr. Henry's laboratory became prominent pioneering sport psychology researchers in Canada: Dr. Rikk Alderman and Dr. Albert Carron. In North America, many sport psychology instructors were trained in motor behaviour in physical education departments.

Nurtured primarily by academics in the movement and sport sciences, sport psychology began to grow in both Canada and the United States during the 1960s and 1970s (Gould & Pick, 1995). This growth corresponded with the establishment of many new universities and junior colleges. At this time, there was limited specialization in exercise psychology. The teaching of sport psychology courses became widespread, and graduate training programs began to appear in the major universities, such as the University of Illinois, the University of Florida, and the University of Alberta. Psychology departments also became more interested in teaching sport psychology, although there seemed to be an overemphasis on abnormal or

Table 1.6 Representative Academic and Professional Sport and Exercise Psychology Textbooks by Canadians

Year	Title	Author
1974	*Psychological Behaviour in Sport*	R. Alderman
1976	*Psychology of Sport: The Behavior, Motivation, Personality and Performance of Athletes*	S. Butt
1980	*Social Psychology of Sport*	A. Carron
1980	*In Pursuit of Excellence*	T. Orlick
1983	*Behavior Modification and Coaching: Principles, Procedures, and Research*	G. L. Martin and D. Hrycaiko
1986	*Psyching for Sport: Mental Training for Athletes*	T. Orlick
1988	*The Mental Game Plan: A Training Program for All Sports*	J. Albinson and S. Bull
1998	*Exercising Your Way to Better Mental Health*	L.M. Leith
1998	*Group Dynamics in Sport*	A. Carron and H. Hausenblas
2003	*The Psychology of Physical Activity*	A. Carron, H. Hausenblas, and P. Estabrooks
2003	*Sport Psychology: Practical Guidelines from Behavior Analysis*	G. L. Martin
2007	*Sport Psychology: A Canadian Perspective*	P. R. E. Crocker

problem behaviour. For example, in 1966, clinical psychologists Bruce Ogilvie and Thomas Tutko published the influential textbook *Problem Athletes and How to Handle Them*. See Table 1.6 for a list of some important sport and exercise psychology textbooks by Canadians.

In Canada, Dr. Rikk Alderman at the University of Alberta developed the first PhD program. Along with Dr. Albert Carron, Alderman could be considered one of the modern parents of sport and exercise psychology in Canada. Under the guidance of Dr. Alderman and Dr. Robert Wilberg (a motor behaviour specialist), the University of Alberta program produced several influential Canadian sport psychology researchers and practitioners in the 1970s. They include John Salmela (Université de Montréal, University of Ottawa), Terry Orlick (University of Ottawa), Cal Botterill (University of Winnipeg), Len Wankel (University of Alberta), and Peter Klavora (University of Toronto).

Two major scholarly professional organizations were established in the United States and Canada. The North American Society for the Psychology of Sport and Physical Activity (NASPSPA) was formed in 1967. It reflected the close ties between the training of specialists in motor learning and in sport psychology in the 1960s. NASPSPA focused on improving the quality of research and teaching in the psychology of sport, motor development, and motor learning and control. The Canadian Society for Psychomotor Learning and Sport Psychology/Société Canadienne D'Apprentissage Psychomoteur et de Psychologie du Sport (SCAPPS) had its beginnings in Edmonton in 1969 but was founded as a society in Banff, Alberta, in 1977. Its main objectives were similar to those of NASPSPA, with a primary focus on research. Dr. Robert Wilberg was its first unofficial

Canadian Profile
Dr. Albert Carron

Dr. Albert Carron

Photograph courtesy of Dr. A. Carron.

Dr. Albert (Bert) Carron is recognized as one of the modern founders of sport and exercise psychology in Canada. Born in Edmonton, Alberta, he completed his undergraduate physical education degree at the University of Alberta (1963), where he also starred as a football player. In 1967, he completed his EdD degree at the University of California, Berkeley, and became a faculty member at the University of Saskatchewan.

He has been at the University of Western Ontario in the School of Kinesiology since 1974, where he established one of the top sport and exercise psychology research programs in the world. Dr. Carron is widely acknowledged as the world expert on group cohesion and group dynamics in sport and exercise. Dr. Carron collaborated with Dr. Larry Brawley and Dr. Neil Widmeyer to produce the Group Environment Questionnaire, at present the best research instrument to assess group cohesion in sport teams. This work has been cited in more than 100 research studies. He has published 10 books and more than 130 research publications.

His colleagues have recognized his contributions by awarding him Fellow status in three professional organizations: the American Academy of Kinesiology and Physical Education, the Association for Applied Sport Psychology, and the Canadian Society for Psychomotor Learning and Sport Psychology (SCAPPS). A Fellow designation is reserved for top academics who have demonstrated high standards of scholarly practice and made significant contributions to scientific knowledge. SCAPPS has also named its senior scholar presentation in sport and exercise psychology after Dr. Carron.

He has consulted with the Spanish and British Olympic Committees, the London Knights of the Ontario Hockey League, and the University of Western Ontario's men's and women's ice hockey teams. His remarkable career and contributions establish the standard for all sport and exercise scholars.

president in 1969, followed by Dr. Jack Leavitt of the University of Windsor. SCAPPS continues to have a strong influence on the research and academic development of sport and exercise psychology in Canada.

The late 1970s and the 1980s were periods of consolidation in sport psychology as it separated from its motor learning parentage. Many universities had specialists in sport psychology, more graduate programs were established, and quality research flourished. The practice of sport psychology also became more widespread. In the United States, the Olympic Committee developed a sport psychology advisory board around 1980, organized a sport psychology registry, and hired a full-time sport psychologist in 1985 (Weinberg & Gould, 2003). Sport psychology services were increasingly sought by professional and Olympic sport organizations. The 1980s also witnessed the growth of exercise psychology in North America. The APA developed a special division—Division 47: Exercise and Sport Psychology—to bring together psychologists interested in this area. In Canada, sport psychology practices were included in the National Coaching Certification Program (NCCP). Three prominent sport psychology journals were established: *The Journal of Sport Psychology* (1979), *The Sport Psychologist* (1986), and the *Journal of Applied Sport Psychology* (1989).

A key event was the formation of the Association for the Advancement of Applied Sport Psychology (AAASP) in 1986. Many Canadian sport and exercise psychology scholars became active members, with Dr. Larry Brawley (University of Waterloo, University of Saskatchewan) as one of its earliest presidents. This association has changed its name slightly, dropping "Advancement." AASP is now the largest organization devoted to the promotion of applied sport (and exercise) psychology. AASP conferences highlight research and professional issues in sport, exercise, and health psychology, as well as provide continuing education workshops.

Since the 1990s there has been tremendous growth in sport and exercise psychology in North America. There are now numerous opportunities for research, teaching, and practice in this expanded field. Within universities, the growth of sport and exercise psychology has been propelled and shaped by societal concerns about health and health care costs. Many programs currently place an emphasis on health and health promotion through physical activity. One impact of this health movement has been the diversification and expansion of exercise and health psychology. Research topics now increasingly focus on body image, self-esteem, well-being, behavioural change, self-presentation, exercise adherence, eating disorders, and other health behaviours affected by physical activity. Many university programs presently offer undergraduate courses in sport psychology, exercise psychology, exercise and health psychology, behavioural medicine, applied sport and exercise psychology, and the like. Major granting agencies in Canada and the United States are directing significant research funding to sport and exercise psychology researchers, especially if the work is linked to health.

Practitioners are also working with major organizations to provide sport organizations and athletes with better access to certified mental or psychological skills consultants. To this end, the CSPA (www.en.cspa-acps.ca/membership/cspaprofessional.html) and the AASP (http://appliedsportpsych.org/consultants) have developed a process to certify qualified consultants.

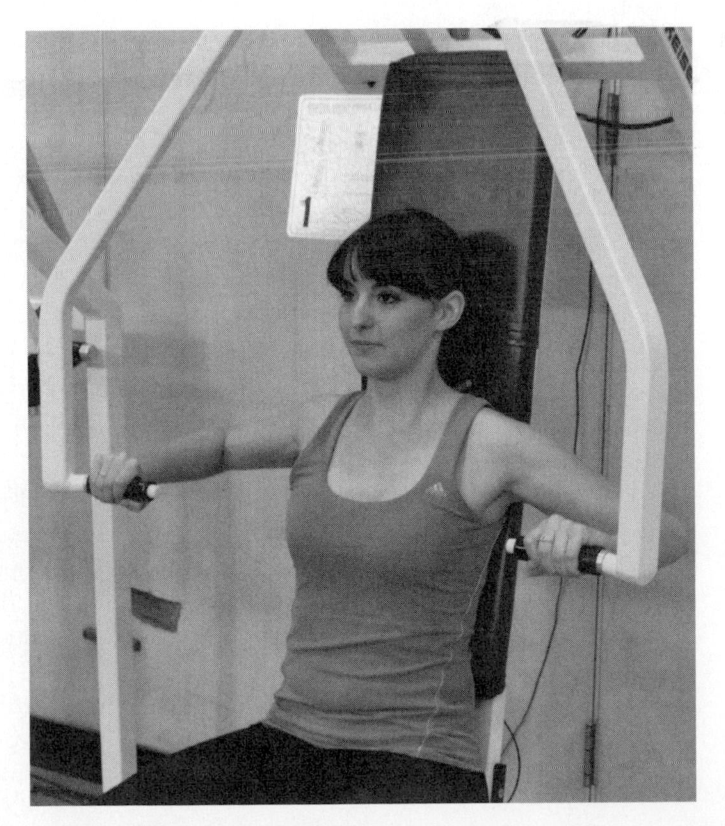

Clients are increasingly utilizing the skills of exercise psychology consultants in Canada.

Photograph by Peter Crocker, University of British Columbia.

SPORT AND EXERCISE PSYCHOLOGY AROUND THE WORLD

The discipline and profession of sport and exercise psychology has witnessed tremendous growth in many parts of the world over the last 25 years. Lidor et al. (2001) estimated there were several thousand sport and exercise psychologists working in numerous countries. Sociocultural, economic, and political forces have shaped the evolution of sport and exercise psychology in various regions. Not surprisingly, sport and exercise psychology is the best developed in the wealthiest economic regions, such as North America, Europe, the United Kingdom, Australia, and Japan. Reviewing the worldwide developments in sport and exercise psychology is beyond the scope of this chapter. We will, however, provide a snapshot of prominent organizations and events. Those students interested in more detail are encouraged to read the third edition of *The World Sport Psychology Sourcebook* by Lidor et al. (2001).

The former Soviet Union boasted one of the first sport psychology programs in the world. Around 1919, the Institute for the Study of Sport and Physical Culture was established in Petrograd (later Leningrad, now St. Petersburg). The Institute developed a systematic approach to the application of sport sciences. Psychologists worked with other sport scientists to develop and apply training and competition principles to maximize performance. This system was adopted by more than 130 sport institutes throughout the former Soviet Union and later in the Soviet-controlled Eastern bloc (Silva, 2002). With the collapse of the Soviet Union beginning in the 1980s, there were insufficient resources and political power to maintain the high level of training and practice of sport psychology.

In the rest of Europe, with the possible exception of Germany, there was little significant support for and development of sport psychology before 1960. However, two major events occurred in the 1960s that played significant roles in the establishment of sport psychology. First, the first World Congress of Sport Psychology was held in Rome in 1965. This led to the formation of the International Society of Sport Psychology (ISSP), with more than 25 countries represented. ISSP also sponsored the first scholarly sport psychology journal, the *International Journal of Sport Psychology*. The second event was the founding of the European Federation of Sport Psychology/Fédération Européenne de Psychologie des Sports et des Activités Corporelles (FEPSAC). In 2005, FEPSAC had representation from more than 24 European sport and exercise psychology organizations. Both ISSP and FEPSAC have had a major impact on the advancement of sport and exercise psychology in Europe and throughout the world.

By 2005, there were many strong academic programs and professional organizations around the world. In Britain, sport and exercise psychology courses are now widespread in the university system. Coaches can learn about sport psychology applications through sports coach UK (formerly the National Coaching Foundation), and the British Association of Sport and Exercise Sciences (BASES) offers individual accreditation in sport psychology. In Australia, psychology departments co-operate with sport science programs to offer graduate training. Sport psychology is well accepted by the Australian sporting community and is fully integrated into the Australian Institute of Sport (www.ausport.gov.au/ais/sssm/psychology). In Asia, the leading countries are Japan, China, and Korea. Major sporting events there

(Olympics, Asian Games) have fuelled the practice of applied sport psychology and other sport sciences. Unfortunately, academic and professional development have been slow in many poorer areas of the world, such as Africa and Central America. Sport and exercise psychology organizations are working with dedicated professionals in these regions to improve educational and professional opportunities in sport and exercise psychology.

Canadian Dr. John Salmela served on the executive of the International Society of Sport Psychology for 16 years.
Photograph courtesy of John Salmela.

KEY HISTORICAL WORLD EVENTS IN SPORT AND EXERCISE PSYCHOLOGY

- Institute for the Study of Sport and Physical Culture established in Soviet Union (1919)
- First World Congress of Sport Psychology held in Rome (1965)
- International Society of Sport Psychology (ISSP) founded (1965)
- European Federation of Sport Psychology/Fédération Européenne de Psychologie des Sports et des Activités Corporelles (FEPSAC) established (1969)
- First issue of the *International Journal of Sport Psychology* (1970)
- Japanese Society of Sport Psychology founded (1973)
- World Congress of Sport Psychology held in Ottawa (1981)
- British Association of Sport Sciences (now British Association of Sport and Exercise Sciences) established a distinct Sport Psychology section (1985)
- Australian Applied Sport Psychology Association founded (1986)
- German Association for Sport Psychology formed in 1969, but first meeting after unification held in Cologne (1991)
- First Congress of Asian and South Pacific Association for Sport Psychology (1991)
- First issue of *Psychology of Sport and Exercise*, a FEPSAC journal (2000)
- ISSP sponsors *International Journal of Sport and Exercise Psychology* (2004)

PREDICTED TRENDS AND ISSUES IN CANADA

Sport and exercise psychology is an interdisciplinary field involving researchers, educators, and practitioners from both the sport sciences and psychology. Many social, economic, and political forces have shaped the present state of sport and exercise psychology in Canada. It has faced many challenges and growing pains but has made very impressive gains in the last two decades. So what does the future hold? We believe there are a number of trends and issues that will dominate the advancement of sport and exercise psychology over the next 20 years.

Increased Specialization and Diversification

Federal and provincial/territorial health initiatives and policies, combined with knowledge development, will drive increased specialization and diversification. Much of the growth in the field will be in exercise related to health, primarily because physical activity is an effective, and relatively inexpensive, way to maintain or improve health. Hot topics are likely to be exercise adherence, obesity, aging, well-being, and youth development. There will be continued expansion of sport and exercise psychology principles in clinical settings, such as the study and treatment of cancer, stroke, spinal cord injuries, and Parkinson's disease.

Increased Research and Teaching Opportunities

Most Canadian universities and colleges offer sport and exercise psychology courses. Because of continued specialization and diversification, the number and types of courses will continue to grow at both the undergraduate and graduate level. Research opportunities will increase as major funding agencies—Social Sciences and Humanities Research Council (SSHRC) of Canada, Canadian Institutes of Health Research (CIHR), and the Heart and Stroke Foundation of Canada—recognize the quality and applicability of sport and exercise psychology research. Although funding for sport-related research has improved in the last few years, the major focus for increased funding will be on health-related research.

Increased Demands for Training in Clinical and Counselling Psychology

Working in diverse sport and exercise settings will require a range of sport science and psychological competencies. Students will demand and require counselling training and possibly clinical psychology training. Unfortunately, Canadian (and US) universities have been slow to respond to this demand. Kinesiology and exercise science programs largely focus on research and teaching, and few psychology departments offer sport and exercise psychology programs. This leaves students with two choices. First, students in kinesiology programs can supplement their training by taking appropriate counselling courses in psychology or educational psychology programs. However, seldom is the opportunity available for supervised internships in applied sport and exercise psychology. Second, students can do a graduate degree in clinical or counselling psychology. An advantage to this route is generalized training that is applicable to many domains. Unfortunately, most clinical and counselling programs lack a critical mass of faculty trained in applied sport and exercise psychology.

Interdepartmental Collaboration in Teaching, Research, and Practice

As the field of sport and exercise psychology expands, there will be a need for faculty to collaborate across departments of sport science, psychology, education, public health, and rehabilitation sciences. There is a need to break down traditional and artificial academic barriers and to create joint or multidepartmental programs. A major challenge, however, is determining the necessary requisite courses and experiences for specific careers at undergraduate and graduate levels.

Ethics and Competencies

There will be increased pressure on practitioners to adhere to professional standards of conduct when working with clients. Regulatory bodies are likely to become more vigilant in monitoring the use of the title *sport psychologist* or *exercise psychologist* as well as the practices of sport and exercise psychology consultants. Consultants from both sport science education and clinical and counselling psychology backgrounds will need to acquire and demonstrate competencies to work with specific populations in sport and exercise.

Working in Performance Enhancement Teams

Though opportunities are still limited, there is beginning to be an increased demand for applied sport psychology services by national and provincial sport organizations. Some of these services are being provided through the various Canadian Sport Centres. These centres provide sport science support to national team athletes or those athletes identified as potential national team members. Within this environment, sport psychology consultants are asked to be accountable for the effectiveness of their services: consultants must find some way to measure the effectiveness of their consulting. A second demand is for the consultants to work in collaboration with other sport science professionals, including biomechanists, nutritionists, and physiologists. Rather than working alone, sport psychology consultants must devise methods of integrating members of these performance enhancement teams in order to most effectively service the athletes.

Online Consulting and Service Provision

In attempts to service more athletes and exercisers, particularly those outside of urban centres, there is a growing trend toward online consultation and service provision. Although this is an effective method of transmitting knowledge to a greater number of clients, sport and exercise psychologists must be especially vigilant that what they want to communicate is being received correctly, that they adhere to an ethical code, that they are not misrepresenting their competencies, and, most importantly, that the privacy and confidentiality of the client are being upheld. The CPA has recently devised ethical guidelines for online consulting (www.cpa.ca/aboutcpa/boardofdirectors/committees/ethics/ethicalguidelines/).

Consulting with Athletes and Exercisers with Disabilities

Government health initiatives are on the rise as activity levels of Canadians continue to decline and obesity rates increase. The lowest rates of physical activity participation continue to be among individuals with disabilities. There will be increased demand on sport and exercise psychologists to involve individuals with disabilities in sport and exercise programs in order to improve overall health. One reason for this is that the profile of the Paralympics, both in Canada and on the world stage, is rapidly increasing. The Paralympic Games are now held immediately following the Olympic Games rather than as completely separate games as they previously were. This increased profile will likely result in increased government funding, sponsorship, and demand for sport psychology services.

Knowledge Translation

There is a critical need to bridge the gap between research evidence and professional practice in sport and exercise psychology. Knowledge must be accessible, understandable, and useful for practitioners such as applied sport psychologists, physical educators, coaches, rehabilitation specialists, and fitness specialists. Traditional knowledge translation methods have been primarily of a top-down nature. These methods have included university courses, textbooks, coaching manuals, and workshops taught by specialists. However, these traditional methods are not always effective. Partnerships among researchers, educators, and practitioners are required—partnerships that produce an exchange and ethically based application of sport and exercise psychology knowledge.

CHAPTER SUMMARY

Sport and exercise psychology is an interdisciplinary field that is recognized in Canada as a core discipline within kinesiology and physical education programs. Sport and exercise psychology specialists are involved in teaching, research, and consulting roles, although most specialists in Canada are employed in universities and colleges. Various educational pathways involve training in the sport sciences or in clinical or counselling psychology. Specific training is often dependent on career objectives, whether as an academic (in either sport sciences or psychology) or as a practitioner. Some scholarly organizations, such as CSPA, do provide a certification process for consultants. However, provincial and territorial bodies regulate the use of the term *psychologist* as well as the specific training and examinations required to become a registered psychologist. All sport and exercise psychology consultants are guided by standards of conduct set out by organizations such as the CPA, AASP, and CSPA. Although the term *psychologist* has a specific legal meaning, throughout this book we will use the term *sport and exercise psychologist* to refer to specialists in the three areas of teaching, research, and consulting.

The state of sport and exercise psychology in Canada, including its strengths and controversies, has been shaped by its parentage. In North America, sport and exercise psychology has been nurtured primarily in the sport sciences. The major Canadian scholarly professional organization is SCAPPS, although many academics and practitioners also affiliate with NASPSPA and AASP. At the applied level, CSPA is likely to have a major impact over the next decade, although the re-emergence (2006) of a sport and exercise psychology section within the CPA could influence future certification and training requirements. At present, sport and exercise psychology is taught in most universities, and research is flourishing. There is increased diversification into health and clinical populations. Sport and exercise psychology also continues to flourish around the world, with major academic organizations in Europe, Australia, New Zealand, the United Kingdom, and Asia.

The next 20 years should witness several major trends, including increased specialization, diversification, research, and teaching opportunities. There will be pressure to improve educational opportunities and training of specific competencies for applied sport and exercise psychology services. It is hoped that faculty in programs in psychology, educational psychology, and sport science will collaborate to enhance the future development of sport and exercise psychology. Lastly, there is a critical need to bridge the gap between research evidence and professional practice in sport and exercise psychology. This process will require effective partnerships among practitioners, educators, and researchers so that sport and exercise principles can be effectively applied across multiple physical activity settings to enhance performance, increase participation, and improve well-being.

Common Myths about Sport and Exercise Psychology Revisited

MYTH: Only athletes or exercisers with serious mental problems need a sport or exercise psychologist.

Any athlete or person wanting to become more physically active can benefit from the services of a qualified sport and exercise psychology specialist. First, specialists design the majority of interventions to prepare athletes to manage the demands of training and competition and to enhance their well-being. Athletes can learn to develop and apply effective psychological skills to manage stress, focus attention, and augment motivation. These are discussed in greater detail in the chapters on motivation (Chapter 4), anxiety (Chapter 5), stress and coping (Chapter 6), and sport psychology interventions (Chapter 14). In addition, specialists can teach coaches how to develop more effective training environments (see Chapters 9 and 11). Second, there are many effective interventions that can help people adopt and maintain healthy levels of physical activity. These issues are discussed in more detail in the chapters on motivation (Chapter 4), exercise and mental health (Chapter 12), and physical activity interventions (Chapter 13).

MYTH: All sport psychology specialists work with elite athletes to enhance their performance.

This is a restrictive view of sport psychology. In Canada, the majority of sport psychology specialists work in universities and colleges, primarily as teachers and researchers. Others may work as independent consultants, in schools, in government, or in private clinical and counselling settings. Many of these professionals do provide services to athletes to facilitate performance and promote psychological growth and development. The athletes range from young to old, and the athletes perform at developmental to elite competitive levels. Furthermore, sport and exercise psychology specialists are increasingly working with people in other areas of physical activity, including physical fitness and rehabilitation.

Review Questions

1. What are the three major roles of a sport and exercise psychology specialist? Are different types of training needed for the three roles?
2. What is positive psychology, and how is it relevant to the study and practice of sport and exercise psychology?
3. What are the differences between a sport and exercise psychology specialist trained in sport sciences and one trained in clinical or counselling psychology?
4. Is a counselling psychologist able to work with athletes to provide performance enhancement strategies? What standards of conduct guide such decisions?
5. How would the principles of Integrity in Relationships and Respect for the Dignity of Persons help guide your decision to reveal information about an athlete's psychological state to a coach who demands it?

6. What are three major sport and exercise psychology organizations around the world? What is the major Canadian organization that promotes sport and exercise psychology research?
7. What is knowledge translation, and why is it important for the advancement of sport and exercise psychology?

Suggested Reading

Feltz, D. L., & Kontos, A. P. (2002). *The nature of sport psychology. In T. Horn (Ed.), Advances in sport psychology* (2nd ed., pp. 3–19). Champaign, IL: Human Kinetics.

Moore, Z. E. (2003). Ethical dilemmas in sport psychology: Discussion and recommendations for practice. *Professional Psychology: Research & Practice, 34*, 601–610.

Weiss, M. R. (2008). "Riding the wave": Transforming sport and exercise psychology within an interdisciplinary vision. *Quest, 60*, 63–84.

References

Albinson, J. G., & Bull, S. J. (1988). *The mental game plan: A training program for all sports*. London, ON: Spodym.

Alderman, R. (1974). *Psychological behaviour in sport*. Toronto, ON: W. B. Saunders.

Anshel, M. H. (2003). *Sport psychology: From theory to practice* (4th ed.). San Francisco: Benjamin Cummings.

Baldwin, M. K., & Courneya, K. S. (1997). Exercise and self-esteem in breast cancer survivors: An application of the Exercise and Self-Esteem Model. *The Journal of Sport and Exercise Psychology, 19*, 347–359.

Butt, D. S. (1976). *Psychology of sport: The behavior, motivation, personality and performance of athletes*. New York: Van Nostrand Reinhold.

Carron, A. V. (1980). *Social psychology of sport*. Ithaca, NY: Mouvement.

Carron, A. V., & Hausenblas, H. A. (1998). *Group dynamics in sport*. Morgantown, WV: Fitness Information Technology.

Carron, A. V., Hausenblas, H. A., & Estabrooks, P. A. (2003). *The psychology of physical activity*. St Louis, MO: McGraw-Hill.

Cox, R. H. (1998). *Sport psychology: Concepts and applications* (4th ed.). Boston: McGraw-Hill.

Crocker, P.R.E. (2007). *Sport psychology. A Canadian perspective*. Toronto, ON: Pearson Education Canada.

Feltz, D. L., & Kontos, A. P. (2002). The nature of sport psychology. In T. Horn (Ed.), *Advances in sport psychology* (2nd ed., pp. 3–19). Champaign, IL: Human Kinetics.

Gill, D. (2000). *Psychological dynamics of sport and exercise* (2nd ed.). Champaign, IL: Human Kinetics.

Gould, D., & Pick, S. (1995). Sport psychology: The Griffith era, 1920–1940. *The Sport Psychologist, 9*, 391–405.

Griffith, C. R. (1926). *The psychology of coaching*. New York: Scribner's.

Griffith, C. R. (1928). *Psychology and athletics*. New York: Scribner's.

Jackson, S. (1992). Athletes in flow: A qualitative investigation of flow states in elite figure skaters. *Journal of Applied Sport Psychology, 4*, 161–180.

Latimer, A. E., Martin Ginis, K. A., Hicks, A. L., & McCartney, N. (2004). An examination of mechanisms of exercise-induced change in pain and physical and psychological well-being among people with spinal cord injury. *Journal of Rehabilitation Research and Development, 41*, 643–652.

Leith, L. M. (1998). *Exercising your way to better mental health: Combat stress, fight depression and improve your overall mood and self-concept with these simple exercises*. Morgantown, WV: Fitness Information Technology.

Lidor, R., Morris, T., Bardaxoglou, N., & Becker, B. (2001). *The world sport psychology sourcebook* (3rd ed.). Morgantown, WV: Fitness Information Technology.

Martin, G. L. (2003). *Sport psychology: Practical guidelines from behavior analysis*. Winnipeg, MB: Sport Science Press.

Martin, G. L., & Hrycaiko, D. (1983). *Behavior modification and coaching: Principles, procedures, and research*. Springfield, IL: C. C. Thomas.

Moore, Z. E. (2003). Ethical dilemmas in sport psychology: Discussion and recommendations for practice. *Professional Psychology: Research & Practice*, *34*, 601–610.

Ogilvie, B. C., & Tutko, T. A. (1966). *Problem athletes and how to handle them*. London, UK: Pelham Books.

Orlick, T. (1980). *In pursuit of excellence*. Champaign, IL: Human Kinetics.

Orlick, T. (1986). *Psyching for sport: Mental training for athletes*. Champaign, IL: Leisure Press.

Orlick, T., & Botterill, C. (1975). *Every kid can win*. Chicago, IL: Nelson-Hall.

Petitpas, A. J. (1996). Counseling interventions in applied sport psychology. In J. L. Van Raalte, & B. W. Brewer (Eds.), *Exploring sport and exercise psychology* (pp. 189–204). Washington, DC: American Psychological Association.

Sabiston, C. M., McDonough, M. H., & Crocker, P. R. E. (2007). Psycho-social experiences of breast cancer survivors involved in a dragon boat program: Exploring links to positive psychological growth. *Journal of Sport & Exercise Psychology*, *29*, 419–438.

Seligman, M. E. P. (2002). *Authentic happiness*. New York: Free Press.

Seligman, M. E. P., & Csikszentmihalyi, M. (2000). Positive psychology: An introduction. *American Psychologist*, *55*, 5–14.

Silva, J. M. (2002). The evolution of sport psychology. In J. M. Silva, & D. E. Stevens (Eds.), *Psychological foundation of sport*. Toronto, ON: Allyn and Bacon.

Vealey, R. S. (2006). Smock and jocks outside the box: The paradigmatic evolution of sport and exercise psychology. *Quest*, *58*, 128–159.

Weinberg, R., & Gould, D. (2003). *Foundations of sport and exercise psychology* (3rd ed.). Champaign, IL: Human Kinetics.

Weiss, M. R. (2008). "Riding the wave": Transforming sport and exercise psychology within an interdisciplinary vision. *Quest*, *60*, 63–84.

Whelan, J. P., Meyers, A. W., & Elkin, T. D. (2002). Ethics in sport and exercise psychology. In J. L. Van Raalte (Ed.), *Exploring sport and exercise psychology* (2nd ed., pp. 503–523). Washington, DC: American Psychological Association.

Chapter 2

Research Perspectives in Sport and Exercise Psychology

Philip M. Wilson

Enrique García Bengoechea

Chapter Objectives

After reading this chapter, you should be able to do the following:

1 Differentiate scientific research from other sources of knowledge.

2 Apply the basic terms and concepts of the research process.

3 Discuss the importance of ethics in scientific research.

4 Explain the role of measurement in the research process.

5 Explain the importance of sampling and design in sport and exercise psychology research.

6 Discuss the utility of qualitative inquiry in sport and exercise psychology research.

---

*We would like to acknowledge the mentorship of Dr. W. Todd Rogers (Professor, Centre for Research in Applied Measurement and Evaluation, University of Alberta) and Dr. Marcel Bouffard (Professor, Faculty of Physical Education and Recreation, University of Alberta). Together, they shaped our own interests in research during our sojourns in Edmonton. Both of them bring personal meaning for us to Sir Isaac Newton's 1676 dictum, "If I have seen a little further, it is by standing on the shoulders of giants."

Coach Etheridge is the director of Niagara Pitch, a high-performance basketball team that provides a forum for young players in the Niagara region to develop their athletic abilities. In her role of overseeing athletes in the Niagara region, Coach Etheridge has covered all aspects of player development from the grassroots to the professional levels. During her time in charge, Coach Etheridge has watched some of the finest basketball players emerge from the region and go on to participate in the Olympic Games and World Cup finals. Despite her enthusiasm for player development, Coach Etheridge is frustrated by the poor training habits exhibited by some of her most talented players, who exemplify what she calls a "practice player" mentality to training for basketball.

Considering her current team roster, Coach Etheridge ponders why some players give maximum effort during every training session while others seem to be simply going through the motions in a largely unmotivated fashion. Although Coach Etheridge is not a scientist, she has attempted to answer some of her questions by monitoring players' habits during practice (using daily performance diaries) and by completing interviews with her players following game-tape analyses of previous matches.

Coach Etheridge and her staff frequently review each player's data and use it in an attempt to motivate better training habits during their competitive season and for off-season training. Based on her own playing experiences, Coach Etheridge is often convinced that the difference between players is motivational in nature and that some players just "want it" more than others, which drives them to excel in all aspects of sport preparation and ultimately perform at a higher and more consistent level. Several of her coaching staff, however, believe that motivation can be affected by coaching and training methods.

The aforementioned scenario might sound familiar to any youth sport coach or the parent of a gifted young athlete. It is common for coaches to have questions regarding the performance of their players and to seek different (sometimes creative and inventive) ways of collecting evidence that allows the coaching staff to answer those questions. Such answers will often lead to changes in player preparation, training regimens, coach–athlete interactions, or, in some instances, team selection. In other words, the process of acquiring information (or data) that answers relevant questions often serves as the springboard that initiates coaching decisions and roster changes. Sometimes the changes produce the desired effects, but on occasion the changes have undesired consequences on player performances. Based on Coach Etheridge's experiences, this process of seeking answers to important questions will invariably lead the coaching staff to undertake more research regarding player preparation.

The Coach Etheridge scenario depicts the acquisition of knowledge through a sequence of events that is known as the research process. The process of conducting research is considered by many to be the cornerstone of scientific inquiry. This chapter will highlight factors about sport and exercise psychology research that are worth considering. The scenario depicted by Coach Etheridge's predicament raises a number of interesting questions. For example, how will the coach measure training performance? What would be the best way to test Coach Etheridge's hunch that motivation is the major influence on training performance?

Could other factors (e.g., illness, family problems, team chemistry, weather) influence the players' daily training performances? Can the findings derived from Coach Etheridge's observations of her own players be applied to other basketball teams or other sports with players of similar age and gender? Can these observations be applied in other physical activity settings? In this chapter, we will provide you with some guidelines to address these and other questions that contribute to the research process. To gain a greater appreciation for this dynamic area, we will attempt to distinguish scientific research from other forms of knowledge acquisition after examining some pervasive myths about scientific research in sport and exercise psychology.

Common Myths about Research in Sport and Exercise Psychology

MYTH: Research is defined by the goals of an activity or undertaking.

MYTH: Experimentation is the only way to advance sport and exercise psychology research.

MYTH: Qualitative research methods are not as rigorous as quantitative research methods.

INTRODUCTION

International competitions have reinforced the dominant role of science in high-performance sport. Consider a selection of events from the 2008 Summer and 2006 Winter Olympic Games. Swimmers competed against one another wearing aerodynamically efficient bodysuits. Cyclists hurtled around an oval-shaped track wearing drag-reducing helmets. Hockey players used sticks made from various high-tech materials to gain power on their shots. In addition to using these legitimate products of scientific knowledge, some athletes adopt a less scrupulous approach and use banned substances, such as erythropoietin, anabolic steroids, and ephedrine, for performance enhancement. These examples imply that sport and science have become inextricably linked at higher levels of competition. In conjunction with this emphasis on the use of science in high-performance sport, it seems clear from even a cursory glance at the health and fitness industry that science features prominently in many endeavours. Consider for a moment the advances in athletic footwear that permit greater flexibility in movement, the development of fitness clothing that reduces (or retains) body heat and/or promotes accelerated cooling to offset premature exhaustion, and the range of mechanical devices used to monitor the body's internal systems, including heart rate. These examples underscore the prominent role that science plays in our society in the realms of competitive sport and health promotion through regular exercise.

The application of scientific principles to the study of sport performance and exercise participation is hardly novel in applied health sciences. However, the emphasis on promoting healthy levels of physical activity in all Canadians illustrates the importance of scientific research since it provides the evidence required to implement and sustain health promotion efforts. Although some might argue that science and research have no place in health-promotion initiatives, others contend that the current emphasis on evidence-based practice makes scientific research an important component of contemporary sport and exercise psychology (Gill, 1997).

SCIENCE AND SCIENTIFIC RESEARCH

The notion of science is often associated with the stereotypical image of a scientist as a nerdy, middle-aged, spectacled person running around a laboratory with test tubes emitting various gases, screaming "Eureka!" ("I've found it!"). Considerable debate exists surrounding the notions of science and scientific inquiry (Bouffard, 1997); however, **science** can be defined as a dynamic yet imperfect process of knowledge accumulation through research (Kerlinger, 1979). In a perfect world, such research endeavours would fall nicely into one of two distinct categories that are often used to classify research in sport and exercise psychology (Baumgartner, Strong, & Hensley, 2002).

The first category is **basic research**. It deals with testing fundamental mechanisms that produce conditions or events, without undue concern for the practical utility of such mechanisms. Conversely, **applied research** focuses on generating solutions to immediate problems irrespective of mechanistic details that form the focus of basic research. Although some researchers have found it useful to dichotomize research into these two camps, we suspect that the majority of sport and exercise psychology research falls somewhere between these two extremes. Perhaps an example of basic research will help illustrate this point. Consider a sport psychologist who is interested in determining the utility of a psychological skills training intervention (PSTI) with a university hockey team. The sport psychologist could set up a variety of motor performance tasks in a controlled laboratory setting, provide half the athletes with the PSTI and the other half with a placebo (a treatment with no known effect on the motor performance tasks), and then observe differences in the athletes' performance on the motor tasks. Although it would be illuminating to find that the intervention group outperformed the placebo group on the motor tasks, the finding may be useless unless those differences translate into variation in on-ice performance. Although the study is a useful (albeit hypothetical) example of basic research, it seems likely that the majority of sport and exercise psychology issues (e.g., determining what factors account for persistence behaviour) call for more practical endpoints. Therefore, we believe it is useful to think about basic and applied research as two ends of a continuum, with most research falling between these two points.

Scientific approaches to knowledge acquisition differ from other sources of information that athletes, coaches, and personal trainers could easily resort to in the pursuit of optimizing performance or sustaining involvement in exercise. These alternative sources of knowledge include intuition, tradition, authorities, and logic (Pelham & Blanton, 2003). **Intuition** refers to the development of an implicit understanding of the phenomena of interest in the absence of formal training. **Tradition** concerns knowledge that is historically rooted, with no emphasis on current information. **Authorities** are experts whose opinions are considered the final word in knowledge acquisition (i.e., "What the

Most sport and exercise psychology research falls between the extreme categories of basic and applied research.

Photograph by Richard Lam, courtesy of University of British Columbia Athletics.

expert says, goes!"). Finally, **logic** involves knowledge generated through the application of formal rules of reasoning to the problem in question. Rules of logic could be derived inductively (moving from a specific observation to a general principle) or deductively (moving from a general principle to a specific observation) depending on how logic is applied to the problem.

REFLECTIONS 2.1

Alex Bauman's record in major international competitions would make him (in most people's estimation) an expert coach. During his illustrious swimming career, Bauman held the world record in the 200 m and 400 m individual medley events, and won two Olympic gold medals in 1984, along with a silver and a bronze medal in the World Championships in 1986. Bauman was inducted into Canada's Sports Hall of Fame in 1987. What sources of knowledge do you think he will rely on most when making (1) team selection decisions and (2) tactical changes? Can you provide two examples for intuition, tradition, authority, and logic that Bauman may use when making selection or tactical decisions during his coaching career?

In contrast to these approaches, most sport and exercise psychology researchers interested in evidence-based knowledge advocate using an approach commonly referred to as the **scientific method**. The scientific method is an omnibus term that includes a series of steps that are executed sequentially to generate knowledge (Baumgartner et al., 2002); however, experts disagree on the level of objectivity and the total number of steps involved in the scientific method. Nevertheless, it is generally accepted that this approach is an attempt to find the best solutions to solvable questions (e.g., "What's the effect of 30 minutes of aerobic exercise performed three times/week on children's body fat distribution?" as opposed to "Are humans inherently good or evil?"). Despite a lack of consensus about the components of this approach, it is important to recognize that the scientific method is guided by the sequential nature of research unfolding over time rather than governed by dogmatic adherence to a formalized set of prohibitive steps. Common steps in the scientific method often include identification of a research problem, generation of a hypothesis, collection and analysis of data, and integration of conclusions with directions for additional study (Okasha, 2002).

The majority of researchers in sport and exercise psychology attempt to describe, predict, or explain phenomena of interest. **Descriptive research** provides an in-depth portrayal of a phenomenon of interest, either in general or for specific participant groups. A useful example of descriptive research in sport psychology is a study that describes athletes' use of imagery in sport (Munroe, Giacobbi, Hall, & Weinberg, 2000). In contrast to descriptive research, **predictive research** is concerned with establishing directional relationships among phenomena of interest. For example, Crocker and colleagues examined the relationship between changes in physical self-perceptions and health-related behaviours in adolescent girls over a three-year period (Crocker, Sabiston, Kowalski, McDonough, & Kowalski, 2006). The results suggested that specific physical self-perceptions in young women were linked with physical activity, dietary restraint, and emotions about the body.

Although descriptive and predictive studies are useful, the overall goal of most scientific research is explanation. Research to explain phenomena moves beyond mere description and prediction and includes arguments for why particular observations occurred. Typically, scientists couch their research within a **theory**. In scientific inquiry, a theory is an interconnected set of concepts that explains how and why discrete phenomena work together (Okasha, 2002). For example, a study by Wilson and colleagues provides a good example of exercise psychology research that embraces theory testing in an attempt to explain participation in regular exercise and feelings of physical self-worth (Wilson, Rodgers, Loitz, & Scime, 2006). In this study, the researchers tested propositions from self-determination theory (Deci & Ryan, 1985) with data collected from regular exercisers to explain persistence behaviours and feelings of adequacy about the physical self. Consistent with propositions in self-determination theory, the researchers noted that exercise behaviour and positive physical self-perceptions were explained by motives for behavioural participation that were more self-determined in nature. This motivation theory is described in more detail in Chapter 4.

Basic Research Terminology

Consider for a moment the following conversation between two old friends:

Bruce: "Yeah. Since my injury I prefer to adopt a less arduous training regimen and usually complete three sets of 10–13 reps at 40%–55% of my 1RM."

Rachel: "Really? I prefer to work through a series of ballistic exercises stressing antagonistic muscle groups using a high-sets (4–6) low-reps (2–4) approach at 80% of my 1RM."

We suspect that such terms as *sets*, *reps*, *1RM*, *ballistic exercises*, and *antagonistic* may seem foreign to some of you depending on your familiarity with resistance training. Consistent with other occupations and cultures, scientific research has a unique vocabulary that forms a common language, allowing scholars to converse (Trochim, 2001). Some terms and concepts common to scientific research require our attention before we proceed to more advanced topics in the research process.

One term commonly used by members of the research community is **variable**. A variable is any attribute or characteristic that can change, or vary, thereby taking on more than one value. In sport and exercise psychology research, variables could include such things as motivation, confidence, arousal, anxiety, and performance. In the context of research, variables can generally be identified as one of two types. The first is the **independent variable**, which is the manipulated variable explaining (or causing) the study outcomes. In contrast, the **dependent variable** is the phenomenon of interest that is expected to change as a result of manipulating the independent variable.

Perhaps an example from a study by Elston and Martin-Ginis (2004) will clarify the distinction between independent and dependent variables. The researchers compared the effects of two different goal-setting conditions (independent variable) on participants' self-efficacy to perform a strength exercise (dependent variable). In one condition, participants set their own goals (the experimental group); in the other condition, the investigators assigned goals to each participant (the comparison group). They noted that the experimental group reported higher levels of self-efficacy post-intervention than the comparison group. However, is it possible that other variables could influence self-efficacy to perform strength-related tasks? The answer is yes. Such factors might conceivably include past experiences with exercise activities designed to increase physical strength, age, gender, and current state of physical fitness, to name a few. Researchers refer to such factors as **extraneous variables** (or confounding variables). An extraneous variable is any variable other than the independent variable that could influence the dependent variable in a research study.

REFLECTIONS 2.2

Consider for a moment your own physical activity experiences. What extraneous variables other than goal setting do you think could influence your confidence to perform a strength-related task?

A second term commonly found in the research literature is **nomothetic**, which concerns attempts to isolate rules or observations that pertain to most cases on most occasions or in most contexts (Bouffard, 1997). For example, a recent study by Janssen and associates examined the unique influences of physical activity and obesity on health complaints, with the intent of discovering a general pattern of relationships that could be applied on most occasions to the majority of Canadian youth (Janssen, Katzmarzyk, Boyce, & Pickett, 2004). By contrast, the term **idiographic** is used when research concerns a special or unique case that does not apply to most people on the majority of occasions. Sport psychologists have become interested in studying career termination as it pertains to movement out of elite sport. For example, a study by Lotysz and Short (2004), using an autobiographical account, examines the experiences of a former professional athlete who had his career terminated prematurely because of complications associated with a knee injury. The insights into this athlete's experiences would be individual in nature and represent information derived from a single person about one incident in his career.

The third term commonly used in research is **hypothesis**. A hypothesis is an educated guess regarding the outcome of a research study (Trochim, 2001). Although some variation exists in the use of the word *hypothesis*, the most common application pertains to the testing of a hypothesis using statistics. In a study, the **null hypothesis** indicates that there is no relationship between the variables under study or that there is no difference anticipated between the groups receiving the different conditions of the independent variable. In contrast, the **alternative (or research) hypothesis** is the researchers' educated guess regarding what they expect to find when conducting the study. A study of prostate cancer survivors may help clarify the difference between these hypotheses. In this study, the authors were interested in determining if a 12-week structured exercise program would improve fitness parameters and quality of life in men living with prostate cancer (Culos-Reed, Robinson, Lau, O'Connor, & Keats, 2007). The null hypothesis stated that an individual's exercise habits had no effect on fitness or quality of life variables, whereas the alternative hypothesis stated that exercise participation would alter physical fitness and quality of life in prostate cancer survivors.

A fourth term (and one of the most contentious in science) often used in the research methods literature is **causal**. This word implies a relationship between the independent and dependent variables. It refers to identifying agents that, when manipulated, bring about changes in the dependent variables of interest (Trochim, 2001). Generally, three conditions are necessary before researchers can make a causal inference in scientific research. First, the proposed cause (independent variable) must be correlated with the observed effect (dependent variable). This condition is sometimes called *systematic covariation*. Second, the proposed cause must precede the effect, or there must be evidence of what methodologists refer to as *temporal precedence*. Finally, all other possible extraneous variables must be systematically ruled out as the causal mechanism.

Here is a hypothetical case to serve as an example in determining causation. Suppose Dr. Reed, a well-known sport psychologist in the Niagara region, is interested in helping Coach Etheridge improve her squad's performances in major tournaments. Considering her options carefully, Dr. Reed implements a goal-setting program designed specifically to enhance team performance, which will be measured by the team's win–loss record obtained from competitive matches during the regular season. This seems like a credible idea given the large volume of sport psychology literature that suggests goal setting can have a positive effect on sport performance (Burton, Naylor, & Holliday, 2000). At the end of the competitive season, Dr. Reed compares the performances of Coach Etheridge's team with those of another basketball team in the same league that did not get the intervention but is similar in terms of both age and gender. Coach Etheridge's team outperformed the comparison group on all dependent variables examined in Dr. Reed's study. Confidently, she concludes that the goal-setting intervention caused the observed differences in the teams' performances. But, wait just a minute! Did Dr. Reed satisfy all of the conditions needed to make a causal inference? Let us take a closer look at what happened in her study.

The first condition of causation is that a relationship exists between the proposed cause and the effect. A relationship is often established by examining the correlation between scores on two or more sets of variables (Vogt, 2005). This is perhaps the easiest of the conditions to satisfy, and some literature does suggest that goal setting can influence sport performance (Burton et al., 2000). Understanding this aspect of the cause–effect debate, Dr. Reed collected data that confirmed through a manipulation check that the intervention group (Coach Etheridge's team) set goals that had a positive relationship with team performance, as indexed by the ratio of games won to lost over the season.

An effective coaching style can enhance athletes' enjoyment of sport. This is determined by examining the covariation between scores on coaching style measures and scores on athlete enjoyment scales.

Photograph © Photodisc/Getty Images.

The second condition is that the presumed cause (independent variable) precedes the observation of the effect (dependent variable). Given that Dr. Reed introduced the goal-setting intervention during the team's pre-season training camp and then monitored their performances across the entire season, it does seem reasonable to claim that the proposed cause did precede the effect. Moreover, it seems reasonable to suggest that the first two conditions of causation have been satisfied within Dr. Reed's study.

Is the third condition of causation satisfied? This condition requires that all other possible causal factors be systematically ruled out. Although the goal-setting sport-performance hypothesis seems tenable at first glance, extraneous variables, including psychological characteristics (e.g., personality, confidence, motivation, cohesion) and contextual considerations (e.g., friendship networks, luck, weather, league schedule), may have contributed to the changes in the team's performance. Given that we cannot typically rule out the influence of extraneous variables in a single study, it would be wise to be cautious about accepting the causal inferences derived from Dr. Reed's study prior to its replication and extension in future research.

Ethical Approval for Sport and Exercise Psychology Research

As in other areas of research, most sport and exercise psychology researchers require approval from an administrative body prior to initiating data collection with humans or animals. In Canada, the relevant administrative body is a university-based **research ethics board (REB)**. The REB ensures that research is conducted in a manner that protects the

Table 2.1 Types of Research and Ethical Review Requirements

Research Requiring Ethical Review	Sport/Exercise Psychology Examples
Any research involving human participants	Intervention studies examining the effects of imagery on sport performance
	Non-experimental studies examining the association between psychological need satisfaction and well-being
Any research using biophysical specimens or human remains	Tracking studies examining the relationship between mood disturbances and performance-enhancing drugs in athletes
	Non-experimental studies testing relationship between physique anxiety and salivary cortisol
Research Not Requiring Ethical Review	**Sport/Exercise Psychology Examples**
Studies using data that are available exclusively in the public domain	Research testing the home-venue advantages in professional sport teams using archival data
	Research exploring the content of images depicted in popular fitness magazines to determine key messages portrayed by the media

integrity and safety of the participants and the researchers. However, does all research require REB approval? The answer is that it depends on whether the activity undertaken meets the criteria for exemption outlined in the *Tri-Council Policy Statement: Ethical Conduct for Research Involving Humans* developed by the Interagency Advisory Panel on Research Ethics. Table 2.1 contains a summary of research that either does or does not require REB approval.

Assuming that the majority of sport and exercise psychology research involves collecting data directly from sport or exercise participants, it seems reasonable to suggest that most sport and exercise psychologists will need to familiarize themselves with REB requirements for ethical review prior to undertaking any research. The *Tri-Council Policy Statement* highlights all aspects of the research process that a sport and exercise psychologist should attend to, and it amalgamates information from key ethical documents that guide decision making in scientific research (www.pre.ethics.gc.ca/english/policystatement/policystatement.cfm). Three broad issues emanating from this report are central to good ethical conduct in scientific research and warrant careful consideration for sport and exercise psychology research.

The first issue is that of respecting participants, and it concerns the anonymity and confidentiality of participant data. **Anonymity** refers to the inability to identify a participant involved in a research project, whereas **confidentiality** refers to the retention of all participant data in confidence so that an individual's data are not identifiable by others. It is appropriate in scientific research to make participants aware of the degree to which their anonymity will be compromised as a result of participating in a research project. Participants are fully informed of their rights and responsibilities during the research project and must agree to participate. This process is referred to as **informed consent**, and it indicates that the research participants have been informed of what their participation will entail and how the data provided will be treated during the research project. Students interested in finding out more about key features of the informed consent process could consult the Interagency Advisory Panel on Research Ethics (www.pre.ethics.gc.ca).

Does the process of respecting participants raise concerns for sport and exercise psychology research? Consider for a moment a hypothetical publication, titled *Wrestling with the Psychology of Elite Female Performance: An Olympian's Perspective*, in which a sport psychologist describes the results of an interview with a female athlete who won Canada's first Olympic gold medal in wrestling. Though the name of the athlete is not disclosed, sufficient information is provided to allow the reader to identify the athlete, thereby breaching confidentiality, assuming that the interviewee was assured of confidentiality in the informed consent process. Respecting the rights and privileges of all participants is the responsibility of the researcher and is the hallmark of good ethical practice in research.

The second major ethical issue is **beneficence**, which concerns the degree to which the proposed research will maximize the potential benefits while minimizing the possible harm to the research participants. This principle does not guarantee that participants face no risk, given that even non-invasive research carries risks such as disclosure of personal information or heightened emotions. This principle does contend that it is the responsibility of the researcher to ensure that the benefits of the study (either to the participant directly or to the scientific community at large) come with the assumption of justifiable risk and thereby outweigh the costs of the research.

The third key ethical issue associated with scientific research is concerned with the notion of **justice** that pertains directly to the selection of participants for research. Central to this idea of justice is the notion that participants in a research study should be the ones who derive the benefits from the results of the study. For example, consider a scenario in which a sport psychologist is interested in understanding the effects of Canada's coaching education program on moral development in youth-sport participants. Imagine that the sport psychologist is housed in a West Coast university but is able (through former connections in his home province) to collect all of the data from Wolfville, Nova Scotia. If all of the participants were active in youth-sport programs in Wolfville but the applications of the research were to be promoted only on the West Coast, then the principle of justice is likely violated given that the participants providing the data will never reap the benefits of any changes made to the coaching education program.

REFLECTIONS 2.3

Think back to a research study that you have read about in the media. What information do you think the research team would have needed to provide prior to enrolling participants in the study? What benefits and risks do you think would be associated with participation in the study? In what way would the results of this study benefit other people beyond the sample under study?

MEASUREMENT IN THE RESEARCH PROCESS

The practice of measurement in sport and exercise psychology research is considered particularly difficult given that most of the variables are invisible to the naked eye. What do we mean by this? Consider for a moment the major variables discussed in other chapters of this book. Variables such as arousal, anxiety, confidence, motivation, personality, and stress are all important psychological concepts that are not observed directly. To illustrate this fact, consider the concept of gravity for a moment. Many of you may be wondering what gravity has to do with the variables of interest to a sport and exercise psychologist. Well, can you actually see gravity? Moreover, could you show your friends gravity if we asked you to? Our guess is that you might throw a pen into the air and say, "Look! Gravity!" But if you stop and think about it, you are not seeing gravity but merely observing what we believe to be gravity's effect on the pen when it is pulled back to the Earth. The key point to keep in mind here is quite simple: Most of the things we are interested in measuring in sport and exercise psychology are not much different from other variables in the sense that they cannot be directly observed with our senses. Nevertheless, this does not mean that we cannot measure them; it only means that we have to take some leaps of faith (scientists often call these assumptions) when measuring variables in research.

Levels of Measurement

Irrespective of the nature of the research question, measurement issues will arise during any research project that attempts to quantify variables. In the classic sense, **measurement** refers to the process of assigning numbers to variables according to specific rules (Stevens, 1946). **Levels of measurement** represent different ways of assigning numbers to variables. The most rudimentary level of measurement is referred to as **nominal**. When numbers are assigned to variables in a nominal fashion, they represent measurement only as labels. In other words, the number 15 assigned to Kara Lang (Canada's women's national soccer team) does not mean that she is three times better than number 5, Andrea Neil. The numbers simply represent a unique label used to identify a soccer player.

The next level of measurement is termed **ordinal** and reflects the assignment of numbers in such a fashion that the variable can be ranked. An example is the assignment of medals representing first, second, and third places on the Olympic medal podium. The distance between the gold and silver medal winners does not have to be equivalent to the distance between the silver and bronze medal winners. The numbers simply reflect the order in which the athletes finished.

The third level of measurement is called **interval** and reflects the assignment of numbers to variables so that the distances between consecutive numbers are equal. For example, daily temperature records throughout events, such as the World Cup, represent interval level measurement. The distance from 25°C to 30°C is the same as from 30°C to 35°C.

The final and most useful level of measurement is **ratio** and concerns the assignment of numbers in such a manner that a true zero exists, representing a complete absence of the variable under study. In this case, a ratio (or fraction) can be constructed. One example of ratio level measurement in exercise psychology is the number of training sessions attended by an individual enrolled in a program with a personal trainer as a measure of adherence. If the individual attends none of the prescribed sessions, then he or she has a complete absence of the variable measuring adherence.

REFLECTIONS 2.4

Keeping in mind the levels of measurement outlined in the previous section, consider some of the variables involved in sports, exercise, or physical activity (e.g., speed, strength, goals, points, motivation, confidence, arousal, anxiety, reps, sets). How is each variable typically measured? What level of measurement is represented by each variable?

Basic Measurement Concepts

The subject of measurement is vast and covers a broad spectrum of issues within several disciplines, most notably the field of **psychometrics**, which is concerned with the assessment of psychological variables using numbers. There are two concepts associated with measurement of variables that warrant consideration: reliability and validity. These concepts form the cornerstone of sound measurement practice in research. Although they will be presented separately in the following sections, these concepts are inextricably linked in research. Our discussion of these concepts will be succinct, so the interested student is directed to the Web Center for Social Research Methods for further insights (www.socialresearchmethods.net).

Reliability **Reliability** concerns the consistency or stability of scores derived from single or multiple tests or measurement procedures (Vogt, 2005). Along these lines, reliability is concerned with the degree of precision inherent in a particular score or set of scores. But what does it really mean for a score on a test to be considered reliable? Perhaps an example of the model that scientists have traditionally used to estimate reliability will help address this question.

The classic approach to estimating reliability is known as the true score model since reliability is concerned with knowing how precisely we can measure a person's true score on a variable of interest. According to the true score model, every **observed score** is composed of two components that provide a numerical index of test-score reliability. The observed score is the actual numerical value derived from the test (i.e., the participant's data). The observed score is composed of the person's **true score** (actual ability) on the variable of interest plus some **error of measurement**, which is inadvertently introduced by the act of measuring a variable (see Figure 2.1).

Let us consider an example that might enhance your understanding of the classical true score model. Imagine a personal trainer is interested in monitoring clients' responses to training and decides to use blood pressure as a key variable. After each training session, the personal trainer measures the client's blood pressure to determine the consistency of each person's response to the demands of training. The trainer has 20 clients under his guidance

Figure 2.1 Classical true score model of reliability

Observed Score = True Score + Measurement Error

who all complete 10 training sessions, resulting in a total of 200 blood pressure recordings. These are the observed scores. Think about the factors that could influence the accuracy of each blood pressure measurement. Scores are likely to be influenced by the auditory ability and experience of the person taking the blood pressure readings and by environmental noise. Participant non-compliance, improper use of the sphygmomanometer, and physiological nuances of the exerciser might also influence the precision with which the each client's blood pressure is measured. This means that each blood pressure value is an observed score that is composed of the exerciser's true blood pressure value plus some measurement error.

Validity The second concept that forms the cornerstone of sound measurement practice is validity. Whereas reliability is concerned with the accuracy or precision inherent in scores used to measure a variable, **validity** is concerned with meaningfulness of the inferences that can be drawn from the numbers once they have been generated (Messick, 1995). Put slightly differently, validity refers to the extent to which test scores, when interpreted, serve their intended function. Consider the simple example of height (measured in metres) and weight (measured in kilograms). The instrument used to measure body weight (a scale) could produce reliable scores. Would those scores be useful in determining how tall a person is at the time of data collection? They would not be useful in that way because scores representing a person's weight were never intended to be interpreted as an index of a person's height. Although this may seem straightforward, validity is one of the most controversial topics in applied measurement and evaluation research today (Downing, 2003; Messick, 1995). Let us look at some sources of validity information used in sport and exercise psychology research.

Evidence of validity has traditionally been collected from multiple sources in the sport and exercise psychology literature (see Figure 2.2). One source is referred to as **content validity**, which assesses the degree to which test items (e.g., survey questions) are relevant to, and fully represent, the focal variable of interest. Content validity is usually assessed by expert review (Dunn, Bouffard, & Rogers, 1999). Another source of validity evidence is known as **criterion validity**, which assesses the degree to which test scores (e.g., responses to the Psychological Need Satisfaction in Exercise scale) are associated with a criterion of interest (e.g., indices of well-being, such as depression and vitality). This can be accomplished by using an approach in which scores on the test in question are collected before the measurement of the criterion. For example, a test measuring aggressiveness (the test) is administered to hockey players and then aggressive actions (the criterion) are recorded for the next 10 weeks. In another approach, the sport and exercise psychologist collects data on the test and criterion variables at about the same time (Pedhazur & Schmelkin, 1991). For example, a survey (the test) assessing how much weekly physical activity people with spinal

Figure 2.2 Sources of data contributing to construct validity evidence

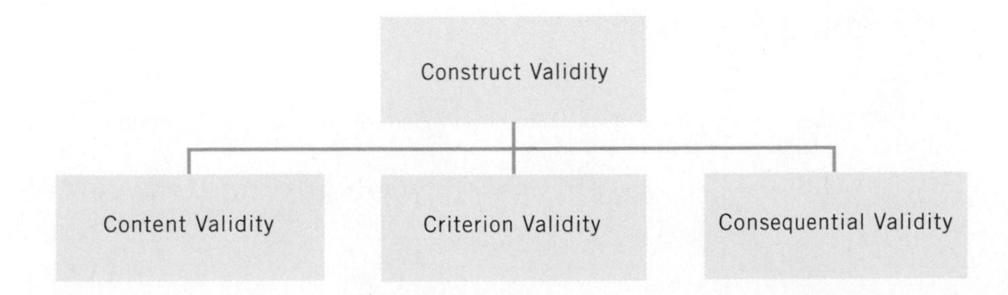

cord injuries do on a regular basis can be administered at the same time as a fitness test (the criterion). Yet another source of validity evidence is **consequential validity**, which involves the actual and potential consequences stemming from test score use (Messick, 1995). Although these sources of evidence can be examined individually, a contemporary view of construct validation contends that the combined sources of evidence reflect the overall validity of test scores (Messick, 1995).

SAMPLING IN SPORT AND EXERCISE PSYCHOLOGY RESEARCH

Sampling refers to the process of selecting observations from a population for the purposes of a research study (Babbie, 1995). We suspect that many of you are very familiar with the concept of sampling and engage in sampling procedures regularly. The media (including the Internet) are constantly polling people about their opinions. These polls include such topics as whether hockey fights should be banned, what form of fitness attire and equipment is most suitable for men and women, and whether funding should be increased for women's sports. Clearly, the intent of such informal opinion polls is to represent the opinions of the public. However, do the opinions of the sample represent the opinions of all people? This underscores the basic idea behind sampling, which involves studying a small yet representative portion of a larger group to answer research questions. However, attention to detail in sampling is critical! Research conclusions and policy decisions affecting many people are made according to findings generated from samples which may or may not represent larger populations. Let us look at some of the terms and concepts associated with sampling and then examine some of the common approaches to collecting samples used in sport and exercise psychology research.

The literature on sampling is comprised of a specialized vocabulary. A **sample** is a selection of observations from a larger population (Babbie, 1995). A **population** can be a **theoretical population** (all of the possible elements) or a **study population** (all of the accessible elements). An obvious question here is "Why sample from a population?" Well, there are several advantages to sampling—namely, cost reduction, speed, feasibility, and accuracy. Sampling allows researchers to make inferences about the study population as a whole without having to study the whole population. How then does the sport and exercise psychologist collect a sample to conduct research? Figure 2.3 provides a schematic overview of the sampling process for the purposes of research.

Figure 2.3 Overview of the sampling process

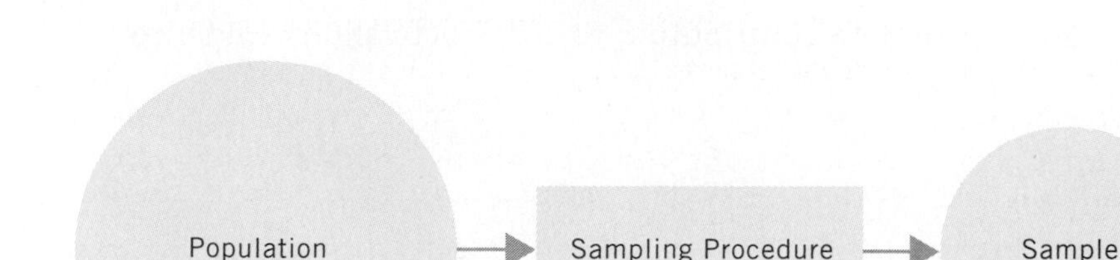

REFLECTIONS 2.5

Fitness magazines often use different images to advertise and promote various pieces of fitness equipment and training programs to the public. You want to identify the most common images used to advertise fitness equipment in Canada. Which elements would comprise your (1) theoretical population, (2) study population, and (3) sample? Could you provide a rationale for the composition of both populations and the sample and give the strengths and weaknesses associated with the approach you have decided to take?

RESEARCH DESIGN: A BLUEPRINT FOR ACTION

Design is an integral portion of the research process in sport and exercise psychology. A **research design** is a plan that the sport and exercise psychology researcher will follow to execute the study (Vogt, 2005). Perhaps a simple analogy will help solidify the importance of the research design. Imagine trying to assemble a piece of furniture (purchased from IKEA perhaps) without the instructions that provide you with an idea of which piece goes where, how they fit together, and what the finished product should look like. Well, the research design is similar to assembly instructions in the sense that it provides a blueprint for action that will guide the proposed study to completion.

Why is research design so important? The answer to this query lies at the heart of what the sport and exercise psychologist is interested in concluding once the study has been completed. Most sport and exercise psychology researchers are interested in understanding what causes events or behaviours to happen. Such questions as "Why did he choke under pressure?" or "Why does she exercise more frequently in January than in August?" are examples of questions that researchers seek to answer about the underlying cause of a person's behaviour. In the language of research design, **internal validity** concerns the extent to which the results of a study can be attributed to a treatment or intervention rather than to a design flaw (Vogt, 2005). If we stop for a moment to consider the types of questions most sport and exercise psychologists seek to answer, we would suspect that the vast majority of those questions are causal in nature. As such, the choice of research design is critically important because some designs provide better evidence for causation than others (Trochim, 2001).

Some designs are more prone to validity threats than others by virtue of their composition. An **internal validity threat** represents another plausible explanation for the study findings, irrespective of the treatment or independent variable manipulated in the study. In the language of research methods, internal validity threats are extraneous variables that represent plausible alternative explanations for changes in the dependent variable. Table 2.2 contains a summary of common threats to internal validity and suggests their implications for causal inference in the research process.

Let us take a closer look at the three major categories of research design proposed in the research methods literature, along with some sport and exercise psychology examples.

Table 2.2 Common Internal Validity Threats in Sport and Exercise Psychology Research

Threat	Nature of Threat
Maturation	Change in participants as a function of biological growth or development, or of fatigue
History	Influence of an unusual yet powerful external event
Selection	Non-random placement of participants into the groups for an intervention research study
Mortality	Departure of participants from studies that use repeated assessments of the dependent variables
Testing	Influence of earlier test scores on later scores when a test is administered on multiple occasions
Instrumentation	Alterations in the nature or reliability of the test used to measure the dependent variable
Regression to the mean	Natural tendency of extreme scores to "regress" closer to the typical population value during subsequent testing
Diffusion of treatment	Adoption of intervention-type responses by participants in the control group when they learn of the treatment provided to the intervention group
Resentful demoralization	Resentment by participants in the control group when they learn of the treatment administered to the intervention group but not to them

Randomized Experimental Designs

The first research designs that offer the strongest evidence for causality are known as randomized experimental designs. **Randomized experimental designs** have two hallmark characteristics that distinguish them from other designs (Trochim, 2001). The first is that they randomly assign study participants to different conditions (sometimes referred to as different levels of the independent variable). The second hallmark characteristic is the manipulation of the independent variable(s). Recall from our earlier discussion that the independent variable is the proposed causal agent inherent in the research project. Within the category of randomized experimental designs, a variety of approaches could be taken depending on resources, time, and available expertise.

What does a randomized experimental design look like in practice? A study conducted by Blanchard, Rodgers, Wilson, and Bell (2004) serves as a useful example of how such randomized experimental designs can be tailored to examine exercise psychology issues. Blanchard et al. examined the influence of two different training conditions on participants' feeling states while equating the total volume of work in the conditions. Participants were community residents who were randomly assigned to either a high-intensity, short-duration or low-intensity, long-duration supervised exercise program for 12 weeks. In essence, this study manipulated exercise training across multiple levels (intensity and duration). The study indicated that positive changes in feeling states were reported from pre-test to post-test in both experimental groups, after equating for total volume of work completed within each condition.

Quasi-experimental Designs

The second approach to designing research studies is known collectively as **quasi-experimental designs**. These designs attempt to unearth the cause of change in the dependent variables without randomly assigning participants to different conditions within the study (Trochim, 2001). Why not randomize? Well, in some instances, random assignment is not possible, practical, or even desirable. For example, if a sport psychologist were interested in comparing the influence of a coaching development program on soccer coaches residing in British Columbia and Ontario, it is neither possible nor desirable to assign participants to either province.

Stevens and Bloom (2003) provide a useful example of a study using a quasi-experimental design. They examined the effectiveness of a sport psychology intervention program designed to enhance team effectiveness in collegiate softball players. One team was exposed to a multifaceted intervention designed to enhance team effectiveness; the other team served as a comparison group and did not receive the intervention.

Examination of post-intervention differences in scores from the Group Integration subscales of the Group Environment Questionnaire (Carron, Widmeyer, & Brawley, 1985) indicated higher levels of task and social group integration (indicative of greater team effectiveness) reported by the team in the intervention condition compared with the team in the comparison condition.

REFLECTIONS 2.6

Considering the study conducted by Stevens and Bloom (2003), what threats to internal validity do you believe could influence the interpretation of their data? Consider each threat presented in Table 2.2 as a possible extraneous variable. To what extent do you think it could have explained the findings of this study?

Non-experimental Designs

The final design category, which is more common in sport and exercise psychology research than the previous two categories, is known as **non-experimental designs** (Trochim, 2001). These designs establish patterns of relationships between the variables of interest in the absence of group assignment or variable manipulation. In non-experimental designs, researchers place emphasis on testing arguments derived from theory or predicting criterion variables of interest to the sport psychologist, rather than on establishing causality. Often in the sport and exercise psychology literature, these designs are labelled as passive observational or correlational designs given that the intent of collecting data in this manner is to establish relationships between variables of interest rather than to identify the causal mechanisms that influence a given dependent variable.

One example of a non-experimental design is a study examining predictors of leisure-time exercise behaviour in Canadian university students (Wilson & Muon, 2008). In this study, perceptions of oneself as an exerciser (particularly one's role identity) were associated with more frequent participation in weekly exercise after controlling for the influence attributable to age, gender, and body mass index. The data indicated that perceptions of the role one has as an exerciser in physical activity settings appear to be an important factor in terms of how much exercise a person engages in each week.

Does this study satisfy the conditions required to claim with confidence that role identity perceptions cause exercise behaviour? Let us examine the evidence in relation to the criteria required for causality presented earlier in this chapter. First, the data support the presence of a relationship between role identity perceptions and exercise participation. Second, all of the data were collected at the same point in time, making it difficult to satisfy the assumption of temporal precedence. Finally, all possible factors contributing to exercise behaviour were not included or controlled for in this study; therefore, it is possible that variables other than role identity beliefs could influence exercise participation in these university students. Considering these points carefully in relation to the criteria for causality, we cannot say with confidence that role identity beliefs cause exercise behaviour in university students. The key point to keep in mind here is that causation requires more than the demonstration of an association between two or more variables, or, as some might argue, "Correlation does not equal causation!"

QUALITATIVE RESEARCH IN SPORT AND EXERCISE PSYCHOLOGY

Much of the aforementioned discussion on measurement, sampling, and design is consistent with what is labelled quantitative research. **Quantitative inquiry** is an approach to research that focuses on quantifying or counting the amount of a particular variable or set of variables (Vogt, 2005). However, in recent years, there has been growing advocacy for the use of qualitative inquiry in sport and exercise psychology research. **Qualitative inquiry** encompasses a set of practices through which researchers seek to understand the world from the perspectives of those being studied, or, as Merriam (1998) points out, to understand the phenomenon of interest from the participants' point of view (e.g., Coach Etheridge and her players). This participant-centred approach is sometimes referred to as attempting to capture the emic, or insider's perspective, as opposed to the etic, or outsider's view. Part of the appeal of qualitative inquiry is that such methods provide a wealth of detailed information and a depth of understanding not typically found in quantitative inquiry (Gould, 1996). Consequently, during the last decade, there has been an increase in the number of studies using qualitative methods published in sport and exercise psychology journals.

A comparative summary of the characteristics defining qualitative and quantitative approaches to research is provided in Table 2.3.

Characteristics of Qualitative Inquiry

Qualitative inquiry has traditionally been associated with various disciplines, such as anthropology, sociology, and clinical psychology (Merriam, 1998). More recently, however,

Table 2.3 Qualitative versus Quantitative Approaches to Research

Research Component	Qualitative Approach	Quantitative Approach
Major assumptions	Accepting the important subjective role of a researcher's background and perspective; providing descriptions of behaviour or building theories inductively	Striving for scientific theories that are objective and confirmable; collating data that corroborate pre-existing theoretical arguments
Sampling	Non-probability-based, typically purposive sampling; generalization to a larger population not important	Non-probability- and probability-based; generalization to a larger population in most instances
Context	The environment in which behaviour naturally occurs because behaviour is context bound	Laboratories in which behaviour is best studied by being isolated from contextual interferences
Data	Text derived from interviews, documents, or personal observations that are trustworthy	Numbers derived from standardized instruments that meet acceptable standards of psychometric rigour
Design	Non-experimental design that is flexible and open to any necessary changes during data collection	Randomized, quasi-experimental, and non-experimental designs, most of which are fixed prior to data collection
Data analysis	Focus on description and inductive interpretation	Focus on hypothesis testing and statistical properties

there has been a proliferation of approaches emerging from such areas as cultural and feminist studies that have been embraced by scholars interested in qualitative research (Denzin & Lincoln, 2003). Although the notions of what constitutes qualitative inquiry are divergent given the multidisciplinary roots of this approach to research, experts in this area of inquiry have reached some consensus on the hallmark characteristics of qualitative inquiry.

Let us look at a core group of characteristics (see Table 2.3) that provide a common thread among the different approaches to qualitative inquiry found in sport and exercise psychology research. Core characteristics common to many qualitative research approaches include observances that occur in naturalistic contexts using multiple methods of inquiry to interpret phenomena of interest (Denzin & Lincoln, 2003). This means that researchers are interested in people's experiences and their associated meanings in the real, natural settings of everyday life—the home, the school, the workplace, or the gymnasium. Moreover, qualitative inquiry is not method bound. It draws from a variety of data collection practices, such as formal and informal interviews, field observations, and document gathering, to enhance understanding of the issues studied (Patton, 2002).

Another important characteristic common to most forms of qualitative inquiry is that participants are sampled because of their potential to offer informative and illustrative manifestations of the phenomenon of interest. Sampling, then, is purposeful or theoretical rather than random in nature. Consequently, qualitative research often involves an in-depth study of a small number of participants.

Marnie McBean won several Olympic and world championship medals in rowing. Qualitative methods could help researchers to understand her experiences in the world of sport.
Photograph © The Canadian Press (Frank Gunn).

Common Approaches to Doing Qualitative Research

Qualitative research is characterized by a remarkable variety of approaches and dynamism, which is considered one of its strengths. Irrespective of this diversity, a number of approaches appear to be gaining prominence in the sport and exercise psychology literature as academics embrace qualitative methods as a viable approach to research. The following section examines some of the common approaches to qualitative research in sport and exercise psychology.

Basic Interpretive Qualitative Studies

Basic interpretive qualitative studies are used by researchers who seek to understand a particular phenomenon or process, the perspectives and perceptions of the participants, or a combination of these (Merriam, 2002). Typically, the researcher collects data through interviews, observations, or document examination and analyzes the data to identify patterns and themes. The researcher then presents a descriptive account of the findings and discusses them in reference to the literature that initially framed the study. For example, García Bengoechea and Strean's (2007) study of the role afforded interpersonal contexts in adolescent sport motivation is one example of qualitative inquiry that used a basic interpretative approach. In-depth, semi-structured interviews revealed that adolescent athletes perceived other people to play five key roles with respect to their motivation for sport participation, including providing support, being a source of pressure/control, offering competence-based information, conveying values with reference to achievement, and acting as a role model. Furthermore, athletes reported that other individuals beyond merely coaches and parents were integral in the motivational architecture of sport participation during adolescence.

Phenomenology

Phenomenology is a philosophical tradition that concerns the structure or essence of a lived experience (phenomenon) for an individual or group of people (Merriam, 2002). In this approach, the researcher has to temporarily put aside his or her preconceptions and beliefs about the phenomenon or experience being studied. In a study by Fitzpatrick and Watkinson (2003), data from retrospective interviews with adults elaborated on what it meant to be physically awkward as a child (i.e., the lived experience). The data generated from this phenomenological approach provided useful insights, encouraging teachers, coaches, and personal trainers to be aware of the emotional and social consequences stemming from physical awkwardness.

REFLECTIONS 2.7

Consider for a moment what the phrase "hitting the wall" means to a competitive runner. An exercise physiologist would describe this phenomenon as a result of glycogen depletion that reduces the energy available for the body to meet the demands of activity. How do you think a phenomenologist would describe the experience of "hitting the wall"?

Grounded Theory The term **grounded theory** refers to a specific approach to qualitative inquiry in which the researcher develops a theory that is inductively derived from (or "grounded" in) the participants' data. Grounded theory developed from the work of sociologists Glaser and Strauss (1967). The development of grounded theory is assisted by analytic procedures, such as different forms of coding the data, and the constant comparison method, which involves comparing one participant's experiences with another participant's experiences using an iterative process. The type of theory developed is usually substantive in nature, as opposed to an omnibus theory that attempts to explain a broad array of phenomena. **Substantive theory** is "localized, dealing with particular real-world situations" (Merriam, 2002, p. 7). For example, Sabiston and colleagues used a grounded theory approach to examine the issue of psychological growth in cancer patients (Sabiston, McDonough, & Crocker, 2007). These researchers indicated that post-trauma positive psychological growth in cancer survivors was linked with social support and a shared sense of survivorship among female dragon boaters. According to the reports of these cancer survivors, physical activity also provided opportunities for exercising personal control, establishing or reformulating identities, and overcoming personal challenges.

Case Studies **Case studies** refer to "intensive descriptions and analyses of a single unit or bounded system such as an individual, program, event, group, intervention, or community" (Merriam, 1998, p. 19). Case studies can and often do incorporate a variety of disciplinary and methodological perspectives. Faulkner and Biddle (2004) used a case study approach to understand the motives and barriers to exercise faced by individuals suffering from clinical depression. They developed individual case studies illustrating the centrality of taking into account the wider context of exercise participants' lives, along with their idiosyncratic characteristics, to better comprehend the complex relationship between physical activity and mental well-being.

Ethnography **Ethnography** is concerned with the study of the culture operating within or around a group or team. The term *ethnography* was initially used in anthropology to refer to a set of techniques used to collect data and to the final written product of using ethnographic methods. Ethnography can be distinguished from methods commonly found in ethnographic research (such as participant observation) when the data are interpreted and presented within a sociocultural framework (Merriam, 2002). This point is nicely illustrated in a study by Holt and Sparkes (2001), who used an ethnographic approach to examine issues of team cohesion and chemistry across a competitive season in university-based soccer players. Using multiple forms of data (i.e., participant observation, formal/informal interviews, documentary evidence, field diaries, and reflexive journaling), this study noted that clear and meaningful roles, selfishness/personal sacrifices, communication, and team goals all played a role in how cohesive the team felt across the soccer season.

Narrative Analysis **Narrative analysis** is an approach to qualitative inquiry that collects data for the purposes of presenting a story, and more specifically, a story told in the first person, which distinguishes this method from other presentations of scientific writing. Other terms used to refer to this type of qualitative research are *biography*, *autobiography*, *life story*, *autoethnography*, and *life narratives* (Merriam, 2002). A study by Carless and Douglas (2008) used narrative analysis to explore and describe in depth the identity of men with serious mental illness and the psychological health issues facing them. The results of the study provide a compelling argument against dominant paradigms of mental illness and suggest that issues of action, achievement, and relationships are evident in the sport and exercise narratives of males living with serious mental illness.

Judging the Merit of Qualitative Research

For many years, qualitative researchers have sought to develop criteria to evaluate and judge their work—criteria that are consistent with the fundamental assumptions of the qualitative paradigm or world view (Denzin & Lincoln, 2003). For example, qualitative researchers often assume that there is no single reality "out there" for us to comprehend, but, rather, that multiple subjective realities exist and are worthwhile. Thus, in qualitative research, such criteria as credibility, rigour, and usefulness of the study (Rossman & Rallis, 2003) typically substitute for validity and reliability claims made with quantitative approaches to research. Some strategies that qualitative researchers employ to ensure credibility of the findings and methodological rigour include triangulation (use of multiple data sources or perspectives), prolonged fieldwork, member checking (participant confirmation of a researcher's data interpretation), and use of a "peer debriefer" to check assumptions and conclusions as the study proceeds.

CHAPTER SUMMARY

At the outset of this chapter on research perspectives in sport and exercise psychology, we introduced Coach Etheridge and the "practice player" problem. Now, it might be prudent to return to this scenario and provide an answer to the perplexed coach regarding how to improve the training habits of her basketball players. A single answer to Coach Etheridge's question may be inappropriate given the variety of research approaches that could generate information regarding the coach's quandary.

A naive methodologist may be inclined to be bold in giving advice to Coach Etheridge. Those researchers indoctrinated within the quantitative tradition might suggest that Coach Etheridge randomly assign her players to separate conditions and administer a psychological skills training intervention to one group of players in an attempt to establish the scientific credence of such techniques. Alternatively, others who have heeded Martens' (1987) call for methodological diversity might advocate a phenomenological approach to the problem whereby athletes exemplifying both good and poor practice habits are interviewed to help Coach Etheridge understand her players' viewpoints. In her article examining the "state of the union" in sport and exercise psychology research, Gill (1997) lamented about the proliferation of authoritative advice treated as dogmatic gospel with this statement: "Give us a hammer, and everything looks like a nail" (p. 50). Methodological advances, including the diversification of approaches to science, offer the sport and exercise psychologist numerous options (and challenging decisions) in addressing questions with inherent practical appeal, such as those faced by Coach Etheridge. Rather than stamping any single approach (or combination of approaches) as the "gateway to acceptability" (Gill, p. 50), we recommend that newcomers to research consider what question(s) they seek to answer and select the most useful approach available, perhaps even combining some of the methods presented in this chapter.

Our brief journey through the methodological literature has described and illustrated various issues and components of the research process that have bearing on Coach Etheridge's predicament. Offering a solitary answer to Coach Etheridge's situation would seem trite and trivialize what we have tried to convey about the nature of research and science in this chapter. Perhaps a famous quote from former British Prime Minister Winston Churchill puts it best: "This is not the end. It is not even the beginning of the end. But it is, perhaps, the end of the beginning." Churchill's words encapsulate quite nicely the food for thought we would like you to consider after reading this chapter—namely, that any journey (or research in sport and exercise psychology) starts with an interesting question but in essence does not require a final destination, merely a path to traverse and a direction to follow.

Common Myths about Research in Sport and Exercise Psychology Revisited

MYTH: Research is defined by the goals of an activity or undertaking.

Many people believe that scientific research in sport and exercise psychology is defined by the outcomes of the research process used to generate new knowledge. Research has produced an assortment of outcomes, including methods of masking anabolic steroid use in sport (which is considered cheating), and guidelines for physical activity that for most people will ensure longer and healthier lives. Considering the various outcomes associated with scientific research, defining the process of research in sport and exercise psychology by the goals of this enterprise is not a viable or useful approach.

MYTH: Experimentation is the only way to advance sport and exercise psychology research.

It is often assumed that experimenting by manipulating a variable (or variables) of interest is the only method to advance knowledge in sport and exercise psychology. A large body of literature supports the use of multiple methods and even mixed methods to address complicated questions associated with human performance and behavioural persistence that do not always lend themselves easily to manipulation. As we saw in this chapter, a number of methods are available to the sport and exercise psychologist interested in conducting research, with the most suitable method typically dictated by the question under investigation.

MYTH: Qualitative research methods are not as rigorous as quantitative research methods.

When thinking about qualitative research, some people believe it is a less rigorous form of inquiry than its quantitative counterpart. However, qualitative research is a demanding, systematic, and time-consuming process that requires careful planning and decision making. Sport and exercise psychologists using qualitative methods are guided by a set of standards or criteria to judge the quality of their work, much like their colleagues using quantitative methods in their research.

Review Questions

1. Discuss and contrast the different sources of knowledge that could be used in the process of knowledge production in science.
2. Classify and provide examples of the types of variables used in sport and exercise psychology research.
3. Define and discuss the major principles associated with measurement in sport and exercise psychology research. Provide examples that illustrate your understanding of the key components involved in the measurement process.
4. Define and discuss some of the major ethical principles guiding research in sport and exercise psychology. Describe two examples of activities that require ethical approval.
5. What types of research design could an applied sport and exercise psychologist use to determine the effectiveness of mental skills training programs? Provide a rationale for using each type of research design in sport and exercise psychology research.
6. What differences and similarities exist between the various approaches to qualitative research presented in this chapter?

Suggested Reading

Berg, B. L. (2004). *Qualitative research methods for the social sciences* (5th ed.). Toronto, ON: Allyn & Bacon.

Shadish, W. R., Cook, T. D., & Campbell, D. T. (2002). *Experimental and quasi-experimental designs for generalized causal inference*. New York: Houghton Mifflin.

Trochim, W. (2001). *The research methods knowledge base* (2nd ed.). Cincinnati, OH: Atomic Dog.

References

Babbie, E. (1995). *The practice of social research* (7th ed.). Toronto, ON: Wadsworth.

Baumgartner, T. A., Strong, C. H., & Hensley, L. D. (2002). *Conducting and reading research in health and human performance* (3rd ed.). Montreal, QC: McGraw-Hill.

Blanchard, C. M., Rodgers, W. M., Wilson, P. M., & Bell, G. J. (2004). Does equating total volume of work between two different exercise conditions matter when examining exercise-induced feeling states? *Research Quarterly for Exercise & Sport*, *75*, 209–215.

Bouffard, M. (1997). Using old research ideas to study contemporary problems in adapted physical activity. *Adapted Physical Activity Quarterly*, *1*, 71–87.

Burton, D., Naylor, S., & Holliday, B. (2000). Goal setting in sport: Investigating the goal effectiveness paradox. In R. N. Singer, H. A. Hausenblas, & C. M. Janelle (Eds.), *Handbook of sport psychology* (2nd ed., pp. 497–528). New York: Wiley.

Carless, D., & Douglas, K. (2008). Narrative, identity, and mental health: How men with serious mental illness re-story their lives through sport and exercise. *Psychology of Sport & Exercise*, *9*, 576–594.

Carron, A. V., Widmeyer, W. N., & Brawley, L. R. (1985). The development of an instrument to assess cohesion in sport teams: The group environment questionnaire. *Journal of Sport Psychology*, *7*, 244–266.

Crocker, L., & Algina, L. (1986). *Introduction to classical and modern test theory*. New York: Holt, Rinehart and Winston.

Crocker P. R. E., Sabiston, C. M., Kowalski, K. C., McDonough, M. H., & Kowalski, N. (2006). Longitudinal assessment of the relationship between physical self-concept and health related behaviour and emotion in adolescent girls. *Journal of Applied Sport Psychology*, *18*, 185–200.

Culos-Reed, S. N., Robinson, J. L., Lau, H., O'Connor, K., & Keats, M. R. (2007). Benefits of physical activity intervention for men with prostate cancer. *Journal of Sport & Exercise Psychology, 29*, 118–127.

Deci, E. L., & Ryan, R. M. (1985). *Intrinsic motivation and self-determination in human behavior*. New York: Plenum.

Denzin, N. K., & Lincoln, Y. (2003). The discipline and practice of qualitative research. In N. K. Denzin, & Y. Lincoln (Eds.), *Strategies of qualitative inquiry* (2nd ed., pp. 1–45). Thousand Oaks, CA: Sage.

Downing, S. M. (2003). Validity: On the meaningful interpretation of assessment data. *Medical Education, 37*, 830–837.

Dunn, J. G. H., Bouffard, M., & Rogers, W. T. (1999). Assessing item content-relevance in sport psychology scale-construction research: Issues and recommendations. *Measurement in Physical Education and Exercise Science, 3*, 15–36.

Elston, T. L., & Martin-Ginis, K. A. (2004). The effects of self-set versus assigned goals on exercisers' self-efficacy for an unfamiliar task. *Journal of Sport & Exercise Psychology, 26*, 500–504.

Faulkner, G., & Biddle, S. J. H. (2004). Exercise and depression: Considering variability and contextuality. *Journal of Sport & Exercise Psychology, 26*, 3–18.

Fitzpatrick, D. A., & Watkinson, E. J. (2003). The lived experience of physical awkwardness: Adults' retrospective views. *Adapted Physical Activity Quarterly, 20*, 279–297.

García Bengoechea, E. G., & Strean, W. B. (2007). On the interpersonal context of adolescents' sport motivation. *Psychology of Sport & Exercise, 8*, 195–217.

Gill, D. L. (1997). Measurement, statistics, and research design issues in sport and exercise psychology. *Measurement in Physical Education & Exercise Science, 1*, 39–53.

Gilmour, H. (2007). Physically active Canadians. *Health Reports, 18*, 45–65.

Glaser, B., & Strauss, A. L. (1967). *The discovery of grounded theory: Strategies for qualitative research.* Chicago, IL: Aldine.

Gould, D. (1996). *Sport psychology: Future directions in youth sport research.* In F. L. Smoll, & R. E. Smith (Eds.), *Children and youth in sport: A biopsychosocial perspective* (pp. 405–422). Dubuque, IA: Brown & Benchmark.

Holt, N. L., & Sparkes, A. C. (2001). An ethnographic study of cohesiveness on a college soccer team over a season. *The Sport Psychologist, 15*, 237–259.

Janssen, I., Katzmarzyk, P. T., Boyce, W. T., & Pickett, W. (2004). The independent influence of physical inactivity and obesity on health complaints in 6th to 10th grade Canadian youth. *Journal of Physical Activity and Health, 1*, 331–343.

Kerlinger, F. N. (1979). *Behavioral research: A conceptual approach.* Toronto, ON: Holt, Rinehart and Winston.

Lotysz, G., & Short, S. (2004, December). "What ever happened to . . . ": The effects of career termination from the National Football League. *Athletic Insight*, 6. Retrieved June 8, 2005, from http://www.athleticinsight.com/Vol6Iss3/WhatEverHappened.htm

Martens, R. (1987). Science, knowledge, and sport psychology. *The Sport Psychologist, 1*, 29–55.

Merriam, S. B. (1998). *Qualitative research and case study applications in education.* San Francisco: Jossey-Bass.

Merriam, S. B. (2002). *Qualitative research in practice: Examples for discussion and analysis.* San Francisco: Jossey-Bass.

Messick, S. (1995). Validity of psychological assessment: Validation of inferences from persons' responses and performances as scientific inquiry into score meaning. *American Psychologist, 50*, 741–749.

Munroe, K. J., Giacobbi, P. R., Hall, C. R., & Weinberg, R. S. (2000). The four w's of imagery use: Where, when, why, and what? *The Sport Psychologist, 14*, 119–137.

Okasha, S. (2002). *Philosophy of science: A very short introduction.* Oxford, UK: Oxford University Press.

Patton, M. Q. (2002). *Qualitative research evaluation and methods* (3rd ed.). Thousand Oaks, CA: Sage.
Pedhazur, E. J., & Schmelkin, L. P. (1991). *Measurement, design & analysis: An integrated approach.* Mahwah, NJ: Lawrence Erlbaum.
Pelham, B. W., & Blanton, H. (2003). *Conducting research in psychology: Measuring the weight of smoke* (2nd ed.). Pacific Grove, CA: International Thompson.
Rossman, G. B., & Rallis, S. F. (2003). *Learning in the field: An introduction to qualitative research* (2nd ed.). Thousand Oaks, CA: Sage.
Sabiston, C., McDonough, M. H., & Crocker, P. R. E. (2007). Psychosocial experiences of breast cancer survivors involved in a dragon boat program: Exploring links to positive psychological growth. *Journal of Sport & Exercise Psychology, 29*, 419–438.
Stevens, D. E., & Bloom, G. A. (2003). The effect of team building on cohesion. *Avante*, 9, 43–54.
Stevens, S. S. (1946). On the theory of scales of measurement. *Science, 103*, 677–680.
Trochim, W. (2001). *The research methods knowledge base* (2nd ed.). Cincinnati, OH: Atomic Dog.
Vogt, W. P. (2005). *Dictionary of statistics and methodology: A nontechnical guide for the social sciences* (3rd ed.). Thousand Oaks, CA: Sage.
Wilson, P. M., & Muon, S. (2008). Psychometric properties of the Exercise Identity Scale in a university sample. *International Journal of Sport & Exercise Psychology*, 6, 115–131.
Wilson, P. M., Rodgers, W. M., Loitz, C. C., & Scime, G. (2006). "It's who I am . . . really!" The importance of integrated regulation in exercise contexts. *Journal of Applied Biobehavioral Research, 11*, 243–264.

Chapter 3

Personality in Sport and Exercise

Whitney A. Sedgwick
Peter R. E. Crocker
Ryan E. Rhodes

Chapter Objectives

After reading this chapter, you should be able to do the following:

1. Define personality and incorporate the concept of individual differences.
2. Describe traits and various perspectives on traits such as the Big Five.
3. Briefly explain personality measurement tools, including sport-specific measures and related ethical issues.
4. Differentiate how personality might develop, involving psychodynamic, humanistic, and cognitive-behaviour perspectives.
5. Explain recent personality research findings in sport and exercise psychology.
6. Discuss the limitations of personality in explaining athletic and exercise behaviours and performance.

Subha and Bob play Rep Bantam Hockey for the New Westminster Bobcats. They are a contrast in personalities. Subha is highly competitive on and off the ice in all achievement-related activities. On the ice, Subha is a skilled and swift forward, a tenacious checker, and is third on the team in penalties.

Her coach, and even opposing coaches, love her playing style. Subha exclaims, "Hockey just brings out the fire in me! I love the speed and contact. Maybe it's from all those nights of watching Hockey Night in Canada and listening to Don Cherry. The boys seem surprised that a girl can be so good. Every night I try to play my best and improve. I can be a little hard on myself when I am not playing well. I hope to play for Canada's Olympic team one day. You have to set high standards for yourself in whatever activity you choose."

Bob is a physical presence, standing at over 1.90 m and weighing close to 100 kg. He has a happy-go-lucky, friendly disposition both on and off the ice. He has many friends and is a good student. Bob is the biggest, fastest, and most skilled Bobcat player, but his coach sees him as an underachiever. He seldom challenges opposing players who constantly rough him up. Bob often jokes with opposing players, and all of his teammates like hanging around with him. These qualities describe his personality in all achievement settings.

Bob states, "I like hockey and hanging with my friends, but it's not the only thing in the world. Coaches and some of the parents are always pressuring me to play tougher. I hate the rough stuff and all the pressure. Who needs that crap? Why are adults always trying to change you? All they talk about is the need to get drafted by a junior team, scholarships, and the NHL. I wish they would all back off and just let me enjoy hockey."

Coach Hartley has strong opinions about both Bob and Subha. "Bob has such great physical potential but doesn't have the right personality for hockey," he says. "Subha, on the other hand, has the right stuff. She is aggressive, confident, never gives up—a real fighter. She will go a long way." Manager Campbell says, "I think Subha's aggressiveness is genetic. Her father was a tough nut back in his hockey days. Her mother was also a high-level gymnast. Bob is soft, no mental toughness." Bob's dad feels his son is doing all right. "Bob is a good kid. Because he is so big, the coaches expect too much. They always compare him to Subha. They are different kids. I think the coaches can develop Bob's on-ice personality. They just don't know how."

In the above scenario, a number of different descriptors are used to describe the behaviours of Subha and Bob. We often describe people in terms of specific traits, with words like *shy*, *aggressive*, *submissive*, *perfectionistic*, *sensitive*, *happy-go-lucky*, and *social.* In many cases, such descriptors imply that we expect people to behave or display these characteristics across time. In the scenario, coaches and parents attempt to understand and explain the two athletes' sport performance and motivation by referring to the construct of personality. The coach goes even further by suggesting that there is a right type of personality for hockey. Such thinking is not unusual and also extends to other sport and physical activity settings.

The above scenario raises a number of questions when we consider personality in sport, questions that also have application to exercise and physical activity. Is the uniqueness of a person consistent across situations, or can a person be different in different contexts, like sport and school? Can personality predict sport performance or exercise choice? Is there a distinct sport or exercise personality? Does personality interact with the environment to influence sport and/or exercise performance? How does personality interact with motivation? For that matter, what is personality? In this chapter we will address these and several other questions related to personality in sport and exercise.

Some Common Myths about Personality in Sport and Exercise

MYTH: A distinct elite athlete personality profile exists.

MYTH: People choose physical activities and remain in these activities based on their personality.

MYTH: Contact-sport athletes consistently score high on aggression measures.

INTRODUCTION

Personality is a complex, integral part of human individuality. Although researchers find personality challenging to define, the average person freely uses descriptors to describe others' (and their own) personalities. In Canadian sport, spectators and the media might use *cheerful* to describe golfer Lori Kane and *dedicated*to describe hockey player Sydney Crosby. Olympic wrestling gold medalist Carol Huynh was described as aggressive and confident. Not surprisingly, sport researchers have been interested in personality for many decades. Over the last 30 years, researchers have also been interested in the potential link between personality and regular exercise (Rhodes, 2006). Students should realize that there are many complex questions regarding personality in sport, and there are many disagreements among sport researchers and consultants about the importance of personality in sport (for more detailed discussions see Crust, 2007; Vanden Auweele, De Cuyper, Van Mele, & Rzewnicki, 1993; Vanden Auweele, Nys, Rzewnicki, & Van Mele, 2001; Vealey, 2002). In the 1970s and 1980s, there was a heated debate, termed the credulous-skeptical argument, about the ability to use personality to predict sport behaviour and success. However, as with most arguments, extreme positions do not really capture the relevance of personality in sport research in the 21st century. Sport-personality research dropped off in the 1980s and 1990s because of perceived difficulties in measuring personality and disagreements about the importance of personality in sport. Yet many psychological factors investigated in sport psychology today are related to personality. These include, among many others, trait confidence, trait anxiety, identity, attentional style, mental toughness, hardiness, optimism, competitiveness, ego and mastery goal orientation, perfectionism, sensation seeking, conscientiousness, and extroversion. You will see many of these psychological terms throughout this book.

WHAT IS PERSONALITY?

When we use the term *personality*, we are referring primarily to the consistency of social behaviour, thoughts, and emotions. A useful definition of **personality** is "the overall organization of psychological characteristics—thinking, feeling, and behaving—that

Sport researchers have long been interested in studying the personalities of sport performers.

Photograph by Richard Lam, courtesy of University of British Columbia Athletics.

differentiates us from others and leads us to act consistently across time and situations" (Lindsay, Paulhas, & Nairne, 2008, p. 472). This definition clearly puts the emphasis on individual differences. Each person is thought to be somewhat unique. Reflect back to the vignette at the beginning of the chapter. Both Subha and Bob seem to have unique ways of meeting the challenges presented by hockey and other achievement domains.

Another term often used in sport-personality research is **disposition**, defined as "broad, pervasive, encompassing ways of relating to particular types of people . . . or situations" (Lazarus & Folkman, 1984, p. 120). For example, to say that a teammate has a cheerful disposition would mean that this person is typically upbeat, regardless of whom he or she is talking with or the environment he or she is in. In sport research, *disposition* has often been applied to behaviours, thoughts, and emotions that are relatively stable, such as competitiveness, optimism, and motivational orientation.

REFLECTIONS 3.1

Carefully consider the definition of personality provided above. Think about Canadian golfer Mike Weir when he made a crucial 2 m putt on the 18th hole to get into the playoffs in the 2003 Masters. On observing his behaviour throughout 18 holes, *Globe and Mail* columnist Lorne Rubenstein stated, "All day he had been a study in tenacity." Can you make inferences about an athlete's personality simply by watching him or her in specific situations? What types of information would you need to determine an athlete's personality?

Personality Traits

Think about the numerous behavioural expressions that can exist in sport and exercise settings. Work in the 1930s identified over 4000 adjectives that described observable behaviours that could be considered relatively permanent (Lindsay et al., 2008). How can we make sense of the enormous number of combinations such that we can come up with a science of personality? The most common way scientists do this is by using statistical methods to look at clusters of behaviours that are related or correlated. These clusters of behavioural (plus cognitive and emotional) expressions are called **traits**, the central element of personality (Lindsay et al., 2008). Most students have probably heard of personality traits. A trait is a relatively stable characteristic or quality that is a portion of one's personality. For example, perfectionism consists of a cluster of expressions that includes being organized, compulsive, socially precise, controlled, self-disciplined, and self-critical. Individuals can vary in these attributes; however, a person scoring high in perfectionism should demonstrate many of these expressions. Conversely, a person scoring low in perfectionism might be characterized as tolerant of disorder, flexible, undisciplined, impulsive, careless of social rules, and uncontrolled. As you will see, the study of traits has had a major impact on personality research in sport and exercise.

Contrary to traits, **states** refer to momentary feelings and thoughts that change depending on the situation and time. Take the following example. In a 2007 NHL hockey game, the New York Islanders' Chris Simon cross-checked Ryan Hollweg of the New York Rangers in the face. Simon was later suspended for the season by the NHL. Were Simon's actions representative of the trait of aggression, or were they the result of a temporary atypical state? This is a very difficult question. Your opinions may differ, but the example highlights questions regarding athletic personality (not to mention the influence of game situations, societal influences or expectations, and the nature of the sport).

A common assumption in many trait models of personality is that traits have a normal distribution throughout the population. This means that most people have moderate levels of a specific trait, with only a small percentage having extremely low or extremely high levels of the trait. What makes the prediction of behaviour difficult, however, is that personality is composed of several different traits that combine to influence specific behaviours.

Various trait models have been developed over time, with many having been applied in sport and exercise psychology research. Two example models are Cattell's (1946, 1995) trait personality model and Digman's five factor model (1990). Cattell's model proposes that there are 16 personality factors, called source traits, that capture personality. These factors are warmth, reasoning, dominance, liveliness, social boldness, rule consciousness, sensitivity, vigilance, abstractedness, privateness, apprehension, openness to change, self-reliance, perfectionism, tension, and emotional stability. Cattell's work was a primary source for many sport psychology studies in the 1960s and 1970s. Some sport psychologists went as far as to argue that successful athletes shared specific traits, like dominance and emotional stability, but over time researchers have realized that there is little consistent evidence for an elite athletic personality profile (Vanden Auweele et al., 2001).

Digman (1990) suggests that all people can be described in terms of the prevalence of five global factors (nicknamed the "Big Five"): **openness to experience** (opposite of closed-mindedness, curious), **conscientiousness** (achievement-striving, self-discipline), **extroversion** (assertiveness, energetic approach to the world), **agreeableness** (compliance, positive approach toward others), and **neuroticism** (feelings of tension and nervousness). A useful acronym to remember these factors is OCEAN. This model has become a pre-eminent theory in personality psychology, though to date there has been limited sport psychology research applying the theory. However, researchers in exercise psychology have been exploring the usefulness of the Big Five to help understand examined exercise behaviour (e.g., Courneya & Hellsten, 1998; Rhodes & Smith, 2006). For example, research in exercise psychology by Rhodes, Courneya, and Hayduk (2002) suggests that personality variables may moderate motivational variables in the prediction of exercise behaviour. Individuals higher in extroversion and conscientiousness are more likely to meet their intentions to exercise.

REFLECTIONS 3.2

Look closely at the factors associated with the five factor model of personality. How might these characteristics affect training and competitive behaviours of athletes? How would you rate yourself on these characteristics? Are they consistent across various aspects of your life?

HOW DOES PERSONALITY DEVELOP?

The study of personality has been shaped by various viewpoints, ranging from biological to sociocultural. An in-depth review of the various ways that personality can develop is more appropriately covered in an advanced personality course. However, we will provide a brief review of three perspectives that capture approaches to studying the development of personality in sport and exercise psychology. These three perspectives are psychodynamic, humanistic, and cognitive-behavioural.

Psychodynamics

The psychodynamic approach to personality grew out of the psychoanalytic movement founded and practised by Sigmund Freud. A key aspect of Freud's work is that he argued there was a strong biological mechanism driving motivated behaviour. The **psychodynamic approach** suggests that all behaviour is interconnected and driven by unconscious forces. As well, Freud's work contained an underlying theme that thoughts and feelings motivate our behaviours—a premise that is widely held to this day. Freud devised a structure of personality that includes the id, the ego, and the superego. The **id** is considered the instinctual and driving force of personality, the pleasure principle centre. The **ego** mediates the individual's relationship with the environment, the reality principle. Finally, the **superego** is the voice of the conscience and morality, the should/should not principle. The ego is considered a mediator, or the reality tester, between the id and superego. Freud proposed that all behaviour stems from conflict and compromise, among the wants of the id, the defences of the ego, and the morality of the superego. Psychodynamics also held that psychological energy was constant and thus had to be directed toward socially acceptable activities such as sport and physical education. The discharge of this energy was called catharsis.

Although the theories of Freud and those who followed him contributed major elements to the advancement of the study of personality, there is little application to current sport performance enhancement and exercise psychology. However, ideas related to psychodynamics are still used by some sport commentators to explain and justify aggression in sport.

Humanistic Psychology

In contrast to the inner drives of psychodynamics, **humanistic psychology** focuses more on personal responsibility, human growth, personal striving, and individual dignity. In this approach, each person's experiences, beliefs, values, and perceptions are emphasized in the present moment. One often sees the term *self-actualization* associated with humanistic approaches. Certainly in competitive athletics, athletes are trying to be the best they can be, to reach their potential; this is a quick way to summarize **self-actualization**.

Figure 3.1 Maslow's hierarchy of needs pyramid

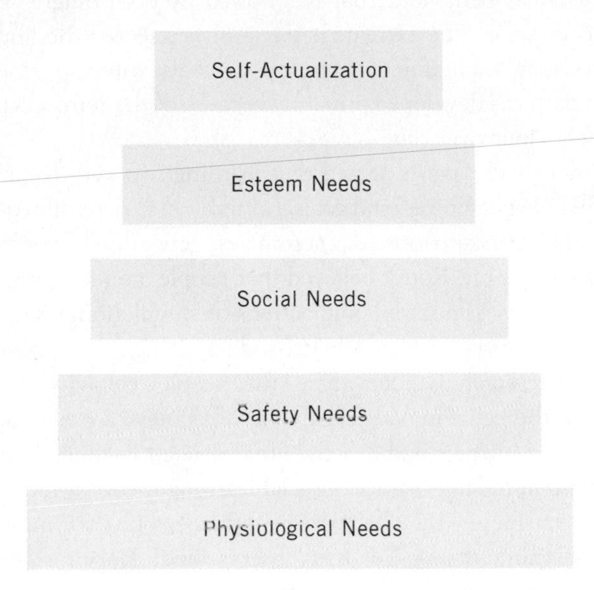

Dr. Terry Orlick of the University of Ottawa has been a strong proponent of humanistic approaches to sport psychology consulting. He emphasizes that it is important to understand the needs and desires of athletes, to respect their perceptions and ideas, and to view their athletic participation in the bigger picture of personal growth (Orlick, 1989).

Carl Rogers (1959) was a humanist psychologist who contributed greatly to the field of personality study. Rogers believed that when there is a discrepancy between a person's self-perceptions and what is being experienced, this person might deny what is actually happening. Abraham Maslow (1943) was another of the founding humanist psychologists. He published a hierarchy of needs in a five-tiered triangular model (see Figure 3.1), which suggests that as our basic human needs (lower tiers of the pyramid) are met, we strive to meet higher needs. The base of the triangle represents physiological needs, such as food, water, sleep, and shelter. The second tier represents safety needs, provided in personal and social settings. If physiological and safety needs are met, then the individual moves to the third tier to satisfy social needs: feelings of belonging, connections to others, the acts of giving and receiving love. The fourth tier of the pyramid is for esteem needs, which can be internal (i.e., self-respect and achievement) or external (i.e., recognition and status). Self-actualization, at the top of the pyramid, refers to the constant striving to make the most of one's special abilities. Olympic champions or individuals who have succeeded in spite of physical or mental disabilities, such as Terry Fox and Rick Hansen, could be considered self-actualized.

Cognitive-Behavioural Approach

Early learning theories suggested that behaviour was not determined by inner drives but by interactions (involving reward and punishment) with the environment. The learning perspective suggests that all behaviour is learned through experience, and it discards notions of disposition, drives, or instincts proposed by other personality theories. B.F. Skinner

(1999) argued that behaviour that is followed by a reward would increase in probability of reoccurrence, whereas behaviour that is followed by punishment would decrease in probability of reoccurrence. The extreme behaviourists rejected the importance of internal causes of behaviour, including such factors as goals, intentions, and expectancies. Thus, behavioural patterns developed primarily because of the reinforcement and punishment of specific behaviour over time.

Over time, other psychologists argued that learning was very complex and involved such aspects as beliefs, expectancies, and goals. Rotter (1954) determined that three factors would influence behaviour: situational expectancies, generalized expectancies, and reinforcement value. More simply, Rotter believed that people are motivated to seek out positive stimulation and to avoid negative interactions or stimulation. Over the last 30 years, other social learning theorists, such as Albert Bandura (1977, 1997), have influenced contemporary personality research. Bandura argued that people's behaviour is highly influenced by their **self-efficacy**, the belief in one's capabilities to achieve a goal or an outcome. (Self-efficacy and motivation in sport and exercise are described in more detail in Chapter 4.) Bandura also emphasized the importance of **social learning theory**, which suggests that people are active agents in shaping their behaviours, influenced by their inner drives and environments. Social learning theory involves **observational learning (modelling)**, which occurs through observing, retaining, and at times replicating others' behaviours. Bandura determined that individuals can learn simply by being reinforced or punished for behaviours, as well as by being exposed to, or observing, the behaviours of others. For example, watching the behaviours of an athlete can influence a person's future behaviour. Bandura's work demonstrated that people can and do learn from multiple sources, such as television, magazines, and social interactions. We know that individuals are more likely to adopt behaviour if the behaviour results in valued outcomes. If a person engages in exercise behaviour and the behaviour results in him or her being perceived as more attractive, then an observer is likely to imitate that behaviour in a similar exercise setting.

Learning theories focus on how situations and individuals reciprocally influence each other. If a situation has an influence on an individual (or vice versa), this influence could subsequently have a lasting effect on his or her personality. Simply put, the strict learning behaviourists suggest that personality is the sum of all that you do, not of what you think or feel. However, social learning theorists believe that people are active agents in shaping their behaviour, with many factors determining a person's actions. It should not be surprising then, that there are multiple applications of social learning theory in sport and exercise. These ideas are explored in many chapters in this book.

REFLECTIONS 3.3

Bandura argued that through observing role models, people learn that specific types of behaviour are acceptable. In many commercials, men and women are presented as working hard to shape their bodies. These images are often associated with socially desirable outcomes such as being happy and being socially and sexually attractive. People may learn that this type of behaviour is expected and valued. Do you think that people can adopt exercise personalities by this process of modelling and imitation? Think of your own behaviour. Who are your role models, and are your sport or exercise behaviours similar to those of your role models?

Interactionist Approach: Dealing with the Person–Situation Debate

A controversy in the area of human behaviour is the person–situation debate. As you can see from the perspectives described above, some psychologists argued that behaviour was driven by internal person forces (the person side of the debate), whereas others argued for the central role of the environment (the situation side of the debate). One major issue in the debate concerned the cross-situational consistency of behaviour. Research in the 1960s suggested that personality was a weak predictor of behaviour in specific situations (Mischel, 1968). Thus, behavioural psychologists argued that "personality traits" were not very useful in understanding behaviour. However, research in the 1970s also indicated that situations were equally inept at predicting behaviour (Epstein, 1979). To make a long story short, the end result of this debate was to recognize that both personal and situational factors impact behaviour in a predictive fashion.

Thus, the interactionist perspective came into vogue in the 1970s in response to perceived limitations of the person-versus-environment approaches. According to Endler and Magnusson's (1976) interactionist approach, it is the situational interplay between the person and the environment that determines the specific behaviours of an individual. Most current research of personality in sport and exercise emphasizes an **interactionist approach** (Vanden Auweele et al., 2001). This acknowledges that each person brings specific dispositions, experiences, and genetic variables to a physical activity situation. The majority of behaviour is best understood by considering the interaction of personality and the environment.

Instead of searching for stability of behaviour across all situations, interactionist researchers are trying to understand how various traits or dispositions affect behaviour depending on the sport or exercise context. In this view, we can consider the interplay among the stable characteristics of the person, the goals and motivations of the person, and the opportunities for and appropriateness of specific behaviours in a given context. The expression of personality is most evident during specific situations that are relevant

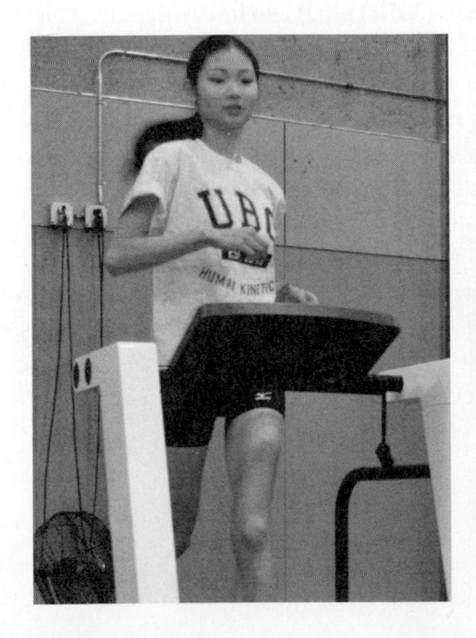

Athletes and exercisers can demonstrate different behaviours depending on their personality and the competitive context.
Photographs by Peter Crocker, University of British Columbia (left) and Richard Lam, courtesy of University of British Columbia Athletics (right).

and important to the person (Lindsay et al., 2008). For example, Ann is a talented player on her university varsity volleyball team. She is known by her teammates as being very competitive. Coming into the last game, her play seems overly relaxed, and the team is losing the match. During the last portion of the final game, Ann's game becomes quick, determined, and driven, and she perceives herself to be competent and up to the challenge. She works hard on the offence and repeatedly hits winning shots to tie the score at 25–25. This is a hypothetical example of how it is important to consider the person's typical pattern of behaviour (Ann's competitiveness) with the goals or expectancies that become activated during game contexts (importance of team success), along with the types of behaviours that are deemed appropriate in this context. In the next chapter on motivation, you will see many instances where sport and exercise psychology examines both personal and environmental factors in an aim to understanding specific types of behaviour.

THE MEASUREMENT OF PERSONALITY

Many inventories have been developed to measure personality and have been used across genders, populations, and cultures worldwide. Because many varied tests are available, it follows that the applicability and relevance of these tests to athletes will vary. Some sport and exercise psychology researchers have been critical of how psychologists and sporting teams have used personality tests in sport (see Vealey, 2002). Before we discuss the ethics of testing, it will be useful to discuss the various types of measures used in personality research and then talk about some sport-specific measures.

Measures of personality can be divided into projective and objective categories. **Projective tests** contain open-ended questions, which provide a subjective perspective. The test taker is not provided with possible answers to the test questions. Researchers believe that the questions will reveal an individual's hidden feelings and thoughts. These tests are not typically used in sport personality research. **Objective tests**, on the other hand, are highly standardized tests that do not require the tester to interpret the meaning of the participant's responses. Examples of objective, standardized tests that present individuals with a choice of responses are Cattell's 16 Personality Factors (16PF) test (Cattell, 1946) and the Neuroticism Extroversion Openness Five Factor Inventory (NEO-FFI; Costa & McCrae, 1994).

Two important issues to consider in the measurement of personality are whether the test is appropriate for physical activity settings and whether the research questions are specific to certain sport or exercise populations. Not surprisingly, trait measures of personality have been very popular in sport and exercise research. The 16PF combines both the state and the trait approach to personality study and assesses different personality trait dichotomies. The majority of studies using the 16PF in sport research occurred between 1960 and 1980, but there was still research in the 1990s using this measure to attempt to differentiate between different levels of sport performers. Since then, there has been a decline in personality-related sport research. It should be noted that the vast majority of personality-based research in physical activity settings has occurred in sport. Thus, many of the specific examples that follow are based on sport populations.

Sport-Specific Measures

The majority of personality research in sport today uses measures that have been developed specifically for sport. There are numerous sport-specific measures that are used to measure either global or specific aspects of athletes' personalities, many of which relate to motivation, anxiety, stress, physical self-perceptions, self-esteem, and aggression, and will be discussed in later chapters. Many of these measures are documented in detail in Ostrow's (2002) *Directory of Psychological Tests in the Sport & Exercise Sciences*. We will address three representative measures that attempt to assess various aspects of personality in sport: (1) the Athletic Motivation Inventory (Tutko, Lyon, & Ogilvie, 1969), (2) the Sport Competition Anxiety Test (Martens, 1977), and (3) the Profile of Mood States (McNair, Lorr, & Droppleman, 1971, 1992).

Athletic Motivation Inventory The Athletic Motivation Inventory (AMI) was designed to measure the personality and motivation of athletes participating in competitive sports. It was the first sport-specific psychological test to be developed, and it measures personality traits within a specific sport, such as ability to cope with emotional stress, dedication to the coach and sport, and traits predictive of athletic success. The inventory was correlated with the variables on the 16PF, including emotional control, aggression, leadership, conscientiousness, tough-mindedness, trust, self-confidence, and guilt-proneness.

Research using the AMI provides equivocal results in terms of validity. For example, researchers Thomas and Sinclair (1978) examined Canadian women intercollegiate basketball players using both the AMI and the 16PF. The results indicated that, when compared with controls, athletes were slightly above average in mental toughness and self-confidence. However, the AMI was later critiqued by Hap Davis (1991), a Canadian sport psychologist based in Calgary. He examined the validity of the instrument by having hockey scouts rate the NHL draft players' psychological strengths by observing their on-ice play. Davis found that only a small number of the hockey players' on-ice behaviours representing psychological strength were related to what the AMI measured. This type of research has implications for draft screening procedures and for determining whether the use of instruments, such as the AMI, is optimal in assessing athletes' psychological strengths.

Sport Competition Anxiety Test The Sport Competition Anxiety Test (SCAT), developed by Martens (1977), is a sport-specific measure designed to capture competitive trait anxiety. **Trait anxiety** refers to a general disposition to respond to a variety of situations with feelings of concern or worry, along with having heightened physiological arousal. According to Martens, athletes who have high competitive trait anxiety would be more likely to experience anxiety across many competitive situations, regardless of situational variables. The SCAT contains 10 statements to measure sport competitive trait anxiety. An example is, "Before I compete I get a queasy feeling in my stomach." The SCAT has been used in many studies to investigate numerous research questions related to trait anxiety in sport. Trait anxiety is discussed in more detail in Chapter 5.

Profile of Mood States A predominant instrument used in sport personality and mood research is the Profile of Mood States (POMS) developed by McNair et al. (1971, 1992). Interestingly, the POMS is not really a stable personality type test since it was designed to assess state affect in psychiatric populations. Yet, it became popular in sport psychology based on the work of Morgan and colleagues (Morgan, 1980; Morgan & Pollock, 1977). The POMS assesses six discrete affective states: tension-anxiety (TEN), depression-dejection (DEP), anger-hostility (ANG), vigour (VIG), fatigue (FAT), and confusion-bewilderment (CON). A total mood score can be calculated by subtracting the score for vigour from the sum of the other five scores.

Figure 3.2 Example of an iceberg profile for successful and unsuccessful athletes

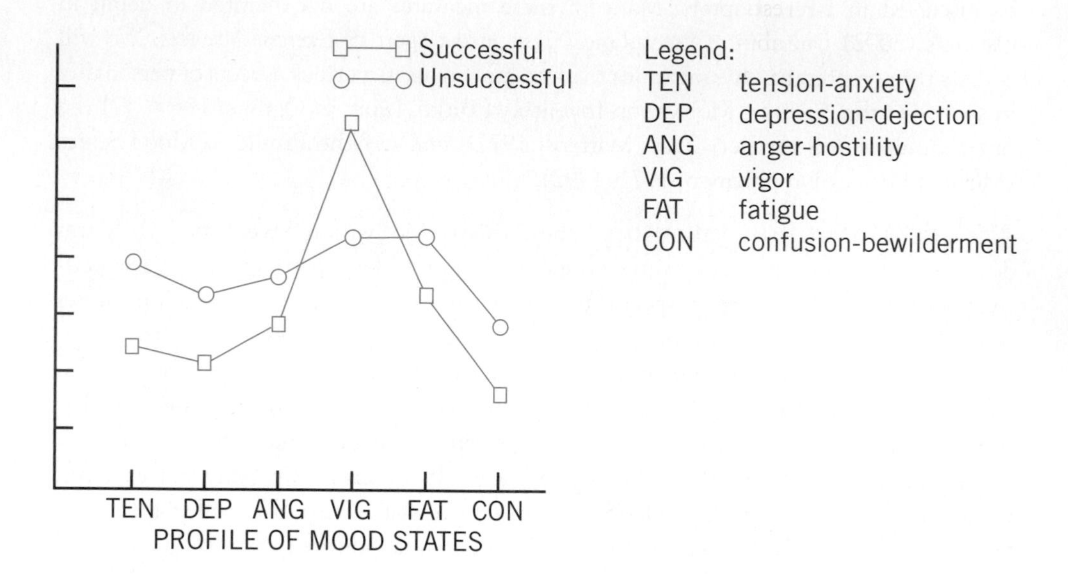

Note: From Wann, Daniel L., SPORT PSYCHOLOGY, Fig. "Example of an iceberg profile for successful and unsuccessful athletes" p. 65, © 1997 Macmillan Publishing Company. Reproduced by permission of Pearson Education, Inc.

Participants in the initial sport study of the POMS (Morgan & Pollock, 1977) included rowers, distance runners, and wrestlers. The research findings suggested that elite athletes with positive affect reported what has been termed an *iceberg profile*, scoring low on tension, depression, anger, fatigue, and confusion but high on vigour (see Figure 3.2). This makes sense because it would be more challenging to perform well—and even harder to aim for a personal best—if one were feeling down, frustrated, tired, or uncertain. If your energy levels are high, you would likely rate your vigour as high, which can aid in creating a positive mood and ultimately positively influence performance.

Morgan and Pollock's work (1977) generated great interest in the link between scores on the POMS and sport performance. However, subsequent research on the iceberg profile has reached mixed conclusions, with many studies failing to support the profile. Rowley, Landers, Kyllo, and Etnier (1995) conducted a **meta-analysis** (a research technique in which the results of many studies are combined) on studies that had used the POMS. They determined that there was weak support for Morgan and Pollock's findings of the iceberg profile (findings showing that, across studies, successful athletes did report more positive affect); the difference between successful and unsuccessful athletes was very small. The meta-analysis results indicated that mood accounted for less than 1% of the athletes' performances! Nevertheless, there still appears to be much interest in the POMS and sport performance, with the *Journal of Applied Sport Psychology* devoting an entire volume in 2000 to research on the POMS.

Ethical Considerations of Personality Measurement

There are multiple tools to measure personality characteristics of athletes, but certain questions should be considered when using such tools. For example, under what conditions should a personality test be used? Should these tests be utilized to screen or select athletes? How should the test (i.e., objective, projective, sport-specific) be selected and then administered? Some tests have been developed and validated for specific populations and contexts, and only qualified professionals should administer and assess scores from certain measurement tools. You wouldn't want a layperson to give you a medical exam and diagnosis, so the same standard should hold for the use of psychological assessments.

Ethical principles are typically devised by a specific organization and used by members of that organization to shape professional judgment and behaviour. Integrity and the responsibility to protect the public's well-being are examples of ethical issues. With respect to psychological testing, individuals need to be informed of the nature of tests, how the results will be used, and who will have access to the results. Using tests or inventories for team selection is frowned upon since there is little evidence to support the validity of such use. Some professional teams have used psychological tests in team selection or to explore an athlete's personality. However, many professional organizations, like the NFL Players Association, have forbidden the use of such tests with its members. Breaches in confidentiality and the potential financial cost of testing athletes are also considerations when using psychological tests with athletic populations. As well, the person administering the test must be qualified. This person must be competent, meaning that he or she has a broad range of experience administering, scoring, and interpreting the particular test. Licensed psychologists or individuals with specialized training in test administration are usually the best resources for psychological testing and interpretation. For students wanting more information, there are some good discussions of ethics in assessment and testing in sport and exercise psychology (see Etzel, Yura, & Perna, 1998; Etzel, Watson, & Zizzi, 2004).

REFLECTIONS 3.4

You are an undergraduate student working with a high-school soccer team. The team is struggling, and the coach is searching for solutions to improve their performance. The coach believes that specific personalities are needed for this sport. He asks you to administer a personality test to determine the personality profile of each player. What would you do? What are the ethical issues involved? Would these same issues be relevant in exercise settings?

PERSONALITY RESEARCH IN SPORT AND EXERCISE

Personality research in sport and exercise has a long history. In sport, much of the research in the 1960s and 1970s was directed toward determining if sporting performance could be predicted by personality traits. There was associated research that also examined if athletes had different personalities than non-athletes or whether personality could predict the types of sports (team versus individual sports) athletes selected. Overall, the research has indicated that there is little evidence that personality can predict performance, athletes from non-athletes, or the type of sport people will select. Most studies that have found relationships between personality and sport or exercise participation have demonstrated small effects (see Rhodes, 2006; Vanden Auweele et al., 2001). That is, personality is only a small part of the story. However, this does not mean that personality traits have no place in the study of sport and exercise. Indeed, you will

Sport research indicates that there does not appear to be a distinct elite sport personality.

Photographs by Richard Lam, courtesy of University of British Columbia Athletics.

see that sport and exercise psychology researchers are finding that personality can predict various types of behaviours.

In the following section, we will provide some examples of sport and exercise research studies that have emphasized a personality approach. We have selected representative research from specific areas that give students an idea of how specific personality factors might affect sport and exercise behaviour. These research areas are risk taking/sensation seeking, competitiveness, perfectionism, and mental toughness. This will be followed by a specific discussion on whether there is a specific personality associated with exercise.

Risk Taking and Sensation Seeking

When you consider Canadian Olympic divers Emilie Heymans and Blythe Hartley, 10 m platform silver medalists at the Olympic Games in Athens, they epitomize sensation-seeking athletes. To stand on a tower 10 metres high, the equivalent of a three-storey building, and then execute a complicated routine with somersaults and twists and enter the water flawlessly is a challenging feat. Or, consider Lori-Ann Muenzer, Athens Olympic gold medalist in cycling, who, in that particular race, averaged 56 km/h on a bicycle with no brakes and her feet attached to the pedals. These athletes became experts in sports in which the thrill of height and speed is inherent.

The term **risk taking** involves narrowing the margin of safety, both physically and psychologically (Anshel, 2003). The elements of danger and possibility of bodily harm, injury, and physical loss are inherent in some sports, such as skydiving, race-car driving, and downhill skiing. Do the athletes who participate in these sports have different personalities from those who remain rooted to the ground, participating in what might be considered safer sports?**Sensation (stimulus) seeking** has been defined as "the seeking of varied, novel, complex and intense sensations and experiences, and the willingness to take physical, social, legal and financial risks for the sake of such experiences" (Zuckerman, 1994, p. 27). Malone (1985) characterized stimulus seeking as a motivational factor for athletes to not only participate in sport but also to engage in risk-taking behaviours. There is research that suggests that stimulus seekers have higher physiological activation levels or chronic levels of high excitation, which are rewarded when they take risks in sport.

Although males generally score higher in sensation seeking, there are many females who compete in high-risk physical activity.
Photograph © Photodisc/Getty Images.

Malone (1985) conducted a review of the literature on risk taking in sport and concluded that the perception of danger creates excitement in athletes. Athletes also have a desire to conquer the situation. This is seen in the results of a study of the personalities of Iditasport (Alaskan ultramarathon) athletes (Hughes, Case, Stuempfle, & Evans, 2003). As well, the personalities of high-risk athletes were examined by Kajtna, Tuscaronak, Baricacute, and Burnik (2004). They compared high-risk athletes (e.g., skydivers, white water kayakers, and ski jumpers) to non-risk athletes (e.g., swimmers, Nordic skiers, and track athletes). Using an instrument associated with the Big Five personality model, they found that high-risk athletes scored highest in emotional stability, conscientiousness, and energy, while openness was highest in non-risk athletes (with no significant differences for acceptability). Finally, Llewellyn and Sanchez (2008) studied individual differences and risk taking in rock climbers. They found that male climbers and individuals high in self-efficacy were more likely to take increased risks; however, they caution against assuming that all people take risks across domains due to elevated sensation seeking needs (i.e., there may be other reasons individuals take risks).

Other researchers have been interested in particular aspects of sensation seeking, such as thrill and adventure seeking, experience seeking, boredom susceptibility, and disinhibition. With respect to gender and age, it would appear that sensation seeking declines with age and that males are more drawn to high-risk sports than are females (Butkovic & Bratko, 2003). Nevertheless, many women excel in high-risk sport; examples are Canadian mountain bikers Marie-Hélène Prémont and Alison Sydor.

Competitiveness

We all know athletes who seem to possess that "killer instinct," those athletes who attack competition and even regular training workouts with high levels of intensity. These athletes want to succeed and are determined to do everything within their power to achieve this goal. Canadian athletes, such as Carol Huynh, have demonstrated such competitiveness and positive determination. Huynh was the Olympic gold medalist in wrestling in the 2008 Beijing Games. Canada's national team coach, Leigh Vierling, described Huynh as dangerous and praised her attacking skills and intensity.

Competitiveness is conceptualized as a desire to engage in and strive for success in sport achievement situations (Gill & Deeter, 1988). Gill and Deeter devised the Sport Orientation Questionnaire to measure athletes' desire to win along three specific dimensions. These dimensions are competitiveness, win orientation, and goal orientation. These researchers compared non-athletes and athletes and found that athletes scored higher on all three dimensions and that males scored higher than females. Interestingly, Gill and Dzewaltowski (1988) found that high-level athletes enjoy performing successfully and place more emphasis on performance, or personal best goals, than on outcome, or winning goals.

As well, Gould, Dieffenbach, and Moffett (2002) have studied competitiveness as a psychological characteristic of Olympic champions. They found competitiveness, adaptive perfectionism, mental toughness, and mental resiliency to be present in Olympic medal winners. Durand-Bush and Salmela (2002), sport researchers from the University of Ottawa, conducted interviews with Canadian World or Olympic medalists. Their research indicated that competitiveness was an important characteristic of these elite athletes. Not surprisingly, the research results across studies are varied with respect to gender differences and competitiveness.

Simply put, competitiveness involves how motivated one is toward achievement. Gender, sport level, and cultural differences have been studied in relation to competitiveness, with varying results. Again, individual differences should not be discounted because people can interpret the notion of competitiveness differently. As you will see in the following chapter on motivation, there are various ways to describe the dispositions related to achieving goals and success in sport.

Perfectionism

Catriona LeMay Doan, Olympic speed-skating champion, and Helen Simard, Paralympic gold medallist in wheelchair tennis, are examples of two outstanding Canadian athletes who trained for numerous years to achieve sporting excellence. Success at this elite level would seem to require that athletes (1) set high personal standards for performance, (2) monitor progress toward these standards, (3) be highly organized, and (4) manage the pressure and expectations of significant others, such as parents, coaches, teammates, and partners. But what about athletes who incur psychological or physical costs while engaging in the drive for success? The danger is that setting unrealistic, high standards could lead to stress and anxiety and could subsequently result in maladaptive behaviours.

Perfectionism is a relatively stable personality construct that involves unrealistic, high standards, inappropriate levels of expectation, and high self-criticism (Flett & Hewitt, 2005; Frost, Marten, Lahart, & Rosenblate, 1990). Psychology researchers have recognized that perfectionism has multiple dimensions that can involve both the self and expectations of significant others. Frost et al. (1990) state that self-perfectionism involves high personal standards, doubts about actions, high concern over mistakes, and organization. Given that many of these behaviours are present in competitive sport, it is not surprising that perfectionism is being more frequently studied in athletes.

It sounds as if perfectionism might lead to destructive behaviour patterns in athletes. Some sport and health psychology researchers believe that there are both healthy and unhealthy aspects of perfectionism (Anshel & Eom, 2003; Dunn, Causgrove, Dunn, &

Syrotuik, 2002). **Maladaptive** or **unhealthy perfectionism** would involve excessive, unrealistic standards of performance, high doubt, high self-criticism, fear of failure, and high distress. **Adaptive** or **healthy perfectionism** consists of realistic goal setting, judging success through personal improvement and effort (task orientation), self-discipline, and achievement striving. Indeed, many of the behaviours associated with healthy perfectionism are the same as for conscientiousness and achievement striving. Sport and exercise research has generally found that extreme or unhealthy perfectionism is associated with negative emotions, social anxiety related to the body, exercise dependence, dropping out, poor or maladaptive coping, perceptions of low competence, and emotional exhaustion (Anshel & Eom, 2003; Giacobbi, Hausenblas, & Frye, 2005; Lemyre, Hall, & Roberts, 2008).

Dr. John Dunn of the University of Alberta has recently been investigating healthy and unhealthy perfectionism in sport. Dunn et al. (2002) studied the link between perfectionism, ego motivation, and task achievement motivation in high-school football players. Ego motivation involves judging success in terms of being better than others. Task achievement motivation involves judging success in terms of personal improvement and effort. (These concepts will be more thoroughly described in Chapter 4.) Dunn et al. defined unhealthy, or maladaptive, perfectionism as having high personal standards, high concerns with mistakes, and high concern with coach and parent pressure. Healthy, or adaptive, perfectionism was reflected by moderate standards and low concern with mistakes and low pressure from coaches and parents. They found that unhealthy perfectionism was positively related to an ego orientation, whereas healthy perfectionism was associated with a task orientation. Vallence, Dunn, and Causgrove-Dunn (2006) found that male youth hockey

Perfectionism in sport can be both healthy and unhealthy.
Photograph by Richard Lam, courtesy of University of British Columbia Athletics.

Canadian Profile
Silken Laumann

In 1992, Canadian rower Silken Laumann looked as if she had the world in her hands. She was the reigning World rowing champion and was highly favoured for gold in the Barcelona Olympics. Shockingly, 10 weeks before the Olympics she suffered serious leg injuries as a result of a boat collision during a race warm-up.

Her Olympic dreams, and possibly her rowing career, seemed shattered. Nevertheless, with the assistance of a special brace to stabilize her leg, Silken endured incredible pain to finish third in the 1992 Olympics (see www.silkenlaumann.com). Sport commentators spoke glowingly about her courage and mental toughness.

players with perfectionist orientations also demonstrated heightened competitive trait anger. Lastly, in a study of competitive figure skaters, Dunham, Dunn, and Hogg (2002) found that negative attitudes toward body image were associated with maladaptive perfectionism, whereas adaptive perfectionists had more positive attitudes.

Researchers at the University of Ottawa have also examined aspects of dispositional perfectionism and links to life satisfaction, motivation, and managing stress. Gaudreau and Anti (2008) examined the two broad dimensions of perfectionism, namely, personal standards perfectionism (PSP) and evaluative concerns perfectionism (ECP). The PSP is similar to healthy perfectionism in which people set highly demanding standards and strive for goal attainment. ECP is related to unhealthy perfectionism in that people are highly self-critical, have high doubts about ability to obtained desired outcomes, and also believe others require them to be perfect. Gaudreau and Anti found that ECP was related to managing stress using avoidance or distraction coping strategies and subsequently to low levels of attaining athletic goals and life satisfaction. PSP, on the other hand, was linked to using task-related coping (effort, problem solving) to manage stress and subsequently to higher levels of goal attainment. Stress and coping are discussed in more detail in Chapter 6.

Mental Toughness

Mental toughness has been identified as one of the most critical psychological characteristics for achieving excellence in elite sport (Connaughton, Wadey, Hanton, & Jones, 2007; Crust, 2007; Gucciardi, Gordon, & Dimmock, 2009; Jones, Hanton, & Connaughton, 2002; Loehr, 1995). For example, in a special issue of the *Journal of Applied Sport Psychology* on athletic excellence, three separate articles identified mental toughness as a personal characteristic of elite performers (Durand-Bush & Salmela, 2002; Gould et al., 2002; Jones et al., 2002). What is mental toughness? Is it a personality variable or a motivational factor? Jones et al. found that **mental toughness** has been described as a personality trait, an outward expression of an inner commitment, and as a collection of psychological attributes and skills. Psychological characteristics associated with mental toughness include control, competitiveness, concentration, confidence, commitment, determination, desire, focus, persistence, and optimism (see Goldberg, 1998; Gould, Hodge, Peterson, & Petlichkoff, 1987; Jones et al., 2002; Loehr, 1995; Mack & Ragan, 2008).

In an attempt to better understand athletes' perspectives on mental toughness, Jones et al. (2002) had 10 international athletes (7 men and 3 women) identify the qualities

High-level performance requires athletes to be mentally tough.
Photograph by Richard Lam, courtesy of University of British Columbia Athletics.

and characteristics of mental toughness. Using qualitative research methods for focus groups, they found many similarities with the results of previous research. Mental toughness was a skill that allowed athletes to cope with competition demands better than their opponents. Some athletes thought that this skill was innate, whereas others believed mental toughness could be developed over time with the right competitive experiences. Ten key characteristics in three broad categories were identified: (1) very strong self-confidence and motivation, (2) ability to manage the stress of competition and training, and (3) ability to maintain or regain focus in the face of distraction.

The key characteristics identified by Jones et al. (2002) are consistent with findings on athletic excellence in Canadian athletes. In a follow-up study, Connaughton, Wadey, Hanton, and Jones (2008) examined whether mental toughness requires maintenance. After interviewing seven elite performers (representing six sports), these researchers found that demonstrating mental toughness involves the motivational climate (i.e., enjoyment, mastery), various individuals (e.g., peers, coaches), experiences in and outside sport, psychological skills and strategies, and insatiable desire and internalized motives to succeed. These results suggest that athletes need to continue to practise psychological skills within a positively supportive network to enhance their desire and internal motivation.

Orlick and Partington's (1988) early research with Olympians found that high levels of commitment and the ability to focus and refocus when confronted with distractions were two elements that distinguish more-successful athletes from less-successful athletes. Durand-Bush and Salmela's (2002) interviews with 10 World or Olympic champions revealed that competitiveness, self-confidence, and motivation were important personal characteristics of excellence. They also found that athletes reported the use of psychological skills to help manage stress and allow a strong competition and training focus.

In summary, the research indicates that mental toughness involves a number of personal characteristics and psychological skills that allow athletes to cope with stress and anxiety while remaining focused on competition demands. The chapters on motivation, anxiety, stress and coping, and sport psychology interventions will discuss many of these areas in more detail.

PERSONALITY TRAITS AND EXERCISE: IS THERE AN EXERCISE PERSONALITY?

Are some people more predisposed to exercise simply because of their personality? Think of how two people can be exposed to the same gym environment but walk away with a different perception of the experience. Alternatively, some people seem to be able to juggle and organize several daily tasks, including getting regular exercise, while others struggle. Might this be attributed to personality? Rhodes and Smith (2006) conducted a meta-analysis on 35 studies that examined the correlation between major personality traits and physical activity. Their results suggested that extroversion and conscientiousness had a positive association with exercise, while neuroticism had a negative relationship. These researchers point out, however, that the relationships were small, suggesting that personality has a relatively minor association with exercise and physical activity. Personality traits like openness to experience, agreeableness, and psychoticism did not have a relationship with exercise. There is also evidence that conscientiousness may affect the successful translation of good exercise intentions into behaviour. Researchers have shown that more-conscientious individuals have larger plans to exercise than their less-conscientious counterparts, which relates to their exercise behaviours (Rhodes et al., 2002; Conner, Rodgers, & Murray, 2007). It has been suggested that the organization and self-discipline marked by those high in conscientiousness translate into these individuals planning and executing exercise behaviours compared to individuals who do not plan as conscientiously.

Targeting Exercise Programs Based on Personality

Exercise professionals are generally interested in promoting physical activity and healthy living, so a link between personality and exercise may have limited practical value. If one subscribes to the view that personality traits are enduring and stable, it also suggests that traits are essentially unchangeable. How can the findings of personality research be used to promote exercise if you can't change personality? Rhodes (2006) suggests that this line of research may help to identify at-risk personalities—people who may struggle with adhering to a new exercise program. In turn, these people may need extra intervention in order to succeed. Some other research has focused on whether preferences for exercise differ by personality. This line of reasoning suggests that different programs could be targeted to various personalities to create a good match (Rhodes, 2006). Courneya and Hellsten (1998) examined several exercise preferences and their relationship with traits from the five factor model. Of interest, extroverts preferred exercises with company, presumably because of the social element of the experience. Those who were open to experience preferred outdoor activities rather than exercising at home or in a fitness centre.

Personality has also shown different relationships with modes of physical activity. Howard, Cunningham, and Rechnitzer (1987) evaluated the relationship of extroversion to several different modes of activity. These researchers found that extroverts were more likely to engage in swimming, aerobic conditioning, dancing, and tennis. In contrast, introverts were more inclined to engage in gardening and home improvement, while no differences were identified for walking, jogging, golf, and cycling. Overall, the relationship between preferences for exercise and personality is interesting, but limited research has actually been performed to assess whether a personality match for exercise is actually effective in improving adherence.

CHAPTER SUMMARY

You were introduced to many ideas in this chapter. From these ideas and concepts, what is known about personality in sport and exercise? Most researchers would probably accept the following key points about personality in sport and exercise today.

Personality is a very complex subject, and numerous theories represent various conceptual approaches. There has been a shift from grand, or global, theories toward more specific key aspects of personality. Investigations and viewpoints are influenced by the particular conceptualizations of personality. Furthermore, researchers are investigating how specific personality factors interact with other psychological factors in specific physical activity contexts.

Measurement of personality requires careful ethical considerations. Sport researchers have generally utilized both general objective personality tests and sport-specific tests to assess personality variables. Personality tests should be administered and interpreted only by individuals with appropriate qualifications. Personality tests generally should not be used to select athletes for teams or positions within teams.

There is no distinct athletic personality, and there is little evidence that a specific personality profile describes successful athletes. Athletes have varied personality profiles. Personality, however, will interact with the competition environment to influence behaviour, cognitions, and emotions. Exercise is positively associated with extroversion and conscientiousness and negatively associated with neuroticism, but the links are weak.

There is no consistent personality trait profile that separates one group of athletes from another, whether it be athletes on teams or in individual sports, athletes in contact sports or non-contact sports, or athletes who are successful or unsuccessful. Furthermore, no consistent personality trait separates athletes from non-athletes. Studies showing statistically significant group differences in a particular trait or cluster of personality traits tend to find that the differences are small (practically meaningless). In many cases, the findings of these studies cannot be replicated. However, large individual differences in personality traits are commonly found among athletes.

Some aspects of personality can be shaped by experience. This implies that sport can change personality. However, research indicates that sport has little impact on core personality traits. This research finding may be due to two reasons. First, to determine the long-term impact of sport on personality would require extensive longitudinal research covering many years. Such research does not exist. Second, many youths enter intensive competitive sport in later adolescence. They bring many years of socialization that have already had a major influence on their personality development.

Personality can influence the behaviour of individual athletes in various contexts. Predicting the strength of personality influence on specific behaviours across athletes or even within a specific athlete across multiple events is often difficult because of contextual and unstable personal factors. Contextual factors include sociocultural norms, the culture and structure of a given sport, and the specific dynamics within a particular sporting event. Unstable personal factors might be physiological states, emotional states, psychological strategies, and motivation. These latter factors will be covered in the following chapters.

Common Myths about Personality in Sport and Exercise Revisited

MYTH: A distinct elite athlete personality profile exists.

The reality is that despite multiple research studies, finding specific characteristics common to elite athletes remains elusive (Vealey, 2002). There are many individual differences among elite athletes both within and across sports and genders. Some people believe that competitiveness and self-confidence are necessary qualities for elite athletes to rise to the highest levels of sport. This seemingly logical belief has only been partially supported in the literature (Gould, Dieffenbach, & Moffett, 2002). This means that some world champions and Olympic gold medallists do not rank themselves high on self-confidence or competitiveness scales. Furthermore, some relatively unsuccessful athletes rate themselves high in self-confidence and competitiveness.

MYTH: People choose physical activities and remain in these activities based on their personality.

There is little evidence that engagement in any particular activity is related to a particular personality profile. There is some evidence that individuals scoring high on sensation seeking might be more likely to engage in high-risk activities, but the strength of this relationship is weak. The research evidence suggests that both activity choice and activity maintenance are regulated by a number of complex factors. Personality is only a small piece of this puzzle. These issues are discussed in more detail in Chapter 4.

MYTH: Contact-sport athletes consistently score high on aggression measures.

If you've played a contact team sport, take a moment to consider your teammates. It is likely that they varied in aggressiveness. The reality is that not all football and rugby players are aggressive on and off the playing field. Some contact-sport athletes may play more aggressively or accrue more fouls or penalties, but this does not necessarily mean that they possess high aggression as a trait.

Review Questions

1. How does the definition ofpersonality differ from that of disposition?
2. Is there an exercise personality? How does conscientiousness influence exercise behaviours?
3. Compare and contrast the state perspective with the trait perspective of personality. Why do you think the trait perspective has had a greater impact on research in sport psychology?

4. What is the interactionist approach to personality in sport? Create an example considering one of your favourite athletes.
5. How might personality interact with exercise motivation?
6. What are the advantages of sport-specific tests of personality?
7. Can exercise programs be matched to meet different personalities?
8. Can a personality test tell you which athletes are going to be successful in a specific sport? Why or why not?
9. What are the differences between competitiveness and sensation seeking?
10. What are the differences between maladaptive and adaptive perfectionism?
11. List the attributes of mental toughness. Try to identify an athlete who has demonstrated all or most of these attributes.

Suggested Reading

Rhodes, R. E., & Smith, N. E. I. (2006). Personality correlates of physical activity: A review and meta-analysis. *British Journal of Sports Medicine, 40*, 958–965.

Vanden Auweele, Y., Nys, K., Rzewnicki, R., & Van Mele, V. (2001). Personality and the athlete. In R. N. Singer, H. A. Hausenblas, & C. M. Janelle (Eds.), *Handbook of sport psychology* (2nd ed., pp. 239–268). New York: Wiley.

Vealey, R. S. (2002). Personality and sport behavior. In T. Horn (Ed.), *Advances in sport psychology* (2nd ed., pp. 43–82). Champaign, IL: Human Kinetics.

References

Anshel, M. H. (2003). *Sport psychology: From theory to practice* (4th ed.). San Francisco: Benjamin Cummings.

Anshel, M. H., & Eom, H. J. (2003). Exploring the dimensions of perfectionism in sport. *International Journal of Sport Psychology, 34*, 255–271.

Bandura, A. (1977). *Social learning theory*. New York. General Learning Press.

Bandura, A. (1997). *Self-efficacy: The exercise of control*. New York: W. H. Freeman.

Butkovic, A., & Bratko, D. (2003). Generation and sex differences in sensation seeking: Results of the family study. *Perceptual and Motor Skills, 97*, 965–970.

Cattell, R. B. (1946). *Description and measurement of personality*. New York: Harcourt, Brace & World.

Cattell, R. B. (1995). Personality structure and the new fifth edition of the 16PF. *Educational & Psychological Measurement, 55*, 926–937.

Connaughton, D., Wadey, R., Hanton, S. & Jones, G. G. (2008). The development and maintenance of mental toughness: Perceptions of elite performers. *Journal of Sports Sciences, 26*, 83–95.

Conner, M., Rodgers, W., & Murray, T. (2007). Conscientiousness and the intention–behavior relationship: Predicting exercise behavior. *Journal of Sport and Exercise Psychology, 29*, 518–533.

Costa, P. T., Jr., & McCrae, R. R. (1994). *Neuroticism Extroversion Openness (NEO) Five Factor Inventory*. Lutz, FL: Psychological Assessment Resources.

Courneya, K. S., & Hellsten, L. A. (1998). Personality correlates of exercise behavior, motives, barriers and preferences: An application of the five-factor model. *Personality and Individual Differences, 24*, 625–633.

Crust, L. (2007). Mental toughness in sport: A review. *International Journal of Sport and Exercise Psychology,5*, 270–290.

Davis, H. (1991). Criterion validity of the Athletic Motivation Inventory: Issues in professional sport. *Journal of Applied Sport Psychology, 3*, 176–182.

Digman, J. M. (1990). Personality structure: Emergence of the five-factor model. *Annual Review of Psychology*, *41*, 417–440.

Dunham, J. M., Dunn, J. G. H., & Hogg, J. M. (2002, October). *Perfectionism and attitudinal body image in competitive female figure skaters*. Paper presented at the annual conference of the Association for the Advancement of Applied Sport Psychology, Tucson, AZ.

Dunn, J. G. H., Causgrove, J., Dunn, J., & Syrotuik, D. G. (2002). Relationship between multidimensional perfectionism and goal orientations in sport. *Journal of Sport & Exercise Psychology*, *24*, 376–395.

Durand-Bush, N., & Salmela, J. H. (2002). The development and maintenance of expert athletic performance: Perceptions of World & Olympic Champions. *Journal of Applied Sport Psychology*, *14*, 154–171.

Endler, N. S., & Magnusson, D. (1976). Toward an interactional psychology of personality. *Psychological Bulletin*, *83*, 956–974.

Epstein, S. (1979). The stability of behaviour: On predicting most of the people much of the time. *Journal of Personality and Social Psychology*, *37*, 1097–1126.

Etzel, E., Watson, J. C., II, & Zizzi, S. (2004). A Web-based survey of AAASP members' ethical beliefs and behaviours in the new Millennium. *Journal of Applied Sport Psychology*, *16*, 236–250.

Etzel, E., Yura, M. T., & Perna, F. (1998). Ethics in assessment and testing in sport and exercise psychology. In J. L. Duda (Ed.), *Advances in sport and exercise psychology measurement* (pp. 423–432). Morgantown, WV: Fitness Information Technology.

Flett, G. L., & Hewitt, P. L. (2005). Perfectionism and maladjustment: An overview of theoretical delinational, and treatment issues. In G. L. Flett, & P. L. Hewitt (Eds.), *Perfectionism: Theory, research, and treatment* (pp. 5–31). Washington, DC: American Psychological Association.

Frost, R. O., Marten, P., Lahart, C., & Rosenblate, R. (1990). The dimensions of perfectionism. *Cognitive Therapy and Research*, *14*, 449–468.

Gaudreau, P., & Anti, S. (2008). Athletes' broad dimensions of dispositional perfectionism: Examining changes in life satisfaction and the mediating role of sport related motivation and coping. *Journal of Sport and Exercise Psychology*, *30*, 356–382.

Giacobbi, P. R., Jr., Hausenblas, H. A., & Frye, N. (2005). A naturalistic assessment of the relationship between personality, daily life events, leisure-time physical activity, and mood. *Psychology of Sport and Exercise*, *6*, 67–81.

Gill, D. L., & Deeter, T. E. (1988). Development of the sport orientation questionnaire. *Research Quarterly for Exercise and Sport*, *59*, 191–202.

Gill, D. L., & Dzewaltowski, D. A. (1988). Competitive orientations among intercollegiate athletes: Is winning the only thing? *The Sport Psychologist*, *2*, 212–221.

Goldberg, A. S. (1998). Sports slump busting: 10 steps to mental toughness and peak performance. Champaign, IL: Human Kinetics.

Gould, D., Dieffenbach, K., & Moffett, A. (2002). Personal characteristics and their development in Olympic Champions. *Journal of Applied Sport Psychology*, *14*, 172–204.

Gould, D., Hodge, K., Peterson, K., & Petlichkoff, L. (1987). Psychological foundations of coaching: Similarities and differences among intercollegiate wrestling coaches. *The Sport Psychologist*, *1*, 293–308.

Gucciardi, D. F., Gordon, S., & Dimmock, J. A. (2009). Advancing mental toughness research and theory using personal construct psychology. *International Review of Sport and Exercise Psychology*, *2*, 54–72.

Howard, J. H., Cunningham, D. A., & Rechnitzer, P. A. (1987). Personality and fitness decline in middle-aged men. *International Journal of Sport Psychology*, *18*, 100–111.

Hughes, S. L., Case, H. S., Stuempfle, K. J., & Evans, D. S. (2003). Personality profiles of Iditasport ultra-marathon participants. *Journal of Applied Sport Psychology*, *15*, 256–261.

Jones, G., Hanton, S., & Connaughton, D. (2002). What is this thing called mental toughness? An investigation of elite sports performers. *Journal of Applied Sport Psychology*, *14*, 205–218.

Kajtna, T., Tuscaronak, M., Baricacute, R., & Burnik, S. (2004). Personality in high-risk sports athletes. *Kinesiology, 36*, 24–35.

Lazarus, R. S., & Folkman, S. (1984). *Stress, appraisal and coping*. New York: Springer.

Lemyre, P. N., Hall, H. K., & Roberts, G. C. (2008). A social cognitive approach to burnout in athletes. *Scandinavian Journal of Medicine and Science in Sports, 18*, 221–234.

Lindsay, D. S., Paulhus, D. L., & Nairne, J. (2008). *Psychology: The adaptive mind*(3rd Canadian ed.). Toronto, ON: Nelson.

Llewellyn, D. J., & Sanchez, X. (2008). Individual differences and risk taking in rock climbing. *Psychology of Sport and Exercise, 9*, 413–428.

Loehr, J. E. (1995). *The new toughness training for sports*. New York: Plume.

Mack, M. G., & Ragan, B. G. (2008). Development of the Mental, Emotional and Bodily Toughness Inventory in collegiate athletes and nonathletes. *Journal of Athletic Training, 43*, 125–133.

Malone, C. (1985). Risk-taking in sport. In L. K. Bunker, R. J. Rotella, & A. S. Reilly (Eds.), *Sport psychology: Psychological considerations in maximizing sport performance* (pp. 264–281). Ithaca, NY: Mouvement.

Martens, R. (1977). *Sport competition anxiety test*. Champaign, IL: Human Kinetics.

Maslow, A. H. (1943). A theory of human motivation. *Psychological Review, 50*, 370–396.

McNair, D. M., Lorr, M., & Droppleman, L. F. (1971). *Profile of Mood States*. San Diego, CA: Educational and Industrial Testing Service.

McNair, D. M., Lorr, M., & Droppleman, L. F. (1992). *Revised manual for the Profile of Mood States*. San Diego, CA: Educational and Industrial Testing Service.

Mischel, W. (1968). *Personality and assessment*. New York: Wiley.

Morgan, W. P. (1980). Personality dynamics and sport. In R. Suinn (Ed.), *Psychology in sport—methods and application* (pp. 145–155). Minneapolis, MN: Burgess.

Morgan, W. P., & Pollock, M. L. (1977). Psychological characterization of the elite distance runner. *Annals of the New York Academy of Science, 301*, 382–403.

Orlick, T. (1989). Reflections on sport psychology consulting with individual and team sport athletes at summer and winter Olympic Games. *The Sport Psychologist, 3*, 358–365.

Orlick, T., & Partington, J. (1988). Mental links to excellence. *The Sport Psychologist, 2*, 105–130.

Ostrow, A. C. (2002). *Directory of psychological tests in the sport & exercise sciences* (2nd ed.). Morgantown, WV: Fitness Information Technology.

Rhodes, R. E. (2006). The built-in environment: The role of personality with physical activity. *Exercise and Sport Sciences Reviews, 34*, 83–88.

Rhodes, R. E., Courneya, K. E., & Hayduk, L. A. (2002). Does personality moderate the theory of planned behavior in the exercise domain? *Journal of Sport & Exercise Psychology, 24*, 120–132.

Rhodes, R. E., & Smith, N. E. I. (2006). Personality correlates of physical activity: A review and meta-analysis. *British Journal of Sports Medicine, 40*, 958–965.

Rogers, C. R. (1959). A theory of therapy, personality and interpersonal relationships as developed in the client-centered framework. In S. Koch (Ed.), *Psychology: A study of a science: Vol. III. Formulations of the person and the social context* (pp. 184–256). New York: McGraw-Hill.

Rotter, J. B. (1954). *Social learning and clinical psychology*. New York: Prentice-Hall.

Rowley, A. J., Landers, D. M., Kyllo, L. B., & Etnier, J. L. (1995). Does the iceberg profile discriminate between successful and less successful athletes? A meta-analysis. *Journal of Sport & Exercise Psychology, 17*, 185–199.

Skinner, B.F. (1999). *The Behavior of Organisms: An Experimental Analysis*. New York: D. Appleton Century. (Original work published 1938)

Thomas, G. C., & Sinclair, G. D. (1978). Relationship between personality and performance of Canadian women intercollegiate basketball players. In *Human performance and behaviour*. Banff, AB: University of Calgary. Retrieved from the SIRC SportDiscus database.

Tutko, T. A., Lyon, L. P., & Ogilvie, B. C. (1969). *Athletic Motivation Inventory*. San Jose, CA: Institute for the Study of Athletic Motivation.

Vallence, J. K. H., Dunn, J. G. H., & Causgrove-Dunn, J. L. (2006). Perfectionism, anger and situation criticality in competitive youth ice hockey. *Journal of Sport and Exercise Psychology*, *28*, 383–407.

Vanden Auweele, Y., De Cuyper, B., Van Mele, V., & Rzewnicki, R. (1993). Elite performance and personality: From description and prediction to diagnosis and intervention. In R. N. Singer, M. Murphey, & L. K. Tenant (Eds.), *Handbook of research in sport psychology* (pp. 257–289). New York: Macmillan.

Vanden Auweele, Y., Nys, K., Rzewnicki, R., & Van Mele, V. (2001). Personality and the athlete. In R. N. Singer, H. A. Hausenblas, & C. M. Janelle (Eds.), *Handbook of sport psychology* (2nd ed., pp. 239–268). New York: Wiley.

Vealey, R. S. (2002). Personality and sport behaviour. In T. Horn (Ed.), *Advances in sport psychology* (2nd ed., pp. 43–82). Champaign, IL: Human Kinetics.

Zuckerman, M. (1994). Behavioral expressions and biosocial bases of sensation seeking. New York: Cambridge University Press.

Chapter 4

Motivation and Behavioural Change

Diane E. Mack
Catherine M. Sabiston
Meghan H. McDonough
Philip M. Wilson
David M. Paskevich

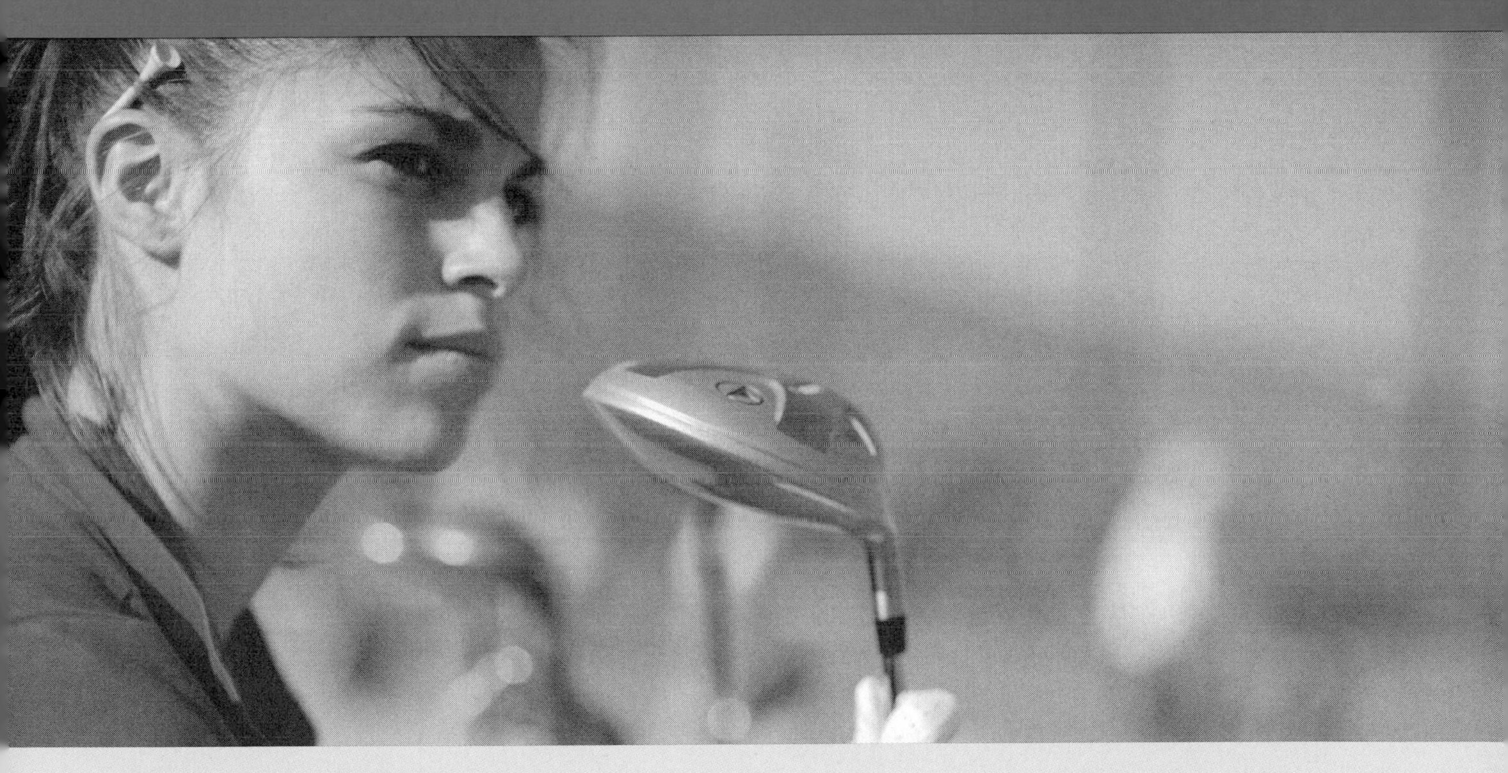

Chapter Objectives

After reading this chapter, you should be able to do the following:

1. Define motivation and apply the definition to your own physical activity behaviour.
2. Describe the different approaches to understanding motivation as applied to behavioural change.
3. Apply select theories and models of motivation to your sport or exercise behaviour.
4. Understand how various social influences, including family and peers, affect motivation for physical activity.
5. Discuss similarities and differences in the theories and models of motivation.

Canadian triathlete Simon Whitfield earned a silver medal at the 2008 Olympics in Beijing to add to the gold he won at the Sydney Olympics in 2000. Although the triathlon is often thought of as an individual event, Whitfield credited teammate (and training partner) Colin Jenkins for much of his success. Prior to the Olympic games, Jenkins was asked to sacrifice personal aspirations to assist Whitfield in his Olympic medal pursuit. By helping Whitfield to conserve energy in the swimming and biking portions of the event, Jenkins permitted Whitfield to focus on his strength—the running portion of the competition. Triathlon Canada was criticized for naming Jenkins to the Olympic team in the role of "domestique," or servant, since other Canadian triathletes were ranked ahead of him. Whitfield endured considerable scrutiny for his vocal request and endorsement of Jenkins' appointment and role—criticism that was likely hard to endure for a Canadian icon in his chosen sport. While Whitfield celebrated his Olympic success, a very different celebration awaited Jenkins, who punched the air in celebration as he crossed the finish line in last place, but who also accomplished his Olympic objective: to help Whitfield win an Olympic medal!

Most of us reading this story will never know the Olympic experience as a competitor. Yet, certain themes may be applicable to your own physical activity history. What have you endured to achieve your physical activity goals? Did you receive criticism, yet persist in your athletic pursuits? Were you ever asked to sacrifice your personal goals for those of your team? Did your motives for continuing to train or compete change as a consequence? With reflection, you may develop an understanding of how motivational processes are key to understanding initiation, maintenance, and termination of all forms of physical activity behaviour.

Common Myths about Motivation and Behavioural Change

MYTH: Motivation is a trait. You are either a motivated individual or you are not.

MYTH: Competence is the main motivator for engaging in physical activity.

MYTH: Enjoyment is the best motive to help us understand physical activity behaviour.

INTRODUCTION

What motivates you? You have likely considered this question on more than one occasion for various aspects of your life. Although various definitions can be found in the literature, **motivation** can be simply defined as the reasons why you do the things you do (Reeve, 2005). To help you fully understand what motivates you, consider addressing each of the questions in Table 4.1. You will see how intricate and daunting it can be to understand motivation.

With thoughtful consideration of these questions, you will gain an understanding of the complexity of (and ongoing fascination with) the topic of motivation among scholars, athletes, coaches, and those interested in health promotion. The examples provided should make it obvious that personal, cognitive, and environmental factors coexist to influence physical activity behaviour.

Table 4.1 Questions to Help Understand Motivation

General Question	Sport and Exercise Examples
Why did you start engaging in sport/exercise?	Who influenced your decision not only to participate in sport, but what sport you competed in? Was it a parent? Was the choice of sport determined in part because you had siblings who were also participating in that sport?
Why did (or do) you persist in sport/exercise?	Was it simply because you enjoyed it? Did you experience personal and competitive success? Did the expectations of others influence your decision to continue?
Why is your behaviour directed toward certain physical activity goals rather than others?	Goals impose priorities on our behaviour. How have your goals for your sport/exercise participation changed over time? Do your goals include any of the following: Fun? Personal success? Competitive success? Lean and fit body? Having the identity of an athlete?
Why did your sport/exercise behaviour change?	Are you still a competitive athlete? Do you still compete at a level similar to what you did a few years ago? Or, has your sport participation transformed into behaviour more consistent with regular exercise?
Why does your sport/ exercise behaviour vary in intensity?	Were you always fired up to train? Compete? Or, were there times when training was tedious or frustrating? How did various external sources (e.g., coaches, family, exercise buddy) influence the intensity of your motivation?
In the short or long term, why did your sport/exercise behaviour stop?	What may have influenced your decision to stop being physically active? Was it loss of interest, injury, no accessibility to facilities, or a change in lifestyle (e.g., parenthood)?

Note: Adapted from Reeve, J. M. (2005). *Understanding motivation and emotion* (4th ed.). Hoboken, NJ: Wiley & Sons.

APPROACHES TO UNDERSTANDING MOTIVATION FOR BEHAVIOURAL CHANGE

How would you describe yourself? As a person who is highly motivated? Someone who internalizes criticism? One who is strongly influenced by rewards? Or, does your motivation vary depending on the situation you are in? In the chapter on personality (Chapter 3), the authors discuss how relatively stable traits or dispositions could influence behaviour. But what about the influence of the environment and/or how one evaluates the environment? Three approaches are described briefly below to help understand motivation as it applies to behavioural change.

Behavioural Approaches

The **behavioural approach** to understanding motivation focuses on conditioning, or learning from the environment. Fathers of behaviourism, including Watson and Skinner, believed that learning from the environment, not personality or free will, determined people's actions.

Basic features of behavioural approaches to understanding motivation include operant conditioning, vicarious conditioning, and operant strategies.

In operant conditioning, the athlete/exerciser associates behaviours with consequences that are learned though coincidental reinforcement (i.e., any factor that is associated with and increases the frequency of a behaviour) or punishment (i.e., any factor that decreases the probability of a behaviour reoccurring) following a specific behaviour. Positive reinforcement involves any factor (usually a reward) that increases behaviour. Negative reinforcement involves the removal of any factor (usually something aversive like criticism) that increases behaviour. Punishment is any factor that decreases the behaviour.

Vicarious conditioning results from observing others. If, through watching our friends be physically active, we observe changes in their energy and appearance, we may be more likely to engage in physical activity, assuming that the changes are valued outcomes. Or, children may model the post-scoring celebrations of professional athletes like Steve Nash because they respect and admire those athletes.

Operant strategies, such as self-monitoring, are effective strategies for developing and maintaining skills. Self-monitoring involves actually recording your own behaviour in specific situations.

Cognitive Approaches

Aaron Beck, the founder of the **cognitive approach**, emphasized the role of thought patterns and cognitive habits as determinants of behaviour. In contrast to the behavioural approach, in the cognitive approach the individual is viewed as an active participant such that it is his or her interpretation of the external environment (as opposed to the external environment itself) that exerts a powerful influence on behaviour. A basic premise is the belief that automatic thought processes (e.g., saying "I messed up again" following a disappointing performance), cognitive errors (e.g., personalization of negative events, all-or-none thinking), and core beliefs (e.g., low self-esteem) can be altered with continued persistence. Alteration of thought patterns is based on recognition and identification of one's systematic thought biases, automatic thoughts, and basic beliefs. Once thought processes have been recognized, they can be challenged and changed to more accurately reflect reality. The cognitive approach teaches people to use rational thought, logic, and empiricism to reform thought patterns. The emphasis on cognition and cognitive evaluation is a key feature of many of the motivational models covered in this chapter.

Cognitive-behavioural Approaches

University of Waterloo professor Donald Meichenbaum is credited with being the founder of **cognitive-behavioural approaches** to changing behaviour. Cognitive-behavioural approaches to understanding motivated behaviour are based on two central tenets: (1) our cognitions influence our emotions and behaviour, and (2) our behaviour can affect our thought patterns and emotions. Cognitive-behavioural approaches, including self-monitoring, goal setting, feedback, and decision making, have been found to be effective for increasing self-reported exercise behaviour (Brawley, Rejeski, & Lutes, 2000). These approaches are covered in more detail in Chapter 13 (Physical Activity Interventions) and Chapter 14 (Sport Psychology Interventions).

REFLECTIONS 4.1

Michael is a 20-year-old minor league professional baseball player. Michael excelled as a semi-pro player, and it was rumoured that he would be invited to the Toronto Blue Jays spring training camp. His shot at the pros! With the pressure to perform mounting, his troubles began, and they continued through the rest of the season. Consequently, he was not invited to spring training camp. He was demoted to a lower division and struggled the following season with shoulder injuries and technical problems, including loss of pitching control. Michael has subsequently experienced a loss of self-confidence, negative thinking, and doubts of the future. He has no understanding of the cause of his difficulties. Reflect on how cognitive-behavioural approaches apply to Michael's concerns.

MODELS OF MOTIVATION AND BEHAVIOURAL CHANGE

Campaigns to get people more physically active, like ParticipACTION (www.participaction.com), are based on an understanding of the factors that shape the behavioural decisions people make about their health. The primary application of motivational models has been either to predict physical activity behaviour or to describe the thoughts and feelings of people who have engaged in a particular pattern (i.e., fluctuations in physical activity) of behaviour. More recently, researchers have used motivational models of behavioural change to develop interventions designed to get people more physically active (e.g., VERB, www.cdc.gov/YouthCampaign; Wheeling Walks, www.wheelingwalks.org). In the next section, we outline various approaches that are thought to motivate people to engage in physical activity and the research supporting these approaches. Implications of this knowledge for the design and implementation of initiatives to promote physical activity behaviour are briefly discussed. Many of these models and associated concepts appear throughout the rest of the textbook.

Transtheoretical Model

The transtheoretical model, or TM (Prochaska & DiClemente, 1986), has emerged as a framework to understand how individuals initiate and adopt regular physical activity. The TM proposes that individuals move through a temporal sequence of five stages: (1) **pre-contemplation** (individuals do not consider exercising in the next six months), (2) **contemplation** (individuals seriously consider beginning exercise in the next six months), (3) **preparation** (individuals have made small changes toward becoming more physically active), (4) **action** (individuals have begun exercising in the past six months), and (5) **maintenance** (individuals exercise and have done so for more than six months). Stage progress is not necessarily linear, and people can enter the process at any stage and may relapse (or regress) to a previous stage, particularly for behaviours that are difficult to change—like physical activity.

One simplistic way of understanding the TM is through the intention–behaviour continuum. The first two stages of change (pre-contemplation and contemplation) are defined by an individual's intent to engage in physical activity (Marcus, Eaton, Rossi,

& Harlow, 1994), whereas preparation combines intentional and behavioural criteria (Prochaska & Marcus, 1994). The action and maintenance stages are defined exclusively by behavioural criteria, that is, the length of time performing the behaviour at the appropriate level. For more detailed information on the TM, consult www.uri.edu/research/cprc/transtheoretical.htm.

Factors Influencing Stage Progression The TM identifies different factors that influence individuals' decisions to become more physically active at each stage(Prochaska & DiClemente, 1986). The first factor is **self-efficacy**, or the belief in one's capabilities to organize and execute the course of action required to produce specific outcomes. Self-efficacy is less salient in earlier stages but increases with stage progression (Plotnikoff, Hotz, Birkett, & Courneya, 2001). Based on expectancy theory, **decisional balance** is a multidimensional set of values linked with advantages and disadvantages of behavioural change. As a general rule, the disadvantages of physical activity outweigh the benefits for those who are inactive, whereas the opposite is true for those who are engaging in physical activity (Prochaska & Velicer, 1997). Finally, **processes of change** reflect strategies that individuals use to progress through the stages (Marcus & Simkin, 1994) and are divided into two dimensions that serve as targets for intervention programs. The first dimension, experiential or cognitive processes, includes strategies used to help an individual modify thought patterns. Typically used in the pre-activity stages, experiential processes include information seeking, reconsidering the consequences of inactivity, the expression of feelings about inactivity, and evaluating the consequences of engaging in physical activity for others (e.g., spouse, children). The second dimension, behavioural processes, includes increased social support for behavioural engagement, the use of rewards and reinforcement, and the use of appropriate cues for maintaining behaviour (e.g., running shoes placed by front door). The use of behavioural processes is greatest in the action and maintenance stages.

Research on the Transtheoretical Model in Exercise Psychology Demographic and health-related variables have been examined for their association with a particular stage of physical activity. Using population health data from the United States, Garber, Allsworth, Marcus, Hesser, and Lapane (2008) noted that 58% of people reported being in the maintenance stage. Being female, being of non-Caucasian ethnicity, and having completed a lower level of education were generally associated with lower stages of change. Age, marital status, and current smoking status were not associated with stage of change. In a meta-analytic review of the application of the TM to exercise behaviour, Marshall and Biddle (2001) found that as stage increased, so did reported physical activity.

Canadian researchers have also examined the TM to determine its use in physical activity settings. Here is a sample of this research:

- Rhodes and Plotnikoff (2006) found that, in a large Canadian sample, self-efficacy and behavioural processes discriminated between those who intended to engage in physical activity and those who did not.
- Berry and colleagues demonstrated that the greatest risk for relapse was found in the preparation stage, with primary barriers including time, access to facilities, and limited opportunities outside physical education (Berry, Naylor, & Wharf-Higgins, 2005).
- Plotnikoff and colleagues (2007) found that female employees who received physical activity information targeted for their individual stage of change increased their physical activity compared to those who did not receive stage-matched information.

Table 4.2 Transtheoretical Model: Key Concepts and Physical Activity Examples

Stage	Potential Change Strategies	Examples
Pre-contemplation	Increase awareness of need for change; personalize information about risks and benefits.	Health communication activities Health risk appraisals/health screening Increase perceived susceptibility and perceived severity
Contemplation	Motivate; encourage making specific plans.	Incentives Encouragement from significant others Supportive policies (e.g., reduced gym membership fees for those who enrol)
Preparation	Assist with goal development and progression to achieve targeted behaviour.	Guidelines to change behaviour Individual and environmental support approach for behaviour change
Action	Assist with feedback, problem solving, social support, and reinforcement.	Continued social and environmental support Incentives for reaching behavioural goals Self-efficacy awareness
Maintenance	Assist with coping, reminders, finding alternatives, and avoiding slips/relapses.	Relapse-prevention techniques Continued social, environmental, and policy support

Note: Adapted from Table 3, pg. 15 in National Cancer Institute, *Theories at a Glance: A Guide for Health Promotion Practice*, 2nd ed., NIH publication no. 05-3896, September 2005. www.cancer.gov/PDF/481f5d53-63df-41bc-bfaf-5aa48ee1da4d/TAAG3.pdf

Applications of the Transtheoretical Model The TM holds considerable appeal at an individual and population health level since it includes guidelines on what information to provide at each stage of behaviour. Indeed, one of the basic principles of stage-matched interventions is to attract the attention of individuals by exposing them to messages that are specific to their motivation to act (see Table 4.2).

Theory of Planned Behaviour

The **theory of planned behaviour**, or TPB (Ajzen, 1985), highlights personal and social factors as influences of behaviour. The TPB stipulates that the most proximal determinant of behaviour is **intention**, that is, a person's readiness to perform a behaviour (see Figure 4.1). More simply put, if an overweight man has no intention of exercising three times a week, he is not likely to do so. The intention–physical activity behaviour relationship demonstrates temporal fluctuation, with weaker relationships between intention and behaviour occurring with distal measures (e.g., Do you intend to exercise in the next three months?)

Figure 4.1 Theory of planned behaviour

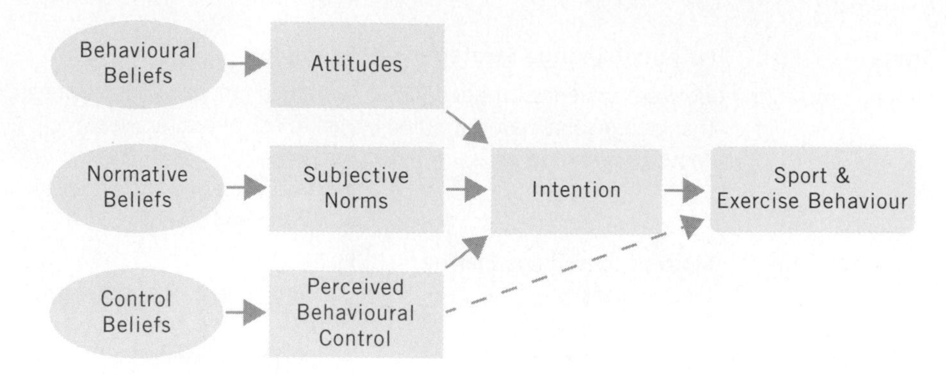

Source: Adapted from Figure 1, pg. 182 in *Organizational Behavior and Human Decision Processes* 50 (December), Ajzen, I. The Theory of Planned Behavior, 179-211, © 1991 with permission from Elsevier.

versus proximal measures (e.g., Do you intend to exercise in the next week?; Symons Downs & Hausenblas, 2005). While not often used in sport research, the TPB is a popular theory in accounting for exercise and leisure time physical activity behaviour.

As a means of understanding the forces influencing behavioural intention, the TPB posits three main factors. **Attitude** reflects the positive or negative evaluation of engaging in a behaviour. **Subjective norms** reflect perceived social pressures to perform a behaviour that stem from various personal (e.g., family, physicians) or environmental (e.g., media) sources. **Perceived behavioural control** reflects the extent to which behaviour is volitional and is thought to indirectly affect behaviour through intention as well as being a direct influence.

Each of the three factors predictive of intention is reflected in a set of underlying beliefs. **Behavioural beliefs** suggest that being physically active will lead to certain consequences (e.g., losing weight) and an evaluation of the consequences (e.g., weight loss is important and will have many positive health benefits). Common behavioural beliefs include that exercise enhances fitness and health, improves physical appearance, is fun

Exercise can facilitate both physical and mental health. Behavioural beliefs, normative beliefs, and control beliefs have been shown to influence attitudes, subjective norms, and perceived behavioural control, which are linked to intention and exercise behaviour.

Photograph courtesy of Peter Crocker, University of British Columbia.

and enjoyable, and promotes social interactions. **Normative beliefs** reflect perceptions of significant others and the value that they place on physical activity behaviour and consequences. Common social pressures for exercise include family and friends, medical professionals, and the media. **Control beliefs** are the perceived barriers (e.g., resources) and facilitators (e.g., opportunities) of engaging in a behaviour. According to the Canadian Fitness and Lifestyle Research Institute (www.cflri.ca/eng/index.php), common control beliefs for exercise include lack of time, lack of energy, and weather.

REFLECTIONS 4.2

You are a fitness consultant hired by a large Canadian organization to improve physical activity levels in the workplace. Before contacting you, the manager conducted a survey on how many of her employees intended to either start an exercise program or increase the challenge of their existing program. The results showed that 35% of the men and 28% of the women intended to start exercising or improve their current program. Based on the TPB, what intervention strategies would you use to help increase physical activity levels in the workplace? Describe differences that you may implement for those employees initiating exercise compared to those who want to increase the challenge of their existing program.

Research on the Theory of Planned Behaviour in Sport and Exercise Psychology Reviews of the TPB literature support the relationships described in the model framework. More specifically, attitude and perceived behavioural control are strong correlates of exercise intentions (Hagger, Chatzisarantis, & Biddle, 2002). Subjective norms has generally shown weaker (but still meaningful) associations with exercise intentions (Hausenblas, Carron, & Mack, 1997). Finally, Godin and Kok (1996) reported that the intention to engage in physical activity explained just over one-third of the individual differences in exercise behaviour.

Given the strong support for the TPB, it is not surprising that researchers in Canada have turned to this theory to develop research studies and explore intervention techniques. Here are just a few examples:

- Researchers have demonstrated the utility of the TPB across gender (Rhodes, Blanchard, & Blacklock, 2008), age (Nguyen, Potvin, & Otis, 1997), and ethnicity (Blanchard et al., 2007).
- There is considerable evidence of the ability of the TPB to predict physical activity behaviour in diverse clinical populations, including colorectal and breast cancer survivors (Courneya & Friedenreich, 1997, 1999), individuals with spinal cord injuries (Latimer & Martin Ginis, 2005), and individuals showing symptoms of peripheral artery disease (Galea & Bray, 2006).
- Data from home-based cardiac rehabilitation patients (Blanchard, 2008) demonstrated that various behavioural beliefs (e.g., get in shape, strengthen heart muscle, and feel more energetic) and control beliefs (e.g., back pain, side effects associated with medication, time, and weather) were associated with exercise behaviour six months after engagement in exercise.

Applications of the Theory of Planned Behaviour Given the influence of intention on behaviour, intervention strategies need to focus on enhancing an individual's intention to exercise. For those wanting to change their exercise behaviour, attitude toward physical activity may be increased by increasing the knowledge of the benefits of exercise and the importance of those benefits. Education can occur at multiple levels, including government health messages, public service announcements, news stories and other media outlets, research findings, and tips posted in fitness facilities. To address changing an individual's intentions to exercise, interventions need to target subjective norms. This can be done by helping individuals identify exercise environments where everyone is physically active or by eliciting the support of others who are physically active.

Finally, target the individual's perceived behavioural control through a range of strategies, such as highlighting coping skills for dealing with barriers. For example, to address the commonly cited barrier of "no time," an individual could do a greater number of shorter bouts of exercise (e.g., 10 minutes three times a day) to fit their schedule as opposed to one long bout (e.g., 30 minutes once a day).

Social Cognitive Theory

Social cognitive theory, or SCT (Bandura, 1997), is a widely used theory that describes the factors that affect and determine behaviour. SCT isrooted in the belief that individuals are proactively engaged in their own development, with motivation viewed as the product of a dynamic interplay of personal (i.e., expectations, values, beliefs, attitudes), behavioural (i.e., effort, persistence, and choice in sport and exercise), and environmental (i.e., social pressures, motivational climate, physical space, and opportunities) influences (see Figure 4.2). How athletes interpret their behaviour informs and alters their environments and the personal factors they possess, which in turn informs and alters subsequent behaviours.

The main constructs embedded within SCT are summarized below:

- **Observational learning:** Individuals learn and acquire behaviour by watching the actions and outcomes of others' behaviours.
- **Goals:** Behaviour is directed by the goals that individuals have.
- **Outcome expectations:** Behaviour is a function of the expected positive and negative consequences associated with a particular behaviour.
- **Outcome expectancies:** The expectations that an outcome that is valuable for the individual will follow a given behaviour.

Figure 4.2 Social cognitive theory

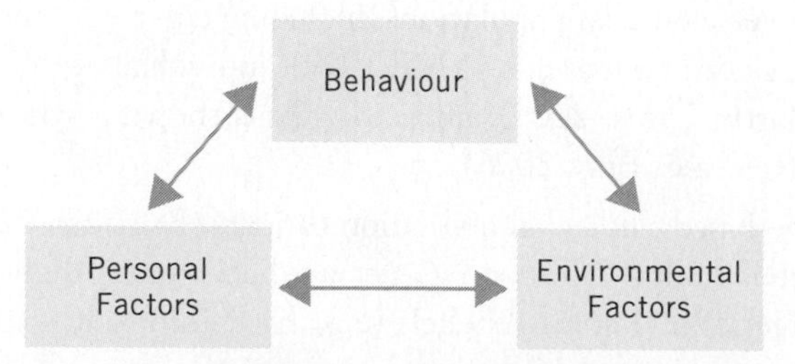

Source: Adapted from Figure 1.1, pg. 6, Adapted from Bandura, A. (1997). *Self-efficacy: The exercise of control.* New York: W.H. Freeman.

- **Self-regulation:** Behaviour is self-directed and is initiated, monitored, and evaluated by the individual in a way that is consistent with accomplishing his or her goals.
- **Behavioural outcomes:** Behaviour is dependent on the individual's knowledge and skills for performing that behaviour.
- **Self-efficacy:** Belief in one's capabilities to organize and execute the course of action required to produce given attainments.

Social Cognitive Theory: A Focus on Self-efficacy At the very core of SCT are self-efficacy beliefs, which serve as the foundation for human motivation, well-being, and personal accomplishment. Self-efficacy is a situation-specific form of self-confidence that focuses on the extent to which an individual feels he or she will be successful in producing a specific outcome given their skills and the situation. For example, self-efficacy would explain how confident a Canadian athlete is that he will win a gold medal at the Vancouver 2010 Olympics (specific outcome) given his training and preparation (skills) and the pressure to perform in front of a home crowd (the situation). Bandura recognized four main personal and environmental ways to change an individual's self-efficacy beliefs: **mastery experience, vicarious experience, social persuasion,** and **physiological and affective states** (see Table 4.3).

Table 4.3 Sources of Self-efficacy

Source	Definition	Example
Mastery experience	Past performance success and failures for similar behaviours	A woman who signs up for a marathon training program at Runner's World may derive her self-efficacy beliefs from her previous experiences with walking or jogging.
Vicarious experience	Modelled behaviours associated with development of and change in self-efficacy, including imagery use and target similarity as key features	A trauma patient at Sunnybrook Health Sciences Centre in Toronto could watch a fellow patient successfully complete a series of exercises in a strength training program.
Social persuasion	Verbal and non-verbal feedback from significant, knowledgeable others	Personal strategies such as self-talk may be used to provide persuasion. Feedback from coaches, friends, fitness trainers, and/or medical professionals also serves as a good source.
Physiological and affective states	Physical and emotional cues associated with performance and behaviour	Physical signs and feelings, such as pain or fatigue, may lead an exerciser to doubt his or her capability to successfully run on the treadmill for 45 minutes. Personal coping strategies (e.g., rhythmic breathing, relaxation, or meditation) may be used to help decrease physiological and affective states.

Note: Adapted from Chapter 3, pp. 79–113, from Bandura, A. (1997). *Self-efficacy: The exercise of control.* New York: W.H. Freeman.

REFLECTIONS 4.3

The coach for a local volleyball team has asked you for advice to help increase the confidence of her star player's spiking ability at home games. How would you describe the sources of self-efficacy to this coach? Provide examples of each source that will help this coach develop strategies to work with her player.

Photograph by Richard Lam, courtesy of University of British Columbia Athletics.

Research Linking Social Cognitive Theory Constructs and Sport and Exercise Behaviour Research in sport and exercise psychology has rarely included all SCT dimensions when examining their influence on behaviour. For those that have examined multiple (but not all) SCT constructs, the included variables have accounted for between 40% and 55% of physical activity behaviour (McAuley, Jerome, Elavsky, Marquez, & Ramsey, 2003). Reviews have supported the unique role of outcome expectancies (Williams, Anderson, & Winett, 2005), goal setting (Shilts, Horowitz, & Townsend, 2004), and self-efficacy in sport and exercise settings (Moritz, Feltz, Fahrbach, & Mack, 2000; Standage & Duda, 2004).

Canadian researchers have contributed to the sport and exercise literature specific to SCT across diverse study populations. A sample of this research is offered below:

- Plotnikoff and colleagues demonstrated that SCT variables of self-efficacy, outcome expectations, impediments, and social support predicted over 50% of the individual differences in physical activity behaviour goals across a six-month period in a population-based sample of Canadian diabetics (Plotnikoff, Lippke, Courneya, Birkett, & Sigal, 2008).
- Self-efficacy is linked to behavioural outcomes, such as sport performance (Beauchamp, Bray, & Albinson, 2002), exercise adherence (Rodgers & Brawley, 1993), energy expenditure in children (Foley et al., 2008), and physical activity participation in individuals attending cardiac rehabilitation (Woodgate & Brawley, 2008).
- Rodgers and colleagues (2008) examined three types of self-efficacy to help understand women's behaviour engagement in a 12-week exercise program. Task efficacy (efficacy to produce enduring behaviour), coping efficacy (efficacy to overcome challenging circumstances), and scheduling efficacy (confidence in exercising regularly despite other time demands) were assessed. Coping and scheduling efficacy increased over time, whereas task efficacy remained stable.

Social-cognitive Theory in Practice SCT has also been used as the basis for informing intervention strategies aimed at increasing physical activity levels. The reciprocal nature of the determinants in SCT makes it possible for coaches or health promotion specialists to intervene at personal, environmental, or behavioural levels. For example, using SCT as a guiding framework, coaches can work to improve athletes' emotional states and correct faulty self-beliefs (personal factors), improve athletic skills and self-regulatory practices (behaviour), and alter the sporting environment (e.g., more skill-focused training environment as opposed to outcome focused) that may undermine achievement (environmental factors).

SCT is also used in the health sector. Many health messages and mission statements from Canadian organizations and agencies are founded on SCT-based evidence. For example, the Public Health Agency of Canada's Healthy Living Unit (www.phac-aspc.gc.ca/pau-uap/fitness/about.html) has the following goals:

- To encourage and assist all Canadians to be physically active by increasing their awareness and understanding about the benefits of physical activity and the range of opportunities to be physically active in daily life
- To influence positive social and physical environments and opportunities that facilitate the integration of physical activity into daily life, and that are accessible to, and equitable for, all Canadians
- To establish partnerships with government and non-governmental agencies across levels and sectors, and encourage and support collaborative action and increased capacity to foster physical activity in Canada

In line with these goals, *Canada's Physical Activity Guide to Healthy Active Living* (www.phac-aspc.gc.ca/pau-uap/paguide/index.html) highlights the benefits of physical activity and informs Canadians of the amount of physical activity they should strive to do and how to get started.

Self-determination Theory

Self-determination theory, or SDT (Deci & Ryan, 1985, 2002), is a global theory of human motivation and development that has evolved from the pioneering work of psychologists Edward L. Deci and Richard M. Ryan (www.psych.rochester.edu/SDT). The main focus of the SDT framework is the extent to which behaviours such as sport and exercise participation are undertaken volitionally as opposed to being controlled by some external agent (e.g., coach, physician) or contingency (e.g., rewards, deadlines; Ryan & Deci, 2007). SDT asserts that people are naturally endowed with innate tendencies for personal growth and development that flourish when social environments provide optimal conditions (Deci & Ryan, 2002). SDT is comprised of four "mini theories" that collectively inform our understanding of motivated behaviour, cognition, and affective experiences in various life domains (see Figure 4.3).

Figure 4.3 Self-determination theory

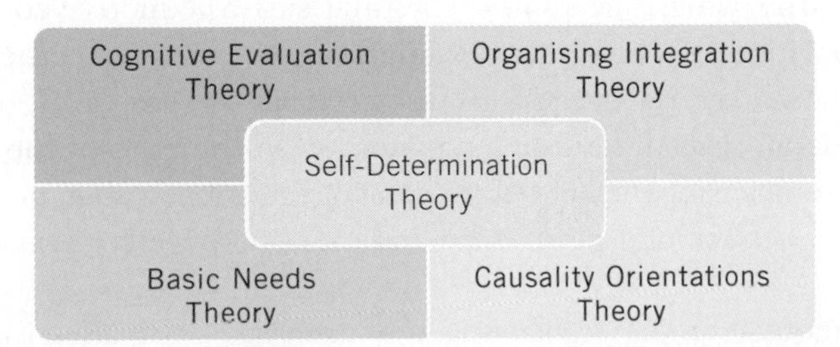

Source: Adapted from Chapter 1 in Deci, E.L., & Ryan, R.M. (2002). *Handbook of self-determination research.* Rochester, NY: University of Rochester Press.

Much of the early work in SDT focused on **cognitive evaluation theory** (CET), which specifies how various conditions shape (or thwart) the development of intrinsic motivation (Deci & Ryan, 2002). Given that not all behaviour is intrinsically motivated, **organismic integration theory** (OIT) describes the extent to which behaviour is motivated for different extrinsic reasons that represent varying degrees of internalization. Within the SDT framework, extrinsic motives can range from being highly autonomous (also called "self-determined") to more controlling in nature. **Causality orientations theory**(COT) uses personality-level constructs to describe individual differences in the degree to which people are self-determined as opposed to controlled. **Basic needs theory** (BNT) is the fourth subcomponent of the SDT framework and is concerned with the nature and function of psychological needs for competence, autonomy, and relatedness in relation to motivation and well-being.

Self-determination Theory: A Focus on Organismic Integration and Basic Needs Theories Important concepts within both OIT and BNT deserve additional attention because they deal with the special nature of motivation in contexts such as sport and exercise, and the manner in which motivation is developed (or internalized) by athletes and exercisers. Deci and Ryan propose within the framework of OIT that motivation is best understood as a multidimensional concept that ranges along a continuum of self-determination (see Table 4.4). At one end of the continuum is **amotivation**, or the absence of motivation, which occurs when individuals perceive no connection between their actions and the outcomes to be derived from the activity. At the other end of the motivational continuum is intrinsic regulation. **Intrinsic regulation** is concerned with athletes and exercisers engaging in activity because it is enjoyable, interesting, stimulating, or autotelic (self-rewarding).

Four different forms of extrinsic motivation (see Table 4.4) are proposed to exist along SDT's motivational continuum (Deci & Ryan, 2002). **External regulation**is the least self-determined form of extrinsic motivation and is concerned with exercising or playing sport to fulfill some external contingency or demand, such as appeasing another person (e.g., trainer, coach) or winning a trophy. The next form of extrinsic motivation is **introjected regulation**. People who engage in exercise or play sport for introjected reasons are attempting to avoid negative emotions (e.g., guilt, shame) or maintain a fragile sense of self-worth. **Identified regulation** occurs when participation in sport or exercise is linked to personally important and valued goals that stem from participation. For example, an athlete might train hard because he realizes how important practice is to improved performance even if he does not like training, or an exerciser may engage in weight training because she realizes that it is an important part of being healthy, which she values. The final extrinsic motive comprising SDT's motivational continuum is **integrated regulation**, which is concerned with participating in sport or exercise because these activities are symbolic of the person's identity. Extrinsic motives differ from one another on the basis of the degree of self-determination accompanying their development and regulation, with more self-determined motives linked to behavioural persistence and more positive cognitive and affective feelings.

The type of motivation that regulates sport or exercise participation is, at least in part, a function of the degree to which athletes and exercisers fulfill their basic psychological

Table 4.4 Self-determination Theory's Motivational Continuum

Level of Self-determination		Behavioural Regulation	Sample Statement
Lower ↑	Non-self-determined or controlled	Amotivation	I don't see why I should have to exercise. I participate in my sport, but I question why I am putting myself through this.
		External regulation	I exercise because other people say I should. I participate in my sport because people push me to play.
		Introjected regulation	I feel guilty when I don't exercise. I participate in my sport because I would feel guilty if I quit.
	Self-determined or autonomous	Identified regulation	It's important to me to exercise regularly. I participate in my sport because the benefits of sport are important to me.
		Integrated regulation	I consider exercise a fundamental part of who I am. I participate in my sport because it's a part of who I am.
↓ Higher		Intrinsic regulation	I enjoy my exercise sessions. I participate in my sport because I enjoy it.

Note: Adapted from Lonsdale, C., Hodge, K., & Rose, E. A. (2008). The Behavioral Regulation in Sport Questionnaire (BRSQ): Instrument development and initial validity evidence. *Journal of Sport & Exercise Psychology, 30,* 323–355; Markland, D., & Tobin, V. (2004). A modification to the Behavioural Regulation in Exercise Questionnaire to include an assessment of a motivation. *Journal of Sport & Exercise Psychology, 26,* 191–196; Wilson, P. M., et al. (2006). The Psychological Needs Satisfaction in Exercise Scale. *Journal of Sport & Exercise Psychology, 28,* 231–251.

needs. According to Deci and Ryan (2002), all humans have three basic psychological needs that when authentically fulfilled facilitate the internalization of behavioural regulation via more self-determined than controlled motives. **Competence** is concerned with feeling effective and capable when undertaking challenging tasks. **Autonomy** is concerned with feeling ownership over behaviour such that one's actions stem from a sense of perceived choice and internal control. The third need, **relatedness**, is concerned with feeling meaningful connections with others in environments such as sport and exercise.

Research Linking Self-determination Theory and Sport and Exercise Behaviour Physical activity research has supported Deci and Ryan's arguments given the observations that greater endorsement of self-determined motives is associated with increased effort in physical education classes and intention to be physically active (Standage, Duda, & Ntoumanis, 2003), exercise intensity (Edmunds, Ntoumanis, & Duda, 2006), and training outcomes such as burnout in elite rugby athletes (Creswell & Eklund, 2005). According to basic needs theory (Deci & Ryan, 2002), the fulfillment of each psychological need is most likely to be associated with greater internalization and more self-determined than controlled motivation. This supposition has been supported in various physical activity contexts, including physical education (Standage et al., 2003), exercise (Wilson, Rodgers, Blanchard, & Gessell, 2003), and sport (Sarrazin, Vallerand, Guillet, Pelletier, & Cury, 2002).

Examples of Canadian research examining different components of the SDT framework are summarized below:

- Consistent with CET, Medic and colleagues demonstrated that the provision of athletic scholarships would reduce intrinsic motivation in Canadian university sport athletes who did not have funding support for their sport participation (Medic, Mack, Wilson, & Starkes, 2007).
- Consistent with OIT, Wilson and colleagues have demonstrated that more self-determined motives for exercise are associated with more frequent weekly exercise behaviour, greater effort expended to exercise regularly, and stronger intentions to continue exercising in the future (Wilson, Rodgers, Fraser, & Murray, 2004).
- Consistent with COT, a recent investigation of cardiac patients demonstrated that those who approached life with a more autonomous than controlled personality reported more self-determined motives for exercise participation, which in turn was linked with stronger intentions to continue exercising in the future (Slovinec D'Angelo, Reid, & Pelletier, 2007).
- Consistent with BNT, a recent study of dragon boat racers from Western Canada by McDonough and Crocker (2007) indicated that more self-determined motivation was evident in racers who experienced a greater sense of competence, autonomy, and relatedness when engaged in sport.

Self-determination Theory in Practice Applications of SDT attempting to initiate and sustain behavioural change in either sport or exercise can focus on the interactional style used by the coach or fitness professional to work with athletes or exercise clients (see Table 4.5). Deci and Ryan contend that a supportive interactional style is characterized by the use of autonomy support, structure, and involvement. This is in direct contrast to a controlling interpersonal style that is typified by telling others what to do and pressurizing people to perform in restrictive ways. **Autonomy support** refers to the provision of choices and options and the reduction of pressure, while **structure** concerns the provision of appropriate feedback and the clarification of expectations to be derived from behaviour. **Involvement** refers to the extent to which individuals (such as athletes or exercisers) feel others are genuinely invested in their health and well-being.

Table 4.5 Developing Supportive Interactional Styles

Supportive Style	Description	Physical Activity Example
Autonomy support	Avoid pressurizing language.	"Attack the ball this way!"
	Provide a variety of options that athletes/ fitness clients can select from.	"Here are three exercises that all work the quadriceps muscle group in a comparable fashion. Try them and select one or two that you like the most for your workout."
Structure	Interact with athletes/ exercisers with empathy, especially when overcoming barriers.	"I understand how difficult this must be for you at the moment."
	Promote realistic self-referenced standards that provide a path for future individually tailored development.	"If you are able to read your opponent's line of vision and the manner in which he opens his body up on approaching the penalty shot, you might have a better chance of guessing the correct direction to dive."
Involvement	Encourage small group activities that foster a sense of involvement, which are expressed with empathy and authentic concern for the individuals' development.	"I know you are having difficulty striking the ball with your left foot. Using a different foot is never easy at the best of times. Remember the basic mechanics of staying on top of the ball and planting your non-kicking foot. With time and practice, you will be able to clip that ball down the line with both feet. Remember that working on all aspects of our game makes us better players and a stronger team. Don't expect to get this right away."

REFLECTIONS 4.4

Think about your own experiences in a particular sport or exercise context. What types of motivational regulation were driving specific motivated behaviour? Was all your motivated behaviour driven by highly self-determined or even intrinsic motivation? What types of behaviour were regulated more by external regulation? Introjected regulation?

Photograph courtesy of Peter Crocker, University of British Columbia.

Achievement Goal Theory

Inherent within many models of motivational change is the understanding of the role of competence or ability. Competence, whether defined as a psychological need, self-efficacy, or perceived behavioural control, is a central motive for behavioural change. Nicholls (1984, 1989) proposed that competence could be described as **achievement goal orientations**, which are two disposition-oriented dimensions based on how people define success and failure. **Task goal orientation** involves reference to one's own past performance or knowledge as the origin of competence feelings. For those demonstrating a task goal orientation, sport is perceived as providing opportunities for personal growth and mastery, the belief that success emanates from hard work, learning, and collaboration (Duda & Nicholls, 1992). Conversely, an **ego goal orientation** (sometimes called a performance orientation) is based on comparisons with others and has been associated with the belief that sport provides opportunities for gaining social status and wealth and that success emanates from outperforming others (Duda & Nichols, 1992).

Whether a person is in a state of ego involvement or task involvement depends not only on dispositional goal orientation but also on developmental and situational factors (Roberts, 2001). First, young children are unable to distinguish between effort and ability, often equating the two. With cognitive maturity, children by the age of 12 or 13 years are able to differentiate between effort and ability. Second, the perceived motivational climate can change the person's psychological achievement goal state. Motivational climate refers to athletes' perceptions of state achievement goals promoted by coaches (and significant others such as parents). Coaches and instructors can structure the teaching setting to emphasize various state achievement goals (Ames, 1992). Environments that stress interpersonal competition, winning, and social comparison tend to evoke ego involvement. On the other hand, an emphasis on mastery learning, effort, individual improvement, and co-operation tends to evoke task involvement (Roberts, 2001).

Research on the Achievement Goal Theory in Sport and Exercise Psychology Considerable research has examined the correlates of achievement goal orientations in sport and physical education settings and, to a lesser extent, structured exercise contexts. In an attempt to synthesize this research, Biddle, Wang, Kavussanu, and Spray (2003) conducted a review of existing literature. A pattern was identified that demonstrated some general differences, as well as some similarities, between those individuals with more of a taskorientation as opposed to an ego orientation (see Table 4.6).

It may be naive to think that any individual could be classified as being either just task oriented or just ego oriented as opposed to the consideration of both goal orientations in combination. This approach has been termed goal profiling, which reflects the relative tendencies of task and ego involvement in combination with socialization. Goal profiling results in individuals being classified into one of four high–low combinations (i.e., high-task/high-ego, high-task/low-ego, etc). Research generally demonstrates that moderate-to-high task orientation in combination with similar levels of ego orientation can be beneficial (Hodge & Petlichkoff, 2000). Consequently, having a high ego orientation is not detrimental when combined with a moderate-to-high task orientation.

Table 4.6 Characteristics Associated with Task and Ego Orientation

Task Goal Orientation	Ego Goal Orientation
Greater belief that effort results in success	Greater belief that ability results in success
Greater endorsement that sport and physical education is associated with mastery experiences, co-operation, fitness/health, and self-esteem	Greater endorsement that sport is associated with the procurement of social status
Linked to adaptive achievement strategies (e.g., persistence in practice)	No clear relationship with adaptive achievement strategies
Associated with perceptions of competence	Associated with perceptions of competence
Associated with greater positive affect but no relationship with negative affect	No relationship with positive and negative affect
Positively related to sportsperson-like behaviours (e.g., fair play)	Positively related to unsportspersonlike behaviours (e.g., intentional injury)
Effort, intention to continue	Lower effort and less intent to continue

Note: Adapted from Biddle, S., Wang, J., Kavussanu, M., & Spray, C. (2003). Correlates of achievement goal orientations in physical activity: A systematic review of research. *European Journal of Sport Science, 3,* (5): 1–20, pp.12–13.

Researchers have attempted to expand the ideas in achievement goal theory by examining the role of approach goals and avoidance goals (Elliott & Church, 1997; Roberts, 2001). Avoidance goals involve actively moving away from situations, often to avoid failing or demonstrating incompetence. Approach goals, in contrast, involve active engagement with the environment. The trichotomous model of achievement motivation involves examining three conditions. The first condition is performance-approach, which is concerned with making good impressions by demonstrating high ability relative to others. The second is performance-avoidance, which centres on avoiding making poor impressions, primarily through avoiding situations in which one would perform worse relative to others. Mastery is the third condition, and is the same as described above. Recently, Elliot and Conroy (2005) have suggested that a 2 × 2 achievement motivation framework (ego goal/mastery goal × approach/avoidance) could advance understanding in sport and exercise. Three of the four factors are the same in the trichotomous model. In addition, mastery avoidance is characterized by the fear that one may be not able to master a sporting or exercise task or make the best of the situation. It is likely that both the trichotomous and 2 × 2 achievement goal frameworks are likely to influence much research in the coming years.

Canadian researchers have examined goal orientations in combination with both individual and situational characteristics:

- Dunn, Causgrove Dunn, and Sytotuik (2002) demonstrated that ego orientation was associated with maladaptive perfectionism (e.g., concerns over mistakes and parental criticism) in a sample of high-school football players. Endorsement of a task orientation was associated with a more adaptive style of perfectionism (e.g., set high standards for performance but allow for mistakes).

Table 4.7 Recommendations for Creating a Mastery Motivational Climate

Thoughtfully select tasks that foster and maximize task involvement.
Distribute authority to shift the locus of responsibility to the learner.
Reinforce task-involved behaviours.
Emphasize individual and co-operative goals over competitive goals.
Reinforce personal performance evaluations based on effort and personal improvement.
Use time-management skills to consider the influence of instruction and physical practice on motivation.

Note: Adapted from Ames, C. (1992). Classrooms: goals, structures, and student motivation. *Journal of Educational Psychology, 84,* (3): 261–271. Copyright © 1992 by the American Psychological Association. Adapted with permission.

- The dispositional tendency to adopt task-involved goals was positively related (1) to the perception of a situational emphasis on personal improvement and learning, and (2) to perceived competence in a sample of children with movement difficulties (Causgrove Dunn, 2000). Environments that emphasized performance were associated with ego orientation.
- Cumming, Hall, Harwood, and Gammage (2002) found the most adaptive profile for sport achievement in competitive swimmers was moderate-task/high-ego.

Achievement Goal Theory in Practice The consistent beneficial outcomes associated with a high task orientation (alone or in combination with high ego orientation) have varied instructional implications for physical education teachers and coaches that emphasize an environment conducive to mastery performance. Ames (1992) has outlined six practical recommendations (see Table 4.7). However, relatively little research has evaluated these recommendation in physical activity settings. The research that has been done (e.g., Harwood & Swain, 2002) has shown that environments promoting a task learning style resulted in increased self-regulatory behaviour and more positive cognitions.

Theory of Competence Motivation

Many of the motivational models we have covered have identified competence as a critical factor. In the 1970s and 1980s, Susan Harter developed a competence-based theory of motivation that focused on children. Her work with children was based on White's (1959) argument that behaviour is directed, selective, and owing to "an intrinsic need to deal (effectively) with the environment" (p. 318); White called this concept **effectance motivation**. Harter (1978, 1982) concluded that individuals are innately motivated to be competent in all areas of human achievement, with sport being one such area. Her theory of effectance, or theory of competence motivation, provides a framework for examining motivation in children and adolescents. Basically, this theory holds that perceptions of one's competence and control in a particular activity that is perceived as valuable or important will produce motivation to continue participating in that activity. Harter's theory has had a major impact on sport research in children and adolescents (see Weiss & Williams, 2004).

A key aspect of Harter's (1982) ideas on competence motivation was that self-concept was multidimensional, that is, that people have a number of domains that comprise their sense

Figure 4.4 Basic tenets of Harter's (1978, 1982) theory of competence motivation

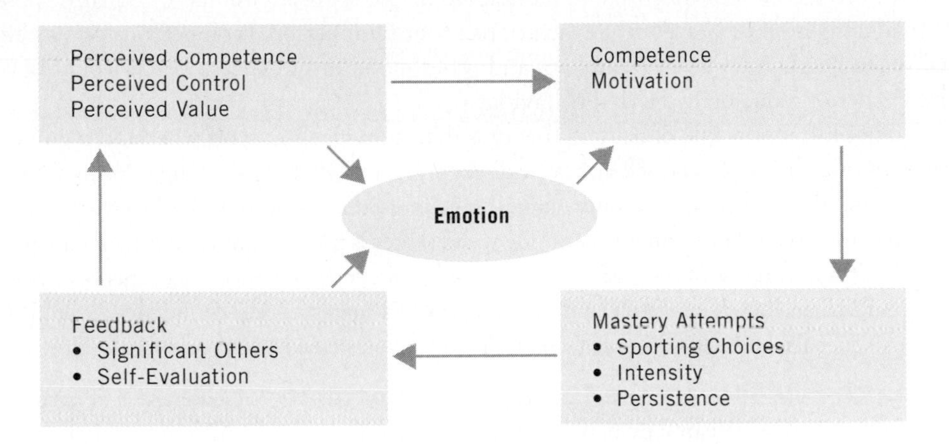

Source: Adapted from Harter, S. (1978). Effectance motivation reconsidered: Toward a developmental model. *Human Development, 21,* 34–64 and Harter, S. (1982). The perceived competence scale for children. *Child Development, 53,* 87–97.

of self. In children, these include social, athletic, physical appearance, behavioural conduct, and academic domains. As people mature cognitively, the number of domains increases and they become more differentiated to include such areas as romantic appeal, close friendships, and job competence. Perceptions of competence and value in these domains contribute to feelings of self-worth or self-esteem and to motivation to continue pursuing activities in those domains. Another feature of Harter's theory is that perceptions of competence in a particular domain will enhance self-worth and subsequent motivation if the individual values competence in that domain. For example, if an adolescent sees herself as having exceptional athletic skills and values competence in sport, she will have high perceptions of self-worth. If she perceives her athletic competence as low and values sport, her self-worth will be low.

The basic components of Harter's theory are shown in Figure 4.4. A young athlete's perceptions of athletic competence and control will lead to emotional states, which combine to facilitate motivation to engage in specific sporting behaviour. If the athlete experiences success in his or her endeavours, then these sporting experiences lead to positive emotional states (e.g., pride, happiness, enjoyment). The sporting experiences will also

Positive feedback can increase perceived competence and motivated behaviour.

Photograph © Photodisc/Getty Images.

impact feedback received from significant others (e.g., coaches, parents, teammates) as well as self-evaluation. The result is that, in a cyclical fashion, these feelings and feedback will lead to a recurrent incentive to participate in the sport environment. Equally, those individuals who receive negative evaluations about their personal competence or mastery will have heightened levels of anxiety and other mood disturbances, which would have the impact of reducing motivated behaviour.

The central principle of Harter's theory is that individuals in sport who hold high perceptions of competence and self-control will exert greater effort, persist longer in the face of failure, and experience more positive affect than individuals who hold lower levels of perceived competence. For example, if a young speed skater is training hard and is receiving positive feedback in terms of successful attempts and in feelings of competence, this behaviour will result in an increase in pride and happiness. With increased self-confidence, it is likely that this speed skater will continue to participate with increased vigour and motivation.

Research Evidence for the Theory of Competence Motivation There is a substantial body of research evidence supporting various aspects of the competence motivation theory in sport. There is strong evidence that positive feedback increases perceived physical competence and that motivated sport and physical activity behaviour is related to perceptions of athletic and physical competence (see Weiss & Williams, 2004). Physical competence and enjoyment are related, and they both impact motivated behaviour (Weiss, 1993). Indeed, enjoyment has consistently been found to be a strong predictor of motivated behaviour in children (see Crocker, Hoar, McDonough, Kowalski, & Niefer, 2004). Enjoyment is not only related to physical competence, but also to personal control, mastery-focused teaching environments, team friendships, pleasing significant others, and being involved in challenging activities (see Crocker et al., 2004; Weiss & Stuntz, 2004). Parents' behaviour can also influence motivated behaviour. Greater levels of parental encouragement and enjoyment are related to higher perceptions of competence and attraction to physical activity in children (Brustad, 1996).

REFLECTIONS 4.5

If you were coaching a community baseball team, what type of feedback and reinforcement would you provide to your athletes to maximize their perceived competence and sense of control? If one of your athletes were unhappy, could you use the framework of competence motivation theory to help explain the behaviour and plan a course of action that could positively affect the athlete's happiness and enjoyment?

Theory of Competence Motivation in Practice Harter's model has a number of practical implications that coaches and parents can use to facilitate motivation in children. First, children often will attempt to engage in physical activities. Positive feedback from coaches, parents, and peers will enhance both positive emotions and perceptions of competence. This increase in perceptions of competence will, in turn, enhance subsequent motivation. As children get older, they develop the ability to form their own internal standards of what is good ability and effort. Perceptions of control and perceived value of the activity will also facilitate competence motivation. Allowing children to have choices and placing them in sporting situations in which they can demonstrate competence will enhance their motivation. Remember that the activities the child or adolescent values may be different from those of the parent. Youth are influenced by multiple sources (e.g., media, peers) in determining what is valued. Overall, the message from the theory of competence motivation is clear: Motivation will be driven by perception of competence, control, and value in an activity. Positive feedback from significant others will often create positive emotions and enhance competence motivation, enhancing future motivation in the activity.

Sport Commitment Model

Would anyone doubt that success in sport or exercise pursuits (most notably long-standing success) clearly requires commitment? **Sport commitment** is defined as "the psychological state representing the desire or resolve to continue sport participation" (Scanlan, Carpenter, Schmidt, Simons, & Keeler, 1993, p. 6) and can include both feelings of wanting to and having to continue participation. The sport commitment model, or SCM (Scanlan et al., 1993), was developed to explain how five factors predict or determine sport commitment: sport enjoyment, involvement alternatives, personal investments, social constraints, and involvement opportunities (see Figure 4.5). **Sport enjoyment** includes positive emotions about participating (e.g., pleasure, fun) and is often found to be the strongest predictor of commitment. **Involvement alternatives** refer to other activities and how attractive they are compared to sport or exercise. **Personal investments** are resources that the person has put into the activity, such as time, effort, or money. **Social constraints** are pressure and expectations from others or norms that make one feel obligated to participate. **Involvement opportunities** refers to things that the athlete or exerciser is able to do only if he or she continues participation, such as getting recognition, developing skill and fitness, travelling, and being with friends.

Research on the Sport Commitment Model in Sport and Exercise Psychology According to Scanlan, Carpenter, et al. (1993), sport commitment is determined by greater enjoyment, personal investments, involvement opportunities, social

Figure 4.5 Sport commitment model

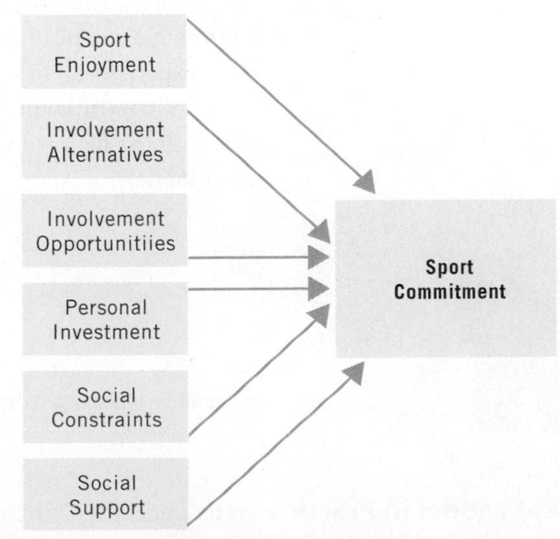

Source: Adapted from Scanlan, T. K., Simons, J. P., Carpenter, P. J., Schmidt, G. W., & Keeler, B. (1993). The sport commitment model: Measurement development for the youth-sport domain. *Journal of Sport & Exercise Psychology, 15,* 16 -38.

constraints, and lower involvement alternatives. Originally developed and tested with youth-sport athletes, considerable support for this supposition has been found (see Carpenter & Coleman, 1998; Carpenter & Scanlan, 1998; Scanlan, Simons, et al., 1993; Scanlan, Carpenter, et al., 1993). Research with elite adult athletes also generally supports the SCM (Scanlan, Russell, Beals, & Scanlan, 2003). Other researchers have been looking at ways to modify the SCM by examining additional factors, like social support, or by viewing commitment from various dimensions, such as obligated commitment (have to), entrapment commitment (committed for negative reasons), and attracted commitment (want to for positive reasons) (Weiss, Kimmel, & Smith, 2001; Weiss & Weiss, 2006, 2007; Wilson et al., 2004).

Canadian researchers have also examined the determinants of physical activity involvement identified in the SCM. Examples of this research include the following:

- Wilson and colleagues (2004) adapted the SCM to the exercise domain. The determinants identified in the SCM were generally supported as being applicable to exercise contexts. Collectively, the dimensions of exercise commitment predicted 12% of exercise behaviour.
- Martin and Hausenblas (1998) examined female aerobic instructors' commitment to exercise. Higher commitment scores were associated with eating disorder symptoms, suggesting that increased psychological commitment may be one risk factor linking exercise participation with eating disorders.
- Crocker and Augaitis (in press) examined gender differences in commitment of adult triathletes. Although no gender differences emerged, the study did find that personal investment, involvement alternatives, and involvement opportunities were significant predictors of sport commitment.

REFLECTIONS 4.6

Several key determinants shape an athlete's commitment to sport. Think of your own experiences in sport. What were some key determinants? Are these consistent with the factors in the sport commitment model?

Photograph by Richard Lam, courtesy of University of British Columbia Athletics.

Sport Commitment Model in Practice In practice, the SCM is helpful in understanding why athletes and exercisers persist, sometimes even in situations where they are not enjoying the activity or their participation is associated with maladaptive outcomes (e.g., Martin & Hausenblas, 1998). However, interventions targeting factors associated with the model have not been directly tested in the sport or exercise literature. Additional variables, such as social support, have also been identified as facilitating commitment (Carpenter & Colman, 1998). A thorough knowledge of the determinants of commitment can help practitioners focus on promoting healthy, adaptive commitment to sport and exercise among their athletes or exercise clients.

MOVING BEYOND INDIVIDUAL APPROACHES TO SOCIAL APPROACHES TO MOTIVATION

Several motivational theories reviewed thus far have highlighted the important role that influential social factors can have on an individual's behaviour. In general, these motivational theories suggest that other people can influence behaviour through modelling, social norms, and providing support for the behaviour. However, the focus has been largely on individual cognitive factors (e.g., perceptions of competence) in physical activity contexts. Features of sport or exercise contexts, including interpersonal relationships, also play an important role in motivation (King, Stokols, Talen, & Brassington, 2002) and deserve attention in this chapter. There is considerable evidence that people need frequent, positive contact with others within stable, mutual relationships (Baumeister & Leary, 1995) and that nurturing such relationships could enhance motivation and consequent behavioural factors.

Research Linking Social Influences to Motivational Outcomes and Behaviour

Evidence is mounting that social relationships with significant others such as coaches, parents, peers, and siblings play an important role in motivational processes for youth. Coaches who are more autonomy-supportive and less controlling of their athletes, who create a mastery/task motivational climate, and who provide positive performance–contingent feedback promote more adaptive forms of motivation on their teams (Duda, 2001). Peer relationship characteristics, such as being accepted and supported by the peer group, friendship quality, and having physically active peers, predict physical activity behaviour among youth (Smith & McDonough, 2008). Furthermore, there is evidence to suggest that the combination of different aspects of peer relationships and the combined effects of social relationships with parents and peers may have an impact on youth-sport and physical activity motivation (Smith, Ullrich-French, Walker, & Hurley, 2006; Ullrich-French & Smith, 2006). Social support for exercise has also been shown to be a contributor to motivation for exercise in research with older adults (Resnick, Orwig, Magaziner, & Wynne, 2002).

Canadian researchers have considered social influence variables on motivation and physical activity participation as part of their program of research:

- Leatherdale and Wong (2008) examined characteristics associated with physical activity and sedentary behaviours in approximately 25,000 Ontario youths. Parents were more likely to strongly encourage males to be active and to be very supportive of males being physically active compared with females. Males were also more likely to have more active friends than females.

- Carron and colleagues (1996) found a small, moderate effect of social influence, including important others, family, and exercise class members, on adherence behaviour in exercise settings.
- Shields and colleagues (2008) found that family social influence taken at one time point predicted 9.5% of youth and adolescent physical activity behaviour four months later.
- Sabiston and Crocker (2008) examined the individual and collective influence of best friend and family social influence on adolescent leisure time physical activity behaviour. Parents remained an influence on adolescent physical activity behaviour, but their influence was slightly less than that from a best friend.

Social Influence in Practice

Of particular interest to practitioners, we still need to learn more about how to effectively promote and support positive social relationships in sport and exercise that foster adaptive motivation. From a practical perspective, it is key to note that social interactions and relationships matter for the motivation of many participants. Coaches can work to provide positive, contingent, instructional feedback and build more supportive relationships with their athletes. Parents can give their kids the resources to be active, discuss their child's sport experiences with them in a positive, supportive light, and participate in activity themselves. And all those involved can provide the time and feedback to help nurture positive relationships among participants. Parents can promote sport and activity motivation by acting as role models (i.e., participating in activity themselves), helping their children interpret their sport and activity experiences in an adaptive way, and providing physical activity opportunities to their children (Fredricks & Eccles, 2004).

CHAPTER SUMMARY

Few topics are so intricate yet universally applicable as the study of motivation. Motivation was simply described as the reasons why we do the things we do; however, this chapter has outlined the complexity of understanding motivational processes. The main factors that influence our motivation are personal, cognitive (i.e., what we think), and environmental factors. There are three broad approaches to help understand motivation as it applies to behavioural change: behavioural, cognitive, and cognitive-behavioural. The main objective of this chapter was to highlight various theories and models that individuals interested in sport and exercise psychology have devised to understand how motivational processes influence physical activity behaviour. As seen with these theories, understanding motivation as applied to behavioural change is a complex interplay of personal and environmental considerations. For those interested in facilitating behavioural change, various practical strategies were identified. While many approaches to understanding motivation were outlined in this chapter, it is not fully inclusive of all the ways that motivation in physical activity contexts has been studied (e.g., social-ecological models and environmental approaches to understanding physical activity behaviour have gained prominence in the literature in recent years).

Common Myths about Motivation and Behavioural Change Revisited

MYTH: Motivation is a trait. You either are a motivated individual or you are not.
The belief that motivation is a trait stems from the person-centred approach. Certainly, personal characteristics do influence our motivation, but it is naive to think that there is nothing else that can influence motivated behaviour. In this chapter, you have been introduced to how changing environmental influences, the support of important others, and intervention strategies can be targeted to influence motivational processes.

MYTH: Competence is the main motivator for engaging in physical activity.
Of course people are motivated to do things in which they feel they are competent. While understanding how competent an individual feels is important for understanding the motivation–behaviour relationship, it should not be considered to the exclusion of other variables. In this chapter, you were introduced to the role of attitudes, social influences, and perceptions of autonomy as important constructs to consider when understanding how to motivate behaviour.

MYTH: Enjoyment is the best motive to help us understand physical activity behaviour.
Engaging in sport and exercise for enjoyment (or intrinsic reasons) is one, but not the only, factor of continued involvement. There are many other reasons why people persist. For example, physical activity has been linked to various health outcomes. Understanding the role of self-determined motives (e.g., valuing the outcome or identity maintenance) may help those interested in health promotion better work with their clients.

Review Questions

1. You have been hired by Ms. Norma Etheridge (Chief Executive Officer of Etheridge International, a manufacturing conglomerate that designs and builds customized home exercise equipment) to reduce employee absenteeism and improve productivity. Ms. Etheridge has identified research evidence that suggests exercise can be beneficial to corporate employees, and she would like you to design an intervention that increases the exercise-related activities of her 5000 employees worldwide. Select a theory that was discussed in this chapter and design an intervention that links theoretical concepts with the target behaviour, namely increased and sustained exercise participation in Etheridge International employees.
2. Select a range of popular health (n = 5) and fitness (n = 5) magazines in which the topic of motivation is discussed. Conduct a key-words-in-context analysis of the magazines to identify the central terms used in the text when discussing motivation.
3. The Centers for Disease Control and Prevention in the United States has developed a communication campaign to encourage people with arthritis to be physically active. The campaign is called "Physical Activity. The Arthritis Pain Reliever." Go to the following link and review the brochure: ftp://ftp.cdc.gov/pub/Publications/arthritis/brochure1_nat_4c.pdf. Can you determine what (if any) motivational approach to behavioural change informed the development of this brochure?
4. Which of the theories of motivation are consistent with the cognitive-behavioural approach to understanding behaviour?

5. Competence is a pervasive construct in many of the approaches to understanding motivated behaviour. Indicate which approaches to understanding motivation include perceived competence.
6. Understanding the role of others (e.g., social approaches) in motivation in sport and exercise is valuable. Which theories include consideration of the influence of others?

Suggested Reading

Hagger, M., & Chatzisarantis, N. (2007). *Intrinsic motivation and self-determination in exercise and sport*. Champaign, IL: Human Kinetics.

Smith, A. L. (2007). Youth peer relationships in sport. In S. Jowett, & D. Lavallee (Eds.), *Social psychology in sport* (pp. 41–54). Champaign, IL: Human Kinetics.

Standage, M., & Duda, J. L. (2004). Motivational processes among older adults in sport and exercise settings. In M. R. Weiss (Ed.), *Developmental sport and exercise psychology: A lifespan perspective* (pp. 357–381). Morgantown, WV: Fitness Information Technology.

References

Ajzen, I. (1985). From intention to actions: A theory of planned behavior. In J. Kuhl, & J. Beckman (Eds.), *Action control: From cognition to behavior* (pp. 11–39). Heidelberg, Germany: Springer.

Ames, C. (1992). Classrooms: goals, structures, and student motivation. *Journal of Educational Psychology, 84*, 261–271.

Bandura, A. (1997). *Self-efficacy: The exercise of control.*New York: W. H. Freeman.

Baumeister, R. F., & Leary, M. R. (1995). The need to belong: Desire for interpersonal attachments as a fundamental human motivation. *Psychological Bulletin, 117*, 497–529.

Beauchamp, M. R., Bray, S. R., & Albinson, J. G. (2002) Pre-competition imagery, self-efficacy and performance in collegiate golfers. *Journal of Sports Sciences, 20*, 697–705.

Berry, T., Naylor, P. J., & Wharf-Higgins, J. (2005). Stages of change in adolescents: An examination of self-efficacy, decisional balance, and reasons for relapse. *Journal of Adolescent Health, 37*, 452–459.

Biddle, S., Wang, J., Kavussanu, M., & Spray, C. (2003). Correlates of achievement goal orientations in physical activity: A systematic review of research. *European Journal of Sport Science, 3*, 1–20.

Blanchard, C. (2008). Understanding exercise behaviour during home-based cardiac rehabilitation: A theory of planned behaviour perspective. *Canadian Journal of Physiological Pharmacology, 86*, 8–15.

Blanchard, C. M., Kupperman, J., Sparling, P., Nehl, E., Rhodes, R. E., Courneya, K. S., Baker, F., & Hunt, T. (2007). Ethnicity as a moderator of the theory of planned behavior and physical activity in college students. *Research Quarterly for Exercise & Sport, 78*, 531–541.

Brawley, L. R., Rejeski, W. J., & Lutes, L. (2000). A group-mediated cognitive behavioral intervention for increasing adherence to physical activity in older adults. *Journal of Applied Behavior Research, 5*, 47–65.

Brustad, R. J. (1996). Parental and peer influences on children's psychological development through sport. In F. L. Smoll, & R. E. Smith (Eds.), *Children and youth in sport: A biopsychosocial perspective* (pp. 112–124). Toronto, ON: Brown & Benchmark.

Carpenter, P. J., & Coleman, R. (1998). A longitudinal study of elite youth cricketers' commitment. *International Journal of Sport Psychology, 29*,195–210.

Carpenter, P. J., & Scanlan, T. K. (1998). Changes over time in the determinants of sport commitment. *Pediatric Exercise Science, 10*, 356–365.

Carron, A. V., Hausenblas, H. A., & Mack, D. (1996). Social influence and exercise: A meta-analysis. *Journal of Sport & Exercise Psychology, 18*, 1–16.

Causgrove Dunn, J. (2000). Goal orientations, perceptions of the motivational climate, and perceived competence of children with movement difficulties. *Adapted Physical Activity Quarterly, 17*, 1–19.

Courneya, K. S., & Friedenreich, C. M. (1997). Determinants of exercise behavior during colorectal cancer treatment: An application of the theory of planned behavior. *Oncology Nursing Forum, 24*, 1715–1723.

Courneya, K. S., & Friedenreich, C. M. (1999). Utility of the theory of planned behavior for understanding exercise during breast cancer treatment. *Psycho-Oncology, 8*,112–122.

Creswell, S. L., & Eklund, R. C. (2005). Motivation and burnout among top amateur rugby players. *Medicine & Science in Sports & Exercise, 37*, 469–477.

Crocker, P. R. E., & Augaitis, L. (in press). Commitment in age class adult triathletes: Examining gender differences in the Sport Commitment Model. *International Journal of Sport Psychology*.

Crocker, P. R. E., Hoar, S. D., McDonough, M. H., Kowalski, K. C., & Niefer, C. B. (2004). Emotional experience in youth sport. In M. R. Weiss (Ed.), *Developmental sport and exercise psychology: A lifespan perspective* (pp. 197–222). Morgantown, WV: Fitness Information Technology.

Cumming, J., Hall, C., Harwood, C., & Gammage, K. (2002). Motivational orientations and imagery use: A goal profiling analysis. *Journal of Sport Sciences, 20*, 127–136.

Deci, E. L., & Ryan, R. M. (1985). *Intrinsic motivation and self-determination in human behavior*. New York: Plenum Press.

Deci, E. L., & Ryan, R. M. (2002). *Handbook of self-determination research*. Rochester, NY: University of Rochester Press.

Duda, J. L. (2001). Achievement goal research in sport: Pushing the boundaries and clarifying some misunderstandings. In G. C. Roberts (Ed.), *Advances in motivation in sport and exercise* (pp. 129–182). Champaign, IL: Human Kinetics.

Duda, J. L., & Nicholls, J. (1992). Dimensions of achievement motivation in schoolwork and sport. *Journal of Educational Psychology, 84*, 290–299.

Dunn, J., Causgrove Dunn, J., & Sytotuik, D. (2002). Relationship between multidimensional perfectionism and goal orientations in sport. *Journal of Sport & Exercise Psychology, 24*, 376–395.

Edmunds, J., Ntoumanis, N., & Duda, J. L. (2006). A test of self-determination theory in exercise domain. *Journal of Applied Social Psychology, 36*, 2240–2265.

Elliot, A. J., & Conroy, D. E. (2005). Beyond the dichotomous model of achievement goals in sport and exercise psychology. *Sport and Exercise Reviews, 1*, 17–25.

Elliot, A. J., & Church, M. A. (1997). A hierarchical model of approach and avoidance achievement motivation. *Journal of Personality and Social Psychology, 72*, 218–232.

Foley, L., Prapavessis, H., Maddison, R., Burke, S., McGowan, E., & Gillanders, L. (2008). Predicting physical activity intention and behavior in school-age children. *Pediatric Exercise Science, 20*, 342–356.

Fredricks, J. A., & Eccles, J. S. (2004). Parental influences on youth involvement in sports. In M. R. Weiss (Ed.), *Developmental sport and exercise psychology: A lifespan perspective* (pp. 145–164). Morgantown, WV: Fitness Information Technology.

Galea, M. N., & Bray, S. R. (2006). Predicting walking intentions and exercise in individuals with intermittent claudication: An application of the theory of planned behavior. *Rehabilitation Psychology, 51*, 299–305.

Garber, C. E., Allsworth, J. E., Marcus, B. H., Hesser, J., & Lapane, K. L. (2008). Correlates of the stages of change for physical activity in a population survey. *American Journal of Public Health, 98*, 897–904.

Godin, G., & Kok, G. (1996). The theory of planned behavior: A review of its applications to health-related behaviors. *American Journal of Health Promotion, 11*, 87–98.

Hagger, M. S., & Chatzisarantis, N. L. D. (2007). *Intrinsic motivation and self-determination in exercise and sport*. Champaign, IL: Human Kinetics.

Hagger, M. S., Chatzisarantis, N. L. D., & Biddle, S. J. H. (2002). A meta-analytic review of the theories of reasoned action and planned behavior in physical activity: Predictive validity and the contribution of additional variables. *Journal of Sport & Exercise Psychology, 24*, 3–32.

Harter, S. (1978).Effectance motivation reconsidered: Toward a developmental model. *Human Development, 21*, 34–64.

Harter, S. (1982). The perceived competence scale for children. *Child Development*, *53*,87–97.

Harwood, C. G., & Swain, A. B. (2002). The development and activation of achievement goals in tennis: II. *The Sport Psychologist*, *16*,111–138.

Hausenblas, H. A., Carron, A. V., & Mack, D. E. (1997). The theory of reasoned action and planned behavior in exercise behavior: A meta-analysis. *Journal of Sport & Exercise Psychology*, *19*, 36–51.

Hodge, K., & Petlichkoff, L. M. (2000). Goal "profiles" in sport: A cluster analysis. *Journal of Sport & Exercise Psychology*, *22*, 256–272.

King, A. C., Stokols, D., Talen, E., & Brassington, G. S. (2002). Theoretical approaches to the promotion of physical activity: Forging a transdisciplinary paradigm. *American Journal of Preventive Medicine*, *23*, 15–25.

Latimer, A. E., & Martin Ginis, K. A. (2005). The theory of planned behavior in prediction of leisure time physical activity among individuals with spinal cord injury. *Rehabilitation Psychology*, *50*,389–396.

Leatherdale, S. T., & Wong, S. L. (2008). Modifiable characteristics associated with sedentary behaviours among youth. *International Journal of Pediatric Obesity*, *3*, 93–101.

Lonsdale, C., Hodge, K., & Rose, E. A. (2008). The Behavioral Regulation in Sport Questionnaire (BRSQ): Instrument development and initial validity evidence. *Journal of Sport & Exercise Psychology*, *30*, 323–355.

Marcus, B. H., Eaton, C. A., Rossi, J. S., & Harlow, L. L. (1994). Self-efficacy, decision making, and stages of change: An integrative model of physical exercise. *Journal of Applied Social Psychology*, *24*, 489–508.

Marcus, B. H., & Simkin, L. R. (1994). The transtheoretical model: Application to exercise. In R. K. Dishman (Ed.), *Advances in exercise adherence*(pp. 1400–1444). Champaign IL: Human Kinetics.

Markland, D., & Tobin, V. (2004). A modification to the Behavioural Regulation in Exercise Questionnaire to include an assessment of amotivation. *Journal of Sport & Exercise Psychology*, *26*, 191–196.

Martin, K. A., & Hausenblaus, H. A. (1998). Psychological commitment to exercise and eating disorder symptomology among female aerobic instructors. *The Sport Psychologist*, *12*, 180–190.

Marshall, S. J., & Biddle, S. J. H. (2001), The transtheoretical model of behavior change: A meta-analysis of applications to physical activity and exercise. *Annals of Behavioral Medicine*, *234*, 229–246.

McAuley, E., Jerome, G. J., Elavsky, S., Marquez, D. X., & Ramsey, S. N. (2003). Predicting long-term maintenance of physical activity in older adults. *Preventive Medicine*, *37*, 110– 118.

McDonough, M. H., & Crocker, P. R. E. (2007). Testing self-determined motivation as a mediator of the relationship between psychological needs and affective and behavioral outcomes. *Journal of Sport & Exercise Psychology*, *29*, 645–663.

Medic,N., Mack, D. E., Wilson, P, M., & Starkes,J. (2007). The effects of athletic scholarships on motivation in sport. *Journal of Sport Behavior*, *30*, 292–306.

Moritz, S. E., Feltz, D. L., Fahrbach, K. R., & Mack, D. E. (2000). The relation of self-efficacy measures to sport performance: A meta-analytic review. *Research Quarterly for Exercise & Sport*, *71*, 280–300.

Nicholls, J. G. (1984). *The development of achievement motivation*. Greenwich, CN: JAI Press.

Nicholls, J. G. (1989). *The competitive ethos and democratic education*. Cambridge, MA: Harvard University Press.

Nguyen, M. N., Potvin, L., & Otis, J. (1997). Regular exercise in 30- to 60-year-old men: Combining the stages-of-change model and the theory of planned behavior to identify determinants for targeting heart health interventions. *Journal of Community Health*, *22*, 233–245.

Partridge, J. A., Brustad, R. J., & Babkes Stellino, M. (2008). Social influence in sport. In T. S. Horn (Ed.), *Advances in sport psychology*(3rd ed., pp. 269–291). Champaign, IL: Human Kinetics.

Plotnikoff, R. C., Hotz, S. B., Birkett, N. J., & Courneya, K. S. (2001). Exercise and the Transtheoretical Model: A longitudinal test of a population sample. *Preventive Medicine*, *33*, 441–452.

Plotnikoff, R. C., Lippke, S., Courneya, K. S., Birkett, N., & Sigal, R. J. (2008). Physical activity and social cognitive theory: A test in a population sample of adults with Type 1 or Type 2 diabetes. *Applied Psychology: An International Review, 57*, 628–643.

Plotnikoff, R. C., Brunet, S., Courneya, K. S., Spence, J. C., Birkett, N. J., Marcus, B., Whiteley, J. (2007). The efficacy of stage-matched and standard public health materials for promoting physical activity in the workplace: the Physical Activity Workplace Study (PAWS). *American Journal of Health Promotion, 21*, 501–509.

Prochaska, J. O., & DiClemente, C. C. (1986). Towards a comprehensive model of change. In W. R. Miller, & N. Heather (Eds.), *Treating addictive behaviours: Processes of change*. New York: Plenum Press.

Prochaska, J. O.,& Marcus,B. H.(1994). The transtheoretical model: Applications to exercise. In R. K. Dishman (Ed.), *Advances in exercise adherence*(pp. 161–180). Champaign, IL: Human Kinetics.

Prochaska, J. O., & Velicer, W. F. (1997). The transtheoretical model of health behavior change. *American Journal of Health Promotion, 12*, 11–12.

Reeve, J. M. (2005). *Understanding motivation and emotion*(4th ed.). Hoboken, NJ: Wiley & Sons.

Resnick, B., Orwig, D., Magaziner, J., & Wynne, C. (2002). The effect of social support on exercise behavior in older adults. *Clinical Nursing Research, 11*, 52–70.

Rhodes, R. E., Blanchard, C. M., & Blacklock, R. E. (2008). Do physical activity beliefs differ by age and gender? *Journal of Sport & Exercise Psychology, 30*, 412–423.

Rhodes, R. E., & Plotnikoff, R. C. (2006). Understanding action control: Predicting physical activity intention-behavior profiles across 6 months in a Canadian sample. *Health Psychology, 25*, 292–299.

Roberts, G. C. (2001). Understanding the dynamics of motivation in physical activity: The influence of achievement goals on motivational processes. In G. C. Roberts (Ed.), *Advances in motivation in sport and exercise*(pp. 1–50). Champaign, IL: Human Kinetics.

Rodgers, W. M., & Brawley, L. R. (1993). Using both self-efficacy theory and the theory of planned behavior to discriminate adherers and dropouts from structured programs. *Journal of Applied Sport Psychology*, 5,195–206.

Rodgers, W. M., Wilson, P. M., Hall, C. R., Fraser, S. N., & Murray, T. C. (2008). Evidence for a multidimensional self-efficacy for exercise scale. *Research Quarterly for Exercise & Sport, 79*, 222–234.

Ryan, R. M., & Deci, E. L. (2007). Active human nature: Self-determination theory and the promotion and maintenance of sport, exercise, and health. In M. S. Hagger, & N. L. D. Chatzisarantis (Eds.), *Intrinsic motivation and self-determination in exercise and sport* (pp. 1–19). Champaign, IL: Human Kinetics.

Sabiston, C., & Crocker, P. R. E. (2008). Exploring self-perceptions and social influences as correlates of adolescent leisure time physical activity. *Journal of Sport & Exercise Psychology*, 30, 3–22.

Sarrazin, P., Vallerand, R. J., Guillet, E., Pelletier, L. G., & Cury, F. (2002). Motivation and dropout in female handballers: A 21-month prospective study. *European Journal of Social Psychology*, 32, 395–418.

Scanlan, T. K., Carpenter, P. J., Schmidt, G. W., Simons, J. P., & Keeler, B. (1993). An introduction to the sport commitment model. *Journal of Sport & Exercise Psychology, 15*,1–15.

Scanlan, T. K., Russell, D. G., Beals, K. P., & Scanlan, L. A. (2003). Project on elite athlete commitment (PEAK): II. A direct test and expansion of the sport commitment model with elite amateur sportsmen. *Journal of Sport & Exercise Psychology, 25*, 377–401.

Scanlan, T. K., Simons, J. P., Carpenter, P. J., Schmidt, G. W., & Keeler, B. (1993). The sport commitment model: Measurement development for the youth-sport domain. *Journal of Sport & Exercise Psychology, 15*, 16–38.

Shields, C. A., Spink, K. S., Chad, K., Mahajarine, N., Humbert, L., & Odnokon, P. (2008). Youth and adolescent physical activity lapsers: Examining self-efficacy as a mediator of the relationship between family social influence and physical activity. *Journal of Health Psychology, 13*, 121–130.

Shilts, M. K., Horowitz, M., & Townsend, M. (2004). Goal setting as a strategy for dietary and physical activity behavior change: A review. *American Journal of Health Promotion, 19*, 81–93.

Slovinec D'Angelo, M., Reid, R. D., & Pelletier, L. G. (2007). A model for exercise behavior change regulation in patients with heart disease. *Journal of Sport & Exercise Psychology, 29*, 208–224.

Smith, A. L. (2007). Youth peer relationships in sport. In S. Jowett, & D. Lavallee (Eds.), *Social psychology in sport*(pp. 41–54). Champaign, IL: Human Kinetics.

Smith, A. L., & McDonough, M. H. (2008). Peers. In A. L. Smith, & S. J. H. Biddle (Eds.), *Youth physical activity and sedentary behavior: Challenges and solutions* (pp. 295–320). Champaign, IL: Human Kinetics.

Smith, A. L., Ullrich-French, S., Walker, E., & Hurley, K. S. (2006). Peer relationship profiles and motivation in youth sport. *Journal of Sport & Exercise Psychology, 28*, 362–382.

Standage, M., & Duda, J. L. (2004). Motivation processes among older adults in sport and exercise settings. In M. R. Weiss (Ed.), *Developmental sport and exercise psychology: A lifespan perspective* (pp. 357–381). Morgantown, WV: Fitness Information Technology.

Standage, M., Duda, J. L., & Ntoumanis, N. (2003). A model of contextual motivation in physical education: Using constructs and tenets from self-determination and goal perspective theories to predict leisure-time exercise intentions. *Journal of Educational Psychology*, 95, 97–110.

Symons Downs, D., & Hausenblas, H. A. (2005). The theories of reasoned action and planned behavior applied to exercise: A meta-analytic update. *Journal of Physical Activity & Health, 2*, 76–97.

Ullrich-French, S., & Smith, A. L. (2006). Perceptions of relationships with parents and peers in youth sport: Independent and combined prediction of motivational outcomes. *Psychology of Sport & Exercise, 7*, 193–214.

Weiss, M. R. (1993). Children's participation in physical activity: Are we having fun yet? *Pediatric Exercise Science, 5*, 205–209.

Weiss, M. R., Kimmel, L. A., & Smith, A. L. (2001). Determinants of sport commitment among junior tennis players: Enjoyment as a mediating variable. *Pediatric Exercise Science, 13*, 131–144.

Weiss, M. R., & Stuntz, C. P. (2004). A little friendly competition: Peer relationships and psychosocial development in youth sport and physical activity contexts. In M. R. Weiss (Ed.), *Developmental sport and exercise psychology: A lifespan perspective*(pp. 165–196). Morgantown, WV: Fitness Information Technology.

Weiss, M. R., & Williams, L. (2004). The why of youth sport involvement: A developmental perspective on motivational processes. In M. R. Weiss (Ed.), *Developmental sport and exercise psychology: A lifespan perspective*(pp. 223–268). Morgantown, WV: Fitness Information Technology.

Weiss, W. M., & Weiss, M. R. (2006). A longitudinal analysis of commitment among competitive female gymnasts. *Psychology of Sport & Exercise, 7*,309–323.

Weiss, W. M., & Weiss, M. R. (2007). Sport commitment among competitive female gymnasts: A developmental perspective. *Research Quarterly for Exercise & Sport, 78*, 90–102.

White, R. W. (1959). Motivation reconsidered: The concept of competence. *Psychological Review*, 66, 297–333.

Williams, D. M., Anderson, E. S., & Winett, R. A. (2005). A review of the outcome expectancy construct in physical activity research. *Annals of Behavioral Medicine, 29*, 70–79.

Wilson, P. M, Rodgers, W. M, Blanchard, C. M., & Gessell, J. (2003). The relationship between psychological needs, self-determined motivation, exercise attitudes, and physical fitness. *Journal of Applied Social Psychology, 33*, 2373–2392.

Wilson, P. M., Rogers, W. T., Rodgers, W. M., & Wild, T. C. (2006). The Psychological Needs Satisfaction in Exercise Scale. *Journal of Sport & Exercise Psychology, 28*, 231–251.

Wilson, P. M., & Muon, S. (2008). Psychometric properties of the Exercise Identity Scale in a university sample. *International Journal of Sport & Exercise Psychology*, 6, 115–131.

Wilson, P. M., Rodgers, W. M., Fraser, S. N., & Murray, T. C. (2004). The relationship between exercise regulations and motivational consequences. *Research Quarterly for Exercise & Sport, 75*, 81–91.

Woodgate, J., & Brawley, L. R. (2008). Self-efficacy for exercise in cardiac rehabilitation: Review and recommendations. *Journal of Health Psychology, 13*, 366–387.

Chapter 5

Anxiety in Sport and Exercise

Sharleen D. Hoar
Kimberley L. Gammage

Chapter Objectives

After reading this chapter, you should be able to do the following:

1. Define and differentiate among different anxiety-related concepts, such as arousal, trait anxiety, social physique anxiety, state anxiety, social anxiety, competitive anxiety, cognitive anxiety, and somatic anxiety.
2. List and describe the dimensions of an anxiety response, such as intensity, frequency of cognitive intrusions, and directional interpretation of anxiety.
3. List and describe personal sources of anxiety in sport and exercise settings.
4. Discuss how anxiety is specific to competitive and exercise settings and state the personal sources of anxiety that affect anxiety responses in those settings.
5. Describe how anxiety affects exercise behaviour.
6. Explain how anxiety affects sport performance using three different theories.
7. Describe the cognitive and physiological mechanisms that are affected by anxiety, which, in turn, affects sport performance.

Naomi, a starting collegiate volleyball player, began her morning thinking, "Today is game day." She had her ritual game-day breakfast and proceeded to get ready for her morning classes. She was able to arrange her school schedule so that she had Friday classes only in the morning. For home games, she needed the afternoons to rest and prepare for the Friday matches.

Thinking about the match, Naomi knew that a win that night was important. They were playing a rival school team, and both teams were even in points in the standings. That meant that this was going to be a challenging match, and, as a starting player for the team, she told herself that it was her responsibility to be on her game in order to lead the team to a win. Her teammates depended on her. Also, her parents were travelling three hours to watch her play that night. She didn't want to disappoint her teammates or her parents.

Naomi tried to concentrate in class, but her thoughts kept drifting off to critical game points. She visualized herself making a series of perfect serves. In her mind she saw herself making important blocks and defensive digs. She imagined the feelings of excitement as her team gained momentum going into the final set. After classes were over, Naomi performed her ritual pre-game routine as she waited for the 6:30 p.m. start. First she went into the gym to burn off some nervous energy. She spent 25 minutes on the elliptical trainer, all the while trying to avoid looking at herself in the mirror by looking at the pictures of the magazine she had picked up. After her workout, she went home to her apartment and took a nap. She had her pre-game meal around 3:00 p.m. She then just tried to relax by watching TV and talking to her roommates.

Arriving at the team room at the gym at 5:30 p.m., Naomi began to feel the physical and mental sensations of nervousness. Her thoughts were racing, and she couldn't focus on the game plan. Her stomach was feeling queasy, her hands were slightly sweaty, and her heart was beating faster than normal. "This doesn't feel too good," she thought to herself. "I hope that things go all right for me on the court tonight, but if I keep feeling this way, I'm not too sure they will!"

Anxiety is often a part of physical activity. It is often described by exercisers, athletes, trainers, coaches, sports writers, and sport and exercise psychology researchers in different ways. For example, Mike Weir explains that what he felt in the final round of the 2003 Masters Tournament was "gut wrenching" (Jarrett, 2003, p. 40). Other terms that are commonly used to refer to this psychological state include *nervous*, *emotional basket case*, *stressed*, *self-conscious*, *pumped*, and *psyched*. Feelings of anxiety can result from hundreds of different events that occur prior to, during, and after participation in physical activity. In the opening vignette, Naomi felt pressure because of the perceived importance of the match, teammate and parent expectations, and the need to play perfectly. Many exercisers can also fall victim to feelings of anxiety. There are, however, instances when performers thrive in their anxious states to produce personal-best performances. Canadian rower Adam Kreek, a 2008 Olympic gold medallist, wrote on his blog in the hours leading up to his race at the 2008 Beijing Olympic Games: "Today is a very special day. It is race day. Shortly after waking up this morning, I could feel the mini-nuclear reactor in my stomach starting to fire up, getting ready to turn the turbines. I run into my teammates in the hotel room hallway and I can sense that they are feeling the same thing. Again" (Kreek, 2008). In this chapter, the following questions will be addressed: What is anxiety? What causes anxiety in sport and exercise settings? What effect does anxiety have on exercise and athletic performance?

Common Myths about Anxiety in Sport and Exercise

MYTH: Anxiety symptoms are generally the same for all sport and exercise participants.

MYTH: Exercise always helps to reduce anxiety.

MYTH: Pre-competitive anxiety always negatively affects sport performance.

INTRODUCTION

Feelings of anxiousness have been of great interest to athletes, coaches, exercisers, exercise trainers, and sport and exercise psychology researchers for many years (Ekkakakis & Petruzzello, 2000; Smith, Smoll, & Wiechman, 1998). It is often thought that the difference between successful performances (e.g., a personal best, a winning performance, or adherence to an exercise class) and those performances which are evaluated to be failures lies in the performers' ability to manage their nervousness or anxiety. Because it has been assumed that elevated levels of anxiety are debilitating for sport and exercise performance, sport and exercise psychology scientists have sought to better understand the causes and consequences of this psychological state.

REFLECTIONS 5.1

Sport and exercise researchers have long been interested in the causes and consequences of anxiety. Think about when you felt nervous or under pressure prior to an important competitive event or exercise session. What caused you to feel nervous? How did the anxiety affect your performance in that setting?

Photograph by Richard Lam, courtesy of University of British Columbia Athletics.

DEFINITIONS AND BASIC CONCEPTS OF ANXIETY

Today, sport and exercise psychology researchers emphasize the importance of developing precise definitions for emotion-related terminology, including *anxiety* (Ekkekakis & Petruzzello, 2000). In this section, we define what is meant by *anxiety* in the physical activity literature.

Anxiety Is Not Arousal

Arousal is a blend of physiological and psychological activation of an individual's autonomic nervous system. Generally, this state varies in intensity on a continuum ranging from deep sleep to peak activation or frenzy (Gould, Greenleaf, & Krane, 2002). At the high end of the arousal continuum, high-arousal athletes commonly exhibit both physiological and psychological symptoms. For example, a highly aroused athlete is likely to have a racing heart, shallow breathing, sweaty palms, as well as tunnel vision and possibly confusion. Arousal is thought to be neither a pleasant nor an unpleasant experience. Increases in arousal states can occur from positive and exciting events as well as from negative and potentially threatening events. Early sport psychology research examining the influence of anxiety on sport performance viewed anxiety as a unidimensional construct equivalent to that of arousal (Cerin, Szabo, Hunt, & Williams, 2000). More recently, anxiety is observed to be considerably more complex in nature than arousal.

Anxiety Is an Emotion and Is Multidimensional in Nature

Anxiety is most commonly understood as a negative emotion. Anxiety is proposed to have the following characteristics: (1) it is elicited following an appraisal (i.e., evaluation) of a specific situation or event, (2) it is universally observed across people of all cultures, (3) it has a distinct physiology, (4) it is observed through a discrete facial expression, and (5) it is associated with a unique set of behaviours that are called action tendencies (Lazarus, 2000).

Sport and exercise psychology researchers have investigated anxiety from a multidimensional perspective (Martens, Vealey, & Burton, 1990). Anxiety might be experienced by physical activity performers in different ways. Some performers report feeling nauseated or having heavy legs, while others report images of disaster. For example, Canadian Olympic diver Blythe Hartley joked about how viewers at home would be able to identify her: "I'm pretty much a nervous wreck the whole competition . . . . I don't look happy, but that's what works for me" (Gatehouse, 2004, p. 28).

Within this multidimensional framework, anxiety is composed of two components, a mental and a physical component. The mental component is called **cognitive anxiety**, and it reflects the athlete's concerns or worries and the reduced ability to focus or concentrate (Krane, 1994). The other component, called **somatic anxiety**, is defined as "the physiological and affective elements of the anxiety experience that develop directly from autonomic arousal" (Martens et al., 1990, p. 6). Somatic anxiety is distinct from arousal in that somatic anxiety is not merely a reflection of the level of physiological arousal that is experienced. Rather, somatic anxiety is the *perception* of the symptom manifestations of arousal. Thus, somatic anxiety is only experienced to the degree that the athlete becomes aware of arousal symptoms, such as clammy hands and a racing heartbeat. Although cognitive and somatic anxiety are conceptualized to be independent and distinct, cognitive and somatic anxiety responses are moderately interrelated and levels of both anxiety responses are experienced in most competitive events.

Anxiety is experienced in different ways, such as feelings of worry, a racing heartbeat, or shaky hands.
Photograph © The Canadian Press/AP Photo/Jack Dempsey.

REFLECTIONS 5.2

Reflect on a time when you watched an important sporting competition. Were the players jittery and fidgeting? Did they appear to be distracted, concentrating on something other than the national anthem? Considering the multidimensional nature of anxiety, what mental and physical symptoms of anxiety were present?

Anxiety Is Context Specific

Social anxiety is a specific type of anxiety that occurs during social situations. For instance, speaking in front of a large group of people, competing in a stadium full of fans, or working out at the local gym are all situations in which anxiety may arise due to interactions with other people. Specifically, social anxiety occurs when people experience, or think that they will experience, evaluations from other people (Leary, 1992). Athletes may feel anxious that their coach or teammates are evaluating their performance during games; exercisers may feel anxious if they think others will be judging their appearance. Some researchers have suggested that **competitive anxiety** is a form of social anxiety (Leary, 1992). In this form of anxiety, athletes may be concerned about their body, their performance, their fitness level, or their skills being evaluated by spectators, teammates, coaches, family, or friends. In the exercise context, **social physique anxiety** is most commonly studied. Social physique anxiety is the tendency to experience anxiety as a result of perceiving that others may evaluate one's physique in social settings (Hart, Leary, & Rejeski, 1989).

Anxiety Has Both Trait and State Components

Anxiety is both a part of our personality and a response that fluctuates from situation to situation. **State anxiety** is the type of anxiety that is associated with worries and apprehension that change from moment to moment (Speilberger, 1966). For example, an exerciser may experience mild symptoms of anxiety when entering the locker room, with symptoms increasing in intensity in the moments waiting in the exercise studio for her leader to begin the aerobic class. During the warm-up, the anxiety symptoms may subside and the exerciser may feel more comfortable in the setting and be distracted by the aerobic routine. In contrast, **trait anxiety** is a stable part of an individual's personality, predisposing the individual to perceive situations as physically or psychologically threatening.

REFLECTIONS 5.3

Think about the times you have been in an exercise setting, such as a gym. What factors could make people feel anxious? Think about the physical surroundings, the other exercisers, and the exercise itself.

Dimensions of the Anxiety Response

What does it mean to state that one exerciser or sport participant has more anxiety than another? *More* could be referring to the intensity of the anxiety symptoms, the number (or frequency) of anxiety-related thoughts or physical symptoms, as well as the directional interpretations of anxiety symptoms for sport performance or exercise behaviour (Mellalieu, Hanton, & Fletcher, 2006).

Intensity of Symptoms Most of the sport and exercise research investigating anxiety has exclusively examined the intensity of symptoms (Mellalieu et al., 2006). This dimension of anxiety examines the amount or level of symptoms experienced by physical activity and sport participants.

Frequency of Cognitive Intrusions The frequency of cognitive intrusions/symptoms refers to the amount of time (expressed as a percentage) that thoughts and feelings about the competition occupy an individual's mind (Mellalieu et al., 2006). This dimension of anxiety is deemed to be important for understanding the temporal nature of the anxiety response. Few sport and exercise psychology researchers have investigated anxiety from this perspective.

Directional Interpretation of Symptoms Most sport and exercise psychology researchers agree that negative emotions do not always negatively affect performance (Uphill, 2008). There are times when anxiety is perceived to have a positive influence on sport and exercise behaviours. Think about how two elite Canadian athletes describe the implications of their anxiety symptoms for future athletic performances. Blythe Hartley (Olympic diver) stated that the feelings of being a "nervous wreck" are positively interpreted as being in a state of readiness for competition. Alternatively, Steve Podborski (Olympic ski racer) referred to a specific intensity of "nervousness" that, if reached, resulted in poor performance. The third dimension of an anxiety response, the directional interpretation of symptoms, refers to the extent to which the intensity of the cognitive and somatic anxiety symptoms are labelled as either facilitative (i.e., positive) or debilitative (i.e., negative) to sport or physical activity performance (Jones & Swain, 1992).

SOURCES OF ANXIETY

Anxiety responses are experienced by virtually all physical activity participants at different times. Over the years, many environmental and personal sources of anxiety have been identified. A complete review of this work is beyond the scope of this chapter. (Interested readers are directed to Mellalieu et al., 2006.) Instead, we highlight select personal sources of anxiety and then draw attention to certain aspects of the sport and exercise environment that interact with personal sources to elicit participants' anxiety.

Personal Sources of Anxiety

Sport and exercise psychology researchers have identified several important personal sources of anxiety. In this section, we discuss the research findings on five of the most-studied personal sources of anxiety, including (1) age, experience, and skill level, (2) gender, (3) trait anxiety, (4) self-confidence and self-presentational beliefs, and (5) self-regulation strategies.

Age, Experience, and Skill Level Early research examining individual differences in anxiety responses came from the laboratory of Walter Fenz and his associates from the University of Waterloo. They demonstrated that novice parachute jumpers differed in their arousal responses to jumping from an airplane compared to expert parachute jumpers (Fenz & Epstein, 1967; Fenz & Jones, 1972). Although their work focused on arousal, it stimulated research investigating anxiety differences among expert and novice participants. However, the results of this research have been equivocal (Hanton, Cropley, Neil, Mellalieu, & Miles, 2007). Some studies revealed anxiety differences between expert and novice athletes, whereas others found no differences (e.g., Gould, Petlichokoff, & Weinberg, 1984; Hanton & Jones, 1997). A limitation of this research was the way in which "expert" and "novice" athletes were defined. In many early studies, expertise was measured as differences in age, years at a sport, familiarity with the environment, and competitive status.

In consideration of these limitations, Jones and his colleagues (Hanton & Jones, 1997; Hanton & Jones, 1999; Jones & Swain, 1995) investigated anxiety response differences among athletes at different skill levels. This work demonstrated that athletes of different skill abilities do not differ in the intensity of anxiety symptoms prior to competition. Rather, more skilled athletes view anxiety symptoms to be facilitative for performance. In contrast, less skilled athletes view anxiety symptoms to be debilitative or harmful for sport performance.

Competitive experience may be a more sensitive indicator related to differences in athletes' experience of anxiety. Mellalieu et al. (2006) observed that, although higher skilled performers are assumed to possess a greater number of competitive experiences, it is possible for a highly skilled athlete to have little experience at a given competitive level due to a sudden rise in performance level (e.g., to international level competition). The results from studies that use "competitive experience" as an operation of expertise reveal that more-experienced performers report lower intensities of pre-competitive anxiety and evaluate anxiety to be more facilitative for sport performance compared to the less experienced performers.

Gender The sport research on gender differences has been inconsistent. Early research provided some evidence that female athletes report higher intensities of trait and state anxiety symptoms prior to competition in comparison with male athletes (Krane & Williams, 1994). More recent research, however, has failed to find differences between male and female competitive anxiety responses (e.g., Hammermeister & Burton, 2004). In exercise and other physical activity settings, females consistently experience higher levels of social physique anxiety compared to males (Crocker, Sabiston, Kowalski, McDonough, & Kowalski, 2006; Hart et al., 1989). In addition, researchers have found that different factors may be related to social physique anxiety for men and women (Hausenblas & Fallon, 2002; Mack, Strong, Kowalski, & Crocker, 2007). Hausenblas found that body mass index (BMI) was the strongest predictor of social physique anxiety for college women, whereas exercise behaviour was the strongest factor for college men. In a study of peer influences on social physique anxiety, Mack and colleagues (2007) found that peer pressure and relative attractiveness of peers were predictors of social physique anxiety in both adolescent males and females. However, the extent to which individuals identified with the peer network was also an important predictor only for females. There are two important points to note. First, although both males and females experience social physique anxiety, it is a greater concern for women. Second, different factors are related to social physique anxiety for males and females.

Trait Anxiety A number of personality traits, or dispositions, are known to influence an individual's level of competitive state anxiety and social physique anxiety. These characteristics include competitiveness, extroversion, hardiness, neuroticism, optimism/pessimism, perfectionism, self-consciousness, and self-esteem. Of the personality traits that have been investigated, trait anxiety (i.e., **competitive trait anxiety**, the tendency to experience anxiety during competitive situations, and social physique anxiety) has received the most attention by sport and exercise psychology researchers. It is proposed that an individual's level of trait anxiety directly affects the perception of threat in competitive and exercise situations and, subsequently, state anxiety intensity levels (Martens et al., 1990). Interestingly, this effect appears to be restricted to the intensity of anxiety symptoms and does not extend to the interpretations of symptoms as facilitative or debilitative to performance. That is, low trait anxious and high trait anxious athletes interpret state anxiety symptoms in a similar manner for affecting sport performance.

Self-confidence and Self-presentational Beliefs An individual's personal beliefs about her or his capability to achieve sport success as well as being able to present his or her body in a favourable manner are critical sources of anxiety for sport and exercise participants. Research with sport competitors reveals that positive beliefs about competence (i.e., self-confidence), readiness for competition, ability to exert control in the competition, and ability to perform better than one's opponent are related to lower levels of state anxiety (Bray, Martin, & Widmeyer, 2000; Hanton & Jones, 1997). Canadian researchers have also identified that beliefs relating to the competitive success of the group or team also influence athletes' pre-competitive anxiety responses. Specifically, athletes who hold positive beliefs about their group's ability to work together to achieve success report having less pre-competitive state anxiety compared with those athletes whose beliefs are negative (Eys, Hardy, Carron, & Beauchamp, 2003; Prapavessis & Carron, 1996).

Self-confident athletes are also more likely to view state anxiety symptoms as facilitative for performance despite the intensity of anxiety symptoms felt (Hanton, Neil, & Mellalieu, 2008). That is, if an athlete believes in his ability to be successful, he is likely to view any level of anxiety symptoms (i.e., low or high) as favourable for performance. Perhaps an elevation in anxiety symptoms is viewed to be evidence that the athlete is ready to compete. Take the example of an Olympic swimmer: "I mean, you have to get nervous to swim well . . . . If you're not bothered by it, you are not going to swim well . . . . I think that the nerves bring out the best in you, and I soon realized that I wanted to feel this way" (Hanton & Jones, 1999b, p. 9). Furthermore, elevations in self-confidence are purported to assist highly worried (i.e., cognitively anxious) athletes to tolerate elevations in physiological arousal that would otherwise disrupt sport performance. This latter point will be discussed further when we address how anxiety affects sport performance.

Self-confidence is not the only type of belief important to athletes' anxiety. During competition, athletes' skill level, fitness, preparedness, and ability to handle pressure are on constant display for others to evaluate. Uphill and Jones (2007) interviewed 12 elite college-aged athletes from a variety of sports and found that a significant source of anxiety was **self-presentation**, which is the process by which people attempt to monitor and control the impressions that other people hold of them (Leary, 1992). The thoughts of the elite athletes centred on what others would think about them; the athletes did not want to make fools of themselves in front of others. McGowen, Prapavessis, and Wesch (2008) confirmed these results with a large sample of over 300 male and female athletes. Their study revealed that poor **self-presentation beliefs** (i.e., the beliefs that one will present one's physical self to others in a negative way) were related to elevations in competitive trait and state anxiety intensity.

Self-presentation beliefs are also a source of anxiety for many exercisers. Sabiston and colleagues investigated body image and exercise motivation as sources contributing to social physique anxiety in college women (Sabiston, Crocker, & Monroe-Chandler, 2005). They found that the discrepancy between women's current and ideal shape was positively associated with social physique anxiety. That is, as the difference between the current and ideal body shape increased (i.e., as the women became more dissatisfied with their bodies), social physique anxiety increased. Studies also reveal that as people exercise more to control their weight and appearance, social physique anxiety is also increased (Frederick & Morrison, 1996; Sabiston et al., 2005).

Exercise psychology researchers have recently begun to investigate the role that self-efficacy (see Chapter 4) may have on anxiety in exercise settings. One particular type of self-efficacy is **self-presentational self-efficacy**, which is the confidence in one's ability to present images of being an exerciser. It may be particularly important in the relationship between social physique anxiety and exercise behaviour. In a study with university women, Gammage and colleagues reported that women who believed they would be exercising in an environment while wearing loose-fitting T-shirts and shorts, with no mirrors or windows present, and no men present (i.e., high self-presentational self-efficacy) showed decreased levels of social anxiety and social physique anxiety (Gammage, Hall, & Martin Ginis, 2004). In contrast, those who believed they would be exercising in revealing clothing, in front of mirrors, and with a man videotaping them close-up (i.e., low self-presentational self-efficacy) reported increases in social anxiety and social physique anxiety. Thus, different forms of self-confidence beliefs are important sources of anxiety.

Self-regulation Strategies What a physical activity participant does to manage anxiety symptoms has been identified as another important source of anxiety. Canadian researchers have been instrumental in studying the influence of specific coping skills that athletes use to manage their pre-competitive anxiety symptoms (e.g., Crocker, Alderman, & Smith, 1988; Haney, 2004; Kowalski, Mack, Crocker, Niefer, & Fleming, 2006). Some coping skills are specific behaviours or actions that an athlete or exerciser can use to adjust physiological arousal and the degree of worry or concern that is experienced. Common coping skills used by athletes are relaxation skills, self-talk and cognitive restructuring, and imagery. Research with Canadian Olympic athletes revealed that the most important factor distinguishing medal winners from non-medal-winners was the ability to use coping skills to manage anxiety responses prior to and during competitive performances (Orlick & Partington, 1988). Haney (2004) studied the effectiveness of a six-month coping skills intervention with 47 Canadian female adult athletes. She found that sport performers in coping skills training groups reduced their pre-competitive somatic and cognitive anxiety responses. Coping is described in greater detail in Chapter 6.

A series of recent studies to identify the ways in which male and female adolescents manage social physique anxiety revealed that adolescents coped by engaging in exercise behaviour (Kowalski et al., 2006; Sabiston, Sedgwick, Crocker, Kowalski, & Stevens, 2007). In fact, physical activity as a coping strategy was reported by approximately 12% of the adolescents (Kowalski et al., 2006). This result should not be surprising since exercise is recommended by physicians as an important strategy for managing anxiety (see Chapter 12).

Another self-regulation strategy that has received attention by sport researchers is the use of **self-handicapping**. Self-handicapping is defined as "any action or choice of performance setting that enhances the opportunity to externalize (or excuse) failure and internalize (reasonably accept credit for) success" (Berglas & Jones, 1978, p. 406). Athletes who use self-handicapping strategies are likely to diminish efforts during competition, select unattainable goals to achieve, exaggerate the pain associated with an injury, or complain illegitimately about the fairness of the referee in order to confuse whether performance failure is due to athletic ability or due to external problems that the athlete had to manage (Coudevylle, Martin Ginis, Famose, & Gernigon, 2008; Prapavessis, Grove, Maddison, & Zillmann, 2003). These athletes also have higher intensity levels of trait and state anxiety. Interestingly, the anxiety symptoms are more likely to be viewed as facilitative for performance (Coudevylle et al., 2008; Ferrand, Champely, & Brunel, 2005).

In sum, physical activity participants' anxiety responses are related to a number of sources that are specific to the person. We highlighted only those personal sources that have received the most attention by sport and exercise researchers. Most of the research has examined anxiety responses in light of the intensity of symptoms experienced. Some research has examined select personal sources that affect athletes' interpretation of anxiety symptoms as facilitative or debilitative for sport performance. It can be generally concluded that elevations in the intensity of anxiety responses in athletes and exercisers are associated with (1) novice expertise, (2) being female, (3) high trait anxiety, (4) low self-confidence (and low self-efficacy) in individual and team competencies, (5) negative or poor self-presentational beliefs, (6) poor self-regulatory skills, and (7) the use of self-handicapping strategies.

Case Study 5.1

Identifying Personal Sources of Competitive Anxiety for an Elite Athlete

Consider Kyle Shewfelt's comments in his blog entry prior to the 2008 Olympic Games in Beijing. What personal sources are likely to be contributing to Kyle's anxiety?

"This morning when I woke up I was a little panicked. The thought that I am actually leaving for Beijing and the Olympic Games felt very real and it freaked me out . . . .

Am I ready? Will I be able to deliver the performance I need to? Will I be able to withstand the Olympic pressure? Have I worked hard enough? Have I done enough routines? Do I need more time? Will my legs hold up? Is my difficulty high enough? What if I don't win again? What if I mess up during the qualification? What if I can't get my second vault? What if I forget how to do gymnastics . . . ?

Feeling the crunch

I am feeling the crunch. The expectation I have of myself and the pressure of the Olympic Games are beginning to build . . . . It's almost as if every moment that I am not in the gym and proving to myself that I can do gymnastics, I am doubting my ability. I am only getting relief and confirmation when I am physically there and going through the motions.

I find myself worrying about the thoughts that are going to go through my head when it's time to compete. I want to be focused and prepared and not wishing that I could escape the moment and run away and hide.

When the sharks attack

I am so scared that my physical, emotional and mental selves are not going to align at the moment I need them to. What if I completely destroy my performance? What if I stand there waiting to compete and I don't trust the work I have done? What if I let the sharks attack and I am left with severed limbs and a devastating experience?

I think these thoughts are normal . . . " (Shewfelt, 2008).

Source: Used with permission of Kyle Shewfelt.

Environment-based Sources of Anxiety

Sport and exercise psychology research also reveals that individuals' anxiety responses are related not only to personal sources. The environment also uniquely contributes to anxiety in physical activity participants. In sport, athletes' anxiety is related to the temporal period within competitive events. In the exercise context, exercisers' anxiety responses are related to specific aspects of the exercise setting, including mirrors, clothing, other participants, and leadership characteristics.

Temporal Patterning in the Sport Environment The intensity of an athlete's anxiety response changes during the lead-up to a competitive event as well as over the course of the event. Martens and colleagues (1990) offered several predictions about the temporal changes in the intensity of cognitive and somatic anxiety symptoms over a competitive event (see Figure 5.1). First, somatic anxiety remains at a low intensity until several hours prior to competition, after which there is a sharp rise until the onset of performance. Second, during and after competition, the intensity level of somatic anxiety decreases. Third, cognitive anxiety demonstrates a different pattern. Unless there is a change in the athlete's evaluation of the potential for success prior to competition, no changes in the intensity level of cognitive anxiety are expected to occur prior to competition. After the onset of competition, there is a steady decline in the intensity of cognitive anxiety. In general, empirical research has broadly supported these propositions (Martens et al., 1990; Swain & Jones, 1993; Wiggins, 1998).

Figure 5.1 Hypothesized temporal patterning of cognitive anxiety and somatic anxiety before and after a sport performance

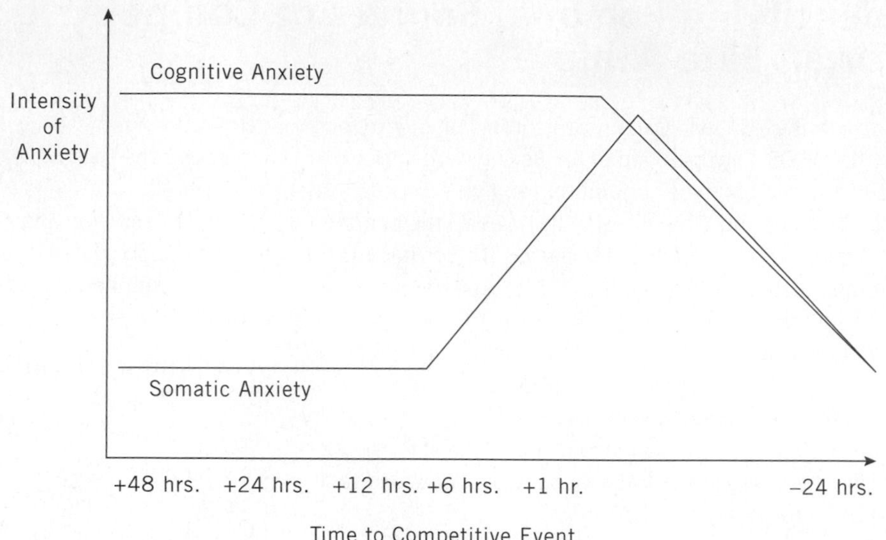

Note: From Parfitt, G., Jones, J. G., & Hardy, L. (1990). Multidimensional anxiety and performance. In J. G. Jones, & L. Hardy (Eds.), *Stress and performance in sport* (p. 48). New York: John Wiley & Sons Limited. Reproduced with permission.

More recently, sport psychology researchers acknowledge that the intensity of competitive anxiety responses is not just affected by the temporal phase of competition. Research has also revealed that a number of personal variables interact with the temporal phase to moderate or influence the exact nature of the temporal patterning of anxiety intensity. These variables include sex and gender role endorsement, skill level, sport type, level of competition, competitiveness, success and failure, and perceived ability. A key feature of many of these variables is that any factor that increases the perceived threat of the situation tends to increase anxiety.

Temporal patterning of competitive anxiety has also been studied according to the frequency of cognitive intrusions/symptoms as well as the directional interpretation of anxiety symptoms. Swain and Jones (1993) found that while the intensity of cognitive anxiety remained stable, the frequency of cognitive intrusions increased as competition nears. Conclusions drawn from the research examining changes in directional interpretation across the competitive temporal phases suggest that directional perceptions of cognitive anxiety become less facilitative as the competition draws nearer (Cerin et al., 2000; Rich, Mellalieu, Hanton, & Mitchell, 2007).

Mirrors in the Exercise Environment Studies have suggested that the presence of mirrors during exercise may increase the levels of state anxiety and social anxiety experienced (Focht & Hausenblas, 2004). This may be particularly true in women who are already high in trait social physique anxiety and for those who are novice exercisers. Research suggests that the effects of mirrors on anxiety are more complex. Raedeke, Focht, and Scales (2007) suggested that mirrors might be useful in providing performance information for more complex tasks or for regular exercisers because they provide an opportunity to watch one's performance rather than appearance. In these conditions, mirrors may not

Anxiety changes over the different phases of a competition. The ability to control anxiety prior to, during, and after competition is critical for competitive success.
Photograph © Corbis RF/Jupiter Images

increase anxiety. However, when tasks are simple, or exercisers are inexperienced, there may be an increase in the tendency to view one's body, thus increasing anxiety.

Clothing in the Exercise Environment The type of clothing worn in the exercise environment is also associated with anxiety, particularly social anxiety. Generally, more revealing clothing is associated with higher levels of social anxiety during exercise. Gammage et al. (2004) told a group of female college students that they would be exercising. Some were told that they would be exercising in front of mirrors and would be wearing revealing clothing—spandex shorts and a jogging bra—while others were told that they would be exercising in a room with no mirrors, wearing a loose-fitting T-shirt and pair of shorts. They found that the women who thought they would be exercising in revealing clothing reported higher social physique anxiety, higher anxiety about exercising in front of others, and higher anxiety about specific body parts (e.g., hips, abdomen). Further, in a series of studies, women who engaged in little physical activity and who were high in social physique anxiety preferred less-revealing attire, while those lower in social physique anxiety preferred more-revealing clothing. However, in participants who were already active, this difference disappeared (Crawford & Eklund, 1994; Eklund & Crawford, 1994).

Characteristics of Other Exercisers Simply exercising in the presence of others can increase anxiety in women. For instance, Focht and Hausenblas (2004) found that women who were higher in social physique anxiety and who exercised when other people were present experienced greater state anxiety during exercise than those who exercised in a lab setting by themselves. In addition to the mere presence of others, there are specific characteristics of other exercisers that are important to consider for anxiety responses. Having other participants be interactive, positive, and enthusiastic during an exercise class ("enriched" participants) was associated with greater social anxiety levels than when other participants did not interact with one another and were not enthusiastic about the exercise class ("bland" participants; Martin & Fox, 2001). Why would a friendlier environment be associated with more anxiety? The authors suggested that the exercisers wanted the other class participants to like them and cared more about what others thought about them, which may have increased their social anxiety. In addition, because the exercisers were interacting with other participants more, they may also have believed that others were watching their performance and were perhaps evaluating it more closely.

Another factor that seems to lead to anxiety in women, but not in men, is the gender of the other exercise participants. Specifically, women who exercise in mixed-gender rather than all-female settings report higher levels of social physique anxiety. One reason is women's perceptions that men are likely to evaluate women's bodies during exercise (Walton & Finkenberg, 2002).

Exercise Leader Characteristics The characteristics of the exercise leader may affect the anxiety experienced during exercise. However, unlike studies that have shown that highly interactive and enthusiastic participants may lead to increases in anxiety, an enriched leadership style may have the opposite effect. Martin and Fox (2001) found that when the instructor used an enriched style (in which she interacted with participants and was encouraging and energetic), participants experienced less social anxiety than when she used a bland style (in which she did not interact with participants, gave vague and negative comments and instruction, and was not encouraging). Why might this style have led to decreases in social anxiety? Perhaps when the instructor is more interactive and positive, participants feel less intimidated and are less worried about being judged negatively.

In addition to leadership style, the appearance of the exercise leader may also affect anxiety. For instance, one study examined the impact that the clothing worn by the instructor in an exercise video had on women's anxiety. However, contradictory to what they had expected, they found that when the instructor wore revealing clothing that emphasized her body, women's anxiety was no different than when the instructor wore less-revealing clothing. This study did find that women who thought they had less attractive bodies than the instructor experienced greater social physique anxiety than those who thought they were just as or more attractive than the instructor (Martin Ginis, Prapavessis, & Haase, 2008). Therefore, the comparisons women make to instructors in exercise classes may be more important than the actual appearance of the instructor.

ANXIETY INFLUENCES ON EXERCISE BEHAVIOUR AND SPORT PERFORMANCE

What effect does anxiety have on exercisers and sport participants? One obvious consequence of anxiety is its potential effect on exercise behaviour and sport performance. Exercisers who experience excessive levels of anxiety are likely to feel uncomfortable in the exercise environment and may not engage in exercise behaviour in the future. Similarly, athletes who consistently experience high levels of worry and apprehension prior to sport competition also tend to have lowered levels of enjoyment with sport, increased susceptibility to athletic injury, enhanced feelings of burnout, and increased dropout rates (Smith et al., 1998). Although these outcomes are important to understand, most of the scientific study of anxiety consequences has focused on exercise adherence and athletic performance. Thus, we will focus on the research investigating the relationship between anxiety and these physical activity behaviours.

The Influence of Anxiety on Exercise Behaviours

Most anxiety research has attempted to determine how various forms of anxiety may influence exercise-related behaviours and cognitions. This research has examined the relationship between social anxiety and exercise primarily through a self-presentational framework. Self-presentation occurs when people try to control how others see them (Leary, 1992). For example, if you want people to see you as fit, you could tell them that you exercise, you could wear exercise clothing, or you could actually exercise. Leary suggested that at very high levels, social anxiety may prevent people from exercising altogether. This idea makes some sense. If people experience anxiety when exercising—or even when thinking about exercising—they may do everything they can to avoid it. Therefore, it is important to understand how anxiety can affect exercise-related behaviours and cognitions. Much of this research has examined the influence of social physique anxiety.

Individuals high in social physique anxiety may exercise more as a way to improve their bodies and therefore receive positive evaluations from others. However, individuals high in social physique anxiety might also avoid exercise, to avoid situations in which others could evaluate their bodies. So which hypothesis is correct? Researchers have found support for both! Some research has found that those higher in social physique anxiety actually exercise more (Frederick & Morrison, 1996), other research indicates that they exercise less (Culos-Reed, Brawley, Martin, & Leary, 2002), and still other research has found no relationship between the two (Crocker et al., 2006; Lantz, Hardy, & Ainsworth, 1997).

Because of the mixed findings, researchers have attempted to examine other variables that may influence this relationship. For example, Angove and her colleagues (2003) investigated the exercise behaviours of older women who were and were not confident in their ability to be seen positively in an exercise setting (i.e., high self-presentation self-efficacy). The results revealed that social physique anxiety led to lower levels of physical activity only in women with low levels of self-presentation efficacy.

One exercise related health risk behaviour that may be related to self-presentational concerns is excessive exercise. For instance, Martin and Leary (2001) found that men often over-lifted at the gym in order to be seen as brave and attractive by others. However, in contrast, Hausenblas and Fallon (2002) found that social physique anxiety was not significantly related to symptoms of exercise dependence when the BMI, gender, and exercise behaviour of the individual was taken into consideration.

REFLECTIONS 5.4

Think about your experiences of anxiety associated with different exercise behaviours. Describe the types of environments that provoked a weak and/or strong anxiety response. In what ways was your exercise behaviour enhanced or hindered by your anxiety?

Photograph © Radius/Jupiter Images.

Anxiety–Sport Performance Relationship Models

Much of the research on anxiety and physical activity has occurred in the sport performance field. Early explanations about the influence of competitive anxiety on sport performance, such as the drive theory and inverted-U theory (see Woodman & Hardy, 2001), were based on anxiety being equivalent to arousal. Since 1990, sport research has largely ignored these explanations in favour of more complex theories that examine anxiety from a multidimensional perspective. Three theories have been prominent in the sport psychology research: multidimensional anxiety theory (Martens et al., 1990), zones of optimal functioning (Hanin, 1980), and cusp catastrophe theory (Fazey & Hardy, 1988; Hardy, 1990).

Multidimensional Anxiety Theory The multidimensional anxiety theory, or MAT (Martens et al., 1990), describes the relationships between components of anxiety and sport performance. The first set of predictions addresses the relationship between cognitive and somatic components of anxiety and sport performance. The second set of predictions addresses how the relationship between the component of competitive anxiety and sport performance may change across different temporal phases of a competition. It is proposed that somatic anxiety has an inverted curvilinear (i.e., inverted U) relationship with performance. That is, as the intensity of somatic anxiety symptoms increases, sport performance should be enhanced, but only up to a certain point. Somatic anxiety beyond a moderate intensity level is proposed to be debilitative for sport performance. This hypothesis was based on research findings that moderate muscular tension levels were associated with best or optimal sport performance (Weinberg, 1978). Cognitive anxiety is proposed to have a negative linear relationship with sport performance. As the intensity of worry and apprehension increases, sport performance is expected to diminish. Martens and colleagues (1990) argued that worrying takes up limited cognitive resources that are then not available for performance execution.

The strength of MAT is its capacity to describe a very complex three-dimensional relationship (between cognitive anxiety, somatic anxiety, and sport performance) in a series of simpler two-dimensional relationships (Uphill, 2008). Unfortunately, the results of studies examining MAT have been somewhat inconsistent (Cerin et al., 2000).

Zones of Optimal Functioning Theory In his work with Russian athletes, Yuri Hanin (1980) noted that athletes demonstrated considerable variability in the level of pre-competitive state anxiety that was associated with optimal athletic performance. Some athletes performed best with high levels of state anxiety, while others achieved superior performances with moderate or low levels of state anxiety. These observations led Hanin to contend that best performances are more likely to occur with optimal levels of state anxiety. Further, Hanin argued that optimal state anxiety is a bandwidth, or zone, of state anxiety intensity scores (not a specific value) that is specific to the individual athlete and is not dependent on motor skill requirements of the sport or the athlete's skill level (Raglin & Hanin, 2000).

Practically speaking, this theory suggests that the optimal intensity zone of competitive state anxiety required for optimal performance from members of a sport team is likely to differ among the players. For example, some hockey players may play their best even if there are large fluctuations in the intensity of anxiety symptoms (i.e., a wide zone of competitive state anxiety), whereas others may play best when the intensity of state anxiety stays constant (i.e., a narrow zone of competitive state anxiety). Moreover, some of the team members may require a low to moderate intensity band of competitive state anxiety,

Case Study 5.2

Using Theory to Explain the Influence of Anxiety on Sport Performance

Carefully consider the tenets of the different competitive-anxiety performance models. Can we explain Perdita Felicien's performance in her final race at the 2004 Olympic Games in Athens? She was ranked No. 1 in the world in the 110 m hurdles. At the Olympic Games, she performed well in her heats and easily qualified for the finals. However, what happened in the final race was what she described as "my worst nightmare come true" ("This is," 2004, p. 2). A few metres into the race, she missed a hurdle, hitting the barrier instead. Losing her balance, she fell into another competitor and fell to the ground. She could not complete her race and was disqualified.

How might each of the models presented in this chapter describe Felicien's competitive anxiety in relation to her performance?

while others display personal best performances when experiencing moderate to high levels of competitive anxiety. The point is that each hockey player's optimal intensity band of competitive state anxiety is individual and is dependent on the player, not the type of sport or sport skills that the athlete is to perform.

Thus, the central tenet of the Zones of Optimal Functioning (ZOF) hypothesis is that an athlete who is within his or her identified competitive state anxiety zone will be more likely to have a best athletic performance. If the athlete has anxiety that is outside of his or her optimal zone (either too low or too high), performance is likely to be impaired (Robazza, 2006). The ZOF hypothesis has been tested in a number of investigations with athletes from a wide variety of countries. The research reveals that, in general, athletes who are within personally identified optimal zones of competitive state anxiety are more likely to have best performances compared with athletes who are outside the determined optimal zone (Jokela & Hanin, 1999). Hanin has expanded the theory to investigate multiple emotional states on sport performance (see Robazza, 2006). This theory has been important for understanding (1) how the relationship between anxiety and performance differs between athletes, and (2) that anxiety is not always detrimental to sport performance.

Cusp Catastrophe Theory The cusp catastrophe theory attempts to describe the combined, or interactive, influences of the multiple components of competitive anxiety and physiological arousal on athletic performance (Fazey & Hardy, 1988; Hardy, 1990). It is emphasized that physiological arousal, rather than somatic anxiety, is included in this theory because arousal is argued to have both a direct and indirect effect on sport performance. Few sport psychology researchers have applied this model to understand the relationship between anxiety and sport performance, and it has been criticized for being overly complex (e.g., Gill, 1994). But why would one expect anxiety and performance relationships to be simple? Canadian downhill ski racer Steve Podborski describes how his competitive anxiety affected his athletic performance: "I discovered that after a certain point of nervousness, I would start to deteriorate pretty rapidly. There was a real drop-off point in my ability to perform if I got too nervous . . . so it was just being able to find that little narrow comfort zone" (Orlick & Partington, 1986, p. 162).

The advantage to using the cusp catastrophe theory is that it recognizes that anxiety has a complex relationship with athletic performance (see Case Study 5.2). Further, unlike MAT, catastrophe theory predicts that under certain circumstances, elevation in

Figure 5.2 Cusp catastrophe theory describing the interactions of cognitive state anxiety, physiological arousal, and sport performance

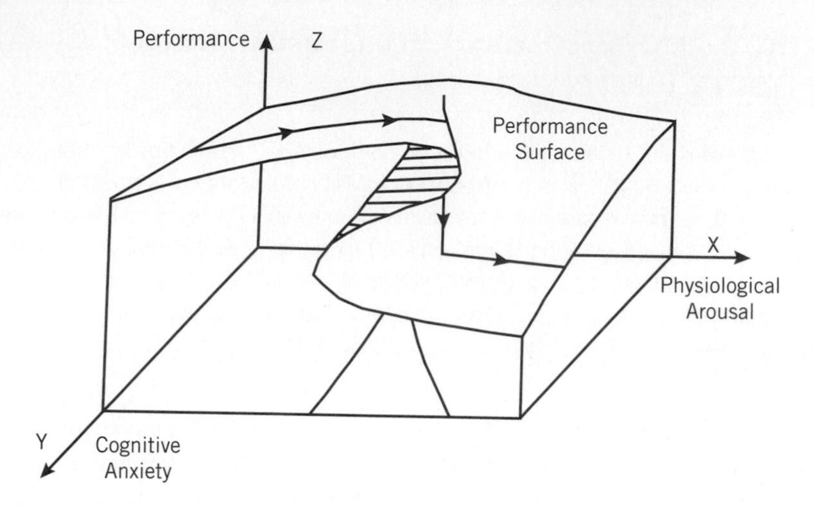

Note: From Hardy, L. (1990). "A catastrophe model of performance in sport." In J. G. Jones, & L. Hardy (eds.), *Stress and Performance in Sport*. John Wiley & Sons Limited, pg. 88. Reproduced with permission.

the intensity of anxiety is not always detrimental for performance. Essentially, this model makes five predictions (Woodman & Hardy, 2005).

1. When cognitive state anxiety is low, the relationship between physiological arousal and performance is uniform or an inverted-U shape (as shown by the back face of Figure 5.2).
2. When physiological arousal is low, elevations in cognitive state anxiety are associated with enhanced performance relative to baseline (as shown by the left side of Figure 5.2).
3. When physiological arousal is high, elevations in cognitive state anxiety are associated with declines in performance (as shown by the right side of Figure 5.2).
4. When cognitive state anxiety is high (as shown by the front face of Figure 5.2), the effects of elevations in physiological arousal can be positive or negative for performance (relative to baseline performance). It is proposed that the combined effect of high cognitive state anxiety and moderately low levels of physiological arousal should produce more successful performances (compared with those produced under conditions of low cognitive anxiety). This proposition implies that a high level of cognitive anxiety is not always detrimental to sport performance. For athletes who are able to sustain moderately low levels of physiological arousal, an increase in worry and concern can function to enhance athletic performance.
5. When physiological arousal is moderately high and cognitive state anxiety is high, it is predicted that a dramatic performance drop (similar to that described by Steve Podborski), called a *catastrophe*, will occur. To improve performance after the catastrophe, a decrease in physiological arousal is required. A performance catastrophe is not proposed to occur when cognitive state anxiety is low.

Studies investigating the proposed relationships of the catastrophe model have produced results that support these predictions across a range of sports (e.g., Edwards & Hardy, 1995; Woodman & Hardy, 2005).

Underlying Mechanisms of the Anxiety–Performance Relationship

Despite important advancements in documenting anxiety and performance relationships, sport psychology researchers still do not completely know why this relationship forms at all. That is, the question "Why does competitive anxiety affect athletic performance?" still remains unanswered. To answer this question, it is important to consider the critical components of sport skill execution. Optimal performance of any motor skill requires at least the following: (1) the cognitive processing of relevant amounts and types of information from the environment, and (2) the appropriate levels and coordination of muscle activation. Consider wheelchair athlete Chantal Petitclerc, Canada's 2008 athlete of the year, who completed her Paralympic career by winning five gold medals at the Beijing Games. In a 1500 m race, she must focus her attention on numerous external stimuli, such as the condition of the track, the position of other racers, her position on the track (straightway or curve), and the actual stage of the race. Throughout the race, she must also generate the correct action plans for generating specific forces and translate these plans into movement programs to produce the appropriate movements. If there are problems in either the action plans or the movement programs, she will not have effective actions. Sport researchers believe that competitive anxiety and arousal processes affect sport performance through interfering either with the cognitive informational processes (i.e., processing of external and internal stimuli) and/or with the neuromuscular control systems (Jones & Uphill, 2004).

Cognitive Mechanisms A number of cognitive functions that are important for sport performance are affected by elevated levels of competitive anxiety. Specifically, results from studies have demonstrated that competitive anxiety affects the amount and the type of information that is processed (i.e., task relevant versus task irrelevant) and the type of cognitive processing (i.e., conscious control versus automatic) that occurs during competitive sport performances.

First, one attentional focus problem associated with elevations in competitive anxiety is called the **attentional focus and selectivity hypothesis**. This hypothesis holds that an elevation in competitive state anxiety reduces the ability to attend to and process large amounts of information (Easterbrook, 1959). Likened to travelling down a tunnel, an increase in competitive state anxiety is associated with the narrowing of attentional focus (Naylor, Burton, & Crocker, 2002). The consequence of this hypothesis is that performance may be improved by increases in competitive anxiety if unimportant distracting cues are blocked out for the athlete. However, it is also possible that the athlete's performance may be diminished if elevated competitive anxiety results in important task-relevant cues being missed.

The second attentional focus problem associated with elevated competitive anxiety is the type of information that is processed. Research has demonstrated that highly anxious athletes attend to threatening task-irrelevant information to a greater extent than low anxious athletes. For example, Moran and colleagues (2002) studied the attentional focus of gymnasts while performing a balance beam routine at different heights (to simulate low-, average-, and high-threat conditions). Results revealed that during the high-threat condition, gymnasts attended more to threat-related peripheral cues deemed irrelevant for performance. In general, the results from this line of research show that the information attended to by highly anxious athletes is governed by the subjective importance of the cues (i.e., threat) rather than the location of the cues in the visual field (Jones & Uphill, 2004). The implication of these findings for sport performers is that attention that is selectively focused to task-irrelevant cues when the athlete is anxious is detrimental for sport performance.

The third attentional focus problem that occurs in the presence of competitive anxiety is the shifting to a conscious, controlled processing system (Liao & Masters, 2002; Maxwell, Masters, & Poolton, 2006). This phenomenon is likened to "a paralysis by analysis" and has been used to explain **choking**, or significant decreases in sport performance when under pressure (Moran, 2004). It is proposed that during high-pressure sport situations, heightened anxiety is associated with increases in a performer's self-conscious awareness about performing successfully, which becomes disruptive for expert performance of motor skills. This can be illustrated in an example of a university basketball player's free-throw shots at the end of regulation time with the score tied. In this situation, the basketball player is likely to experience elevations in anxiety (i.e., due to the increased importance of making a successful shot) that are associated with increased attention paid to the mechanics of the shot. Although increasing attention to the shot mechanics may seem like the right thing to do in order to increase the likelihood of success, research demonstrates that it has a paradoxical effect (Masters, 1992; Mullen, Hardy, & Tattersall, 2005). Heightened conscious control of a previously automatic skilled behaviour disrupts the coordinated fluidity that is associated with a well-learned skill.

Physiological Mechanisms The relationship between competitive anxiety and athletic performance can also be explained through anxiety-related changes to the functional patterns of muscle activation (Parfitt, Jones, & Hardy, 1990). Traditionally, it has been proposed that increased physiological arousal disrupts the performance of motor skills that require manual dexterity and fine motor control. Elevated physiological arousal can increase anaerobic power, which, in turn, may enhance the performance of simple tasks such as jumping (Parfitt & Pates, 1999). Jones and Uphill (2004) state that caution is warranted in suggesting that arousal elevations associated with competitive anxiety states have a unitary response on sport performance. Arousal is likely to impact an athlete's physical functioning in a number of ways. Notebook and his colleagues provide empirical evidence that high levels of arousal can decrease performance on fine motor tasks through increasing muscular tension, which can impact motor control (Notebook, Fleschner, & Enoka, 2001). High arousal has also been associated with difficulties in coordination of movement among soldiers required to do stepping tasks and weightlifters performing a snatch lift (Collins, Jones, Fairweather, Doolan, & Priestley, 2001). The implication of this research is that elevations in anxiety result in less fluid movement patterns and lowered sport performance. It was suggested that the elevated anxiety state of the sport performers may predispose the athlete to injury.

REFLECTIONS 5.5

Think about your own competitive performance errors. When were the errors primarily a result of missed cues within the situation? When were the errors primarily a result of overactivation of your muscles?

Photograph © Photodisc/Getty Images.

CHAPTER SUMMARY

Physical activity is associated with anxiety. What does more than 40 years of research reveal to us about anxiety-related emotions in sport and exercise? The following key points are conclusions that are generally accepted by sport and exercise psychology researchers about the effects of anxiety in sport and physical activity.

Anxiety is a complex, multidimensional psychological construct. A number of conceptual terms have been identified and delineated to describe competitive anxiety. Anxiety includes trait anxiety, social physique anxiety, somatic anxiety, cognitive anxiety, and arousal. It is important to distinguish among these different components of anxiety in order to understand what causes competitive anxiety to occur and what effects competitive anxiety has on physical activity performance and other important outcomes.

Several dimensions of the anxiety response can be examined. Most of the research within sport and exercise psychology has investigated anxiety responses according to the intensity of anxiety symptoms. However, it is acknowledged that anxiety can be observed in forms other than intensity. Specifically, sport psychology researchers also examine anxiety responses according to the frequency of anxiety-related thoughts and the directional interpretation of anxiety for performance.

Anxiety is related to different aspects of the person. Specific attributes of an individual are related to who will experience anxiety in specific sport and exercise situations as well as to the differences that are observed in individuals' anxiety responses to the same physical activity situation. In this chapter, five personal variables (i.e., expertise, gender, trait anxiety, self-confidence and self-presentation beliefs, and self-regulation strategies) were discussed.

Anxiety responses are related to specific aspects of the environment. There are unique aspects of sport and exercise environments that contribute to anxiety responses. For example, in sport, the time period leading up to a competitive event is proposed to affect athletes' anxiety responses in different ways. In the exercise environment, mirrors, clothing, other exercisers, and leadership contribute to anxiety responses of exercisers. Also, it is recognized that different performers in similar environments may vary in their anxiety response. This is attributed to the interaction of the environment with personal factors.

Anxiety experienced in the exercise setting is related to poor exercise adherence and excessive exercise behaviours. Exercise psychology research has produced evidence that some individuals who are high in social physique anxiety exercise less, while others high in social physique anxiety exercise more than individuals who are not high in social physique anxiety.

High levels of competitive anxiety may lead to a host of negative outcomes for sport performers, including poor athletic performance. Competitive anxiety has a complex relationship with sport performance that is individual for each athlete. Recent advances in sport psychology researchers' understanding of this relationship reveal that multidimensional anxiety theory, zones of optimal functioning, and cusp catastrophe theory are appropriate in explaining how competitive anxiety influences sport performance. Competitive anxiety is not necessarily debilitating for all athletes.

Changes to cognitive processes and neuromuscular control systems explain why competitive anxiety affects athletic performance. Competitive anxiety affects how athletes process the information they receive from internal and external environments. Research also demonstrates that anxiety-related emotion affects the tension and coordination of muscle action. Both mechanisms are directly related to sport performance.

Common Myths about Anxiety in Sport and Exercise Revisited

MYTH: Anxiety symptoms are generally the same for all sport and exercise participants.
The reality is that the exact anxiety response to a sport or exercise event is specific to the individual. Sport and exercise psychology researchers state that anxiety symptoms can differ with respect to the kind of symptom (e.g., "gut wrenching," concerns about past failed performance), intensity of anxiety (e.g., high or low), frequency of symptoms, and duration of the felt anxiety (Jones, 1995). The individual anxiety response displayed by physical activity participants is important to understanding how anxiety affects performance.

MYTH: Exercise always helps to reduce anxiety.
Although exercise may help people to cope with anxiety, certain characteristics of individuals and certain factors in the exercise environment can actually increase anxiety. Therefore, it is important to understand each individual and structure the environment to minimize anxiety.

MYTH: Pre-competitive anxiety always negatively affects sport performance.
Traditional research efforts assumed that elevated levels of pre-competitive anxiety were always detrimental to athletic performance. However, for many athletes this assumption is false! There are many examples in which Canadian athletes have excelled in elite competition despite their feelings of pre-competitive nervousness. If you reflect on your own competitive sport performances, it is likely that you can recall a time when you enjoyed the benefits of competitive anxiety. Today, most sport psychology researchers agree that pre-competitive anxiety can have both positive (e.g., facilitative) and negative (e.g., debilitative) consequences for sport performance.

Review Questions

1. Compare and contrast the following concepts of anxiety: arousal, social anxiety, competitive anxiety, trait anxiety, social physique anxiety, state anxiety, cognitive anxiety, and somatic anxiety.
2. Describe the dimensions of anxiety that are studied by sport and exercise psychology researchers.
3. Summarize five personal sources contributing to a performer's anxiety response.
4. Describe how the temporal phase of competition affects cognitive and somatic anxiety responses of athletes. How would the expertise or gender of an athlete affect the anxiety response exhibited prior to and during a competition?
5. Discuss four attributes of the exercise environment that are related to exercisers' anxiety response. Which personal sources of anxiety affect the anxiety response of exercisers in different exercise environments?
6. Discuss the major differences in how the following theories explain how competitive anxiety affects sport performance: multidimensional anxiety theory, zones of optimal functioning, and cusp catastrophe theory.
7. Describe two mechanisms that are likely responsible for the relationship between competitive anxiety and sport performance.

Suggested Reading

Jones, M. V. (2003). Controlling emotions in sport. *The Sport Psychologist, 17*, 471–486.

Lox, C. L., Martin Ginis, K. A., & Petruzzello, S. J. (2006). Anxiety and exercise. The psychology of exercise: *Integrating theory and practice* (2nd ed., pp. 295–320). Scottsdale, AZ: Holcomb Hathway.

Mellalieu, S. D., Hanton, S., & Fletcher, D. (2006). A competitive anxiety review: Recent directions in sport psychology research. In S. Hanton, & S. D. Mellalieu (Eds.), *Literature reviews in sport psychology* (pp. 1–45). New York: Nova Science Publishers.

References

Angove, J., Martin Ginis, K. A., Sinden, A. R. (2003). Physical activity and social physique anxiety in older women: The moderating effects of self-presentation efficacy. *Journal of Applied Biobehavioral Research, 8*, 116–127.

Berglas, S., & Jones, E. E. (1978). Drug choice as a self-handicapping strategy in response to non contingent success. *Journal of Personality and Social Psychology, 36*, 405–417.

Bray, S. R., Martin, K. A., & Widmeyer, W. N. (2000). The relationship between evaluative concerns and sport competition state anxiety among youth skiers. *Journal of Sport Sciences, 18*, 353–361.

Cerin, E., Szabo, A., Hunt, N., & Williams, C. (2000). Temporal patterning of competitive emotions: A critical review. *Journal of Sports Sciences, 18*, 605–626.

Collins, D., Jones, B., Fairweather, M., Doolan, S., & Priestley, N. (2001). Examining anxiety associated changes in movement patterns. *International Journal of Sport Psychology, 31*, 223–242.

Coudevylle, G. R., Martin Ginis, K. A., Famose, J. P., & Gernigon, C. (2008). Effects of self-handicapping strategies on anxiety before athletic competition. *The Sport Psychologist, 22*, 304–315.

Crawford, S., & Eklund, R.C. (1994). Social physique anxiety, reasons for exercise, and attitudes toward exercise settings. *Journal of Sport and Exercise Psychology, 16*, 70–82.

Crocker, P. R. E., Alderman, R. B., & Smith, F. M. R. (1988). Cognitive-affective stress management training with high performance youth volleyball players: Effects on affect, cognition, and performance. *Journal of Sport & Exercise Psychology, 10*, 448–460.

Crocker, P.R. E., Sabiston, C., Kowalski, K., McDonough, M., & Kowalski, N. (2006). Longitudinal assessment of the relationship between physical self-concept and health-related behavior and emotion in adolescent girls. *Journal of Applied Sport Psychology, 18*, 185–200.

Culos-Reed, S. N., Brawley, L. R., Martin, K. A., Leary, M. R. (2002). Self-presentation concerns and health behaviors among cosmetic treatment patients. *Journal of Applied Social Psychology, 32*, 560–569.

Easterbrook, J. A. (1959). The effect of emotion on cue utilization and the organization of behavior. *Psychological Review, 66*, 183–201.

Edwards, T. C., & Hardy, L. (1995). Interactive affects of facilitators and debilitators of cognitive and somatic anxiety, self-confidence, and performance. *Journal of Sports Sciences, 13*, 28–36.

Ekkakakis, P., & Petruzzello, S. J. (2000). Analysis of the affect measurement conundrum in exercise psychology. I. Fundamental issues. *Psychology of Sport & Exercise, 1*, 71–88.

Eklund, R. C., & Crawford, S. (1994). Active women, social physique anxiety, and exercise. *Journal of Sport and Exercise Psychology, 16*, 431–448.

Eys, M. A., Hardy, J., Carron, A. V., & Beauchamp, M. R. (2003). The relationship between task cohesion and competitive state anxiety. *Journal of Sport & Exercise Psychology, 25*, 66–76.

Fazey, J. A., & Hardy, L. (1988). *The inverted-U hypothesis: A catastrophe for sport psychology?* (British Association of Sports Sciences Monograph, 1). Leeds, UK: White Line Press.

Fenz, W. D., & Epstein, S. (1967). Gradients of physiological arousal in parachutists as a function of an approaching jump. *Psychosomatic Medicine, 29*, 33–51.

Fenz, W. D., & Jones, G. B. (1972). Individual differences in physiologic arousal and performance in sport parachutists. *Psychosomatic Medicine, 34*, 1–8.

Ferrand, C., Champely, S., & Brunel, S. (2005). Relations between female students' personality traits and reported handicaps to rhythmic gymnastics performance. *Psychological Reports*, 96, 361–373.

Focht, B. C., & Hausenblas, H. A. (2004). Baseline anxiety and perceptions of evaluative threat influence state anxiety during exercise in women with high social physique anxiety. *Journal of Applied Sport Psychology, 16*, 361–368.

Frederick, C. J., & Morrison, C. S. (1996). Social physique anxiety: Personality constructs, motivations, exercise attitudes, and behaviors. *Perceptual and Motor Skills, 82*, 963–972.

Gammage, K. L., Hall, C. R., & Martin-Ginis, K. A. (2004). Self-presentation in exercise contexts: Differences between high and low frequency exercisers. *Journal of Applied Social Psychology, 34*, 1638–1651.

Gammage, K., Martin Ginis, K. A., & Hall, C. R. (2004). Self-presentational efficacy expectancy: Its influence on anxiety in an exercise context. *Journal of Sport and Exercise Psychology, 26*, 179–190.

Gatehouse, J. (2004, August 16). Athens '04. *Maclean's, 117*, 26–35.

Gill, D. L. (1994). A sport and exercise psychology perspective on stress. *Quest, 46*, 20–27.

Gould, D., Greenleaf, C., & Krane, V. (2002). Arousal-anxiety and sport behavior. In T. Horn (Ed.), *Advances in sport psychology* (2nd ed., pp. 207–241). Champaign, IL: Human Kinetics.

Gould, D., Petlichkoff, L., & Weinberg, R. S. (1984). Antecedents of, temporal changes in, and relationships between CSAI-2 subcomponents. *Journal of Sport Psychology,* 6, 289–304.

Hammermeister, J., & Burton, D. (2004). Gender differences in coping with endurance sport stress: Are men from Mars and women from Venus? *Journal of Sport Behavior, 27*, 148–164.

Haney, C. J. (2004). Stress-management interventions for female athletes: Relaxation and cognitive restructuring. *International Journal of Sport Psychology, 35*, 109–118.

Hanin, Y. (1980). A study of anxiety in sports. In W. F. Straub (Ed.), *Sport psychology: An analysis of athlete behaviour* (pp. 236–249). Ithaca, NY: Mouvement.

Hanton, S., Cropley, B., Mellalieu, S. D., Neil, R., & Miles, A. (2007). Experience in sport and its relationship with competitive anxiety. *International Journal of Sport and Exercise Psychology, 5*, 28–53.

Hanton, S., & Jones, G. (1997). Antecedents of intensity and direction dimensions of competitive anxiety as a function of skill. *Psychological Reports, 81*, 1139–1147.

Hanton, S., & Jones, G. (1999a). The acquisition and development of cognitive skills and strategies. I: Making the butterflies fly in formation. *The Sport Psychologist, 13*, 1–21.

Hanton, S., & Jones, G. (1999b). The effects of a multimodal intervention program on performers. II: Training the butterflies to fly in formation. *The Sport Psychologist, 13*, 22–41.

Hanton, S., Neil, R., & Mellalieu, S. D. (2008). Recent developments in competitive anxiety direction and competition stress research. *International Review of Sport and Exercise Psychology, 1*, 45–57.

Hardy, L. (1990). A catastrophe model of performance in sport. In J. G. Jones, & L. Hardy (Eds.), *Stress and performance in sport* (pp. 81–106). New York: Wiley.

Hardy, L. (1996). Testing the predictions of the cusp catastrophe model of anxiety and performance. *The Sport Psychologist, 10*, 140–156.

Hart, E. H., Leary, M. R., & Rejeski, W. J. (1989). The measurement of social physique anxiety. *Journal of Sport and Exercise Psychology, 11*, 94–104.

Hausenblas, H. A., & Fallon, E. A. (2002). Relationship among body image, exercise behavior, and exercise dependence symptoms. *International Journal of Eating Disorders, 32*, 179–185.

Jarrett, R. (2003, April 21). New man of the moment. *Sports Illustrated*, 98, 38–44.

Jokela, M., & Hanin, Y. L. (1999). Does the Individual Zones of Optimal Functioning model discriminate between successful and less successful athletes? A meta-analysis. *Journal of Sports Sciences, 17*, 873–887.

Jones, G. (1995). More than just a game: Research developments and issues in competitive anxiety in sport. *British Journal of Psychology*, *86*, 449–478.

Jones, G., & Swain, A. B. J. (1992). Intensity and direction dimensions of competitive state anxiety and relationships with competitiveness. *Perceptual and Motor Skills*, *74*, 467–472.

Jones, G., & Swain, A.B. J. (1995). Predispositions to experience debilitative and facilitative anxiety in elite and nonelite performers. *The Sport Psychologist*, 9, 201–211.

Jones, M. V., & Uphill, M. (2004). Emotion in sport: Antecedents and performance consequences. In D. Lavallee, J. Thatcher, & M. V. Jones (Eds.), *Coping and emotion in sport* (pp. 9–28). Hauppauge, NY: Nova Science Publishers.

Kowalski, K. C., Mack, D. E., Crocker, P. R. E., Niefer, C. B., & Fleming T. L. (2006). Coping with social physique anxiety in adolescence. *Journal of Adolescent Health*, *39*, 275.e9–275.e16.

Krane, V. (1994). The mental readiness form as a measure of competitive state anxiety. *The Sport Psychologist*, 8, 189–202.

Krane, V., & Williams, J. M. (1994). Cognitive anxiety, somatic anxiety, and confidence in track and field athletes: The impact of gender, competitive level, and task characteristics. *International Journal of Sport Psychology*, *25*, 203–217.

Kreek, A. (2008, August 11). Race day. CBC. Beijing: The Olympic Games 2008. Columns, Blogs and Diaries. Message posted to http://www.cbc.ca/olympics/blog/athletes/adam_kreek/race_drama.html#more

Landers, D. M., & Arent, S. M. (2001). Arousal-performance relationships. In J. Williams (Ed.), *Applied sport psychology* (4th ed., pp. 164–184). Palo Alto, CA: Mayfield.

Lane, A. M., Sewell, D. F., Terry, P. C., Bartman, D., & Nesti, M. S. (1999). Confirmatory factor analysis of the competitive state anxiety inventory-2. *Journal of Sports Sciences*, *17*, 505–512.

Lantz, C. D., Hardy, C. J., & Ainsworth, B. E. (1997). Social physique anxiety and perceived exercise behavior. *Journal of Sport Behavior*, *20*, 83–93.

Lazarus, R. S. (2000). Cognitive-motivational-relational theory of emotion. In Y. L. Hanin (Ed.), *Emotions in sport* (pp. 39–63). Champaign, IL: Human Kinetics.

Leary, M. R. (1992). Self-presentational processes in exercise and sport. *Journal of Sport and Exercise Psychology*, *14*, 339–351.

Liao, C., & Masters, R. S. W. (2002). Self-focused attention and performance failure under psychological stress. *Journal of Sport and Exercise Psychology*, *24*, 289–305.

Mack, D. E., Strong, H., Kowalski, K. C., & Crocker, P. R. E. (2007). Does friendship matter? An examination of social physique anxiety in adolescence. *Journal of Applied Social Psychology*, *37*, 1248–1264.

Martens, R., Vealey, R. S., & Burton, D. (Eds.). (1990). *Competitive anxiety in sport*. Champaign, IL: Human Kinetics.

Martin, K. A., & Fox, L. D. (2001). (References and further reading may be available for this article. To view references and further reading you must purchase this article.) Group and leadership effects on social anxiety experienced during an exercise class. *Journal of Applied Social Psychology*, *31*, 1000–1016.

Martin, K. A., & Leary, M. R. (2001). Self-presentational determinants of health risk behavior among college freshmen. *Psychology and Health*, *15*, 1–11.

Martin Ginis, K. A., Prapavessis, H., & Haase, A. (2008). The effects of physique-salient and physique non-salient exercise videos on women's body image, self-presentational concerns, and exercise motivation. *Body Image*, *5*, 164–172.

Masters, R. S. W. (1992). Knowledge, knerves, and know-how: The role of explicit versus implicit knowledge in the breakdown of a complex motor skill under pressure. *British Journal of Psychology*, *83*, 343–358.

Maxwell, J. P., Masters, R. S. W., & Poolton, J. M. (2006). Performance breakdown in sport: The roles of reinvestment and verbal knowledge. *Research Quarterly for Exercise and Sport*, *77*, 271–276.

McGowan, E., Prapavessis, H., & Wesch, N. (2008). Self-presentational concerns and competitive anxiety. *Journal of Sport & Exercise Psychology, 30*, 383–400.

Mellalieu, S. D., Hanton, S., & Fletcher, D. (2006). A competitive anxiety review: Recent directions in sport psychology research. In S. Hanton, & S. D. Mellalieu (Eds.), *Literature reviews in sport psychology* (pp. 1–45). New York: Nova Science Publishers.

Moran, A. (2004). *Sport and exercise psychology: A critical introduction*. London, UK: Routledge.

Moran, A., Byrne, A., & McGlade, N. (2002). The effects of anxiety and strategic planning on visual search behavior. *Journal of Sports Sciences, 20*, 225–236.

Mullen, R., Hardy, L., & Tattersall, A. (2005). The effects of anxiety on motor performance: A test of the conscious processing hypothesis. *Journal of Sport and Exercise Psychology, 27*, 212–225.

Naylor, S., Burton, D., & Crocker, P. R. E. (2002). Competitive anxiety and sport performance. In J. M. Silva III, & D. E. Stevens (Eds.), *Psychological foundations of sport* (pp. 132–154). Boston: Allyn & Bacon.

Notebook, J. T., Fleshner, M., & Enoka, R. M. (2001). Activation of the arousal response can impair performance on a simple motor task. *Journal of Applied Physiology, 91*, 821–831.

Orlick, T., & Partington, J. (1986). *Inner views of winning: Psyched*. Ottawa, ON: Coaching Association of Canada.

Orlick, T., & Partington, J. (1988). Mental links to excellence. *The Sport Psychologist, 2*, 105–130.

Parfitt, G., Jones, J. G., & Hardy, L. (1990). Multidimensional anxiety and performance. In J. G. Jones, & L. Hardy (Eds.), *Stress and performance in sport* (pp. 43–80). New York: Wiley.

Parfitt, G., & Pates, J. (1999). The effects of cognitive and somatic anxiety and self-confidence on components of performance during competition. *Journal of Sports Sciences, 17*, 351–356.

Prapavessis, H., & Carron, A. V. (1996). The effect of group cohesion on competitive state anxiety. *Journal of Sport & Exercise Psychology, 18*, 64–74.

Prapavessis, H., Grove, J. R., Maddison, R., & Zillmann, N. (2003). Self-handicapping tendencies, coping, and anxiety responses among athletes. *Psychology of Sport and Exercise, 4*, 357–375.

Raedeke, T. D., Focht, B., & Scales, D. (2007). Social environmental factors and psychological responses to acute exercise for socially physique anxious females. *Psychology of Exercise and Sport, 8*, 463–476.

Raglin, J. S., & Hanin, Y. L. (2000). Competitive anxiety. In Y. Hanin (Ed.), *Emotions in sport* (pp. 93–112). Champaign, IL: Human Kinetics.

Rich, N., Mellalieu, S. D., Hanton, S., & Mitchell, I. (2007). Temporal patterning of precompetitive state anxiety symptoms in female netballers. *Journal of Sport & Exercise Psychology, 29*, S193.

Robazza, C. (2006). Emotion in sport: An IZOF perspective. In S. Hanton, & S. D. Mellalieu (Eds.), *Literature reviews in sport psychology*(pp. 127–158). New York: Nova Science Publishers.

Sabiston, C. M., Crocker, P. R. E., & Monroe-Chandler, K. J. (2005). Examining current-ideal discrepancy scores and exercise motivations as predictors of social physique anxiety in exercising females. *Journal of Sport Behavior, 28*, 68–85.

Sabiston, C. M., Sedgwick, W. A., Crocker, P. R. E., Kowalski, K. C., & Stevens, D. (2007). Social physique anxiety in adolescents: An examination of influences, coping strategies and health behaviours. *Journal of Adolescent Research, 22*, 78–101.

Schlenker, B. R., & Leary, M. R. (1982). Social anxiety and self-presentation: A conceptualization and model. *Psychological Bulletin, 92*, 641–669.

Shewfelt, K. (2008, July 15). It's starting to get scary. CBC. Beijing: The Olympic Games 2008. Columns, Blogs and Diaries. Message posted to http://www.cbc.ca/olympics/blog/athletes/kyle_shewfelt/its_starting_to_get_scary.html#more

Smith, R. E., Smoll, F. L., & Wiechman, S. A. (1998). Measurement of trait anxiety in sport. In J. Duda (Ed.), *Advancement in sport and exercise psychology measurement* (pp. 105–127). Morgantown, WV: Fitness Information Technology.

Speilberger, C. D. (1966). Theory and research on anxiety. In C. D. Speilberger (Ed.), *Anxiety and behaviour*(pp. 3–22). New York: Academic.

Swain, A. B. J., & Jones, G. (1993). Intensity and frequency dimensions of competitive state anxiety. *Journal of Sports Sciences*, *11*, 533–542.

"This is my worst nightmare come true": Felicien. (2004, August 25). CBC. Retrieved January 31, 2005, from http://www.cbc.ca/olympics/story/2004/08/24/perdita040824.html

Uphill, M. (2008). Anxiety and sport: Should we be worried or excited? In A. M. Lane (Ed.), *Sport and exercise psychology: Topics in applied psychology* (pp. 35–52). Hachette Livre, UK: Hodder Education.

Uphill, M. A., & Jones, M. V. (2007). Antecedents of emotions in elite athletes: A cognitive motivational relational theory perspective. *Research Quarterly for Exercise and Sport*, *78*, 79–89.

Walton, V. R., & Finkenberg, M. E. (2002). Women's anxiety about social and exercise settings. Perceptual and Motor Skills, 94, 700–702.

Weinberg, R. S. (1978). The effects of success and failure on the patterning of neuromuscular energy. *Journal of Motor Behavior*, *10*, 53–61.

Wiggins, M. S. (1998). Anxiety intensity and direction: Preperformance temporal patterns and expectations in athletes. *Journal of Applied Sport Psychology*, *10*, 201–211.

Woodman, T., & Hardy, L. (2001). Stress and anxiety. In R. Singer, H. A. Hausenblas, & C. M. Janelle (Eds.), *Handbook of research on sport psychology* (pp. 290–318). New York: Wiley.

Woodman, T. & Hardy, L. (2005). Tenebaum and Becker's critique: Much ado about nothing. *Journal of Sport & Exercise Psychology*, *27*, 382–392.

Chapter 6

Stress and Coping in Sport and Exercise

Kent C. Kowalski
Patrick Gaudreau

Many of the truths we cling to depend greatly on our point of view.

—Obi-Wan Kenobi, Star Wars

Chapter Objectives

After reading this chapter, you should be able to do the following:

1. Define the concepts of stress and coping.
2. Describe the relationship between stress and emotions.
3. Illustrate the role of cognitive appraisal and coping in the stress process.
4. Describe typical sources of stress in sport and exercise.
5. Identify predictors of coping in sport.

Jessica, a 20-year-old undergraduate student in kinesiology, finds going to the gym a stressful experience. Although she certainly recognizes the benefits of exercise to her health, more often than not she dreads going to the gym. She grew up playing sports like basketball and volleyball, but her physical activity really declined throughout her high-school years, to the point where her family now (somewhat) affectionately refers to her as the "couch potato princess."

Jessica finds many things about going to the gym stressful. First, she feels a great deal of anxiety and is quite uncomfortable working out at the university facility. According to her, "Everyone looks like they should be playing beach volleyball." Second, because she has not been active in such a long time, she feels that everyone at the gym thinks she is not skilled enough to be there. Jessica explains it this way: "I don't really know whether or not anyone even notices me, but it sure feels like they're all looking at me and thinking I'm not good at anything. I see these other women running at 20 km/h or something like that, and here I am walking every 30 seconds because I'm going to pass out." Third, she does not like the way the exercise instructors in the classes are always making her do things that she thinks are too difficult for her. "Sure, if I was 80 pounds this stuff would be easy. But I'm not, so I just get angry when I'm there."

Jessica has tried a number of strategies in the past to try to deal with her stress. At one point, instead of working out at the university, she got a membership at Ron's Fitness World. The attendees there represented a much broader range of physical appearances and fitness levels compared to the students at the university fitness centre. However, as she explains, "That only lasted about a week because I found travelling an extra hour each day to get there and back was taking up time that I didn't have. It was just making school more stressful because I couldn't get my work done." As a result, her next strategy was to resume her workouts at the university, but this time having her best friend Sonya as a workout partner. Unfortunately, that too was not very successful because, as Jessica said, "All Sonya did was complain, and she was absolutely no fun to be there with." Although that did not quite work out as planned, Jessica liked having someone else to train with. So, next, she hired a personal trainer. While somewhat effective for her, she could not afford a personal trainer very often because she was "already stressed to the max about the cost of books, tuition, rent, gas, food, a new laptop computer, coffee, ..."

The use of the term *stress* is commonplace in modern Canadian society. Although it certainly is not an experience limited to sport and exercise, the ability to manage stress is often thought to be critical to elite performance and adherence to, as well as enjoyment of, exercise. But what does it mean when someone says that he or she is stressed? And what role does coping play in the experience of stress? Jessica's story provides us with some insight into the complexity of stress and the coping process. There are many facets to a person's life that are often competing with one another and making the management of stress extremely challenging. Such is the case with Jessica and her attempts to manage her exercise stress in a way that does not create other academic or financial stress. In addition, seldom are situations easily resolved. Often they play out over a long period of time and significantly strain people's personal resources as they attempt to cope.

Canadians have played a prominent role in stress and coping research in recent years (see Figure 6.1). The work of Peter Crocker in the late 1980s acted as a catalyst for coping research, particularly sport coping research, in Canada over the past two decades (e.g., Crocker, 1989; Crocker, Alderman, & Smith, 1988). Contributions to the field have been made by many scholars. In this chapter, the concepts of stress and coping in sport

Figure 6.1 Over the past two decades, stress and coping have been a focus of research in Canada to help *sport and exercise professionals* help *people* deal more effectively with the many demands of sport and exercise

Illustration by Kent Kowalski.

and exercise will be explored, with special emphasis on Canadian perspectives and examples. Although definitions of stress and coping have changed over time, one constant theme is that these two concepts are intimately linked.

Common Myths about Stress and Coping in Sport and Exercise

MYTH: Elite sport is inherently stressful.

MYTH: Exercise always reduces stress.

MYTH: Dropping out of sport or stopping exercise is an ineffective coping strategy.

INTRODUCTION

Any conversation about stress and coping in sport and exercise needs to begin by addressing the basic question: What is stress? Is competing in mixed martial arts stressful? Is it stressful to have to work out in a gym where everyone else is better than you? Is it stressful as a student to find the time to read a chapter about stress in sport and exercise in order to prepare for an academic class? The answer to these questions is a resounding "maybe." As we will discuss, situations are not inherently stressful. Instead, people play an active role in how they interpret the situations they face, and it is often very difficult to predict when stress will occur. For example, early in the 2008 Canadian Football League season, Toronto Argonauts quarterback Kerry Joseph returned to Regina to play against the Saskatchewan Roughriders, a team he lead to a Grey Cup victory the previous season. When asked about what he expected, he said in an interview with TSN, "I know that it's going to be a hostile environment, but it's going to be fun" (Joseph leads Argos, 2008). If leading a new team into an environment with thousands of "hostile" fans is not stressful, then defining stress is clearly not a simple matter!

THE CONCEPT OF STRESS

Carpenter (1992) described how the concept of stress most often has one of two meanings. First, stress can represent what is often referred to as the **stress response**, which consists of our physiological, cognitive, affective, and behavioural reactions when we are faced with heavy demands. For example, if a hitter in baseball sees a fastball coming straight toward his head, he experiences increased blood pressure, heart rate, and perspiration, as well as the fight-or-flight reaction (e.g., ducking out of the way). This response serves a very adaptive function for human beings, and athletes are more able to get pumped up or get the adrenaline flowing to achieve peak performance when there is sympathetic nervous system arousal (Aldwin, 2000; see Buckworth & Dishman, 2002 for an overview of the physiological mechanisms of the stress response).

A second approach to defining stress is to consider it as a process that links situational demands to an individual's reactions to the outcomes of that experience. This second definition is consistent with cognitive-based models of stress that emphasize the dynamic interrelationships between the environment and people's thoughts and behaviours in that environment. What is stressful for one person might not be stressful for another or even for that same person at another time (Aldwin, 2000). Hence, **stress** can be defined as an experience that is produced through a person–situation relationship that is perceived as taxing or exceeding the person's resources.

Stressors, on the other hand, are the external events, forces, and situations that have the potential to be interpreted as stressful. Examples of potential stressors include playing in a championship match, getting injured, being yelled at by a coach or personal trainer, and losing national team funding or facing increased fitness club fees. The implication is that each athlete or exerciser might interpret situations and stressors in unique ways. For example, although working out in the university gym was a very stressful experience for Jessica in the chapter vignette, for someone else it might be more stressful not to go.

As we can see from the definition of stress, **cognitive appraisal**, or someone's interpretation of a situation, is a key concept. Richard Lazarus (1991, 2000a, 2000b) distinguished between primary and secondary cognitive appraisal. **Primary appraisal** is an evaluation of what is at stake for a person in a situation. Whether or not something is at stake depends on whether what is happening is relevant to that person's goals and whether the situation is interpreted as having the potential to be beneficial or harmful. Alternatively, **secondary appraisal** is an evaluation of what can be done in the situation, which will depend on an individual's available resources, level of perceived control, and expectations regarding what is likely to occur in the future.

The cognitive appraisal process can result in various kinds of stress, including harm/loss, threat, and challenge. **Harm/loss** refers to an appraisal of a situation in which psychological damage has already been done and the loss is irrevocable. For example, a university athlete might experience stress over not being able to play Canadian interuniversity sport as a result of using up her five years of eligibility. Her personal identity might be strongly tied to being a member of the university team, and once that identity is taken away she could really struggle in her search for a new identity. A **threat** appraisal refers to the anticipation of harm that might occur or is likely to occur. An example would be a weightlifter who is fearful of maximum weight testing because of the potential for injury or the embarrassment of lifting a maximum weight that is lighter than it is for everyone else. **Challenge**, on the other hand, stems from the interpretation of potential benefits from succeeding in a situation that presents difficult demands. For example, University of Victoria field hockey player Ali Lee said before the championship game, "My body is so tired, I've got bruises and scratches and everything. But your mind can carry you a lot further than your body can. We have a great rivalry with UBC and U of A, so doesn't matter who, I just want to win this the right way and earn this" (Lowther, 2008). Although the outcome of the game was unknown to her at that time, it is clear that she was looking forward to the opportunities that the final game presented.

When different types of stress are considered, it seems clear that not all stress is negative and to be avoided. The potential for stress to be both beneficial and harmful has long been recognized. Hans Selye (1993) was one of the pioneers of the stress concept in the 20th century and was a professor at McGill University and the Université de Montréal. He distinguished between **eustress** (good stress) and **distress** (bad stress). He suggested that stress can be useful for performance and well-being (eustress) but that at a certain point it becomes too high (distress) and results in various mental, emotional, and physiological limitations. Thus, we really need to consider the type of stress that people are experiencing because this knowledge informs us of how situations are being interpreted and the potential consequences of the stressful experience. It is also important to note that we will experience stress only if the situation is meaningful or important to us. If an athlete or exerciser does not really care about what happens, then the situation will not be perceived as stressful. An example would be a young goalkeeper who gets scored on in a game of soccer but is indifferent to letting in a goal or losing the competition. However, if the game was important, then letting in a goal, especially if she felt blamed for it, would indeed likely be a source of stress. Similarly, missing a workout would only be stressful to an exerciser if missing workouts mattered to him.

REFLECTIONS 6.1

What makes a situation stressful for an athlete or exerciser? What types of situations are more likely to be interpreted as stressful?

Illustration by Kent Kowalski.

STRESS AND EMOTION

It is important to point out that the concept of stress is closely tied to the concept of emotion (Lazarus, 1999). Richard Lazarus provided a framework for the way in which many researchers study and interpret stress and coping. He suggested that the concepts of stress and emotion are similar; however, he also said that we can learn more about what an individual is experiencing, what a situation means to an individual, and how the individual is likely to respond by looking at the specific emotion that is experienced rather than by looking at the more general concept of stress. He stated the following:

> "Despite these subdivisions of stress types (harm/loss, threat, and challenge), the typical idea of stress is much simpler than that of the emotions. Either as a single dimension, or with only a few functional categories, stress tells us relatively little about the details of a person's struggle to adapt. Emotion, conversely, includes at least 15 different varieties, greatly increasing the richness of what can be said about a person's adaptational struggle" (Lazarus, 1999, p. 33).

The 15 emotions Lazarus identified, including both positive and negative emotions, are shown in Table 6.1. Each of these emotions is important because there is a core relational theme for each emotion that describes the nature of the relationship between a person and his or her environment. For example, the core relational theme of anxiety is that the person is facing an uncertain, existential threat, suggesting that when someone is experiencing anxiety, he or she is not sure of what will happen, when it will happen, or even what can be done about it (Lazarus, 2000a). If we look at competitive anxiety in sport, much of the stress that is experienced is simply the result of not knowing what the outcome will be (e.g., "Will I perform well today?"). We can also see an example of this in the chapter vignette, where much of Jessica's anxiety stems from being unsure of what others in the gym think of her. Examples of sport and exercise situations demonstrating when each of the emotions might be experienced are also provided in Table 6.1; however, it is important to remember that situations do not necessarily lead to particular emotions. Similar to stress, the emotion that is experienced depends a lot on what is at stake for the individual and his or her perceived resources to cope with the situation (Lazarus, 1999). Clearly, knowing about a specific emotion does tell us more about what is going on for someone than just knowing that he or she is stressed.

Although in the past stress has been considered to be centred primarily on the negative emotions, it is becoming increasingly clear that the positive emotions also play a very important role in the stress process (Folkman, 2008). However, despite Lazarus' recommendation to focus more on specific emotions, as opposed to general stress relationships, there is an abundance of sport and exercise psychology research on general aspects of stress. A major focus of research has been on identifying the sources of stress.

SOURCES OF STRESS IN SPORT

Think about the complexity inherent in the numerous types and competitive levels of sport. To help understand the various sources of stress, researchers have proposed the use of general dimensions or concerns. In their research with American national champion figure skaters and national teams for alpine and freestyle skiers, Daniel Gould and his colleagues

Table 6.1 Core Relational Themes for Emotions, with Sport and Exercise Examples

Emotion	Theme	Sport and Exercise Examples (demonstrating when emotion might be experienced)
Anger	A demeaning offence against me and mine.	David experiences anger when he feels that a bad call by a basketball official caused him to foul out of an important game.
Anxiety	Facing uncertain, existential threat.	Susan, a football player, experiences anxiety because of not knowing how she will perform in the championship game.
Fright	An immediate, concrete, and overwhelming physical danger.	Gymnast Mark experiences fright when he loses his grip on the parallel bars.
Guilt	Having transgressed a moral imperative.	Irene experiences guilt when she realizes it is wrong to make fun of someone else at the gym.
Shame	Failing to live up to an ego ideal.	Phillip, a discus thrower, experiences shame when he comes last in a competition that he is expected to win.
Sadness	Having experienced an irrevocable loss.	Ronald experiences sadness when he realizes that he will not be able to run again because of an injury.
Envy	Wanting what someone else has and feeling deprived of it but justified in having it.	Stephan, a rookie NHL player, experiences envy when he wants the same ice time and money as other team members because he feels he deserves it.
Jealousy	Resenting a third party for loss of or threat to another's affection or favour.	Speed skater Ivan experiences jealousy when his coach decides not to continue to coach him because a better athlete has come into the program.
Happiness	Making reasonable progress toward the realization of a goal.	Sheila experiences happiness when she accomplishes her goal to run her first marathon.
Pride	Enhancement of one's ego identity by taking credit for a valued object or accomplishment, either one's own or that of someone or a group with whom one identifies.	Evan, a volleyball player, experiences pride when he believes that the team won because of his blocking ability.
Relief	A distressing goal-incongruent condition that has changed for the better or gone away.	Joan, a race-car driver, experiences relief by escaping a crash without injury when she thought there was no she was going to avoid crashing hard into way the wall.
Hope	Fearing the worst but yearning for better and believing the improvement is possible.	Peter experiences hope when, despite his poor performances on the golf course to date, getting a birdie helps him believe that he can get better.
Love	Desiring or participating in affection, usually but not necessarily reciprocated.	Karen, a swimmer, experiences love when she desires a teammate's affection.
Gratitude	Appreciating an altruistic gift that provides personal benefit.	William, a young goalkeeper, experiences gratitude when he is helped by a veteran goalkeeper to develop his skills, even though the veteran might lose his starting position to the younger goalkeeper.
Compassion	Being moved by another's suffering and wanting to help.	Irena, a boxer, experiences compassion when she sees another boxer injured and is concerned for her safety.

Note: Table 3.4, (p.122), modified from *Emotion and Adaptation* by Richard S. Lazarus copyright © 1991 by Oxford University Press, Inc. Used by permission of Oxford University Press, Inc.

found that general sources of stress identified by athletes included (1) psychological concerns, such as competitive stress, self-doubt, losing, fear of injury, and mental readiness to perform, (2) physical concerns, such as injury, body weight, pain, and physical inactivity, (3) social concerns, such as negative relationships with others, lack of attention, coaching changes, and others' expectations, (4) environmental concerns, such as financial stress and media demands, and (5) career and life direction concerns (Gould, Finch, & Jackson, 1993; Gould, Udry, Bridges, & Beck, 1997).

A group of Canadian researchers studied sources of stress for members of a women's national soccer team during preparations for the 1999 women's soccer World Cup finals (Holt & Hogg, 2002). They wanted to know about sources of stress in a team sport during a six-week preparation camp leading up to the World Cup event, in part because most of the previous research had been with individual sports. They found four main categories of stressors: coaches' communication, demands of international soccer, competitive stressors, and distractions. Examples of coaches' communication stressors included a negative, punitive coach–player interaction during training and negative, excessive feedback during the games. Demands of international soccer that they identified revolved primarily around the need to adjust to the technical and tactical demands of a fast-paced international game. A number of competitive stressors were identified by the players, including having pre-game anxiety, having high expectations of going to the Olympics, making mistakes, coming off the bench, fearing being cut from the team, and getting evaluations of their performance. The two primary distractions that the athletes mentioned were the fatigue from practising twice a day during camp and opponent aggression. As Holt and Hogg identified, one of the unique aspects of their study was finding that many of the stressors were related to the social interactions that are part of a team environment.

Types of Stressors

Three distinctions have been made in the literature in an attempt to categorize types of sport stress, including acute versus chronic stressors, expected versus unexpected stressors, and competitive versus non-competitive stressors. **Chronic stress** occurs over a long period of time, such as in the case of ongoing harassment, relationship issues, and chronic pain; **acute stress** occurs over a shorter period of time, and its onset is much more sudden. Mark Anshel and his colleagues have identified a number of acute stressors that athletes might face, such as making a physical or mental error, being criticized or reprimanded by a coach, observing an opponent cheating, sustaining pain or injury, receiving a bad call by an official, seeing an opponent play really well, performing poorly because of bad weather or substandard playing conditions, and being distracted by a crowd (Anshel, 2001; Anshel, Jamieson, & Raviv, 2001). If acute stressors are not managed effectively, they can lead to long-term chronic stress and burnout (Anshel, Kim, Kim, Chang, & Eom, 2001). For example, we all have probably seen situations in which a coach makes a negative comment to an athlete during a practice or competition, but nothing is done to resolve the conflict; then, later on, many other relationship issues develop between the coach and the athlete.

A second distinction that has been made is between expected and unexpected stressors (Dugdale, Eklund, & Gordon, 2002). An **expected stressor** is one that an athlete plans or prepares for, whereas an **unexpected stressor** is one that is not anticipated. Dugdale and colleagues asked 91 athletes representing New Zealand at the 1998 Commonwealth Games (ages 14 to 46) to identify the most stressful experience they had prior to or during the Games. The experiences were then rated as expected or unexpected. They found that more than two-thirds of athletes who reported stress said that the source of stress was unexpected. Examples given by the athletes included things like transportation delays, poor food, and bad refereeing decisions. One of the study's most interesting findings was that the athletes perceived the unexpected stressors to be more threatening than the expected ones, suggesting that athletes might experience more or less stress depending on the type of stress source they face. Surely the extreme distress that Canadian track-and-field hurdler Perdita Felicien (and the nation) experienced after her fall in the 2004 Olympic final 100 m hurdles was a result of not only the importance of the race but also of the unexpectedness of her fall, based on her previous performances.

A third distinction that has been made is between competitive and non-competitive stressors (Dugdale et al., 2002; Gould, Eklund, & Jackson, 1993; Noblet & Gifford, 2002). **Competitive stressors** would be those that are experienced prior to, during, or immediately following competition; they include injury, poor officiating, and expectations from others. **Non-competitive stressors**would be those that are related to sport but are not directly part of an actual competition performance; they include having to deal with the media, travel, rehabilitation, and team meetings. For example, Noblet and Gifford (2002) interviewed professional Australian Football League players who reported competitive stressors like poor technique, constant pressure to perform, and high performance expectations, as well as a wide variety of non-competitive stressors, including job insecurity, long training sessions, lack of feedback, constant public scrutiny, and difficulty balancing sport with other commitments. For student athletes who compete in university sport, it can be quite challenging to balance the competitive and non-competitive stressors that arise from the many demands of athletics and academics. The stress can be especially high during the competitive season when a commitment to sport can often require the athlete being away from the classroom.

It is also important to recognize that specific sports might have unique sources of stress. For example, the professional Australian Football League players in the Noblet and Gifford (2002) study had to deal with stressors associated with being in a professional, high-profile league—specifically, job insecurity and constant public scrutiny—that other athletes might not have to face. Another example of sport-specific stressors is provided by Campbell and Jones (2002), who looked at stress experienced by male wheelchair basketball players. They interviewed 10 members of Great Britain's men's wheelchair basketball team and found a variety of common sources of stress, including pre-event concerns, negative match preparation, on-court concerns, post-match performance concerns, negative aspects of a major event, poor group interaction and communication, negative coaching style or behaviour, and relationship issues. However, they also found stressors that many athletes in other sports do not have to contend with, such as the demands or costs of wheelchair basketball and people's lack of disability awareness.

The idea that there are a number of stressors that are common to many athletes but unique to specific sports has been supported in research with UK track athletes. McKay and colleagues (2008) interviewed 12 elite athletes and found that many of the sources of strain they face are common to athletes in previous research, including competitive concerns, pressure to perform, lifestyle demands, and negative aspects of interpersonal relationships, but that there are sources of strain that might be specifically relevant to track athletes, such as social evaluation and self-presentational concerns. However, no one strain was reported by all of the participants in their study, demonstrating the key role of the individual in the experience of stress. Also note that they used the term strain quite intentionally to reflect an important distinction between the environmental demands of a situation (stressors) and the psychological, physical, and behavioral responses to stressors (strain).

REFLECTIONS 6.2

Think back to your own experiences in sport. What different types of acute/chronic, expected/unexpected, and competitive/non-competitive sources of stress have you witnessed as an athlete, a spectator, or a coach?

SELF-PRESENTATION AND EXERCISE

Self-presentation is one of the most discussed and studied sources of stress experienced in the exercise setting. The vignette of Jessica to begin this chapter highlights a number of self-presentational concerns that can occur in the exercise setting. In her case, sources of stress included things like her family calling her a "couch potato princess," the increased focus on the appearance of her body at the gym, and others' judgments of her exercise skills and competencies. Leary and Kowalski (1990) described **self-presentation**, often referred to as impression management, as "the process by which individuals attempt to control the impressions others form of them" (p. 34). As social beings, people are often concerned about the impressions being formed about them by others; hence, exercise, particularly when done in a public setting, can be a source of self-presentational concern and stress for many people. In his review of self-presentation in exercise and sport, Leary (1992) described how simply engaging in exercise can reflect self-presentational motives, such as attempting to improve or maintain a desired physical appearance or an identity as a fit or athletic person. However, these same types of self-presentational concerns can make people worried about how they appear when doing physical activity, whether due to concern over the attire they wear while working out or appearing unskilled, both of which can lead to an avoidance of the exercise setting.

In 2004, the *Journal of Applied Sport Psychology* published a special issue dedicated specifically to self-presentation in exercise and sport. In that issue, Hausenblas and colleagues (2004) discussed how self-presentation can influence a wide range of exercise cognitions, attitudes, and behaviours. Speaking to the relevance of self-presentational motives to exercise participation, they wrote, "It is not surprising that some people are motivated to exercise for those self-presentational reasons considering that positive self-presentation is strongly influenced by the aesthetic-ideal physique" (p. 6). They suggested that self-presentational concerns can also deter participation in exercise for those who doubt that they can appear attractive to others. Also, the choices people make as to how and where they exercise, such as in public or private settings, are often driven by self-presentation motives and concerns.

Among the emotions most relevant to self-presentational stress, social anxiety is probably the most common because it arises when there is a desire to project a particular image to others but also a doubt as to whether or not that desired image will be made successfully. Within the exercise and sport domain, a subtype of social anxiety, called **social physique anxiety**, has garnered much attention over the past 20 years. As described in Chapter 5, social physique anxiety is experienced by someone when there is a concern that her or his physique will be negatively evaluated by others. But what kinds of situations lead to the experience of social physique anxiety? This question was addressed directly by Sabiston, Sedgwick, Crocker, Kowalski, and Mack (2007), who, through interviews with young women, found that some of the most common antecedents of social physique anxiety included social situations and events (e.g., going to the beach or swimming pool, change rooms), as well as messages about appearance received from others (e.g., peers, media, mothers). Quotes from that study, such as "Everything's based on appearance" (p. 87), speak to the pervasiveness of the potential for experiencing stressful evaluations of the body and appearance in today's society. The exercise setting, which not only highlights the salience of the physique, often puts the body on display for evaluation. Is it any wonder that the exercise setting can be a source of stress?

REFLECTIONS 6.3

If you were an owner of a fitness facility and wanted to reduce self-presentational stress for those who worked out there, what would your gym look like? Would there be mirrors? Who would be the instructors? Would there be a "dress code" of some type? Would your membership be restricted? What factors other than self-presentational concerns would you need to consider in your answers to these questions (e.g., ethical, financial, emotional)?

THE CONCEPT OF COPING

When people are faced with stress and emotion, how they attempt to manage their experiences can take many forms. First, if athletes or exercisers believe that they can effectively manage a situation, they will be less likely to experience stress and negative emotions to begin with. Second, the ways in which people attempt to cope with stress can affect both the level and the type of stress and emotion that they experience. Essentially, if stress and emotion are experienced when a situation taxes someone's perceived resources (i.e., an important goal is harmed/lost, threatened, or challenged), then coping is the way in which he or she attempts to deal with that psychological stress and emotion (Lazarus, 1999).

Thus, an important question to start with is, "What is coping?" A formal definition of coping was provided by Lazarus (1991), who described **coping** as "cognitive and behavioural efforts to manage specific external or internal demands (and conflicts between them) that are appraised as taxing or exceeding the resources of the person" (p. 112). Consequently, although coping does include actual physical actions, it is not limited to them. For example, if Jessica from the opening vignette tries to convince herself that nobody is looking at her while exercising, it is as much an effort to cope as is changing her workout attire to something that hides her body. However, within Lazarus' definition, it is important to also point out that coping has to be an effortful process to manage stress. If athletes engage in behaviours that are routine but that still help them to avoid problems, such as going to practice every day, it is not coping per se. Instead, routine behaviours are probably more appropriately viewed as **management skills** that help prevent stress from happening in the first place, although these management skills themselves might have developed initially as ways of coping (Aldwin, 2000). For example, a soccer player might have initially begun wearing shin pads to cope with the frustration of being kicked; however, once that behaviour (wearing shin pads) becomes relatively automatic, it is better considered a management skill rather than actual coping. Most importantly, what Lazarus' definition of coping suggests is that efforts to manage stress are constantly changing and are extremely complex. People's coping will depend, in part, on available coping resources and expectations. Their coping efforts then must shift as the effectiveness of particular strategies becomes evident and as the situation itself changes over time. Sometimes the changing dynamics of a situation can require all the effort that one can muster, such as Simon Whitfield's inspirational finishing sprint in the triathlon at the 2008 Beijing Olympics. Following his silver medal performance, he reported to CBC, "I kind of fought my way on there, and I thought there's no time like the present. I tried to make it a battle of pure willpower. I gave it everything I had" (Canada's Whitfield, 2008).

MICRO- AND MACRO-ANALYTIC LEVELS OF COPING

One common notion across models of coping is that coping can be studied at different levels of analysis. A **micro-analytic** approach to coping involves the specific coping strategies, or families of coping strategies, that people engage in to cope with stress. An example of a micro-analytic approach to coping is provided by Crocker and Graham (1995). They assessed the coping strategies of 377 competitive athletes who had used the strategies in a recent athletic situation—either a practice or a game—in which there was a performance difficulty or pressure to perform. The strategies Crocker and Graham assessed were active coping, seeking social support for instrumental or emotional reasons, planning, denial, humour, behavioural disengagement, venting of emotion, and suppression of competing activities.

The micro-analytical approach provides a rich description of the diversified coping repertoire of athletes and exercisers. A major challenge in the sport coping literature, in particular, is that there is no consistent set of micro-level coping strategies across studies. However, not only does this lack of consistency reflect the difficulty in understanding the coping process, but it also seems that a variety of strategies is necessary in order to understand coping in different sports or situations. For example, a coping strategy, such as on-field task communication, might be entirely appropriate for international level soccer, but it might be entirely inappropriate for singles figure skating or gymnastics in which communication with teammates during the actual performance is absent and irrelevant. Thus, researchers are always trying to find the delicate balance between including coping strategies that are appropriate for their population and sport but still allowing for comparison between athletes and sports. Another limitation with the micro-level approach is that knowing the specific coping strategies being used tells us little about why athletes are using those particular strategies or what goals they are trying to accomplish via their coping efforts.

Alternatively, the **macro-analytic** approach to coping considers the goals or functions of the strategies used by athletes or exercisers. An important macro-level distinction that is often made in the literature is between problem-focused coping and emotion-focused coping. **Problem-focused coping** refers to efforts that help people change the actual situation in some way. For example, a few years ago many Canadian speed skaters began using clap skates (skates with a spring-loaded hinge under the heel) in order to more effectively deal with the stress of increasing performance demands in world-class speed skating. Catriona Le May Doan, a Canadian speed skater who won a number of Olympic medals and broke many world records, had to adjust to clap skates during her career and had a great deal of success with them. An exercise example of problem-focused coping would be someone hiring a personal trainer to learn how to do exercises with proper technique. **Emotion-focused coping**, on the other hand, is an attempt to change the way a situation is attended to or interpreted. For example, an athlete might be comforted by a parent who tells her that the coach is only trying to get the best out of her athletes through her punitive behaviour. Another example of emotion-focused coping would be an exerciser who tries to convince himself that no one in the gym actually cares about the exercises he is doing or how he is doing them. A third distinct type of coping often included in the literature is **avoidance coping**, in which athletes attempt to remove themselves from the stressful situation (e.g., Endler & Parker, 1994; Kowalski & Crocker, 2001). A common example of avoidance coping in sport would be an athlete abandoning the pursuit of an important personal goal. As mentioned earlier, avoidance of exercise settings, or particular types of exercise settings, is one of the strategies people often use to deal with self-presentation concerns.

Some researchers have attempted to merge micro- and macro-analytic approaches. For example, Gaudreau and Blondin (2002, 2004a) developed a framework for coping that consists of 10 micro-level coping strategies regrouped under three macro-level dimensions of coping: (1) task-oriented coping (micro-level coping includes thought control, mental imagery, relaxation, effort expenditure, logical analysis, and seeking support), (2) distraction-oriented coping (micro-level coping includes distancing and mental distraction), and (3) disengagement coping (micro-level coping includes venting and disengagement/resignation).

COPING STYLE

Researchers are undecided about whether coping should be treated as a stable characteristic of the individual (i.e., trait) or as a changing response varying across situations (i.e., state). The trait approach to coping states that people attempt to cope in similar ways across different situations and over time. In other words, athletes and exercisers have preferred **coping styles** that make them consistent in the ways they attempt to manage stress. For example, an athlete with a dispositional tendency to use humour as a mode of coping is likely to use this strategy regardless of whether the stress is a conflict with a coach, an upcoming important competition, or a bad call by an official. Coping style is contrasted with a state-like, or situational, approach that emphasizes coping changes depending on the situation. A state-like view of coping would predict coping to be much more variable since someone experiencing stress would attempt to match their coping strategy to the specific stressor, rather than having a tendency to rely on a consistent coping style.

There is a growing body of literature on coping styles in the sport domain. In support of a state-like view of coping, Bouffard and Crocker (1992) found that individuals with physical disabilities did not consistently use the same coping strategies across three challenging physical activity settings. However, in a subsequent study with 25 youth swimmers,

People appear to have preferred ways of coping with stress; however, coping requires flexibility to select strategies that best match the situation.

Photograph courtesy of Kent Kowalski.

Crocker and Isaak (1997) showed that there was evidence of a coping style for training sessions but not for competitions. They suggested that one reason this difference might occur is that competitions are less consistent in their demands than workouts in practice, which tend to be fairly repetitious. Competitions often differ in their importance, in other swimmers in the race, and in who is watching the race. As a result, a more diverse way of coping is needed in competition than during practice.

Taken together, the results are somewhat mixed regarding the existence of a coping style in sport; however, there seems to be support for both a coping-style view and a state-like view. Louvet and colleagues have reoriented this debate by showing that some athletes are coping in a consistent manner across time, whereas other athletes are changing their use of coping (Louvet, Gaudreau, Menaut, Genty, & Deneuve, 2007). For instance, 55% of the soccer players participating in their study maintained a moderate level of task-oriented coping over a six-month period, whereas 5% and 40% increased and decreased, respectively, their use of task-oriented coping. These results are consistent with Lazarus' (1991) view of coping as an idiosyncratic process, that is, that distinct subtypes of athletes are likely to interpret the source of stress in a dissimilar manner and to differ in their attempts to meet the changing demands of a situation.

DISTINGUISHING BETWEEN COPING AND OUTCOMES OF COPING

An important distinction to be made when trying to understand coping in sport and exercise is the distinction between the concept of coping and the outcomes of the coping process. Coping is an effort to deal with stress. An **outcome of coping** is the result (good or bad)

more likely to make progress in the pursuit of their goals. Of particular interest, the positive role of distraction-oriented coping was also evident in a study with a sample of Canadian amateur elite golfers participating in a provincial championship (Gaudreau & Blondin, 2004a). Specifically, momentarily focusing on things unrelated to the competition during the golf round was associated with greater likelihood of goal attainment, but only for athletes who were also using task-oriented coping to a large extent. In a similar study of French Canadian athletes participating in various sports, the debilitative effect of disengagement-oriented coping was attenuated when athletes were also using high levels of task-oriented coping (Gaudreau & Blondin, 2004b).

The most common outcomes in sport coping research are emotional states. Generally, problem-focused coping strategies, like active coping and planning, are positively related to positive affect, enjoyment, feelings of sport satisfaction, and even to general feelings of life satisfaction. Emotion-focused strategies, like seeking social support for emotional reasons, and avoidance-oriented strategies are more related to negative affect (e.g., Crocker & Graham, 1995; Gaudreau & Blondin, 2002). Amiot and colleagues used a longitudinal design in which affective states were assessed a few days before a competition and a few days after the competition among a sample of Canadian athletes (Amiot, Gaudreau, & Blanchard, 2004). The goal of the study was to determine whether the affective states of athletes would change after the competition, compared to before the competition, as a result of their use of coping strategies. Using task-oriented coping during a competition resulted in increased positive affect, whereas disengagement-oriented coping was associated with increased negative affect. These results were replicated in a similar study examining the relationship between coping and changes in life satisfaction (Gaudreau & Antl, 2008). Athletes using task-oriented coping were more satisfied about their life after a competition (as compared to their initial level of life satisfaction), thus implying that the mere effort of actively pursuing one's goal can lead to a substantial change in emotional well-being.

Not surprisingly, coping has been recognized as an important factor by sport trainers and athletic therapists for effective injury rehabilitation (Ford & Gordon, 1998), and there is some evidence to suggest that coping can contribute to a more rapid return to competition and a lower chance of repeat injuries (Udry, 1997). Stress, particularly the negative life events experienced by an athlete, has often been portrayed as a significant risk factor for sport injuries. However, a study by Smith, Smoll, and Ptacek (1990) indicated that the deleterious effect of negative life events on subsequent injuries can be attenuated for athletes possessing good coping skills and a rich social support network.

Knowing which specific strategies lead to a more effective recovery from injury is a more difficult question to answer. A key element to a successful recovery from sport-related injuries is adherence to the rehabilitation program. In a study of 107 injured athletes from the United Kingdom, the use of active coping, planning, and seeking instrumental social support increased the likelihood of attending rehabilitation sessions over a three-week period (Hagger, Chatzisarantis, Griffin, & Thatcher, 2005). Different strategies might be needed at distinct stages of the rehabilitation process. Consistent with the suggestion of Cornelius (2002), it is likely that both problem-focused and emotion-focused coping strategies are important for athletes to facilitate the rehabilitation process.

Case Study 6.1

The Case of the Injured Basketball Player

You are a coach of an under-19 women's basketball team, and your best athlete, Amy, suffers a significant knee injury. She is a top-ranked and highly recruited player who was going to be captain of the provincial team this summer and play university basketball in the fall. She comes to you and says that she is having a very difficult time dealing with her injury. She has been told by her doctor and physiotherapist that she will not be able to participate in any team basketball drills for at least three months and that, at best, her knee will be at 80% for university tryouts in the fall. Amy describes her rehabilitation to date as "slow, frustrating, and boring." You can also tell that she has lost confidence in her ability to play at an elite level. What are the key issues in this case study that you need to be aware of as a coach? What would you say to Amy in your next conversation with her? What resources would you recommend to her that could help her more effectively manage the stress of her injury?

Athletic burnout has received mounting attention from sport scientists in recent years. Burnout is a syndrome composed of physical exhaustion, devaluation of one's sport, and reduced sense of accomplishment (Raedeke & Smith, 2001). These symptoms, at least in part, result from the inability to effectively manage excessive demands in training and competition. As such, Raedeke and Smith (2004) reported that general coping skills such as taking quiet time each day and effective management of time were associated with lower levels of physical exhaustion, sport devaluation, and reduced sense of accomplishment. However, it is not only athletes who experience burnout in sport. Coaches and athletic directors are also at risk because of the many demands of sport and the challenges of balancing sport involvement with their occupational and family life (Kelley, Eklund, & Ritter, 1999).

After reading the preceding discussion, you probably came to the conclusion that some forms of coping strategies represent good news coping ways to promote good outcomes while preventing injuries, relapses from rehabilitation, and burnout. Coaches, parents, and even the athletes themselves want to know how they can create winning conditions that could facilitate the utilization of these good news coping strategies. In this section, we will present two groups of variables considered to be antecedents leading the way to coping utilization in sport: sociodemographic and individual factors.

Sociodemographic Factors

Gender Studies that look at gender differences in coping have been of great interest to sport researchers, especially over the last 10 years. This literature has demonstrated one of the most consistent findings in the sport coping literature: males and females do appear to cope differently in sport. Overall, females tend to use more social support, help-seeking, increased effort, and emotion-focused coping than do males to manage sport stress (e.g., Kowalski & Crocker, 2001; Maniar, Curry, Sommers-Flanagan, & Walsh, 2001). In general, the combined sport and general psychology literature has shown that females tend to use more coping strategies than males (Tamres, Janicki, & Helgeson, 2002). However, these differences might be due to differences in the types of stressors males and females face.

Role constraint theory states that differences in stress are primarily the result of the different roles men and women play in society, as opposed to any inherent gender differences (Tamres, Janicki, & Helgeson, 2002). Beach volleyball provides a good example because the women might have to develop coping strategies to manage self-presentation concerns that the men do not, simply because of the expectations of what they wear in competition. On the other hand, the **gender socialization hypothesis** predicts that males and females learn to use different coping strategies to manage the same types of situations (Hoar et al., 2006). Through sex-role stereotyping and role expectations, females more than males are generally encouraged to express their emotions and turn to others for emotional support. All in all, although the finding of gender differences is one of the most consistent results in sport coping research, why males and females differ is less clear.

REFLECTIONS 6.4

Although there is a growing body of evidence to suggest that males and females cope differently with stress in sport, we do not really know why they are coping differently. Two possible explanations are that (1) males and females experience different sources of stress, and (2) there are socially defined expectations as to what are acceptable ways of coping for males and females. What particular aspects of Canadian culture strengthen or weaken gender differences in coping?

Culture Cross-cultural psychology is a discipline examining cultural differences in psychological functioning. Limited attention has been devoted to direct comparisons of coping across groups of athletes from different countries and cultures. Nonetheless, research on sport coping has been conducted with athletes from different areas of the world, thus providing some indirect evidence about cross-cultural coping differences. For example, a number of studies have shown the particular importance of prayer as a coping strategy for Korean athletes (Kim & Duda, 2003; Park, 2000; Yoo, 2001). There have been surprisingly few studies to see if Canadians have a particular way of coping with stress in sport, as well as a limited number of coping studies within more well-defined cultures in Canada.

Individual Factors

Throughout this chapter, the importance of people's cognitive appraisal in the experience of stress and subsequent coping efforts has been emphasized. Yet, other individual factors are worth considering in the prediction of coping. As discussed in Chapter 3, **trait anxiety** represents a general tendency to feel anxious, worried, and preoccupied in the competitive sport arena. Research has indicated that trait-anxious athletes are more likely to use disengagement-oriented forms of coping such as self-blame, denial, wishful thinking, and behavioural disengagement (Eubank & Collins, 2000; Giacobbi & Weinberg, 2000). However, perceiving anxiety as facilitative before a sport competition has recently been associated with greater usage of problem-focused coping and lesser usage of disengagement-oriented coping during competition among a sample of 39 swimmers with international competitive experience (Hatzigeorgiadis & Chroni, 2007).

Some athletes are more prone to outburst of anger; they possess a high level of **dispositional anger**. Anger is useful to protect the self and to attack whenever a threatening situation challenges one's physical security. Unfortunately, anger can also be detrimental, such as when it leads to unnecessary roughness and injures an opponent. Results of a 2008 study indicated that athletes with a tendency to experience frequent and intense outbursts of anger are less likely to use emotion-focused coping strategies when confronted with an anger-provocative situation (Bolgar, Janelle, & Giacobbi, 2008). In contrast, athletes with a tendency to control their impulsive behaviours are more likely to use both problem-focused and emotion-focused coping during anger-provocative situations.

Optimism, which is the tendency to believe that good things will happen in the future, has been studied in the context of performance slumps. Grove and Heard (1997) showed that both trait self-confidence and optimism were positively associated with usage of problem-focused coping and with lesser use of emotion-focused coping. The importance of optimism is not limited to coping. In a study of Canadian competitive golfers, Gaudreau and Blondin (2004a) found that optimistic athletes were more likely to attain their performance goals and to experience subjective well-being following a competition. In their study, task-oriented coping was an important factor because optimistic athletes were using strategies like increased effort, mental imagery, and relaxation, which, in turn, positively related to goal attainment and positive affect. Similar results were obtained in studying **dispositional perfectionism** of athletes. Athletes pursuing perfectionistic standards to please significant others have been found to experience lower levels of well-being (Flett & Hewitt, 2005). In a study of Canadian athletes from various sports, socially prescribed perfectionism was associated with the use of disengagement-oriented coping, which was related to lower levels of life-satisfaction (Gaudreau & Antl, 2008). However, some athletes pursue perfectionistic goals without feeling pressured by their significant others. These self-oriented perfectionistic athletes use task-oriented coping during the course of competition, which facilitates both goal attainment and increased life-satisfaction.

Level of expertise has also been shown to influence the use of coping strategies, with more proficient athletes using more task-oriented coping (Gaudreau & Blondin, 2002). For instance, in a study with a large sample of athletes from the United Kingdom, international and national athletes were more likely to use problem-solving, planning, increased effort, and relaxation than their counterparts competing at the county, university, and club level (Nicholls, Polman, Levy, Taylor, & Cobley, 2007). Despite these results, future research should try to follow the same group of athletes during a transition from provincial to national and from national to international levels of competition to determine how coping efforts change (or do not change) to meet the increasing demands of sport.

REFLECTIONS 6.5

It is important to distinguish between *coping* and *outcomes of coping*. Reflecting on your own experiences, in what ways has your involvement in sport and exercise been a stress release? In what ways has it just been another source of stress in your life?

COPING INTERVENTIONS

Three prominent coping interventions that have been used in sport are stress inoculation training, stress management training, and COPE training. The development of an athlete's coping resources combined with an application of those skills in practice and competition is a key component of all these programs. It is really the manner of the application that makes them distinct from one another. In Meichenbaum's (1993) stress inoculation training, athletes learn to develop and rehearse a wide range of coping skills or learn to better use the coping skills that they already have. It is called **stress inoculation training** because when athletes practise their coping skills, they start with small manageable doses of stress and gradually progress to more stress-inducing situations (see www.apa.org/divisions/div12/rev_est/sit_stress.html for more information and references).

In Smith's (1980) **stress management training**, athletes develop an **integrated coping response**, which can be used across a wide variety of stressful situations in sport and generally consists of muscular relaxation and self-talk statements. In stress management training, contrary to stress inoculation training, athletes do not practise coping with gradually increasing stress. Instead, the training uses a procedure called **induced affect** in which athletes learn to turn off a high level of stress via the implementation of their integrated coping response.

Finally, Anshel's (1990) **COPE training** is similar to the other two interventions in that athletes learn coping strategies in a planned sequence while recognizing that different strategies are going to be more or less effective depending on the specific situation. However, a specific emphasis of COPE training is on the management of acute stress, as opposed to chronic stress.

Research has generally confirmed the effectiveness of these programs in helping athletes cope with stress in sport (see Crocker, Kowalski, & Graham, 2002; Hoar et al., 2006). In addition, although not specifically termed coping materials, Canadian sporting bodies have resource materials that help facilitate a positive emotional environment for parents, coaches, and athletes. Examples include the Children in Sport skill development program (www.sasksport.sk.ca/cis/cis.html) and the Canadian Sport for Life (CS4L) program (www.canadiansportforlife.ca). These programs aim to make the sporting environment a positive experience for all involved in youth sport, and they challenge our current sport models, which often make sport a stressful experience for young athletes.

A more specific problem-focused type of coping intervention has been implemented with tennis players to help them overcome the disruptive thoughts, feelings, and physiological states likely to interfere with their preparation for competition (Achtziger, Gollwitzer, & Sheeran, 2008). The day before a competition, athletes were asked to identity up to four negative inner states from a predetermined list (e.g., problem concentrating, exhaustion, frustration) and to create a plan of action in the form of if–then contingencies ("Whenever ________, I will _______"). For instance, a tennis player could create the following strategy: "Whenever I feel frustrated, I will close my eyes and take a couple of deep breaths."

Similar interventions have been proposed for exercise behaviour. Various researchers have reported an increase in physical activity following the creation of action plans designed to determine where, when, and how to perform physical activity (Gollwitzer & Sheeran, 2006). However, two notes of concern are warranted when implementing these intervention programs. First, planning interventions have the potential to be deleterious when used by clients with high levels of socially prescribed perfectionism since they already have a tendency to strive toward their goals in an unduly rigid and inflexible manner (Powers, Koestner, & Topciu, 2005). Second, planning interventions are more optimal when clients do not feel pressured to adhere to the planning strategy (Koestner et al., 2006). Providing meaningful choices and encouraging the clients to formulate a personalized plan that fits their lifestyle can go a long way in maximizing the usefulness of these coping interventions.

REFLECTIONS 6.6

Psychological skills act as coping resources that people draw upon to use as strategies to cope with stress in sport and exercise. What psychological skills do you possess that help you cope with stress? What skills do you need to develop or enhance in order to improve your ability to cope with stress in sport and exercise?

Photograph © Jon Feingersh/Masterfile.

CHAPTER SUMMARY

If we reflect on the opening vignette of the chapter, we can see the complexity of stress and coping. Exercise is obviously important to Jessica, and, as a result, she is dealing with a number of stress sources, ranging from time management and financial concerns to concerns about being evaluated by others. Her ways of coping are numerous, with efforts ranging from changing her fitness facility, to finding a workout partner, to hiring a personal trainer. Maybe most importantly, it clearly demonstrates that coping with stress is a process that plays out over time, often with no simple resolution.

Cognitive appraisal is a key component of the stress experience. How people interpret the situations they face in sport and exercise is now generally considered as important as the situations themselves. People are not passive agents who must succumb to the demands placed upon them. Instead, they interpret situations in relation to their goals and their perceived coping options. General sources of stress that are often reported as threatening, challenging, or as a harm/loss include various psychological, physical, social, environmental, and career demands. These general sources include acute and chronic stressors, expected and unexpected stressors, and competitive and non-competitive stressors.

Coping is a dynamic process. It is a response to stress that includes a wide variety of cognitive and behavioural efforts. These efforts can range from accepting the situation, to making a plan of action, to leaving the situation altogether. Often, multiple coping efforts are made in any given situation as someone tries to figure out the most effective way to manage the demands he or she faces. These coping efforts themselves then reshape the situation and possibly the person's cognitive appraisal of the situation, making new coping attempts necessary (if stress remains). The distinction between micro- and macro-analytic approaches to coping is useful to understanding the dynamic process of coping, because not only will specific coping strategies change, but so too might the goals of the strategies.

Coping seems to reflect both coping styles and characteristics of the situation. There is growing evidence that athletes might have preferences for coping in specific ways, but that despite these preferences, coping can still be quite variable across different situations. Whether or not a particular coping style can be used across different situations likely depends on how similar those situations are to one another and whether the coping style is appropriate for the situations. One of the limitations in many situations is that there are constraints on what can be done to cope; thus, people must often seek out alternative ways to manage the demands placed upon them.

Coping strategies are neither inherently effective nor ineffective. Whether or not a coping strategy is effective depends on the fit between the coping efforts and the stress that is experienced. Although there is some evidence to suggest that, in general, problem-focused coping efforts are most effective in the long term, ultimately the effectiveness of coping needs to be considered in relation to a person's goals and well-being, which sometimes contradict each other.

Much more work is needed in establishing predictors of coping in sport and exercise. The challenge is that all situations seem to be relatively unique at some level because not only do the characteristics of situations change, but so too do individuals' appraisals of those situations. Researchers have only begun to look at consistencies across situations that might help establish whether strong predictors of coping can be established.

Despite the many unknowns regarding stress and coping in sport and exercise, coping intervention programs seem to be effective in helping people manage stress. Coping interventions, such as stress inoculation training, stress management training, and COPE training, all seem to have a great deal of potential for helping people develop a set of resources that allow them to more effectively meet the demands of sport and exercise. Ultimately, however, an interest in stress and coping in sport and exercise stems from a desire not only to help people meet the demands of sport and exercise in a healthy way but also to promote a lifetime of enjoyable physical activity involvement.

Common Myths about Stress and Coping in Sport and Exercise Revisited

MYTH: Elite sport is inherently stressful.

How athletes interpret specific situations is the key factor that will determine whether or not they experience stress (and what level of stress). Even situations that one might think should be stressful might not cause stress, depending on a particular athlete's goals and interpretation of what is happening. Two track-and-field event favourites in the 2008 Olympic Summer Games were Russian pole vaulter Yelena Isinbayeva and Portuguese long-jumper Naide Gomes. Heading into the Olympics, Isinbayeva was the only woman to clear 5 m in pole vault, and Gomes was the only woman among those competing with a season-best long jump heading into the Olympics beyond 7 m. Isinbayeva went on to win the Olympic gold medal and set a new world record; she said of the spotlight, "I love it so much. I feel like an actress" (Butcher, 2008). Alternatively, Gomes reported to CBC, "I lacked confidence and felt a lot of pressure" (Canada's Charles, 2008). Gomes failed to qualify for the long-jump final.

MYTH: Exercise always reduces stress.
While in a lot of cases exercise is indeed a good way to cope with stress, for some people, as the chapter vignette suggests, exercise is the primary source of stress. Many times the exercise setting is abound with potential triggers, such as mirrors, crowded gyms, and revealing attire, that can lead to self-presentation concerns. Or, for others, exercise simply is not a very enjoyable experience. As Berger (1994) recognized over 15 years ago in her review on using exercise as a way to cope with stress, "Physical activity is an ideal way to both raise and lower one's stress levels" (p. 101). Thus, in many cases, we need to work with people to develop coping strategies to deal with their exercise participation, in addition to encouraging them to use exercise as a coping strategy to deal with other life stresses.

MYTH: Dropping out of sport or stopping exercise is an ineffective coping strategy.
Although in many cases dropping out of sport or stopping exercise may not be the best or preferable option to manage stress, in some cases these actions might well be the most effective coping strategy. Coping strategies are not inherently good or bad. Effective coping depends on the match between the situation, the person's goals and values, and the strategies that are used.

Review Questions

1. What does it mean to describe stress as a "process"?
2. What roles do cognitive appraisal and coping play in the experience of stress?
3. How are the concepts of stress and emotion related?
4. Discuss why it is important to distinguish between *coping* and *outcomes of coping*.
5. Compare and contrast micro- and macro-analytic level dimensions of coping.
6. What predictors of coping in sport were discussed in the chapter? What relationship do they have to coping?
7. Discuss challenges to understanding stress and coping in sport and exercise.

Suggested Reading

Hoar, S. D., Kowalski, K. C., Gaudreau, P., & Crocker, P. R. E. (2006). A review of coping in sport. In S. Hanton, & S. Mellalieu (Eds.), *Literature reviews in sport psychology* (pp. 47–90). New York: Nova Science.

Lazarus, R. S. (2000b). How emotions influence performance in competitive sports. *The Sport Psychologist*, *14*, 229–252.

Nicholls, A. R., & Polman, R. C. J. (2007). Coping in sport: A systematic review. *Journal of Sports Sciences*, *25*, 11–31.

References

Achtziger, A., Gollwitzer, P. M., & Sheeran, P. (2008). Implementation intentions and shielding goal striving from unwanted thoughts and feelings. *Personality and Social Psychology Bulletin, 34*, 381–393.

Aldwin, C. M. (2000). *Stress, coping, and development: An integrative perspective*. New York: Guildford.

Amiot, C. E., Gaudreau, P., & Blanchard, C. M. (2004). Self-determination, coping, and goal attainment in sport. *Journal of Sport & Exercise Psychology, 26*, 386–411.

Anshel, M. H. (1990). Toward validation of a model for coping with acute stress in sport. *International Journal of Sport Psychology, 21*, 58–83.

Anshel, M. H. (2001). Qualitative validation of a model for coping with acute stress in sport. *Journal of Sport Behavior, 24*, 223–245.

Anshel, M. H., Jamieson, J., & Raviv, S. (2001). Coping with acute stress among male and female Israeli athletes. *International Journal of Sport Psychology, 32*, 271–289.

Anshel, M. H., Kim, K., Kim, B., Chang, K., & Eom, H. (2001). A model for coping with stressful events in sport: Theory, application, and future directions. *International Journal of Sport Psychology, 32*, 43–75.

Berger, B. G. (1994). Coping with stress: The effectiveness of exercise and other techniques. *Quest, 46*, 100–119.

Bolgar, M. R., Janelle, C., & Giacobbi, P. R., Jr. (2008). Trait anger, appraisal, and coping differences among adolescent tennis players. *Journal of Applied Sport Psychology, 20*, 73–87.

Bouffard, M., & Crocker, P. R. E. (1992). Coping by individuals with physical disabilities with perceived challenge in physical activity: Are people consistent? *Research Quarterly for Exercise and Sport, 63*, 410–417.

Buckworth, J., & Dishman, R. K. (2002). *Exercise psychology*. Champaign, IL: Human Kinetics.

Butcher, P. (2008, August 19). Isinbayeva puts on a show. IAAF. Retrieved August 19, 2008, from www.iaaf.org

Campbell, E., & Jones, G. (2002). Cognitive appraisal of sources of stress experienced by elite male wheelchair basketball players. *Adapted Physical Activity Quarterly, 19*, 100–108.

Canada's Charles leaps into long jump final. (2008, August 19). CBC Sports. Retrieved August 19, 2008, from www.cbc.ca

Canada's Whitfield takes silver in triathalon. (2008, August 19). CBC Sports. Retrieved August 19, 2008, from www.cbc.ca

Carpenter, B. N. (1992). Issues and advances in coping research. In B. N. Carpenter (Ed.), *Personal coping: Theory, research, and application*(pp. 1–13). Westport, CT: Praeger.

Conroy, D. E., Elliot, A. J., & Hofer, S. M. (2003). A 2x2 achievement goal questionnaire for sport: Evidence for factorial invariance, temporal stability, and external validity. *Journal of Sport & Exercise Psychology, 25*, 456–476.

Cornelius, A. (2002). Psychological interventions for the injured athlete. In J. M. Silva III, & D. E. Stevens (Eds.), *Psychological foundations of sport* (pp. 224–246). Boston: Allyn & Bacon.

Crocker, P. R. E. (1989). Evaluating stress management training under competition conditions. *International Journal of Sport Psychology, 20*, 191–204.

Crocker, P. R. E., Alderman, R. B., & Smith, F. M. (1988). Cognitive-affective stress management training with high performance youth volleyball players: Effects on affect, cognition, and performance. *Journal of Sport & Exercise Psychology, 10*, 448–460.

Crocker, P. R. E., & Graham, T. R. (1995). Coping by competitive athletes with performance stress: Gender differences and relationships with affect. *The Sport Psychologist, 9*, 325–338.

Crocker, P. R. E., & Isaak, K. (1997). Coping during competitions and training sessions: Are youth swimmers consistent? *International Journal of Sport Psychology, 28*, 355–369.

Crocker, P. R. E., Kowalski, K. C., & Graham, T. R. (1998). Measurement of coping strategies in sport. In J. L. Duda (Ed.), *Advances in sport and exercise psychology measurement* (pp. 149–161). Morgantown, WV: Fitness Information Technology.

Crocker, P. R. E., Kowalski, K. C., & Graham, T. R. (2002). Emotional control and intervention. In J. M. Silva III, & D. E. Stevens (Eds.), *Psychological foundations of sport* (pp. 155–176). Boston: Allyn & Bacon.

Dugdale, J. R., Eklund, R. C., & Gordon, S. (2002). Expected and unexpected stressors in major international competition: Appraisal, coping, and performance. *The Sport Psychologist, 16*, 20–33.

Endler, N. S., & Parker, J. D. (1994). Assessment of multidimensional coping: Task, emotion, and avoidance strategies. *Psychological Assessment, 6*, 50–60.

Eubank, M., & Collins, D. (2000). Coping with pre- and in-event fluctuations in competitive state anxiety: A longitudinal approach. *Journal of Sports Sciences, 18*, 121–131.

Filaire, E., Maso, F., Sagnol, M., Lac, G., & Ferrand, C. (2001). Anxiety, hormonal responses and coping during a judo competition. *Aggressive Behavior, 27*, 55–63.

Flett, G. L., & Hewitt, P. L. (2005). The perils of perfectionism in sports and exercise. *Current Directions in Psychological Science, 14*, 14–18.

Folkman, S. (1992). Making the case for coping. In B. N. Carpenter (Ed.), *Personal coping: Theory, research, and application*(pp. 31–46). Westport, CT: Praeger.

Folkman, S. (2008). The case for positive emotions in the stress process. *Anxiety, Stress, and Coping, 21*, 3–14.

Ford, I. W., & Gordon, S. (1998). Perspective of sport trainers and athletic therapists on the psychological content of their practice and training. *Journal of Sport Rehabilitation, 7*, 79–94.

Frey, M., Laguna, P. L., & Ravizza, K. (2003). Collegiate athletes' mental skill use and perceptions of success: An exploration of the practice and competition settings. *Journal of Applied Sport Psychology, 15*, 115–128.

Gaudreau, P., & Antl, S. (2008). Athletes' broad dimensions of dispositional perfectionism: Examining changes in life-satisfaction and the mediating role of sport-related motivation and coping. *Journal of Sport & Exercise Psychology, 30*, 356–382.

Gaudreau, P., & Blondin, J. P. (2002). Development of a questionnaire for the assessment of coping strategies employed by athletes in competitive sport settings. *Psychology of Sport and Exercise, 3*, 1–34.

Gaudreau, P., & Blondin, J. P. (2004a). Different athletes cope differently: A cluster analysis of coping. *Personality and Individual Differences, 36*, 1865–1877.

Gaudreau, P., & Blondin, J. P. (2004b). The differential associations of dispositional optimism and pessimism with coping, goal attainment, and emotional adjustment during a sport competition. *International Journal of Stress Management, 11*, 245–269.

Giacobbi, P. R., Jr., & Weinberg, R. S. (2000). An examination of coping in sports: Individual trait anxiety differences and situational consistency. *The Sport Psychologist, 14*, 42–62.

Gollwitzer, P. M., & Sheeran, P. (2006). Implementation intentions and goal achievement: A meta-analysis of effects and processes. *Advances in Experimental Social Psychology, 38*, 69–119.

Gould, D., Eklund, R. C., & Jackson, S. A. (1993). Coping strategies used by U.S. Olympic wrestlers. *Research Quarterly for Exercise and Sport, 64*, 83–93.

Gould, D., Finch, L. M., & Jackson, S. A. (1993). Coping strategies used by national champion figure skaters. *Research Quarterly for Exercise and Sport, 64*, 453–468.

Gould, D., Udry, E., Bridges, D., & Beck, L. (1997). Stress sources encountered when rehabilitating from season-ending ski injuries. *The Sport Psychologist, 11*, 361–378.

Grove, J., & Heard, P. N. (1997). Optimism and sport confidence as correlates of slump-related coping among athletes. *The Sport Psychologist, 11*, 400–410.

Hagger, M. S., Chatzisarantis, N. L., Griffin, M., & Thatcher, J. (2005). Injury representations, coping, emotions, and functional outcomes in athletes with sports-related injuries: A test of self-regulation theory. *Journal of Applied Social Psychology, 35*, 2345–2374.

Hatzigeorgiadis, A., & Chroni, S. (2007). Pre-competition anxiety and in-competition coping in experienced male swimmers. *International Journal of Sports Science & Coaching, 2*, 181–189.

Hausenblas, H. A., Brewer, B. W., & Van Raalte, J. L. (2004). Self-presentation and exercise. *Journal of Applied Sport Psychology, 16*, 3–18.

Hoar, S. D., Kowalski, K. C., Gaudreau, P., & Crocker, P. R. E. (2006). A review of coping in sport. In S. Hanton, & S. Mellalieu (Eds.), *Literature reviews in sport psychology* (pp. 47–90). New York: Nova Science.

Holt, N. L., & Hogg, J. M. (2002). Perceptions of stress and coping during preparations for the 1999 women's soccer World Cup finals. *The Sport Psychologist, 16*, 251–271.

Joseph leads Argos in return to Regina. (2008, July 27). TSN. Retrieved August 19, 2008, from www.tsn.ca

Kelley, B. C., Eklund, R. C., & Ritter, T. M. (1999). Stress and burnout among collegiate tennis coaches. *Journal of Sport & Exercise Psychology, 21*, 113–130.

Kim, M. S., & Duda, J. L. (2003). The coping process: Cognitive appraisals of stress, coping strategies, and coping effectiveness. *The Sport Psychologist, 17*, 406–425.

Koestner, R., Horberg, E. J., Gaudreau, P., Powers, T. A., Di Dio, L., Bryan, C., et al. (2006). Bolstering implementation plans for long haul: The benefits of simultaneously boosting self-concordance and self-efficacy. *Personality and Social Psychology Bulletin, 32*, 1547–1558.

Kowalski, K. C., & Crocker, P. R. E. (2001). Development and validation of the coping function questionnaire for adolescents in sport. *Journal of Sport & Exercise Psychology, 23*, 136–155.

Kowalski, K. C., Mack, D. E., Crocker, P. R. E., Niefer, C. B., & Fleming, T.-L. (2006). Coping with social physique anxiety in adolescence. *Journal of Adolescent Health, 39*, 275.e9–275.e16.

Lazarus, R. S. (1991). *Emotion and adaptation*. New York: Oxford University Press.

Lazarus, R. S. (1999). *Stress and emotion: A new synthesis*. New York: Springer.

Lazarus, R. S. (2000a). Cognitive-motivational-relational theory of emotion. In Y. L. Hanin (Ed.), *Emotions in sport* (pp. 39–63). Champaign, IL: Human Kinetics.

Lazarus, R. S. (2000b). How emotions influence performance in competitive sports. *The Sport Psychologist, 14*, 229–252.

Leary, M. R. (1992). Self-presentational processes in exercise and sport. *Journal of Sport and Exercise Psychology, 14*, 339–351.

Leary, M. R., & Kowalski, R. M. (1990). Impression management: A literature review and two-component model. *Psychological Bulletin, 107*, 34–47.

Louvet, B., Gaudreau, P., Menaut, A., Genty, J., & Deneuve, P. (2007). Longitudinal patterns of stability and change in coping across three competitions: A latent class growth analysis. *Journal of Sport & Exercise Psychology, 29*, 99–116.

Lowther, N. (2008, November 1). GAME 9 CIS championship: Vikes clinch berth in final, 'Birds have to wait. CIS. Retrieved May 2, 2009, from www.cisport.ca/e/championships/w_fieldhockey/2008

Maniar, S. D., Curry, L. A., Sommers-Flanagan, J., & Walsh, J. A. (2001). Student-athlete preferences in seeking help when confronted with sport performance problems. *The Sport Psychologist, 15*, 205–223.

McKay, J., Niven, A. G., Lavallee, D., & White, A. (2008). Sources of strain among elite UK track athletes. *The Sport Psychologist, 22*, 143–163.

Meichenbaum, D. (1993). Stress inoculation training: A 20-year update. In P. M. Lehrer, & R. L. Woolfolk (Eds.), *Principles and practices of stress management* (2nd ed., pp. 373–406). New York: Guildford.

Nicholls, A. R., & Polman, R. C. J. (2007). Coping in sport: A systematic review. *Journal of Sports Sciences, 25*, 11–31.

Nicholls, A. R., Polman, R., Levy, A. R., Taylor, J., & Cobley, S. (2007). Stressors, coping, and coping effectiveness: Gender, type of sport, and skill differences. *Journal of Sports Sciences, 25*, 1521–1530.

Noblet, A. J., & Gifford, S. M. (2002). The sources of stress experienced by professional Australian footballers. *Journal of Applied Sport Psychology, 14*, 1–13.

Park, J. K. (2000). Coping strategies used by Korean national athletes. *The Sport Psychologist, 14,* 63–80.

Powers, T. A., Koestner, R., & Topciu, R. A. (2005). Implementation intentions, perfectionism and goal progress: Perhaps the road to hell is paved with good intentions. *Personality and Social Psychology Bulletin, 31,* 902–912.

Raedeke, T. D., & Smith, A. L. (2001). Development and preliminary validation of an Athlete Burnout Measure. *Journal of sport and Exercise Psychology, 23,* 281–306.

Raedeke, T. D., & Smith, A. L. (2004). Coping resources and athlete burnout: An examination of stress mediated and moderation hypotheses. *Journal of Sport & Exercise Psychology, 26,* 525–541.

Sabiston, C. M., Sedgwick, W. A., Crocker, P. R. E., Kowalski, K. C., & Mack, D. E. (2007). Social physique anxiety in adolescence: An exploration of influences, coping strategies, and health behaviors. *Journal of Adolescent Research, 22,* 78–101.

Selye, H. (1993). History of the stress concept. In L. Goldberger, & S. Breznitz (Eds.), *Handbook of stress: Theoretical and clinical aspects* (2nd ed., pp. 7–17). New York: The Free Press.

Skinner, E. A., Edge, K., Altman, J., & Sherwood, H. (2003). Searching for the structure of coping: A review and critique of category systems for classifying ways of coping. *Psychological Bulletin, 129,* 216–269.

Smith, R. E. (1980). A cognitive-affective approach to stress management training for athletes. In C. Nadeau, W. Halliwell, K. Newell, & G. Roberts (Eds.), *Psychology of motor behavior and sport—1979* (pp. 54–73). Champaign, IL: Human Kinetics.

Smith, R. E., Smoll, F. L., & Ptacek, J. (1990). Conjunctive moderator variables in vulnerability and resiliency research: Life stress, social support and coping skills, and adolescent sport injuries. *Journal of Personality and Social Psychology, 58,* 360–370.

Tamres, L. K., Janicki, D., & Helgeson, V. S. (2002). Sex differences in coping behavior: A meta-analytic review and an examination of relative coping. *Personality and Social Psychology Review, 6,* 2–30.

Udry, E. (1997). Coping and social support among injured athletes following surgery. *Journal of Sport & Exercise Psychology, 19,* 71–90.

Wipfli, B. M., Rethorst, C. D., & Landers, D. M. (2008). The anxiolytic effects of exercise: A meta-analysis of randomized trials and dose-response analysis. *Journal of Sport and Exercise Psychology, 30,* 392–410.

Yi, J. P., Smith, R. E., & Vitaliano, P. P. (2005). Stress-resilience, illness, and coping: A person-focused investigation of young women athletes. *Journal of Behavioral Medicine, 28,* 257–265.

Yoo, J. (2001). Coping profile of Korean competitive athletes. *International Journal of Sport Psychology, 32,* 290–303.

Chapter 7

Group Cohesion in Sport and Exercise

Kevin S. Spink

Chapter Objectives

After reading this chapter, you should be able to do the following:

1. Explain why the study of groups is important.
2. Provide a definition of group dynamics.
3. Identify group processes associated with group effectiveness.
4. Provide a definition of group cohesion.
5. Explain how to measure group cohesion.
6. Describe the conceptual model of group cohesion.
7. Explain the important correlates of group cohesion.

---

* I would like to thank Carly Priebe and Kathleen Wilson for their feedback and excellent suggestions for cohesion examples that were included in this chapter.

The Apple Hill Hockey Executive has been told that a team from Europe will be touring at the end of the season and a request has been made by the "Euros" to play a team from the Apple Hill league in an exhibition series. The Executive has been charged with selecting a team to play the Euros. Although the task seems a bit daunting, two common suggestions come forward. One of the suggestions comes from Marion, who thinks that the team that wins the league championship should be the one to play in the series. The other suggestion that receives support comes from Joan, who thinks that the league should put together an All Star team to play the touring Euros.

Those supporting the idea of using an All Star team offer positive support. Kenton makes the point that the Euros will be highly skilled, so stocking a team with league All Stars, who are the most skilled players at each of the positions, makes the best sense. Dwayne adds to this idea when he says, "There is no substitute for skill." Ana-Grace continues on with this theme when she suggests that the best players are likely the ones who will be able to adapt quickest to the new style required to play in a series such as this. This sentiment is echoed by Tanner, who says, "There will be few second chances, so the team that adapts the fastest should emerge victorious."

Those on the side of sending the team that wins the league championship see this issue differently. They do not dispute the fact that skill will be required to compete successfully against the Euros. However, their main argument for supporting the league champion revolves around the idea that hockey is a team game, so the group must factor highly into the decision. Tyler supports the league champion idea when he says, "Players who have played together all year as a group will be better at communicating with each other, so it will be easier for them to make adjustments on the fly that lead to successful plays than for players who have not played with each other before." To this, Tyson adds, "To be successful in a team sport, you need to be willing to contribute to the team's overall goal at the expense of your own personal agenda, and players on a championship team have already learned to put their egos aside and make sacrifices for the team, whereas league All Stars might not be able to do this as easily."

As you can see in the vignette, both sides have put up valid points. What would you do? After reading this chapter about groups and how they function, you should be in a better position to make an informed decision as to which team you would put forward to play the Euros.

Common Myths about Group Cohesion in Sport and Exercise

MYTH: Team harmony is required for cohesion to develop.

MYTH: There is no "I" in team.

MYTH: High cohesion is always a good thing.

The task in this chapter is to give an explanation of the group cohesion construct. However, before group cohesion is presented, the importance of groups, in general and in sport, will be discussed.

INTRODUCTION

You do not have to think very long to recognize that a lot of sport participation occurs in group settings. Sport groups come in the obvious guises of a hockey, football, soccer, basketball, volleyball, or baseball team. Although typically classified as individual sports, track and field, swimming, triathlon, and wrestling involve participation in teams. Group participation also occurs in many exercise activities, including aerobic, spin, or aqua fitness classes. The fact that we participate in a lot of activity groups parallels the fact that participation in group activities permeates most aspects of our non-sport lives as well, be it involvement in a drama club, debating group, band, choir, or local Mensa group.

The reality is that we all belong to a number of different groups. Given that groups form a large part of our lives, it may not be surprising that a field of study has emerged that focuses on the behaviour of groups. The field is called *group dynamics*, and it is viewed as a major branch of social psychology. According to Cartwright and Zander (1968), **group dynamics** focuses on gaining knowledge about the nature of groups and their development and on understanding the interrelationships between groups and individuals, between groups, and between groups and larger institutions.

Implicit in the above description is the idea that a group is different from a mere collection of individuals. It has been known for many years that group composition, for instance, is an important variable in group settings. The term **assembly effect** refers to variations in group behaviour that are a function of the particular combinations of individuals in the group. Rosenberg, Erlick, and Berkowitz (1955) found that individuals contributed differently to a group's outcome depending on the particular other individuals with whom they were grouped.

Although this difference (between a group and a collection of individuals) is recognized in the academic community, its significance is not lost on the sporting community. Brad Gushue, skip of the Canadian men's 2006 Olympic gold curling team, acknowledged this difference when he said, "At this level, chemistry is the most important thing. Take all the curlers here [at the Brier]: Everyone can make all the shots. The deciding factor is each team working to get the most out of each other. Some teams are just better together than they are individually" (Maki, 2009). Similarly, Michael Jordan, retired basketball player, wrote, "Me, I'd rather have five guys with less talent who are willing to come together as a team than five guys who consider themselves stars and aren't willing to sacrifice" (Jordan, 1994, p. 24).

As the preceding quotes illustrate, there appears to be a strong connection between team effectiveness and group behaviour in the sport setting. Research supports this as there are a number of group processes associated with how effective a group becomes. One of the key group processes involved with team effectiveness is how a group communicates. This is obviously important in the sport context. For example, the failure of a linebacker and a defensive lineman to communicate on a stunt may be the difference between a quarterback sack and a big play for the offence. Recognizing the importance of team communication, Sullivan and Feltz (2003) have developed the Scale for Effective Communication in Team Sports (SECTS), which identifies distinctiveness, acceptance, positive conflict, and negative conflict as four factors of effective communication in teams. Using SECTS, a strong positive relationship also has been found between communication and athlete satisfaction (Sullivan & Gee, 2007). Since satisfaction has been related to performance (Riemer & Chelladurai, 1998), this suggests that increasing team communication could lead to better team performance.

To enhance communication in sport teams, Carron and colleagues have suggested a number of strategies, such as providing opportunities to socialize to increase comfort levels among players, arranging the dressing room so that players are close enough to talk to each other easily, encouraging players to modify any dissenting ideas, and promoting cooperation and reducing rivalry by focusing on group goals and de-emphasizing personal goals and objectives (Carron, Hausenblas, & Eys, 2005).

This latter point is particularly important given the suggestion that team members will typically set goals for both themselves and the team (Zander, 1971), which is a finding that emerged when Canadian varsity athletes were questioned about the goals they set (Dawson, Bray, & Widmeyer, 2002). When team and personal goals are set, it has been suggested that team goals will be more effective when the sport requires a high degree of coordination and co-operation (Locke & Latham, 1984).

Another group process associated with team effectiveness involves how decisions are made. Common wisdom suggests that a decision made by the group should be better than one made by individuals because it is generally believed that the group possesses more resources to inform a decision than any one individual member (i.e., two heads are better than one). However, this assumes that the group process is effective at getting all members to share their thoughts honestly and then is able to integrate the information meaningfully. Research has found that groups who use the **majority rule**, which is based on the simple principle of equal participation and equal power, tend to make more successful decisions (Hastie & Kameda, 2005). Unfortunately, the use of the majority rule does not always occur since members sometimes provide thoughts that reflect conformity rather than true personal beliefs. In this instance, groups are likely to make poorer decisions because of what is termed *groupthink* (Janis, 2007). **Groupthink** occurs when concurrence-seeking becomes so dominant in a cohesive group that it tends to overshadow realistic appraisals of alternative courses of action. Based on this, one can see how a team should be very aware of the process it uses to solicit information because this can contribute greatly to the effectiveness of the decision being made.

In terms of understanding why teams become effective, another key factor that emerges concerns the forces that bind members to their groups. The binding property that has been identified as fundamental to understanding groups is cohesion. In fact, cohesion has been described as the most important small group variable (Lott & Lott, 1965). This suggestion makes sense when one considers that most researchers who use the term cohesion agree that it refers to the degree to which members are motivated to stay in the group (Shaw, 1976).

The recognition that cohesion is the glue that keeps the group together may be enough justification to examine the construct; however, there are other important reasons. One of the most important reasons is that the study of cohesion has revealed that enhanced levels of cohesion are associated with key outcomes for both the individual and the team in the sport setting. Consider the recognition of the importance of cohesion for team outcomes by one of the best individual basketball players of all time, Michael Jordan:

> "Naturally, there are going to be ups and downs, particularly if you are trying to achieve at a high level. But when we stepped between the lines, we knew what we were capable of doing. When a pressure situation presented itself, we were plugged into one another as a cohesive unit. That's why we were able to beat more talented teams" (Jordan, 1994, p. 23).

THE NATURE OF GROUP COHESION

There is some general understanding that cohesion is the glue that binds members in a group. However, in terms of specific scientific definitions, many ideas have been expressed. Over the years, cohesion has been defined in various ways, including attraction to the group, level of motivation evidenced by group members, and coordination of group members (Shaw, 1976). One of the seminal definitions of cohesion stated that it is "the resultant of all forces acting on members to remain in the group" (Festinger, 1950, p. 274). In outlining his ideas, Festinger suggested that there are many reasons why individuals would want to remain in a group, including attractions to other members of the group, the specific activities of the group, and the prestige of the group. Although this important definition highlighted the multidimensional nature of cohesion, numerous studies that followed assumed that cohesion was unidimensional, with interpersonal attraction being the most common definition used in the early days of cohesion research (Lott & Lott, 1965). With so many definitions, it may not be a surprise that after reviewing 50 years of empirical research on cohesion, Mudrack (1989) concluded that the construct of cohesion was difficult to define precisely or consistently.

Although Mudrack (1989) noted the confusion in defining cohesion, he did identify one definition as being important. It was one forwarded by Canadian sport psychology researcher Bert Carron, who defined cohesion as a "dynamic process which is reflected in the tendency for a group to stick together and remain united in the pursuit of its goals and objectives" (Carron, 1982, p. 124). Since this definition was formulated, Carron and two of his Canadian colleagues, Larry Brawley and Neil Widmeyer, have refined and revised the definition of cohesion to state that it is, "the dynamic process which is reflected in the tendency for a group to stick together and remain united in the pursuit of its instrumental objectives and/or for the satisfaction of member affective needs" (Carron et al., 1998, p. 213). This is currently the most accepted definition of group cohesion in sport.

REFLECTIONS 7.1

Examine the definition of cohesion outlined by Carron and colleagues (1998). Does their definition differ from what you think cohesion is? In what ways is it similar or different?

Carron and colleagues (2005) noted that this definition captures the four key characteristics of cohesion: dynamic, multidimensional, instrumental, and affective. One of the important characteristics of cohesion is that it is dynamic, not static. This characteristic acknowledges that reasons for cohesion can change over time. For instance, team members may be drawn to a team in its early stages because it is very task oriented but stay with the group because they have all become good friends.

This definition also reflects the fact that the factors that hold the group together can be varied and numerous, thus highlighting its multidimensional nature. Further, these factors can also vary between groups. For instance, there could be two highly cohesive intramural hockey teams that are being held together for very different reasons. On the first team, the members remain in the group because the team is highly united around winning the intramural championship (i.e., task reasons). On the other hand, the members of the second team stay together, not because they will win games, let alone the championship, but because they are very socially compatible (i.e., social reasons).

Another important characteristic captured in the definition is the instrumental nature of cohesion. This characteristic reflects the most basic of facts, namely, that all groups form for a reason. Whether it be a professional football team staying together to pursue the Grey Cup or the "beer" league hockey team staying together to maintain lifelong friendships, all groups form for a purpose. As such, it is important to keep in mind this instrumental basis of cohesion when trying to define the construct.

Finally, affective relationships are important in understanding cohesion. Outside of the instrumental reasons for members remaining in a group, sometimes groups stay together because there are strong emotional ties among the individuals in the group. For instance, a curling team may stay together because the members make each other laugh and feel comfortable. Likewise, members of a football team may form a tight bond because they have all gone through a gruelling initiation process in which those who could not take it quit, and those who made it through developed a greater respect for one another. A good example of this was portrayed in the movie *Remember the Titans*, in which a new coach, to make a racially diverse football team very cohesive, unites them by exposing them to a series of very demanding tasks (e.g., early morning runs).

MEASURING GROUP COHESION

Numerous general measures have been used to assess cohesion in the sport setting. These measures have included assumed similarity (Fiedler, 1954), esteem for teammates (Myers, 1962), interpersonal relationships (McGrath, 1962), social and leadership choices (Lenk, 1969), and attraction to the group (Klein & Christiansen, 1969). In addition to these all-purpose measures, there have been sport-specific questionnaires developed to assess cohesion, including the Sport Cohesiveness Questionnaire (Martens, Landers, & Loy, 1972) and the Group Environment Questionnaire (GEQ; www.fitinfotech.com/geq/geqadmin.tpl) developed by the Canadian trio of Carron, Widmeyer, and Brawley (1985). The GEQ has been, by far, the most extensively used of the sport-specific cohesion instruments developed to date. Although there could be a number of reasons for the extensive use and longevity of the GEQ in the sport setting, its major strength likely stems from the fact that it is based on an accepted definition of cohesion (Carron, 1982) as well as an accepted conceptual framework of cohesion by Carron et al. (1985). Prior to the development of the GEQ, the theoretical basis for cohesion was not well developed, so to address this shortcoming, Carron et al. (1985) developed the conceptual model that served as the basis for operationalizing the GEQ.

CONCEPTUAL MODEL OF GROUP COHESION

The conceptual model of cohesion developed by Carron et al. (1985) portrays cohesion as a multidimensional construct that includes individual and group aspects. The individual aspect refers to the beliefs each member holds about personal benefits of group membership; the group aspect refers to the beliefs each member holds about the group as a collective. These two aspects each divide into task and social cohesion. Task cohesion refers to the orientation toward achieving the group's objectives; social cohesion refers to the orientation toward developing and maintaining social relationships within the group. This construct results in four factors of cohesion in sport groups: (1) individual attractions to the group-task, (2) individual attractions to the group-social, (3) group integration-task, and (4) group integration-social (see Figure 7.1). These four related facets act together to create an integrated perception

Figure 7.1 Conceptual model of group cohesion

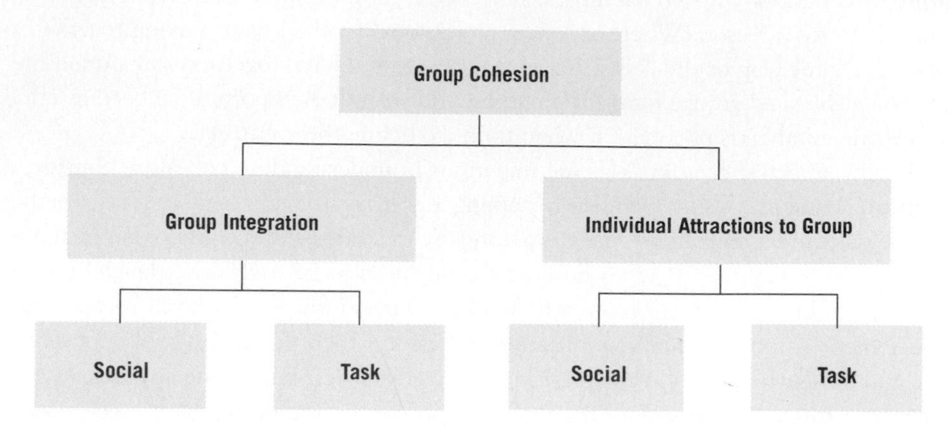

Note: From Carron A. V., Widmeyer W. N., & Brawley, L. R. (1985). The development of an instrument to assess cohesion in sport teams: the Group Environment Questionnaire. *Journal of Sport Psychology, 7,* 248, Figure 2. © 1985 by Human Kinetics Publishers, Inc. Reprinted with permission from Human Kinetics (Champaign, IL).

of cohesion. Although developed for the sport setting, this conceptualization of cohesion has broad acceptance in settings outside of sport (Cota, Evans, Dion, Kilik, & Longman, 1995).

REFLECTIONS 7.2

How do you think having a conceptual framework in place helped the development of the GEQ?

It is from this two-dimensional (group/individual, task/social) conceptual model formulated by Carron et al. (1985) that the GEQ was developed to assess cohesion in the sport setting. The GEQ instrument contains 18 questions that are divided into four subscales, which reflect the four factors identified in the conceptual model.

The GEQ has been used extensively in the sport setting and has generally received good psychometric support across a wide range of teams and situations (see Carron et al., 1998). Although the instrument is psychometrically sound, further adjustments, including positively rewording the negative items in the scale, have served to refine the GEQ (Eys, Carron, Bray, & Brawley, 2007). In addition, it has been modified for use in an exercise setting (Carron & Spink, 1992; Carron, Widmeyer, & Brawley, 1988, Study 1). Using the conceptual model of cohesion (see Figure 7.1), Estabrooks and Carron (2000) further developed a measure called the Physical Activity Group Environment Questionnaire to assess cohesion in the exercise setting. There is preliminary evidence for the utility of this questionnaire as a test of cohesion in exercise groups (Estabrooks & Carron, 2000; Watson, Martin Ginis, & Spink, 2004).

CORRELATES OF GROUP COHESION

Now that we have some sense of what cohesion is and how to go about measuring it, let us turn our attention to factors that have been associated with cohesion. A framework outlined by Carron, Hausenblas, and Eys (2005) illustrates the factors that correlate with

Figure 7.2 A general framework for examining the correlates of cohesion in sport and exercise groups

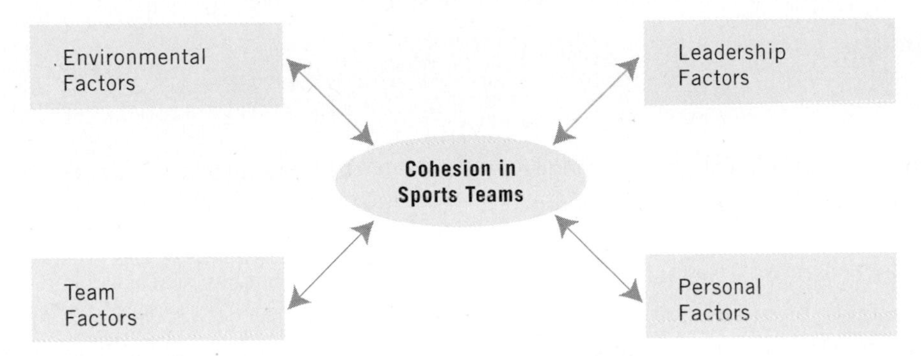

Note: From *Group Dynamics in Sport,* 3rd ed., (p. 242), by A. V. Carron, H. A. Hausenblas, and M.A. Eys, 2005, Morgantown, WV: Fitness Information Technology. Reprinted with permission.

group cohesion (see Figure 7.2). The use of the term *correlate* is intentional, given that most research in group cohesion is of a correlational nature rather than a cause-and-effect nature (see Chapter 2). In fact, it is likely that many of the relationships between cohesion and these correlates are bidirectional. For instance, it is just as likely that cohesion will influence satisfaction as it is that satisfaction will influence cohesion (Spink, Nickel, Wilson, & Odnokon, 2005). Similarly, it is equally likely that cohesion will influence intention to return to a group as intention to return will influence cohesion (Spink, 1995).

In Figure 7.2, four categories of correlates are illustrated: environmental, leadership, personal, and team factors. In this chapter, selected studies will illustrate the different factors in each category. In keeping with the intentions of Carron, Hausenblas, and Eys (2005) for the use of the framework, two caveats are worth noting. First, the four categories outlined in Figure 7.2 are not intended to be independent; that is, factors within different categories may be related. Second, the placement of factors within the categories was not intended to be absolute but was based on what was perceived to be a good fit. The factors and studies selected to illustrate the categories were chosen to give the reader a sense of what has been examined over the years and were not intended to be inclusive of all the research that has been conducted to study cohesion. Also, it is worth mentioning that the majority of the studies that will be reported involve sports. This should not be taken as a sign that cohesion is not important in exercise settings, but rather as a reflection of what appears in the literature. Relevant exercise studies are reported when they are available.

Environmental Correlates of Group Cohesion

Group Size Researchers and theoreticians alike have had a long-standing interest in the association between group size and cohesion. For the most part, an inverse relationship has emerged between cohesion and group size, both generally and specifically within sport and exercise. In terms of examining groups generally, the results of a **meta-analysis** across a wide range of groups led Mullen and Copper (1994) to conclude that the smaller the group, the greater the level of cohesion. (A meta-analysis is a literature review wherein a number of studies in an area that meet criteria specified by the researcher are quantified to allow the use of statistical techniques as a means of analysis [Glass, 1976].) This inverse relationship has been documented in both sport (Widmeyer, Brawley, & Carron, 1990) and exercise settings (Carron & Spink, 1995, Studies 1 & 2), with increases in group size being associated with decreases in task cohesion.

REFLECTIONS 7.3

Why do you think cohesion goes down as the size of the group increases? Do you think anything could be done to change this?

Specific Activity Setting Another environmental factor that has been associated with cohesion is the specific setting, or context, in which the activity occurs. As noted previously, cohesion is perceived to be multidimensional, and, as such, it might be expected that the factors that hold the group together might change across situations. Given that individuals likely come to different situations with different expectations, one might wonder whether a specific setting (context) would affect the perceptions of cohesiveness that develop. Research in the sport setting suggests that this may be the case. For example, Granito and Rainey (1988) found that high-school football players endorsed task cohesion significantly more than university football players.

The effects of context on cohesion also appear to play out in the exercise setting. In two Canadian studies in the exercise setting, the type of exercise context (i.e., university versus private fitness club) tended to moderate the relationship between cohesion and adherence to an exercise program (Carron & Spink, 1995, Studies 1 & 2). Specifically, in the university context, those attending regularly reported perceiving greater levels of task cohesion in the class than did eventual dropouts. On the other hand, in the private club context, regular attendees held greater perceptions of social cohesion than did eventual dropouts. The finding that task-cohesion factors were more salient to adherence in the university context while social-cohesion factors were more related to adherence in the private club context lends credibility to the suggestion that the specific context within the general setting may affect the type of cohesion that emerges.

REFLECTIONS 7.4

What might be different between the private club and university exercise settings that would explain why social-cohesion factors were more salient in the former and task-cohesion factors were more important in the latter?

Leadership Correlates of Group Cohesion

In sport, it might be expected that the development of cohesiveness would be associated with the behaviour of the coach. Research in the sport setting has provided abundant empirical support for the proposed association between coaching factors and cohesion across many different sports, including basketball (Pease & Kozub, 1994), football (Westre & Weiss, 1991), softball/baseball (Gardner, Shields, Bredemeier, & Bostrom, 1996), soccer (Murray, 2006), and ringette (Spink, 1998). In addition to researchers acknowledging the importance of the cohesion–leadership relationship, coaches also have recognized the importance of cohesion and their role in developing it. For instance, in one study using Canadian intercollegiate coaches, the role of the coach in developing cohesion was specifically addressed. The findings revealed that coaches clearly recognized the relationship between cohesion and performance and their important role in developing cohesion (Bloom, Stevens, & Wickmire, 2003).

Leader's Behaviour In the leadership literature, examining the relationship between specific leader behaviour patterns and such criteria as member satisfaction and performance has been very important in determining leadership effectiveness. A similar tactic has been taken when examining the association between leadership and cohesion. Leadership behaviours have been assessed primarily through the Leadership Scale for Sports (LSS) developed by Chelladurai and Saleh (1980). The LSS contains five leadership subscales, with three of them reflecting behaviours (training and instruction, social support, and positive feedback) and the remaining two reflecting decision style (autocratic style and democratic style). The behaviour subscales will be discussed in this section, and the decision style subscales will be included in the next section.

According to Chelladurai and Saleh (1980), **training and instruction** was captured in behaviours by the coach that were geared to improving the team members' performance by emphasizing and facilitating hard training; providing instruction in skills, techniques, and tactics; clarifying the relationship among team members; and structuring and coordinating the activities of the team members. **Social support**, on the other hand, involved leader behaviours that were characterized by a concern for the welfare of the individual athletes, the fostering of a positive group atmosphere, and warm relationships with team members. Finally, behaviours by the coach that reinforced an athlete by recognizing and rewarding strong performance were categorized as **positive feedback**.

In several sport studies, it has been demonstrated that coaches who were perceived to engage in training and instruction, social support, and positive feedback behaviours had teams that were both more socially cohesive (Gardner et al., 1996; Murray, 2006; Spink, 1998) and task cohesive (Jowett & Chaundy, 2004; Murray, 2006; Westre & Weiss, 1991).

Leader's Decision Style Another leader variable that has received attention in the cohesion literature is the leader's decision style. **Decision style** refers to the degree to which a leader allows participation by subordinates in decision making. Much of the research examining leaders' decision style in the sport setting has used the LSS. As noted above, the LSS includes two decision-style subscales (Chelladurai & Saleh, 1980). One is the **autocratic style**, which signifies behaviour by the leader that involves independent decision making and stresses personal authority on the part of the leader. This translates into the leader making decisions alone. The other is the **democratic style**, which signifies behaviour by the leader that allows greater participation by the athletes in decisions relating to team goals, practice methods, and game tactics and strategies. In this approach, the final decision is made jointly, with the leader having no more or no less input into the final decision than any of the team members.

There appears to be some consensus in the cohesion literature that the more democratic the leader style, the greater the tendency for cohesion to develop. This relationship has been found across several sports (Brawley, Carron, & Widmeyer, 1993; Gardner et al., 1996; Jowett & Chaundy, 2004; Westre & Weiss, 1991).

Based on the studies outlined above, it appears that the cohesion of a team is associated with specific coaching behaviours and styles. Cohesion within a team tends to be associated with coaches who allow athletes' input into team decisions, exhibit positive feedback, and provide solid instruction and training.

REFLECTIONS 7.5

It has been found consistently that higher levels of cohesion within a sport team tend to be associated with a more democratic style of leadership. Do you think a democratic style exhibited by a leader would be associated with enhanced cohesion in an exercise setting? Why?

Team-building Activities In the research reported on leadership, the focus was on studies that examined simple associations between cohesion and leadership variables. In this section, the focus will be on research in which attempts were made to use the leader to create cohesion through the implementation of team-building protocols. Before we present the research, a few terms require clarification. First, what is meant by *team building*? Although it has been defined in numerous ways, the definition by Newman (1984) forms the basis of many team-building programs in activity settings. According to Newman, **team building** refers to programs that are geared toward promoting an increased sense of team unity and cohesiveness, which then enables the team to function together more smoothly and effectively.

It is important to note that in the research presented here, the intervention created was filtered through the coach or exercise leader (cf. Carron, Spink, & Prapavessis, 1997). This is an indirect form of team building because the intervention was done through a third party; it contrasts with more direct forms of team building in which the intervention is presented directly to the team members. In direct approaches, the intervention specialist works directly with the team members to provide them with greater insight and greater independence. It is assumed that, through the contact and education, team members will become more intrinsically motivated to team-build as a result of their enhanced competence and self-determination (Carron et al., 1998). One example of a direct team-building approach is outlined by Yukelson (1997) in his description of the program run in the athletics department at Penn State University. Stevens and Bloom (2003) also described a team-building intervention that combined both a direct and an indirect approach by involving both softball coaches and their athletes. Although examples of direct (and combined) interventions are interesting and can be effective forms of team building, they will not be included here since the focus in this section of the chapter is on the relationship between leadership and cohesion. Thus, only those studies in which the coach or exercise leader is the sole delivery agent of the intervention (i.e., indirect team building) will be presented.

Canadian researchers have created and implemented a four-stage team-building model (introduction, conceptual, practical, and interventions) using the coach or exercise leader as the agent of delivery (Bruner & Spink, 2007, 2008; Carron & Spink, 1993, 1995; Prapavessis, Carron, & Spink, 1996; Spink & Carron, 1993; Watson et al., 2004). The first three stages of the team-building model occur in a workshop conducted by the team-building specialist with coaches or exercise leaders. The final stage involves the coaches or leaders going back to their team or group and implementing the team-building strategies that were formulated during the workshop.

In the first stage of the team-building model, coaches or leaders are presented with a brief overview of the benefits of cohesion to their specific setting. For instance, coaches hear about the relationship between perceptions of cohesiveness and improved team outcomes as identified in the literature (Carron, Colman, Wheeler, & Stevens, 2002). On the other hand, if exercise leaders are being addressed, they hear about the benefits associated with cohesion in specific exercise settings. For instance, if the leaders run exercise classes for older adults, they hear about the positive relationships that have been established between elderly exercisers who perceive their group as more cohesive and better exercise class attendance (Estabrooks & Carron, 1999; Watson et al., 2004).

The second stage provides a frame of reference for the participants. This is accomplished by introducing a conceptual model. In the conceptual model, cohesion within the group is viewed as an output (or product) of conditions that arise from three different categories of group characteristics. Two categories are inputs: the environment of the group and the structure of the group; and one category is a throughput: group processes. Furthermore, within each of the three categories, specific factors are identified that have previously emerged as being associated with enhanced group cohesiveness. The conceptual model that is used in the Carron and Spink (1993) team-building program in the exercise setting is presented in Figure 7.3.

Figure 7.3 Conceptual framework used as a basis for the implementation of a team-building program in exercise classes

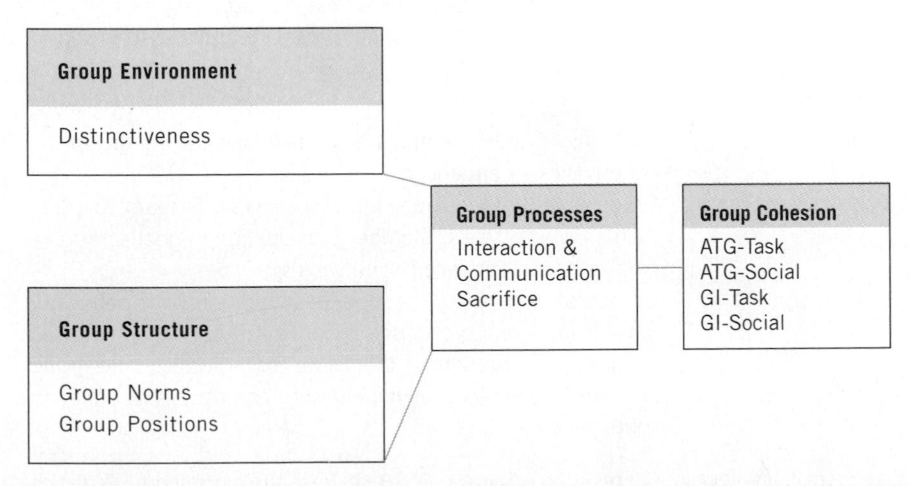

Note: From Carron A. V., & Spink, K. S. (1993). Team building in an exercise setting. *The Sport Psychologist, 7*, 11, Figure 1. © 1993 by Human Kinetics Publishers, Inc. Reprinted with permission from Human Kinetics (Champaign, IL).

As noted in Figure 7.3, distinctiveness has been identified in the group environment category as one factor to be manipulated to enhance cohesion in the exercise setting. When this is presented to the exercise leaders, they are told that when something in the group's environment is somehow made distinctive, members develop a stronger sense of "we," more readily distinguish themselves from non-members of the group, and ultimately develop stronger perceptions of cohesiveness (Carron & Spink, 1993). This procedure of presenting the leader with a research-based rationale justifying the inclusion of each factor is repeated for all factors outlined in Figure 7.3.

Although a similar conceptual model is used in the sport setting, the specific factors that are highlighted are different from those in the exercise setting, which is consistent with Brawley and Paskevich's (1997) suggestion that team-building factors may differ across situations because the importance of fundamental group processes changes across groups. As one example, under the group (or team) environment category in the sport setting (see Table 7.1), togetherness and distinctiveness are both factors to be

Table 7.1 Principles Underlying the Team-building Program in a Sport Setting

Category	Principle
Team Structure	
Role clarity and acceptance	When group members clearly understand their role in the group, cohesiveness is enhanced. When group members are satisfied and accept their roles in the group, cohesiveness is enhanced.
Leadership	Task and social cohesiveness in the group are influenced by the behaviour of the team leaders. A participative style of coaching leadership contributes to enhanced cohesiveness.
Conformity to standards	Conformity to group social and task norms contribute to enhanced cohesiveness. Group norms are highly resistant to change.
Team Environment	
Togetherness	When group members are repetitively put in close physical proximity, feelings of cohesiveness increase.
Distinctiveness	The presence of group distinctiveness contributes to group cohesiveness.
Team Processes	
Sacrifices	When high-status members make sacrifices for the group, cohesiveness is enhanced.
Goals and objectives	Group goals are more strongly associated with team success than individual goals. Member participation in goal setting contributes to enhanced cohesiveness.
Co-operation	Co-operative behaviour is superior to individualistic behaviour for individual and group performance. Co-operative behaviour is superior to competitive behaviour for individuals and group performance. Co-operative behaviour contributes to enhanced cohesiveness.

Note: From Prapavessis, H., Carron, A. V., & Spink, K. S. (1996). Team building in sport. *International Journal of Sport Psychology, 27*, p. 275. Used with permission from Edizioni Luigi Pozzi.

manipulated, whereas under the same category in the exercise setting, only distinctiveness appears.

The practical stage is the final part of the workshop. The main purpose of this stage is to have the coaches and exercise leaders become active agents in developing practical strategies that they will use in their own group settings (Carron & Spink, 1993). This is done by having them use the conceptual framework to brainstorm as many specific techniques, procedures, or protocols as possible to be used for team building in their own groups. In the case of exercise groups, the leaders are asked to use distinctiveness, norms, positions, sacrifice, and communication/interaction as frames of reference for generating their techniques. Some representative examples of the specific strategies suggested by the leaders to enhance group cohesiveness in exercise classes are presented in Table 7.2. From the lists of practical suggestions generated, each coach or leader is free to take the suggestions that he or she feels would work best.

Table 7.2 Examples of Specific Strategies Suggested by Leaders to Enhance Group Cohesiveness in Exercise Classes

Category	Examples of Specific Strategies
Group Environment	
Distinctiveness	Have a group name. Make up a group T-shirt. Hand out neon head bands and/or shoelaces.
Group Structure	
Individual positions	Have signs to label parts of the group. Use specific positions for low-, medium-, and high-impact exercisers. Let them pick their own spot and encourage them to remain in it throughout the year.
Group norms	Encourage members to become fitness friends. Establish a goal to lose weight together. Promote a smart work ethic as a group characteristic.
Group Processes	
Sacrifices	Ask two or three people for a goal for the day. Ask regulars to help new people (as fitness friends). Ask people who aren't concerned with weight loss to make a sacrifice for the group on some days (more aerobics), and ask people who are concerned with weight loss to make a sacrifice on other days (more mat work).
Interaction and communication	Use partner work and have them introduce themselves to the person on the right and left. Work in groups of five and take turns showing a move. Use more partner activities.

Note: From Carron A. V., & Spink, K. S. (1993). Team building in an exercise setting. *The Sport Psychologist, 7*, 13, Table 1.

The results supported the conclusion that reports of individual sacrifice and teammate sacrifice contributed to team task and social cohesion. In terms of specific findings, internal sacrifices made by individuals and teammates had the most powerful effect on cohesion. One can only imagine the level of cohesion that existed on the 2008 Canadian Olympic triathlon team, given the sacrifice made by Colin Jenkins for teammate Simon Whitfield. Jenkins appeared to sacrifice his final placing in the Olympics by riding and swimming very hard to allow teammate Whitfield to draft behind him and remain with the lead pack coming into the final run stage of the triathlon, which was Whitfield's strength. After racing hard for the first two legs, Jenkins had nothing left in the tank and finished last overall. However, due in part to the sacrifices of his teammate, Whitfield was able to finish with the Olympic silver medal.

Self-handicapping In terms of personal factors, it has also been found that what the individual brings to the group can affect cohesiveness. One such factor is the tendency to self-handicap. If you have ever remarked to a teammate before a big game that you may not play well because you were up all night with a cold, you may have been using a **self-handicapping** strategy. According to Jones and Berglas (1978), self-handicapping involves using strategies that protect one's self-esteem by providing excuses for forthcoming events (see Chapter 5). This is done by providing explanations wherein potential failure can be attributed to external factors (e.g., "I was up all night") rather than to internal factors (e.g., "I'm not prepared").

The relationship between team cohesiveness and self-handicapping has been examined in the sport setting (Carron, Prapavessis, & Grove, 1994; Hausenblas & Carron, 1996). In one study examining male athletes from a number of different sports, a negative relationship was found between the self-handicapping trait and perceptions of task cohesion (Carron et al., 1994). One possibility to explain this relationship might be that the self-handicapper's perception of low task cohesion might be ego protective. If the team fails, the athlete can fall back on the thought, "I'm okay, but I'm not so sure about the team." The athlete externalizes the failure by blaming the team.

The purpose of another sport study conducted by Canadian researchers was to examine whether cohesion would moderate the use of self-handicapping strategies prior to competition (Hausenblas & Carron, 1996). Studying elite male and female athletes from a number of sports, Hausenblas and Carron found that athletes who scored high on self-handicapping and who perceived their team as more cohesive had a greater tendency to make excuses (i.e., self-handicap) before competition. On the other hand, when cohesion of their team was perceived as low, no relationship was found between the self-handicapping trait and the tendency to make excuses. In the case of the self-handicapper, the tendency to make more excuses may simply reflect the fact that members on more-cohesive teams feel a greater responsibility to the group and the use of prior claims of hindrances acts like an ego-protective mechanism in case the team fails.

Team Correlates of Group Cohesion

In team correlates, the final category of correlates of group cohesion, the focus is on those factors that are associated with the team as a unit. Without doubt, the team factor that has been most associated with cohesion over the years is team outcome (team success). The assumption is that when team cohesion is strong, the group is motivated to perform well and is better able to coordinate activities that will lead to a positive team outcome (Cartwright, 1968).

Team Success Given the insight provided by researchers (Cartwright, 1968) and the claims by coaches and athletes (see earlier quotes by Brad Gushue and Michael Jordan on page 168) about the proposed association between team cohesion and team success, it may come as a surprise that the research findings in this area have been mixed. There are studies showing that greater levels of team cohesion lead to success in intercollegiate ice hockey (Ball & Carron, 1976), studies showing that lesser levels of team cohesion lead to success in international rowing teams (Lenk, 1969), and studies showing no relationship between cohesion and team success in intramural basketball teams (Melnick & Chemers, 1974).

Based on the results of a meta-analysis, Mullen and Copper (1994) concluded that a small but significant positive relationship exists between cohesion and performance across many groups and tasks. Three other specific suggestions from their analysis were the following. First, the cohesion–performance relationship was strongest when cohesion was measured as task commitment (similar to task cohesion) rather than as social cohesion. Second, the cohesion–performance relationship was stronger in real groups than in artificial groups. Third, within real groups, the link was strongest in sport teams.

Canadian researchers Carron et al. (2002) conducted a more focused meta-analysis wherein they examined the cohesion–performance relationship using only studies conducted with sport teams. Based on their analysis of 46 sport studies, they concluded that there was a moderate to large relationship between cohesion and performance. This is consistent with Mullen and Copper's (1994) suggestion that the cohesion–performance relationship is strongest in real groups, especially sport teams. In a third meta-analysis, Beal, Cohen, Burke, and McLendon (2003) also found that task and social cohesion related to performance across multiple group settings. They also reported that the relationship between cohesion and performance was stronger when performance was defined as **behaviour** (i.e., actions relevant to achieving the outcome) as opposed to **outcome** (i.e., results of behaviours).

Despite the mixed results from past research, the results from these three meta-analyses provide some strong evidence that cohesion and performance are related. Although this relationship appears to be established, one question still remains: Which is stronger, cohesion leading to performance or performance leading to cohesion?

This is an important question because it captures the essence of that age-old belief of coaches and athletes alike—having more cohesiveness will lead to more wins. Unfortunately, at the present time, the research does not support this belief. From the results of Mullen and Copper's (1994) meta-analysis, it was concluded that there was more support for success leading to cohesion than for cohesion leading to success. The results from the Carron et al. (2002) meta-analysis using only sport teams found no difference. However, the results from a qualitative analysis of English soccer teams found that players believed that strong team cohesion had a positive influence on performance (Pain & Harwood, 2007). Despite these mixed results, the fact still remains that there is some evidence that task and social cohesion are associated with better performance.

Collective Efficacy for Cohesion Performance (team success) is the team correlate that has received the most attention in the research literature; however, there are other proposed correlates of team cohesion. One such correlate is **collective efficacy**.

The term was coined by Bandura (1977) to capture the idea that groups often have collective expectations for success. There has been speculation that different properties of a group, such as cohesion, have great potential to contribute to a team's sense of efficacy (Spink, 1990a), and this has been borne out in the sport literature. In one Canadian study examining the relationship between cohesion and collective efficacy in volleyball teams, it was found that teams high in collective efficacy rated task and social cohesion higher than teams lower in collective efficacy (Spink, 1990b). Of interest, this relationship was found only for elite teams, not for recreational teams. In another study, which also examined volleyball teams in Canada, task cohesion measures differentiated between athletes who were low or high in their perception of their team's overall collective efficacy (Paskevich, Brawley, Dorsch, & Widmeyer, 1999).

Support for the relationship between cohesion and collective efficacy was also found by Kozub and McDonnell (2001) in a study involving rugby teams. They found that cohesion measures were highly associated with collective efficacy measures, with task cohesion having the strongest relationship with cohesion, thus supporting the results from the other sport studies mentioned previously (Paskevich et al., 1999; Spink, 1990b).

Psychological Momentum The "Big Mo" is another team factor that appears to be related to team cohesion. **Psychological momentum** refers to a perception on the part of team members that the team is progressing toward its goal. This definition was adapted from one posited for individual behaviour by Vallerand, Colavecchio, and Pelletier (1988). The idea that cohesion and psychological momentum might be linked is not new. In one of the first works to discuss the effect of psychological momentum in sport events, Adler (1981) suggested that perceptions of psychological momentum and cohesion are linked. He went further by suggesting that coaches in team sports should attempt to develop a perception of cohesion in order to create a team climate favourable to momentum.

In the only test of this possible relationship in the sport setting, the relationship between perceptions of task cohesion and psychological momentum in high-school volleyball teams was examined (Eisler & Spink, 1998). Results revealed that members of highly cohesive teams rated their team as possessing more psychological momentum than did the members of teams perceived as less cohesive. This finding supports Adler's (1981) contention that the development of cohesion creates a climate favourable to the perception of psychological momentum.

Athlete's Starting Status Another team factor linked to cohesion is the impact of an athlete's starting status. In one of the first studies to examine this relationship, Granito and Rainey (1988) found that players at both the high-school and college levels who were selected to start games scored higher on measures of task cohesion than players who were not selected to start. In an extension of this result, an examination was undertaken of the perceived cohesion levels of starters and non-starters on less successful and more successful Canadian volleyball teams (Spink, 1992). Results revealed that starters perceived more task cohesion on their team than did non-starters, which supports the Granito and Rainey (1988) result. However, this occurred only on teams that were less successful. On teams that were more successful, there were no differences in the levels of perceived cohesion between the starters and non-starters. From the results of this study, it appears that team success might serve to ameliorate the possible negative impact of not starting and help to maintain task cohesion.

REFLECTIONS 7.9

Spink (1992) found that it was only on less-successful teams that starters and non-starters differed in their perceptions of team cohesion. Do you think this finding has any implications for the examination of the cohesion–success relationship? Explain how.

Photograph © Feng Li/Getty Images

GROUP COHESION AS A MEDIATOR

Mediators are mechanisms that account for the effect of one variable on another variable. There has been a call by theoreticians for more research examining group-level mediators, such as cohesion, to help understand important relationships (Baron & Kenny, 1986). Since that call, examples have appeared in the literature that illustrate that cohesion does, in fact, act as a mediator in a number of important relationships.

We have already come across one important example of cohesion acting as a mediator, and that involved team-building research. As you will recall, in the Carron and Spink (1993) team-building model, it was stated that team building impacts adherence through the mechanism of cohesion. Although initial research established a relationship between team building and cohesion (Carron & Spink, 1993), this has now been extended to include the actual team-building processes used in the model (see Case Study 7.1).

In another study in the sport setting, the researcher examined whether social cohesion would mediate the relationship between leadership behaviour and intention to return to sport (Spink, 1998). Using female ringette players, it was found that specific forms of leadership behaviour (i.e., training and instruction) predicted who intended to return to the sport the next season, but the effect was minimized when social cohesion was added to the prediction. The fact that the relationship between leadership and intention to return disappeared when social cohesion was entered suggests that social cohesion was the mechanism through which leadership behaviour was affecting intention to return (see Figure 7.4).

Two studies by Canadian researchers in the exercise setting provide further support for cohesion as an important mediator. The first study revealed that task cohesion mediated the relationship between an exercise leader's behaviours (i.e., availability, motivation, and enthusiasm) and both attendance and perceived exertion in older adult exercisers (Loughead, Colman, & Carron, 2001). This suggests that exercise leaders need to engage in availability, motivation, and enthusiasm to increase the group's task cohesion, which, in turn, will improve the attendance and perceived exertion of older exercisers.

Case Study 7.1

Evaluating Cohesion as the Mediator in a Team-building Intervention in the Exercise Setting

As mentioned previously, within the three distinct categories (structure, environment, and processes) in the Carron and Spink (1993) team-building conceptual model, there are a number of attendant factors that have been identified as contributing to the enhancement of cohesion within an exercise setting. These include highlighting group distinctiveness (group environment), fostering group norms and individual positions (group structure), and increasing communication/interaction and individual sacrifices (group processes). While each of the five team-building factors identified above have been viewed as contributing collectively to the cohesion of a group, the effect of these factors themselves on cohesion (i.e., the mediator on the intervention targets) had not been evaluated.

To address this issue, a study was conducted to examine whether targeted team-building factors would differentiate participants in team-building and control groups (Bruner & Spink, 2007). To do this, a group-based activity intervention designed for high-school students was conducted. The intervention was comprised of high-school physical activity clubs that were created to run outside of regular school hours. The schools were randomly assigned to either a team-building or control condition. In the team-building condition, trained teachers implemented a team-building protocol focused on the five factors of group distinctiveness, individual positions, group norms, communication/interaction, and individual sacrifices identified in the Carron and Spink (1993) team-building model.

Results revealed that the team-building factors manipulated in the model significantly differentiated the team-building groups from control groups. Further analysis revealed that the five manipulated team-building factors collectively contributed to the prediction of the proposed mechanism of task cohesion after controlling for group membership and baseline levels of task cohesion.

The second study examined whether task cohesion would mediate the relationship between fitness leader behaviours and an exerciser's affective state (Loughead, Patterson, & Carron, 2008). Results revealed that task cohesion mediated the relationship between the leader behaviour of task interaction and both the positive and negative affect experienced by the participant. The results from these three studies suggest that cohesion can be an important mechanism in mediating important relationships in the sport and exercise settings.

Figure 7.4 Proposed mediation model

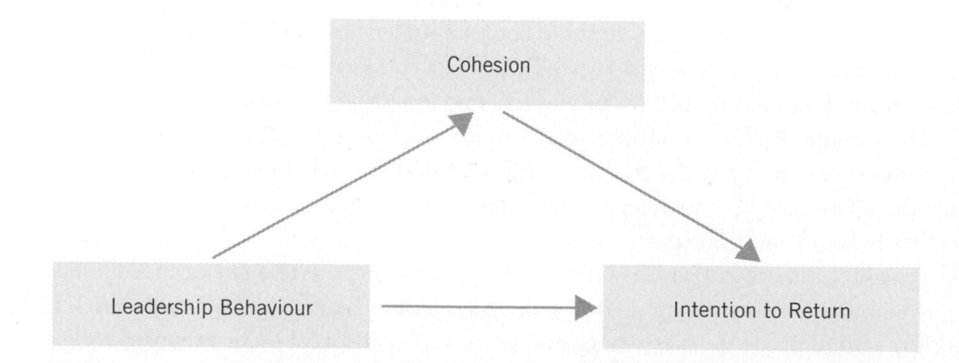

REFLECTIONS 7.10

Cohesion has been identified as a possible mediator in the relationship between leadership and both adherence and affective measures. Identify two other relationships in which you think cohesion might act as a mediator.

CHAPTER SUMMARY

After reading this chapter, it should be quite clear that a team is much more than the sum of its individual members and that there are a number of group processes associated with the effectiveness of a team. It also should be clear why team cohesion is often portrayed as the key group element that is associated with many factors that are of consequence to the group and the individual. Also, the importance of understanding cohesion goes well beyond examining its relationship to team performance. There is still much more to understand about cohesion as it relates to sport and physical activity, so more research is needed. In particular, one area that seems to be missing concerns the examination of gender differences. As males and females may have different reasons for joining a team or an exercise group, it is possible that this might translate into differences in perceptions of cohesion. This awaits future research. Despite the need for more research, several points about group cohesion have strong support within the research community. Cohesion has moved from being viewed as a unidimensional construct to being viewed as a multidimensional construct that incorporates at least two dimensions: the individual/group orientation and a task/social distinction. To assess cohesion in the sport setting, the Group Environment Questionnaire is the instrument of choice. The research literature is replete with examples demonstrating that cohesion is related to a number of important environmental, leadership, personal, and team factors. There is also evidence that team-building strategies implemented by exercise leaders or coaches can enhance cohesion in both the exercise and sport setting.

Although it is typically believed by coaches and athletes that cohesion will increase team success, this is not fully supported in the research literature; however, the fact remains that there is some evidence that task and social cohesion contribute to better performance. There is also emerging evidence that cohesion can be used to account for other important relationships. For instance, some research has demonstrated that cohesion is one mechanism to explain why various leadership behaviours may be related to a number of important outcomes, including attendance, intention to return, perceived exertion, and affective states.

Common Myths about Group Cohesion in Sport and Exercise Revisited

MYTH: Team harmony is required for cohesion to develop.

For many coaches, team harmony is synonymous with team cohesion. Conversely, they see slim chances of cohesion developing within a team if there is any form of intrateam conflict.

Although this has a nice intuitive feel, research suggests otherwise. As an example, a study by Sullivan and Feltz (2001) with ice hockey teams revealed that negative (destructive) intrateam conflict was associated with lower cohesion but that positive (constructive) intrateam conflict was associated with higher team cohesion.

MYTH: There is no "I" in team.

The standard locker-room fare of "there is no 'I' in team" makes good press, but it does not hold up well in the scientific literature. This statement implies that members of a group are generally less important than the group as a collective; however, there is little scientific evidence to support this contention. It is generally accepted by the scientific community that cohesion is a multidimensional construct that incorporates both group and individual components (Carron, Widmeyer, & Brawley, 1985). Individuals join and remain in groups for many reasons, and it has been acknowledged that the cognitions that individuals hold about the cohesiveness of their team reflect the overall group as well as the manner in which the group satisfies individual needs (Carron, Brawley, & Widmeyer, 1998), suggesting that the needs and wants of the individual must be recognized when one examines group cohesion.

MYTH: High cohesion is always a good thing.

There is an old saying that "if a little is good, then more is better." For many people, this saying certainly applies to cohesion since there is a general understanding among lay people that a team and its members glean more benefits as the cohesiveness of the group increases. While it would make life simpler for those who wanted to use the power of group closeness to increase benefits to the team and individuals alike, research suggests that there might be disadvantages to being in a highly cohesive group. In one study examining the consequences of high levels of cohesiveness in sports teams, 56% of the athletes questioned reported possible disadvantages associated with social cohesion, and 31% reported possible disadvantages associated with being on a team high in task cohesion (Hardy, Eys, & Carron, 2005).

Review Questions

1. Why is it important to study groups?
2. What is the definition of *group dynamics*?
3. What are three suggestions for improving team communication?
4. What is the definition of *groupthink*? How might groupthink hinder the performance of a group?
5. What are the main differences between the two definitions of cohesion advanced by Bert Carron?
6. Identify the four key characteristics of cohesion.
7. Identify and briefly describe the sport-specific questionnaires that have been used to assess cohesion. Which is the most useful one, and why?
8. Briefly outline the conceptual model of group cohesion.
9. What is the main difference between direct and indirect team-building procedures? Which approach would you use if you were trying to enhance cohesion in a basketball team? Why?

10. Outline the four stages in the team-building model.
11. Identify and briefly explain the relationship between cohesion and the six personal correlates.
12. Identify and describe two relationships in which cohesion has been examined as a mediator.

Suggested Reading

Carron, A. V., Hausenblas, H. A., & Eys, M. A. (2005). *Group dynamics in sport* (3rd ed.). Morgantown, WV: Fitness Information Technology.

Carron, A. V., Spink, K. S., & Prapavessis, H. (1997). Team building and cohesiveness in the sport and exercise setting: Use of indirect interventions. *Journal of Applied Sport Psychology*, 9, 61–72.

References

Adler, P. (1981). *Momentum: A theory of social action*. Beverly Hills, CA: Sage.

Ball, J. R., & Carron, A. V. (1976). The influence of team cohesion and participation motivation upon performance success in intercollegiate ice hockey. *Canadian Journal of Applied Sport Sciences*, *1*, 271–275.

Bandura, A. (1977). Self-efficacy: Toward a unifying theory of behavioural change. *Psychological Review*, *84*, 191–215.

Baron, R. M., & Kenny, D. A. (1986). The moderator-mediator variable distinction in social psychological research: Conceptual, strategic, and statistical considerations. *Journal of Personality & Social Psychology*, *51*, 1173–1182.

Beal, D. J., Cohen, R., Burke, M. J., & McLendon, C. L. (2003). Cohesion and performance in groups: A meta-analytic clarification of construct relations. *Journal of Applied Psychology*, *88*, 989–1004.

Bloom, G. A., Stevens, D. E., & Wickmire, T. L. (2003). Expert coaches' perceptions of team building. *Journal of Applied Sport Psychology*, *15*, 129–143.

Brawley, L. R., Carron, A. V., & Widmeyer, W. N. (1993). The influence of the group and its cohesiveness on perceptions of group-related variables. *Journal of Sport & Exercise Psychology*, *15*, 245–260.

Brawley, L. R., & Paskevich, D. M. (1997). Conducting team building research in the context of sport and exercise. *Journal of Applied Sport Psychology*, 9, 11–40.

Bray, C. D., & Whaley, D. E. (2001). Team cohesion, effort, and objective individual performance of high school basketball players. *The Sport Psychologist*, *15*, 260–275.

Bruner, M., & Spink, K. S. (2007). The effects of team building on the adherence patterns of youth exercise participants. *Journal of Sport & Exercise Psychology*, *29*, 149.

Bruner, M., & Spink, K. S. (2008). Examining the effects of team building on group task satisfaction in a youth setting. *Journal of Sport & Exercise Psychology*, *30*, 156.

Carron, A. V. (1982). Cohesiveness in sport groups: Interpretations and considerations. *Journal of Sport Psychology*, *4*, 123–138.

Carron, A. V., Brawley, L. R., & Widmeyer, W. N. (1998). The measurement of cohesiveness in sport groups. In J. L. Duda (Ed.), *Advancements in sport and exercise psychology measurement* (pp. 213–226). Morgantown, WV: Fitness Information Technology.

Carron, A. V., Colman, M. M., Wheeler, J., & Stevens, D. (2002). Cohesion and performance in sport: A meta-analysis. *Journal of Sport & Exercise Psychology*, *24*, 168–188.

Carron, A. V., Hausenblas, H. A., & Eys, M. A. (2005). *Group dynamics in sport* (3rd ed.). Morgantown, WV: Fitness Information Technology.

Carron, A. V., Prapavessis, H., & Grove, J. R. (1994). Group effects and self-handicapping. *Journal of Sport & Exercise Psychology*, *16*, 246–258.

Carron, A. V., & Spink, K. S. (1992). Internal consistency of the Group Environment Questionnaire modified for an exercise setting. *Perceptual and Motor Skills, 74*, 1075–1078.

Carron, A. V., & Spink, K. S. (1993). Team building in an exercise setting. *The Sport Psychologist, 7*, 8–18.

Carron, A. V., & Spink, K. S. (1995). The group size-cohesion relationship in exercise groups. *Small Group Research, 26*, 86–105.

Carron, A. V., Spink, K. S., & Prapavessis, H. (1997). Team building and cohesiveness in the sport and exercise setting: Use of indirect interventions. *Journal of Applied Sport Psychology, 9*, 61–72.

Carron, A. V., Widmeyer, W. N., & Brawley, L. R. (1985). The development of an instrument to assess cohesion in sport teams: The Group Environment Questionnaire. *Journal of Sport Psychology, 7*, 244–266.

Carron, A. V., Widmeyer, W. N., & Brawley, L. R. (1988). Group cohesion and individual adherence to physical activity. *Journal of Sport & Exercise Psychology, 10*, 119–126.

Cartwright, D. (1968). The nature of group cohesiveness. In D. Cartwright, & A. Zander (Eds.), *Group dynamics: Research and theory* (pp. 91–109). New York: Harper & Row.

Cartwright, D., & Zander, A. (1968). *Group dynamics: Research and theory*. New York: Harper & Row.

Chelladurai, P., & Saleh, S. D. (1980). Dimensions of leadership behaviour in sport: Development of a leadership scale. *Journal of Sport Psychology, 2*, 34–45.

Cota, A. A., Evans, C. R., Dion, K. L., Kilik, L., & Longman, R. S. (1995). The structure of group cohesion. *Personality and Social Psychological Bulletin, 21*, 572–580.

Dawson, K. A., Bray, S. R., & Widmeyer, W. N. (2002). Goal setting by intercollegiate sport teams and athletes. *Avante, 8*, 14–23.

Eisler, L., & Spink, K. S. (1998). Effects of scoring configuration and task cohesion on the perception of psychological momentum. *Journal of Sport & Exercise Psychology, 20*, 311–320.

Estabrooks, P. A., & Carron, A. V. (1999). Group cohesion in older adult exercisers: Prediction and intervention effects. *Journal of Behavioral Medicine, 22*, 575–588.

Estabrooks, P. A., & Carron, A. V. (2000). The Physical Activity Group Environment Questionnaire: An instrument for the assessment of cohesion in exercise classes. *Group Dynamics, 4*, 230–243.

Eys, M. A., Carron, A. V., Bray, S. R., & Brawley, L. R. (2007). Item wording and internal consistency of a measure of cohesion: The Group Environment Questionnaire. *Journal of Sport & Exercise Psychology, 29*, 395–402.

Festinger, L. (1950). Informal social communication. *Psychological Review, 57*, 271–282.

Fiedler, F. E. (1954). Assumed similarity measures as predictors of team effectiveness. *Journal of Abnormal and Social Psychology, 49*, 381–388.

Fraser, S., & Spink, K. S. (2002). Examining social support and group cohesion in the compliance behaviour of females in a health-related exercise setting. *Journal of Behavioral Medicine, 25*, 233–249.

Gardner, D. E., Shields, D. L., Bredemeier, B. J., & Bostrom, A. (1996). The relationship between perceived coaching behaviours and team cohesion among baseball and softball players. *The Sport Psychologist, 10*, 367–381.

Glass, G. V. (1976). Primary, secondary, and meta-analysis. *Educational Researcher, 5*, 3–8.

Granito, V. J., & Rainey, D. W. (1988). Differences in cohesion between high school and college football teams and starters and nonstarters. *Perceptual and Motor Skills, 66*, 471–477.

Hardy, J., Eys, M. A., & Carron, A. V. (2005). Exploring the potential disadvantages of high cohesion in sports teams. *Small Group Research, 36*, 166–187.

Hastie, R., & Kameda, T. (2005). The robust beauty of majority rules in group decisions. *Psychological Review, 112*, 494–508.

Hausenblas, H. A., & Carron, A. V. (1996). Group cohesion and self-handicapping in female and male athletes. *Journal of Sport & Exercise Psychology, 18*, 132–143.

Hoigaard, R., Safvenbom, R., & Tonnessen, F. E. (2006). The relationship between group cohesion, group norms, and perceived social loafing in soccer teams. *Small Group Research, 37*, 217–232.

Holt, N. L., & Sparkes, A. C. (2001). An ethnographic study of cohesiveness in a college soccer team over a season. *The Sport Psychologist, 15*, 237–259.

Janis, I. (2007). Groupthink. In R. P. Vecchio (Ed.), *Leadership: Understanding the dynamics of power and influence in organizations* (2nd ed., pp. 157–169). Notre Dame, IN: University of Notre Dame Press.

Jones, E. E., & Berglas, S. (1978). Control of attributions about the self through self-handicapping strategies: The appeal of alcohol and the role of underachievement. *Personality and Social Psychology Bulletin, 4*, 200–206.

Jordan, M. (1994). *I can't accept not trying*. San Francisco: Harper.

Jowett, S., & Chaundy, V. (2004). An investigation into the impact of coach leadership and coach-athlete relationships on group cohesion. *Groups Dynamics*, 8, 302–311.

Karau, S. J., & Williams, K. D. (1993). Social loafing: A meta-analytic review and theoretical integration. *Journal of Personality and Social Psychology, 65*, 681–706.

Klein, M., & Christiansen, G. (1969). Group composition, group structure and group effectiveness of basketball teams. In J. W. Loy, & G. S. Kenyon (Eds.), *Sport, culture and society* (pp. 397–408). New York: Macmillan.

Kozub, S. A., & McDonnell, J. F. (2001). Exploring the relationship between cohesion and collective efficacy in rugby teams. *Journal of Sport Behavior, 23*, 120–129.

Latane, B., Williams, K., & Harkins, S. (1979). Many hands make light the work: The causes and consequences of social loafing. *Journal of Personality and Social Psychology, 37*, 822–832.

Locke, E. A., & Latham, G. P. (1984). *Goal setting: A motivational technique that works*. Englewood Cliffs, NJ: Prentice Hall.

Lenk, H. (1969). Top performance despite internal conflict: An antithesis to a functional proposition. In J. W. Loy, & G. S. Kenyon (Eds.), *Sport, culture and society* (pp. 393–397). New York: Macmillan.

Lott, A. J., & Lott, B. E. (1965). Group cohesiveness as interpersonal attraction: A review of relationships with antecedent and consequent variables. *Psychological Bulletin, 64*, 259–309.

Loughead, T. M., Colman, M. M., & Carron, A. V. (2001). Investigating the mediational relationship of leadership, class cohesion and adherence in an exercise setting. *Small Group Research, 32*, 558–575.

Loughead, T. M., Patterson, M. M., & Carron, A. V. (2008). The impact of fitness leader behavior and cohesion on an exerciser's affective state. *International Journal of Sport and Exercise Psychology*, 6, 53–68.

Maki, A. (2009, March 7). Gushue's rock group unites. CTV Vancouver 2010. Retrieved April 13, 2009, from http://www.ctvolympics.ca/curling/news/newsid=6631.html

Martens, R., Landers, D. M., & Loy, J. W. (1972). *Sport cohesiveness questionnaire*. Washington, DC: AAHPERD Publications.

McGrath, J. E. (1962). The influence of positive interpersonal relations on adjustment and effectiveness in rifle teams. *Journal of Abnormal and Social Psychology*, 65, 365–375.

McKnight, P., Williams, J. M., & Widmeyer, W. N. (1991, October). *The effects of cohesion and identifiability on reducing the likelihood of social loafing*. Paper presented at the annual conference of the Association for the Advancement of Applied Sport Psychology, Savannah, GA.

Melnick, M. J., & Chemers, M. (1974). Effects of group social structure on the success of basketball teams. *Research Quarterly, 45*, 1–8.

Mudrack, P. E. (1989). Defining group cohesiveness. A legacy of confusion? *Small Group Behavior, 20*, 37–49.

Mullen, B., & Copper, C. (1994). The relation between group cohesiveness and performance: An integration. *Psychological Bulletin, 115*, 210–227.

Murray, N. P. (2006). The differential effect of team cohesion and leadership behavior in high school sports. *Individual Differences Research, 4*, 216–222.

Myers, A. (1962). Team competition, success and adjustment of team members. *Journal of Abnormal and Social Psychology, 65*, 325–332.

Newin, J., Bloom, G. A., & Loughead, T. M. (2008). Youth ice hockey coaches' perceptions of a team-building intervention program. *The Sport Psychologist, 22*, 54–72.

Newman, B. (1984). Expediency as benefactor: How team building saves times and gets the job done. *Training and Development Journal, 38*, 26–30.

Pain, M. A., & Harwood, C. (2007). The performance environment of the England youth soccer teams. *Journal of Sports Sciences, 25*, 1307–1324.

Paskevich, D. M., Brawley, L. R., Dorsch, L. R., & Widmeyer, W. N. (1999). Relationships between collective efficacy and team measurement factors. *Group Dynamics, 3*, 210–222.

Pease, D. G., & Kozub, S. A. (1994). Perceived coaching behaviours and team cohesion in high school girls basketball team. *Journal of Sport & Exercise Psychology, 16*, S93.

Prapavessis, H., & Carron, A. V. (1997a). Cohesion and work output. *Small Group Research, 28*, 294–301.

Prapavessis, H., & Carron, A. V. (1997b). Sacrifice, cohesion, and conformity to norms in sport teams. *Group Dynamics, 1*, 231–240.

Prapavessis, H., Carron, A. V., & Spink, K. S. (1996). Team building in sport. *International Journal of Sport Psychology, 27*, 269–285.

Riemer, H. A., & Chelladurai, P. (1998). Development of the Athletic Satisfaction Questionnaire (ASQ). *Journal of Sport & Exercise Psychology, 20*, 127–156.

Rosenberg, S., Erlick, D., & Berkowitz, L. (1955). Some effects of varying combinations of group members on group performance measures and leadership behaviors. *Journal of Abnormal and Social Psychology, 51*, 195–203.

Schinke, R. J., Draper, S. P., & Salmela, J. H. (1997). A conceptualization of team building in high performance sport as a season-long process. *Avante, 3*, 57–72.

Senecal, J., Loughead, T. M., & Bloom, G. A. (2008). A season-long team-building intervention: Examining the effect of team goal setting on cohesion. *Journal of Sport & Exercise Psychology, 30*, 186–199.

Shaw, M. E. (1976). *Group dynamics: The psychology of small group behaviour*. New York: McGraw-Hill.

Spink, K. S. (1990a). Collective efficacy in the sport setting. *International Journal of Sport Psychology, 21*, 380–393.

Spink, K. S. (1990b). Group cohesion and collective efficacy in volleyball teams. *Journal of Sport & Exercise Psychology, 12*, 301–311.

Spink, K. S. (1992). Group cohesion and starting status in successful and less successful elite volleyball teams. *Journal of Sports Sciences, 10*, 379–388.

Spink, K. S. (1995). Cohesion and intention to participate of female sport team athletes. *Journal of Sport & Exercise Psychology, 17*, 416–427.

Spink, K. S. (1998). Mediational effects of social cohesion on the leadership-intention to return relationship in sport. *Group Dynamics, 2*, 92–100.

Spink, K. S., & Carron, A. V. (1992). Group cohesion and adherence in exercise classes. *Journal of Sport & Exercise Psychology, 14*, 78–86.

Spink, K. S., & Carron, A. V. (1993). The effects of team building on the adherence patterns of female exercise participants. *Journal of Sport & Exercise Psychology, 15*, 39–49.

Spink, K. S., & Carron, A. V. (1994). Group cohesion effects in exercise classes. *Small Group Research, 25*, 26–42.

Spink, K. S., Nickel, D., Wilson, K., & Odnokon, P. (2005). Examining the relationship between task cohesion and team task satisfaction in elite ice hockey players: A multilevel approach. *Small Group Research, 36*, 539–554.

Spink, K. S., & Odnokon, P. (2001a). Examining the effect of team cohesion on male ice hockey players' intention to return. *Journal of Sport & Exercise Psychology, 23*, S33.

Spink, K. S., & Odnokon, P. (2001b). Effects of team cohesion on male athletes' perceived effort. *Journal of Sport & Exercise Psychology, 23*, S32.

Steers, R., & Rhodes, S. (1978). Major influences of employee attendance: A process model. *Journal of Applied Psychology, 63*, 391–407.

Stevens, D. E., & Bloom, G. A. (2003). The effect of team building on cohesion. Avante, 9, 43–54.

Sullivan, P., & Feltz, D. (2001). The relationship between intrateam conflict and cohesion within hockey teams. *Small Group Research, 32*, 342–355.

Sullivan, P., & Feltz, D. L. (2003). The preliminary development of the Scale for Effective Communication in Team Sports (SECTS). *Journal of Applied Social Psychology, 33*, 1693–1715.

Sullivan, P., & Gee, C. J. (2007). The relationship between athletic satisfaction and intrateam communication. *Group Dynamics: Theory, Research, and Practice, 11*, 107–116.

Vallerand, R. J., Colavecchio, P. G., & Pelletier, L. G. (1988). Psychological momentum and performance inferences: A preliminary test of the antecedents-consequences psychological momentum model. *Journal of Sport & Exercise Psychology, 10*, 92–108.

Van Raalte, J. L., Cornelius, A. E., Linder, D. E., & Brewer, B. W. (2007). The relationship between hazing and team cohesion. *Journal of Sport Behavior, 30*, 491–507.

Watson, J. D., Martin Ginis, K. A., & Spink, K. S. (2004). Team building in an exercise class for the elderly. *Activities, Adapation, & Aging, 28*, 35–47.

Westre, K. R., & Weiss, M. R. (1991). The relationship between perceived coaching behaviors and group cohesion in high school football teams. *The Sport Psychologist, 5*, 41–54.

Widmeyer, W. N., Brawley, L. R., & Carron, A. V. (1990). The effects of group size in sport. *Journal of Sport & Exercise Psychology, 12*, 177–190.

Williams, K. D., Nida, S. A., Baca, L. D., & Latane, B. (1989). Social loafing and swimming: Effects of identifiability on individual and relay performance of intercollegiate swimmers. *Basic and Applied Social Psychology, 10*, 73–81.

Yukelson, D. (1997). Principles of effective team building interventions in sport: A direct services approach at Penn State University. *Journal of Applied Sport Psychology, 9*, 73–96.

Zander, A. (1971). *Motives and goals in groups*. New York: Academic Press.

Chapter 8

Aggression and Moral Behaviour in Sport

Todd M. Loughead
Kim D. Dorsch

Chapter Objectives

After reading this chapter, you should be able to do the following:

1 Explain how moral behaviour develops and what its impact is in sport.
2 Discuss the factors that influence the development of moral behaviours.
3 Define aggression and differentiate it from other terms, such as *assertion* and *violence*.
4 Discuss key theories useful for understanding why people behave aggressively.
5 Outline how some of the personal, situational, and group factors influence aggressive behaviour.
6 Understand the consequences of aggressive behaviour on athletes and spectators.
7 Discuss ways to reduce aggressive behaviour in sport.

On March 8, 2004, the Colorado Avalanche of the NHL played the Vancouver Canucks. Late in the third period, Todd Bertuzzi of Vancouver followed Steve Moore of Colorado around the ice attempting to engage the latter in a fight. Moore ignored the advances made by Bertuzzi. Finally, Bertuzzi grabbed Moore's jersey from behind and punched Moore to the side of the head. As Moore fell to the ice, Bertuzzi and other players from both teams landed on top of Moore. Once the players were removed from the pile, Moore remained lying on the ice for several minutes until he was removed with the help of a stretcher. As a result of this brutal incident, Moore suffered three fractured vertebrae in his neck, a severe concussion, vertebral ligament damage, nerve damage, and facial cuts. To date, Moore has not appeared in another professional hockey game. For his actions, Bertuzzi was suspended indefinitely by the NHL. He was later reinstated after sitting out 20 games. On June 24, 2004, the criminal justice branch of the British Columbia Ministry of the Attorney General announced that Bertuzzi was formally charged with assault causing bodily harm. On December 22, 2004, Bertuzzi pleaded guilty to the assault charge after arranging a plea bargain with prosecutors. He was given a conditional discharge and one year's probation. During sentencing, Bertuzzi said in a pre-recorded video statement that was played in court, "I made a terrible mistake that I wish I could take back. I crossed the line that professional hockey players, like anyone else, should never cross" (Girard, 2004, p. A01). In another video statement released to the media, Bertuzzi said that "what happened that night in March is not who I am. One thing I want to do for the game is to let everyone know how important it is to respect the limits of what can be tolerated. Those of us who play the game at all levels—professional and amateur—never do anything intended to cause each other serious bodily harm. When we do that, it's not hockey" (Girard, 2004, p. A01).

The incident described above is one of many that can occur in ice hockey. But acts of aggression have also tarnished sports other than hockey. In baseball, we often see bench-clearing brawls, brush-back pitches, or deliberate "beanings" of hitters. In basketball, elbows are thrown and players assault their coaches. For example, Latrell Sprewell of the Golden State Warriors in the NBA allegedly choked his coach, P.J. Carlesimo. Basketball players also get into altercations with fans; Ron Artest, then of the Indiana Pacers, was banned for the 2004/05 season for attacking a fan who reportedly threw a beverage on him during a game. Aggressive behaviours occur so often in sport that Russell (1993) suggested that "outside of wartime, sports is perhaps the only setting in which acts of interpersonal aggression are not only tolerated but enthusiastically applauded by large segments of society" (p. 191).

There are also aggressive behaviours in individual sports, such as tennis. An extremely aggressive act in tennis occurred in April of 1993 when a fan stabbed Monica Seles, who was then ranked number one in women's play. The fan did it because he wanted Steffi Graf to regain her number one ranking. Then, approximately eight months later, an assailant struck figure skater Nancy Kerrigan, a 1992 Olympic bronze medalist, on the knee just before the 1994 Winter Olympic Games. Also, consider the incident that occurred during the men's marathon in the 2004 Summer Olympic Games held in Athens, Greece. With only 5 km to go, a spectator grabbed the leader of the race, Vanderlei de Lima of Brazil, and pulled him into the crowd. Even though other spectators rescued de Lima, he lost valuable time and was slightly injured, but still managed to win the bronze medal.

Common Myths about Aggression and Moral Behaviour in Sport

MYTH: Aggression in sport is a good characteristic. It is something to be encouraged in players.

MYTH: Aggression is only a physical behaviour.

MYTH: Athletes are born with certain moral behaviours.

MYTH: Participating in physical sports will decrease the desire to behave aggressively.

INTRODUCTION

It is because we hear and see incidents such as those described at the beginning of the chapter that we need to become aware of aggression and moral behaviour in sport. We need to become aware of what aggression is, why it occurs, what some of the factors are, such as morality, that may cause people to behave aggressively, and, perhaps most importantly, what we can do to try to change these behaviours. In this chapter, we will address these issues with respect to aggression and moral behaviour in sport.

It is common for people to say that sport builds character and helps develop moral values. This notion is based on the belief that sport provides opportunity for its participants to learn how to co-operate with teammates, develop self-control, and play fair (Shields & Bredemeier, 1995). A great example of this occurred when Central Washington University played against Western Oregon University in intercollegiate softball. On April 26, 2008, Sara Tucholsky hit her first-ever collegiate home run. Overjoyed by the occasion, Tucholsky missed first base, and when she turned back to touch it, her knee gave out and she suffered a torn anterior cruciate ligament (ACL), rendering her unable to touch the remaining bases and having her first home run turn into a single. However, two players from Central Washington University asked if they could carry the injured player around the bases. In a remarkable display of sportspersonship, Mallory Holtman and Liz Wallace lifted Tucholsky and carried her from base to base, allowing her to touch each base with her foot.

DEVELOPMENT OF MORAL CHARACTER

How can we explain the behaviour of Mallory Holtman and Liz Wallace? While there are diverging perspectives about how an athlete's character develops, two distinct perspectives are the most widely accepted: structural-developmental and social learning.

Structural-developmental Perspective

Structural-developmental theorists (e.g., Haan, 1991; Kohlberg, 1984) view **moral development** as the change in reasoning patterns that are related to a person's cognitive growth and development. Lawrence Kohlberg (1984) suggested that in contrast to Piaget's theory of cognitive development, moral reasoning develops and progresses well into adulthood. Based on his testing through interviews using hypothetical moral dilemma scenarios, Kohlberg arrived at six developmental stages of moral judgment, grouped into three levels. The first level was labelled as pre-conventional morality, in which children abide by rules in fear of punishment

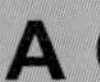

(stage 1) or in hopes of receiving rewards (stage 2). The second level is conventional morality, whereby individuals will conform to avoid disapproval of others (stage 3) and will uphold laws and social rules (stage 4). The final level, post-conventional morality, is established as individuals' moral reasoning is no longer confined by the strict boundaries of rules. That is, actions are guided by principles commonly agreed on as being essential (stage 5), and these actions are self-selected and guided by ethical principles (stage 6). According to Kohlberg, the majority of people, including athletes, will never progress beyond the second level, and less than 10% of individuals display stage 6 moral reasoning.

Social Learning Perspective

The social learning perspective maintains that **moral behaviour**—the carrying out of an action that is deemed right or wrong—is learned through the processes of reinforcement and modelling. This perspective would then suggest that participation in sport teaches and/or reinforces sportspersonship behaviours. In fact, some people argue that athletes tend to be more unsportspersonlike than their non-athlete counterparts, and that sports which contain physical contact (e.g., hockey, football) negatively impact an athlete's moral reasoning (Bloom & Smith, 1996). On the one hand, Beller and Stoll (1995) found that non-athletes in high school had higher moral reasoning scores than did athletes in high school. On the other hand, Wandzilak, Carroll, and Ansorge (1988) conducted a season-long intervention with 20 male junior high-school basketball players and found improved moral reasoning and sportspersonship behaviours when the players were positively reinforced for all sportspersonlike behaviours and sanctioned for any unsportspersonlike behaviours.

So, how can we explain the differences in the research findings? The following section will examine some of the factors that influence, or shape, our moral behaviours.

FACTORS INFLUENCING MORAL BEHAVIOUR

Sport Environment

The sport environment is an important context in which moral behaviours can be developed by providing opportunities for moral practice and development (Arnold, 2001). Sport enables individuals to learn rules and appropriate conduct of fair play. According to Meakin (1981), sport can act as an environment where moral behaviours can flourish by the promotion of co-operation, team loyalty, fair play, respect for opponents, and perseverance when faced with adversity. Meakin also points out that sport can have the opposite effect, whereby negative influences such as the opportunity for unfair play, illegitimate aggression, and intimidation can also present themselves to athletes.

Treasure (2002) suggested that the type of coaching impacts an athlete's moral development. A coach can prohibit acts that disrespect or violate rules and encourage conduct that demonstrates respect and fair play. In addition, being a positive role model for athletes can help promote positive moral behaviour development. Athletes who learn morally appropriate behaviours in sport are more likely to transfer these positive behaviours to other activities and aspects outside the sporting environment (Bloom & Smith, 1996). However, coaches who display a lack of proper leadership, by emphasizing winning or encouraging immoral actions, can promote an environment that is more conducive to unsportspersonlike and aggressive behaviours.

violence of a murderer, it ought to be dropped or more closely defined" (p. x). What he meant is that we often hear the word *aggression* used in everyday society in a variety of ways. In sport settings in particular, we often hear about a baseball player aggressively running the bases or a volleyball player aggressively digging the ball. From a sport psychology perspective, however, this is not the correct use of the term. In an attempt to try to define the term more closely, Silva (1980) suggested that **aggression** is any overt verbal or physical act that is intended to psychologically or physically injure another living organism. A **violent behaviour** is an extreme act of physical aggression that bears "no direct relationship to the competitive goals of sport, and relates to incidents of uncontrolled aggression outside the rules of sport" (Terry & Jackson, 1985, p. 27). Keep in mind that because the aggressive action is directed at another living organism, there is always an aggressor and a victim in any aggressive or violent act.

Using Silva's (1980) definition, the term *aggression* is not appropriate for the description of the baseball and volleyball players' behaviours provided above. Sport psychologists prefer to describe those behaviours as *assertive*. The difference between an aggressive and an assertive action is that the latter behaviour does not include the intent to harm another living being. **Assertive behaviours** are those actions that are forceful, vigorous, and legitimate, but the individual performing these behaviours does not intend to injure an opponent (e.g., a hard tackle in football). Therefore, when a coach or parent tells an athlete or child to play more aggressively, in most situations what they are encouraging is behaviour that is more assertive.

Consequently, defining aggressive behaviour involves four key points:

1. It is a behaviour (i.e., an act), not an emotion or a feeling.
2. It can be verbal or physical.
3. It is intended to physically or psychologically harm.
4. It is directed toward another living organism.

Let's go back to the image of aggression in sport that was presented at the beginning of this chapter. Todd Bertuzzi "sucker-punched" Steve Moore to the side of the head. Based on the definition of aggression provided above, this behaviour would be considered aggressive because the intent to harm was present.

Sport psychologists make one further distinction in defining acts of aggression based on the reason why the individual behaved in such a way—that is, what they wanted to accomplish. As a result, two kinds of aggression have been identified in the sport psychology literature: instrumental aggression and hostile or reactive aggression. In both types of aggression, the intent is to harm. However, there is a distinction in terms of the goals being sought. **Instrumental aggression** serves as the means to a particular goal, such as winning, money, or prestige, in which injury to the opponent is involved. This type of injury is impersonal and designed to limit the effectiveness of the opponent. A hockey example for instrumental aggression would be when a player bodychecks his or her opponent, who is driving hard to the net trying to score a goal. The player who delivered the bodycheck has the intention of intimidating, or psychologically harming, the opponent so that next time, the opponent will think twice before driving to the net. This type of aggression is instrumental in helping the team achieve its goal of winning the game. On the other hand, the primary objective of **hostile (or reactive) aggression** is to injure another person deliberately. The intent is to make the victim suffer, either physically, psychologically, or both. For instance, the Todd Bertuzzi sucker-punch on Steve Moore was a clear attempt to deliberately injure—the goal was to cause suffering.

REFLECTIONS 8.1

The following are scenarios that could occur in sport. Using the definitional criteria of aggressive behaviour, decide whether the behaviours are aggressive or not.

1. After striking out, Kanya, a baseball player, throws her bat into the dugout where it hits the coach.
2. Samantha, a left-winger in soccer, purposely kicks an opposing player in the shin in retaliation for it being done to her.
3. In order to win a game of dodge ball, Assad deliberately aims for Jake's face and throws the ball as hard as he can, but Jake ducks out of the way, so the ball misses.
4. With 3.2 seconds left in the championship game and the opposing team, down by one, at the free-throw line, Coach Hoeber calls a time out in order to make the shooter worry and think about missing the shot.
5. After missing the tournament-winning putt, Steve wraps his putter around the light pole.

Answers

1. Not aggressive. The act was not intended to injure anyone; it was an accident.
2. Aggressive. Because Samantha's goal was to hurt another player, it is an act of hostile/reactive aggression.
3. Aggressive. Despite the fact that the ball did not hit Jake, Assad still wanted to injure him in order to win the game; therefore, it is a case of instrumental aggression.
4. Aggressive. The intent of Coach Hoeber was to instill anxiety in the opposing team's shooter (i.e., a form of psychological harm); therefore, it was an act of instrumental aggression.
5. Not aggressive. Although he was probably angry, Steve did not intend to harm another living being.

Although the act definitely has to contain the aggressor's intent to injure, some researchers suggest that the behaviour also has to go against the prevailing norms within the sport-specific culture (Mummendey, Linneweber, & Löschper, 1984a). Each sport has its own written and unwritten rules. It is through socialization and experience gained through participation in the sport that the participants become knowledgeable regarding the normative standards (i.e., unwritten rules) of that sport. Therefore, acts that may be aggressive in one sport are not necessarily considered aggressive in another sport. Fighting in ice hockey is a prime example of this. Many people involved within the subculture of ice hockey (e.g., players and coaches) do not believe that fights are an aggressive action (Colburn, 1986). These individuals believe that fighting is not an attempt to injure, but an attempt to control some of the more potentially harmful behaviours, like stick work, kicking, or kneeing. Players like Marty McSorley have stated that "fighting is not only accepted but an important part of NHL hockey. The job of a tough guy is to inspire team-mates and to ensure the team's skilled players are not intimidated" (Meant no harm, 2000). Should this same act occur in another sport, like volleyball or basketball, where the unwritten rules do not sanction fighting, the perception of the act as non-aggressive would definitely change.

REFLECTIONS 8.2

Think about the role of fighting in different types of sports. Some coaches talk about "controlled" aggression. Do you think there is a place for aggression in sport? What place is there for aggression in sport?

Another factor that influences the perception of aggression is the viewpoint from which one is involved in the behaviour. The actor (alleged aggressor) will usually view the action as appropriate and not aggressive, whereas the actor's opponent (alleged victim) will usually perceive the behaviour as inappropriate or aggressive (Mummendey, Linneweber, & Löschper, 1984b). For example, a wrestler may subtly "work against the joint," intentionally inflicting pain on the opponent in order to pin him or her on the mat. While the athlete may think that he or she is just doing what it takes to win, the opponent more than likely believes that it was a deliberate attempt to cause injury and may subsequently question the "attacker's" sportspersonship.

Another factor that tends to influence a person's perception of whether or not an act is aggressive is the outcome of the act (i.e., did someone get hurt?). However, if you refer back to the definition of aggression, the key point is the intent to harm another living being. This description does not mean that the actor has to succeed in harming an opponent, only that he or she intended to harm the other individual. If an act was committed with the intent of psychologically intimidating an opponent but does not succeed, it is still an aggressive behaviour. Let us revisit the action of Assad described in the Reflections 8.1 box. He tried to physically injure Jake by throwing the ball at his face. Just because Jake dodged the ball, rendering Assad's attempt futile, that does not negate the fact that Assad's actions were aggressive. The intent to do harm was present.

REFLECTIONS 8.3

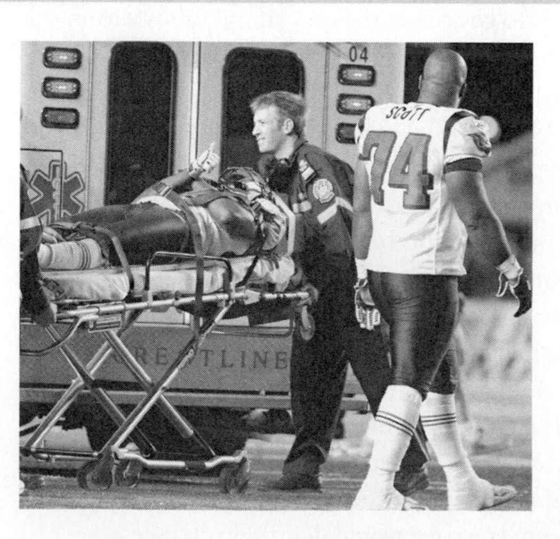

If you were in charge of handing out suspensions for a sport governing body, on what evidence would you base the length of time of the suspension?

Photograph © The Canadian Press (Marianne Helm).

THEORIES OF AGGRESSION

What are the reasons some athletes lose control and act aggressively? Are people born to be aggressive, or are they products of their environment? In order to explain what causes athletes to be aggressive, scientists have advanced several theories and explanations. These theories and explanations can be classified into five groups: psychodynamics, frustration-aggression theory, physiological explanations, social learning theory, and moral disengagement.

Psychodynamics

The basic tenets of psychodynamics were covered in the chapter on personality (Chapter 3). This theory holds that humans are born with certain psychic drives (i.e., instincts) that will cause them to act in certain ways. For example, Freud (1925) believed that aggressive behaviour was an innate, natural response that evolved primarily through a struggle for survival. Aggression builds up naturally and must be released. Freud believed that numerous socially approved methods existed for releasing this pent-up aggression. Sport is one such socially acceptable activity that could curtail the negative results of aggression. This releasing process was termed **catharsis**, a word derived from the Greek term *katharsis*, which means to purge/cleanse the body. According to this theory, hitting an opponent in sport serves as a catharsis or release of built-up aggression.

Psychodynamic theory has far more detractors than supporters. Bandura (1973) noted that a large body of research, involving either direct or vicarious aggressive experiences, has demonstrated that aggression will actually be maintained rather than reduced. Further, the probability of subsequent aggression will increase rather than diminish! These findings are also apparent in a sport setting, where research has found no draining of aggressive tendencies through participation in physical activities. In fact, many sport researchers have argued that exposure to violence in sports serves as a reinforcer, not as a catharsis. Thus, many scientists have rejected this theory for understanding aggression in sport.

Frustration-Aggression Theory

Rejecting Freud's notion of an aggressive instinct, Dollard, Miller, Doob, Mowrer, and Sears first proposed the frustration-aggression theory in 1939. This theory viewed aggression as a natural response to frustration. Originally, it was hypothesized that all aggression was due to frustration and that frustration always leads to aggression. For instance, a rugby player who has been tackled high and hard might become frustrated and punch his opponent in retaliation. Although this theory has intuitive appeal because it seems reasonable that most aggression occurs when individuals are frustrated, the frustration-aggression theory has some definite shortcomings. For example, individuals are able to deal with their frustrations in non-aggressive ways. Consequently, Berkowitz (1989) proposed a **revised frustration-aggression theory**, recognizing that aggression can have causes other than frustration and that frustration can lead to behaviours other than aggression, such as withdrawal from sport. Berkowitz suggested that when an individual is frustrated, an emotional reaction of anger is produced that does not automatically lead to aggression but rather to a readiness to be aggressive. Some scientists have been reluctant to accept this theory since it implies an instinctual mechanism that accounts for the frustration–anger link.

REFLECTIONS 8.4

What are some of the ways in which a person could deal with her or his frustration?

Physiological Explanations

Proponents who believe that aggression is physiological in nature use two supportive mechanisms: brain pathology and blood chemistry. Insofar as brain pathology is concerned, research has shown that aggressive behaviour is often characteristic of people with brain tumours. In these people, aggressive behaviours can be elicited by stimulating various parts of the brain. As for blood chemistry, aggression has been linked primarily to the hormone testosterone. Although researchers have found a link between testosterone and aggressive behaviour in animal species, the relationship is less consistent in humans. That is, testosterone may cause individuals to be aggressive, but it is difficult to explain why people who possess high levels of this hormone are aggressive in some situations and not in others. As well, it is hard to explain why people, such as females, who possess little or low amounts of testosterone can act aggressively.

Although physiological explanations have been used to explain aggression in animal species, rarely has this explanation been forwarded as a cause of aggression in sport. One exception concerns the use of steroids by athletes, most notably athletes in power and strength sports like weightlifting, football, baseball, and track and field. The links between steroid use and feelings of aggressiveness, and between steroid use and aggressive behaviour, have been frequently documented among athletes (e.g., Yates, Perry, & Murray, 1992). For instance, studies have shown that athletes who take steroids have higher levels of aggression toward objects, of verbal aggression, and of aggressiveness while training. It should be pointed out that when the athletes stopped using steroids, these characteristics disappeared (Parrott, Choi, & Davies, 1994).

Social Learning Theory

The most supported explanation of why aggression occurs is social learning theory. The leading advocate for this theory, relative to aggression, is Albert Bandura. According to social learning theory, a person is neither driven by inner forces nor controlled solely by environmental influences. Instead, Bandura (1973) believes that people are aggressive because they have learned that aggression pays. In other words, the use of aggressive behaviours can lead to success.

Bandura (1973) theorized that two forms of social interaction lead to the development of aggressive behaviours. The first form of interaction involves modelling. In its simplest form, modelling suggests that people can acquire aggressive behaviours from observing aggressive models and can retain these aggressive tendencies over time. For instance, Michael Smith (1983) has suggested that youth hockey players learn to be aggressive by watching their role models from professional leagues, like the NHL.

The other form of interaction involves learning or acquiring new responses because of reinforcement. When an action is performed and then positively reinforced (i.e., rewarded), the behaviour is strengthened. The behaviour will be discontinued if it is not rewarded or is punished. For example, research has suggested that parents, teammates, and coaches are the most influential providers of social reinforcement, especially for young athletes (Smith, 1979). Smith surveyed minor hockey players and found that those who engaged in fighting believed that their parents, teammates, and coaches approved of this behaviour. Specifically, Smith found that 31% of players said that their father would approve of fighting, and 21% said that their mothers would approve. Similarly, hockey players said that 64% of their teammates and 26% of their coaches approved of fighting.

Approval is not the only possible reinforcer of aggression. The belief that aggression is related to success also can influence aggressive behaviours. Luxbacher (1986) investigated the influence of the coach's attitude toward winning on aggression in youth soccer. The findings showed that players who perceived their coach to have a win-at-all-costs attitude expressed higher levels of aggression and were more willing to use illegal, aggressive tactics to win.

In short, social learning theory is a strong force in contemporary research, linking aggression to the environment and the individual. It is a model that contains provisions for direct learning and for vicarious learning. Furthermore, Bandura's (1973) theory contains a cognitive dimension that had been previously missing from other theories regarding aggression. Finally, since aggression allegedly does not originate internally and its environmental determinants are alterable, social learning theory holds a more optimistic view of reducing aggression in humans.

Moral Disengagement

It should be noted that the moral disengagement view is an extension of social learning theory that has been developed to specifically address moral behaviour. Bandura (1999) attempted to explain how people who are engaged in a deviant behaviour such as aggression justify their choices. According to moral disengagement, individuals tend to refrain from engaging in behaviour that violates their own moral standards. That is to say, if a hockey player believes that fighting is an unacceptable behaviour, he or she may not engage in that behaviour since it violates his or her moral beliefs. However, these standards or beliefs do not necessarily function as fixed internal controls of aggression. That is, athletes do not always behave the way they should. Going back to our fighting example, an athlete may engage in this behaviour even if it is against his or her standards. In fact, there are eight methods by which individuals attempt to disengage themselves from the behaviour. Bandura refers to these as the mechanisms of moral disengagement.

The first method is moral justification, whereby an individual reconsiders aggression as being a negative behaviour and makes it acceptable by portraying this behaviour as facilitating a social or moral purpose. For instance, a hockey player could argue that he or she fought an opponent to protect a teammate. Euphemistic labelling involves changing the language to make the aggressive behaviour seem less harmful. For example, those involved in hockey often justify the existence of fighting by claiming that fighting allows players to "let off some steam." Advantageous comparison is another way of making aggression seem acceptable. This involves comparing an aggressive behaviour with something that is more reprehensible. You will often hear athletes say, "We didn't do bad stuff, and if we did, it wasn't as bad as what the other team did." Displacement of responsibility occurs when athletes shift the blame for their aggressive behaviours to other individuals. For instance, a baseball pitcher could say that the coach wanted her to go and throw a brush-back pitch at the hitter. By shifting the responsibility to the coach, athletes can employ these types of tactics when

The social learning theory suggests that since aggressive behaviour is learned, it can be unlearned.

Photograph © The Canadian Press (Darryl Dyck).

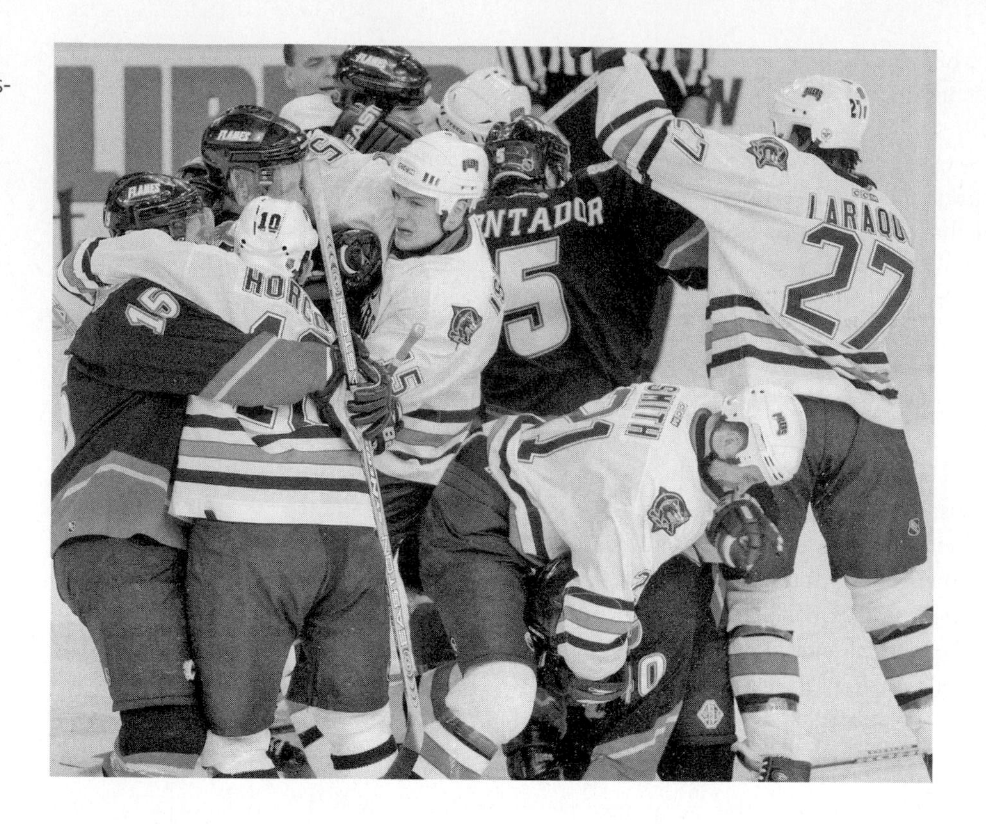

they wouldn't normally contemplate using them. Diffusion of responsibility involves team members making a group decision to use aggressive behaviours. By making the decision to act aggressively as a team, no single athlete feels personally responsible. Distortion of consequences is achieved when an athlete minimizes the harm caused by his or her actions. For instance, let us say a football player tackles his opponent and the opponent hits his head on the turf and suffers a concussion. The football player who delivered the hit may say that it was not that bad and that the concussion resulted from contact with the field and not from the hit itself. Dehumanization involves cognitively removing people of their human qualities. In sport, athletes are often portrayed as "goons," "animals," and "beasts." When athletes describe their opponents as such, they no longer view them as people but as subhuman objects. Attribution of blame occurs when athletes see themselves as the victim and not the aggressor. This sort of behaviour occurs when athletes retaliate against their opponent and use this type of excuse as a way of justifying their behaviour.

Summary of Theories of Aggression

Several major theoretical frameworks have been utilized in the study of aggressive behaviour. These theoretical frameworks have attempted to explain or predict an individual's aggressive behaviour. We often hear people trying to explain aggression by saying such things as "boys will be boys" or "they are just blowing off steam." The belief in the basic tenets of psychodynamic theory and the frustration-aggression theory has had an impact on the sporting sphere. People will often justify aggression as natural and necessary. These justifications occur even though research indicates that these theories are not effective means of explaining aggressive behaviour. Bandura's attempt to explain aggression from a moral disengagement viewpoint is

Table 8.1 Theories Regarding Aggressive Behaviour

Theory	Major Tenet
Psychodynamic theory	Humans are born with the instinct for aggression.
Frustration-aggression theory	A blocked goal causes the individual to become frustrated, and frustration produces aggression.
Revised frustration-aggression theory	A blocked goal causes emotional reactions (e.g., anger), which lead to a readiness to behave aggressively; appropriate environmental cues cause this readiness to develop into aggression.
Physiological theories	Aggressive behaviour occurs because individuals have either a brain pathology or excess testosterone.
Moral disengagement	Aggressive behaviour occurs through individuals changing their morality under certain conditions.
Social learning theory	Individuals use aggression because they have learned that aggression pays.

still in its infancy, but this perspective gives us another useful avenue to use in our quest for understanding. Up to this point, social learning theory provides the most plausible and empirically supported foundation for describing, understanding, predicting, and ultimately controlling aggressive behaviour in sport (see Table 8.1).

REFLECTIONS 8.5

Think back to a time when you behaved aggressively, saw someone behaving aggressively, or were a victim of another's aggressive action. Using the theories just discussed, try to explain why you or the other individual behaved in this manner.

FACTORS INFLUENCING AGGRESSION

Being frustrated or wanting reinforcement may partially explain why athletes behave aggressively. There are, however, other personal, situational, and group factors that help us to understand when aggression is more likely to occur. In this section, we will briefly discuss some of these factors. The findings for many of these factors will be equivocal, considering the lack of research done in the sport setting and the many ways in which researchers have examined aggression.

Personal Factors Influencing Aggression

Gender Historically, the majority of research examining aggression in sport has primarily examined male athletes. Recently, there has been more interest shown in sport behaviours exhibited by women, particularly aggressive behaviours. In ice hockey, female athletes have also shown a tendency to engage in aggressive behaviours, similar to their male counterparts.

For instance, a 15-year-old female hockey player was charged with assault after she repeatedly punched an opponent in the head, causing her opponent to suffer whiplash and neck bruises (McGregor, 2002).

Given that female athletes appear to be displaying similar aggressive behaviours as their male counterparts, Canadian researchers Todd Loughead, Gordon Bloom, and their colleagues (Bloom & Vanier, 2004; Shapcott, Bloom, & Loughead, 2007; Vanier, Bloom, & Loughead, 2005) have conducted a series of studies specifically examining aggression in women's hockey. They discovered that the majority of aggressive behaviour in women's hockey occurs to (1) protect the goalie, (2) gain a competitive advantage, and (3) get the opponent to retaliate and draw a penalty. They also found that these women tended to rely more on psychological aggression than on physical aggression in the form of verbally taunting and provoking their opponents into taking retaliatory penalties.

Shapcott et al. (2007) videotaped and then individually queried female university hockey players from one team about their aggressive intentions during game play. The results of these interviews revealed that female players used aggression for five reasons. The most frequent reason was to obtain the puck from their opponent even if it meant using aggression to do it. The second intention was related to strategy: the players indicated that their coach taught them various aggressive behaviours as a method of impeding their opponents' progress; another strategy used by the players was to utilize aggression as a way of preventing the opposition from scoring and as a way to draw penalties. A third reason for using aggression was to protect themselves or their teammates from being hit by the opposition. A fourth reason was to intimidate their opponents; this included using verbal and physical aggression. The fifth reason was for no other purpose than simply to hit their opponent. Interestingly, all the players indicated that they never intended to physically injure anyone.

REFLECTIONS 8.6

Would boxing be considered aggressive behaviour? When and why do women behave aggressively in sport?

Photograph © The Canadian Press (Andrew Vaughan).

Age No conclusive statement can be made regarding the relationship between age and aggressive behaviour considering that not many studies have looked at age as the specific variable of interest. One study by Loughead and Leith (2001) compared aggressive behaviours of Atom (i.e., aged 10–11 years), Pee-Wee (i.e., aged 12–13 years), and Bantam (i.e., aged 14–15 years) hockey players. The results indicated that Atom players were more approving of instrumental aggression than their older Pee-Wee and Bantam counterparts. However, Pee-Wee and Bantam players were more approving of hostile aggression than were Atom players. Visek and Watson (2005) examined the perceived legitimacy of aggression in male ice hockey players at the youth, high-school, varsity, and professional levels. The results showed that as players aged (from youth to professional), they endorsed the use of both instrumental and hostile aggression to a greater extent.

There are contrary findings to the argument that there is a positive relationship between age and aggressive behaviour. Several studies have examined statements regarding the desire to behave aggressively among male Pee-Wee ice hockey players (Dorsch, 1992), high-school ice hockey players (Sanszole, 1995), and university ice hockey players (Brice, 1990). As can be seen in Figure 8.1, desire to physically and psychologically injure

Figure 8.1 Age and aggressive behaviour

At different levels of competition, the desire of male ice hockey players to physically and psychologically injure an opponent at least once per period

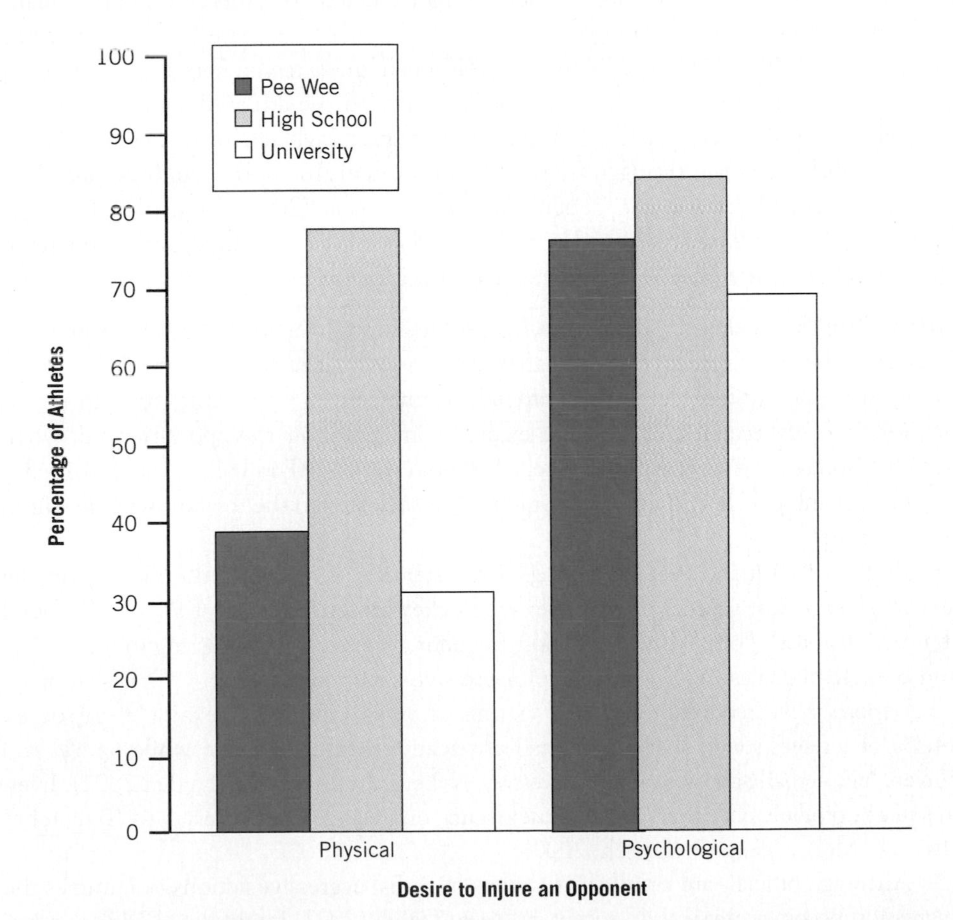

Note: Data from Brice, J. G. (1990). *Frustration in ice hockey: Extent, antecedents and consequences.* Unpublished master's thesis, University of Waterloo, Waterloo, ON, Canada; Dorsch, K. D. (1992).*The extent and antecedents of aggression in PeeWee hockey.* Unpublished manuscript, University of Waterloo, Waterloo, ON, Canada; Sanszole, M. (1995). *The extent, antecedents and response to sport frustration by high school students.* Unpublished manuscript, University of Waterloo, Waterloo, ON, Canada.

opposing players peaks during the middle years. Consequently, we cannot definitively state the direction of the relationship between age and aggressive behaviour until more research examines this variable.

Physical Size One might think that bigger players are more likely to use their size to their advantage; however, one could also imagine that larger athletes may be aware of their size and not want to engage in activities that may injure an opponent. In one study looking at Pee-Wee hockey players, Dorsch (1992) found that both height and weight positively correlated to the number of aggressive penalties. This size–aggression relationship was supported by Lemieux, McKelvie, and Stout (2002), who compared the aggressive behaviour of athletes involved in contact sports (e.g., football and rugby), athletes involved in non-contact sports (e.g., track, baseball, golf, and volleyball), and individuals not involved in any sports. They found that regardless of whether an individual was an athlete or not, the bigger the person, the more he reported being involved in a fight in a non-sport setting.

Retaliation Motives Brice's (1990) study of university ice hockey players and Sanszole's (1995) study involving a variety of male and female athletes found that many athletes expressed wanting to physically harm an opponent because the opponent had attempted to injure them or a teammate. Although these researchers did not directly examine the link between these retaliation motives and the athletes' aggressive behaviour, Harrell (1980) did find the strongest predictor of high-school basketball players' aggressive behaviour was the aggression of their opponent. In another study of basketball and ice hockey players, Kirker, Tenenbaum, and Mattson (2000) found that the most severe aggressive acts were preceded by aggressive acts, often committed by the opponent. These retaliatory acts often led to further acts of aggression.

Annoyances Widmeyer, Bray, Dorsch, and McGuire (2002) suggested that some athletes might become aggressive because they are annoyed. Annoyances in sport could take the form of inconsistent calls by an official, mannerisms of opponents, or taunting by opposing players, coaches, or fans. For example, imagine how the opposition felt when Terrell Owens, then of the San Francisco 49ers (National Football League), scored a touchdown and pulled a Sharpie marker out of his sock to sign the football—while still in the end zone!

Brice (1990) found that officiating inconsistencies were one of the most annoying and most prevalent sources of anger for ice hockey athletes. Kirker et al. (2000) found that verbal abuse of officials was the most frequent aggressive act occurring in ice hockey and basketball games (30% and 26% of aggressive acts, respectively). Officials in many other sports have reported being the victims of verbal abuse. For example, in soccer, 24.3% of referees stated that players had physically threatened them, while 63.6% said players had verbally abused them (Folkesson, Nyberg, Archer, & Norlander, 2002). Even in squash, officials state that verbal abuse occurs, on average, once every 5 to 10 matches (Dorsch, McAuliffe, & Paskevich, 2000).

Although officials are usually the victims of verbal aggressive actions, sometimes the aggression becomes physical. In soccer, Folkesson et al. (2002) found that 12.1% of referees had suffered some form of physical aggression from players. In baseball and softball, Rainey (1994) discovered that 11% of umpires reported some form of assault, usually pushing, shoving, grabbing, hitting, or punching.

Self-presentation Sport psychologists often refer to **self-presentation** as the way individuals present themselves (i.e., behave, dress) in social situations. Some sport psychologists believe that some athletes may behave aggressively in order to convey or maintain an image of toughness to opponents and observers, particularly within contact sports, such as football, basketball, and ice hockey (Widmeyer et al., 2002). In support of this notion, Wann and Porcher (1998) found that intercollegiate ice hockey and football players whose names were printed on the backs of their jerseys were more aggressive. They surmised that because the players were now identifiable to others, they needed to portray a certain image. Similarly, McGuire (1990) found that professional ice hockey players who did not wear facemasks were more aggressive than those who did. A possible explanation for this finding is that because the players' identities are more apparent without the facial protection, the need to present themselves in a manner consistent with the norms of the game becomes more prevalent.

The contrasting viewpoint would suggest that aggressive impulses are increased when the individual feels less identifiable, a process known as **deindividuation**. Rehm, Steinleitner, and Lilli (1987) found that handball teams whose members wore the same jersey and consequently appeared similar to each other (i.e., high anonymity) committed more aggressive acts than the team in which each individual wore his own shirt. This finding supports the assumption that higher levels of anonymity contribute to actions that are more aggressive. However, there are few other studies that have systematically examined deindividuation in sport.

REFLECTIONS 8.7

Consider the findings on self-presentation. Most of these studies use correlational research methods. Thinking back to what you read in Chapter 2, what are the limitations of this research in drawing conclusive causal statements about identifiability and aggression?

Situational Factors Influencing Aggression

Frequency of Competition It is not a stretch to think that the number of times competitors meet may have an impact on the amount of aggressive behaviour demonstrated in the matches. Indeed, Widmeyer and McGuire (1997) did find that aggressive behaviours occurred more often in intradivisional professional ice hockey games (i.e., teams competing in the same division) than in interdivisional games (i.e., teams competing in different divisions). For instance, in the NHL, teams competing within their division (e.g., Montreal Canadiens and Toronto Maple Leafs) had higher incidences of aggression than did teams competing outside their divisions (e.g., Montreal Canadiens and Edmonton Oilers).

Home Advantage An archival study by McGuire, Courneya, Widmeyer, and Carron (1992) examined whether home teams in ice hockey exhibited more aggressive behaviours than visiting teams and whether or not this type of behaviour had an impact on the outcome of the game. They found that there was indeed a home advantage, with the home teams winning 58.5% of decided games. Furthermore, home teams received more aggressive penalties in games they won, while visiting teams incurred more aggressive penalties in games they lost. Using an observational methodology, Jones, Bray, and Olivier (2005) found no difference in the frequency of aggression between the home and visiting teams in professional rugby. However, the authors found that the visiting team engaged in more aggressive behaviours when they lost compared to when they won.

Point Differentials Losing is often thought to be a frustrating situation. If this assumption is true, then according to the frustration-aggression theory, individuals should behave in an aggressive manner when they are losing. In general, when researchers examined the influence of losing during a game and took into account the score when an aggressive act occurred, these situations were not related to aggressive behaviours (Lefebvre & Passer, 1974; McGuire, 1990). Despite the fact that there does not seem to be a relationship between aggressive behaviour and losing situations in general, there does seem to be some support for the occurrence of aggressive behaviours and various specific losing situations. For example, several studies in ice hockey (e.g., Kirker et al., 2000; Wankel, 1973) have found that teams losing late in the game tend to be more aggressive. Other researchers have found that teams losing by a large margin tend to display more aggressive actions (Harrel, 1980; McGuire, 1990; Wankel, 1973).

Group Factors Influencing Aggression

As discussed previously in this chapter, the psychological closeness of an observer to an aggressor will influence the observer's perception of the aggressor's intent. Similarly, belonging to a group will have an impact on an individual's willingness to behave aggressively. Within a group, such factors as the role the individual plays, team norms, group cohesion, and the group's **collective efficacy for aggression** (perception of the ability to use aggressive behaviour as a tactic or strategy) will impact the individual's and consequently the team's aggressive behaviour.

Individual's Role Individuals who occupy a specific role on a team are generally expected to behave in a manner consistent with the behaviours expected of that role. Within sports like ice hockey, we often see players designated as the "enforcer" or "policeman." The players who fill these roles are expected, and may even be recruited, to behave in an aggressive manner. As Marty McSorley, former Boston Bruin enforcer, stated, "The job of a tough guy is to inspire team-mates and to ensure the team's skilled players are not intimidated" (Meant no harm, 2000).

Team Norms As discussed earlier, team norms are the standards for the behaviour that is expected of members of the group. Typically referred to as the unwritten rules of the game, team norms provide the player with the information necessary to know what is or is not acceptable behaviour. Stephens (2000) found that the best predictor of girls' likelihood to engage in aggressive behaviours in a soccer game was their belief that their teammates would play unfairly. It is this expectation of unfair play as being the team norm that subsequently guided the athletes' behaviours.

Collective Efficacy for Aggression As teams develop an acceptance of aggressive behaviour and subsequent expectation that it is needed for success, they develop a perception of their ability to use aggression as a tactic or strategy within the game. This perception of their ability to use aggression as a strategy (i.e., collective efficacy for aggression) is similar to the sense of collective competence they feel for their offensive or defensive skills. A study of Canadian university and junior ice hockey teams by Dorsch (1997) found that collective efficacy for strategic aggression did predict future team aggressive behaviours. Furthermore, these perceptions were more similar among team members than between teams, suggesting that it is a group perception.

Group Cohesion Dorsch, Widmeyer, Paskevich, and Brawley (1996) examined perceptions of team cohesion and aggressive behaviour among Canadian junior ice hockey teams. They found that as the teams became more united in pursuit of their goals and objectives (i.e., more cohesive; Carron, 1988), they exhibited more aggressive behaviours. In a study of youth minor hockey, Bessette and Loughead (2007) found further support to suggest that both task and social cohesion predicted team norms regarding the use of physical aggression. Together these studies lead to the suggestion that group cohesion may in fact be a group factor that influences aggressive behaviour.

REFLECTIONS 8.8

As a sport psychology consultant, you have been asked by a youth hockey league to help reduce aggression levels. Which factors—personal, situational, or both—would you target, and why?

CONSEQUENCES OF AGGRESSIVE BEHAVIOUR

All aggressive acts have both an aggressor and a victim. Furthermore, most of these acts in a sport setting also have at least one observer. Consequently, within an aggressive interaction there can be consequences to the aggressor, victim, and observer. The most obvious of these consequences to the individuals involved in the altercation is injury. While many studies have examined the incidence of injury in sports, few have related the cause of the injury to the aggressive behaviour. In an attempt to address this limitation, Katorji and Cahoon (1992) reported that trainers and players in Canadian Junior B hockey said that approximately 59% of injuries occurred because of an opponent's aggressive act. Katorji and Cahoon also found that of the injuries that occurred to the aggressor, approximately 27% occurred when the actor was attempting to harm his opponent.

Falling back on the definition of an aggressive behaviour, intimidation or psychological harm is another possible consequence of an aggressive altercation. Even though it is very difficult to measure the amount of psychological harm that occurs within a sporting event, we can sometimes infer from a player's behaviour that the aggressor's intent has succeeded. For example, if we see the football receiver hesitate or alter his pattern to avoid the safety, or if we see that an ice hockey forward is afraid to go into the corners to get the puck, we assume that these players have been intimidated. The difficulty is that the athlete may have been intimidated by an assertive behaviour and not by an aggressive behaviour.

Regardless of whether one is attacked or is the attacker, another possible consequence of the altercation is an elevated arousal level. Anger or other emotions are often associated with involvement in an aggressive incident. Coupled closely with these emotions is an alteration in the individual's arousal level. The impact this altered state of arousal will have on the performance of the athlete was more fully discussed in the chapter on anxiety (Chapter 5). In support of this suggestion, NHL referee Brad Watson was quoted as saying, "I find that a fight is, more times than not, a way to fire a team up" (Tuchman, 2000, p. 7).

Finally, penalization is the most common consequence that can occur to the aggressor and the team. In most sports, penalization is designed to discourage aggressive behaviour by reducing the individual's or team's chances of success.

REFLECTIONS 8.9

What are the various ways to reduce intimidation in sport?

Photograph © Joe McBride/Corbis.

FAN VIOLENCE

What happens to the observer of aggression in sport? Research suggests that fans like violence in their sports (Bryant, Comisky, & Zillman, 1981; Bryant, Brown, Comisky, & Zillman, 1982). One sports journalist stated, "The two loudest cheers you ever hear in a hockey game are when the home team scores a goal and when there is a fight" (Tuchman, 2000, p. 17).

Some people go to sport events not only to watch the aggressive behaviours of athletes but also even to instigate aggressive altercations themselves. Gord Russell of the University of Lethbridge (1995) and Russell and Arms (1995) found that individuals who are most likely to take part in aggressive behaviours in the stands at ice hockey games are young males who travel in groups, have a recent history of fighting, like to watch fights, attend hockey games in hopes of seeing fights, react impulsively, and score high on the trait of aggressiveness. These researchers have suggested that the individuals who tend to instigate aggression among fans have a false belief about the willingness of other fans to join in these acts of aggression. They refer to this perception as the **false consensus effect**.

In order to see how willing spectators actually are to become involved, the researchers asked fans at ice hockey games what they would do if a fight were to break out nearby in the stands. Of their respondents, 61% said that they would watch, 26% said that they would try to stop the fight, 7% said that they would applaud or join in, and the remaining 6% said that they would leave the area. The small percentage of people who indicated that they would become involved gives support to the notion of the false consensus effect.

In addition to aggressive incidents that occur among the observers of athletic contests, there are many reports of altercations occurring between fans and athletes. Incidents of verbal abuse or the throwing of objects at athletes, coaches, or officials would be considered acts of hostile aggression if the intent of the fan is to physically or psychologically injure those individuals. Even if the intent is to gain an advantage for the fan's team by distracting the opposition, this could be considered an act of instrumental aggression (Tenenbaum, Stewart, Singer, & Duda, 1996).

We may believe that the majority of the aggressive acts that occur between fans and athletes happen at the professional level; however, a particularly disturbing incident occurred on January 16, 2005, between a father of a 9-year-old ice hockey player in Toronto and the child's coach. The team's policy was that if a player missed a practice, he would sit out for a couple of shifts during the next game. While the child was sitting on the bench, his father, who disagreed with the rule, reached over the glass partition, grabbed the coach by the neck, and choked the coach until he became unconscious.

REFLECTIONS 8.10

Tie Domi, former Toronto Maple Leafs enforcer, stated, "When fans try to get involved in our work they gotta be ready to pay the price" (Fans vs. athletes: 10 ugly incidents, 2004). What do you think should happen to fans who physically or psychologically abuse athletes?

Photograph © The Canadian Press (AP Photo/Miles Kennedy).

REDUCING AGGRESSION IN SPORT

Before we can even attempt to reduce aggressive behaviours in sport, we have to understand why they occur. By reading the chapter up to this point, you should have a clear understanding of some of the theories concerning why people behave aggressively and some of the personal, situational, and group factors that may influence a person's intent to physically or psychologically harm another individual. Based on what we have discussed so far and on suggestions presented elsewhere in the literature (e.g., Tenenbaum et al., 1996;

Widmeyer, 2002), we are suggesting five broad methods that may be useful in helping individuals participating in, or even observing, sports to curb their aggressive behaviours. These methods are not necessarily directed specifically at the athletes. Interventions targeted toward other individuals involved in the sporting system (e.g., coaches, parents, officials, and the media) may also prove to be beneficial in accomplishing successful behavioural change.

Punishment and Encouragement

Social learning theory suggests to us that people learn that aggression pays. Therefore, teaching individuals that aggression does not pay would be paramount for behavioural change. In order to make this shift, the individuals who strongly influence the athletes' learning process (i.e., coaches and parents) need to ensure that the penalty or punishment athletes receive for an act of aggression is more meaningful to them than any reinforcement they may receive. To this end, coaches must emphasize the value of fair play, and encourage and reward such behaviours as great moves, strong effort, unselfish play, teamwork, and courage. Parents also need to reinforce these assertive behaviours. Outside the field of play, parents should also focus on developing their child's ability to utilize a task goal orientation instead of an ego goal orientation. Finally, parents and coaches need to provide young athletes with positive role models, ones who demonstrate non-aggressive, yet effective, assertive behaviours.

In an attempt to ensure that positive behaviours are modelled by parents, the minister responsible for amateur sport in British Columbia was considering having parents of all young athletes in the province sign a contract ensuring that they (1) encourage their child to play by the rules and to resolve conflicts without resorting to hostility or violence, (2) never ridicule or yell at their child for making a mistake or losing a competition, and (3) never question the official's judgment or honesty in public (Contracts for parents?, 2000, p. 1). A similar contract was used with athletes participating in the 2002 Arctic Winter Games. The rules for these Games included good sportspersonship, no violence, no racial slurs, no gender bashing, no drugs, and no alcohol (Games code of conduct introduced, 2002, p. 1).

Educational Interventions

One way we can help those involved in sport understand that aggression does not pay is through educational interventions. Some associations in Florida built upon the contract suggested by British Columbia and required parents to take classes on how to behave at sporting events (Zarrella, 2000, p. 1). Similarly, in 2005, Major League Baseball collaborated with Northeastern University's Center for the Study of Sport in Society to offer this professional league's first violence-prevention training partnership. These workshops teach athletes, parents, coaches, officials, media personnel, and authority figures the meaning of aggression, why it occurs, the cost of aggressive acts, and how to control aggression.

Another aspect of educational programs should be the teaching of psychological skills. Such programs should not just focus on technical skills but also on teaching athletes to expect frustration, annoyance, and attack. Inherent in any sporting situation is an opponent's attempt to stop the athlete's ultimate goal of winning. The athlete has to be able to deal with these situations in an effective, yet non-aggressive, manner. The chapters on stress and coping (Chapter 6) and sport psychology interventions (Chapter 14) review the different types of psychological skills. Another feature any educational program should focus on is the consequences of anabolic steroid use. Athletes, parents, and coaches need to become more familiar with the extremely negative impacts that the use of these drugs has on the future health of the user.

Behavioural Modification Practices

In the International Society of Sport Psychology's position on aggression and violence in sport, Tenenbaum et al. (1996) state, "The tightening of rules, imposing of harsher penalties and changing of reinforcement patterns are only part of the answer to inhibiting aggression in sport. Ultimately, the athlete must assume responsibility for his/her behaviour" (p. 234). Part of assisting the athlete to assume this responsibility could involve the athlete's participation in programs designed to help reduce the desire to behave aggressively. As part of daily training, athletes should work on self-awareness and develop their strategies and coping skills.

When committing an instrumentally aggressive behaviour, a player has more control over his or her behaviour because the act is deliberate and is a means to an end; the player chooses to use aggression in those situations. Pure hostile aggression, however, may be slightly more difficult to curtail because this type of aggression typically occurs in a reactive manner, in a heightened state of arousal, and independent of meaningful cognitive processes. The aggressor needs to develop coping strategies to modify these behaviours (see Chapter 6). Brunelle, Janelle, and Tennant (1999) examined a promising method of dealing with anger and its subsequent behaviours in soccer. They found that a role-playing intervention, in which athletes simulated and practised strategies for dealing with angry feelings, was helpful in controlling these feelings and the typically aggressive behaviours that resulted from them.

Tenenbaum and colleagues (1996) also recognized that "like players, officials are placed under great stress during games" (p. 233). Consequently, they suggest that officials take measures to improve their psychological skills, for example, their ability to concentrate, to control unnecessary arousal, and to cope with pressure. Ultimately, the development of these skills will enable officials to become more competent and consistent in enforcing the rules of sport. According to Tenenbaum et al., the subsequent decline in the incidence of errors will help decrease athletes', coaches', and fans' levels of frustration, while also promoting fair play and minimizing aggressive behaviour.

Changes to the Sporting Environment

Even though we did not mention the use of alcohol previously, it is readily accepted that the ingestion of alcohol lowers an individual's inhibitions and consequently makes that individual more prone to act aggressively. Therefore, the use of alcoholic beverages at sporting events should be banned, or at the very least, limited and controlled. Cox (2002) suggests that "athletic events should be promoted and encouraged as family affairs" (p. 316). Sporting events should be an enjoyable experience, where parents and their children can learn about fair play.

Aggressive Behaviour in the Media

Previously we acknowledged the fact that fans like aggression in the sports they observe. Bryant and Zillman (1983) suggest that the media exploits this desire by (1) sensationalizing and replaying acts of aggression repeatedly, (2) focusing on and glorifying aggression in feature stories, and (3) promoting previous aggressive behaviours between competitors to encourage future attendance. Instead of making aggressive behaviours the highlights, the media should promote a campaign to decrease aggressive behaviours in sport, which would be more beneficial. The assertive (not aggressive) plays and players should be glorified and those players held up as role models in order to promote these acceptable behaviours.

CHAPTER SUMMARY

The information we discussed in this chapter deals with the reasons that an individual may behave in an aggressive manner, including the role of moral behaviour in influencing aggression. In order for us to truly understand and attempt to control aggressive behaviour in sport, we must include other scientific disciplines (e.g., sociology, anthropology) in this quest. However, from a psychological viewpoint, we know the following points regarding aggressive and moral behaviour in sport.

Aggressive behaviour is *not* something we want to encourage or reinforce in athletes because the definition of aggression includes the intent to physically or psychologically harm another. We want to teach and encourage athletes to play assertively (i.e., with legitimate force and energy).

The notion that sport builds character has been and will continue to be a popular viewpoint, and terms such as *sportspersonship*, *character building*, and *moral development* will be pervasive in school textbooks and in the mainstream media. The study of moral behaviour within the context of sport is in its infancy. Nonetheless, this chapter introduced two classic paradigms in which moral behaviours have been studied—structural-developmental and social learning—and some of the factors that influence how we behave.

Many factors influence aggressive behaviour. Although many theories have helped us understand why people behave aggressively, the theory that provides the most promise for helping us control this behaviour in sport suggests that people behave aggressively because they have learned that aggression pays. Even though the social learning theory gives us a foundation from which to work, we need to be aware of many other personal, situational, and group factors that influence aggressive behaviour.

Reducing aggressive behaviour in sport involves everyone. Controlling aggression is not just an individual athlete's task. Many other actions or interventions could be implemented by, or even targeted at, other sport participants. Coaches, parents, officials, and the media are key stakeholders in the process of behaviour change.

Common Myths about Aggression and Moral Behaviour in Sport Revisited

MYTH: Aggression in sport is a good characteristic. It is something to be encouraged in players.

Most coaches, when asked what kind of player they want on their team, would include *aggressive* in their description of the ideal player. However, from a sport psychology perspective, aggression is not a good thing. An aggressive act is one in which the player intentionally tries to hurt his or her opponent. The behaviours that coaches and parents should try to encourage in their athletes and children are correctly labelled *assertive* behaviours.

MYTH: Aggression is only a physical behaviour.
A classic scene in the movie *Slapshot* exemplifies this myth. An opponent was trying to get the Chiefs' goalie off of his game, so he skated by the goalie and said something insulting about a member of the goalie's family. The Chiefs' goalie then skated after the opposing player, trying to slash him with his stick. A verbal insult like trash talking can be considered an aggressive act since it is an intentional attempt to psychologically hurt (i.e., distract or intimidate) a person.

MYTH: Athletes are born with certain moral behaviours.
Similar to other behaviours in sport, moral behaviours are influenced by our environment. Coaches, parents, and teammates play a key role in how athletes will behave during competition.

MYTH: Participating in physical sports will decrease the desire to behave aggressively.
It is widely believed that people can get rid of their aggressive urges by participating in a sport that has a lot of physical contact (e.g., football, hockey) and through this participation be able to reduce aggressive behaviour. However, this notion of catharsis has not found any support in the literature.

Review Questions

1. Discuss the differences among aggression, assertion, and violence.
2. What are the two classic perspectives for examining the development of moral behaviour in sport?
3. Discuss the four factors that influence the development of moral behaviours in sport and provide a sport example of each.
4. Explain the difference between instrumental and hostile aggression.
5. Hockey Canada hires you as a consultant to offer workshops to their players, coaches, and officials regarding the appropriateness of aggression in hockey. What will you tell them during the workshops?
6. As the sport psychology consultant for a Major Junior A team, you notice that one of the players frequently takes retaliation-type penalties after being bodychecked by an opposing player. How will you help the player understand why he behaves this way, and help him change his behaviour?
7. Describe four group factors that influence aggression in sport.

Suggested Reading

Shields, D. L., & Bredemier, B. L. (2007). Can sports build character? In D. Smith, & M. Bar-Eli (Eds.), *Essential readings in sport and exercise psychology* (pp. 423–432). Champaign, IL: Human Kinetics.

Widmeyer, W. N., Bray, S. R., Dorsch, K. D., & McGuire, E. J. (2002). Explanations for the occurrence of aggression: Theories and research. In J. M. Silva, & D. E. Stevens (Eds.), *Psychological foundations of sport* (pp. 352–379). Boston: Allyn & Bacon.

References

Arnold, P. J. (2001). Sport, moral development, and the role of the teacher: Implications for research and moral education. *Quest, 53*, 135–150.

Bandura, A. (1973). *Aggression: A social learning analysis*. Englewood Cliffs, NJ: Prentice-Hall.

Bandura, A. (1999). Moral disengagement in the perpetration of inhumanities. *Personality and Social Psychology Review, 3*, 193–209.

Beller, J. M., & Stoll, S. K. (1995). Moral reasoning of high school student athletes and general students: An empirical study versus personal testimony. *Pediatric Exercise Science, 7*, 352–363.

Berkowitz, L. (1989). Frustration-aggression hypothesis: Examination and reformulation. *Psychological Bulletin, 106*, 59–73.

Berkowitz, L. (1990). On the formation and regulation of anger and aggression. A cognitive-neoassociationistic analysis. *American Psychologist, 45*, 494–503.

Bessette, N., & Loughead, T. M. (2007, November). *The examination of cohesion and norms for aggression on perceived belonging in youth minor hockey*. Paper presented to the Canadian Society for Psychomotor Learning and Sport Psychology Conference, Windsor, ON.

Bloom, G. A., & Smith, M. D. (1996). Hockey violence: A test of cultural spillover theory. *Sociology of Sport Journal, 13*, 65–77.

Bloom, G. A., & Vanier, J. L. (2004). Coaches' perceptions of aggression in elite women's ice hockey. In D. J. Pearsall, & A. B. Ashare (Eds.), *Safety in ice hockey: Fourth Volume* (pp. 12–25). Philadelphia: American Society for Testing and Materials.

Brice, J. G. (1990). *Frustration in ice hockey: Extent, antecedents and consequences*. Unpublished master's thesis, University of Waterloo, Waterloo, Ontario, Canada.

Brunelle, J. P., Janelle, C. M., & Tennant, L. K. (1999). Controlling competitive anger among male soccer players. *Journal of Applied Sport Psychology, 11*, 283–297.

Bryant, J., Brown, D., Comisky, P. W., & Zillman, D. (1982). Sports and spectators: Commentary and appreciation. *Journal of Communications, 32*, 109–119.

Bryant, J., Comisky, P. W., & Zillman, D. (1981). The appeal of rough-and-tumble play in televised football. *Communication Quarterly, 29*, 256–262.

Bryant, J., & Zillman, D. (1983). Sports violence and the media. In J. Goldstein (Ed.), *Sport violence* (pp. 195–211). New York: Springer Verlag.

Bushman, B. J. (2002). Does venting anger feed or extinguish the flame? Catharsis, rumination, distraction, anger, and aggressive responding. *Personality and Social Psychology Bulletin, 28*, 724–731.

Carron, A. V. (1988). *Group dynamics in sport*. London, ON: Spodym.

Colburn, K. (1986). Deviance and legitimacy in ice-hockey: A microstructural theory of violence. *The Sociological Quarterly, 27*, 63–74.

Contracts for parents? (2000, October 3). CBC. Retrieved September 15, 2009, from www.cbc.ca/news/story/2000/10/03/bc_parentscontracts001003.html

Cox, R. H. (2002). *Sport psychology: Concepts and applications* (5th ed.). New York: McGraw Hill.

Dollard, J. C., Doob, L., Miller, N., Mowrer, O. H., & Sears, R. R. (1939). *Frustration and aggression*. New Haven, CT: Yale University Press.

Dorsch, K. D. (1992). *The extent and antecedents of aggression in PeeWee hockey*. Unpublished manuscript, University of Waterloo, Waterloo, Ontario, Canada.

Dorsch, K. D. (1997). *Examining aggressive behaviour from a group perspective*. Unpublished doctoral dissertation, University of Waterloo, Waterloo, Ontario, Canada.

Dorsch, K. D., McAuliffe, J., & Paskevich, D. M. (2000, April). Perceived stress, burnout, coping styles, and intentions to terminate among Canadian squash officials. *The Squash Official*, 6–7.

Dorsch, K. D., Riemer, H. A., Kolmel, W., Hoeber, L., Howald, S., Park, I., Baxter-Jones, A., & Alfano, D. P. (2004, October). *Perceptions of aggressive behaviour in Atom ice hockey*. Paper presented at the meeting of the Canadian Society for Psychomotor Learning and Sport Psychology, Saskatoon, SK.

Dorsch, K. D., Widmeyer, W. N., Paskevich, D. M., & Brawley, L. R. (1996). Exploring relationships among collective efficacy, norms for aggression, cohesion, and aggressive behaviour in Junior hockey. *Journal of Applied Sport Psychology, 8*, 55.

Fans vs athletes: 10 ugly incidents. (2004, November 24). CBC. Retrieved January 8, 2005, from www.cbc.ca/sports/columns/top10/fan_violence.html

Folkesson, P., Nyberg, C., Archer, T., & Norlander, T. (2002). Soccer referees' experience of threat and aggression: Effects of age, experience, and life orientation on outcome of coping strategy. *Aggressive Behavior, 28*, 317–327.

Forsythe, D. R. (1999). *Group dynamics* (3rd ed.). Belmont, CA: Brooks/Cole.

Freud, S. (1925). *Collected papers*. London, UK: Hogarth Press.

Games code of conduct introduced. (2002, February 5). CBC. Retrieved January 8, 2005 from http://north.cbc.ca/regional/servlet/View?filename=fe5conduct

Giebink, M. P., & McKenzie, T. L. (1985). Teaching sportsmanship in physical education and recreation: An analysis of interventions and generalizations effects. *Journal of Teaching in Physical Education, 4*,167–177.

Girard, D. (2004, December 23). Canucks superstar; Gets discharge for brutal attack on Colorado's Moore. *Toronto Star*, p. A01.

Haan, N. (1991). Moral development and action from a social constructivist perspective. In W. M. Kurtines, & J. L. Gewirtz (Eds.), *Handbook of moral behavior and development: Vol. 1. Theory* (pp. 251–273). Hillsdale, NJ: Erlbaum.

Harrell, W. A. (1980). Aggression by high school basketball players: An observational study of the effects of opponents' aggression and frustration inducing factors. *International Journal of Sport Psychology, 11*, 290–298.

Hastorf, A. H., & Cantril, H. (1954). They saw a game: A case study. *Journal of Abnormal and Social Psychology, 59*, 129–134.

Jones, M. V., Bray, S. R., & Olivier, S. (2005). Game location and aggression in rugby league. *Journal of Sports Sciences, 23*, 387–393.

Katorji, J. K., & Cahoon, M. A. (1992). *The relationship between aggression and injury in Junior B hockey*. Unpublished manuscript, University of Waterloo, Waterloo, ON, Canada.

Kavussanu, M., & Roberts, G. C. (2001). Moral functioning in sport: An achievement goal perspective. *Journal of Sport & Exercise Psychology, 23*, 37–54.

Kavussanu, M., Seal, A. R., & Phillips, D. R. (2006). Observed prosocial and antisocial behaviors in male soccer teams: Age differences across adolescence and the role of motivational variables. *Journal of Applied Sport Psychology, 18*, 326–344.

Kirker, B., Tenenbaum, G., & Mattson, J. (2000). An investigation of the dynamics of aggression: Direct observations in ice hockey and basketball. *Research Quarterly for Exercise and Sport, 71*, 373–386.

Kohlberg, L. (1984). *Essays on moral development: Vol 1. The philosophy of moral development*. San Francisco: Harper & Row.

Lefebvre, L. M., & Passer, M. W. (1974). The effects of game location and importance on aggression in team sport. *International Journal of Sport Psychology, 5*, 102–110.

Lemieux, P., McKelvie, S. J., & Stout, D. (2002, December). Self-reported hostile aggression in contact athletes, no contact athletes and non-athletes. *Athletic Insight: The Online Journal of Sport Psychology, 4*. Retrieved December 29, 2004, from www.athleticinsight.com/Vol4Iss3/SelfReportedAggression.htm

Loughead, T. M., & Leith, L. M. (2001). Hockey coaches' and players' perceptions of aggression and the aggressive behavior of players. *Journal of Sport Behavior, 24*, 394–407.

Luxbacher, J. (1986). Violence in sport: An examination of the theories of aggression, and how the coach can influence the degree of violence in sport. *Coaching Review, 9*,14–17.

McGregor, J. (2002). Girl charged in hockey scuffle. *The Toronto Star*. Retrieved April 3, 2002, from www.thestar.com/NASApp/cs

McGuire, E. J. (1990). *Antecedents of aggressive behaviour in professional ice hockey*. Unpublished doctoral dissertation, University of Waterloo, Waterloo, ON, Canada.

McGuire, E. J., Courneya, K. S., Widmeyer, W. N., & Carron, A. V. (1992). Aggression as a potential mediator of the home advantage in professional ice hockey. *Journal of Sport and Exercise Psychology, 14*, 148–158.

Meakin, D. C. (1981). Physical education: An agency of moral education. *Journal of the Philosophy of Education, 15*, 241–253.

Meant no harm. (2000, September 28). *Sports Illustrated*. Retrieved January 3, 2005, from http://sportsillustrated.cnn.com/hockey/nhl/news/2000/09/27/mcsorley_ap

Mummendey, A., Bornewasser, M., Löschper, G., & Linneweber, V. (1982). Defining interactions as aggressive in specific social contexts. *Aggressive Behavior, 8*, 224–228.

Mummendey, A., Linneweber, V., & Löschper, G. (1984a). Aggression: From act to interaction. In A. Mummendey (Ed.), *Social psychology of aggression: From individual behaviour to social interaction*. Berlin, Germany: Springer-Verlag.

Mummendey, A., Linneweber, V., & Löschper, G. (1984b). Actor of victim of aggression: Divergent perspectives – divergent evaluations. *European Journal of Social Psychology, 14*, 297–311.

Nicholls, J. G. (1989). *The competitive ethos and democratic education*. Cambridge, MA: Harvard University Press.

Parrott, A., Choi, P., & Davies, M. (1994). Anabolic steroid use by amateur athletes: Effects upon psychological mood states. *Journal of Sports Medicine and Physical Fitness, 34*, 292–298.

Piaget, J. (1932). *The moral judgement of the child*. New York: Harcourt & Brace.

Rainey, D. W. (1994). Assaults on umpires: A statewide survey. *Journal of Sport Behavior, 17*, 148–155.

Rehm, J., Steinleitner, M., & Lilli, W. (1987). Wearing uniforms and aggression – A field experiment. *European Journal of Social Psychology, 17*, 357–360.

Riefman, A. S., Larrick, R. P., & Fein, S. (1991). Temper and temperature on the diamond: The heat-aggression relationship in major league baseball. *Personality and Social Psychology Bulletin, 17*, 580–585.

Russell, G. W. (1993). *The social psychology of sport*. New York: Springer Verlag.

Russell, G. W. (1995). Personalities in the crowd: Those who would escalate a sports riot. *Aggressive Behavior, 21*, 91–100.

Russell, G. W., & Arms, R. L. (1995). False consensus effect, physical aggression, anger, and a willingness to escalate a disturbance. *Aggressive Behavior, 21*, 381–386.

Sanszole, M. (1995). *The extent, antecedents and response to sport frustration by high school students*. Unpublished manuscript, University of Waterloo, Waterloo, ON, Canada.

Shapcott, K. M., Bloom, G. A., & Loughead, T. M. (2007). Factors influencing aggressive and assertive intentions of women ice hockey players. *International Journal of Sport Psychology, 38*, 145–162.

Shields, D. L., & Bredemeier, B. J. (1995). *Character development and physical activity*. Champaign, IL: Human Kinetics.

Shield, D. L., LaVoi, N. M., Bredemeier, B. L., & Power, F. C. (2007). Predictors of poor sportspersonship in youth sports: Personal attitudes and social influences. *Journal of Sport & Exercise Psychology, 29*, 747–762.

Silva, J. M. (1980). Understanding aggressive behavior and its effects upon athletic performance. In W. F. Straub (Ed.), *Sport psychology: An analysis of athlete behavior*. Ithaca, NY: Mouvement Publications.

Smith, M. D. (1979). Social determinants of violence in hockey. *Canadian Journal of Applied Sport Sciences, 4*, 76–82.

Smith, M. D. (1983). *Violence and sport*. Toronto, ON: Butterworth.

Stephens, D. E. (2000). Predictors of likelihood to aggress in youth soccer: An examination of coed and all-girls teams. *Journal of Sport Behavior, 23*, 311–325.

Stephens, D. E. (2004, Winter). Moral atmosphere and aggression in collegiate intramural sport. *International Sports Journal*, 65–75.

Stephens, D. E., & Kavanagh, B. (2003, Summer). Aggression in Canadian youth ice hockey: The role of moral atmosphere. *International Sports Journal*, 109–119.

Storr, A. (1968). *Human aggression*. London, UK: Penguin.

Stuart, M. E., & Ebbeck, V. (1995). The influence of perceived social approval on moral development in youth sport. *Pediatric Exercise Science*, *7*, 270–280.

Tenenbaum, G., Stewart, E., Singer, R. N., & Duda, J. (1996). Aggression and violence in sport: An ISSP position stand. *International Journal of Sport Psychology*, *27*, 229–236.

Terry, P. C., & Jackson, J. J. (1985). The determinants and control of violence in sport. *Quest*, *37*, 27–37.

Treasure, D. (2002). Teaching ethics via sports. *The Futurist*, *36*, 2–3.

Tuchman, G. (2000, September 26). Hockey player goes on trial for on-ice assault. CNN. Retrieved January 3, 2005, from http://archives.cnn.com/2000/LAW/criminal/09/25/mcsorley.trial.02/

Vanier, J., Bloom, G. A., & Loughead, T. M. (2005). Personal experiences, rules, procedures, and aspectsof aggression in competitive women's ice hockey. *Avante*, *11*, 66–82.

Visek, A., & Watson, J. (2005). Ice hockey players' legitimacy of aggression and professionalization of attitudes. *The Sport Psychologist*, *19*, 178–192.

Wandzilak, T., Carroll, T., & Ansorge, C. J. (1988). Values development through physical activity: Promoting sportsmanlike behaviors, perceptions, and moral reasoning. *Journal of Teaching Physical Education*, *8*, 13–22.

Wankel, L. M. (1973, October). An examination of illegal aggression in intercollegiate hockey. In *Proceedings: Fourth Canadian psycho-motor learning and sport psychology symposium* (pp. 531–544). Waterloo, ON: University of Waterloo.

Wann, D. L. & Porcher, B. J. (1998). The relationship between players' names on uniforms and athletic aggression. *International Sports Journal*, *2*, 28–35.

Widmeyer, W. N. (2002). Reducing aggression in sport. In J. M. Silva, & D. E. Stevens (Eds.), *Psychological foundations of sport* (pp. 380–395). Boston: Allyn & Bacon.

Widmeyer, W. N., Bray, S. R., Dorsch, K. D., & McGuire, E. J. (2002). Explanations for the occurrence of aggression: Theories and research. In J. M. Silva, & D. E. Stevens (Eds.), *Psychological foundations of sport* (pp. 352–379). Boston: Allyn & Bacon.

Widmeyer, W. N., & McGuire, E. J. (1997). Frequency of competition and aggression in professional ice hockey. *International Journal of Sport Psychology*, *26*, 57–60.

Yates, W. R., Perry, P. J., & Murray, S. (1992). Aggression and hostility in anabolic steroid users. *Biological Psychiatry*, *31*, 1232–1234.

Zarrella, J. (2000, July 10). Florida youth league requires parents to learn sportsmanship. CNN. Retrieved January 3, 2005, from http://archives.cnn.com/2000/HEALTH/07/10/kids.sports.parents/index.html

Chapter 9

Youth Involvement and Positive Development in Sport

Jean Côté

Jessica Fraser-Thomas

Chapter Objectives

After reading this chapter, you should be able to do the following:

1. Define the objectives of youth sport.
2. Describe the positive and negative outcomes that can result from youth-sport participation.
3. Understand the principles of positive youth development as applied to youth sport.
4. Discuss youth-sport programs and the types of activities likely to lead to positive sport experiences.
5. Discuss how coaches and parents can influence positive youth-sport participation.
6. Understand the major theoretical frameworks of youth-sport motivation and development.

---

* Support for the writing of this chapter was provided through a Standard Research Grant from the Social Sciences and Humanities Research Council of Canada (SSHRC Grant 410-08-1266). The authors are grateful to Kristin Côté, Dany MacDonald, and Leisha Strachan for their helpful comments in the preparation of this chapter.

From ages 7 to 12, Sebastian and Olivia were neighbours and played on the same local hockey team. In the summer, they played soccer and tennis. They also liked swimming and playing pickup basketball and street hockey in their free time. Their soccer coach, Nick, was a physical education teacher and had many years of experience coaching youth sport. As a coach, Nick taught sport skills sequentially and logically, providing informative, positive, and constructive feedback to his players. Nick believed that sports offered children opportunities to learn important life skills, such as co-operation, responsibility, empathy, respect, and self-control. Accordingly, he used time during practices and games to deliberately teach and discuss these life skills with his players. Nick's teams were never the best in the league; however, Nick's goal was to make sure that all his players loved the game and felt good about their sport participation. At age 30, Sebastian and Olivia attribute many of their current successes to the values they learned through their youth-sport participation. Sebastian is now an award-winning teacher and a recreational tennis player. Olivia obtained a graduate degree in kinesiology, played university hockey, and is now a member of the women's national hockey team.

Two other children, Madelyn and Rachel, had very different experiences from each other in youth sports. They played hockey year round from ages 5 to 12. They were highly involved as early as age 5 in extra hockey training, such as power skating lessons and hockey schools. At age 13, Madelyn dropped out of hockey and did not get involved in any other sports. Now, at age 30, she has a successful career but is not regularly involved in any type of physical activity. She does not have particularly positive memories of her youth-sport experiences. Rachel, on the other hand, also 30, is now playing on a line with Olivia on the women's national hockey team. Rachel's life has always revolved around hockey, and she has not yet had a chance to think about what she will do when she retires from hockey.

The final example is Michael: he never had the opportunity to participate in youth sport or other extracurricular activities, such as music or art. He spent much of his youth in unstructured leisure activities, such as watching television or hanging out with friends. At age 30, he has a sedentary lifestyle, is overweight, and is struggling to find a meaningful career.

These scenarios describe a number of different youth-sport experiences and outcomes. Sebastian and Olivia were fortunate to experience various sports during their childhood. They had coaches who taught them skills while being caring and understanding. For Sebastian, his youth-sport experiences did not lead to elite performance; however, his positive sport experiences helped him to understand the value of regular physical activity and health and gave him assets that helped his personal and professional development. Madelyn and Rachel were intensely involved in one sport from ages 5 to 12 and accordingly developed high-level skills. Rachel persisted with her training and eventually was selected for the national team; on the other hand, Madelyn showed signs of burnout and completely dropped out of hockey and other sports at age 13. Madelyn's intense training at a young age reduced her enjoyment of hockey and eventually led her to an inactive lifestyle. Unfortunately, Michael did not have opportunities to get involved in sports or other extracurricular activities. Spending less time in constructive leisure activities, such as sports, may have limited the number of developmental assets that Michael acquired as a child, which in turn may have led him to a more apathetic lifestyle.

The above scenarios illustrate explicit experiences and outcomes of youth sport that are not always evident. Nevertheless, the scenarios provide examples that raise a number of questions about youth-sport participation. What is the goal of youth sport? What are the best contexts and training patterns for youth-sport participation? How should contexts and training patterns change according to children's age and development? In this chapter, we will provide answers to these and other questions related to youth-sport participation.

Common Myths about Youth Involvement in Sport

MYTH: Involvement in youth sport builds character.

MYTH: Involvement in sport leads to negative outcomes, such as violence and aggression.

MYTH: To become elite athletes, children must specialize in their sport by age six or seven.

MYTH: Parents should limit their involvement in their children's sport.

MYTH: Youth-sport coaches should be specialists in the sport that they are coaching.

INTRODUCTION

Data from Statistics Canada show that two million Canadian children aged 5 to 14 (51%) regularly take part in organized sports (Clark, 2008). The significance of sport involvement for youth is considerable given that most children typically begin their involvement in organized sport when they are in their formative years (De Knop, Engström, & Skirstad, 1996; Smith & Smoll, 1990). The significance of sport as an integral avenue for youth development has been formally recognized as an important global issue. In 1999, the United Nations Educational, Scientific and Cultural Organization (UNESCO) organized the Third International Conference of Ministers and Senior Officials Responsible for Physical Education and Sport (MINEPS III). At the conference, a declaration was made to start a global movement toward youth sport and physical education participation. This declaration supports the significance of sport in the life of youth by acknowledging that sport is an essential and integral part of education and of individual and social development (UNESCO, 1999). Following this, the European Union proclaimed 2004 as the European Year of Education through Sport. Furthermore, the United Nations General Assembly adopted a resolution proclaiming 2005 as the International Year of Sport and Physical Education as a means to promote education, health, development, and peace.

These organizations' recognition of the health and developmental benefits of youth sport comes at a critical time, as cultures around the world are experiencing the institutionalization of youth sport (De Knop et al., 1996). Socioeconomic status and environmental factors are becoming greater barriers to youth-sport opportunities given that programs are becoming increasingly expensive, competitive, and elitist. In this chapter, we highlight how sport must continue to be embraced and promoted as an activity that provides children with a chance to experience enjoyment and acquire positive outcomes, such as enhancing physical and mental health, meeting challenges, experiencing social interaction, and developing new skills.

OBJECTIVES OF YOUTH SPORT

Youth sport has the potential to accomplish three important objectives in children's development. First, sport programs provide youth with opportunities to be physically active, which can lead to improved physical health. Second, youth-sport programs have long been considered important to youth's psychosocial development, providing opportunities to learn important life skills such as co-operation, discipline, leadership, and self-control. Third, youth-sport programs are critical for the learning ofmotor skills; these motor skills serve as a foundation for future national sport stars and recreational adult-sport participants.

These three objectives may appear to conflict; however, it is important that youth-sport programs focus on all three objectives rather than just one or two at the cost of the others. For example, a youth-sport program that focuses solely on the learning of sport skills at the cost of children's physical health and psychosocial development would be inefficient. Similarly, a sole focus on children's physical health at the cost of developing fundamental sport skills and children's psychosocial assets would limit the potential influence of sport on children's overall development. Instead, youth-sport programs that focus on fun, skill development, and maximum participation encourage people to stay involved and achieve success at all developmental stages of life and at all levels of sport. To promote a culture of sport participation and performance, the roles of physical education, school sports, recreational sports, and performance sports should all be linked because the independent development of these programs is expensive and ineffective. Thus, by focusing on the common building blocks that all young people need, we can reduce costs and increase the benefits associated with sport participation.

REFLECTIONS 9.1

There are three primary objectives of youth sport: to improve children's physical health, to promote positive psychosocial development among children, and to teach children motor skills. Think of your experiences in youth sport. How well did sport contribute to each of the above objectives? Describe how children's sport programs can promote these three objectives equally.

Photograph © Stockbyte.

Clearly, youth-sport programs have the potential to contribute to positive youth outcomes, but these positive outcomes do not occur automatically through youth-sport involvement. In the next section we will briefly review the positive and negative physical, psychological, emotional, and social outcomes that have been associated with youth-sport participation. The rest of this chapter will focus on developmental activities and contexts of sport programs that are likely to lead to improved health, psychosocial development, and the learning of motor skills among youth.

OUTCOMES ASSOCIATED WITH YOUTH-SPORT PARTICIPATION

For the most part, we hear of the positive outcomes associated with youth-sport involvement: health benefits, increased self-esteem, friendships, discipline, teamwork, and competence. However, more and more frequently, we are hearing of more negative youth-sport experiences: insensitive coaches, pressure from parents, peer victimization, aggression, and decreased self-esteem. Although no studies have empirically shown a cause–effect relationship between youth-sport participation and developmental outcomes (due to methodological and ethical difficulties), Table 9.1 outlines the positive

Table 9.1 Positive and Negative Outcomes of Youth Sport

	Positive Outcomes	Negative Outcomes
Physical health	• Cardiovascular fitness • Weight control • Muscular strength/endurance • Adult physical activity • Decreased risk of adult heart disease • Decreased risk of diabetes • Decreased risk of osteoporosis • Decreased risk of cancer	• Overuse injuries • Eating disorders
Psychological development	• Fun and enjoyable experiences • Challenging experiences • Increased self-esteem • Decreased stress • Increased life satisfaction • Increased happiness	• Decreased self-perceptions • Decreased confidence/self-esteem • Experience of isolation from teammates • Experience of excessive pressure • Burnout
Social development	• Positive intergroup and peer relationships • Citizenship • Social status and success • Social mobility • Leadership skills • Increased academic performance • Enhanced adult career achievement • Decreased school dropout • Decreased delinquent behaviour	• Aggression • Assault • Poor sportspersonship • Decreased moral reasoning • Increased drinking

and negative outcomes associated with youth sport based on research in the areas of physical health, psychological development, and social development (see Fraser-Thomas, Côté, & Deakin, 2005, for a review).

As Table 9.1 shows, sport involvement can contribute to physical health and positive psychological and social development; however, there is also evidence of less-desirable relationships between sport participation and youth development. A key to understanding whether youth-sport programs foster positive outcomes is to first identify the processes that occur within them. Youth-sport programs provide a platform for positive youth development, and, if structured appropriately, they can have direct effects on youth's present and future development and productivity. There is a growing body of literature in developmental psychology recognizing the importance of sports as prosocial activities that can contribute to youth's positive life trajectories and more civil societies (Eccles & Barber, 1999; Larson, 2000). Before discussing sport-specific contexts that are likely to lead to positive outcomes in youth, we will discuss major principles of positive youth development that could potentially be helpful in promoting the health, psychosocial development, and learning of motor skills in youth.

REFLECTIONS 9.2

Many sport programs aim to promote positive youth development. Examine the websites of these organizations and programs below. What are the goals and values of these organizations? What kinds of environments do these programs aim to create?

Ottawa Lions Track and Field Club: www.ottawalions.com
YMCA Canada: www.ymca.ca
Barrie Women's Hockey Association: www.bwha.ca
Halifax County United Soccer Club: www.hcusoccer.ca
Stampede City Gymnastic Club: www.stampedecitygym.com
Church Athletic League of Kingston: www.calkingston.org
True Sport: www.truesportpur.ca

PRINCIPLES OF POSITIVE YOUTH DEVELOPMENT

Developmental Assets

Benson (1997) has outlined 40 **developmental assets**, commonly termed the "building blocks" for human development (see Table 9.2). The development of these assets in youth embodies a broad vision of communities and youth interacting in positive and effective manners. The assets fall into two broad categories: external assets and internal assets. Within each of these two broad categories, four types of assets exist. **External assets** comprise support, empowerment, boundaries and expectations, and constructive use of time. **Internal assets** comprise commitment to learning, positive values, social competencies, and positive identity. Benson and others (Benson, 1997; Scales & Leffert, 1999) found that the more developmental assets an adolescent possesses, the greater his or her likelihood of

Table 9.2 Forty Developmental Assets for Human Development

Category	Type	Assets
External assets (1–20)	Support (1–6)	1. Family support
		2. Positive family communication
		3. Other adult relationships
		4. Caring neighbourhood
		5. Caring school climate
		6. Parent involvement in schooling
	Empowerment (7–10)	7. Community values youth
		8. Youth as resources
		9. Service to others
		10. Safety
	Boundaries and expectations (11–16)	11. Family boundaries
		12. School boundaries
		13. Neighbourhood boundaries
		14. Adult role models
		15. Positive peer influence
		16. High expectations
	Constructive use of time (17–20)	17. Creative activities
		18. Youth programs
		19. Religious community
		20. Time at home
Internal assets (21–40)	Commitment to learning (21–25)	21. Achievement motivation
		22. School engagement
		23. Homework
		24. Bonding to school
		25. Reading for pleasure
	Positive values (26–31)	26. Caring
		27. Equality and social justice
		28. Integrity
		29. Honesty
		30. Responsibility
		31. Restraint
	Social competencies (32–36)	32. Planning and decision making
		33. Interpersonal competence
		34. Cultural competence
		35. Resistance skills
		36. Peaceful conflict resolution
	Positive identity (37–40)	37. Personal power
		38. Self-esteem
		39. Sense of purpose
		40. Positive view of personal future

Note: Adapted from P. L. Benson, (2006). *All Kids Are Our Kids: What Communities Must Do to Raise Caring and Responsible Children and Adolescents.* 2nd ed. San Francisco: Jossey-Bass, pp.75–76. Adapted with permission of John Wiley & Sons, Inc.

developing in a positive and healthy manner. Specifically, the more assets an adolescent possesses, the more likely that he or she will "thrive" (e.g., show leadership, volunteer, get good grades) and the less likely that he or she will use alcohol or be depressed, suicidal, or violent.

Programs fostering Benson's 40 developmental assets have been found to lead to positive youth development. While sport programs cannot be expected to foster all 40 assets, Petitpas and colleagues (Petitpas, Cornelius, Van Raalte, & Jones, 2005; Petitpas, Cornelius, & Van Raalte, 2008) offer a framework for planning sport programs that foster psychosocial development, with an emphasis on internal and external developmental assets. We believe that sport programs have the potential to contribute to many developmental assets. For example, involvement in sport programs can foster external assets in the areas of constructive use of time, emotional support from family, empowerment, positive social relationships, and high expectations. Past research also indicates that youth-sport programs have the potential to foster numerous internal assets, such as achievement motivation, school engagement, caring, responsibility, social competencies, conflict resolution skills, and a sense of positive identity (Benson, 1997; Scales & Leffert, 1999).

Desirable Youth-Sport Program Settings

The National Research Council (NRC) and Institute of Medicine (IOM) in the United States (NRC & IOM, 2002) outlined eight features of settings that are most likely to foster positive assets in youth. All these features should be considered by policy makers, sport organizations, parents, and coaches when they are designing and implementing youth-sport programs. These eight features are shown in Table 9.3.

First, the NRC and IOM suggest that physical and psychological safety and security are essential to any setting aimed at promoting positive youth development. Although a child's physical safety is often a concern in sport settings, children's psychological and emotional sense of security must not be overlooked. If programs are implemented inappropriately, sport environments can often be intimidating or even frightening to youth. Second, settings must provide clear and consistent (age-appropriate) structure and appropriate adult supervision. All too often in youth-sport settings, coaches are volunteers with insufficient knowledge of youth's developmental capabilities. The third and fourth setting features are supportive adult relationships (with parents and coaches) and opportunities to belong. Again, these relationships and opportunities must be worked toward, rather than assumed to occur.

Table 9.3 Features of Positive Development Settings for Youth

Physical and psychological safety
Appropriate structure
Supportive relationships
Opportunities to belong
Positive social norms
Support for efficacy and mattering
Opportunities for skill building
Integration of family, school, and community efforts

Note: Adapted from National Research Council (NRC) and Institute of Medicine (IOM). (2002). *Community programs to promote youth development.* Washington, DC: National Academy Press.

The fifth setting feature, positive social norms, is usually assumed to be facilitated by youth-sport programs; however, much research continues to indicate that many programs promote exaggerated masculinity, aggression, and competitiveness (Eder & Parker, 1987). For the sixth feature, the NRC and IOM suggest that settings support youth's efficacy and sense of mattering. More specifically, youth-sport programs must be child-centred and promote empowerment, autonomy, and opportunities to experience challenge. The seventh setting feature concerns skill-building opportunities, which are often provided in sport but occur only through developmentally appropriate program designs and coaching. Finally, programs that integrate family, school, and community create optimal environments for positive youth development because this integration creates opportunities for meaningful communication between different settings in youth's lives.

Fostering Initiative through Constructive Activities

Researchers have also taken an interest in the type of activities that lead to positive youth development. Children's activities have been classified into two categories: relaxed leisure activities and constructive leisure activities. **Relaxed leisure activities** (e.g., watching television, hanging out) are activities that are enjoyable but not demanding in terms of effort. **Constructive leisure activities** (e.g., sport, music, art) can also be enjoyable but require sustained effort toward the achievement of a clear goal. Larson (2000) argues that constructive leisure activities, rather than relaxed leisure activities, foster initiative development in children. He suggests that **initiative** (the ability to be motivated from within and to direct attention and effort toward a challenging goal over time) is a core quality of positive physical, psychological, and social development in children. As such, activities promoting initiative development must have three essential elements. First, they must be intrinsically motivating. Second, they must involve concerted attention toward specific goals. Third, they must occur over an extended period of time (i.e., regular involvement). Larson argues that constructive leisure activities provide these three elements and thus foster initiative.

When reviewing how youth spend their time around the world, Larson and Verma (1999) found sport participation to be the most popular constructive leisure activity for youth in North America and Europe. In addition, Larson and Kleiber (1993) reported that youth devote more attention to sports and games than to other daily life activities, such as schoolwork or watching television. These findings suggest that for many young people, sport may be more important than any other daily activity in contributing to positive development and the growth of critical adult skills, such as initiative and the capacity for autonomous action. Danish and colleagues (Danish, 2002; Theokas, Danish, Hodge, Ihirangi, & Forneris, 2008) have done extensive work on teaching life skills in youth sport settings. They have developed a program called SUPER (Sports United to Promote Education and Recreation) to teach life skills to young athletes through a peer-led series of 18 modules taught like sport clinics. SUPER sport programs also provide opportunities for coaches and athletes to demonstrate, model, and practise what they are teaching and learning.Unfortunately, the principles of SUPER programs are not always reproduced within community or school sport systems. Not all community and school sport programs create enjoyable and challenging environments that are able to develop initiative and life skills in youth while sustaining their engagement over time.

Five C's of Positive Youth Development

A final framework of positive youth development is reflected in five desired outcomes of youth, or five C's of positive youth development: competence, character, connection, confidence, and caring (or compassion; Jelicic, Bobek, Phelps, Lerner, & Lerner, 2007). This developmental theory of positive youth development suggests that policies must be implemented to allow families and programs to foster and promote positive development. If this occurs, youth will demonstrate the five C's of positive youth development. Collectively, these processes will lead to a sixth C of positive youth development: contribution. As healthy youth become adults, they will choose to contribute, or give back, to family, community, and civil society. In doing so, they will be promoting the positive development of the next generation of youth.

REFLECTIONS 9.3

Take a moment and look at major periods in your development in sport from early childhood until now. Assess the different sport programs you were involved in, in terms of how they promoted the 40 developmental assets and fostered the five C's of positive youth development. Provide practical examples of how a youth-sport coach could create a setting among athletes that integrates the eight features of positive youth development.

Photography © Stockbyte.

CONSIDERATIONS FOR YOUTH-SPORT PROGRAMS

The work of researchers in positive youth development constitutes a solid foundation on which youth-sport programs can be based. Developmental assets, setting features, and the five C's of positive youth development should be considered when sport programs are being constructed in order to support the development of youth's health, psychosocial attributes, and motor skills. Although it can be assumed that most youth-sport programs intend to foster positive youth development, the research behind Table 9.1 indicates that many programs may be failing. This raises the challenging question: How do sport organizations, coaches, and parents ensure the concerted benefits of improved health, psychosocial development, and the learning of sport skills through sport participation? To do this most effectively, it is important to first examine two primary factors contributing to positive and negative experiences in youth sport, as identified in the literature: program activities and adult influences.

Youth-sport Program Activities

When coaches develop activities for youth practices and when sport organizations design youth-sport programs, they must consider the three objectives of youth sport (health, psychosocial development, and the learning of motor skills). In particular, coaches and programmers must consider the differing implications of deliberate play, deliberate practice, and early specialization.

Deliberate Play, Deliberate Practice, and Early Specialization A common trend among adults involved in regular sport and physical activity is that they were involved in a broad range of organized sports and deliberate play activities during their youth. Côté and colleagues (Côté & Hay, 2002; Côté, Baker, & Abernethy, 2003, 2007) define **deliberate play** activities in sport as those designed to maximize inherent enjoyment. These activities are regulated by flexible rules adapted from standardized sport rules and are set up and monitored by the children or by an involved adult. Children typically modify rules to find a point where their game most resembles the actual sport but still allows for play at their level. For example, children may change soccer and basketball rules to suit their environment and their needs (e.g., playing in the street, on a playing field, or in someone's backyard). When involved in deliberate play activities, children are less concerned with the outcome of their behaviour than with the behaviour. On the other hand, Ericsson, Krampe, and Tesch-Römer (1993) suggest that the most effective learning occurs through involvement in highly structured activities defined as deliberate practice. **Deliberate practice** activities require effort, generate no immediate rewards, and are motivated by the goal of improving performance rather than the goal of enjoyment. Early specialization is often characterized by high amounts of deliberate practice and low amounts of deliberate play. **Early specialization** is defined as limiting participation to one sport that is practised on a year-round basis.

Early specialization is one of the most controversial areas in youth sport. Many parents believe that early specialization will enhance their child's prospects for later elite performance.
Photography courtesy of Peter Crocker.

The two concepts of deliberate play and deliberate practice could be placed at opposite ends of a continuum. Behaviours could be located along the continuum, from those that are primarily motivated by a process-experimentation perspective (deliberate play) to those that are motivated by a goal-directed perspective (deliberate practice). When individuals are involved in deliberate play, they experiment with new or different combinations of behaviours, but not necessarily in the most effective way to improve performance.

In contrast, when individuals are involved in deliberate practice, they exhibit behaviour focused on improving performance by the most effective means available. For example, the backhand skill in tennis could be learned and improved over time by playing matches or by creating fun practice situations. However, players could more effectively improve their backhand performance by practising drills that might be considered less enjoyable. Although the drills used in deliberate practice might not be the most enjoyable, they might be the most relevant to improving performance. When one is considering the optimal amount of deliberate play, deliberate practice, and involvement in other sports that children should have in their early years, one has to consider the three objectives of youth sport: health, psychosocial development, and the learning of motor skills.

REFLECTIONS 9.4

Consider a children's sport program with which you are quite familiar. Does the program focus primarily on deliberate practice or deliberate play? Does the program's focus align with its stated objectives? Discuss how involvement during childhood and adolescence in several different sports, deliberate play activities, and deliberate practice activities may contribute to continued sport involvement or dropout.

Early Specialization and Deliberate Practice Considerations From a health perspective, an overemphasis on deliberate practice at a young age and early specialization can lead to dropout, muscle overuse, injury, and athletes' failure to develop transferable skills (Abernethy, Baker, & Côté, 2005; Fraser-Thomas, Côté, & Deakin, 2008a; Hollander, Meyers, & LeUnes, 1995; Law, Côté, & Ericsson, 2007; Wall & Côté 2007). Early specialization often has harmful effects on emotional and psychological development. For example, early specialization can lead to decreased enjoyment, disappointment, discouragement, and burnout since youth may experience a sense of failure if they are unable to meet their goals after investing so heavily (Boyd & Yin, 1996; Fraser-Thomas, Côté, & Deakin, 2008b). Early specialization is also a concern for youth's social development because it can lead to missed social opportunities experienced through early diversification (Wright & Côté, 2003).

From a skill-acquisition perspective, there is evidence that early specialization and an increased focus on deliberate practice activities during the early years can be effective in producing elite performers (Law, Côté, & Ericsson, 2007); however, as outlined above, there are many costs associated with this pattern of activities. It appears that deliberate play and involvement in various sporting activities may serve as a more cost-effective way for youth to explore their physical capacities in various contexts and to develop their sport skills. Analyses of elite athletes' early involvement in sports show that deliberate play activities and early diversification in sport activities are important during the first few years of sport participation. For example, Soberlak and Côté (2003) showed that elite ice hockey players spent slightly more time in deliberate play activities than deliberate practice activities before age 20. Although much research suggests that involvement in deliberate practice is a consistent factor that differentiates elite from non-elite athletes (e.g., Helsen, Starkes, & Hodges, 1998), the difference of time invested in deliberate practice activities generally occurs during the adolescent and adult years. Baker and Côté (2006) suggest that reducing the acquisition of sport skills

Table 9.4 Benefits and Costs of Early Specialization in Sport

Dimension of Sport Involvement	Benefits	Costs
Physical	Sport-specific skills learned	Increased injuries and reduced health
Psychosocial	Self-confidence in one sport	Lack of diverse experiences
		Reduced enjoyment
		Parental expectations/pressure
		Coaching expectations/pressure
		Dropout
		Burnout

to a single dimension (i.e., deliberate practice) fails to acknowledge important developmental, motivational, and psychosocial aspects of human abilities. However, the peak age in some sports, such as female gymnastics and figure skating, tends to be quite young. Athletes in these sports are sometimes required to specialize early in order to reach the highest levels. In these sports, extreme caution should be used. Training programs must always consider children's physical, psychological, social, and cognitive development.

Overall, early specialization and too much emphasis on deliberate practice activities during the early years of sport involvement may lead to health problems or withdrawal. Instead, an emphasis on various sport activities and deliberate play activities during childhood is likely to have immediate developmental and long-term health benefits. Some of the benefits and costs of early specialization are outlined in Table 9.4.

Many youth-sport programs are inherently designed to eventually expect specialization as athletes age and mature. Although this is a path that many young athletes choose to follow, it is not a route for all youth. Given that a lot of research attributes adolescent sport withdrawal to required time commitment and competitive focus (Linder, Johns, & Butcher, 1991; Petlichkoff, 1993), sport programmers should aim to offer both specialization (deliberate practice) and recreational programs (deliberate play) so that all adolescents can continue to enjoy and participate in sport.

REFLECTIONS 9.5

Looking back on your involvement in sport, recall all the activities that constituted your sporting experiences throughout development. Consider each sport program's focus on deliberate practice, deliberate play, and competition. Describe how the number of activities and the nature of your sporting activities changed during your development.

Role of Coaches

Coaches are a major adult influence in children's sport participation. They influence children's competence beliefs, life-skill development, sport enjoyment, and motivation for sport participation (Gould, Collins, Lauer, & Chung, 2007). However, youth coaches who place primary emphasis on winning sometimes exploit their athletes rather than consider their psychological and social best interests (Gilbert, Gilbert, & Trudel, 2001a, 2001b). As Peterson (2004) points out, youth development programs, such as sport, have the potential to "build a better kid," but the personal characteristics of group leaders are critical to the success of all youth development programs. Côté (2002) suggests that studies examining coaches' influences on youth can be categorized into three main areas: psychological growth, social skills, and motor development.

Coaches' Roles in Children's Psychological Growth The most influential studies examining coaches' influences on children's psychological growth were conducted by Ronald Smith and Frank Smoll and their colleagues at the University of Washington (see Smoll & Smith, 2002, for a review of their work). Their research took place in two phases and was centred on the development and assessment of a program called coach effectiveness training (CET), which was aimed at improving coaches' ability to interact effectively with their young athletes. Results from different studies generally showed that trained coaches were more supportive, provided more reinforcement and encouragement, and were less punitive than non-trained coaches. Additionally, participants who played for trained coaches exhibited a significant increase in self-esteem and a decrease in anxiety throughout the season compared with participants from a control group. More recent studies have demonstrated that the CET program can also help to create more positive and cohesive team atmospheres in youth sport and reduce attrition rates among young athletes (Barnett, Smoll, & Smith, 1992; Smith & Smoll, 1997).

The coach–athlete relationship also has an important influence on young athletes' experiences of sport. Jowett and her colleague (Jowett, 2003; Jowett & Timson-Katchis, 2005) have shown that three components are important to consider in the coach–athlete relationship (the three C's model): (1) closeness (i.e., feelings of trust and respect), (2) co-orientation (i.e., commitment to maintain relationships), and (3) complementarity (i.e., co-operative and supportive behaviours). Gould et al. (2007) found evidence that these three C's were the foundation of award-winning high-school coaches' ability to teach life skills to young athletes.

Coaches' Roles in Developing Children's Social Skills Youth-sport coaches are in a prime position to increase children's prosocial behaviours, such as co-operation and responsibility, and decrease children's antisocial behaviours, such as cheating and aggression (Arnold, 2001). Hellison and colleagues (Hellison, 2003; Hellison, Martinek, & Walsh, 2008) provide a framework for teaching personal and social responsibility through physical activity, and this framework can guide positive youth-development coaching. Hellison highlights the roles of integration, transfer, empowerment, and coach–athlete relationships in leading youth from irresponsibility to respect, participation, self-direction, and caring. He also provides preliminary teaching strategies, including counselling time, awareness talks, group meetings, and reflection time. In a recent review of the literature, Gould and Carson (2008) suggested that coaches' direct and indirect teaching strategies, such as the ones proposed by Hellison, are determinants of young athletes' psychosocial development and positive outcomes through sports.

Unfortunately, studies observing youth-sport coaches in real-life situations indicate that most coaches do not explicitly teach players appropriate social behaviours. Despite valuing social skills, coaches often behave in manners that conflict with children's development of appropriate social behaviours. For example, McCallister, Blinde, and Weiss (2000) explored youth-sport coaches' philosophies and values, and while coaches believed they were successful at facilitating a wide range of positive values and life skills, they struggled to articulate exactly how they did so, and their observed behaviours were often inconsistent with their stated values and philosophies. Furthermore, several authors have reported that youth-sport coaches' behaviours during games are directed primarily toward winning rather than toward players' actions and the development of players' social skills (Gilbert, Trudel, & Haughian, 1999; Wilcox & Trudel, 1998). In addition, youth-sport coaches sometimes set poor examples of fair play. In their study of Canadian youth-sport coaches during ice hockey games, Côté et al. showed that when coaches were losing, they became hostile and shouted their grievances at referees significantly more than when they were winning (Côté, Trudel, Bernard, Boileau, & Marcotte, 1993).

In the realm of youth sport, coaches play a crucial role in enabling young athletes to become self-controlled, constructive members of a team and, ultimately, productive members of society. Unfortunately, for many young athletes, sport settings stimulate a change in social values and moral reasoning patterns. For example, children tend to believe violent acts are acceptable and would be supported by coaches and parents in game situations. Youth-sport coaches should not "use language or techniques that might encourage participants to separate their sport experiences from 'real life'" (Bredemeier & Shields, 1996, p. 396). Youth sport should be seen as a medium through which social values can be learned and transferred to real-life situations.

REFLECTIONS 9.6

Consider your own experiences as a coach or athlete. What behaviours do you demonstrate most frequently as a coach? How would you evaluate your coaches' behaviours during your youth?

Photograph courtesy of Jean Côté.

Coaches' Roles in Developing Children's Motor Skills A goal for youth-sport coaches is to provide a context where all children have opportunities to learn physical skills. Key variables that affect children's learning of physical skills are on-task practice time and the coaches' instructional behaviours. Vickers (1994) presents five steps that are universal to teaching motor skills: (1) assess entry skill, (2) provide instruction, (3) facilitate practice, (4) provide feedback, and (5) evaluate learning. To teach skills effectively, one of these five steps in isolation is not sufficient. Rather, these five steps together compose a teaching process necessary for learning to occur; however, it is beyond the scope of this chapter to outline the appropriate specific pedagogical strategies to teach motor skills. We suggest that the promotion of quality instruction by coaches and participation in various sport contexts will maximize children's learning of fundamental motor skills. In summary, coaches play critical roles in youth-sport participants' learning of motor skills. Further, the environment in which this learning occurs has important implications for later sport investment and recreational participation.

Role of Parents

Hellstedt (1987) suggests that parents' involvement in their children's sport participation can be conceptualized on a continuum from under-involved, to moderately involved, to over-involved. **Under-involved parents** show "a relative lack of emotional, financial, or functional investment" (p. 153). **Moderately involved parents** are characterized by "firm parental direction, but enough flexibility so that the young athlete is allowed significant involvement in decision-making" (p. 153). Finally, **over-involved parents** "have an excessive amount of involvement in the athletic success of their children" (p. 154). Frequent behaviours of over-involved parents include yelling during competitions, disagreeing with coaches about their child's playing time, consistently asking their child to try harder, and coaching their child when unsolicited to do so. Hellstedt suggests that a moderate level of parental involvement promotes the best interests of the child, even if this means that parents must sometimes sacrifice personal interests.

Although a typology of parental involvement in sport, such as the one presented by Hellstedt, is useful, it provides little insight into the specific types of parental behaviours that have the most favourable socialization effects on children in sport. Woolger and Power (1993) identified three dimensions of parent behaviour associated with children's sport socialization, motivation, and behaviour: parental support, modelling, and expectations.

Parental Support Parents' psychosocial support is an essential element in the development of children's self-esteem, competence, and achievement. Côté and Hay (2002) suggest four categories of psychological needs for young athletes: emotional support, informational support, tangible support, and companionship. **Emotional support** is provided through parents' comforting gestures during times of stress and anxiety. When parents give their child positive feedback on his or her ability or express belief in their child's capabilities, the child believes that he or she is cared for. These supportive efforts and gestures can enhance a child's sense of competence and level of self-esteem (Cutrona & Russell, 1990). Children need to believe that what they do with their time, energy, and talent in sport is meaningful to themselves and others.

Informational support refers to parents' provision of advice or guidance in problematic situations. For example, parents can provide general information on how to choose a suitable sport program or provide specific instructions to a child on how to learn a certain technique.

Tangible support refers to concrete assistance given to children in stressful situations; parents provide necessary resources to help their children cope with events. Examples of tangible support include providing the financial assistance or the time commitment necessary for lessons, equipment, and travel associated with sport participation. Overall, tangible support is required for participation in most sport programs, and the lack of it can certainly become a constraint to a child's sport participation.

Companionship, or "network support," reflects casual relationships that enable an individual to engage in various forms of social and recreational activities (Cutrona & Russell, 1990). Parents can be involved in various kinds of companionship related to their child's participation in sport. For instance, parents can develop special relationships with their children through sport by attending their child's competitive events, collecting sports cards for their child, getting involved in deliberate play with their child, or simply by spending time travelling to and from practices with their child (Côté, 1999; Fraser-Thomas & Côté, 2009).

Parental Modelling Research on the role of parental modelling in sport contexts has been mixed. For example, one study found that maternal modelling was positively associated with boys' and girls' enthusiasm for their sport, but paternal modelling was negatively associated with boys' enthusiasm for their sport (Power & Woolger, 1994). Another recent study suggests that parents who were high-level athletes in their youth may indirectly lead to their child's disengagement in sport (Fraser-Thomas et al., 2008a). Collectively, these and other studies suggest that sport-loving families are not a prerequisite for children's motivation in sport. Nevertheless, parents of committed individuals tend to espouse values related to the importance of achievement, hard work, success, being active, and being persistent (Csikszentmihalyi, Rathunde, & Whalen, 1993; Fraser-Thomas & Côté, 2009). Therefore, home environments that offer opportunities for children to witness physically active lifestyles and the successful outcomes of sustained efforts foster positive motivational climates for sport participation.

Parental Expectations Parents' expectations can have a powerful effect on children's emotions and motivation in sport. There is a positive relationship between parental expectations and children's success and enjoyment in sport (Fredericks & Eccles, 2004). On the other hand, parental expectations can also become a source of pressure and stress that interferes with children's participation in sport (Fraser-Thomas et al., 2008b). Power and Woolger (1994) found an inverted U-shaped relationship between parental expectations and children's enthusiasm for swimming. High and low parental expectations were associated with less enthusiasm from children, while an intermediate level of expectation was associated with children's highest level of enthusiasm for swimming. Clearly, parents with inflated expectations can become a source of stress and anxiety for their children. Eccles and Harold (1991) proposed that parental expectations influence children's decisions to engage in particular activities, their intensity of effort expended in these activities, and their actual performance levels. Therefore, parents should be sensitive to the positive and negative impacts their expectations can have on their children's involvement in sport.

In summary, how children feel about themselves is largely related to how they are seen and treated by others, particularly their parents. Parents need to be constantly aware of their child's desire, motivation, and attitude toward sport so that they can modify and adjust their own behaviours.

REFLECTIONS 9.7

In 2005 in Toronto, the father of a nine-year-old boy reached over the Plexiglas at a hockey arena and choked his son's ice hockey coach. Before other parents could intervene, the coach collapsed to the ground. People involved with the team said that the dispute arose when the coach, following team rules, benched the boy for missing a practice earlier in the week. The father was released on $2000 bail and faced charges for choking. He was ordered to take anger management courses and was banned from Toronto hockey arenas. Imagine that you were interviewed by the media as an expert on youth sport, parents, and coaches. Provide your analysis of the situation.

MODELS OF SPORT MOTIVATION

In response to questions about why they play sports, children commonly cite reasons related to enjoyment (e.g., having fun), physical competence (e.g., learning skills), or social influence (e.g., being with friends). However, it is difficult to comprehend what constitutes enjoyment, competence, and positive social influence from a child's perspective. The mediational model of global self-worth and perceived competence (Harter, 1987), the achievement goal theory (Nicholls, 1989), and the self-determination theory (Deci & Ryan, 1985; Ryan & Deci, 2000) are prominent theories of motivation that have undergone substantial investigation to explain why children participate in sport. Aspects of these theories were described in some detail in Chapter 4; however, we will provide a short description of each in this chapter to help explain children's motivation for sport.

Mediational Model of Global Self-worth

The mediational model of global self-worth (Harter, 1987) suggests that children's competence-importance beliefs and their social support predict their sense of a global self-worth and their consequent motivation. For example, if children value sport as an important area for being successful, but are not very competent in sport, then their global self-worth and motivation to participate in sport will be reduced. On the other hand, if children value sport as an important area for being successful and are competent in sport, then their global self-worth and motivation will be enhanced. The social support construct of the model postulates that children's self-worth and subsequent motivation for sport are influenced by their perceptions of what significant others, such as coaches or parents, think of them. Children will have a high self-opinion if they perceive that coaches or parents have a high regard for them in sport. On the other hand, children will have a low self-opinion if they perceive that coaches or parents have a low regard for them in sport, and motivation will be affected.

Achievement Goal Theory

Achievement goal theory (Nicholls, 1989) suggests that children are not able to fully differentiate between ability and luck or between ability and effort until early adolescence. At approximately age 12, children gain a more mature conception of ability and become more capable of displaying task- or ego-involvement tendencies when participating in sports. When children are task-involved in sports, they focus on their own effort and improvement. Ego-involved children are more concerned with comparing themselves to others or with winning. As outlined in Chapter 4, there are multiple benefits to task-involvement in sport. During childhood, these benefits include increased enjoyment, effort, and motivation. Potential risks associated with ego-involvement in sport during childhood include increased anxiety and decreased motivation.

Self-determination Theory

Self-determination theory (Deci & Ryan, 1985; Ryan & Deci, 2000) supports the notion that enjoyable experiences in sport over time will positively affect individuals' overall participation motivation. Ryan and Deci (2000) suggested that building a solid foundation of intrinsic motivation through involvement in activities that promote enjoyment (i.e., deliberate play) is paramount in the development of highly motivated, self-determined individuals. Thus, children's involvement in numerous enjoyable activities can provide them with opportunities to become more self-determined and committed in their future participation in sport.

REFLECTIONS 9.8

Weiss and Williams (2004) proposed four guidelines for motivating children and youth to stay involved in sport. How are these guidelines consistent with the three primary objectives of youth sport discussed at the beginning of the chapter? How are these guidelines reinforced in youth sport?

Photograph © Photodisc/Getty Images.

Weiss and Williams (2004) reviewed some of the motivational theories outlined above and derived four practical guidelines for sustaining children's engagement in sport. First, they suggest that self-perceptions, such as perceived competence and global self-worth, are important determinants of motivated behaviour in youth sport. Therefore, parents and coaches should ensure through proper feedback and encouragement that youth maintain positive competence perceptions. Second, they emphasize that affect, or emotion, is a critical influence on child motivation because it is the final influence. They suggest that positive emotions, such as enjoyment, excitement, and pleasure, increase future motivation participation, whereas negative emotions, such as anxiety, sadness, and disappointment, decrease motivation. To promote positive emotion in sport, coaches should pay special attention to learning environments that encourage enthusiasm and playfulness, focusing on the positive behaviours of athletes and encouraging athletes' improvement (Bengoechea, Strean, & Williams, 2004; McCarthy & Jones, 2007). Third, Weiss and Williams recommend that coaches and parents implement a task-oriented climate, which focuses on self-improvement, instead of an ego-oriented climate, which focuses on comparison with others. This can be done by encouraging effort and improvement and by being careful not to reward excessive competition, physical aggression, and cheating. Finally, they highlight social support from coaches, parents, teachers, and peers as essential for continued engagement in youth sport. Through their behaviours and attitudes, significant adults and peers have an important influence on children's enjoyment, physical competence, self-worth, and, ultimately, their overall motivation to stay in sport.

THE DEVELOPMENTAL MODEL OF SPORT PARTICIPATION

The developmental model of sport participation (DMSP) by Côté and colleagues (Côté, 1999; Côté et al., 2007; Côté & Hay, 2002) emerged from extensive retrospective interviews with athletes in a variety of sports: hockey, baseball, gymnastics, rowing, tennis, and triathlon (see Figure 9.1). The DMSP proposes three possible sport participation trajectories: (1) recreational participation through sampling, (2) elite performance through sampling, and (3) elite performance through early specialization. Two of these trajectories, recreational participation and elite performance through sampling, have the same foundation from ages 6 to 12. After the sampling years, sport participants can choose to either stay involved in sport at a recreational level (recreational years, age 13+) or embark on a path that focuses primarily on performance (specializing years, ages 13–15; investment years, age 16+). These two trajectories have different outcomes in terms of performance but similar psychosocial and physical health benefits. A third possible trajectory consists of elite performance through early specialization (right side of Figure 9.1). Although this trajectory leads to elite performance, it can also result in reduced physical health (i.e., overuse injuries) and enjoyment.

Trajectory 1: Recreational Participation through Sampling

During the sampling years (ages 6–12), athletes participate in a variety of sports with the focus being primarily on deliberate play activities. These years are considered essential building blocks for recreational sport participation. The recreational years (age 13+) are usually

Figure 9.1 Developmental model of sport participation

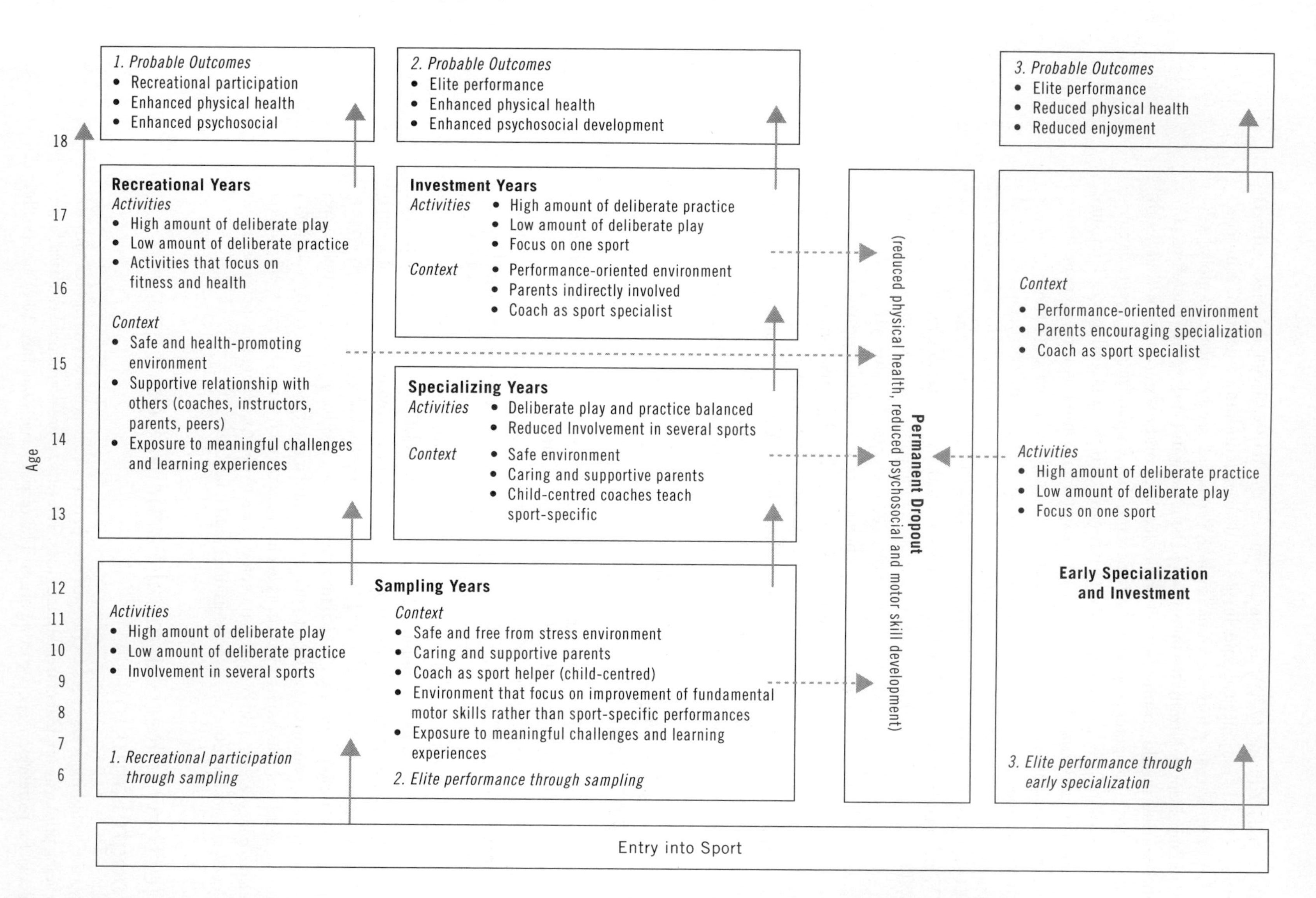

Note: Adapted from Côté, J. (1999). The influence of the family development of talent in sport. *The Sport Psychologist, 13,* 395–417; and Côté, J., & Hay, J. (2002). Children's involvement in sport: A developmental perspective. In J. M. Silva III, & D. E. Stevens (Eds.), *Psychological foundations of sport* (pp. 484–502). Boston: Allyn & Bacon.

Case Study 9.1

Simon Whitfield, Canadian Triathlete

Simon Whitfield, a native of Kingston, Ontario, was almost unknown to Canadians on September 16, 2000, when he came from behind to win Canada's first gold medal of the 2000 Olympics in Sydney, Australia. Consequently, many immediately took an interest in his path to athletic stardom.

Simon participated in many sports from a very young age. As he suggests, he began playing soccer as soon as he could crawl. His parents played a huge role in his early childhood involvement by enrolling and supporting him in a variety of activities. His older sister was also an avid athlete. As she progressed in her sports, and eventually specialized in rowing, Simon looked up to her as a role model and appreciated her support.

Simon was 11 years old when he was first exposed to triathlons, competing in the local Sharbot Lake Kids of Steel triathlon. He raced on a clunky mountain bike in a pair of boxer shorts and recalls the fun he had hanging out on the beach and enjoying a post-race barbecue.

It was not until age 15 that Simon decided to specialize in triathlon. His training increased in volume, intensity, and focus. Eventually, he relocated to the Pacific National Training Centre in British Columbia and spent a year training in Australia. He worked closely with a variety of coaches, focusing especially on his weakness, the swimming component of the triathlon.

During the weeks and months following Simon's 2000 Olympic victory, Canadians sang his praises and were proud to call him their own. His model citizenship was apparent as he travelled the country visiting schools, reaching out to children, and inspiring adults. A natural public speaker, Simon shared his positive sport experiences and served as a spokesperson for active, healthy living and fun-focused children's sport programs.

Since Simon's victory in 2000, participation in Kids of Steel and adult age-group triathlons has grown exponentially, while the depth of triathlon competition on the international stage has increased substantially. Simon remains a focused and dedicated athlete, and he has continued to refine his training regimens, competitive plans, and mental skills. His persistent popularity among Canadians was evidenced by record viewing rates on Canadian networks as he raced to his Olympic silver medal in the 2008 Beijing Olympics. He continues to share his contagious passion for sport, show remarkable respect for his competitors and support network, and claim that fun is the foundation to any successful youth-sport program.

Consider Simon's story in light of the chapter's content. Comment on Simon's sport development path using the models outlined above. Also, using the principles of positive youth development as a guide, comment on Simon's psychosocial development.

seen as an extension of the sampling years, with the primary goals being enjoyment and health. Activities can involve deliberate play and deliberate practice, and sport programs are flexible enough to adapt to individual interests and ages. During the sampling and recreational years, coaches are primarily kind, supportive, and encouraging (McCarthy & Jones, 2007). Parents' roles include introducing their children to sports, enrolling their children in diverse activities, and providing their children with necessary resources and equipment.

Trajectory 2: Elite Performance through Sampling

For youth interested in a more performance-oriented path, a second trajectory of the DMSP suggests that specialization begins around age 13, after the sampling years (see Case Study 9.1). The specializing years (ages 13–15) are seen as a transitional stage to the investment years (age 16+). During the specializing years, youth engage in fewer activities, which are a mix of deliberate play and deliberate practice activities; during the investment years, youth commit to only one activity and engage primarily in deliberate practice. During both the specializing and the investment years, a more reciprocal coach–athlete respect develops, with coaches' styles becoming more skill oriented and technical. Parents become less involved but provide more financial and emotional support by helping their children through challenges and obstacles. Essentially, parents progress from a leadership role during the sampling years to a following and supporting role during the specializing and investment years (Côté, 1999).

Trajectory 3: Elite Performance through Early Specialization

In sports where peak performance is achieved before puberty (e.g., women's gymnastics, figure skating), early specialization is often necessary to reach elite performance. Elite performers in these early-specialization sports usually skip the sampling years and, consequently, do not always experience the most positive psychosocial development. In addition, early specializers often experience overuse injuries, as outlined earlier in this chapter. The early specialization path is characterized by high amounts of deliberate practice and low amounts of deliberate play in a context that focuses on performance.

Other Trajectories

Opportunities for horizontal movement across stages (e.g., going from investment to recreational) should be provided for participants so that individuals can change their level of participation at any age if they so desire. Unfortunately, in many sports it is difficult for a 16-year-old adolescent to invest in a sport if he or she has not been specializing in that sport since approximately age 13; however, in some sports, such as triathlon, investment in adulthood is possible (Baker, Côté, & Deakin, 2005).

Finally, at any stage of development, youth may also choose to disengage from sport and physical activity altogether. If this is the case, their youth-sport programs clearly failed to achieve the first objective of youth-sport programming: the long-term physical health of participants. Unfortunately, many youth-sport programs are failing to reach this objective, as evidenced by current adolescent and adult inactivity rates.

YOUTH-SPORT PROGRAMS: BEST PRACTICES

The following is a list of five "best practices" that sport programmers and coaches should integrate into their programs in order to assure children and young adolescents' healthy personal and sport development.

1. Adopt an inclusive focus as opposed to an exclusive selection policy based on performance.

   Sport programs that focus on play and participation for all have been shown to lead to less dropout, more prolonged participation in sport, and greater elite performance in adulthood. On the other hand, youth-sport programs that are built upon a rigid skill-based model imply early selection of "talented" children and an increase in resources for a special group of athletes; such programs, consequently, exclude several youth from continuing to participate in sport.

2. Promote a task-oriented motivational climate.

   People's motivation to stay involved in sport, either at a recreational or elite level, is largely influenced by their experiences in sport during childhood. Youth-sport programs should be designed on motivational principles that are amenable to children and adolescents' needs. A focus on self-improvement as opposed to performance outcomes such as winning is critical to promote motivation in young athletes.

3. Allow children and young adolescents to take initiative in their learning and development of fundamental motor skills.

   One objective of structured training activities in youth sport is for participants to learn fundamental motor skills. However, the main focus of youth sport should be to let participants experiment with various ways of executing sport skills in various contexts through playful activities and fun involvement. A child's number one reason for getting involved in sports is "fun." As such, coaches should be cautious of teaching motor skills through repetitive and boring drills.

4. Provide opportunities for young athletes to have fun and engage playfully in low-organization games.

   Because children's continued motivation for sport is driven largely by their enjoyment and positive experiences in sport, a supportive environment should be created with ample opportunity for children to engage in low-organization games and other sports. Further, because children and young adolescents don't understand competition and sport performances the same way adults do, coaches should not over-organize competition or overemphasize performance through deliberate practice during childhood.

5. Promote psychosocial development through sport.

   Sport participation can nurture important psychosocial characteristics and life skills that are important within and outside the sport context. Adults involved in youth-sport programs (i.e., coaches and parents) should use sport experiences as a medium to teach skills that can be applied in all aspects of life.

CHAPTER SUMMARY

In this chapter, we outlined three objectives of youth-sport programs: physical health, psychosocial development, and the learning of motor skills. We reviewed the literature highlighting the positive outcomes (e.g., fitness) and negative outcomes (e.g., overuse injuries) of youth sport and suggested how to foster positive youth-sport experiences. Youth-sport programs should be conducted in desirable settings, and they should aim to foster developmental assets, initiative, health, performance, and the five C's of positive youth development (confidence, competence, character, connection, and caring/compassion). To reach these objectives, youth-sport programs should promote participation in diverse activities and focus on deliberate play activities at a young age, rather than requiring children to specialize early and focus on deliberate practice activities. Coaches and parents, through their supportive behaviours and attitudes, have important roles in influencing children's psychological growth, social skills, and motor development.

In the last section of the chapter, we outlined models that help to explain children's motivation and development in sport. Motivation models suggest that children's motivation is linked to their competence beliefs, sport enjoyment, and the social support they receive. The models reinforce the important roles of parents and coaches in building children's competence beliefs, creating task-oriented climates, and facilitating environments that lead to positive emotions. The developmental model of sport participation highlights various factors that lead to prolonged participation, expertise, and dropout. This model shows that youth's health, psychosocial development, and motor skill development must be considered by youth-sport programmers as a whole, instead of as separate entities. Youth should be encouraged to participate in diverse sports and extracurricular activities that focus on fun, play, excitement, recreation, personal involvement, games, friendships, variety, and choice. Activities and contexts that promote regular participation, enjoyment, and skill acquisition are the building blocks of all effective youth-sport programs.

We began this chapter by introducing you to Sebastian, Olivia, Madelyn, Rachel, and Michael, five young adults who had very different sport experiences during their youth, which in turn led them on very different paths. As you read through the chapter, you were introduced to some of the specific factors that caused these individuals to have more-positive or less-positive youth-sport experiences. We hope that you will continue to consider these factors as you progress as professionals, coaches, administrators, programmers, and policy makers, in sport, physical activity, health, and other settings.

Common Myths about Youth Involvement in Sport Revisited

MYTH: Involvement in youth sport builds character.

Character-building through sport is not automatic. Sport programs have to be specifically designed to foster positive development in youth. Positive outcomes depend on children's personal experiences, which are heavily influenced by the sport program activities and the coaches and parents who coordinate these activities.

MYTH: Involvement in sport leads to negative outcomes, such as violence and aggression.

Studies indicate some associations between sport and negative outcomes; however, well-designed programs aimed at promoting positive youth development, coupled with appropriate adult support, are less likely to lead to negative outcomes.

MYTH: To become elite athletes, children must specialize in their sport by age six or seven.

There is evidence that early specialization and sport-specific training are effective in producing elite performers; however, evidence also exists that suggests early involvement in a variety of sporting activities can also lead to elite performance in most sports. Current research suggests that there are many physical, psychological, and social benefits to early diversification, while there are many costs associated with early specialization. For this reason, it appears that, in most sports, early diversification is a healthier path to elite performance.

MYTH: Parents should limit their involvement in their children's sport.
Parents are an important source of various forms of support for their children. In addition, parents can influence their children's involvement through their behaviours and expectations. Sport programs must make a greater effort to proactively involve parents in their children's sport development. Parents should be informed about how their sport-related behaviours and beliefs influence their children's behaviours and beliefs.

MYTH: Youth-sport coaches should be specialists in the sport that they are coaching.
Past research indicates that coaches play a key role in children's competence beliefs, sport enjoyment, motivation for sport participation, and reasons for sport withdrawal. These responsibilities are as important as teaching sport skills. Thus, coaches play a critical role in children's sport involvement, and they must be trained to understand children's physical, cognitive, social, and psychological development.

Review Questions

1. Describe the three objectives of youth sport.
2. Discuss the positive and negative outcomes of youth-sport participation in the areas of health, psychological development, and social development.
3. Differentiate between relaxed leisure activities and constructive leisure activities. Provide examples of each.
4. Using developmental assets and setting features as frameworks, highlight some of the strengths and weaknesses of the youth-sport programs you were involved in during childhood.
5. What are the five C's of positive youth development? Provide a sport example of each C.
6. Outline the two characteristics of youth-sport activities associated with positive youth-sport experiences.
7. What are the three dimensions of parental behaviour that can be associated with children's sport socialization, motivation, and behaviour? Briefly describe how each dimension influences children's sport experiences.
8. Coaches influence children's psychological growth, social skills, and motor development. Briefly describe findings of past studies on coaching in one of these three areas.
9. Outline and discuss the key features of the developmental model of sport participation.

Suggested Reading

Smoll, F. L., & Smith, R. E. (2002). *Children and youth in sport: A biopsychosocial perspective*(2nd ed.). Dubuque, IA: Kendal Hunt.

Weiss, M. R. (Ed.). (2004). *Developmental sport and exercise psychology: A lifespan perspective*. Morgantown, WV: Fitness Information Technology.

References

Abernethy, B., Baker, J., & Côté, J. (2005). Transfer of pattern recall skills as a contributor to the development of sport expertise. *Applied Cognitive Psychology, 19*, 705–718.

Arnold, P. J. (2001). Sport, moral development, and the role of teacher: Implications for research and moral education. *Quest, 53*, 135–150.

Baker, J., & Côté, J. (2006). Shifting training requirements during athlete development: The relationship among deliberate practice, deliberate play and other sport involvement in the acquisition of sport expertise. In D. Hackfort, & G. Tenenbaum (Eds.), *Essential processes for attaining peak performance*(pp. 92–109). Aachen, Germany: Meyer and Meyer.

Baker, J., Côté, J., & Deakin, J. (2005). Expertise in ultra-endurance triathletes: Early sport involvement, training structure, and the theory of deliberate practice. *Journal of Applied Sport Psychology, 17*, 64–78.

Barnett, N. P., Smoll, F. L., & Smith, R. E. (1992). Effects of enhancing coach-athlete relationships on youth sport attrition. *The Sport Psychologist*, 6, 111–127.

Bengoechea, E. G., Strean, W. B., & Williams, D. J. (2004). Understanding and promoting fun in youth sport: Coaches' perspective. *Physical Education and Sport Pedagogy*, 9, 197–214.

Benson, P. L. (1997). *All kids are our kids: What communities must do to raise caring and responsible children and adolescents*. San Francisco: Jossey-Bass.

Boyd, M. P., & Yin, Z. (1996). Cognitive-affective sources of sport enjoyment in adolescent sport participants. *Adolescence, 31*, 383–395.

Bredemeier, B. J. L., & Shields, D. L. L. (1996). Moral development and children's sport. In F. L. Smoll, & R. E. Smith (Eds.), *Children and youth sport: A biopsychosocial perspective* (pp. 381–404). Chicago: Brown & Benchmark.

Clark, W. (2008). Kids' sport. *Canadian Social Trends, 11*, 54–61.

Côté, J. (1999). The influence of the family in the development of talent in sport. *The Sport Psychologist, 13*, 395–417.

Côté, J. (2002). Coach and peer influence on children's development through sport. In J. M. Silva III, & D. E. Stevens (Eds.), *Psychological foundations of sport*(pp. 520–540). Boston: Allyn & Bacon.

Côté, J., Baker, J., & Abernethy, B. (2003). From play to practice: A developmental framework for the acquisition of expertise in team sport. In J. Starkes, & K. A. Ericsson (Eds.), *Recent advances in research on sport expertise*(pp. 89–114). Champaign, IL: Human Kinetics.

Côté, J., Baker, J., & Abernethy, B. (2007). Practice and play in the development of sport expertise. In R. Eklund, & G. Tenenbaum (Eds.), *Handbook of sport psychology*(3rd ed., pp. 184–202). Hoboken, NJ: Wiley.

Côté, J., & Hay, J. (2002). Children's involvement in sport: A developmental perspective. In J. M. Silva III, & D. E. Stevens (Eds.), *Psychological foundations of sport*(pp. 484–502). Boston: Allyn & Bacon.

Côté, J., Trudel, P., Bernard, D., Boileau, R., & Marcotte, G. (1993). Observation of coach behaviors during different game score differentials. In C. R. Castaldi, P. J. Bishop, & E. F. Hoerner (Eds.), *Safety in ice hockey: second volume ASTM STP 1212*(pp. 78–87). Philadelphia: American Society for Testing and Materials.

Csikszentmihalyi, M., Rathunde, K., &Whalen, S. (1993). *Talented teenagers: The roots of success and failure*.Cambridge: Cambridge University Press.

Cutrona, C. E., & Russell, D. W. (1990). Type of social support and specific stress: Toward a theory of optimal matching. In B. R. Sarason, I. G. Sarason, & G. R. Pierce (Eds.), *Social support: An interactional view*(pp. 319–366). New York: Wiley.

Danish, S. (2002). *SUPER (Sports United to Promote Education and Recreation) Program: Leader manual*(3rd ed.). Richmond, VA: Life Skills Centre, Virginia Commonwealth University.

Deci, E. L., & Ryan, R. M. (1985). *Intrinsic motivation and self-determination in human behavior*.New York: Plenum.

De Knop, P., Engström, L.-M., & Skirstad, B. (1996). Worldwide trends in youth sport. In P. De Knop, L.-M. Engström, B. Skirstad, & M. Weiss (Eds.), *Worldwide trends in youth sport* (pp. 276–281). Champaign, IL: Human Kinetics.

Eccles, J. S., & Barber, B. L. (1999). Student council, volunteering, basketball, or marching band: What kind of extracurricular involvement matters? *Journal of Adolescent Research, 14*, 10–43.

Eccles, J. S., & Harold, R. D. (1991). Gender differences in sport involvement: Applying the Eccles expectancy-value model. *Journal of Applied Sport Psychology, 3*, 7–35.

Eder, D., & Parker, S. (1987). The cultural production and reproduction of gender: The effect of extracurricular activities on peer-group culture.*Sociology of Education*, 60,200–213.

Ericsson, K. A., Krampe, R. T., & Tesch-Römer, C. (1993). The role of deliberate practice in the acquisition of expert performance. *Psychological Review, 100*, 363–406.

Fraser-Thomas, J. L., Côté, J., & Deakin, J. (2005). Youth sport programs: An avenue to foster positive youth development. *Physical Education and Sport Pedagogy, 10*,49–70.

Fraser-Thomas, J., & Côté, J. (2009). Understanding adolescents' positive and negative developmental experiences in sport. *The Sport Psychologist, 23*,3–23.

Fraser-Thomas, J., Côté, J., & Deakin, J. (2008a). Examining adolescent sport dropout and prolonged engagement from a developmental perspective. *Journal of Applied Sport Psychology, 20*, 318–333.

Fraser-Thomas, J., Côté, J., & Deakin, J. (2008b). Understanding dropout and prolonged engagement in adolescent competitive sport. *Psychology of Sport and Exercise*, 9, 645–662.

Fredericks, J. A., & Eccles, J. S. (2004). Parental influences on youth involvement in sports. In M. R. Weiss (Ed.), *Developmental sport and exercise psychology: A lifespan perspective*(pp. 145–164). Morgantown, WV: Fitness Information Technology.

Gilbert, W. D., Gilbert, J. N., & Trudel, P. (2001a). Coaching strategies for youth sports. Part 1: Athlete behavior and athlete performance. *Journal of Physical Education, Recreation and Dance, 72*, 29–33.

Gilbert, W. D., Gilbert, J. N., & Trudel, P. (2001b). Coaching strategies for youth sports. Part 2: Personal characteristics, parental influence, and team organization. *Journal of Physical Education, Recreation and Dance, 72*, 41–46.

Gilbert, W. D., Trudel, P., & Haughian, L. P. (1999). Interactive decision making factors considered by coaches of youth ice hockey during games. *Journal of Teaching in Physical Education, 18*, 290–311.

Gould, D., & Carson, S. (2008). Life skills development through sport: Current status and future directions. *International Review of Sport and Exercise Psychology, 1*, 58–78.

Gould, D., Collins, K., Lauer, L., & Chung, Y. (2007). Coaching life skills through football: A study of award winning high school coaches. *Journal of Applied Sport Psychology, 19*, 16–37.

Harter, S. (1987). The determinants and mediational role of global self-worth in children. In N. Eisenberg (Ed.), *Contemporary topics in developmental psychology*(pp. 219–242). New York: Wiley.

Hellison, D. (2003). *Teaching responsibility through physical activity* (2nd ed.). Champaign, IL: Human Kinetics.

Hellison, D., Martinek, T., & Walsh, D. (2008). Sport and responsible leadership among youth. In N. Holt (Ed.), *Positive youth development through sport*(pp. 49–60). New-York: Routlege.

Hellstedt, J. C. (1987). The coach/parent/athlete relationship. *The Sport Psychologist, 1*, 151–160.

Helsen, W. F., Starkes, J. L., & Hodges, N. J. (1998). Team sports and the theory of deliberate practice. *Journal of Sport & Exercise Psychology, 20*, 12–34.

Hollander, D. B., Meyers, M. C., & LeUnes, A. (1995). Psychological factors associated with overtraining: Implications for youth sport coaches. *Journal of Sport Behavior, 18*, 3–18.

Jelicic, H., Bobek, D. L., Phelps, E., Lerner, R. M., & Lerner, J. V. (2007). Using positive youth development to predict contribution and risk behaviors in early adolescence: Findings from the first two waves of the 4-H study of positive youth development. *International Journal of Behavioral Development, 31*, 263–273.

Jowett, S. (2003). When the honeymoon is over: A case study of a coach-athlete relationship in crisis. *The Sport Psychologist, 17*,444–460.

Jowett, S., & Timson-Katchis, M. (2005). Social networks in sport: Parental influence on the coach-athlete relationship. *The Sport Psychologist, 19*,267–287.

Larson, R. W. (2000). Toward a psychology of positive youth development. *American Psychologist, 55*, 170–183.

Larson, R. W., & Kleiber, D. A. (1993). Structured leisure as a context for the development of attention during adolescence. *Society and Leisure, 16*, 77–98.

Larson, R. W., & Verma, S. (1999). How children and adolescents spend time across the world: Work, play, and developmental opportunities. *Psychological Bulletin, 125*, 701–736.

Law, M. P., Côté, J., & Ericsson, K. A. (2007). Characteristics of expert development in rhythmic gymnastics: A retrospective study. *International Journal of Sport and Exercise Psychology, 5*, 82–103.

Linder, K. J., Johns, D. P., & Butcher, J. (1991). Factors in withdrawal from sport: A proposed model. *Journal of Sport Behavior, 14*, 13–18.

McCallister, S. G., Blinde, E. M., & Weiss, W. M. (2000). Teaching values and implementing philosophies: Dilemmas of the youth sport coach. *Physical Educator, 57*, 35–46.

McCarthy, P. J., & Jones, M. V. (2007). A qualitative study of sport enjoyment in the sampling years. *The Sport Psychologist, 21*, 400–416.

National Research Council (NRC) and Institute of Medicine (IOM). (2002). *Community programs to promote youth development*. Washington, DC: National Academy Press.

Nicholls, J. G. (1989). *The competitive ethos and democratic education*. Cambridge, MA: Harvard University Press.

Peterson, C. (2004). Positive social science. *The Annals of the American Academy of Political and Social Science, 591*, 186–201.

Petitpas, A. J., Cornelius, A. E., Van Raalte, J. L., & Jones, T. (2005). A framework for planning youth sport programs that foster psychosocial development. *The Sport Psychologist, 19*, 63–80.

Petitpas, A. J., Cornelius, A. E., Van Raalte, J. L. (2008). Youth development through sport: It's all about relationships. In N. Holt (Ed.), *Positive youth development through sport*(pp. 61–70). New-York: Routlege.

Petlichkoff, L. M. (1993). Coaching children: Understanding the motivational process. *Sport Science Review, 2*, 48–61.

Power, T. G., & Woolger, C. (1994). Parenting practices and age-group swimming: A correlational study.*Research Quarterly for Exercise and Sport, 65*, 59–66.

Ryan, R. M., & Deci, E. L. (2000). Self-determination theory and the facilitation of intrinsic motivation, social development, and well-being. *American Psychologist, 55*, 68–78.

Scales, P., & Leffert, N. (1999). *Developmental assets: A synthesis of the scientific research on adolescent development*. Minneapolis, MN: Search Institute.

Smith, R. E., & Smoll, F. L. (1990). Self-esteem and children's reactions to youth sport coaching behaviors: A field study of self-enhancement processes. *Developmental Psychology, 26*, 987–993.

Smith, R. E., & Smoll, F. L. (1997). Coach-mediated team building in youth sports. *Journal of Applied Sport Psychology*, 9, 114–132.

Smoll, F. L., & Smith, R. E. (2002). Coaching behavior research and intervention in youth sports. In F. L. Smoll, & R. E. Smith (Eds.), *Children and youth in sport: A biopsychosocial perspective* (2nd ed., pp. 211–233). Dubuque, IA: Kendal Hunt.

Soberlak, P., & Côté, J. (2003). Developmental activities of elite ice hockey players. *Journal of Applied Sport Psychology, 15*, 41–49.

Theokas, C., Danish, S., Hodge, K, Ihirangi, H., & Forneris, T. (2008). Enhancing life skills through sport for children and youth. In N. Holt (Ed.), *Positive youth development through sport* (pp. 71–82). New-York: Routlege.

United Nations Educational, Scientific, and Cultural Organization (UNESCO). Third International Conference of Ministers and Senior Officials Responsible for Physical Education and Sport (MINEPS III). (1999). *Draft recommendations*. Punta del Este, Uruguay: United Nations Educational, Scientific, and Cultural Organization.

Vickers, J. N. (1994). Psychological research in sport pedagogy: Exploring the reversal effect. *Sport Science Review, 3*, 28–40.

Wall, M. and Côté, J. (2007). Developmental activities that lead to drop out and investment in sport. *Physical Education and Sport Pedagogy, 12*, 77–87.

Weiss, M. R., & Williams, L. (2004). The *why* of youth sport involvement: A developmental perspective on motivational processes. In M. R. Weiss (Ed.), *Developmental sport and exercise psychology: A lifespan perspective*(pp. 223–268). Morgantown, WV: Fitness Information Technology.

Wilcox, S., & Trudel, P. (1998). Constructing the coaching principles and beliefs of a youth ice hockey coach. *Avante, 4*, 39–66.

Woolger, C., & Power, T. G. (1993). Parent and sport socialization: Views from the achievement literature. *Journal of Sport Behavior, 16*, 171–189.

Wright, A. D., & Côté, J. (2003). A retrospective analysis of leadership development through sport. The Sport Psychologist, 17, 268–291.

Chapter 10

Aging and Involvement in Sport and Physical Activity

Joseph Baker
Sean Horton

Chapter Objectives

After reading this chapter, you should be able to do the following:

1. Present a profile of physical activity and sport involvement in older persons.
2. Understand the consequences of low levels of physical activity in this group.
3. Discuss and differentiate between models of skill maintenance.
4. Discuss the factors influencing sport and physical activity involvement in this group.
5. Consider the impact of societal perceptions of aging on physical and cognitive performance.
6. Identify strategies for increasing sport and physical activity involvement in older populations.
7. Discuss whether the Master athlete is an effective model of successful aging.

---

* Support for this chapter was provided by a standard research grant from the Social Sciences and Humanities Research Council of Canada Sport Participation Research Initiative (grant #862-2007-0002).

Richard grew up working on his family's farm and spent his childhood and adolescence playing a range of school sports. As an adult, he left rural life and moved to a small city to start a family of his own. Recently, Richard found out that he was at increased risk of having a heart attack because he has high cholesterol. His doctor advised him to add some physical activity to his daily routine. This negative bill of health surprised Richard since he'd always been active as a child and adolescent. After decades of inactivity, Richard finds it difficult to make changes to his routine. He tries joining a local fitness club but finds that he has little in common with the club's other members. He inquires about the aerobic and stretching programs available at the club, but the club's personal trainer informs him that their programs are likely too advanced for someone of his age and fitness level.

Richard finally has some success when he begins a walking routine with his friend Nyla. This activity is well suited to their neighbourhood since it has wide sidewalks and minimal traffic. After a few months, Nyla moves to live with her daughter's family, and Richard quickly becomes discouraged walking by himself. At his checkup one year later, Richard still hasn't made any consistent changes to his physical activity habits and remains at increased risk of having a heart attack.

In the above scenario, Richard has difficulty making the necessary changes to add a greater amount of physical activity to his lifestyle. Unfortunately, this situation is commonplace among older adults in Canadian society. In this chapter, we look at the factors influencing physical activity involvement in aging populations to determine the most effective courses of action for optimal health and performance in this group.

Common Myths about Aging and Involvement in Sport and Physical Activity

MYTH: Getting older involves the inevitable loss of the ability to function in society.

MYTH: Stereotypes about "old people" are generally accurate.

MYTH: Participating in competitive sports is too strenuous for older persons.

INTRODUCTION

In 2007, the first wave of the Canadian baby boomer generation turned 60 years of age. Persons over 85 years are the fastest-growing segment of the population, and even very conservative estimates predict a 10-fold increase in the number of people over 100 years of age by 2050. Clearly, this is a section of the population that is of considerable importance in Canadian society.

In the past 160 years, our average life expectancy has increased at a rate of about three months per year. Back in 1840, the average lifespan was approximately 40 years. Some lucky people still lived to an advanced age, but many died young. As medical technology and health care have improved over the years, fewer people die at an early age, and the elderly are living even longer. In fact, the relationship between increasing life expectancy and the passage of time is so consistent that some researchers have considered it to be "the most remarkable regularity of mass endeavor ever observed" (Oeppen & Vaupel, 2002, p. 1029). Although this is an exciting finding since it suggests that we have a longer life to look forward to, an increased lifespan does not necessarily mean a better **quality of life** (overall well-being). In fact, many Canadians run the risk of spending a significant portion of their senior years in states of **morbidity** (being unhealthful) or in complete dependence. A significant factor contributing to this decreased quality of life is physical inactivity.

Data from the Canadian Community Health Survey (CCHS; Statistics Canada, 2005) support a robust and rather unsettling trend in physical activity research—physical activity levels decrease as we get older. These data indicate that among older adults, 68% of women and 53% of men can be classified as inactive or sedentary. Furthermore, only 13% of women and 22% of men meet their recommended daily physical activity requirements. Although there is encouraging news indicating that this trend is improving, the fact remains that the majority of older men and women are not active enough for optimal health.

The most common physical activities for adults over 65 are outlined in Table 10.1. Walking, gardening, and exercising at home have the greatest rates of participation in older adults. These forms of physical activity are excellent avenues for staying active. However, because they are low in aerobic intensity, older adults need to be mindful of performing enough activity to meet their physical activity requirements. (The Canadian Fitness and Lifestyle Research Institute monitors physical activity involvement in various age groups across Canada; www.cflri.ca.)

REFLECTIONS 10.1

Compare the activities you typically see youth participating in with the activities of older adults. What implications do you think these differences have for targeting physical activities interventions for older adults?

Table 10.1 Most Popular Physical Activities among Canadian Adults over 65 Years

Activity	Participation (%)
Walking	66
Gardening	40
Home exercise	23
Swimming	9
Social dancing	9
Bicycling	7
Golf	6
Bowling	4
Fishing	4
Exercise classes	3
Weight training	1

Note: Data from Statistics Canada, *Canadian Community Health Survey, Cycle 3.1* (2005), Public Use Microdata File.

Table 10.2 Benefits of Exercise in Older Adults

Benefits
Increase in cardiovascular function
Decrease in cardiovascular disease risk factors
Increased muscle mass and strength
Improved bone health and decreased risk of osteoporosis
Improved balance and postural stability
Improved flexibility
Improved psychological health

Note: Adapted from American College of Sports Medicine. (2009). Exercise and Physical Activity for Older Adults (position stand), Salem, George J.; Skinner, James S.; Chodzko-Zajko, Wojtek J.; Proctor, David N.; Fiatarone Singh, Maria A.; Minson, Christopher T.; Nigg, Claudio R. *Medicine & Science in Sports & Exercise.* 41(7):1510–1530, July 2009.

Weight training is essential to prevent sarcopenia.
Photograph © Thinkstock/Jupiter Images.

Data indicate that involvement in aerobic exercise is not enough. To reduce the loss of muscle mass (**sarcopenia**) that typically occurs with age, older adults must also regularly participate in exercise that taxes their muscle strength (e.g., weight training). *Canada's Physical Activity Guide to Healthy Active Living for Older Adults* recommends up to 60 minutes of moderate to vigorous physical activity on most days, including a variety of endurance, flexibility, strength, and balance activities (Health Canada, 1999). There is overwhelming support that habitual involvement in these forms of physical activity is related to increased physical and mental health, as well as increased functional autonomy in aging populations (see Table 10.2). Physical activity guidelines for older adults (as well as for other age groups) are available on Health Canada's website (www.phac-aspc.gc.ca/pau-uap/paguide/index.html).

COGNITIVE AND PHYSICAL DECLINE WITH ADVANCING AGE

Examinations of cognitive and physical performance across time indicate that these capacities decline as we get older. Some researchers believe that 0.5% per year is a general rate of decline for *all* skills and capacities after we have reached peak performance.

For example, performance in many aerobic sports such as running, swimming, and rowing appears to decline at this rate (see Bortz & Bortz, 1996). Although there is consistent evidence indicating that physical and cognitive abilities decline as we age, there is conflicting evidence as to whether this is actually due to age. Some researchers have suggested that many of the physical and cognitive declines associated with aging are in fact the result of a "long-standing sedentary lifestyle or disuse" (Maharam, Bauman, Kalman, Skolnik, & Perle, 1999, p. 274). As mentioned earlier, involvement in physical activities also declines as we age. Current thinking is that these two factors—declining involvement and declining ability—are inextricably linked.

Studies of cognitive and motor skills suggest that performance can be maintained at high levels in spite of advancing age provided that there is continued involvement in the activity. For instance, studies of chess players (Charness, 1981), pianists (Krampe & Ericsson, 1996), and typists (Salthouse, 1984) have shown that high levels of performance could be maintained as the performers got older. The maintenance of skilled performance over time has been explained primarily using one of two models, the compensation model (e.g., Salthouse, 1984) or the selective maintenance model (Krampe & Ericsson, 1996).

The Compensation Model of Skill Maintenance

The basis of **compensation theory** is that although individual components of a skill may decline with age, it is possible for overall performance to remain the same because of an increased reliance on other aspects of performance (see Figure 10.1). Put more simply, the theory suggests that skilled performers strategically compensate for a decline in one skill area by developing or improving in another. Two excellent examples of this research come from studies examining chess players and typists. Charness (1981) found that skilled, older chess players could perform at the same level as younger skilled players despite age-related deficiencies in memory ability. Charness explained these results by suggesting that older players compensate for their declining memory by using more efficient information processing; they perform a more systematic search of the problem space and make a better global evaluation of chess positions. In addition, studies have found little decline in expert typing skill with advancing age (Bosman, 1993; Salthouse, 1984). The evidence indicates that expert typists suffer a decline in reaction time, but they compensate by scanning further ahead in the text, which allows them to begin keystroke preparation earlier. As a result of this advanced planning, aging typists can offset a deficiency in one area by their improved performance in another.

Figure 10.1 The compensation model of aging

Although components of performance may decline (A), increases in a compensatory skill (B) allow for stability of performance over time (C)

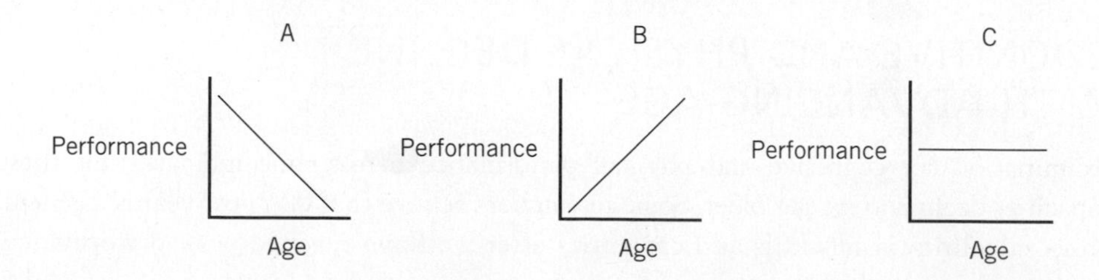

Research indicates that golf skill is resistant to degradation over time.

Photograph © The Canadian Press (AP/Orlin Wagner).

The Selective Maintenance Model of Skill Maintenance

Ericsson and Krampe (Ericsson, 2000; Krampe & Ericsson, 1996) advocate that expert performance in skilled domains is maintained in very specific capacities. In their **selective maintenance model**, this is possible through appropriate attention to deliberate practice (see Chapter 9 for more on deliberate practice). Through extensive focus on this type of practice, experts are able to develop domain-specific mechanisms that allow them to circumvent general age-related limitations, and these mechanisms are more resistant to degradation over time, as long as training persists.

To test this hypothesis, Krampe and Ericsson (1996) compared older and younger pianists on a range of performance-related measures. In addition, they compared performers at the expert and amateur levels (i.e., older expert, older amateur, younger expert, and younger amateur). They found that older performers, both amateur and expert, showed the same pattern of age-related decline on general measures of performance, such as reaction time; however, domain-specific measures of performance, such as finger-tapping speed and quality of performance, were maintained to a greater extent in older experts. In most cases, differences in domain-specific measures of performance between younger and older experts were explained by differences in the amount of training and practice rather than age. Based on these results, the authors concluded that persistent regular involvement in a domain over time would allow aging performers to maintain their skills.

REFLECTIONS 10.2

Gordie Howe, one of the most successful hockey players in history, was able to continue playing in the NHL until he was 51 years of age. Compare explanations of this occurrence according to the compensation model and the selective maintenance model. Put yourself in the role of a researcher examining this issue. What evidence would you need to support each of the models?

Furthermore, the belief that old age is inevitably associated with the gradual loss of physical and cognitive functionality may promote a disengagement from other positive health behaviours. Levy and Myers (2004) used survey data from the Ohio Longitudinal Study of Aging and Retirement to examine this hypothesis. They examined how older adults felt about their own aging and whether those beliefs affected their health behaviours over a 20-year period. Healthy behaviours included wearing a seatbelt, eating a balanced diet, having regular physical examinations, and participating in some form of exercise. Their results revealed that older adults who had more positive self-perceptions of aging were more likely to practise preventive health behaviours.

Although these results point to a strong influence of age-related beliefs in determining physical activity involvement, the issue is complex. Research suggests that exercise can have significant positive effects on measures of emotional and psychological health (see Biddle & Mutrie, 2001 for a review). Thus, there may be a dynamic, reciprocal relationship between physical activity and age beliefs, such that positive age beliefs promote physical activity and physical activity promotes positive age beliefs.

REFLECTIONS 10.4

When you think of a 70-year-old, what words or images come to mind? Are they predominantly negative or positive? Consider ways in which your day-to-day experiences may reinforce negative stereotypes of aging.

DETERMINANTS OF PHYSICAL ACTIVITY AND SPORT INVOLVEMENT IN OLDER ADULTS

The factors influencing (younger) adults' participation in physical activity and sport (e.g., Trost, Owen, Bauman, Sallis, & Brown, 2002) fall into five categories, which are equally suited to describing the factors influencing participation in older adults.

Demographic and Biological Factors

Among Canadian adults, age and gender are the most consistent predictors of physical activity involvement, with rates of participation declining as age increases and males being consistently more active than females (Stephens & Craig, 1990). As a matter of fact, gender is a fundamentally important variable in understanding exercise behaviour among older adults. In addition, other demographic factors also play significant roles. For instance, **socioeconomic status** (i.e., social position) and educational level are two factors that are commonly linked with lifelong physical activity involvement (Dishman, 1990; Rudman, 1986). Older adults with higher socioeconomic status and a higher level of education are more likely to be involved in physical activity than those with lower socioeconomic status and a lower level of education. Research has also linked marital status and occupation with physical activity as an older adult (e.g., Dergance et al., 2003; O'Brien Cousins, 1998), although more research is necessary to determine precisely how these factors affect participation levels.

Behavioural Attributes

Patterns of behaviour throughout the lifespan have been good predictors of physical activity involvement. For instance, alcohol consumption is negatively related to physical activity involvement in older adults; that is, more activity generally means less alcohol use (Smith & Storandt, 1997). Of note, some variables we might expect to be strongly related to adult physical activity level are not; one example is the amount of physical activity performed as a child or adolescent. Researchers involved in tracking studies have found that childhood and adolescent physical activity habits are only weakly correlated with physical activity as an adult (Seefeldt, Malina, & Clark, 2002; Trudeau, Laurencelle, & Shephard, 2004). There is also research that suggests that the strength of the relationship between childhood/adolescent physical activity levels and adult physical activity levels decreases as individuals age (Malina, 2001). For example, childhood physical activity may be a good predictor of involvement for a young adult, but it is not as effective at predicting physical activity for an older adult.

Social and Cultural Factors

Although individual barriers are often the focus of research and interventions, social and cultural barriers also play an important role. For instance, studies have reported that adequate levels of social support are critical to physical activity involvement (Chogahara, O'Brien Cousins, & Wankel, 1998). Researchers have found a variety of sources of support that can affect how much older adults exercise. For instance, endorsement of physical activity by their spouse (Perusse, LeBlanc, & Bouchard, 1988), by members of their immediate family (Spreitzer & Snyder, 1983), by peers (O'Brien Cousins, 1998), or by physicians (Wechsler, Levine, Idelson, Rohman, & Taylor, 1983) can positively affect the likelihood that older adults will initiate and maintain physical activity involvement.

The dynamic interaction among members of an exercise group can also influence physical activity levels. A study by Estabrooks and Carron (2000) used a team-building task to foster group cohesion. Their results showed that groups with greater cohesion had better rates of attendance and better adherence than control groups. Often, the dynamics of the group are influenced by the behaviour of the group's leader. Research examining the role of an exercise leader or class instructor has found that these individuals can have considerable influence on the quality of their participants' experience (McAuley & Jacobson, 1991).

Some expectations about behaviour are rooted in cultural beliefs, and these expectations can significantly impede an older individual's involvement in physical activity and exercise. A group that is particularly disadvantaged by cultural barriers is aging women. As mentioned earlier, women have typically been less physically active than men, and this trend persists as women age. Characterizations of female older adults as fragile or delicate reinforce the notion that physical activity for them is risky, and often these perceptions are reinforced by health-care practitioners (Vertinsky, 1995).

Physical Environment Factors

Factors related to the physical activity environment can also impede exercise involvement in older adults. An investigation by O'Neill and Reid (1991) examined barriers to physical activity in Canadian older adults and reported that between 5% and 15% felt that environmental factors negatively affected their participation. More specifically, the respondents indicated that difficulties getting to the facility, excessive costs of programs, unappealing activities, and inconvenient activity times were significant barriers to involvement. These factors may be less powerful predictors of physical activity participation than others (e.g., gender and age), but they are relatively easy to remedy. Simple changes to the way in which a program is administered can correct many environmental factors impeding physical activity involvement in older adults.

Psychological, Cognitive, and Emotional Factors

This final category of determinants is perhaps most applicable and salient to our discussion of the psychology of the older athlete. Several variables have been identified as important correlates of physical activity in adults, for example, locus of control, expected benefits, knowledge of health and exercise, perceived health or fitness, personality variables, body image, and perceived value of exercise outcomes (Trost et al., 2002). Despite the fact that more research is necessary to determine their relevance in predicting physical activity in older adults, several factors have been identified as central to understanding such activity. The two most common are enjoyment and perceived health and fitness.

Enjoyment Researchers examining the factors that determine involvement in physical activity at any age have found that enjoyment is usually the best predictor (e.g., Lewis, Marcus, Pate, & Dunn, 2002; Salmon, Owen, Crawford, Bauman, & Sallis, 2003). Evidence indicates that this variable is an important predictor of physical activity involvement in older adults (Dergance et al., 2003; McAuley, Jerome, Elavsky, Marquez, & Ramsey, 2003).

Perceived Health and Fitness A powerful barrier to physical activity involvement in older persons is a low perception of their current level of health and fitness. Many older adults believe that they are unable to participate in any type of exercise because of functional limitations (Cohen-Mansfield et al., 2003). Although in many cases these limitations are perceived rather than actual, they still limit older adults' inclination toward physical activities.

It is important to note that there is considerable interaction among the barriers outlined above. For instance, demographic barriers, such as socioeconomic status, affect physical environment barriers (e.g., proximity to exercise facilities) as well as psychological and emotional barriers (e.g., enjoyment and perceived health). These relationships reinforce the view that involvement in physical activity across the lifespan is an enormously complex issue and that successful physical activity programs and interventions should recognize this complexity.

SELF-EFFICACY AND OLDER ADULTS

A criticism of the majority of research available on older adults' motives for participating in sport and physical activity is that the research has been descriptive and atheoretical (Biddle & Nigg, 2000; Standage & Duda, 2004); this means that it is not driven by a theory or hypothesis. Although descriptive studies are enormously important in the initial stages of behavioural research, they are limited in that they do little to explain the motivational processes underlying behaviour.

One theory of motivation that has been considered in aging populations is Bandura's theory of self-efficacy (Bandura, 1986, 1997). As outlined in Chapter 4, **self-efficacy** refers to feelings of self-confidence in a given situation and has been found to be a central factor in explaining individuals' enthusiasm for different activities. Although a significant body of research has been amassed on the power of self-efficacy in predicting physical activity behaviour in youth (e.g., Bungum, Dowda, Weston, Trost, & Pate, 2000; Ryan & Dzewaltowski, 2002), recent research has confirmed its utility in older adults as well (e.g., McAuley et al., 2003).

Bandura's theory is based on the notion that individuals with high feelings of self-efficacy about physical activity are more likely to initiate and continue participation. Researchers examining this assumption in older adults have confirmed the importance of self-efficacy in predicting program initiation (McAuley, 1993), attendance (Estabrooks & Carron, 2000), and adherence (McAuley, Lox, & Duncan, 1993). What is perhaps more interesting is that when older individuals participate in physical activity, their feelings of self-efficacy go up (Li et al., 2001; McAuley et al., 1993; McAuley et al., 1999); however, these levels decline when regular participation stops (McAuley et al., 1999). This finding suggests that feelings of self-efficacy and participation have a reciprocal relationship feelings of self-efficacy promote participation, which promotes increases in self-efficacy.

A positive finding from this research is that feelings of self-efficacy are readily modifiable. This has important implications for program design and interventions intended to promote physical activity in older populations. By focusing on increasing feelings of self-efficacy regarding physical activity, program administrators can support older individuals' exercise involvement in a powerful way.

REFLECTIONS 10.5

Although other theories of motivation have not been examined in aging populations, such theories may still explain the factors that influence older persons' participation in sport and physical activity. Recall one of the other theories discussed in Chapter 4, and consider how it might apply to motivation in older adults.

Canadian Profile

Ed Whitlock, Rewriting the Record Books

Ed Whitlock, marathon runner.

Photograph © The Canadian Press (Tannis Toohey).

In 1896, the Olympic marathon was won in a time of two hours and fifty-six minutes. In 2003, Ed Whitlock, a Canadian marathoner, ran just a few minutes slower than this in the Toronto marathon.

What is remarkable about this feat is that Whitlock was 72 years old when he achieved this performance and became the first person over 70 years of age to break three hours for the marathon distance (two hours, fifty-nine minutes).

Throughout his running career, Whitlock has established numerous age-group records, and he continues to train and compete at the highest levels of competition, regularly representing Canada at international events. As remarkable as Whitlock is, he is not as rare as you might expect. With each passing year, aging athletes are rewriting the sports record books as they demolish previous standards of performance. This aging vanguard forces us to re-evaluate our perspective of what it means to grow older.

SUCCESSFUL AGING

In the fields of gerontology and geriatrics, evidence supporting the maintenance of high levels of functioning into advanced age has motivated many researchers to examine the antecedents of optimal or "successful" aging. Currently, the most popular model of successful aging is the one developed by Rowe and Kahn (1987). Their model suggests that successful aging is the balance of three components: (1) absence of chronic disease, (2) maintenance of cognitive and physical functioning, and (3) active engagement with life. The Rowe and Kahn model, like most models of successful aging, is based on the notion that positive behaviour choices throughout life (e.g., eating a balanced diet, attending regular doctor visits) influence one's likelihood of aging well. In a recent study, Baker, Meisner, Logan, Kungl, and Weir (2009) considered the extent to which involvement in physical activity predicted whether an older person aged successfully. They found a strong **dose-response relationship**, whereby greater involvement in physical activity promoted a greater likelihood of aging successfully. In the section below, we consider whether Master athletes, who are highly involved in competitive sport, are good models of aging well.

THE MASTER ATHLETE: A MODEL OF SUCCESSFUL AGING?

The increasing popularity of Master-level competition is evident in such events as the World Masters Games and the Senior Olympic Games in the United States. These highly competitive events continue to grow with each passing year, providing older athletes with the opportunity to participate in sport at a highly competitive level against the best athletes in the world at their age. Canada has played an important role in the development of Master sport. The first World Masters Games were held in Toronto in 1985, and, in 2005, the sixth World Masters Games were held in Edmonton. Recent games have seen more than 20,000 athletes compete in 27 sports, making the games the largest multi-sport event in the world. (The World Masters Games are governed by the International Masters Games Association; www.imga.ch).

Because of their ability to maintain high levels of physical and cognitive competency, Master athletes represent a unique population that defy the stereotypical views of aging we hold in North America. For instance, Master athletes consistently report high levels of physical and mental health (Shephard, Kavanagh, Mertens, Qureshi, & Clark, 1995).

One criticism of research on Master athletes and the application of that research to models of general aging is that the Master data represent individuals who are often at extraordinarily high levels of performance. Master athletes may not accurately reflect the age-related decline of the average individual. Although this is a valid criticism, this population is still extremely valuable for age-related research, primarily because it reflects a group of individuals who have maintained involvement in physical activity and exercise for extended periods of time. Data from Master athletes represent the performance levels possible for adults who perform high amounts of physical activity throughout their lifespan. In general, research on Master athletes indicates that maintaining a high level of involvement in physical activity as we age allows us to maintain high levels of ability. As a result, Master athletes appear to represent an important model of successful aging.

Master athletes may also serve as role models (e.g., as stereotype busters) for society as a whole. Individuals who attempt amazing athletic feats at late ages are often profiled in the popular press and force us to re-evaluate our notions of what is possible for older people to accomplish. While there are anecdotal examples of how these athletes affect society's perceptions of aging, there has been little in the way of systematic research in this area. This is an intriguing field of inquiry for future researchers.

There has been some investigation into the effect that elite Master athletes have on those in their peer group. Some researchers (e.g., Ory et al., 2003) have suggested that older elite athletes are more likely to intimidate their peers rather than inspire them to be more active in their own lives. The authors noted that most older adults would have trouble relating to individuals with such an extreme level of fitness. They suggested that it is likely more effective to portray average older people doing average things, out walking with friends, for example. A more recent study (Horton, Baker, Côté, & Deakin, 2008) has added some complexity to this argument, however. The findings suggested that, while some older adults will indeed find elite Master athletes intimidating, others will find inspiration in their example. This may be tied to current physical activity levels—older adults who are already somewhat active in their own lives may be more likely to find master athletes to be appropriate role models. Once again, however, this research is in its very early stages.

Questions remain with respect to how positive role models of aging can best be used to motivate older adults to engage in physical activity. Considering how negative stereotypes can discourage older adults from engaging in exercise, it is important to discover ways of challenging those stereotypes. Positive role models, whether they are Master athletes or older adults performing at high levels in other areas, have the potential to challenge and change the most negative stereotypes of aging.

Although Master-level competition has been around for quite some time, we actually know very little about those who compete at this level compared with performers at younger levels of competition. However, some general conclusions can be made from research conducted to date.

Participant Motives in Master Sport

An exploratory investigation of participant motives of Master track athletes found that the top-ranked motives were "to be physically fit" and "to meet new friends," while the lowest-ranked motives were "to get out of the house" and "to get rid of energy" (Fung, Ha, Louie, & Poon, 1992). These findings were echoed in a study of marathon runners by Ogles and Masters (2000), who found the primary motivation for older runners was to improve general health, to deal with weight concerns, to give meaning to their lives, and to affiliate with other runners. In addition, the researchers found that the motives of younger and older runners for participating were appreciably different. While older runners were motivated by physical and social benefits of participation, younger athletes were more motivated by personal goal achievement (e.g., running a personal best, improving overall running speed).

Master-level Competitors versus Non-competitor Older Athletes

Master runners have higher self-esteem, lower consumption of alcohol, better sleep patterns, and fewer physical problems than their non-active contemporaries (Morgan & Costill,

1996). In addition, Master athletes view their participation as an effective way to deal with stress and improve mood (Smith & Storandt, 1997).

Early Sport Involvement

An investigation of competitors, non-competitors (i.e., physically active but not competitive older athletes), and non-exercisers found that there was no difference among the groups with regard to activity levels during childhood and adolescence (Smith & Storandt, 1997). However, a critical time for Master athletes seems to be their 20s, when many adults are focusing on establishing families and careers. Master athletes were more likely to maintain involvement in sport and physical activity during this period, while non-competitors and non-exercisers were less likely to.

Mood and Personality

In the past, researchers have examined the relationships between performance and personality in elite athletes. Similar investigations have been undertaken with Master athletes. Ungerleider, Golding, and Porter (1989) found that, similar to other athletes examined, Master track-and-field athletes demonstrated an iceberg profile: lower scores on tension, depression, fatigue, and confusion and higher scores on vigour than normative samples. In addition, the Master athletes' profile was also lower in depression and anger than reported by other athletes. A single study examining measures of personality (Smith & Storandt, 1997) found little difference between Master-level competitors and non-competitors.

General Recommendations for Working with Master Athletes

Although many of the sport psychology concepts covered in this text are equally applicable to Master-level performers (e.g., goal setting and imagery), some concepts require an approach specifically designed with older athletes in mind. First, the specific needs of this population should be recognized. The psychological needs of Master athletes are unique; therefore, training programs and interventions must be designed to address and meet those needs. Second, the athlete's experience and knowledge should be acknowledged. In the majority of cases, Master athletes will have an enormous depth of experience in their sport, in many cases superior to the knowledge of the sport psychologist working with them. Rather than attempting to learn as much or more than the athlete they are working with, sport psychologists should consider ways in which they can access and incorporate the athlete's knowledge. This will reduce the amount of background reading needed and improve the rapport between the sport psychologist and the Master athlete. Third, one's attitudes toward older adults should be assessed for stereotypes. North American society reinforces a predominantly negative perspective of the aging process, and, as a result, this may be entrenched in your own outlook about aging. Changing your outlook to something more positive (and more accurate) is, unfortunately, not done overnight. Being aware of any preconceived beliefs you have will assist you in dealing with older athletes.

CHAPTER SUMMARY

The focus of this chapter has been on physical activity and sport involvement in older persons. Unfortunately, there is a continuing trend among Canadians toward a decreasing level of physical activity as we age. There is, however, growing support for the notion that much of the cognitive and physical decline seen in aging populations is a result of disuse, rather than aging per se. The variables influencing involvement in physical activity in older adults include demographic and biological factors, behavioural attributes, social and cultural factors, physical environment factors, and psychological, cognitive, and emotional factors. In addition, negative cultural stereotypes about aging are unique barriers for older adults in our society.

One group of older adults seems to defy the typical profile of aging—Master athletes. This group has been able to maintain high levels of ability in the face of advancing age. Researchers examining these athletes have indicated that they are unique, different from sedentary older adults and younger athletes in several areas (e.g., mood, self-esteem, and motives). Further research is clearly required to describe the factors influencing sport involvement and competitive performance in this group.

Common Myths about Aging and Involvement in Sport and Physical Activity Revisited

MYTH: Getting older involves the inevitable loss of the ability to function in society.
Although a certain degree of ability loss appears to be inevitable with age, most of this loss is due to decreased participation in cognitively and physically stimulating activities. With continued involvement in challenging activities, older adults can maintain (and even increase) physical and cognitive abilities.

MYTH: Stereotypes about "old people" are generally accurate.
The stereotype commonly endorsed in North America is that older adults have diminished capacities, almost as though they are reverting to child-like levels of development. In fact, the majority of stereotypes about older adults promoted in our society have no basis in empirical research.

MYTH: Participating in competitive sports is too strenuous for older persons.
The field of competitive sports for aging populations is rapidly growing. Master-level competition is now possible in a wide range of organized sports throughout the world, and competitors regularly participate at the regional, national, and international level.

Review Questions

1. Compare and contrast the compensation model and the selective maintenance model of skill maintenance.
2. Describe four characteristics of Master-level performers.
3. Briefly explain the influence negative cultural stereotypes of aging may have on older adults.
4. Define *sarcopenia* and explain why older adults should be aware of this condition.
5. Describe the typical profile of physical activity involvement in older adults.
6. Provide a list of barriers to physical activity involvement in older adults and provide a possible strategy to address these barriers.

Suggested Reading

Baker, J., Horton, S., & Weir, P. (2010). *Masters athletes: Understanding the role of exercise in optimizing aging*. London, UK: Routledge.

O'Brien Cousins, S. (1998). *Exercise, aging, and health: Overcoming barriers to an active old age*. Philadelphia: Taylor and Francis.

O'Brien Cousins, S., & Horne, T. (1999). *Active living among older adults: Health benefits and outcomes*. Philadelphia: Taylor and Francis.

References

American College of Sports Medicine (ACSM). (1998). Exercise and physical activity in older adults (Position Stand). *Medicine and Science in Sports and Exercise*, *30*, 992–1008.

Baker, J., Horton, S., Pearce, W., & Deakin, J. (2005). A longitudinal examination of performance decline in champion golfers. *High Ability Studies*, *16*, 179–185.

Baker, J., Meisner, B., Logan, J., Kungl, A. M., & Weir, P. (2009). Physical activity and successful aging in Canadian seniors. *Journal of Aging and Physical Activity*, *17*, 223–235.

Bandura, A. (1986). *Social foundations of thought and action: A social cognitive theory*. Englewood Cliffs, NJ: Prentice Hall.

Bandura, A. (1997). *Self-efficacy: The exercise of control*. New York: Freeman.

Biddle, S., & Mutrie, N. (2001). *Psychology of physical activity: Determinants, well-being, and interventions*. Oxford, UK: Routledge.

Biddle, S. J. H., & Nigg, C. R. (2000). Theories of exercise behavior. *International Journal of Sports Psychology*, *31*, 290–304.

Bortz, W. M., & Bortz, W. M. (1996). How fast do we age? Exercise performance over time as a biomarker. *Journal of Gerontology: Medical Sciences*, *51*, 223–225.

Bosman, E. A. (1993). Age-related differences in the motoric aspects of transcription typing skill. *Psychology and Aging*, *8*, 87–102.

Bungum, T., Dowda, M., Weston, A., Trost, S. G., & Pate, R. R. (2000). Correlates of physical activity in male and female youth. *Pediatric Exercise Science*, *12*, 71–79.

Charness, N. (1981). Search in chess: Age and skill differences. *Journal of Experimental Psychology: Human Perception and Performance*, *7*, 467–476.

Chogahara, M., O'Brien Cousins, S., & Wankel, L. M. (1998). Positive and negative social influences on the physical activity of older adults. *Journal of Aging and Physical Activity*, *6*, 1–17.

Cohen-Mansfield, J., Marx, M. S., & Guralnik, J. M. (2003). Motivators and barriers to exercise in an older community-dwelling population. *Journal of Aging and Physical Activity*, *11*, 242–253.

Dergance, J. M., Calmbach, W. L., Dhanda, R., Miles, T. P., Hazuda, H. P., & Mouton, C. P. (2003). Barriers to and benefits of leisure time physical activity in the elderly: Differences across cultures. *Journal of the American Geriatrics Society*, *51*, 863–868.

Dishman, R. K. (1990). Determinants of participation in physical activity. In C. Bouchard, R. J. Shephard, T. Stephens, J. R. Sutton, & B. D. McPherson (Eds.), *Exercise, fitness and health: Consensus of current knowledge* (pp. 75–101). Champaign, IL: Human Kinetics.

Ericsson, K. A. (2000). How experts attain and maintain superior performance: Implications for the enhancement of skilled performance in older individuals. *Journal of Aging and Physical Activity*, *8*, 346–352.

Ericsson, K. A., Krampe, R. T., & Tesch-Römer, C. (1993). The role of deliberate practice in the acquisition of expert performance. *Psychological Review*, *100*, 363–406.

Estabrooks, P. A., & Carron, A. V. (2000). Predicting scheduling self-efficacy in older adult exercisers: The role of task cohesion. *Journal of Aging and Physical Activity*, *8*, 41–50.

Fung, L., Ha, A., Louie, L., & Poon, F. (1992). Sport participation motives among veteran track and field athletes. *Journal of the International Council for Health Physical Education and Recreation, 29*, 24–28.

Hausdorff, J. M., Levy, B. R., & Wei, J. Y. (1999). The power of ageism on physical function of older persons: Reversibility of age-related gait changes. *Journal of the American Geriatric Society, 47*, 1346–1349.

Health Canada. (1999). *Canada's physical activity guide to healthy active living for older adults*. Ottawa, ON: Canada Communications Group.

Horton, S., Baker, J., Côté, J., & Deakin, J. M. (2008). Understanding seniors' perceptions and stereotypes of aging. *Educational Gerontology, 34*, 997–1017.

Krampe, R. T., & Ericsson, K. A. (1996). Maintaining excellence: Deliberate practice and elite performance in young and older pianists. *Journal of Experimental Psychology: General, 125*, 331–359.

Levy, B. R. (2000). Handwriting as a reflection of aging self-stereotypes. Journal of Geriatric Psychiatry: *A Multidisciplinary Journal of Mental Health*, 33, 81–94.

Levy, B. R., & Banaji, M. R. (2002). Implicit ageism. In T. D. Nelson (Ed.), *Ageism: Stereotyping and prejudice against older persons* (pp. 27–48). Cambridge, MA: MIT Press.

Levy, B. R., & Langer, E. J. (1994). Aging free from negative stereotypes: Successful memory in China and among the American deaf. *Journal of Personality and Social Psychology*, 66, 989–997.

Levy, B. R., & Myers, L. M. (2004). Preventive health behaviors influenced by positive self-perceptions of aging. *Preventive Medicine*, 39, 625–629.

Lewis, B. A., Marcus, B. H., Pate, R. R., & Dunn, A. L. (2002). Psychosocial mediators of physical activity behavior among adults and children. *American Journal of Preventive Medicine*, 23, 26–35.

Li, F., Harmer, P., McAuley, E., Fisher, K. J., Duncan, T. E., & Duncan, S. C. (2001). Tai Chi, self-efficacy and physical function in the elderly. *Prevention Science*, 2, 229–239.

Maharam, L. G., Bauman, P. A., Kalman, D., Skolnik, H., & Perle, S. M. (1999). Masters athletes: Factors affecting performance. *Sports Medicine*, 28, 273–285.

Major, B., Spencer, S., Schmader, T., Wolfe, C., & Crocker, J. (1998). Coping with negative stereotypes about intellectual performance: The role of psychological disengagement. *Personality and Social Psychology Bulletin*, 24, 34–50.

Malina, R. M. (2001). Adherence to physical activity from childhood to adulthood: A perspective from tracking studies. *Quest*, 53, 346–355.

McAuley, E. (1993). Self-efficacy and the maintenance of exercise participation in older adults. *Journal of Behavioral Medicine*, 16, 103–113.

McAuley, E., & Jacobson, L. (1991). Self-efficacy and exercise participation in sedentary adult females. *American Journal of Health Promotion*, 5, 185–191.

McAuley, E., Jerome, G. J., Elavsky, S., Marquez, D. X., & Ramsey, S. N. (2003). Predicting long-term maintenance of physical activity in older adults. *Preventive Medicine, 37*, 110–118.

McAuley, E., Katula, J., Mihalko, S. L., Blissmer, B., Duncan, T., Pena, M., et al. (1999). Mode of physical activity and self-efficacy in older adults: A latent growth curve analysis. *Journal of Gerontology: Psychological Sciences*, 54B, 283–292.

McAuley, E., Lox, C. L., & Duncan, T. (1993). Long-term maintenance of exercise, self-efficacy, and physiological change in older adults. *Journal of Gerontology*, 48, 218–223.

Montepare, J. M., & Zebrowitz, L. A. (2002). A social-developmental view of ageism. In T. D. Nelson (Ed.), *Ageism: Stereotyping and prejudice against older persons* (pp. 77–125). Cambridge, MA: MIT Press.

Morgan, W. P., & Costill, D. L. (1996). Selected psychological characteristics and health behaviors of aging marathon runners: A longitudinal study. *International Journal of Sports Medicine*, 17, 305–312.

O'Brien Cousins, S. (1998). *Exercise, aging and health: Overcoming barriers to an active old age*. Philadelphia: Taylor and Francis.

Chapter 11

Coaching Psychology

Gordon A. Bloom

Chapter Objectives

After reading this chapter, you should be able to do the following:

1 Describe the coach education structure and process in Canada and abroad.

2 Identify the steps to become an elite coach.

3 Describe the common characteristics and coaching principles of youth-sport coaches.

4 Describe the components of Chelladurai's sport leadership model and its relationship to coaching.

5 Define the different components of the coaching model.

6 Describe the coaching model and its relationship to effective coaching.

7 Explain the athlete-centred approach adopted by many non-professional Canadian coaches.

8 Explain the model of coaching efficacy.

Coach C, an aspiring third-year coach of an elite women's basketball team, could not sleep for the past week. She was thinking about her team competing in the upcoming playoffs without her top player and league most valuable player (MVP). With this player, Coach C's team had been ranked as high as first in the province and fifth in the country. They were on a roll, and the playoffs were just around the corner. Coach C wanted to win to establish her reputation as an up-and-coming elite coach.

The loss of this key player was not due to injury, attitude, or academics; rather, it was due to an ethical dilemma that would create the defining moment of this young coach's career. If this athlete played one more game during the season, then she would forfeit a year of eligibility at a NCAA Division 1 university in the United States, for which she was being heavily recruited. Playing at an American Division 1 university would allow this athlete to realize her dream of competing against the best women basketball players in the world and possibly playing basketball for the Canadian national team upon her graduation.

The day before the playoffs began, Coach C received a text message from her athlete indicating her desire to continue playing this year. Would Coach C lessen her chance of coaching a national championship team by not encouraging her star athlete to play in this game? The answer is "yes"; Coach C convinced her league MVP not to play in the game, and the team subsequently lost a close game in the first round of the playoffs. Coach C knew her star athlete's heart was with the team but that deep down she was uncertain and nervous about the consequences of playing and forfeiting a year of NCAA-playing eligibility. Coach C believed that the value of a sound education for a student was far more important than adding a notch to her coaching resume.

This scenario indicates how a coach's decision and behaviour affect many people in different ways. Thus, it is not surprising that research on expert performers in domains ranging from the arts and sciences to sport have found that the quality of teaching or coaching is an important factor contributing to an individual's rise to prominence (Bloom, 1985; Salmela & Moraes, 2003). This may also explain the large amount of time, effort, and energy that some parents of gifted children spend searching for the right coach or teacher to help their child realize his or her potential.

Given this information, why then is so little respect afforded to many of Canada's greatest coaches by both the media and the general population? Possibly with the exception of professional or national team coaches in ice hockey—where the exploits of Toe Blake, Scotty Bowman, Danielle Sauvageau, and Mike Babcock are lauded—many of our elite-level Canadian coaches have received little acclaim or public adoration. For example, how many people in Canada are aware of the accomplishments of former Olympic basketball coaches Kathy Shields or Jack Donohue, or of current national team coaches Michel Larouche in diving and Allison McNeill in basketball, or Paralympic coach Peter Eriksson in athletics?

The relative anonymity of these great coaches leads to many interesting questions: Do people value and understand the importance of a good coach? As well, is there a recipe for coaching development and knowledge acquisition? And, what knowledge is used by coaches to develop successful and well-balanced athletes?

Common Myths about Coaching Psychology

MYTH: Outstanding athletes have an advantage in becoming excellent coaches.

MYTH: Aspiring coaches must emulate the most successful coaches in their sport, regardless of their own personality, beliefs, or philosophy.

MYTH: All elite-level coaches are focused solely on winning at the expense of athlete growth and development.

MYTH: Coaching confidence is determined solely by one's innate personality.

INTRODUCTION

Information presented in this chapter falls under Gilbert and Trudel's (2004) term **coaching science**, which "comprises research on the coaching, learning, and instructional processes as directed by coaches" (p. 389). Gilbert and Trudel compiled and analyzed a database of 611 studies on coaching science published in English-language journals between 1970 and 2001. Among their findings are the following points:

- Coaching science research has increased significantly since 1970, now averaging approximately 30 published articles per year.
- There is a relatively small core of authors who have developed a significant line of research in coaching science.
- Research has branched from solely examining coaching behaviours to looking at coaching behaviours in combination with coaching cognition.
- There is no single resource that lists and evaluates the assessment tools created to study coaching practices.
- Coach gender issues are one of the most frequently studied topics in this field; as well, coaching effectiveness (knowledge) and career issues (e.g., burnout) are starting to receive increased attention.
- Coaching science research has seen a continuous increase in qualitative research studies, especially those incorporating an interview technique.
- There is a virtual absence of studies of coaching science that include athletes, parents, and sport administrators.
- Most coaching scientific studies have focused on both team-sport and school-based coaches; however, this excludes the youth and professional levels of coaching.
- Ninety percent of the studies have not used any criteria of coaching effectiveness.

COACH EDUCATION

The value and impact of coaching has grown tremendously since the word coach first came into existence following the 1860 American Civil War (Coakley, 1990). Yet, the path for becoming a coach is not as clearly laid out as it is for other professionals, such as a teacher, lawyer, or nurse. In Canada, coach education and development is governed by

Figure 11.1 The new coaching education structure in Canada

Community Sport stream	Competition stream	Instruction stream
Initiation CSp-Init **Ongoing participation CSp-Ong**	**Introduction Comp-Int** **Development Comp-Dev** **High performance Comp-HP**	**Beginners Inst-Beg** **Intermediate performers Inst-Imd** **Advanced performers Inst-Adv**
Initiation context Participants of all ages are encouraged to participate in the sport and introduced to sport basics in a fun, safe, and self-esteem building environment regardless of their ability.	**Introduction context** Children and/or adolescents are taught basic sport skills and athletic abilities in a fun and safe environment and are typically prepared for local and/or regional level competitions.	**Beginners context** Participants of all ages, with little or no sport experience, are taught basic sport skills.
Ongoing participation context Participants of all ages are encouraged to continue participating in the sport for fun, fitness, skill development, and social interaction.	**Development context** Adolescents and young adults are coached to refine basic sport skills, to develop more advanced skills and tactics, and are generally prepared for performance at provincial and/or national level competitions.	**Intermediate performers context** Participants, who already have some experience and proficiency in the sport, are taught to refine basic skills and introduced to more complex techniques.
	High performance context Young adults are coached to refine advanced skills and tactics and are typically prepared for performance at national and international level competitions.	**Advanced performers context** Participants who are experienced and already proficient in the sport are taught to refine advanced skills and techniques.

Note: Table from Coaching Association of Canada. Retrieved September 20, 2009, from www.coach.ca/eng/certification/nccp_for_coaches/nccp_model.cfm. Used with permission.

the **Coaching Association of Canada** (**CAC**; www.coach.ca), which was created in 1970 following a task force recommendation on sport in our country. The CAC's mission is to provide the foundation of skills, knowledge, and attitudes needed to ensure effective coaching leadership for Canadian athletes. In 1974, CAC created the **National Coaching Certification Program** (**NCCP**) to meet the needs of all coaches, from beginner to most experienced. Through a series of workshops, the NCCP trains and certifies coaches in more than 60 sports. Most sources have credited Canada's NCCP as being the first widely adopted national coach education program in the world.

The structure of the NCCP has recently been re-developed. The original model was a knowledge- and course-based program run by the CAC with five levels of certification. The new model is structured around a competency-based approach to coach training and education that places more emphasis on coaches' abilities to meet the needs of their participants. As well, more emphasis is placed on the environment or context (particular level) in which the coach is coaching. In layman's terms, the CAC has moved from a "what a coach should know" approach to a "what a coach should do" approach.

The new NCCP model is divided into three streams (see Figure 11.1 and www.coach.ca/eng/certification/nccp_for_coaches/nccp_model.cfm):

1. Community Sport Stream: This stream focuses on broad-based participation at introductory levels of sport (e.g., house league). Coaches in this stream are instructed to introduce sport for fun, to develop skills, and to foster social interaction and life-long participation.

2. Competition Stream: This stream focuses on skill development for participation in competitive contexts (e.g., high-school sport and higher). The coaches are instructed in all areas of athlete training, including physical, technical, tactical, and mental.
3. Instruction Stream: This stream focuses on skill proficiency in non-competitive situations (e.g., tennis camp, golf instructor).

Additional coach education and development information in Canada can be acquired through either the educational system or the National Coaching Institutes. Regarding the former, some universities in Canada (i.e., Victoria, Alberta, and Laval) offer specialized training in coach education. Perhaps the most well known is the Master of Education in Coaching Studies program at the University of Victoria (www.educ.uvic.ca/phed/med_coaching.html). This two-year, non-thesis program caters to those with a particular interest in coaching science and offers both courses and co-operative work terms. It is geared to those with a specific interest in elite coaching. Although not a post-graduate program, Université Laval offers a Baccalauréat en Intervention Sportive (BIS; www.fse.ulaval.ca/reseau-bis) that is also divided into distinct stages that provide both theory (classroom setting) and practical experiences (apprenticeships).

Canada presently has **National Coaching Institutes (NCIs**; www.coach.ca/eng/institutes/index.cfm) located in seven provinces across the country whose mission is to enhance the training environment for high-performance coaches (and athletes) through a variety of services. Successful completion of this program grants students a diploma in High Performance Coaching, which attests to expertise in three main areas: (1) planning, designing, and implementing a sport program that fits within the context of their athletes, (2) knowledge on practical coaching, and (3) leadership skills and ethical coaching strategies. The NCIs integrate classroom study with a coaching apprenticeship under the guidance of a highly qualified master coach. Overall, the program aims to improve one's critical thinking, communication skills, and overall philosophy on coaching elite athletes.

Similar in many ways to Canada, both Australia and the United Kingdom have coach education systems that are fewer than 35 years old and were developed in part with government participation and assistance. Created around the same time as Canada's program, Australia's program (www.ausport.gov.au/participating/coaches) ensures that its 84,000 accredited coaches have received training in coaching principles. The National Coaching Accreditation Scheme (NCAS) is an initiative of the Australian Sports Commission (ASC) and is a progressive coach education program offering courses at various levels, with over 70 sports participating. The ACS has developed an initiative to encourage inexperienced coaches to enter their program and has launched the Beginning Coaching General Principles, a free basic skills course to assist beginner coaches in Australia.

The United Kingdom's coach education program began in 1983 with their National Coaching Foundation, which then changed its name to sports coach UK (www.sportscoachuk.org). Its mandate is to guide the education and development of coaches at every level and to promote and establish coaching as a profession. In 2006, sports coach UK was asked to develop The UK Coaching Framework, an initiative that was designed to enhance the quality of coaching at all levels and to be a world leader in coaching development by 2016. One of the developments of this group is the UK Coaching Certificate

(UKCC), a coach education program in which 21 sports are currently taking part (www.ukcoachingcertificate.org).

A different approach to coach training and education has taken place in the United States. Unlike the three countries already mentioned, the United States does not have one government-based national coaching organization for training its many volunteer and professional coaches, and coach education programs are rarely mandatory. Instead, several coaching development programs were created around the same time as the NCCP and NCAS. For example, the American Coaching Effectiveness Program, founded in 1976, evolved into the American Sport Education Program (ASEP; www.asep.com) and is the most widely used program in the United States (Trudel & Gilbert, 2006). ASEP currently certifies coaches in two streams: volunteer and professional. Positive Coaching Alliance (PCA) is another American organization that is responsible for educating coaches (www.positivecoach.org). Founded in 1998 at Stanford University, PCA provides research-based training workshops and practical tools for coaches.

Recent efforts from the National Association for Sport & Physical Education (www.aahperd.org/naspe), a non-profit organization established in the 2000s, led to the creation of the National Council for the Accreditation of Coach Education in the United States. Its goal is to facilitate the development and accreditation of all coaching education/certification programs based on domain standards that are set across several levels. This project has been endorsed by the United States Olympic Committee, several key youth-sport organizations, and many universities offering coaching education studies.

The government-funded and -supported coaching education programs in Canada, Australia, and the United Kingdom demonstrate that coaching is becoming recognized as an important field that can assist the growth and development of today's amateur and professional athletes. Coach education has grown tremendously in the last 40 years since certified programs were introduced. Presently, coach education is aided by the **International Council for Coach Education (ICCE**; www.icce.ws), whose mission is to improve the quality and exposure of coaching at all levels around the world. Based at the Wingate Institute for Physical Education and Sport in Israel, the ICCE has a membership that includes contacts in over 25 countries. ICCE's mission has undoubtedly been enhanced by the creation of several journals that are particularly geared toward coaching science: *International Journal of Coaching Science*, *International Journal of Sports Science & Coaching*, *Journal of Coaching Education*, *Coaching: An International Journal of Theory, Research, and Practice*. The rapid progress and restructuring of coach education programs around the world, combined with different avenues to disseminate information, indicates that people are beginning to understand and value the importance of the coach in the growth and development of athletes.

Stanley Cup–winning coach Mike Babcock studied physical education at McGill University.

Photograph courtesy of Detroit Red Wings courtesy of McGill Athletics and Recreation Department.

Coaching education programs offered by national organizations (e.g., NCCP), National Coaching Institutes, and higher education institutions can facilitate coaching effectiveness.

REFLECTIONS 11.1

Canada, the United Kingdom, and Australia have well-developed coach education programs that were partly developed with government participation and assistance. What do you think are the advantages of structured coaching education programs? Can you think of any possible drawbacks?

COACH DEVELOPMENT

Despite the efforts of the ICCE and various coach education programs, there has historically been a lack of scientific research on ways of becoming a successful (Canadian) coach. In the last 15 years, a group of Canadian researchers have begun identifying common developmental pathways and characteristics that shed light on what it takes to become a top-level coach in this country (e.g., Carter & Bloom, in press; Erickson, Côté, & Fraser-Thomas, 2007; Gilbert, Côté, & Mallett, 2006; Schinke, Bloom, & Salmela, 1995). As athletes, all of the elite Canadian coaches reported living active and successful sporting lives that began with a love of sport that was often fuelled by the encouragement of family members and accessibility to physical resources. They played and excelled in a number of sports as youths (both team and individual) and often had many leadership positions throughout their athletic careers. Not surprisingly, some researchers have found that elite athletic experiences were found to be an important aspect of expert coaches' career development, knowledge, and perhaps even career success (Cregan, Bloom, & Reid, 2007; Erickson et al., 2007; Gilbert et al., 2006; Schinke et al., 1995). The question that remains unanswered is how much athletic experience is required.

Gilbert and colleagues (2006) found that successful high-school and elite sport coaches accumulated a minimum of several thousand hours of athletic participation, across several sports, for at least 13 years. Erickson and associates (2007) also found that expert coaches had accumulated highly competitive sport experiences. Despite this, neither study was able to identify a minimum standard of athletic excellence required to reach an elite level of coaching, although it was implied that they were "elite" athletes. Carter and Bloom (in press) offered a different viewpoint on the necessity of elite athletic experiences for becoming an expert coach. More specifically, their sample consisted of successful university team-sport coaches who had not competed as athletes at the university level or higher. The coaches in their study demonstrated that, with persistence, it was possible to acquire coaching knowledge without having been an elite athlete. Interestingly, most of their recommendations for acquiring coaching knowledge were similar to other studies on expert coach development (except for the elite athletic experiences):

- Volunteering in the community, either at camps or at youth-sport practices
- Gaining experience as an assistant coach
- Frequently interacting with other coaches
- Observing other coaches
- Studying kinesiology and physical education at university

- Attending coaching clinics
- Reading coaching books and acquiring coaching information via the Internet

One additional area that may be the most important factor in coaches' growth and development is mentoring. There are many professions in which mentoring is a common and expected process. For example, pilots, doctors, and police officers spend years refining their skills with the assistance of experienced and knowledgeable colleagues who ensure that they are allowed to grow and develop in an environment designed to minimize errors and build knowledge and confidence.

An empirical examination of mentoring by researchers Bloom, Durand-Bush, Schinke, and Salmela (1998) found that all of the 21 expert coaches in their sample were mentored both as athletes and as developing coaches by well-respected individuals. The knowledge they acquired from their mentors helped mold their coaching ideas and philosophies. Interestingly, these coaches noted that it was important for them not to imitate everything about their mentors; rather, their own beliefs and personalities affected their coaching style. The importance of mentoring has also been highlighted by researchers in both the United States (Gould, Giannini, Krane, & Hodge, 1990) and the United Kingdom (Jones, Armour, & Potrac, 2003).

Although the NCCP values the importance of receiving advice and training from a respected mentor, a question still remains: How much of an impact does good mentoring have on the growth and development of aspiring coaches? The answer to this question may never be known; however, an examination of the pedigree of some of sport's greatest coaches clearly shows the importance of solid mentoring. Former NHL coach Scotty Bowman learned from the greatest predecessor of his time, Toe Blake. Interestingly, many of Bowman's proteges have assumed top leadership roles in hockey, from Jacques Lemaire to Bob Gainey to Ken Dryden. Likewise, Bill Walsh, the successful coach of the San Francisco

Canadian Profile

Kathy Shields

Kathy Shields has influenced many of Canada's athletes and coaches in basketball for more than 30 years.

Photograph courtesy of University of Victoria Vikes.

No discussion about coach and athlete mentoring in Canada would be complete without mentioning Kathy Shields—a former member of our Olympic basketball team, as well as former assistant coach and head coach for our national basketball team. She finished her coaching duties as head coach at the University of Victoria in 2005, where she compiled an astounding.865 winning percentage over her 25-year coaching career. She received the Order of British Columbia in 2008, the province's highest recognition of excellence. Certified as a master coach in 1986 by the CAC, Shields has influenced nearly all of Canada's elite coaches and athletes in women's basketball for the last 30 years. No fewer than eight of her former players and assistant coaches are or have been head coaches of university teams.

49ers dynasty of the 1980s, apprenticed under a master coach, Paul Brown. Walsh then mentored a number of successful NFL head coaches, including Mike Holmgren, Dennis Green, and George Seifert.

Despite the effort of Kathy Shields and other top women coaches in our country, the data on high-level head coaching positions in Canada indicate that women are underrepresented. More specifically, an unofficial tally of the number of head coaches in Canadian Interuniversity Sport (CIS) in 2008 revealed that only 10% to 15% were women. The data also revealed a clustering effect of coaches in the sports of women's basketball, ice hockey, rugby, and volleyball. While many men were coaching women's teams, only two women were head coaches of men's teams in the CIS in 2008 (i.e., Brenda Willis, volleyball, at Queen's University and Olga Hrycak, basketball, at the Université du Québec à Montréal). At the Olympic level, women are also dramatically underrepresented. For example, women comprised only 21% of Canada's head coaches at the 2002 Salt Lake City Winter Olympics and 10% at the 2000 Sydney Summer Olympics.

REFLECTIONS 11.2

The chapter on motivation (Chapter 4) discussed several factors related to developing confidence in sport. How do you think mentoring fits into enhancing coaching confidence for less-experienced coaches?

YOUTH-SPORT COACHING

Up to this point in the discussion, most information has been slanted toward coaches of elite sport. The context of youth sport has many interesting nuances that distinguish it from other levels of coaching. More specifically, the role of the coach in youth sport may have more important global implications than it does for elite sport. For example, physical inactivity usually begins at a young age; the medical and economic impact of physical inactivity accounts for $5.3 billion in Canadian health-care costs (Katzmarzyk & Janssen, 2004). Only two in every five Canadian children are defined as being active enough for optimal growth and development, and the proportion of children who are overweight has tripled since the 1970s (Cragg, Cameron, Craig, & Russell, 1999; Strong et al., 2005). One way to increase physical activity is to focus on factors that increase motives for youth-sport participation, specifically the nature of the environment surrounding the learning and implementation of physical skills (see Chapter 9 for more details). The person who is responsible for creating this positive youth-sport environment is the coach.

Characteristics of Youth Coaches

Trudel and Gilbert (2006) outlined a number of characteristics of youth-sport coaches:

- Most are male.
- Most are in their mid-30s.
- As few as 10% of these coaches continue coaching for 10 years or more.

- Almost all of these coaches competed in sport, and most were above-average athletes.
- Most of these coaches acquired athletic experience for five years or more in the sport they now coach.
- Love of the sport, wanting to remain associated with the sport, a desire to help young people develop skills, and a desire to serve as a leader and supervisor for young people were the main reasons for coaching.
- Most coaches had a child of their own on the team they coached.
- Just over half of the coaches were university educated.

Research at the University of Ottawa has examined the acquisition and sharing of knowledge of youth-sport coaches (e.g., Culver & Trudel, 2006; Lemyre, Trudel, & Durand-Bush, 2007; Wright, Trudel, & Culver, 2007). Interestingly, this research found that many youth-sport coaches were reluctant to share coaching knowledge with their peers for fear of giving away their secrets. On the other hand, many youth-sport coaches have complained that they operate in isolation and that there are few opportunities to meet and engage with other coaches at their level of competition. These findings support Lemyre et al.'s suggestion that more empirical attention be given to the factors affecting youth-sport coaches—in particular, ways to acquire and share knowledge.

Ideal Behaviours of Youth Coaches

Ideal behaviours for youth-sport coaches have been studied extensively by Smith and Smoll (2002a, 2002b). These researchers believed in the importance of training youth-sport coaches to ensure young athletes had fun, enjoyed being a part of a team, learned skills, and developed and increased their self-esteem. Their research over the past 35 years can be divided into two phases. The first phase involved the development of the mediational model of leadership and the coaching behaviour assessment system (CBAS) to categorize coaching behaviours (Smith, Smoll, & Hunt, 1977). Findings from their research using the CBAS demonstrated that coaching behaviours influenced children's self-perceptions, anxiety, and adherence levels. In addition, Smith, Smoll, and colleagues noted that coaching behaviours could be modified through structured coach training and education programs.

These findings influenced the second phase of their research, which involved the implementation of an intervention program called coach effectiveness training (CET), and the subsequent testing of the program in the youth-sport setting. Applied research using the CET has demonstrated that children playing for trained coaches, as opposed to untrained volunteers, had significant increases in self-esteem, had decreases in anxiety levels, enjoyed their sporting experience more, and evaluated their coach and teammates more favourably, regardless of the win–loss record (Smith & Smoll, 2002a). Results also indicated that children who played for trained coaches were also more likely to return the following season (Smith & Smoll, 2002a). Table 11.1 summarizes the researchers' key recommended coaching behaviours.

Lasting approximately three hours, a CET workshop follows five coaching principles (Smith & Smoll, 2002a; Smoll & Smith, 2002). The first principle is to create a healthy climate that is enjoyable and is focused on mastering skills instead of trying to beat an opponent. As well, coaches must understand that their success or failure is not dependent

Table 11.1 Effective Practices for Coaching Youth Sport

Reinforce effort as much as results.
Give encouragement after a mistake but in positive and encouraging ways.
Establish clear expectations; involve athletes in behavioural guidelines and work to build team unity in achieving them.
Set a good example of behaviour, encourage athletes to be supportive of each other, and reinforce them when they do so.
Always give instructions positively and do so in a clear, concise manner.
Foster two-way communication, and respond to the needs of individual players appropriately.

Note: From Smith, R. E., & Smoll, F. L. (2002). *Way to go coach!: A scientifically-proven approach to youth sports coaching effectiveness* (2nd ed., pp. 31–48). Palo Alto, CA: Warde Publishers.

on the outcome of the game or the win–loss record, but rather on their ability to get their athletes to give maximum effort. The second principle is to utilize a positive approach to coaching that involves positive reinforcement, encouragement, and appropriate instruction. Punitive behaviours are highly discouraged. The third principle is to establish norms that emphasize athletes' obligations to help and support one another, thereby increasing cohesion and personal commitment to the team. Coaches must also model and support these behaviours. The fourth principle is to include athletes in decision-making roles regarding team rules and compliance. The fifth principle is to engage in self-monitoring and assessment in order to focus on positive coaching behaviours.

Smith, Smoll, and Cumming (2007; Smoll, Smith, & Cumming, 2007) recently modified the CET program and renamed it the **Mastery Approach to Coaching (MAC)**. The philosophy of the program remains the same, which is the promotion of team cohesion and a positive coach–athlete interaction that creates an atmosphere that allows for skill development and reduces the fear of failure. As well, the goal of both programs is to increase intrinsic motivation in young athletes. Among the key changes, the five principles

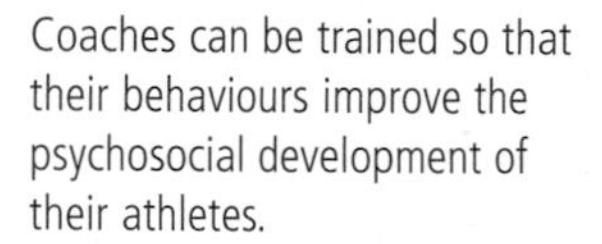

Coaches can be trained so that their behaviours improve the psychosocial development of their athletes.

Photograph courtesy of Henry Gagné.

in the CET were reduced to two themes: emphasizing reinforcement in positive ways and measuring success based on maximum effort. Other differences include the length (75 minutes compared to three hours) and the delivery of material (lecture-based rather than discussion-based).

In summary, many of today's successful high-profile coaches have gone through common developmental patterns that began during their athletic careers and continued as they moved through the coaching ranks. While they were athletes, most of these experts acquired leadership skills and knowledge from their coaches. As well, most acquired information through the NCCP and supplemented this information with a developmental pattern that included exposure to positive role models (mentors). Their initiation into coaching, combined with the encouragement of their own coaches and their burning desire for sport, helped them excel as elite coaches. Although research on youth-sport coaching is comparatively lacking, some common characteristics and ideal coaching principles have been forwarded by experts in this field. As the importance of the youth-sport coach becomes more apparent in the overall physical activity level of adults, one can expect more research on this overlooked sector of coaching.

COACHING KNOWLEDGE

This section will focus on the knowledge of coaches, including their goals, roles, and responsibilities, as well as the extent to which they can affect the learning and performance of their athletes. In order to present this information, three bodies of literature in coaching psychology will be examined: (1) Chelladurai's sport leadership model, (2) Feltz and colleagues' coaching efficacy model, and (3) Côté et al.'s coaching model.

Sport Leadership

Leadership has been defined as "a process whereby an individual influences a group of individuals to achieve a common goal" (Northouse, 2001, p. 3). Given its apparent practical appeal, it is not surprising that leadership has been one of the most studied areas in industrial and organizational psychology (Northouse, 2001). Leadership has been defined, constructed, and researched from numerous theoretical frameworks, such as trait theories or behavioural approaches (Klenke, 1993). In spite of the rich background of research on leadership, this concept is one of the least understood phenomena because almost every finding about leadership (e.g., personality characteristics, gender differences) can be contradicted by other results (Klenke, 1993). In sport, effective leadership has been cited by athletes and coaches as a vital component of achievement (Chelladurai & Riemer, 1998; Dupuis, Bloom, & Loughead, 2006) and athlete satisfaction (Riemer & Chelladurai, 1995). At present, most sport leadership research has focused on coaching effectiveness by identifying personality traits, behavioural attributes, and situational determinants.

Several models of sport leadership have been advanced, the most noteworthy being Chelladurai's (1978, 1993) **multidimensional model of leadership** (MML), a linear model comprising antecedents, leader behaviours, and consequences (see Figure 11.2). Created specifically for sport situations, Chelladurai's MML conceptualizes leadership as an interactional process, and thus it allows researchers to evaluate leadership effectiveness through team member satisfaction and performance of athletes (consequences). These consequences are directly affected by the degree of congruence among the three states of leader behaviours, called required, preferred, and actual. Required leader behaviours are those that are expected of a coach. For example, coaches are not allowed to make physical contact with their athletes. Preferred leader behaviours are how a coach acts and are generally based on the athletes' preferences. For example, most professional coaches do not socialize with their players after games. Finally, actual leader behaviours are the behaviours that a coach exhibits, regardless of team standards. These leader behaviours are influenced by antecedent factors, which can be classified into situational (e.g., team goals, norms), leader (e.g., leader's experience or personality), and team-member characteristics (e.g., gender, ability). To date, the majority of research using this model has been for individuals rather than teams.

Chelladurai's model benefited coaching research because it attributed coaches' success to more than great leadership skills. It stressed that success was a function of coaches' capacity to display actual leadership behaviours that responded to a combination of demands from the environment, the players, and the coaches themselves. Furthermore, successful coaches were able to adjust to these demands by incorporating the required and preferred behaviours into their actual behaviours. The majority of research using the MML has primarily focused on the leadership behaviours of adult coaches of elite sports.

Figure 11.2 Multidimensional model of leadership

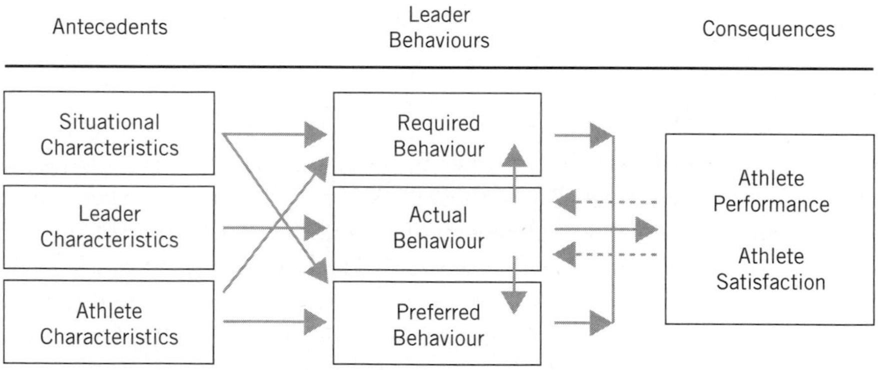

Note: Adapted from Chelladurai, P. (1993). Leadership. In R. N. Singer, M. Murphey, & L. K. Tennant (Eds.), *Handbook of research on sport psychology* (p. 648). New York: Macmillan.

REFLECTIONS 11.3

Who was your favourite coach that you played for? What were his or her actual leader behaviours? Did all players prefer these behaviours? Does the multidimensional model of leadership help explain your own experiences with this coach?

Outside of sport psychology, research in leadership has begun to focus on the nature and effects of transformational leadership in organizations. A series of papers and writings published by Bass and Avolio (Avolio & Bass, 1991; Bass, 1999; Bass & Avolio, 1994) suggest that transformational leaders were, among other things, inspirational motivators who were able to elevate the interest of their followers. **Transformational leadership** contains four leader behaviours that have been shown to influence followers' values, needs, awareness, and performance (Bass & Riggio, 2006). The applicability of this model for understanding coaching leadership styles is apparent. Transformational leadership has slowly begun to enter applied sport psychology research (Charbonneau, Barling, & Kelloway, 2001; Rowold, 2006; Vallée & Bloom, 2005; Zacharatos, Barling, & Kelloway, 2000). So far, the results are encouraging, showing improved athlete functioning in areas such as intrinsic motivation, commitment, and satisfaction for those who were coached by transformational leaders. As well, Vallée and Bloom found that the expert coaches in their sample, who also met the criteria of being transformational leaders, had the ability to elicit extraordinary outcomes from their athletes. The expert coaches accomplished this by investing in their athletes' personal growth and development, articulating a vision for their team, and having their athletes buy into that vision. In summary, while research on transformational leadership in sport is still in its infancy, the success of research using this theory in non-sport settings, combined with its intuitive leadership appeal and applicability to coaching, indicates that this may be a growing area of research in coaching psychology.

Coaching Efficacy

Sport psychology practitioners now generally believe that confidence levels can be changed and improved over time. Thus, the experts would argue that star athletes, like Wayne Gretzky, Clara Hughes, Steve Nash, and Chantal Petitclerc, were not born with exceptionally higher levels of confidence than their competitors. The same analogy can be made with elite coaches. In fact, the topic of confidence has recently been applied to the coaching psychology literature under the title of **coaching efficacy**. This term is defined as "the extent to which coaches believe they have the capacity to affect the learning and performance of their athletes" (Feltz, Chase, Moritz, & Sullivan, 1999, p. 765). The authors have identified four key dimensions at the core of their model:

1. Game strategy: This refers to the degree to which coaches believe they can effectively coach (i.e., devise strategies) during competitions.
2. Motivation: This refers to the degree to which coaches believe they can effectively affect their athletes' psychological attributes.
3. Technique: This refers to the degree to which coaches believe they can teach the effective skills and techniques of their sport and recognize talent.
4. Character building: This refers to the degree to which coaches believe they can instill a sense of respect or fair play in their athletes.

Those coaches who scored high in each of these four areas were said to have teams that performed better with higher winning percentages, were more committed to their profession, used more praise and encouragement, and had more satisfied athletes who had higher levels of confidence. Furthermore, a coach's level of efficacy was affected by

Figure 11.3 Model of coaching efficacy

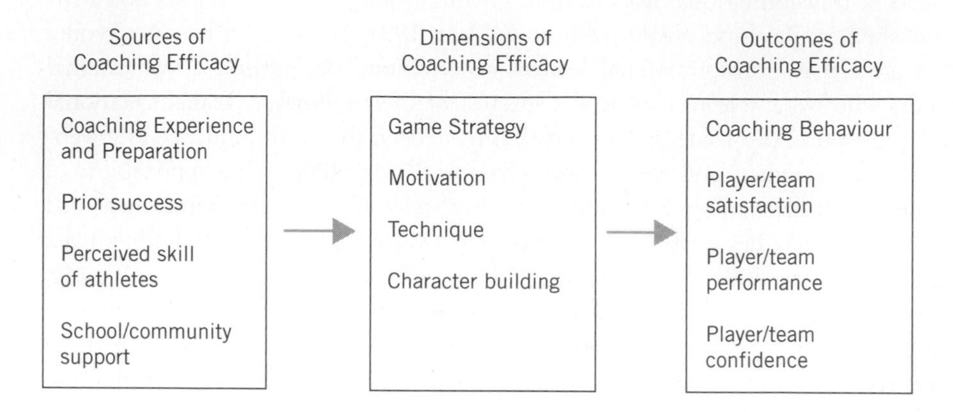

Note: From Sullivan, P. J., & Feltz, D. L. (2002). *The psychological effect of Canada's national coaching education program* (final grant report). Ottawa, ON: Social Sciences and Humanities Research Council of Canada. Reprinted with permission.

four sources: previous experiences and preparation, previous level of success, perceived skill of the athletes, and the level of community support (see Figure 11.3). The most important of these sources was prior success; coaches who had experienced success as either coaches or athletes felt more confident, especially in devising strategy and motivating athletes.

Since the creation of the conceptual model of coaching efficacy, a group of researchers have begun investigating the effects of coach education courses on a coach's level of efficacy (e.g., Campbell & Sullivan, 2005; Malete & Feltz, 2000; Sullivan & Gee, 2008). Among their conclusions, it was found that coaches who completed a coach education course showed an increase in all four dimensions of coaching efficacy. These findings demonstrate how an important coaching dimension (efficacy) can be learned and improved through coach education programs.

Case Study 11.1

Coaching Hiring Committee

As a parent of two athletic, high-school-aged children, you have volunteered as a member of the hiring committee for the new girl's high-school basketball coach. The committee has been unable to reach consensus on the best candidate for the job. They disagree on what characteristics or attributes are most important for a new coach, often looking at winning percentage, number of championships, and/or number of provincial all-stars.

You are growing increasingly frustrated with the committee's lack of progress and decide to take a leadership role. Having taken a class in sport psychology, you recall the value and importance of coaching efficacy. Using the content presented in this chapter, particularly the model of coaching efficacy, draft a one-page summary for your committee that will provide guidance and direction in helping to choose the next coach.

Coaching Model

Côté and colleagues (Côté, Salmela, Trudel, Baria, & Russell, 1995) created a coaching model that allows for connections to be established between the accumulated knowledge of how and why coaches perform as they do (see Figure 11.4). The **coaching model** infers that coaches begin their job by developing a mental model of the potential of their athletes or teams. This mental model is influenced by three peripheral components: coach's personal characteristics, athletes' personal characteristics, and contextual factors. Coaches integrate these three peripheral components into their operational strategies to determine which of the three primary components—organization, training, and competition—must be used to maximize the development of the athlete and the team. The primary components of the coaching model are what distinguish it from other more specific models of coaching, including the MML. Moreover, the coaching model proposes that success includes more than a specific set of personality traits, organizational behaviours, or interpersonal skills of the coach. Overall, coaching success appears to be related to various interpersonal, cognitive, and operational aspects of leadership.

Research for the coaching model was carried out on expert individual-sport coaches in gymnastics (Côté, Salmela, Trudel, et al., 1995). The components of the coaching model were supported in a single case study of an elite university team-sport coach (i.e., hockey coach; Gilbert & Trudel, 2000). Finally, Moraes (1998) used the coaching model as a framework to study expert coaches of combat (martial art) sports. Given this information, it is

Figure 11.4 Coaching model

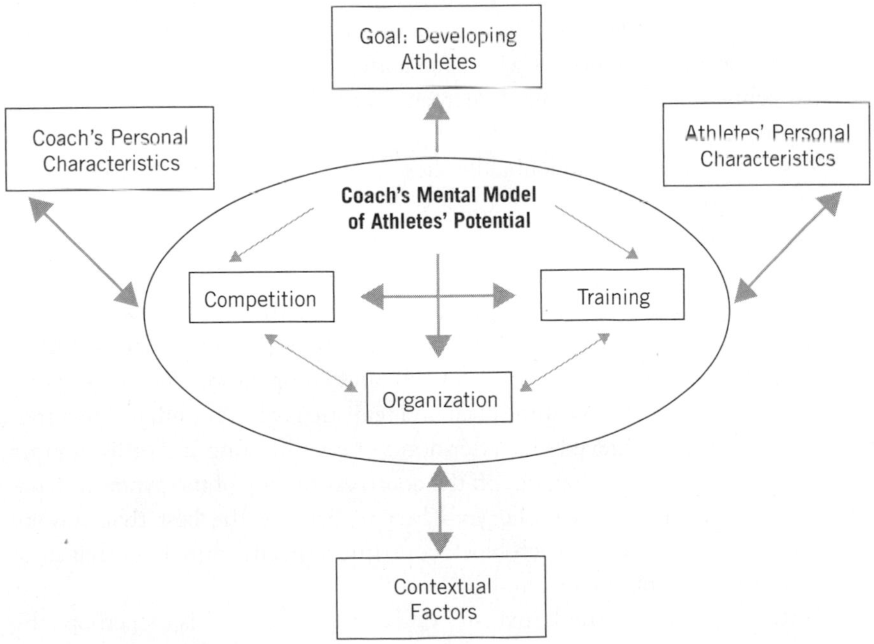

Note: From Côté, J., Salmela, J. H., Trudel, P., Baria, A., & Russell, S. J. (1995). The coaching model: A grounded assessment of expert gymnastics coaches' knowledge. *Journal of Sport & Exercise Psychology, 17,* 10, Figure 1. © 1995 by Human Kinetics Publishers, Inc. Reprinted with permission from Human Kinetics (Champaign, IL).

not surprising that the coaching model has served as a theoretical framework for much research on expert Canadian coaching.

Overall Goal of Coaching Too often, we read the horror stories of coaches who put winning above all else. For example, the coach of a novice hockey team who has a power-play unit for the most skilled players or the youth softball coach who always bats the same two players at the bottom of the batting order. Although this winning-first philosophy may ultimately produce more victories, it certainly does not build the confidence and self-esteem of all the young players. In Canada, a body of research on successful university and Olympic coaches reveals that their main goal of coaching has a very positive, athlete-centred approach (e.g., Côté, Salmela, Trudel, et al., 1995; Gilbert & Trudel, 2000; Miller, Salmela, & Kerr, 2002; Vallée & Bloom, 2005). More specifically, although winning was important to these coaches, they were at least equally concerned with developing their athletes' personal and academic skills.

It is difficult to determine if this holistic approach to athlete development is specific to Canadian amateur sport, from which athletes rarely enter the professional setting (except perhaps for ice hockey). Two coaching books would suggest otherwise (Walton, 1992; Wooden, 1988). Gary Walton (1992) recounted the careers of six great coaches (five Americans) in a variety of sports: John Wooden, James "Doc" Counsilman, Woody Hayes, Vince Lombardi, Brutus Hamilton, and Percy Cerutty. Walton poignantly noted that although this group compiled extraordinary win–loss records and contributions to technical advances in their sports, they were more concerned about their contributions as educators and role models. In the same vein, John Wooden (1988) wrote, "I often told my players that, next to my own flesh and blood, they were the closest to me. They were my children. I got wrapped up in them, their lives, and their problems" (p. 62). Wooden's philosophy is even more impressive, considering the on-court success of his UCLA basketball teams: they set all-time records with four perfect 30-0 seasons, 88 consecutive victories, 38 straight NCAA tournament victories, and 10 national championships, including seven in a row.

Wooden's secret to success undoubtedly lies in his pyramid of success (www.coachwooden.com), which explains the necessary steps to achieve success in basketball and in life. Wooden once explained that no building is better than its structural foundation, and no man is better than his mental foundation. Two foundations at the bottom of the pyramid are industriousness and enthusiasm, which stress the value of each player's consistent hard work in games and practices. These two mental components are linked with teamwork principles, such as loyalty, friendship, and co-operation. Wooden's pyramid also highlights the value of establishing clear and realistic goals. As well, it shows that poise and confidence will be achieved only after hours of conditioning and drills in practice and a commitment to proper behaviour off the court. At the top of the pyramid is success, which is defined as knowing you did your best to become the best that you are capable of becoming. In other words, each block constitutes specific principles that must be in place in order to move up the pyramid.

Pat Summitt, head coach of the University of Tennessee Lady Vols, is perhaps the most widely recognized women's head coach in North America. Besides being a co-captain of the 1976 silver-winning US women's Olympic basketball team, Coach Summitt has won more national basketball championships than any other coach, man or woman, since John Wooden. Further to this, she holds the all-time NCAA record for most wins by a basketball coach, with a win–loss record of 983-182 (www.coachsummitt.com). Interestingly, she has attributed her coaching success to a change of coaching philosophy that involved adopting a more athlete-centred approach, about 10 years into her coaching career. She recounts,

> Then, in 1987, we won our first title. And four more in the next ten years. What changed? For one thing, me. Over the years, I matured and learned from my experiences. I was forced out from behind my desk to deal with drugs, alcohol, injury, broken hearts, and emotional breakdowns of every other description. I was confronted by unwanted pregnancies, drinking problems, a player in a near-fatal car wreck, and countless instances of love gone wrong . . . . I was learning that a coach is far more than a strategist or a disciplinarian. You are a peculiar form of crisis counselor and interim substitute parent (Summitt & Jenkins, 1998, pp. 67–68).

Perhaps it can be concluded that all non-professional coaches in Canada should adopt an athlete-centred approach that includes their athletes' social, academic, and athletic pursuits. As well, an examination of both Pat Summitt's and John Wooden's philosophies clearly indicates that it is also possible for an elite amateur coach in the United States to follow a similar approach, even though media coverage and pressure to win are often greater than they are in Canada.

Primary Components of the Coaching Model **Organization** Côté, Salmela, Trudel, et al. (1995) stipulated that organization involves "applying one's knowledge towards establishing optimal conditions for training and competition by structuring and coordinating the tasks involved in reaching the goal" (p. 9). Desjardins (1996) alluded to the multitude of organizational tasks of team-sport coaches. These included the following seven tasks: creating a vision, establishing a seasonal plan, selecting a team, setting goals, developing team cohesion, working with support staff, and attending to administrative matters. By contrast, Côté and Salmela (1996) identified the following five organizational tasks for their group of expert gymnastics coaches: working with parents, working with assistants, helping gymnasts with personal concerns, planning training, and monitoring gymnasts' weight and aesthetics.

Whether in individual or team sports, organizational tasks are present before, during, and after the season and represent the foundation of the coaches' knowledge base. Moreover, a coach's ability to organize the season and to deal with organizational issues reveals much about his or her coaching and management skills. If a coach is organized, there will be a solid foundation from which to build a championship team. This should lead to more effective training sessions that, in turn, might improve the team's success at competitions.

One of the fundamental elements of organization is creating and selling a **coaching vision**. Desjardins (1996) found that expert coaches began coaching their teams with a vision of where they could go and how they could get there. This vision involved both the long-term goal of program growth and development and the short-term goal of what the coach believed each athlete or the entire team could achieve in any given season. Desjardins stated that once the vision was established, the expert coaches transformed this vision into a **mission statement**, a tangible written statement that gave the team direction for the upcoming year. The mission statement then influenced the seasonal plan, daily practices, training regimens, team selection, and goal setting. Desjardins also mentioned that expert coaches drew up a complete plan for the upcoming season, taking

Establishing optimal conditions for training and competition will help teams attain performance and personal goals.

Photograph courtesy of www.golancers.ca.

into consideration the mental, physical, tactical, and technical aspects of training. In other words, a mission statement was not merely a target to aim for—it was the team's absolute reason for being.

Further evidence about the need for a solid mission statement can be found in a Canadian study on expert university basketball and volleyball coaches (Vallée & Bloom, 2005). The participants in this study all took over losing programs, and, in a short time, they turned the teams into perennial contenders with excellent reputations on and off the court. Although these authors also found that the primary goal of these coaches was the holistic development of their athletes, they found that it was important for the coaches to possess strong organizational and interpersonal skills, including a vision for the team (highlighting personal growth and development). Early on in their appointments, coaches worked at changing past philosophies, setting higher standards and goals, and leading the team in a new direction. Coaches also emphasized the importance of the athletes buying into the vision for the team to achieve success.

REFLECTIONS 11.4

You are asked to develop a vision for a high-school basketball team. What would it be? What factors would you need to consider in developing this vision?

Training Training encompasses the knowledge coaches utilize to maximize their athletes' ability to acquire and perform various skills during practice. Training has been found to include coaches' application of technical training, physical training, mental training, tactical training, and intervention style (Côté, Salmela, Trudel et al., 1995; Durand-Bush, 1996).

Tharp and Gallimore (1976) performed a classic study on the technical skills of expert coaches by observing and analyzing coaching great John Wooden during basketball practice sessions over the course of one season. Results revealed that the majority of Wooden's cues were technical. He was focusing on the basic fundamentals of playing basketball, which in a recent re-analysis accounted for his apparent lack of positive praise (Gallimore & Tharp, 2004). This seemingly successful approach led to a new way of seeing coaching success. According to Tharp and Gallimore, Wooden was successful because of the quality of his teaching, interventions, and instructions. Additionally, research revealed that technical instructions were the most common form of instruction, and coaches stressed the importance of sound technical training to ensure their athletes were prepared for games and practices (Côté, Salmela, & Russell, 1995; Durand-Bush, 1996; Lacy & Darst, 1985).

Physical training focuses on the athletes' physical strength, endurance, and conditioning. With regard to physical training, expert coaches have commented on the uniqueness of each athlete and how they often created individualized training programs to meet their athletes' needs (Durand-Bush, 1996). Many of these coaches have utilized strength and conditioning specialists to work with their teams.

Over the years, there have been mixed messages, both anecdotally and empirically, about the use and importance of mental training by high-level coaches. Some elite coaches have given mental training less attention than physical and technical training (Durand-Bush, 1996). In contrast, some expert coaches have perceived mental training as an equally important component of training (Côté, Salmela, Trudel, et al., 1995; Wrisberg, 1990). These coaches felt that it was beneficial to use a sport psychologist to work with their team on the more specific aspects of mental training, such as motivation, visualization, and controlling anxiety. As well, there are instances of Olympic and professional teams hiring sport psychologists. Thus, it appears that expert coaches are beginning to realize that in order to get the best out of their athletes, they must incorporate mental training, and perhaps the best way to do so is by utilizing the assistance of a sport psychologist.

Research has shown that many expert coaches spend a large portion of practice time on tactical training—offensive and defensive strategies—as well as on creatively inventing drills to improve tactical difficulties (Bloom, Crumpton, & Anderson, 1999; Durand-Bush, 1996). According to Durand-Bush, elite coaches are knowledgeable about their sport and are able to adjust each practice to fit the current needs of their athletes.

Research has revealed that an authoritative intervention style was not present among top-level Canadian gymnastics coaches (Côté, Salmela, & Russell, 1995). However, two European studies present very different perspectives from that of Canadian coaches. For example, d'Arrippe-Longueville, Fournier, and Dubois (1998) reported that French judo coaches were not only authoritarian with their large number of World and Olympic champions, but they also used sarcasm and divisive training strategies to increase rivalry, and they created hostility among players; however, this was associated with great international success. In another European study, Chantal, Guay, Dobreva-Martinova, and Vallerand (1996) found that elite Bulgarian athletes, while being self-determined, were not motivated by needs of inner fulfillment and ownership, but rather by external rewards and medals. In Brazil, especially in soccer, the primary goal is winning; for coaches, the consequence for losing is immediate dismissal (Salmela & Moraes, 2003). Thus, while more research is needed to reach any global conclusions, it appears that Canadian Olympic and university coaches use a different coaching style than some of their European and Brazilian counterparts. As well, there are likely differences based on the sport itself.

Competition This primary component relates to the coaching knowledge applied throughout the day of competition and the tasks performed. Researchers have reported that elite coaches developed pre-match routines for both themselves and their athletes, mastered the contingencies that they could control during a match (e.g., time outs, rapport with officials), and dealt with emotions following the match to better deal with their athletes' performances (Bloom, 1996; Bloom, Durand-Bush, & Salmela, 1997; Côté, Salmela, Trudel et al., 1995). This section on competition will focus on team-sport coaches because of their active role on game day, compared with a more passive approach for individual and combat sport (martial art) coaches.

Pre-competition tasks involve coaches' activities leading up to their arrival on site. Research has indicated that these expert coaches are very meticulous in their plans for both themselves and their athletes on game day. With respect to themselves, coaches need time alone to mentally prepare and rehearse for the game. Often this occurred by taking a game-day jog. With respect to their athletes, coaches wanted them to have set routines so that they were not wasting energy thinking about what to eat or how to get to the competition site. As well, coaches preferred that their athletes spend time together as a way of improving team cohesion.

An interesting finding from the research on expert Canadian coaches focused on the pre-game pep talk (Bloom, 1996; Bloom et al., 1997). Likely because of Hollywood's preoccupation with sensationalizing the pre-game talk (e.g., Knute Rockne's "win one for the Gipper" speech), many outsiders expect coaches to fire up the team prior to every competition. Nothing could be further from the truth, according to the expert Canadian coaches. These coaches preferred a calm, even-tempered pre-game pep talk. The coaches' final words were process-centred and reviewed three or four of the most important points stressed in the previous week's preparation.

Bloom's (1996) research revealed a number of important factors for expert team-sport coaches once competition began. Their coaching required attention to detail, an even-tempered demeanour, and an ability to out-think the opposing coach. This was accomplished in many ways: through strategically using time outs and substitutions, relaying two or three important points of information during intermissions, developing productive relationships with officials, and providing athletes with appropriate playing time. The coaches' understanding of sport went beyond the basic textbook strategies. Some have compared expert team-sport coaches with grand chess masters because both have to think many steps ahead of the opposition. For example, while watching the game, these coaches put their players in the right position to maximize their strengths and minimize their opponents' strengths, and they regularly monitored their own behaviours, all with the goal of helping their team achieve success.

Post-competition activities of expert team-sport coaches dealt with four areas: how the coaches handled the outcome, how they coped with their own emotions, what they did and said in the locker room, and what their post-game evaluation was (Bloom et al., 1997). The content and focus of the post-competition meeting depended on both the outcome and the coaches' perceptions of whether the team played well or poorly. Most coaches gave their teams a few pointers, saving the in-depth analysis for the next practice or team meeting. Winning was the easiest outcome to handle. When the team played well and won, coaches emphasized effort and performance, not just outcome. When the team played poorly but won, coaches stressed areas needing improvement and acknowledged those individuals who gave a solid effort. The coaches did not want to spoil the thrill of victory, no matter how poorly they thought the team had played.

Losses were more demanding on the coaches. Most importantly, they had to decide if their players performed up to their capabilities. For example, when the team played well but lost, the expert team-sport coaches said that it was important to remain encouraging, focusing on the positive aspects of their performance. However, when the team played poorly and lost, most of these coaches felt that it was best to say little to their players because the emotional climate for themselves and their athletes was very high, and they worried about saying something they would later regret.

After any competition, the expert team-sport coaches also had to deal with their own emotions before entering the locker room. Many chose to take some time for themselves in order to "wind down." Most coaches said very little because they realized that both they and their athletes were still very emotional. They were especially aware that they should not single out any individual player. One reason for not analyzing the game in the locker room was that the coaches wanted to complete a thorough post-game evaluation, something that took place within 24 hours of the match. They wanted to consult a number of resources, such as videos, statistics, and assistant coaches, before finalizing their post-game evaluation. Regardless of the outcome, the coaches used every game as a learning experience to help prepare for future contests.

Peripheral Components of the Coaching Model **Coach's Personal Characteristics** Côté, Salmela, Trudel, et al. (1995) defined the coach's personal characteristics as "any variables that are part of the coach's philosophy, perceptions, beliefs, or personal life that could influence the organization, training, or competition components" (p. 11). A study specifically examining the characteristics of expert Canadian coaches was completed by Bloom and Salmela (2000). Their results included coaching preferences, goals, and beliefs. Among the results, it was found that expert coaches have an ongoing quest for personal growth and knowledge acquisition, display a strong work ethic, communicate effectively, empathize with players, and are good teachers. Many of these coaches noted that they work in a very competitive field and that the best way to succeed was by working harder than their colleagues. This involved spending long hours in their offices, which led to less time with their family and close friends. In fact, it also might explain why many expert Canadian coaches have been divorced (Salmela, 1996).

Bloom and Salmela (2000) also noted that a coach's personal characteristics greatly affected his or her ability to coach. They found that coaches who chose to regularly attend clinics or symposia, who shared information with other coaches, and who were willing to self-evaluate likely devoted more time and energy to all other aspects of their profession. Thus, it could be hypothesized that their hard work and attention to detail resulted in more creative practices and perhaps better success at competition.

Interestingly, the expert coaches' personal characteristics mirrored those of high-school teachers who help cultivate their students' talents (Csikszentmihalyi, Rathunde, & Whalen, 1993). Specifically, teachers who created the most ideal learning environments for their students shared three common characteristics. First, the teachers thoroughly enjoyed what they were doing and encouraged their students to excel beyond their current level of performance. Second, teachers created optimal learning conditions so that students were not bored or excessively frustrated, enabling them to maximize their level of concentration, self-esteem, potency, and involvement. Finally, the teachers showed reassuring kindness and genuine concern for the students' overall development, both inside and outside school.

REFLECTIONS 11.5

What is your typical coaching style and philosophy?

Athletes' Personal Characteristics Côté, Salmela, Trudel, et al. (1995) defined the athletes' personal characteristics as any variables relating to the athlete's stage of learning, personal abilities, and other personal characteristics that could affect the three primary components of the model. More specifically, this involved the coach adjusting to the makeup of each athlete, whether this involved the athlete's personality, strengths, or weaknesses. The goal was to maximize their athletes' potential and output. Given the differences between coaching an individual athlete and a group of athletes, one would expect a number of differences to arise between coaches of individual sports and of team sports. Whereas individual-sport coaches can divert all of their attention to one athlete all of the time, and thus create more personal decisions around a single athlete, team-sport coaches must be aware of how their interactions relate to the overall organization and effectiveness of the team.

Perhaps a good example of a coach being able to adapt to his athlete's idiosyncrasies was the legendary Phil Jackson; the athlete was Dennis "The Worm" Rodman. On the court, Rodman was a major rebounding presence throughout his career, although he was suspended for assaulting referees, opponents, and even a photographer. However, his off-court behaviours were far more outlandish and possibly detrimental to the team. Some of Rodman's acts included posing nude, cross-dressing, dying his hair, and acquiring numerous body piercings and tattoos. Coach Phil Jackson obviously did not treat Rodman the same way he did his other notable stars, Michael Jordan and Scottie Pippen. Undoubtedly, his ability to adapt to Rodman, yet still put the team ahead of all else, may partially have contributed to the success of the Chicago Bulls during their NBA championship run in the 1990s.

Contextual Factors Côté, Salmela, Trudel, et al. (1995) defined contextual factors as "unstable factors, aside from the athletes and the coach, such as working conditions, that need to be considered when intervening in the organization, training, and competition components" (p. 12). These could also be defined as situation-specific variables. Within the coaching model, the coaching context has been shown to be a determining factor that shapes all perceptions and behaviours. Available resources, pressures, and general lifestyles determine and affect coaches' views of their world. For example, a high-school team can gain a significant advantage over other schools if it receives more funding for equipment and training facilities than other schools.

Within team sports, Salmela (1996) listed a number of different contextual variables that could affect an elite Canadian coach's win–loss record and, hence, job security. These variables included the availability of athletic scholarships or funding (especially compared

Successful coaches are able to adapt to all of their athletes' differences without disrupting the climate of the team or the performance of each athlete.

Photograph © The Canadian Press (Frank Gunn).

with the United States), the relationship between the coach and management, and the coaching salary. Some of these factors emerged in a study of job satisfaction of elite male coaches at Canadian universities (Davies, Bloom, & Salmela, 2005). These coaches, who had all achieved a fair amount of success, noted that such factors as their relationship with their athletic director, recruiting challenges, lack of publicity, and low salary caused them some job dissatisfaction. However, these factors were more than compensated for by their passion for coaching and helping their athletes grow and mature both on and off the court. As well, these coaches learned how to lead a balanced lifestyle that prioritized their family commitments.

CHAPTER SUMMARY

Coaching science is one of the newest areas of sport psychology research. As such, there is opportunity for empirical research at all levels of coaching, from the grassroots to the highest levels. The chapter began with a discussion of coach education, with particular emphasis on the NCCP program in Canada. Nearly one million Canadians have passed through this certification program.

The chapter presented information pertaining to the knowledge and leadership skills of coaches, as well as how to become a coach. More specifically, a summary of research from a small group of Canadian researchers reported various pathways to becoming an expert coach, including the importance of mentoring and working with top professionals in the sport of interest. Information on youth-sport coaching highlighted the characteristics and ideal behaviours of these coaches.

The attributes of expert coaches were also discussed. One of the most important findings to emerge from research is that coaching is an art that requires years of hard work and practice; it also requires an ability to integrate and translate knowledge effectively to the specific sport environment. Moreover, many of Canada's top Olympic and university coaches were shown to possess an athlete-centred approach to coaching that indicated the primary goal of an elite Canadian coach was to develop the athlete, both as a person outside sport and as a participant inside sport.

Common Myths about Coaching Psychology Revisited

MYTH: Outstanding athletes have an advantage in becoming excellent coaches.
Although many people believe that elite athletes can more easily become elite coaches than less-skilled athletes, the scientific evidence suggests otherwise. Although most expert coaches played at a high level in their sport, few were exceptional performers. Moreover, there are very few Hall of Fame athletes who reach the same level of success as coaches. Finally, some recent research found that it is possible to become an expert coach without any elite sporting background.

MYTH: Aspiring coaches must emulate the most successful coaches in their sport, regardless of their own personality, beliefs, or philosophy.
Studies have found that individuals should create their own coaching style based on their traits, beliefs, and philosophy, rather than emulate someone who has achieved success in their sport.

MYTH: All elite-level coaches are focused solely on winning at the expense of athlete growth and development.
Research on elite Canadian coaches at the university and Olympic levels have found these coaches to be just as concerned about the personal growth and development of their athletes as they are with their athletic growth and development. Similar findings have also emerged with some elite American coaches at similar levels of competition.

MYTH: Coaching confidence is determined solely by one's innate personality.
Coaching confidence can be improved over time with positive performances, coach education seminars, community support, and perceived team ability.

Review Questions

1. Outline some of the methods of knowledge acquisition for becoming an elite coach.
2. Summarize the role of the NCCP in Canada.
3. How is mentoring important in the career progression of an elite coach?
4. An effective practice for coaching youth sport is to give encouragement after a mistake in a positive way. Provide a real-life game example to illustrate this recommendation.
5. List some effective practices for coaching youth sport.
6. Explain how coaching leadership is an interactional process.
7. What is meant by an athlete-centred approach to coaching?
8. What are the four key dimensions of coaching efficacy?
9. What can a coach do to improve the mental component of athlete development?

Suggested Reading

Smith, R. E., & Smoll, F. L. (2002). *Way to go coach!: A scientifically-proven approach to youth sports coaching effectiveness* (2nd ed.). Portola Valley, CA: Waroe.

Trudel, P., & Gilbert, W. D. (2006). Coaching and coach education. In D. Kirk, M. O'Sullivan, & D. McDonald (Eds.), *Handbook of research in physical education* (pp. 516–539). London, UK: Sage.

References

Avolio, B. J., & Bass, B. M. (1991). *The full range of leadership development: Basic and advanced manuals*. Birmingham, NY: Bass, Avolio, & Associates.

Bass, B. M. (1999). Two decades of research and development in transformational leadership. *European Journal of Work and Organizational Psychology, 8*, 9–32.

Bass, B. M., & Avolio, B. J. (1994). *Improving organizational effectiveness through transformational leadership*. Thousand Oaks, CA: Sage.

Bass, B. M., & Riggio, R. E. (2006). *Transformational leadership* (2nd ed.). Mahwah, NJ: Lawrence Erlbaum.

Bloom, B. S. (1985). *Developing talent in young people*. New York: Ballantine.

Bloom, G. A. (1996). Competition: Preparing for and operating in competition. In J. H. Salmela (Ed.), *Great job coach! Getting the edge from proven winners* (pp. 138–179). Ottawa, ON: Potentium.

Bloom, G. A., Crumpton, R., & Anderson, J. E. (1999). A systematic observation study of the teaching behaviors of an expert basketball coach. *The Sport Psychologist, 13*, 157–170.

Bloom, G. A., Durand-Bush, N., & Salmela, J. H. (1997). Pre- and postcompetition routines of expert coaches of team sports. *The Sport Psychologist, 11*, 127–141.

Bloom, G. A., Durand-Bush, N., Schinke, R. J., & Salmela, J. H. (1998). The importance of mentoring in the development of coaches and athletes. *International Journal of Sport Psychology, 29*, 267–281.

Bloom, G. A., & Salmela, J. H. (2000). Personal characteristics of expert team sport coaches. *Journal of Sport Pedagogy, 6*, 56–76.

Campbell, T., & Sullivan, P. J. (2005). The effect of a standardized coaching education program on the efficacy of novice coaches. *Avante, 11*, 56–68.

Carter, A. D. & Bloom, G. A. (in press). Coaching knowledge and success: Going beyond athletic experiences. *Journal of Sport Behavior*.

Chantal, Y., Guay, F., Dobreva-Martinova, T., & Vallerand, R. J. (1996). Motivation and elite performance: An exploratory investigation with Bulgarian athletes. *International Journal of Sport Psychology, 27*,173–182.

Charbonneau, D., Barling, J., & Kelloway, E. K. (2001). Transformational leadership and sports performance: The mediating role of intrinsic motivation. *Journal of Applied Social Psychology, 31*, 1521–1534.

Chelladurai, P. (1978). *A contingency model of leadership in athletics*. Unpublished doctoral dissertation, University of Waterloo, Waterloo, Ontario.

Chelladurai, P. (1993). Leadership. In R. N. Singer, M. Murphey, & L. K. Tennant (Eds.), *Handbook of research on sport psychology* (pp. 647–671). New York: Macmillan.

Chelladurai, P., & Riemer, H. A. (1998). Measurement of leadership in sport. In J. L. Duda (Ed.), *Advances in sport and exercise psychology measurement* (pp. 227–253). Morgantown, WV: Fitness Information Technology.

Chelladurai, P., & Saleh, S. D. (1980). Dimensions of leader behavior in sports: Development of a leadership scale. *Journal of Sport Psychology, 2*, 34–45.

Coakley, J. J. (1990). *Sport in society: Issues and controversies*. Toronto, ON: Times Mirror/Mosby.

Côté, J., & Salmela, J. H. (1996). The organizational tasks of high-performance gymnastic coaches. *The Sport Psychologist, 10*, 247–260.

Côté, J., Salmela, J. H., & Russell, S. J. (1995). The knowledge of high-performance gymnastic coaches: Competition and training considerations. *The Sport Psychologist*, 9, 76–95.

Côté, J., Salmela, J. H., Trudel, P., Baria, A., & Russell, S. J. (1995). The coaching model: A grounded assessment of expert gymnastic coaches' knowledge. *Journal of Sport & Exercise Psychology, 17*, 1–17.

Cragg, S., Cameron, C., Craig, C. L., & Russell, S. J. (1999). *Canada's children and youth: A physical activity profile*. Ottawa, ON: Canada Fitness and Lifestyle Research Institute.

Cregan, K. Bloom, G. A., & Reid, G. (2007). Career evolution and knowledge of elite coaches of swimmers with a physical disability. *Research Quarterly for Exercise and Sport, 78*, 339–350.

Csikszentmihalyi, M., Rathunde, K., & Whalen, S. (1993). *Talented teenagers: The roots of success and failure*. New York: Cambridge.

Culver, D., & Trudel, P. (2006). Cultivating coaches' communities of practice: Developing the potential for learning through interactions. In R. Jones (Ed.), *The sport coach as educator: Reconceptualising sport coaching* (pp. 97–112). London, UK: Routledge.

d'Arrippe-Longueville, F., Fournier, J. F., & Dubois, A. (1998). The perceived effectiveness of interactions between expert French judo coaches and their athletes. *The Sport Psychologist, 12*, 317–332.

Davies, M. J., Bloom, G. A., & Salmela, J. H. (2005). Job satisfaction of accomplished male university basketball coaches: The Canadian context. *International Journal of Sport Psychology, 36*, 173–192.

Desjardins, G., Jr. (1996). The mission. In J. H. Salmela (Ed.), *Great job coach! Getting the edge from proven winners* (pp. 1–35). Ottawa, ON: Potentium.

Douge, B., & Hastie, P. (1993). Coach effectiveness. *Sport Science Review, 2*, 14–29.

Dupuis, M., Bloom, G. A., & Loughead, T. M. (2006). Team captains' perceptions of athlete leadership. *Journal of Sport Behavior, 29*, 60–78.

Durand-Bush, N. (1996). Training: Blood, sweat, and tears. In J. H. Salmela (Ed.), *Great job coach! Getting the edge from proven winners* (pp. 103–139). Ottawa, ON: Potentium.

Erickson, K., Côté, J., & Fraser-Thomas, J. (2007). The sport experiences, milestones, and educational activities associated with the development of high-performance coaches. *The Sport Psychologist, 21*, 302–316.

Feltz, D. L., Chase, M. A., Moritz, S. E., & Sullivan, P. J. (1999). A conceptual model of coaching efficacy: Preliminary investigation and instrument development. *Journal of Educational Psychology, 91*, 765–776.

Gallimore, R., & Tharp, R. (2004). What a coach can teach a teacher, 1975–2004: Reflections and reanalysis of John Wooden's teaching practices. *The Sport Psychologist, 18*, 119–137.

Gilbert, W. D., Côté, J., & Mallett, C. (2006). Developmental pathways and activities of successful sport coaches. *International Journal of Sport Science and Coaching, 1*, 69–76.

Gilbert, W. D., & Trudel, P. (2004). Analysis of coaching science research published from 1970–2001. *Research Quarterly for Exercise and Sport, 75*, 388–399.

Gilbert, W. D., & Trudel, P. (2000). Validation of the coaching model (CM) in a team sport context. *International Sports Journal, 4*, 120–128.

Gould, D., Giannini, J., Krane, V., & Hodge, K. (1990). Educational needs of elite U.S. national team, Pan American, and Olympic coaches. *Journal of Teaching in Physical Education, 9*, 332–344.

Jones, R. L., Armour, K. M., & Potrac, P. (2003). Constructing expert knowledge: A case study of a top-level professional soccer coach. *Sport, Education and Society, 8*, 213–229.

Katzmarzyk, P. T., & Janssen, I. (2004). The economic costs associated with physical inactivity and obesity in Canada: An update. Canadian *Journal of Applied Physiology, 1*, 90–115.

Klenke, K. (1993). Meta-analytic studies of leadership: Added insights or added paradoxes? *Current Psychology: Developmental, Learning, Personality, Social, 12*, 326–343.

Lacy, A. C., & Darst, P. W. (1985). Systematic observation of behaviours of winning high school head football coaches. *Journal of Teaching in Physical Education, 4*, 256–270.

Lemyre, F., Trudel, P., & Durand-Bush, N. (2007). How youth-sport coaches learn to coach. *The Sport Psychologist, 21*, 191–209.

Malete, L., & Feltz, D. (2000). The effect of a coaching education program on coaching efficacy. *The Sport Psychologist, 14*, 410–417.

Miller, P. S., Salmela, J. H., & Kerr, G. (2002). Coaches perceived role in mentoring athletes. International *Journal of Sport Psychology, 33*, 410–430.

Moraes, L. C. (1998). *Influence in the development of beliefs of Canadian expert judo coaches and their impact on action*. Unpublished doctoral dissertation, University of Ottawa, Ottawa, Ontario.

Northouse, P. G. (2001). *Leadership: Theory and practice* (2nd ed.). Thousand Oaks, CA: Sage.

Riemer, H. A., & Chelladurai, P. (1995). Leadership and satisfaction in athletics. *Journal of Sport & Exercise Psychology, 17*, 276–293.

Rowold, J. (2006). Transformational and transactional leadership in martial arts. *Journal of Applied Sport Psychology, 18*, 297–311.

Salmela, J. H. (Ed.). (1996). *Great job coach! Getting the edge from proven winners*. Ottawa, ON: Potentium.

Salmela, J. H., & Moraes, L. C. (2003). Development of expertise: The role of coaching, families and cultural contexts. In J. L. Starkes, & K. A. Ericsson (Eds.), *Expert performance in sports: Advances in research on sport expertise* (pp. 275–296). Champaign, IL: Human Kinetics.

Schinke, R. J., Bloom, G. A., & Salmela, J. H. (1995). *The career stages of elite Canadian basketball coaches*. Avante, 1, 48–62.

Smith, R. E., & Smoll, F. L. (2002a). Youth sport as a behavioral setting for psychosocial interventions. In J. L. Van Raalte, & B. W. Brewers (Eds.), *Exploring sport and exercise psychology* (pp. 341–371). Washington, DC: American Psychological Association.

Smith, R. E, & Smoll, F. L. (2002b). *Way to go coach!: A scientifically-proven approach to youth sports coaching effectiveness* (2nd ed.). Portola Valley, CA: Waroe.

Smith, R. E., Smoll, F. L., & Cumming, S. P. (2007). Effects of a motivational climate intervention for coaches on young athletes' sport performance anxiety. *Journal of Sport & Exercise Psychology, 29*, 39–59.

Smith, R. E., Smoll, F. L., & Hunt, E. (1977). A system for the behavioral assessment of athletic coaches. *Research Quarterly, 48*, 401–407.

Smoll, F. L., & Smith, R. E. (2002). *Children and youth in sport* (2nd ed.). Dubuque, IA: Kendall/Hunt.

Smoll, F. L., Smith, R. E., & Cumming, S. P. (2007). Effects of a motivational climate intervention for coaches on changes in young athletes achievement goal orientations. *Journal of Clinical Sport Psychology, 1*, 23–46.

Strong, W. B., Malina, R. M., Blimkie, C. J. R., Daniels, S. R., Dishman, R. K., Gutin, B., et al., (2005). Evidence-based physical activity for school-age youth. *Journal of Pediatrics, 146*, 732–737.

Sullivan, P. J., & Feltz, D. L. (2002). *The psychological effect of Canada's national coaching education program* (Final Grant Report). Ottawa, ON: Social Sciences and Humanities Research Council of Canada.

Sullivan, P., & Gee, C. (2008). The effect of different coaching education content on the efficacy of coaches. *International Journal of Coaching Science, 2*, 1–8.

Summitt, P., & Jenkins, S. (1998). *Raise the roof*. New York: Broadway.

Tharp, R. G., & Gallimore, R. (1976). What a coach can teach a teacher. *Psychology Today, 9*, 75–78.

Trudel, P., & Gilbert, W. D. (2006). Coaching and coach education. In D. Kirk, M. O'Sullivan, & D. McDonald (Eds.), *Handbook of research in physical education* (pp. 516–539). London, UK: Sage.

Vallée, C. N., & Bloom, G. A. (2005). Building a successful university sport program: Key and common elements of expert coaches. *Journal of Applied Sport Psychology, 17*, 179–196.

Walton, G. M. (1992). *Beyond winning: The timeless wisdom of great philosopher coaches*. Champaign, IL: Human Kinetics.

Werthner, P., & Trudel, P. (2006). A new theoretical perspective for understanding how coaches learn to coach. *The Sport Psychologist, 20*, 198–212.

Wright, T., Trudel, P., & Culver, D. (2007). Learning how to coach: The different learning situations reported by youth sport ice hockey coaches. *Physical Education and Sport Pedagogy, 12*, 1–17.

Wooden, J. (1988). They call me coach. Chicago, IL: Contemporary Books.

Wrisberg, C. A. (1990). An interview with Pat Head Summitt. *The Sport Psychologist, 4*, 181–191.

Zacharatos, A., Barling, J., & Kelloway, E. K. (2000). Development and effects of transformational leadership in adolescents. Leadership Quarterly, 11, 211–226.

Zhang, J., Jensen, B. E., & Mann, B. L. (1997). Modification and revision of the Leadership Scale for Sport. *Journal of Sport Behavior, 20*, 105–122.

Chapter 12

Exercise and Mental Health

Larry M. Leith
Gretchen A. Kerr
Guy E. Faulkner

Chapter Objectives

After reading this chapter, you should be able to do the following:

1. Provide an overview of the prevalence of mental health disorders in Canada.
2. Understand the positive impact of exercise on depression, stress, anxiety, mood, and self-concept.
3. Distinguish among the different mechanisms that could explain the relationship between exercise and mental health.
4. Explain the role of exercise in preventing mental health problems.
5. Provide guidelines for using exercise to improve mental health in both non-clinical and clinical settings.

Over the last several months, Danna's mood seemed to be gradually deteriorating. She felt stressed out and depressed for no apparent reason and had trouble sleeping. Although she didn't feel that her problems were serious enough to see a doctor, she did notice that they were affecting the way she felt during most of the day. The feelings were made worse by her lack of sleep. She didn't have her usual level of energy and worried that this would have a noticeable effect on her university studies. In addition, her worsening mood was starting to undermine her self-confidence. At one point, Danna considered trying some over-the-counter sleeping tablets to see if they might help, but she didn't feel totally comfortable with that idea. One day after class, during a conversation with a close friend, she was told about a book that outlined a program of exercise to improve overall mood and overall psychological well-being. Although this seemed like a somewhat unusual idea, she decided to give it a try. Besides, since coming to university a little over a year ago, her level of physical activity had declined drastically because of her change of lifestyle. She had been telling herself for months to get more physically active, so the news of the exercise and mental health book was just the prompt she needed to start exercising again. In no time, Danna was glad she did. She noticed improvements with her very first exercise session, and, better yet, her feelings continued to improve over the first several weeks of regular exercise. Danna still feels down from time to time, but overall, her mood has been greatly improved by a simple exercise program.

The above vignette highlights the fact that regular exercise has a significant positive effect on elements of mental health. While most individuals know that exercise can improve muscle tone, decrease body fat, lower blood pressure, and decrease the chance of heart attack and stroke, few people realize the potential of exercise to improve mental health. Over the past two decades, a great deal of research has focused on this relationship between exercise and mental health. The bulk of that research suggests that exercise is very effective in improving mental health in both non-clinical and clinical settings (Leith, 2009; Mutrie & Biddle, 1995). In Danna's case, it was her overall mood that improved, but research has shown that exercise is also effective for depression, anxiety, aspects of stress, and self-concept/self-esteem. Each of these mental health states will be discussed separately in this chapter.

The scenario with Danna also raises a number of questions when we consider using exercise to improve mental health. What aspects of mental health have been shown to benefit from a regular exercise program? What are the mechanisms that explain the relationship between exercise and mental health? What types of exercise work best? How often, how hard, and how long must someone exercise to experience the most benefit? How soon can one expect to see positive results after starting an exercise program? Can exercise serve as a preventive intervention as well as a treatment intervention? In this chapter, we will address these and several other questions related to the exercise and mental health relationship.

Common Myths about Exercise and Mental Health

MYTH: Mental health problems are not that common in the general population.

MYTH: Exercise is more effective for treating mental problems in clinical populations than it is for improving or preventing them in non-clinical populations or in asymptomatic participants.

MYTH: In order for exercise to improve mental health, the participant must experience fitness gains by engaging in vigorous physical activity.

INTRODUCTION

Mental health problems are pandemic in modern society. In a recent landmark study investigating Canada's mental health crisis (Centre for Addiction and Mental Health, 2006), the following statistics were reported:

- 333 out of 1000 Canadians in general hospital beds at any given moment are there because of mental illness.
- 210 out of 1000 Canadians will suffer a mental illness over their lifetime.
- 48 in 1000 will experience major depression in any given year.
- 48 in 1000 will be hit with an anxiety disorder.
- 31 in 1000 will abuse substances.
- 10 in 1000 are people with schizophrenia, and six of them will attempt suicide.
- 10 in 1000 will develop bipolar disorder.
- 20 in 1000 deaths each year in Canada are suicides, and 18 of these people had diagnosable mental illness.

Similar statistics are reported in the United States, with the most common mental disorders being anxiety and depression. The World Health Organization supports both the Canadian and American statistics and has projected that depression will be second only to cardiovascular disease as the world's leading cause of death and disability by the year 2020 (Murray & Lopez, 1997).

Traditionally, mental health problems such as these have been treated by psychotherapy and/or psychotropic medication. Although there is scientific merit in both techniques, psychotherapy involves a relatively long time commitment and has a moderate to low efficacy rate, and psychotropic medications are often associated with a host of serious side effects. For this reason, increasing interest has been paid to the use of alternative means of treating and preventing mental health problems. One such non-traditional technique involves the use of long-term exercise programs.

In this chapter, we will thoroughly examine the most recent research investigating the relationship between exercise and a number of psychological states, including depression, stress, anxiety, self-concept, and mood. To a large extent, we will focus on experimental and quasi-experimental studies (as discussed in Chapter 2) but will also cover research using other methodologies. A challenge in understanding the effects of exercise on mental health is that specific components of exercise can vary markedly across studies. These components of exercise include type or modality, frequency, intensity, duration, and length of program. Researchers are often interested in the dose-response gradient,which involves understanding how these components are manipulated. In exercise psychology, the **dose-response gradient** holds that increasing levels of physical activity should correspond with decreased levels of negative psychological states and/or increased levels of positive psychological states. As you will see, there does not seem to be a clear dose-response gradient in exercise psychology. We will also explore the various mechanisms that attempt to explain the exercise and mental health relationship and will conclude the chapter with a discussion of some guidelines for best practice.

REFLECTIONS 12.1

Do you know anyone who has experienced a mental health problem? How did it affect their lives?

DEPRESSION

As an emotional state, depression is experienced by most of us sometime in our lives as we deal with the frustrations and high emotional demands of daily living. It is absolutely normal to experience temporary mood swings. Normal depression is transient and very reactive to situational stressors. Clinical **depression**, however, is less common and is a potentially lethal and debilitating disease. According to the latest version of the *Diagnostic and Statistical Manual of Mental Disorders*(American Psychiatric Association, 2000), a major depressive episode is categorized by either a depressed mood or a loss of interest or pleasure in all or most activities, and the presence of other symptoms for at least a two-week period. At least five of the following associated features are also needed: (1) loss of appetite, (2) weight loss or gain, (3) sleep disturbances, (4) psychomotor agitation or retardation, (5) decrease in energy, (6) sense of worthlessness, (7) guilt, (8) difficulty in concentration, and (9) thoughts of suicide.

Exercise and Depression

Over the years, a significant amount of research has accumulated examining the effects of exercise on depression in both non-clinical and clinical settings. Research has documented the beneficial effects of exercise on reducing depression (Annesi, 2000; Crews, Lochbaum, & Landers, 2004; Waelde, Thompson, & Gallagher-Thompson, 2004), with most studies indicating that exercise performed three times per week is sufficient to significantly lower depression in the participants (Annesi, 2000; Crews et al., 2004). Although isolated studies have successfully employed greater exercise frequencies, there does not appear to be any added advantage with exercise frequencies of greater than three or four times per week. Indeed, by staying within the recommended range, participants will minimize the risk of overuse injury and be more likely to maintain their desire to stay in the program.

At one time, some researchers suggested that significant reductions in depression could not be considered a reliable result among individuals scoring within the clinically normal range of depression (e.g., Brown, 1990; Paluska & Schwenk, 2000). However, empirical research now challenges this viewpoint. Researchers have consistently found significant reductions in depression symptoms following exercise programs in many healthy, asymptomatic populations, including children (Crews et al., 2004), college students (Motl, Birnbaum, Kubik, & Dishman, 2004), and adults (Alfermann & Stoll, 2000; Waelde et al., 2004). These research findings certainly highlight the potential for exercise to benefit those people who fall within a normal range of depression. Let us consider one such study that investigated the effect of six weeks of exercise on depression in grade four Hispanic children (Crews et al., 2004). The children were divided into an aerobic exercise group and a control group that performed no exercise. The exercise program was conducted for six weeks, and the children exercised three times per week. The exercise program consisted of cycling and running and was performed at greater than 60% maximum heart rate for 20 minutes per session. At the end of the six-week program, only the aerobic exercise group experienced significantly lower depression.

Exercise as a Treatment for Depression Exercise has also been found to be an effective means of treating clinical depression. A classic study by Martinsen and Medhus (1989) highlights this. These researchers assessed 43 patients, one to two years after discharge, who had been treated in the hospital for major depression. During their time in the hospital, participants had been randomly assigned to a training group or a control group by block randomization with respect to sex. The training group underwent a six- to nine-week aerobic training program, while the control group attended occupational therapy. Because six participants in the control group started to exercise at the conclusion of the testing period, they were considered a separate control plus training treatment group. When assessed one to two years after discharge from the hospital, the participants were asked to evaluate the different therapeutic modalities they received while at the hospital. These various interventions included medication, community meetings, contact with other patients, group psychotherapy, physical exercise, individual psychotherapy, and contact with the staff. When participants were asked which of these interventions they found most helpful and to rank the top three, they ranked physical exercise as the most important element in their comprehensive treatment program.

More recent evidence further suggests that exercise can serve as an effective adjunct to psychotropic therapy in adults and children (Daley, MacArthur, & Winter, 2007; Faulkner & Biddle, 2004; Stathopoulou et al., 2006). One of these studies (Daley et al., 2007) investigated the effect of a 12-week multi-intervention program involving group pram walking (pushing baby strollers) on postpartum depression. In this study, the subjects were divided into two experimental groups. In both groups, approximately half of the women were receiving medication for their depression, and a small number were receiving counselling. The treatment group used pram walking as an adjunct therapy, and the other group served as a control and did not exercise. At the end of the 12-week program, the women in the pram walking group exhibited a significantly lower depression score compared to their control group counterparts. In addition, women in the treatment group also had significantly improved aerobic fitness post-intervention compared to women in the control group. In this very unique study, pram walking was found to be an effective adjunct therapy for postpartum depression.

Meta-analytic reviews provide us with some tentative conclusions concerning the relationship between exercise and depression (e.g., Crews, Craft, & Landers, 1998; Lawlor & Hopker, 2001; Stathopoulou et al., 2006). Recall that meta-analysis considers the strength of results (called effect sizes) from multiple studies. When all of the meta-analyses are taken together, the following can be concluded:

- Exercise significantly decreased depression, and the antidepressant effects of exercise continued through follow-up measures.
- Subject populations experiencing similar decreases in depression include all age groups, both males and females, as well as clinical and non-clinical populations.
- All modes of exercise, including both aerobic and anaerobic exercise, were effective in decreasing depression.
- The longer the exercise program, the greater the decreases in depression.
- Exercise was at least as effective as other traditional treatments for depression.

Based on these meta-analyses, Stathopoulou and colleagues (2006) concluded that clinicians should seriously consider the role of adjunctive exercise interventions in their clinical practice for the treatment of depression.

More recently, Leith (2009) reviewed over 53 empirical studies that examined the exercise and depression relationship. In summary, perhaps the most obvious observation that can be made is that the vast majority of these studies reported significant improvements in depression following exercise. The observation is heartening and highlights the potential of exercise in the prevention and treatment of depression.

Case Study 12.1

Exercise Prescription for Depression

Consider a scenario in which a sport and exercise psychology consultant is advising a client who has been experiencing problems with depression. The individual tells the consultant that he has heard about the potential of exercise to improve depression, if used correctly. He asks the consultant for advice, and, after discussing the details, the consultant prescribes a walking program to be performed two times per week at mild intensity for 20 to 30 minutes per session.

The exercise prescription was based, in part, on the fact that the client has been relatively physically inactive over the years. During the next scheduled appointment three weeks later, the client reports no noticeable improvement. Consider this scenario in light of what you have learned in this chapter. What might the consultant say to this individual during the second meeting? What questions should the consultant ask? What change in treatment should the consultant suggest, if any, and why?

REFLECTIONS 12.2

Why do you think exercise can be effective in reducing depression symptoms, even in non-clinical populations? How often do people have to exercise to receive any benefits?

Photograph courtesy of Peter Crocker, University of British Columbia.

ANXIETY

In its simplest form, **anxiety** may be defined as a subjective feeling of apprehension and heightened physiological arousal. In Chapter 5, the concept of anxiety in sport and exercise was covered in some detail. As you may recall,periodic anxiety is a normal emotion as long as it remains moderate in frequency and intensity. It is a reaction to the everyday hassles, frustrations, interpersonal relationships, and aspirations that we experience. In some cases, however, the anticipation of real or imaginary problems can become so strong or recurrent that it reaches clinical magnitude. When this happens, the resulting anxiety interferes with family relationships, work, and personal well-being. Maladaptive behaviours often result, and the symptoms become so intense that it often becomes necessary to seek professional help. Problems of this nature are by no means uncommon. Every year in Canada, one out of every 20 individuals will experience an anxiety disorder (Centre for Addiction and Mental Health, 2006). This translates into approximately 1,650,000 Canadians per year. Furthermore, it has been estimated that the prevalence rate of anxiety is approximately 25% across the lifetime (Dishman, Washburn, & Heath, 2004).

There are different ways to define anxiety depending on whether we focus on specific contexts (e.g., test anxiety, social physique anxiety) or situational versus trait aspects of the anxiety experience. You will recall that **state anxiety** refers to the ever-changing mood component of anxiety—it is a "right now" kind of feeling and is very situation specific. **Trait anxiety**, on the other hand, is part of the personality, an acquired disposition that influences our behaviour on a long-term basis. More specifically, trait anxiety predisposes a person to view a wide range of events as threatening, even if that feeling is not objectively warranted by the circumstances. In the sport and exercise psychology literature, both state and trait anxiety have been investigated, although most of the recent exercise literature on interventions has focused on state anxiety.

Anxiety and Exercise

The research demonstrates that state anxiety is significantly reduced by long-term participation in exercise. Landers & Petruzzello (1994) reported that over 80% of all studies completed between 1960 and 1992 found anxiety reduction following exercise. Leith (2009) has reported similar findings, extending the time frame through 2008 and examining only empirical research. It also appears that most exercise modes will produce this beneficial effect. A few examples help demonstrate these relationships. In a study comparing the effects of aerobic and non-aerobic exercise on anxiety, Altchiler and Motta (1994) found that both aerobic and non-aerobic exercise reduced state anxiety. However, state anxiety decreased more for the aerobic exercise group after a single bout of exercise than it did for the non-aerobic group. McAuley, Mihalko, and Bane (1996) reported that both a walking exercise group and a stretching exercise program significantly reduced anxiety compared to a control group who did not exercise. Similarly, Parente (2000) compared aerobic exercise with stretching exercise and found that anxiety was significantly reduced in both groups. Watanabe, Takeshima, Okada, and Inomata (2000) reported that a 70-minute water exercise program and a 50-minute land exercise program both produced significant reductions in state anxiety and that there was no difference between the two exercise groups. Thus, it appears that many exercise modalities produce beneficial reductions in anxiety.

Let us consider the specifics of a particular study that compared two different types of resistance training (Focht, Koltyn, & Bouchard, 2000). In this study, 54 female participants were randomly assigned to a circuit resistance exercise (CRE) condition, multiple set resistance exercise (MSRE) condition, or control (CON) condition. Resistance exercise consisted of performing one set of 10 to 20 reps at 50% of one repetition maximum (1RM) for 12 different exercises in the CRE condition, and three sets of 6 to 10 reps at 75% of 1RM for four different exercises in the MSRE condition. Results indicated that state anxiety was significantly reduced in both exercise conditions. In addition, the study concluded that one session of CRE was associated with reductions in anxiety that were evident 120 and 180 minutes following exercise (see Figure 12.1). Overall, this study is consistent with the majority of studies that have found that different exercise modes are equally effective in reducing anxiety.

Weinberg and Gould (2007) summarized the collective results of three meta-analyses (Landers & Petruzzello, 1994; Long & Van Stavel, 1995; Petruzzello, Landers, Hatfield, Kubitz, & Salazar, 1991) and concluded the following:

- Longer training programs are more effective than shorter ones in producing positive changes.
- Reductions in state anxiety after aerobic exercise may be achieved with exercise intensities between 30% and 70% of maximal heart rate. Earlier research had suggested that exercise intensities of 70% of maximal heart rate were required for positive results.

Figure 12.1 State anxiety and exercise

State anxiety before and after resistance exercise for the circuit, multiple set, and control conditions (mean and standard error)

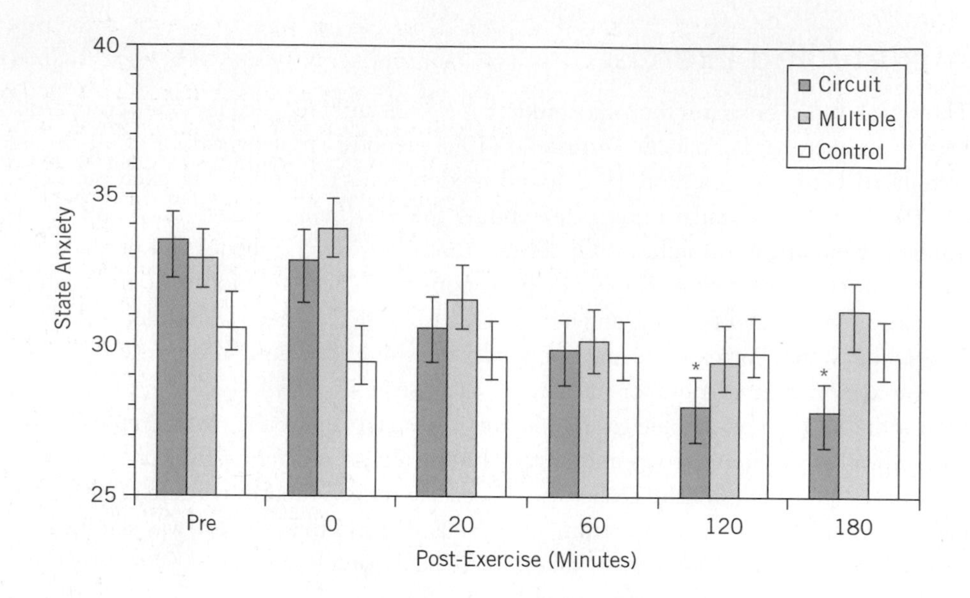

Note: From "State Anxiety and Blood Pressure Responses Following Different Resistance Exercise Sessions" by B.C. Focht, K.F. Koltyn and L.J. Bouchard, 2000, *International Journal of Sport Psychology,* 31, p.376–390. Copyright © 2000 by the International Journal of Sport Psychology. Used with permission.

- For anaerobic exercise, reductions in anxiety appear evident at a lower range (30% to 50%) of maximal heart rate.
- Exercise is particularly effective for individuals who have elevated levels of anxiety, but it also reduces anxiety for individuals with lower levels of anxiety.
- All durations of exercise significantly reduce anxiety, although larger effects were found for periods up to 30 minutes in length.
- State anxiety returns to pre-exercise levels within 24 hours, maybe as quickly as four to six hours.
- Exercise is associated with reductions in muscle tension.
- Reductions in anxiety are not necessarily tied to the physiological gains resulting from exercise.
- Anxiety reduction following exercise occurs regardless of the intensity, duration, or type of exercise, although greater effects have occurred for aerobic versus anaerobic activities.
- Aerobic exercise can produce anxiety reductions similar in magnitude to those seen with other commonly used anxiety treatments.
- Anxiety reduction after exercise occurs for all types of participants (e.g., male or female, fit or unfit, active or inactive, anxious or non-anxious, healthy or unhealthy, younger or older, with or without anxiety disorders).

REFLECTIONS 12.3

Do you remember a time when you were feeling nervous or anxious about an upcoming event and found that going for a walk, jog, bike ride, or swim made you feel much better? If so, why do you think that exercise had the calming effect?

Photograph © Sophieso/Dreamstime.com.

MOOD

Mood can be viewed as a host of transient, fluctuating affective states that can be positive or negative (Berger, Pargman, & Weinberg, 2002). Research suggests mood may be further categorized as having both positive and negative affects. **Positive affect** reflects the individual's level of pleasurable engagement with the environment and is characterized by mental alertness, enthusiasm, energy, and determination. In contrast, **negative affect** reflects the person's general level of subjective distress, as witnessed by anger, guilt, fear, tension, sadness, scorn, and distrust (McIntyre, Watson, & Cunningham, 1990).

Exercise and Mood

Because mood is a multidimensional concept, it is not sufficient merely to report improvements or no improvements in mood following involvement in an exercise program. A more appropriate analysis involves looking at the specific elements of mood affected by the exercise process. The majority of studies examining the exercise and mood association have employed the Profile of Mood States, or POMS (McNair, Lorr, & Droppleman, 1971). The POMS was described in Chapter 3 when discussing the iceberg profile and its relationship with mental health in sport and exercise. An overview of studies employing the POMS reveals that exercise has been consistently associated with improvements in tension-anxiety, depression-dejection, anger-hostility, vigour-activity, fatigue-inertia, and confusion-bewilderment (see McLafferty, Wetzsein, & Hunter, 2004; Motl, Birnbaum, Kubik, & Dishman, 2000; Osei-Tutu & Campagna, 2005; Russell et al., 2003).

Although the POMS is frequently used in exercise and mood studies, some recent research has started to employ other instruments that differentiate between positive and negative aspects of mood. An instrument called the Positive Affect and Negative Affect Schedule, or PANAS (Watson, Clark, & Tellegen, 1988) contains 10-item positive affect and negative affect scales. The positive affect scale consists of mood descriptors that capture active engagement, whereas the negative affect scale consists of mood descriptors capturing aspects of distress. Typically, positive affect and negative affect are not opposite affective states but rather capture different types of mood affects. Let us consider a specific study by McIntyre et al. (1990). Eighteen male and female undergraduate students completed the PANAS at the beginning of a one-week period to establish baseline levels, and they were then administered three additional PANAS within the week. One was given after social interaction, one after exercise, and another prior to a stressful test. Findings revealed that both exercise and social interaction significantly increased positive affect but exerted no influence on negative affect.

The majority of studies investigating the relationship between exercise and mood have used running and/or walking as the mode of physical activity. However, a variety of other types of exercise that have been associated with improvements in mood include swimming, jogging, cycling, yoga, tai chi, tae kwon do, rock climbing, rowing, weightlifting, aerobic dance, as well as unspecified exercise programs (see Leith, 2009 for details). Looking at all of the literature, it appears that the most frequent and consistent mood improvements following exercise have been associated with walking, jogging, cycling, and weightlifting. Although a variety of other physical exercises have resulted in mood improvements, the majority of exercise modes have been aerobic.

In terms of the length of an exercise program required to produce beneficial results, significant improvements in mood have been found following exercise programs lasting various durations. It appears that exercise programs ranging from six weeks to over five months have produced significant improvements in participants' mood scores (Leith, 2009), though the exact length of the exercise program does not appear critical for improvements in mood to be experienced. This viewpoint is further reinforced by the increasing number of studies reporting mood improvements after a single bout of exercise (e.g., Motl et al., 2000; O'Halloran, Murphy, & Webster, 2004; Russell et al., 2003). In one study, significant improvements in mood were reported after one 24-minute bout of rock climbing (Motl et al., 2000). In this particular study, rock climbing resulted in significant improvements in tension, depression, and vigour compared to a control group, as measured by the POMS. Another study (O'Halloran et al., 2004) utilized POMS to assess the mood of 80 regular runners prior to a 60-minute run, at the 10-, 25-, 40-, and 55-minute marks, and then again 10 minutes after the run. The results revealed significant improvements (relative to the control condition) in moods related to composure, energy, elation, and mental clarity during and after the run. Although significant improvements in participant mood scores have been reported after single bouts of exercise, it is tempting to speculate that these changes are likely more transient than those occurring with chronic participation in exercise. This hypothesis remains to be tested.

When examining the impact of exercise frequency, the majority of studies suggest that exercise should be performed a minimum of three or four times per week to experience consistent positive mood changes (Leith, 2009). Although mood improvements have been reported with greater exercise frequencies, this approach has also resulted in mood deterioration in some cases (e.g., Raglin, Eksten, & Garl, 1995).

What about the impact of exercise intensity? Unfortunately, most studies examining the exercise and mood relationship do not report exercise intensities. Of those that do, exercise intensities range from 60% to 85% maximum heart rate. Because the majority of these studies report exercise intensities within a particular range, such as 70% to 85%

(e.g., DiLorenzo et al., 1999), 60% to 80% (e.g., Osei-Tutu & Campagna, 2005), and 50% to 65% (e.g., McAuley et al., 2000) maximum heart rate, it becomes difficult to compare exercise intensities in terms of their mood-elevating effects. At present, no definitive answer exists regarding the best exercise intensity to improve participant mood. However, it appears that moderate-intensity exercise programs have the best potential to impact participant mood states (Leith, 2009). Although high-intensity exercise has also been associated with significant improvements, it has also produced negative results in some instances. In addition, moderate-intensity exercise is safer and more enjoyable for most individuals.

One final consideration involves the duration of exercise in a specific session that is required to produce beneficial effects on mood. Most of the studies reviewed involved exercise sessions of 20 minutes or more, with the majority of studies falling in the 40- to 60-minute range (e.g., Mack, Huddleston, & Dutler, 2000; O'Halloran et al., 2004). Significant improvements in mood have also been reported utilizing exercise durations of 20–30 minutes (Motl et al., 2000; Russell et al., 2003). Only one study was found comparing different exercise durations in terms of their mood-enhancing effects (Osei-Tutu & Campagna, 2005). In this particular study, there were larger changes in total mood disturbance in the long-bout exercise duration treatment when compared to the short-bout exercise treatment and control groups. These results are shown in Figure 12.2.

One excellent recent major review was a meta-analysis on the effect of aerobic exercise on positive affect (Reed & Ones, 2006). This review involved over 150 studies from 1979 to 2005 and over 13,000 participants. The results concluded that the effects were

Figure 12.2 Mood disturbance and exercise

Changes in total mood disturbance from pre-training to mid-training and post-training for the long-bout, short-bout, and control groups

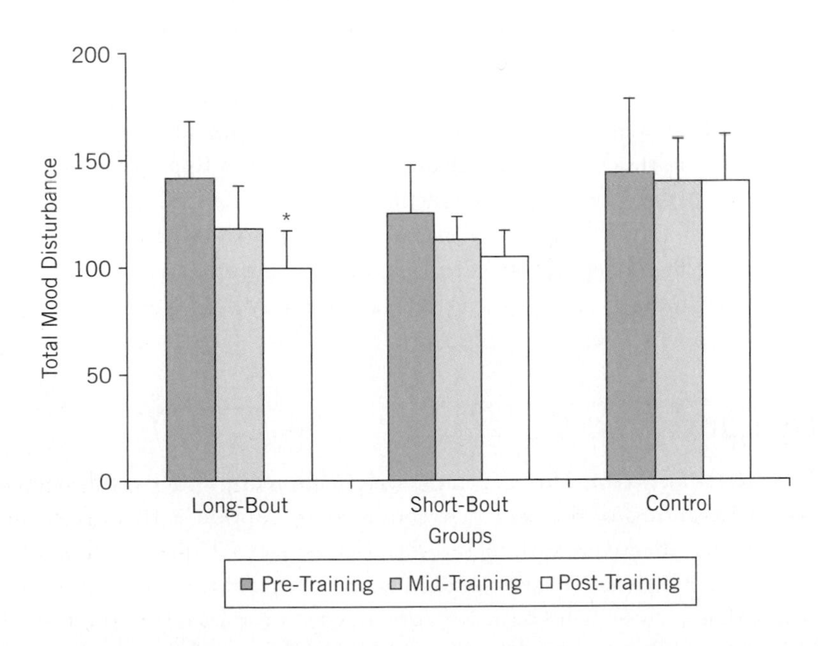

Note: Reprinted from *Preventative Medicine,* 40, by K.B. Osei-Tutu, "The effects of short- vs. long-bout exercise on mood, VO2max., and percent body fat," p. 92–98, Copyright © 2004 by the Institute For Cancer Prevention and Elsevier Inc., with permission from Elsevier.

consistently positive (1) immediately post-exercise, (2) when pre-exercise positive activated affect (PAA) was lower than average, (3) for low-intensity exercise with less than 15% to 35% oxygen uptake reserve, (4) for durations up to 35 minutes, (5) for low- to moderate-intensity exercise, and (6) for at least 30 minutes before returning to baseline.

In summary, the majority of studies reported significant improvements in mood following participation in a regular exercise program. Exercise, therefore, can be viewed as a proactive way to prevent or combat mood-related problems.

REFLECTIONS 12.4

Think back on your own exercise history. How does exercising affect your mood? Were there specific types of exercise that had positive benefits?

STRESS

In today's busy society, everyone claims to experience stress. Discussions about stress are heard in everyday conversations; it's difficult to open a newspaper or magazine without reading something about stress. For some, stress results from commuting and making ends meet financially, while for others, it's associated with writing examinations and public speaking. Regardless of the causes, the stress process affects sleep, concentration, memory, decision making, coordination, blood pressure, and immune function, among other things. In the workplace, billions of dollars are spent every year on stress-related conditions. Among university students in particular, stress has been associated with impaired academic performance and increases in the frequency of colds and upper respiratory and gastrointestinal difficulties during examination periods.

Needless to say, stress is an integral part of the natural fabric of life, and coping with stress is an everyday requirement for normal human growth and development. **Stress** has been defined in a multitude of ways, including as a stimulus, a response, and an interaction between the person and the environment. Stress has also been defined as the nonspecific response of the body to any demand placed upon it, whether the demand is pleasure or pain. The concepts of stress and coping were covered in detail in Chapter 6, but we will review some of the key ideas when we discuss whether exercise has any systematic effect on helping people manage stress.

Exercise and Stress

Much of the literature on stress focuses on the search for predispositions and effective coping strategies. Regardless of the approach, the basic assumption is that given the right tools, one can cope effectively with most forms of stress (see Chapter 6). It is commonly proposed that exercise is an effective stress management tool. However, in spite of the popular belief that exercise helps to manage and/or control stress levels, there are limited empirical data to support such a claim. You might recall from Chapter 6 that one common myth is that exercise always reduces stress.

Numerous studies purport to examine the effects of exercise on stress, but a closer examination of these studies casts doubt on these claims. The main criticisms of this area of research concern the measures used to assess stress, the lack of generalizability from lab-based to real-life stressors, and the failure to account for the individual nature of stress.

With respect to measurement, such studies often employ quantitative surveys that capture only aspects of the entire stress process (as described in Chapter 6). These surveys use scales that assess mood, anxiety, and depression. However, these should be more accurately conceptualized as only part of the stress process, and, in many ways, only a response to stress. Other studies on stress and exercise have assessed stress using scales such as life event checklists and daily hassle inventories. These scales include such items as moving residence, loss of an important relationship, and commuting. These studies more accurately examined the relationship between exercise and potential stressors, but not the experience of stress itself, namely, the person–environment transaction that is deemed threatening to one's well-being. Additionally, they fail to account for individual differences in appraising and coping with stress. Other studies have used the Perceived Stress Scale (PSS; Cohen, Kamarck, & Mermelstein, 1983) to assess the potential stress-reducing benefits of exercise. The PSS instructs respondents to identify the frequency of their feelings and thoughts during the last month and includes items such as feeling nervous or "stressed" and being angry or overwhelmed. These items also reflect possible responses to part of the stress process, so it may be argued that studies that use the PSS accurately assess the relationship between exercise and potential responses to stress, while failing to account for potential stressors, appraisal, and coping.

In addition to surveys, there have also been attempts to study the relationship between stress and exercise using laboratory-based stressors such as the Stroop test, anagrams, and vigilance tasks. These tasks are used to assess and tax an individual's mental cognitive processing and attention capabilities. In many cases, researchers are also interested in how people respond to the stressors, measuring physiological factors such as heart rate, blood pressure, and sweating (see Holmes, 1993). The results allow the researcher to make conclusions about how people respond to particular stressors but cannot speak to how participating in fitness or exercise activities might change one's experience of stress. Further, these short-term, acute stressors have limited generalizability to people's real-life experiences of stress.

Physical fitness may be linked to decreases in physiological reactivity to, and faster recovery from, certain psychosocial stressors as measured by changes in heart rate, blood pressure, cardiac output, stroke volume, and plasma catecholamines (Anshel, 2003; Holmes, 1993). For example, there is evidence that individuals with high aerobic fitness levels may have a slower and lower response in blood pressure when presented with a demanding laboratory-based task (such as a difficult cognitive task) compared to individuals with low aerobic fitness (Holmes, 1993). Nevertheless, questions remain about long-term stress reactivity, reactivity to naturally occurring stressors, the effects of fitness and different exercise conditions, as well as the impact of individual appraisal and coping (Leith, 2009). For example, you might recall from Chapter 6 that the stress experience is heavily influenced by an individual's appraisal and coping skills. It is not clear how aerobic fitness influences this process, if at all. To a large extent, physical fitness seems to have a primary impact on the physiological systems associated with the stress process.

It is possible that exercise can influence the stress process by acting as a coping mechanism (Long, 1993). In Chapter 6, we discussed how coping strategies can reduce distress by regulating emotions (emotion-focused), avoiding possible stressors (avoidance), or by changing the situation or the person (problem-focused). Exercise can also reduce anxiety and enhance mood, thus influencing part of the stress process. Salmon (2001) proposed that regular exercise may afford protection from the harmful effects of the stress response, such as anxiety, depression, and elevated blood pressure. Exercise may also allow individuals to avoid interpersonal stressors, although running away from problems may only act as a temporary solution and result in increased long-term problems. Exercise can also help individuals make specific changes to their bodies by reducing body fat, increasing strength and muscularity, and improving cardiovascular functioning. As discussed in Chapter 5 (Anxiety in Sport and Exercise), many people experience anxiety because of body concerns. Long-term exercise participation may allow people to improve their perceived body appearance, thus reducing body-related anxiety and enhancing self-image. Regular exercise may also allow people to met new friends and enhance social relationships. Recall that in Chapter 4 (Motivation and Behavioural Change), social relationship needs were identified as a key feature of motivation. But it is also important to recall that the demands created in exercise settings and by individuals' expectations can also create psychological threat and set off the stress process. As you can see, exercise has the potential to impact aspects of the stress process that can influence the overall stress process. Nevertheless, there are few studies that have systematically examined the impact of exercise on the whole stress process.

Many people believe that exercise can help reduce stress. However, there is little evidence that exercise changes how people appraise and cope with stressful situations. Nevertheless, exercise may help regulate responses to the stress process, such as by reducing reactivity and anxiety.

Photograph courtesy of Peter Crocker, University of British Columbia.

In conclusion, while several studies have examined the relationship between exercise and stressors or responses to stress, one could propose that none of the existing studies have assessed the effects of exercise on reducing experiences of stress. Given the generally accepted definition of stress, namely, that stress results from the person–environment transaction that is appraised as threatening to one's well-being, none of the extant studies have addressed the appraisal and coping functions that mediate the relationship between stressors and responses. As such, despite the underlying beliefs of exercise advocates that exercise should be an effective stress management strategy, the existing research does not provide strong empirical support for such a claim.

A qualitative approach might provide a better understanding of the relationship between exercise and the stress process. Qualitative methods were covered in Chapter 2. To date, no studies have adopted such an approach. In order to assess the idiosyncratic nature of the experience of stress, including individual appraisals, an argument could be made that interviews of people's experiences is necessary. Such a study may include previously sedentary individuals, some of whom are assigned to an intervention group that engages in prescribed exercise programs, while others remain inactive and serve as controls. Interviews about experiences of stress, including appraisals and coping strategies, would be conducted with both groups prior to, at regular intervals throughout the exercise intervention program, and at specified periods post-intervention to assess potential carry-over effects of exercise. Through a qualitative approach, researchers may be better equipped to understand the individual dynamics involved in the stress process, including the assessment of appraisal and coping, which are deemed to be critical to the experience of stress. As you can see, there is much to learn about the role of exercise in the entire stress experience.

Figure 12.3 Hierarchical structure of self-concept

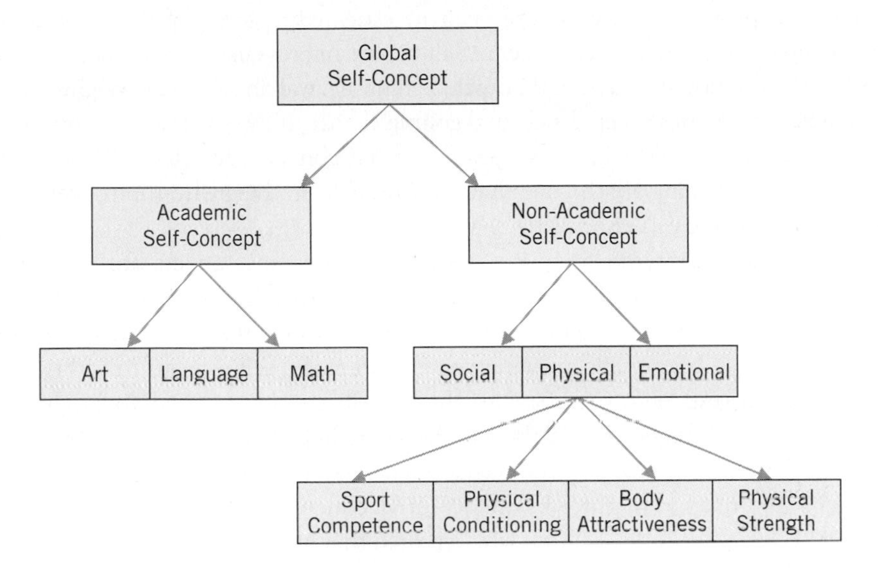

Note: Adapted from "Advances in the Measurement of the Physical Self," by K.R. Fox, 1998. In J.L. Duda (Ed.), Advances in Sport and Exercise Psychology Measurement (pp. 295 – 310). Reprinted by permission of Fitness Information Technology via the Copyright Clearance Center.

SELF-CONCEPT AND SELF-ESTEEM

Self-concept and self-esteem have often been cited as important indicators of psychological well-being. Although the terms *self-concept* and *self-esteem* have been used interchangeably, they are not exactly the same. In the sport and exercise psychology literature, **self-concept** has been defined as the "multitude of attributes and roles through which individuals evaluate themselves to establish self-esteem judgments" (Fox, 1998). Recently, self-concept has come to be viewed as a multiple domain of self-structure, with specific self-concepts for specific roles in life, such as physical, social, emotional, and academic dimensions (Fox, 1997; Harter, 1999; Marsh, 1997). **Self-esteem** has been described as a "personal judgment of worthiness" (Coopersmith, 1967, p. 5). Fox identified self-esteem as "the global and relatively stable evaluative construct reflecting the degree to which an individual feels positive about him- or herself" (1998, p. 296).

Researchers in sport and exercise have also focused on the physical self (Fox & Corbin, 1989). The physical self can be divided into various subdomains, such as sport competence, physical conditioning, body attractiveness, and physical strength. An example of a hierarchical model of the self, including the physical self, is presented in Figure 12.3. Sport and exercise psychology researchers have asserted that physical activity should have a greater impact on physical self domains compared to other domains (e.g., academic) or the more higher-order domains like global self-esteem (Crocker, Kowalski, & Hadd, 2008; Fox, 2000).

Exercise and Self-esteem

Self-esteem has been long identified as the psychological state with the greatest potential to reflect the benefits that can be gained from regular exercise (Folkins & Sime, 1981;

Spence, McGannon, & Poon, 2005; Sonstroem, 1997). The research continues to show that following a regular exercise program results in improved self-concept/self-esteem. A wide range of physical activities have been investigated in terms of their potential to impact people's self-concept/self-esteem. Significant improvements have been reported following participation in activities that include running, walking, cycling, weight-training, cardiopulmonary training, step dance, and golfing (Leith, 2009). It therefore appears that most types of exercise have a positive benefit on self-concept/self-esteem, although running and weight-training are the two that have resulted in the greatest improvements in self-concept/self-esteem (Leith, 2009).

Some caution in interpretation is necessary, however, since a meta-analysis (Spence et al., 2005) shed some skepticism on the conclusion that exercise improves self-esteem in all cases. The authors reviewed 113 empirical research studies and concluded that exercise results in small but significant improvements in global self-esteem. In addition, this meta-analysis suggests that increases in physical fitness are required to produce this improvement in self-esteem. Lastly, these authors conclude that the link between exercise and general self-esteem has been somewhat overstated. Obviously, much more research needs to be performed in this area before definitive conclusions may be drawn. This view is supported by Crocker et al. (2008), who reported that although some evidence suggests that global self-esteem is related to physical activity, other factors may also be involved. For example, the physical self (i.e., ability and appearance) appears to be more important than global self-esteem in determining motivated physical activity behaviour. Crocker and colleagues suggest the following significant gaps in our understanding of the exercise and self-esteem relationship: (1) The causal link between physical self-perceptions and exercise has not been clearly established; (2) Culture is likely an intervening variable, but little research has been conducted that investigates culture, self, and physical activity; and (3) Body appearance is the component of physical self that is most related to global self esteem, but it is a weak predictor of physical activity. The authors concluded that these challenges must be addressed by future researchers.

One of the limiting factors in most of the early research on self-esteem and exercise is that exercise intensity is often not reported or controlled (Leith, 1994). Fortunately, more recent research has been more thorough, with studies documenting significant improvements in self-concept/self-esteem (Alfermann & Stoll, 2000; Asci, 2002; Bodin & Martinsen, 2004; Butki, Rudolph, & Jacobsen, 2001; Crews et al., 2004; Ng & Tam, 2000). It is interesting to point out, however, that exercise intensities ranging from 85% maximum heart rate (Butki et al., 2001) to low-intensity exercise (Ng & Tam, 2000) have all been associated with improved self-concept/self-esteem. A paucity of related research makes it difficult to develop a meaningful guideline in terms of the most appropriate exercise intensity to improve participants' self-concept/self-esteem. It would appear, however, that any level of exercise intensity has the potential to produce significant improvements (Leith, 2009). Until future research confirms this, it might be wise to employ moderate exercise intensities that can also produce changes in physical fitness.

There are also challenges to developing guidelines for exercise duration. Asubstantial number of studies do not report the length of each individual exercise session. Of those that did report this key exercise variable, durations have ranged from less than 20 minutes (Butki et al., 2001) to more than one hour (Alfermann & Stoll, 2000; Bodin & Martinsen, 2004;

Bond, Biddle, & Ntoumanis, 2001). In a review of all empirical studies investigating the relationship between exercise and self-concept/self-esteem, Leith (2009) suggested that exercise durations of an hour or more appear to provide the greatest potential to improve self-concept in the participant. The viewpoint follows earlier suggestions that higher exercise frequencies and longer exercise programs are associated with greater improvements in self-concept. Intuitively, this relationship makes a good deal of sense. When exercise is performed more often, is prolonged, or extends for longer periods of time, the potential for physical changes (e.g., weight loss, increased muscle mass, enhanced cardiovascular functioning) is greatly enhanced. Previous research has suggested that physical changes have been linked to improved body image, with improved body image impacting positively on global self-image (Asci, 2002; Crocker et al., 2008; Fox, 1998; Zion, 1965). It therefore appears that longer exercise sessions are required to produce improvements in self-concept/self-esteem in the participant.

Are fitness gains necessary for an individual to experience improvements in self-concept/self-esteem? It certainly seems reasonable to assume that someone experiencing an objectively measured cardiovascular fitness gain would also experience an improvement in self-esteem. Support for this position can be gleaned from earlier research (Wilfley & Kunce, 1986) as well as more recent reviews (Spence et al., 2005). Let us consider a specific example. Asci (2002) tested the effect of step dance on physical self-perception in male and female university students. The exercise sessions were 50 minutes each, performed three times per week for a total of 10 weeks. The exercise intensity was 60% to 80% maximum heart rate. The results demonstrated that improved fitness gains were associated with improved self-concept. Another study (Annesi, 2000) utilized a 12-week protocol that prescribed low-intensity cardiovascular and resistance training for a sample of obese females. At the conclusion of the exercise program, the subjects had significant increases in maximum volume of oxygen uptake (VO_2max). This improved fitness was also associated with an improvement in body satisfaction. Clearly, fitness changes seem to produce improvements in global self-esteem and likely specific components of physical self-concept such as aerobic conditioning (Spence et al., 2005; Crocker et al., 2008).

It is very likely that some other variables associated with exercise are more directly linked to improvements in self-concept/self-esteem. As reported earlier in this chapter, self-concept is a multidimensional construct, and certain aspects of self-concept (e.g., physical) might be more affected by exercise than others (e.g., social). Consider, for example, that physical self-concept itself is composed of sport competence, physical condition, body attractiveness, and physical strength. Improvements in any one of these categories results in improved self-concept in many cases, but that fact alone does not imply that fitness gains have been achieved. A person suffering from a poor body image due to excess weight could still experience improved self-concept/self-esteem by simply doing long, slow exercise to burn more body fat. This long, slow exercise may not be at a level of intensity to improve VO_2max or resting heart rate.

There is also strong evidence that exercise is related to changes in self-concept in physical activity interventions involving special populations. Significant improvements in self-concept have been reported following exercise for cardiac rehabilitation patients (Ng & Tam, 2000), young children (Planinsec & Fosnaric, 2005), low-income Hispanic children (Crews et al., 2004), obese women (Butki et al., 2001), HIV-1 infected men

Case Study 12.2

Exercise and Self-concept/Self-esteem

You and your friend are currently enrolled in a popular sport and exercise psychology class at a major university. Both you and your classmate absolutely love the course. In fact, your friend likes it so much that she is considering going on to graduate work in the field of sport and exercise psychology. For this reason, she is planning to present a paper at the National Undergraduate Research Conference, held annually at the University of Toronto. The research topic that interests her the most is the relationship between exercise and self-concept/self-esteem.

Because this will be the first time she has ever presented a research paper, she asks for your opinion in developing her research design. She confides in you that she would really like to be able to demonstrate some type of significant improvement following an exercise program but admits that she could use your help in selecting the independent and dependent variables. Based on the material presented in this chapter, what suggestions would you offer, and why?

(Lox, McAuley, & Tucker, 1995), and clinically depressed male and female adults (Bodin & Martinsen, 2004). The psychological, as well as physical, benefits of exercise in special populations are also discussed in the next chapter.

In summary, the majority of studies report significant improvements in self-concept/self-esteem following participation in an exercise program. However, the size of the improvement in self-esteem appears to be small. The relationship between physical activity and the physical self subdomains appear to be stronger; however, there is a lack of systematic experimental work in this area.

Regular exercise can produce significant improvements in physical self-concept and global self-esteem.

Photograph courtesy of Peter Crocker, University of British Columbia.

THE EXERCISE AND MENTAL HEALTH RELATIONSHIP: SUGGESTED MECHANISMS OF CHANGE

Several hypotheses have been advanced to explain why mental health improves following involvement in an exercise program. This section will provide a brief overview of the mechanisms that might explain this relationship, including endorphin, monoamine, thermogenic, and distraction hypotheses. We will also explore several other psychological explanations that have been advanced to explain this relationship.

The Endorphin Hypothesis

Despite the absence of compelling scientific evidence, the **endorphin hypothesis** represents the most popular explanation of the psychological benefits of exercise. When endorphins were discovered (Hughes et al., 1975), they were termed the "brain's own morphine" because of their ability to ease pain, and, in some cases, produce a feeling of euphoria. This latter effect has been referred to as the "runner's high" in the popular literature. This overall euphoria produced by endorphins is believed to be responsible for reducing levels of anxiety, depression, confusion, and a host of other negative mood states.

The term **endorphin** is a general classification label for beta-endorphin. This important body chemical is a peptide and mimics the chemical structure of morphine. It is particularly important in regulating emotion and perceiving pain. Although science is routinely able to measure the activity of beta-endorphin in the brains of rats through examining brain tissue, we obviously cannot examine beta-endorphin receptor site occupancy in humans. Research on the effects of exercise on beta-endorphin levels in humans has been restricted to measuring levels of beta-endorphin and its metabolites in peripheral blood (the blood outside the blood-brain barrier).

Pioneering studies (e.g., Riggs, 1981; Villet, 1978) suggested a positive relationship between exercise and psychological well-being and inferred that the relationship was linked to beta-endorphin levels. Although this early research provided reason for guarded optimism that endorphins may be responsible for the positive benefits of exercise and mental health, several later studies reported opposite findings. Studies performed on humans (e.g., Kraemer, Dzewaltowski, Blair, Rinehardt, & Castracane, 1990) have failed to support a role for endorphins in the exercise and mood relationship. In fact, the Kraemer et al. (1990) study actually demonstrated a decrease in blood plasma endorphins in association with an increase in positive mood. These and other similar findings have led others (Hoffman, 1997) to conclude that while endorphin release into the bloodstream may have an effect on mood changes, there are several other transmitter systems involved that may be responsible for the enhanced mood effects following exercise.

The Monoamine Hypothesis

The **monoamine hypothesis** suggests the improved affect associated with exercise can be explained by changes in one or more of the brain **monoamines** (i.e., the neurotransmitters dopamine, norepinephrine, and serotonin). Until recently, the relationship between our behaviour and brain neurochemistry had remained a mystery. Our brain was considered an inaccessible black box. Although the brain still remains somewhat of a mystery, modern technology has now allowed neurochemists to begin exploring the biological aspects of psychology. It has now been established that certain areas of the brain and particular neural pathways form systems that are associated with mental processes such as anxiety, depression, pleasure, pain, and even organized thought. Each system utilizes particular neurotransmitters (chemical messengers) that transmit signals across synapses (gaps) between neurons making up the system. Messages travel along the neural pathways in the form of electrical energy. When this electrical energy terminates at the end of a presynaptic neuron, it releases neurotransmitters. These neurotransmitters travel across the synaptic gap and bind to specific receptor sites (much as a specific key fits a specific lock) on the postsynaptic neuron. If enough neurotransmitters bind to receptor sites, the message is transmitted. If a sufficient number of neurotransmitters are not present, the message is not transmitted. Of special interest to us is the finding that the number of neurotransmitters available at synapses along each neural pathway is related to our mood, which in turn is affected by such things as drugs and exercise. Because an association exists between exercise and improved mood, researchers have investigated the relationship between physical activity and the monoamines.

Research on the effects of exercise on monoamine activity in humans has been restricted mostly to assessing levels of the urinary metabolite of epinephrine (namely, 3-methoxy-4-hydroxyphenolglycol, or MHPG). Because brain norepinephrine is unable to cross the blood-brain barrier, research has been restricted to the metabolites of norepinephrine found in cerebrospinal fluid, blood, or urine. Although cerebrospinal fluid measures provide the most direct indication of brain levels of norepinephrine, blood and urine samples are safer and easier to obtain. Because the technology required to detect MHPG in blood plasma is relatively recent, most research has utilized the urinary source of MHPG.

There are a number of potential mechanisms that might explain why exercise produces benefits in mental health. These mechanisms include endorphins, brain monoamines, thermogenic changes, psychological distraction, as well as other psychological variables.
Photograph courtesy of Peter Crocker, University of British Columbia.

Pioneer research revealed that regular exercise alters both plasma and urinary levels of MHPG (Doctor & Sharkey, 1971; Pierce, Kupprat, & Harry, 1976). In fact, blood plasma and urinary levels of MHPG have been shown to increase 200% to 600% above normal levels during bouts of acute exercise (Howley, 1981). Another early study on endurance athletes reported that experienced runners competing in a marathon experience norepinephrine and dopamine plasma levels that are 300% above normal (Appenzeller & Schade, 1979). This elevated level is maintained until the 26-mile race ends, then peaks to 600% above normal levels before dropping back to normal levels in about one hour. A study examining the effect of short-term bicycle work at mild, moderate, and heavy workloads also suggests that exercise intensity may be an important variable (Hartley et al., 1972). In this study, mild exercise was found to have little effect on the plasma MHPG, while moderate and heavy workouts resulted in significant elevations.

As in the case of endorphins, we still do not know what happens to monoamine levels in human brains. Although research measurements remain, by necessity, indirect, the hypothesis that exercise impacts mental health by means of monoamine activity is a compelling one. There is ample reason to believe that a monoamine relationship exists between exercise and mental health (Leith, 2009). Future studies will undoubtedly contribute to a more thorough understanding of such a relationship.

The Thermogenic Hypothesis

A somewhat different view of the exercise and mental health relationship is termed the **thermogenic hypothesis**. This idea is by no means a new one. The therapeutic effect of elevating body temperature has been used for many centuries. The practice has been traced back to at least 800 bce in Finland (Morgan, 1997). Scandinavians partake in regular sauna baths for both health benefits and the sensation of well-being. This practice appears to possess a fair degree of merit, because pioneer research has shown that whole-body warming (e.g., warm shower, sauna, or fever therapy) reduces muscle tension (de Vries, Beckman, Huber, & Dieckmeir, 1968).

It is interesting to speculate how elevated body temperature is related to improved mental health. A study by Cannon and Kluger (1983) pointed out that our bodies respond to strenuous exercise in the same manner as when they are invaded by bacteria or viruses. The release of pyrogens (endogenous leukocyte mediators) results in reductions of zinc and iron concentrations in our blood, an increase in leukocytes (white blood cells), and an increase in body temperature (a fever). This combined effect serves to kill off the bacteria and/or virus. It also results in a relaxation effect, just like a sauna or hot shower.

Concurrent research by Horne and Staff (1983) provides additional support for the thermogenic hypothesis. Eight trained subjects were exposed to the following three conditions: (1) two 40-minute treadmill runs at 80% VO_2max, separated by a 30-minute rest period; (2) two 80-minute treadmill runs at 40% VO_2max, separated by a 15-minute rest period; and (3) two 40-minute sessions sitting in a hot bath, separated by a 30-minute rest period. The last experimental condition utilized a water temperature that resulted in the same core rectal temperatures in the subjects as those that were produced with the high-intensity exercise treatment. Horne and Staff concluded that high-intensity exercise and passive heating produce similar increases in slow wave sleep. Because slow wave sleep is that portion of the sleep cycle most conducive to relaxation and renewal effects, exercise may indeed have potential to result in mental health benefits.

On a more practical dimension, Johnsgard (2004) has suggested that the pyrogenic response may explain why regular exercisers (who do not overdo it) report fewer incidences of, and less severity of, the common cold and flu. The pyrogenic effect of exercise, by increasing leukocytes, may kill off the bacteria and viruses associated with these nagging illnesses. If true, this would indeed be an added benefit to the hypothesized thermogenic-produced mental health benefits associated with exercise.

In summary, the research cited above suggests that the thermogenic hypothesis is a tenable explanation for the exercise and mental health relationship. However, as Morgan (1997) and Koltyn (1997) in their excellent reviews of this topic have suggested, the confirmation or refutation of the thermogenic hypothesis awaits future research.

The Distraction Hypothesis

In contrast to the previous three explanations, which use physiological mechanisms to explain the exercise and mental health relationship, Bahrke and Morgan's (1978) **distraction hypothesis** proposes a psychological mechanism. This explanation maintains that being distracted from stressful stimuli, or taking "time out" from daily routine activities, is responsible for the improvements in mental health associated with exercise.

As Morgan (1997) stated, this hypothesis does not dispute the influence of physiological mechanisms, but it suggests that the psychological effects often attributed to exercise may actually be caused by other factors.

It is important for future research to compare the effects of exercise distraction with other forms of distraction, such as reading, watching TV, resting quietly, meditating, or using a variety of relaxation techniques. An experiment of this nature would allow us to determine if it is the exercise, or merely the distraction, that results in positive psychological benefits. Research of this nature, with replicative experiments, is needed to determine the relative value of exercise versus distraction in promoting mental health. Although this has not yet been done, a meta-analysis performed by North and colleagues (North, McCullagh, & Tran, 1990) concluded that chronic exercise is a more powerful and effective treatment for reducing negative mood than the relaxation provided by other distracting, but enjoyable, activities.

Other Possible Psychological Explanations

Several additional psychological variables have also been suggested as potential explanations for the exercise and mental health relationship. **Self-efficacy**, or the strength of belief that one can successfully execute a behaviour, is one such viewpoint (Bandura, 1997). According to Bandura, a person's perception of his or her ability to perform in a demanding situation, such as exercise, affects that person's emotions. Self-efficacy can be improved by past performance accomplishments, vicarious experience, verbal persuasion, or level of arousal. The basic tenet of self-efficacy theory is that as a person engages in exercise and experiences fitness gains or bodily changes, self-efficacy improves. This results in the person feeling better about him- or herself and may partially explain the positive benefits of exercise on mental health. Most readers will be able to identify with the concept of "feeling better" after a workout. The research cited above highlights the fact that a non-exerciser perceives exercise to be a difficult task. When this person ultimately succeeds in becoming a regular exerciser, he or she will experience a feeling of accomplishment and self-efficacy. This, in turn, breaks the negative downward spiral of negative affect, such as depression, anxiety, and other negative mood states. In the final analysis, there is still much to be learned about the mechanisms explaining the exercise and mental health relationship. It is also very likely that an interactive effect exists, whereby a combination of different mechanisms works together to produce improvements in mental health following exercise. Much more empirical research must be conducted before we can generate reasonable and valid conclusions.

EXERCISE AND THE PREVENTION OF MENTAL HEALTH PROBLEMS

The focus of this chapter so far has been on how exercise may be used to promote psychological well-being or treat existing mental health problems. Physical activity may also play a role in *preventing* mental health problems. In terms of psychological well-being, the strongest evidence supporting such a role for physical activity comes in the area of depression. There are at least four epidemiological studies showing that physical inactivity increases the likelihood of developing clinically defined depression (Camacho, Roberts, Lazarus, Kaplan, & Cohen, 1991; Farmer et al., 1988; Paffenbarger, Lee, & Leung, 1994; Strawbridge, Deleger, Roberts, & Kaplan, 2002). These studies involved large numbers of people and measured physical activity status before the incidence of depression. For example, Camacho and colleagues (1991) found an association between inactivity and incidence of depression in a large population from Alameda County in California who were assessed first in 1965 and then again in 1974 and 1983. Physical activity levels of the study participants were categorized as low, medium, or high. In the first wave of follow-up (1974), the probability of developing depression was significantly greater for both men and women who were categorized as low active in 1965 compared to those who were deemed high active.

Although these findings are consistent, they cannot rule out the potential for self-selection. It is possible that individuals who are more physically active represent a selection of people who happened to have greater education, greater financial resources, or social support networks that made them less likely to develop depression, irrespective of their exercise behaviour. However, even when these studies take account of a wide range of possible confounding factors in the statistical modelling (e.g., disability, body mass index, smoking, alcohol, and social status), the relationship between physical activity and a decreased risk of depression remains.

How active should people be to help prevent depression? There are still insufficient data to determine if there is a dose-response relationship, or if there exists an optimal level of activity for prevention of mental illness. However, data from a study of middle-aged Australian women showed that even physical activity at levels below the currently recommended guidelines (i.e., about 60 to 150 minutes of moderate activity per week) may help prevent depression (Brown, Ford, Burton, Marshall, & Dobson, 2005).

How might physical activity prevent mental health problems? A Canadian study (Cairney, Faulkner, Veldhuizen, & Wade, in press) explored whether changes in physical activity were associated with changes in psychological distress, defined as a psychological construct incorporating symptoms of depression and anxiety, in adults 65 years or older over a six-year period using the longitudinal National Population Health Survey (NPHS). They also examined whether this association was mediated by changes in global self-esteem, mastery, and physical health status. In line with the literature exploring physical activity in the prevention of depression, individuals who had a reduction in physical activity after six years showed a dramatic increase in psychological distress. Conversely, those with increases in physical activity showed a decrease in distress over time. It appears that even late-life improvements in physical activity may reduce psychological distress among older adults.

The key finding of this study, however, concerns the other potential mediators in the relationship between physical activity and distress among older adults. The results demonstrated that a substantial part of the association between physical activity and distress (39%) was influenced by changes in self-esteem (see earlier section on mechanisms). That is, higher levels of activity were associated with greater self-esteem, as well as lower levels of psychological distress. Together, these findings suggest that it may be important to target self-esteem and sense of control in physical activity interventions. Framing the promotion of physical activity and structuring physical activity interventions for older adults in ways that target mastery or the enhancement of perceptions of self-worth may better facilitate the alleviation of distress than interventions with a narrow focus on fitness or endurance improvements. These issues are also discussed in the next chapter.

In summary, there is some epidemiological evidence that shows that physical activity is associated with a decreased risk of developing clinically defined depression. There is insufficient evidence to determine the appropriate dose of activity for this preventive role or to link physical inactivity to the onset of other mental health conditions. While further research is required and methodological concerns do exist, we would contend that the potential of physical activity to play a preventive role far outweighs the potential risk that no mental health benefit will occur. Because physical activity is an effective method for improving important aspects of physical health, such as obesity, cardiovascular fitness, and hypertension, the consideration of physical activity as a mental health promotion strategy can be seen as a "win-win" situation, with potentially both mental and physical health benefits accruing (Mutrie & Faulkner, 2004).

REFLECTIONS 12.5

What do you feel is the role of exercise in preventing mental health problems? Can you identify possible mechanisms?

CHAPTER SUMMARY

This chapter reviewed the prevalence of key mental health indicators such as depression, anxiety, mood, aspects of stress, and self-concept and the effectiveness of exercise in improving mental health. We have seen that exercise can be an effective adjunctive therapy in the treatment of several mental health problems as well as help non-clinical populations improve mental health. The literature indicates that a number of different types of exercise are effective in various populations for a wide range of mental health indicators. In regard to type of exercise, aerobic, anaerobic, and non-aerobic activities appear equally effective in producing positive mental health benefits, although studies and narrative reviews suggest that aerobic exercise is most effective. Within these respective categories, no single type of exercise has been shown to be superior, although running has been the most frequently studied activity. The actual dosage of exercise (frequency, intensity, and duration) required to produce beneficial results is not clear. Several mechanisms such as the endorphin, monoamine, thermogenic, and distraction hypotheses have been proposed to underlie the changes in mental health. However, the exact mechanism for specific mental health benefits is still not clear. Nevertheless, there is overwhelming evidence that exercise has beneficial psychological effects across all ages, sexes, and sample populations, although there is some evidence suggesting that clinical populations show the potential for the most improvement. Table 12.1 provides some general guidelines for best practices for exercise and mental health.

Table 12.1 Exercise and Mental Health: Best Practices

1. Regular participation in physical activity/exercise is needed to experience improved mental health. Improvements have been reported for depression, aspects of the stress process, anxiety, mood, and self-concept.
2. It appears that any form of aerobic or anaerobic physical activity is effective in improving mental health, but the best results have been reported with exercises that involve the large muscle groups and are rhythmic in nature.
3. Exercise should be performed approximately three to four times per week for at least 20 to 30 minutes for best results.
4. The exercise program should continue for a minimum of 12 weeks for best results.
5. Either mild- or moderate-intensity activity is recommended since this exercise is being performed for mental health (not fitness) reasons. Although some positive results have been reported with high-intensity exercise, the reverse has also been true.
6. Exercise should be considered as an adjunct treatment in special populations that are clinically symptomatic.
7. Exercise can serve as a mechanism to help prevent mental health disorders.
8. When developing exercise programs to enhance the mental health of others, one must always consider the ethical guidelines that were covered in Chapter 1.

Common Myths about Exercise and Mental Health Revisited

MYTH: Mental health problems are not that common in the general population.
Mental health problems are actually widespread in modern society. For example, one out of three Canadians in hospital beds at any given moment are there for mental health reasons. One out of every five Canadians will experience a mental health problem over the course of their lifetime. This translates into approximately 1,650,000 Canadians. So, in actual fact, mental health problems are very common in the general population.

MYTH: Exercise is more effective for treating mental problems in clinical populations than it is for improving or preventing them in non-clinical or asymptomatic participants.
Although this was the original view, the empirical literature shows that exercise is equally effective for treating mental health problems in individuals who are considered asymptomatic. This is probably because everyone experiences problems with mood, depression, anxiety, and self-concept from time to time. Extensive research has shown exercise to be every bit as effective for reducing these problems in the general population.

MYTH: In order for exercise to improve mental health, the participant must experience fitness gains by engaging in vigorous physical activity.
In the early literature, it was assumed that this was true, but the assumption was not based on solid empirical evidence. A relatively substantial number of empirical studies that have measured fitness gains and another significant number of studies that did not even document this information have shown that we cannot conclude that fitness is a prerequisite for improved

mental health. There is evidence that fitness is related to changes in global self-esteem but not to other mental health indicators such as anxiety, depression, and mood.

Review Questions

1. Why do you feel there is such a prevalence of mental health problems in today's society? Could you draw the conclusion that this is due to low levels of physical activity? Why or why not?
2. In terms of depression, who do you feel would benefit more from an exercise program: clinical or non-clinical populations? Explain your answer.
3. What is the relationship between stress and physical activity? Do you think exercise can reduce stress? Are there particular components of the stress process that seem to respond to exercise? Explain your answer.
4. Can you think of any situations where exercise could actually increase anxiety in the participant? You might want to reflect back to your readings from Chapter 5 (anxiety) and Chapter 6 (stress). If you answered "yes," give some examples and defend your position.
5. Do you think that certain types of exercise have more potential to improve aspects of mood? Explain your answer.
6. How can exercise change global and physical self-esteem? Do you think that specific types of exercise are more effective in changing particular aspects of physical self-concept? How might individual differences in the importance attached to specific dimensions of the physical self (fitness, muscularity/strength, or body appearance) impact self-esteem?
7. What are the three key physiological mechanisms that are believed to be responsible for the positive effect of exercise on mental health? How might each of these be associated with specific changes in depression, anxiety, and mood?

Suggested Reading

Leith, L. M. (2009). *Foundations of exercise and mental health*(2nd ed.). Morgantown, WV: Fitness Information Technology, Inc.

Reed, J., & Ones, D. S. (2006). The effect of acute exercise on positive activated affect: A meta-analysis. *Psychology of Sport and Exercise*, *7*,477–514.

Stathopoulou, G., Powers, M. B., Berry, A. C., Jasper, A. J., Smits, J. A. J., & Otto, M. W. (2006). Exercise interventions for mental health: A quantitative and qualitative review. *Clinical Psychology: Science and Practice*, *13*, 179–193.

References

Alfermann, D., & Stoll, O. (2000). Effects of physical exercise on self-concept and well-being. *International Journal of Sports Psychology*, *30*, 47–65.

Altchiler, L. & Motta, R. (1994). Effects of aerobic and nonaerobic exercise on anxiety, absenteeism, and job satisfaction. *Journal of Clinical Psychology*, *50*, 829–840.

American Psychiatric Association. (2000). *Diagnostic and statistical manual of mental disorders* (4th ed.). Washington, D.C: American Psychiatric Association.

Annesi, J. J. (2000). Effects of minimal exercise and cognitive behavior modification on adherence. Emotion change, self-image, and physical change in obese women. *Perceptual and Motor Skills*, *91*, 322–336.

Anshel, M. H. (2003). *Sport psychology: From theory to practice*.New York: Benjamin Cummings.

Appenzeller, O., & Schade, D. R. (1979). Neurology of endurance training III: Sympathetic activity during a marathon run. *Neurology*, *29*, 542.

Asci, F. H. (2002). The effects of step dance on physical self-perception of female and male university students. *International Journal of Sport Psychology, 33*, 431–442.

Bahrke, M. S., & Morgan, W. P. (1978). Anxiety reduction following exercise and meditation. *Cognitive Therapy and Research, 2*, 323–333.

Bandura, A. (1997). *Self-efficacy: The exercise of control*. New York: Freeman.

Berger, B. G., Pargman, D., & Weinberg, R. (2002). *Foundations of exercise psychology*.Morgantown, WV: Fitness Institute Technology.

Bodin, T., & Martinsen, E. W. (2004). Mood and self-efficacy during acute exercise in clinical depression. A randomized, controlled study. *Journal of Sport and Exercise Psychology, 26*, 623–633.

Bond, K. A., Biddle, S. J. H., & Ntoumanis, N. (2001). Self-efficacy and casual attribution in female golfers. *International Journal of Sport Psychology, 31*, 243–256.

Brown, D. R. (1990). Exercise, fitness, and mental health. In R. Bouchard, R. Shephard, T. Stephens, J. Sutton, & B. McPherson (Eds.), *Exercise, fitness and health*(pp.607–626). Champaign, IL: Human Kinetics.

Brown, W., Ford, J., Burton, N., Marshall, A. L., & Dobson, A. J. (2005). Prospective study of physical activity and depressive symptoms in middle-aged women. *American Journal of Preventive Medicine, 29*, 265–272.

Butki, B. D., Rudolph, D. L., & Jacobsen, H. (2001). Self-efficacy, state anxiety, and cortisol responses to treadmill running. *Perceptual and Motor Skills, 92*, 1129–1138.

Cairney, J., Faulkner, G., Veldhuizen, S., & Wade, T. J. (in press). Changes over time in physical activity and psychological distress among older adults. *Canadian Journal of Psychiatry*.

Camacho, T. C., Roberts, R. E., Lazarus, N. B., Kaplan, G. A., & Cohen, R. D. (1991). Physical activity and depression: Evidence from the Alameda county study. *American Journal of Epidemiology, 134*, 220–231.

Cannon, J. G. & Kluger, M. J. (1983). Endogenous pyrogen activity in human plasma after exercise. *Science, 220*, 617–619.

Centre for Addiction and Mental Health (CAMH). (2006). *The changing faces of mental health and mental illness in Canada*.Toronto, ON: CAMH.

Cohen, S., Kamarck, T., & Mermelstein, R. (1983). Perceived Stress Scale. *Journal of Health and Social Behavior, 24*, 386–396.

Coopersmith, S. (1967). *The antecedents of self esteem*.San Francisco: Freeman.

Crews, D. J., Craft, L. L., & Landers, D. M. (1998). The effect of exercise on clinical depression and depression resulting from mental illness: a meta-analysis. *Journal of Sport and Exercise Psychology, 20*, 339–357.

Crews, D. J., Lochbaum, M. R., & Landers, D. M. (2004). Aerobic physical activity effects on psychological well-being in low-income Hispanic children. *Perceptual and Motor Skills, 98*, 319–324.

Crocker, P. R. E., Kowalski, K., & Hadd, V. (2008). The role of self and identity in physical (in)activity. In A. Smith, & S. J. Biddle (Eds.), *Youth, physical activity and inactivity: Challenges and solutions*(pp. 215–237). Champaign, IL: Human Kinetics.

Daley, A. J., MacArthur, C., & Winter, H. (2007).The role of exercise in treating postpartum depression: A review of the literature. *Journal of Midwifery & Women's Health, 52*, 56–62.

deVries, H. A., Beckman, P., Huber, H., & Dieckmeir, L. (1968).Electromyographic evaluation of the effects of sauna on the neuromuscular system. *Journal of Sports Medicine and Physical Fitness, 8*, 1–11.

DiLorenzo, T. M., Bargman, E. P., Stucky-Ropp, R., Brassington, G. S., Frensch, P. A., & LaFontaine, T. (1999). Long-term effects of aerobic exercise on psychological outcomes. *Preventative Medicine, 28*, 75–85.

Dishman, R. K., Washburn, R. A., & Heath, G. W. (2004). *Physical activity epidemiology*.Champaign, IL: Human Kinetics.

Doctor, R., & Sharkey, B. J. (1971).Note on some physiological and subjective reactions to exercise and training. *Perceptual and Motor Skills, 32*,233–237.

Farmer, M., Locke, B., Moscicki, E., Dannenberg, A., Larson, D., & Radloff, L. (1988). Physical activity and depressive symptoms: The NHANES 1 epidemiological follow-up study. *American Journal of Epidemiology, 128,* 1340–1351.

Faulker, G. E., & Biddle, S. J. H. (2004). Exercise and depression: considering variability and contextuality. *Journal of Sport & Exercise Psychology, 26,* 3–18.

Focht, B. C., Koltyn, K. F., & Bouchard, L. J. (2000). State anxiety and blood pressure responses following different resistance exercise lessons. *International Journal of Sport Psychology, 31,* 376–390.

Folkins, C. H., & Sime, W. E. (1981). Physical fitness training and mental health. *American Psychologist, 35,* 373–389.

Fox, K. (1997). *The physical self: From motivation to well-being.*Champaign, IL: Human Kinetics.

Fox, K. (1998). Advances in the measure of the physical self. In J. L. Duda (Ed.), *Advances in sport and exercise psychology measurement*(pp. 295–310). Morgantown, WV: Fitness Information Technology, Inc.

Fox, K. (2000). The effects of exercise on self-perceptions and self-esteem. In S. J. H. Biddle, K. Fox, & S. Boutcher (Eds.), *Physical activity and psychological well-being*(pp. 88–117). London, UK: Routledge.

Fox, K. R., & Corbin, C. B. (1989). The physical self-perception profile: Development and preliminary validation. *Journal of Sport and Exercise Psychology, 11,*408–430.

Harter, S. (1999). *The construction of the self: A developmental perspective.* New York: Guildford Press.

Hartley, L. H., Mason, J. W., Hogan, R. P., Jones, L. G., Kotchen, T. A., Mougey, E. H., et al. (1972). Multiple hormonal response to graded exercise in relation to physical training. *Journal of Applied Physiology, 33,* 602–606.

Hoffman, P. (1997). The endorphin hypothesis. In W. P. Morgan (Ed.), *Physical activity and mental health*(pp. 163–177). Washington, DC: Taylor & Francis Publisher.

Holmes, D. (1993). Aerobic fitness and the response too psychological stress. In P. Seraganian (Ed.), Exercise psychology: The effects of physical exercise on psychological processes (pp. 39–63). Toronto, ON: John Wiley and Sons.

Horne, J. A., & Staff, C. H. (1983). Exercise and sleep: Body heating effects. *Sleep,* 6,36–46.

Howley, E. T. (1981). The excretion of catecholamines as an index of exercise stress. In F. J. Nagel, & H. J. Montoye (Eds.), *Exercise in health and disease*(pp.22–31). Springfield, IL: Charles C. Thomas.

Hughes, J., Smith, T. W., Kosterlitz, H. W, Fothergill, L. A., Morgan, B. A., & Morris, H. R. (1975). Identification of two related pentapeptides from the brain with potent opiate agonist activity. *Nature, 258,* 577–579.

Johnsgard, K. (2004). *Conquering depression and anxiety through exercise.*Amherst, NY: Prometheus Books.

Koltyn, K. F. (1997). The thermogenic hypothesis. In W. P. Morgan (Ed.), *Physical activity and mental health*(pp. 163–177). Washington, DC: Taylor and Francis.

Kraemer, R. R., Dzewaltowski, D. A., Blair, M. S., Rinehardt, K. F., & Castracane, V. D. (1990). Mood alteration from treadmill running and its relationship to beta-endorphin, coricotrophin, and growth hormone. *The Journal of Sports Medicine and Physical Fitness,* 30, 241–246.

Landers, D. M., & Petruzzello, S. J. (1994). Physical activity, fitness, and anxiety. In C. Bouchard, R. J. Shephard, & T. Stevens (Eds.), *Physical activity, fitness, and health*(pp. 868–882). Champaign, IL: Human Kinetics.

Lawlor, D. A., & Hopker, S. W. (2001). The effectiveness of exercise as an intervention in the management of depression: Systematic review and meta-regression analysis of randomized controlled trials. *British Medical Journal, 322,*763–766.

Leith, L. M. (1994). *Foundations of exercise and mental health.*Morgantown, WV: Fitness Information Technology, Inc.

Leith, L. M. (2009). *Foundations of exercise and mental health*(2nd ed.). Morgantown, WV: Fitness Information Technology, Inc.

Leith, L. M., & Taylor, A. H. (1990). Psychological aspects of exercise: A decade literature review. *Journal of Sport Behavior, 13,*1–22.

Long, B. C. (1993). A cognitive perspective on the stress reducing effects of physical exercise. In P. Seraganian (Ed.), Exercise psychology: The effects of physical exercise on psychological processes (pp. 339–357). Toronto, ON: John Wiley and Sons.

Long, B. C., & Van Stavel, R. (1995). Effects of exercise training on anxiety: A meta-analysis. *Journal of Applied Sport Psychology, 7*,167–189.

Lox, C. L., McAuley, E., & Tucker, R.S. (1995). Exercise as an intervention for enhancing subjective well-being in an HIV-1 population. *Journal of Sport & Exercise Psychology, 17*, 345–362.

Mack, M. G., Huddleston, S., & Dutler, K. E. (2000). Mood state changes of students enrolled in physical activity classes. *Perceptual and Motor Skills*, 90, 911–914.

Marsh, H. W. (1997). The measurement of physical self-concept: A construct validation approach. In K. R. Fox (Ed.), *The physical self: From motivation to well-being*(pp. 27–58). Champaign IL: Human Kinetics.

Martinsen, E. W., & Medhus, A. (1989). Adherence to exercise and patients' evaluation of physical exercise in a comprehensive treatment programme for depression. *Nordisk-Psykiatrisk-Tidsskrift, 43*,411–415.

McAuley, E., Blissmer, B., Marquez, D. X., Jerome, G. J., Kramer, A. F., & Katula, J. (2000). Social relations, physical activity, and well-being in older adults. *Preventative Medicine*, *31*, 608–617.

McAuley, E., Mihalko, S. L., & Bane, S. M. (1996). Acute exercise and anxiety reduction: does the environment matter? *Journal of Sport and Exercise Psychology*, *18*, 408–418.

McIntyre, C. W., Watson, D., & Cunningham, A. C. (1990). The effects of social interaction, exercise, and test stress on positive and negative affect. *Bulletin of the Psychonomic Society, 28*, 141–143.

McLafferty, C. L., Wetzsein, C. J., & Hunter, G. R. (2004). Resistance training is associated with improved mood in healthy older adults. *Perceptual and Motor Skills*, 98, 947–957.

McNair, D. M., Lorr, N., & Droppleman, L. F. (1971). *Manual for the profile of mood states*.San Diego, CA: Education and Industrial Testing Service.

Morgan, W. P. (1997). Methodological considerations. In W. P. Morgan (Ed.), *Physical activity and mental health*(pp. 3–32). Washington, DC: Taylor and Francis.

Motl, R. W., Birnbaum, A. M., Kubik, M. Y., & Dishman, R. K. (2004). Naturally occurring changes in physical activity are inversely related to depressive symptoms during early adolescence. *Psychosomatic Medicine*, *66*, 336–342.

Murray, C. J., & Lopez, A. D. (1997). Alternative projections of mortality and disability by cause 1990–2020: Global Burden of Disease Study. *Lancet*, *349*,1498–1504.

Mutrie, N., & Biddle, S. J. H. (1995). The effects of exercise on mental health of nonclinical populations. In S. J. H. Biddle (Ed.), *European perspectives on exercise and sport psychology*(pp. 50–70). Champaign, IL: Human Kinetics.

Mutrie, N., & Faulkner, G. (2004). Physical activity: Positive psychology in motion. In A. Linley, & S. Joseph (Eds.), *International handbook of positive psychology in practice: From research to application*(pp. 146–164). Toronto, ON : Wiley and Sons, Inc.

Ng, J. Y., & Tam, S. F. (2000). Effect of exercise-based cardiac rehabilitation on mobility and self-esteem of persons after cardiac surgery. *Perceptual and Motor Skills*, *91*, 107–114.

North, T. C., McCullagh, E., & Tran, Z. V. (1990). Effects of exercise on depression. *Exercise and Sport Science Reviews*, *18*, 379–415.

O'Halloran, P. D., Murphy, G. C., & Webster, K. E. (2004). Mood during a 60-minute treadmill run: Timing and type of mood change. *International Journal of Sports Psychology*, *35*, 309–327.

Osei-Tutu, K. B., & Campagna, P. D. (2005). The effects of short- vs. long-bout exercise on mood, VO_2max, and percent body fat. *Preventative Medicine*, *40*, 92–98.

Paffenbarger, R. S., Lee, I.-M., & Leung, R. (1994). Physical activity and personal characteristics associated with depression and suicide in American college men. *Acta Psychiatrica Scandinavica*, 89, 16–22.

Paluska, S. A., & Schwenk, T. L. (2000). Physical activity and mental health: Current concepts. *Sports Medicine*, 29, 167–180.

Parente, D. (2000). Influence of aerobic and stretching exercise on anxiety and sensation-seeking mood state. *Perceptual and Motor Skills, 90*, 347–348.

Petruzzello, S. J., Landers, D. M., Hatfield, B. D., Kubitz, K. A., & Salazar, W. (1991). A meta-analysis on the anxiety-reducing effects of acute and chronic exercise: Outcomes and mechanisms. *Sports Medicine, 11*, 143–182.

Pierce, D., Kupprat, I., & Harry, D. (1976). Urinary epinephrine and norepinephrine levels in women athletes training and competition. *European Journal of Applied Physiology, 36*, 1–6.

Planinsec, J., & Fosnaric, S. (2005). Relationship of perceived self-concept and physical activity level and sex among young children. *Perceptual and Motor Skills, 94*, 349.

Raglin, J. S., Eksten, F., & Garl, T. (1995). Mood state responses to a preseason conditioning program in male collegiate basketball players. *International Journal of Sports Psychology, 26*, 214–225.

Reed, J., & Ones, D. S. (2006). The effect of acute exercise on positive activated affect: A meta-analysis. *Psychology of Sport and Exercise, 7*,477–514.

Riggs, C. E. (1981).Endorphins, neurotransmitters and/or neuromodulators and exercise. In M. H. Sacks, & M. L. Sachs (Eds.), *Psychology of running*(pp. 224–230).Champaign, IL: Human Kinetics.

Russell, W., Pritschet, B., Frost, B., Emmett, J., Pelley, T. J., Black, J., & Owen, J. (2003). A comparison of post-exercise mood enhancement across common exercise distraction activities. *Journal of Sport Behaviour, 26*, 368–383.

Salmon, P. (2001). Effects of physical exercise on anxiety, depression and sensitivity to stress: A unifying theory. *Clinical Psychology Review, 21*, 33–61.

Sonstroem, R. J. (1997). Physical activity and self-esteem. In W. P. Morgan (Ed.), *Physical activity and mental health*(pp. 127–143). Washington, DC: Hemisphere.

Sonstroem, R. J., & Morgan, W. P. (1989). Exercise and self-esteem: Rationale and model. *Medicine and Science in Sports and Exercise, 21*, 329–337.

Spence, J. C., McGannon, K. R., & Poon, P. (2005). The effect of exercise on global self-esteem: A quantitative review. *Journal of Sport & Exercise Psychology, 27*, 311–334.

Stathopoulou, G., Powers, M. B., Berry, A. C., Jasper, A. J., Smits, J. A. J., & Otto, M. W. (2006). Exercise interventions for mental health: A quantitative and qualitative review. *Clinical Psychology: Science and Practice, 13*,179–193.

Stein, E. N., & Motta, R. W. (1992). Effects of aerobic and nonaerobic exercise on depression and self-concept. *Perceptual and Motor Skills, 74*,79–89.

Strawbridge, W. J., Deleger, S., Roberts, R. E., & Kaplan, G. A. (2002). Physical activity reduces the risk of subsequent depression for older adults. *American Journal of Epidemiology, 156*,328–334.

Villet, B. (1978). Opiates of the mind. *The Atlantic, 241*, 82–89.

Waelde, L. C., Thompson, L., & Gallagher-Thompson, D. (2004). A pilot study of a yoga and meditation intervention for dementia caregiver stress. *Journal of Clinical Psychology*, 60,677–687.

Watanabe, E., Takeshima, N., Okada, A., & Inomata, K. (2000). Comparison of water and land-based exercise in the reduction of state anxiety among older adults. *Perceptual & Motor Skills, 91*, 97–104.

Watson, D., Clark, L. A., & Tellegen, A. (1988). Development and validation of brief measures of positive and negative affect: The PANAS scales. *Journal of Personality and Social Psychology, 54*, 1063–1070.

Weinberg, R. S., & Gould, D. (2007). *Foundations of sport and exercise psychology*(4th ed.). Champaign, IL: Human Kinetics.

Wilfley, D., & Kunce, J. (1986). Differential physical and psychological effects of exercise. *Journal of Counseling Psychology, 33*, 337–342.

Zion, L. C. (1965). Body concept as it relates to self-concept. *Research Quarterly*, 36, 490–495.

Chapter 13

Physical Activity Interventions

Kimberley A. Dawson
Jennifer Robertson-Wilson
Kathleen Martin-Ginis

Chapter Objectives

After reading this chapter, you should be able to do the following:

1. Describe how social cognitive theory, theory of planned behaviour, and transtheoretical model have contributed to intervention research.
2. Explain how physical activity can be both an outcome variable and an intervention variable in exercise intervention research.
3. Outline the seven key components that increase the probability of successful physical activity interventions.
4. Appreciate valuable Canadian contributions to physical activity intervention research.
5. Identify the ways physical activity interventions improve the lives of people living with chronic diseases.

Sue and John Brown live in Toronto, Ontario. They have a 16-year-old daughter named Kerri and a 12-year-old son named Carter. John works shifts at the Cadbury Chocolate Company while Sue works part time at St. Joseph's hospital in the laundry department. They earn enough money to meet their living expenses but do not have any money left over for anything else. They do not own a car. John and Sue just had their annual physicals. Their doctor informed Sue that she was 30 pounds overweight with high blood pressure and that John had high cholesterol levels. Neither one participates in physical activity of any kind, and both take public transportation to work. Their doctor has recommended that they both start a regular exercise program to combat their medical problems.

Kerri is in grade 10, her second year of high school. Because her family has never had a lot of expendable cash, she has relied on school sports to keep her active. With school budget cuts, the after-school sports she enjoyed previously are no longer available. She is currently selecting her courses for grade 11 and is thinking that she won't have room in her schedule for physical education because she should be taking more mathematics and computer courses in preparation for university. Her best friend, Anita, just got her driver's licence and a new car from her parents, so they can now drive to school. As a result, Kerri has become more sedentary than ever.

Carter is in grade 6. His favourite thing to do is to play his friend's Xbox. He delivers papers to make spare cash and spends most of it on candy and pop at the 7-Eleven. He has also gained about 40 pounds in the last two years. As he's gained weight, he has become more self-conscious about his body and stopped swimming at the community pools with his friends. He has also decided that he does not really need to participate in gym class in order to obtain a good mark; he's happy to just stand around and get a passing grade.

The Brown family is typical of many families living in Canada. In order to help families like the Browns, researchers have to address political situations (school-board cutbacks), motivational issues (choosing to play video games *about* skateboarding rather than skateboarding itself), economic factors (not making a lot of money for extra things such as gym memberships), work obstacles (working shift work), and peer issues (inactive friends). Successful strategies or **interventions** are based on manipulating the specific factors that affect exercise behaviour. All effective behaviour change is based on understanding the commonalities among people while appreciating the differences that exist between them.

Common Myths about Physical Activity Interventions

MYTH: It is easy to get people to become or stay physically active.

MYTH: Exercise interventions offer long-term effects.

MYTH: If you have a positive attitude toward physical activity, you will always exercise.

MYTH: Individuals with chronic illnesses do not want to exercise because they have other things to worry about.

MYTH: An individual's physical activity level is determined by his or her motivation. It is not dependent on other key factors such as public health policies, incentives, or environmental barriers.

INTRODUCTION

There are many situations in which individuals have specific physical activity needs. You may have come across some of them already in your work, sport, or volunteer experiences. In many cases, people who need to change their exercise behaviour will require the help of trained professionals who understand how to help them successfully fit physical activity into their lives. You have chosen to study kinesiology, physical education, exercise science, or sport and exercise psychology for your own reasons. But if you choose to follow this path and become a teacher, doctor, personal trainer, physiotherapist, or other health and education professional, you can be certain that you will be dealing with people and their relationship with physical activity. Therefore, it is important that you understand how to utilize physical activity and exercise behaviour research to help people maintain a healthy lifestyle (see Table 13.1). Prescribing exercise is the first part of the equation; helping people adhere to or comply with the recommendation is the second.

The overall objective of this chapter is to help you understand what interventions have been successful for increasing physical activity as well as to discuss how physical activity has been used to help individuals with special needs or chronic illness. Recommendations, which you may find useful in your future pursuits, are provided to increase the probability of successfully modifying behaviour in a physical activity context.

THE IMPORTANCE OF MAINTAINING A PHYSICALLY ACTIVE LIFESTYLE

The benefits of an active lifestyle are becoming increasingly well known. You need only watch a nightly news program or read your local paper to hear about the latest research proclaiming the benefits of exercise. The well-established benefits of decreasing the risk

Table 13.1 Occupational Situations that Involve Physical Activity Interventions

Occupation	Situation	Behavioural Recommendation
Medical doctor	Patient with high blood pressure	Cardiovascular exercise three times/week by joining a community exercise program
Physical education teacher	Student with diabetes	Playing in a recreational basketball league
Coach	Player who wants to lose weight	Supplementing playing with running
Physiotherapist	Client with a knee injury	Riding a bicycle three times/week in the clinic
Personal trainer	Client who wants to tone up	Resistance training three times/week

of diabetes, cancer, osteoporosis, obesity, and cardiovascular disease, as well as improving mental health, have been mentioned previously in this text.

In order to accrue these health benefits, however, individuals have to exercise with a high degree of regularity. Unfortunately, the Canadian Fitness and Lifestyle Research Institute (CFLRI; www.cflri.ca), a non-profit national research organization that monitors the physical activity patterns of Canadians, has documented that only 49% of all Canadians (older than 20 years) are classified as at least moderately active, which is defined as walking a total of half an hour per day (Cameron, Wolfe, & Craig, 2007). That leaves 51% of Canadians to be classified as inactive or sedentary.

This is troublesome for two reasons. First, despite the abundant information documenting the benefits of an active lifestyle, Canadians continue to remain largely sedentary. Second, from a public health perspective, Canadians are living longer (Statistics Canada, 2006), and this increased life expectancy will place an increased strain on our health-care system. Work by Katzmarzyk and colleagues also highlights that physical inactivity among Canadians is very costly to our health-care system (Katzmarzyk, Gledhill, & Shepard, 2000). An active lifestyle will help to diminish this burden by keeping more people healthier, longer.

Clearly, there is a need to intervene and help Canadians become more active. Recognizing this priority, many Canadian provinces have targeted physical activity as a key health issue and developed initiatives to encourage behaviour change. Examples include *ACTIVE2010* (www.active2010.ca), developed by the Ontario Ministry of Health Promotion to remove barriers to physical activity. One key objective is to have 55% of all Ontarians complete the equivalent of 30 minutes of daily walking by the year 2010. Other examples of provincial resources promoting physical activity and healthy eating include Alberta's Healthy U (www.healthyalberta.com/default.htm), British Columbia's ActNow BC (www.actnowbc.ca/EN/home), and Saskatchewan's *in motion* (www.saskatchewaninmotion.ca). This is not an exhaustive list. You may be familiar with some programs that we have not listed. The CFLRI website also lists government initiatives.

These initiatives are impressive and timely in their attempts to address the issue of Canada's inactivity. However, many of them do not get at the heart of the problem: *why* Canadians remain inactive, and *how* we can get them to exercise with the frequency, intensity, and duration necessary to realize some of the aforementioned health benefits. In the end, political strategies like the above must be based on the success of researchers addressing these very questions. Fortunately, from 2005 to 2008, there were over 1300 research articles evaluating physical activity and behaviour change! Clearly, this is a hot topic and is likely to remain so.

DETERMINANT AND INTERVENTION RESEARCH

This chapter is primarily dedicated to discussing intervention research, but what exactly do we mean by intervention-based research? There is often confusion regarding what exactly defines an exercise intervention study. The confusion usually revolves around two distinct, yet related fields of research: determinant research and intervention research.

Determinant research is dedicated to evaluating **determinants**, which are the factors that affect exercise behaviour. These determinants are generally based on four factors:

Researchers are working hard to understand the determinants of exercise behaviour and the associated physical and psychological health benefits.

Photograph courtesy of Peter Crocker, University of British Columbia.

individual, psychological, social, and program (Willis & Campbell, 1992). They have also been expanded to include physical features of the environment (Trost, Owen, Bauman, Sallis, & Brown, 2002). **Individual factors** reside within the person. Age, for example, was found to have a generally negative linear association with exercise such that exercise involvement usually declined with age (Fitness Ontario, 1983). **Psychological factors** address what the individual thinks or the traits that he or she may possess. For example, regular exercisers were found to have greater self-confidence than dropouts (Young & Ismail, 1977). **Social factors** involve aspects within the social setting or human interaction. Heinzelmann and Bagley (1970) found that wives' attitudes positively influenced their husbands' adherence patterns. **Program factors** are based on the program context. For example, exercise convenience, a program factor, increases the likelihood of exercise adherence (Goodrick, Hartung, Warren, & Hoepfel, 1984). Physical features of the environment may include things such as the weather, feeling safe in one's neighbourhood, and the accessibility of particular physical activity facilities (Trost et al., 2002).

Intervention research, on the other hand, does not directly alter exercise behaviour but, rather, seeks to manipulate the different factors that affect behaviour. For example, determinant research established that Canadian mothers with young children are the least likely population to exercise (Verthoef, Love, & Rose, 1992). One possible explanation for this sedentary behaviour is the increased barriers associated with becoming a parent. Canadian researchers Cramp and Brawley (2006) designed a successful physical activity intervention to help new moms develop skills to overcome postnatal specific barriers. Mothers in Motion (www.caaws.ca/mothersinmotion/home_e.html) was created to help Canadian moms maintain a physically active lifestyle by providing information on how to overcome child-related barriers.

It is a great accomplishment when research comes full circle. First, factors determining physical activity patterns are established. Second, a successful intervention based on these determinants is completed, and, third, the information is passed on to the public. However, there are major challenges to overcome. One current problem is that there is an abundance of evidence-based exercise intervention research, but only a fraction has been translated into practice settings (Glasgow, Davidson, Dobkin, Ockene, & Spring, 2006; Klesges, Dzewaltowski, & Christensen, 2006).

Figure 13.1 Physical activity as the outcome variable

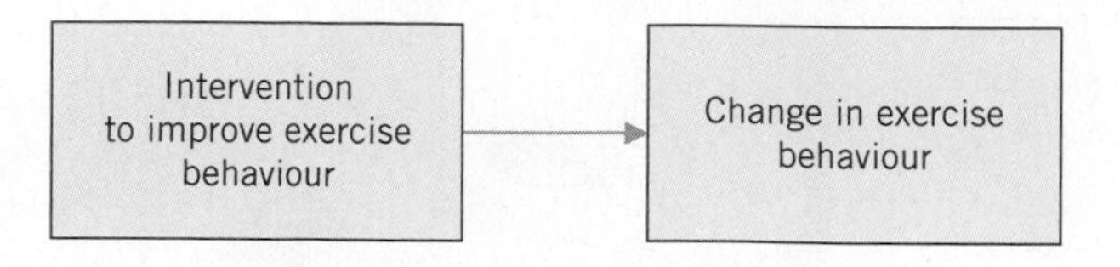

Figure 13.2 Physical activity as the treatment variable

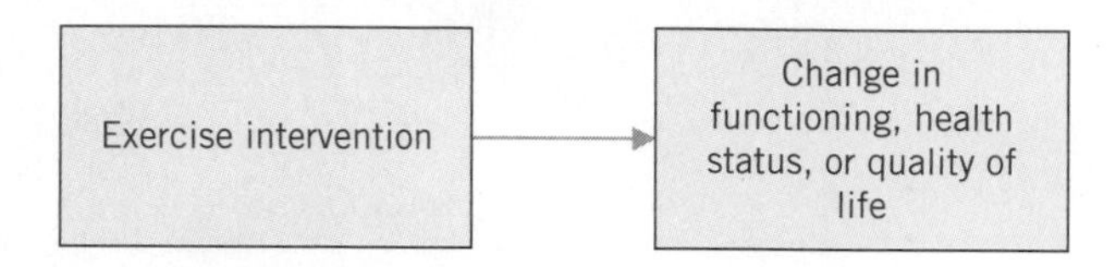

INTERVENTION RESEARCH INVOLVING PHYSICAL ACTIVITY

Individuals reviewing intervention research have tried to classify their studies according to a number of systems. It is important to have a system to make sense of the vast amount of material. To help you better understand the literature, we have chosen to classify research according to the role that physical activity plays within the intervention study.

Research into the role of physical activity can be of two types. The first type, and the one that we will examine in the next section, evaluates physical activity as an outcome variable (see Figure 13.1). The focus of **outcome research** is to develop an intervention and test whether or not it positively affects exercise behaviour. It could be as simple as placing a sign beside an elevator encouraging individuals to take the stairs, or as complex as increasing an individual's confidence to exercise regularly through educational programs. While the intervention strategies are distinct, the goal is the same—to increase physical activity patterns.

The second type of research uses physical activity as the treatment variable (see Figure 13.2). The intent of **treatment research** is to modify an individual's life experience in some way through the use of physical activity. For example, an exercise program could be used to help cancer patients better cope with their disease or the side effects of treatment. In this case, the population may change as well as the factors that are evaluated to see how they were affected by activity participation, but the treatment—physical activity—stays the same.

REFLECTIONS 13.1

You may notice a great number of Canadian researchers have contributed to physical activity intervention research. However, there are areas that lack Canadian content. It is important to keep in mind that not all research conducted with Canadian participants will apply to other countries with different populations, ethnicities, health-care systems, and climate. Nor will research that is conducted elsewhere in the world apply to Canada. Remember this when you are reading research conducted in California—does it apply to people living in the Maritimes in January?

PHYSICAL ACTIVITY AS AN OUTCOME IN INTERVENTION RESEARCH

Numerous approaches have been used to increase physical activity. For the purpose of this chapter, we will highlight the intervention research developed from the theories described earlier in Chapter 4 (Motivation and Behavioural Change). Intervention research can be theory based or non-theory based in nature. **Theory-based research** evaluates relationships among constructs that are proposed by theories or models of behaviour change. **Non-theory-based research** may contain the same constructs outlined by theories, but it is not concerned with testing theoretically proposed relationships. We will highlight the three models that have been given the most attention and show the most promise in leading to effective interventions to change exercise behaviour: the theory of planned behaviour, social cognitive theory, and the transtheoretical model. Because all of these theories were described in Chapter 4, we provide a limited review of aspects of the theories that are most pertinent to designing successful exercise interventions. We will discuss the relevant intervention research based on these theories and will describe some of the general and popular intervention strategies that are not necessarily based on theory but have been used to influence exercise behaviour. We finish the section by providing specific recommendations based on key components of successful interventions.

Theory-based Physical Activity Intervention Research

Theory of Planned Behaviour Recall from Chapter 4 that the theory of planned behaviour (Ajzen, 1985) postulates that the most immediate predictor of behaviouris an individual's intention to complete the behaviour. An intention is determined by an individual's attitude toward the behaviour and the subjective norm. Perceived behavioural control is proposed to affect both the intentions to engage in the behaviour and the behaviour itself.

Symons Downs and Hausenblas (2005) completed a statistical review of the theory of planned behaviour applied to exercise. They concluded that intention and perceived behavioural control were most strongly associated with exercise, and attitude was most strongly associated with intention. These authors suggest that both of these factors are useful for designing exercise intervention studies. Culos-Reed, Gyurcsik, and Brawley (2001) highlighted the importance of addressing the attitude component. Interventions based on this model should focus on changing attitudes toward physical activity(Sallis & Owen, 1999) despite the fact that the theory does not directly tell researchers how to do this (Ajzen & Manstead, 2007). **Persuasive communication** is one way to provoke attitude change and is based on providing specific information regarding beliefs about physical activity (Bright, Manfredo, Fishbein, & Bath, 1993).

REFLECTIONS 13.2

How would you use persuasive communication techniques to try to change someone's mind about exercise so that he or she thought more favourably about it?

Case Study 13.1

Persuasive Communication

Chatzisarantis and Hagger (2005) evaluated the effectiveness of two persuasive communications based on the theory of planned behaviour to promote physical activity attitudes, intentions, and behaviour in teenagers (mean age 14.60 years). One message was relevant to the participants and discussed things that had been found in previous studies to be meaningful to this cohort: physical activity helps you get fit, have fun, and avoid injuries.

The second message targeted benefits of exercise that were found previously to not be meaningful to the youth: physical activity helps you relax, feel better mentally, and help you forget about your cares. Results demonstrated that the relevant persuasive message resulted in more positive attitudes and stronger intentions to be physically active. However, neither group actually increased their physical activity participation.

One new area of research that helps to bridge the intention–behaviour gap addresses implementation intentions. Gollwitzer (1999) describes **implementation intentions** as those strong mental associations that form between a situational cue and a specific behaviour (e.g., "When I get in the car, I will drive to the gym"). Whereas the intention construct captured by the theory of planned behaviour specifies people's general behavioural goals (e.g., "I intend to exercise three times per week"), implementation intentions specify when, where, and how that general goal intention will be translated into action (Gollwitzer, 1999).

Clearly, the theory of planned behaviour has the potential to help guide exercise interventions by focusing on the three beliefs (attitudes, subjective norms, and control) and intentions to exercise. Three aspects of successful behavioural change are a result of applying interventions based on the theory of planned behaviour. First, in order to change behaviour, it is necessary to change attitudes or beliefs surrounding the targeted behaviour. Second, persuasive communication is a successful technique for influencing attitude change. Third, specific implementation intentions can increase the probability of completing the action.

Social Cognitive Theory Social cognitive theory (Bandura, 1986, 1997) is an all-encompassing theory used to describe human behaviour in a number of situations,

Case Study 13.2

Implementation Intentions

In a study conducted at McMaster University, researchers tested whether implementation intentions could help sedentary women increase the number of steps they walked each week (Arbour & Martin Ginis, 2008). Women in the implementation intentions condition were required to choose three days each week over the course of the study, and to specify the time, place, and number of minutes they intended to walk on each of those days.

Women in a control condition did not formulate implementation intentions. All study participants were given a pedometer and were asked to keep track of the number of steps they walked each day for 11 weeks. The implementation intention condition walked more steps over the course of the study than the control condition.

including exercise. As described in Chapter 4, the model is composed of a number of constructs and proposed relationships. Of key importance in this theory is the concept of self-efficacy. Recall, from Chapter 4, that **self-efficacy** describes an individual's belief in his or her ability to produce desired outcomes (Bandura, 1986). Researchers agree that self-efficacy influences exercise behaviour and changes in response to being physically active (Culos-Reed et al., 2001; McAuley & Blissmer, 2002). As self-efficacy increases, so too does desirable behaviour. In response to positive behaviour changes, self-efficacy rises and so continues the cycle.

Exercise behaviour can be enhanced by changing attitudes and developing effective implementation strategies.

Photograph courtesy of Peter Crocker, University of British Columbia.

Targeting and improving self-efficacy will be a large part of any successful intervention. Regardless of the type of intervention, the goal remains the same—to improve individual perceptions of ability. Once an individual feels competent, he or she is more likely to change the targeted behaviour. There are many types of self-efficacy that can be influenced in the exercise setting. Some examples are **barrier self-efficacy** (confidence in one's ability to overcome barriers that may arise when participating in exercise), **scheduling self-efficacy** (confidence in one's ability to plan and organize exercise in one's life), **task self-efficacy** (confidence in one's ability to complete the exercise task), and **exercise self-efficacy** (confidence in one's ability to engage in physical activity).

Similar to how attitudes can be changed through persuasive communication, self-efficacy can also be increased in many ways in an exercise context. Some ways of increasing self-efficacy are through goal setting, encouraging social support, and providing information or educational programs. Recall that Cramp and Brawley (2006) improved the barrier self-efficacy perceptions of postnatal women by having group-based sessions geared toward helping new moms develop skills to manage specific postnatal barriers. Dawson, Tracey, and Berry (2008) increased barrier and exercise self-efficacy through educational programs.

One key component of interventions geared toward changing exercise behaviour will be increasing self-efficacy perceptions. Whatever the means (e.g., educational programs, counselling), it is important to raise an individual's evaluation of their capabilities regarding barriers, scheduling, and the task in order to see effects on behaviour.

Case Study 13.3

Physical Activity Counselling

Blanchard et al. (2007) compared the effects of a physical activity intervention delivered by a primary health-care provider (control group) with the effects of counselling by a **physical activity counsellor (PAC)**, a trained member of the health-care team who used behaviour modification techniques to help individuals overcome barriers to exercise (barrier self-efficacy) and feel confident about exercising (task self-efficacy).

Results suggested that participants in the PAC condition had significantly higher task and barrier self-efficacy than the control group at six weeks, which resulted in significantly more physical activity at week 13.

Canadians face many environmental barriers to regular physical activity. Enhancing self-efficacy to overcome such barriers is a key to increasing physical activity for all Canadians.
Photograph courtesy of Catherine Sabiston.

REFLECTIONS 13.3

Is anyone looking for a career option? Physical activity counsellor is certainly a viable one for individuals trained in kinesiology, physical education, or exercise science. Hopefully, to protect the public and provide recognition of your specific training, certification will soon require you to call yourself a *physical activity counsellor*. What skills do you think you might need? Think back to the ethical and educational issues discussed in Chapter 1.

Transtheoretical Model Recall from Chapter 4 that the transtheoretical model (Prochaska & DiClemente, 1983; Prochaska, DiClemente, & Norcross, 1992) suggests that there are distinct stages that an individual passes through when attempting to change behaviours: pre-contemplation (no intention to make changes), contemplation (intending to make changes within six months), preparation (intending to make changes in the next month), action (starting a new behaviour), maintenance (sustaining the behaviour), and termination(removing relapse potential).

Sallis and Owen (2002) suggested that interventions based on the transtheoretical model should be **stage matched**. This implies that individuals think and behave differently in each stage. They are motivated by different processes. Stage-matching intervention research designs specific intervention strategies that are sensitive to these differences and tailored to the specific needs of the individual. This means that individuals are first evaluated for their current stage on the exercise continuum and are then provided with relevant information for that specific stage. The information is usually based on constructs from the theory of planned behaviour (e.g., attitudes, intentions) and social cognitive theory (e.g., self-efficacy). For example, an individual who is beginning to contemplate exercise should receive an intervention tailored differently than someone in the action stage (see Table 13.2). Stage-targeted activity promotion interventions are more likely to induce changes in motivation than approaches that do not consider stages (Brug & Kremers, 2005).

It is clear that individuals will follow unique paths in their own exercise journeys. Interventions need to be tailored to the specific stage that each individual is currently in. The transtheoretical model does a good job of describing these stages and keeping researchers aware that successful interventions will need to be stage matched in some way.

Case Study 13.4

Stage-matched Physical Activity Intervention

Canadian researchers Dawson, Tracey, and Berry (2008) used a stage-matched approach in their comparison of a traditional group-based intervention with an Internet-based physical activity intervention in an Ontario workplace. Both interventions were based on social cognitive theory integrated with the transtheoretical model. All participants completed a stage of change questionnaire each week (Marcus, Rossi, Selby, Niaura, & Rossi, 1992). This information was used to determine the stage-relevant information that was provided for the participants. Thus, for each week of the 10-week intervention, information was provided that was relevant to the participants' unique motivational and behavioural processes.

Results demonstrated that although the Internet-based intervention attracted more participants, the group-based intervention showed significant increases in exercise and barrier self-efficacy. With respect to stages, more than a statistically expected number of participants in the preparation stage were found in both intervention groups. Also, more individuals in the preparation and maintenance stages of exercise chose the Internet-based intervention over the group-based intervention. This study demonstrates how individuals in different stages might be unique in their preferences for intervention delivery mode and psychological and behavioural factors.

Table 13.2 Using the Transtheoretical Model to Develop Successful Interventions

	Pre-contemplation	Contemplation	Preparation	Action
Stage description	Focused on the costs of exercise	Does not yet fully appreciate the benefits of exercise	Ready to change soon	Engaging in physical activity but not necessarily regularly
	Does not see the benefits of exercise		Starting to see the benefits of exercise	
Tailored advice	Provide lots of information about the benefits of exercise	Ask questions to help individual identify the benefits of exercise	Help individual organize and plan exercise	Provide tips on how to overcome barriers
			Suggest that individual finds social support	Use techniques to increase motivation (e.g., goal setting, contracts)

Note: Adapted from C.L. Lox, K.A. Martin Ginis, and S.J. Petruzello (2006). *The psychology of exercise. Integrating theory and practice* (2nd ed.), pp.83–84. Copyright © 2007 by Holcomb Hathaway, Publishers (Scottsdale, AZ). Used with permission.

REFLECTIONS 13.4

What stage describes your exercise behaviour? Think of interventions that would be effective to change your physical activity. Now think of how you could help someone in the contemplation stage.

Non-theory-based Intervention Research

Recall that we said earlier that some interventions are based on theory while others are not. If we reviewed only theoretically based research, a large part of the intervention picture would be missing. Some intervention research does not include factors or attempt to evaluate the relationships among constructs proposed by the theories that we discussed above. Similarly, some attempts at changing people's exercise behaviour cluster around common areas, while others offer unique approaches. For example, Brown and Rhodes (2006) found that individuals in Victoria, British Columbia, who owned dogs were much more likely to walk regularly than those without dogs, and they suggested that acquiring a dog should be explored as an intervention to get people more physically active. Not a bad idea!

In our attempt to find common clusters to organize this chapter, we found two areas that have received a fair amount of attention: delivery approaches and behavioural approaches. **Delivery approaches** are based on how information is delivered to an individual (e.g., email, telephone, in person). **Behavioural approaches** teach individuals specific management skills necessary for successful maintenance of physical activity. These are specific how-to strategies that individuals complete to help make exercise important in their lives.

There are many ways to get regular health-promoting physical activity that do not involve formal exercise settings.

Photograph courtesy of Catherine Sabiston.

The method of information delivery is an important aspect of the intervention strategy to understand. It is necessary to know this information when determining what format to choose. What form of communication would you use to provide a successful educational package to seniors? Children? Teenagers? Knowing which strategies tend to be most successful will help with these decisions. We have classified the interventions based on the method of delivery used in the intervention. We remind you that content is also important, and although many of these study authors did not intentionally set out to test the theory of planned behaviour or social cognitive theory, some of the content is still based on constructs relevant to these theories (e.g., attitudes, self-efficacy).

Interventions Based on Delivery Approaches

Computer Technology Interventions The computer has become a useful technological advancement for designing exercise interventions. Utilizing website or Internet technology has become so popular that the new term *eHealth* was developed (Eng, 2001). The content included on most physical activity websites usually involves educational information about exercise and techniques to help individuals manage their own activity. Websites are dynamic and interactive, allowing for new information to be updated regularly and for users to log in and track their own unique behaviours, emotions, and thoughts.

Case Study 13.5

Computer Technology

As computer technology has advanced, so too have interventions based on this technology. King and colleagues (2008) described their intervention based on a hand-held personal digital assistant (PDA) as first generational. Thirty-seven healthy, underactive adults (over 50) were randomly assigned to a control group or intervention group and evaluated for changes in physical activity over an eight-week period.

The PDA was programmed to ask twice per day about the amounts and types of physical activity undertaken, as well as to provide information about helpful behavioural strategies. Results demonstrated that intervention participants reported significantly higher levels of physical activity relative to controls.

Computer technology is an exciting and interesting new mode of delivering physical activity interventions. The main advantage of this technology is that it is highly interactive. Researchers are able to give and receive information quickly and directly. Educational information can be delivered to the individual either through a website, email, or personal digital assistant (PDA), and the participants can respond and track their progress. This is a very cost-effective and comprehensive approach to modifying behaviour. Large numbers of people can be serviced with minimal cost. The main disadvantage of computer technology is the lack of face time and accountability it provides. The more anonymity people have, quite often, the less they feel supported or responsible for their individual behaviours.

While computer technology may provide short-term changes in physical activity, it may be less effective in the long run. Vandelanotte, Spathonis, Eakin, and Owen's (2007) review of Web-based physical intervention studies found that effects were short lived, and there was limited evidence of maintenance behaviours. However, it is an exciting time in intervention research, when exercise participants can be contacted individually and immediately to receive or obtain relevant information. When designing successful physical activity interventions, it is important to remember that a large component of behaviour change is based on supportive and positive environments. Oftentimes, computer technology does not provide this component.

Case Study 13.6

Internet-based vs. Group-based Physical Activity Interventions

Tracey, Dawson, and Berry (2009) evaluated two physical activity interventions: Internet-based and group-based. Individuals who completed the group-based intervention described how they liked the accountability and personal aspect of the traditional meeting group. Many exercise friendships were formed that continued after the program.

They also felt that the information provided in the talks by the leader was helpful. Internet-based participants felt that they missed the social contact and that the information provided on the website was not new or relevant to their specific needs. The authors concluded that Internet-based activity interventions lack the social support necessary for successful long-term behaviour change.

REFLECTIONS 13.5

How has computer technology has enhanced your world? How could it be used to help university students maintain an exercise program during busy times such as midterms or final exams?

Telephone Interventions Telephones have become a popular mode of information delivery. The main advantage of telephone interventions is that, like computer technology–based interventions, they are also cost-effective and capable of reaching many people (Marcus, Nigg, Riebe, & Forsyth, 2000). Typical telephone designs involve a trained health educator providing counselling over the phone. Sessions usually involve providing support, physical activity information, and problem solving regarding exercise barriers. After reviewing 16 physical activity telephone interventions, Eakin, Lawler, Vandelanotte, and Owens (2007) concluded that there is solid evidence for telephone interventions to change exercise behaviour. King et al. (2007) also found that an automated telephone delivery system was just as effective as a human phone call for delivering physical activity information and increasing physical activity. While data suggest that more frequent contact is best, it may not matter what is said in the phone call (i.e., talking about physical activity or not). Simply touching base without discussing exercise can also help to increase physical activity (Lombard, Lombard, & Winett, 1995).

Mass Media Interventions **Mass media campaigns** are interventions that attempt to reach large numbers of individuals simultaneously through public forums. Types of mass media are video, television, radio, and print. These techniques reach a potentially greater audience than interventions based on personal contact (Marcus, Owen, Forsyth, Cavill, & Fridinger, 1998).

"It's not going to kill you" is a provocative mass media campaign utilizing television, print, and the Internet, sponsored by the Government of Ontario (www.notgoingtokillyou.ca). It implies that exercise won't hurt you by showing scared kids running away from sporting equipment with the tagline, "It's not going to kill you." Perhaps you've seen on television some ParticipACTION (www.participaction.com) commercials highlighting how "inactive kids may get old before their time." And Hal and JoAnne continue to try and motivate everyone to be active in the Body*Break* commercials (www.bodybreak.com/episodes.php).

One criticism of mass media campaigns is that although they lead to increased population awareness, it has been difficult to show their effects on behaviour change (Marcus et al., 1998). For example, Bauman, Madill, Craig, and Salmon (2004) noted that Canadians had high awareness of ParticipACTION, but they could not attribute physical activity patterns to the campaign. It appears that while media campaigns increase our awareness, future intervention research is necessary to evaluate the long-term effectiveness of this awareness in terms of changes in physical activity.

REFLECTIONS 13.6

Does it motivate you to exercise when you see a television commercial promoting physical activity? Why or why not?

Case Study 13.7

Pedometers

In a recent review, Bravata and colleagues (2007) examined the utility of pedometers in increasing physical activity (rather than just measuring physical activity levels).

They reported that while physical activity (steps) was higher among those using a pedometer, the number of steps taken by those using pedometers was in part influenced by having set a goal for the number of steps to attain as well as by keeping a diary recording the number of steps taken.

Interventions Based on Behavioural Approaches Three behavioural approaches to changing physical activity include goal setting, behaviour monitoring, and signing a physical activity contract (Berger, Pargman, & Weinberg, 2002; Buckworth & Dishman, 2002; Lox, Martin Ginis, & Petruzello, 2006). **Goal setting** involves identifying what an individual would like to work toward in terms of his or her physical activity participation. The SMART principles of specificity, measurability, adjustability, realism, and timeliness also apply when considering how to effectively optimize physical activity goals (see Chapter 14). For instance, an individual who has been infrequently physically active may set a New Year's resolution or goal to "get physically active in the New Year." However, this is not a SMART goal. A better example of a SMART goal is "to walk with my spouse five nights a week in the neighbourhood for at least half an hour over the next six months."

This goal is specific in terms of the frequency, type, and duration of physical activity identified. The goal can be measured in terms of time and frequency and is flexible to accommodate the individual's evening schedule and other concerns like the weather. This goal appears realistic for the individual; just like Goldilocks, to be successful you want to set a goal that is "just right," not too hard and not too easy. Finally, a timeline for the goal has been set (six months), at which time the individual may alter the goal based on the progress made.

In addition to goal setting, another strategy to facilitate physical activity behaviour change is **behaviour monitoring**, or keeping track of the desired physical activity behaviour (and even related emotions and cognitions). Monitoring can be achieved by keeping a physical activity diary, chart, or calendar that records daily or weekly physical activity (Buckworth & Dishman, 2002) and any details related to physical activity, for example, what type of physical activity was engaged in, the duration and location of the activity, or how one felt afterward (e.g., energetic, tired, sore; Lox et al., 2006). Both goal setting and monitoring are linked to models of self-regulation (e.g., Baumeister, Heatherton, & Tice, 1994). Part of the difficulty in regulating one's behaviour (like physical activity) has been linked to the absence of standards (or goals) and lack of monitoring (Baumeister & Heatherton, 1996).

Physical activity contracts are another strategy to promote physical activity. Contracts are thought to enhance an individual's commitment and motivation to attain the physical activity goal. Cress and colleagues (2005) list contracts as one of several "best practice" strategies to foster physical activity among older adults. A physical activity contract specifies in writing the physical activity behaviour to be achieved. The individual and another person (e.g., physical activity counsellor, physician, personal trainer, significant other) then sign the contract (Haber & Looney, 2000). In addition to identifying the physical activity goal a person agrees to, a physical activity contract may also include other details like rewards (e.g., a dinner out) to be received for fulfilling the contract (Berger et al., 2002; Buckworth & Dishman, 2002; Lox et al., 2006).

Conclusions about Interventions Used to Increase Physical Activity

The most successful interventions will be based on many of the key components that we've discussed throughout this chapter. By implementing these recommendations, the probability of the intervention being successful is increased. Key components to remember when attempting to change individuals' exercise behaviour are as follows:

1. Base the intervention on trying to change an individual's attitude toward exercise. In order to change an individual's attitude, it is important to use specific information that is based on his or her unique beliefs about physical activity.
2. Have individuals identify a specific implementation intention so that they attach activity-related behaviour to a situational cue that is relevant in their life.
3. Use creative ways to increase individuals' perceptions of their ability to partake in physical activity and to overcome specific barriers that are unique to their situation.
4. Be sensitive to the exercise stage that an individual is currently in. Use strategies that are helpful at each stage. For example, if someone has not exercised previously, provide him or her with information highlighting the benefits of exercise. Conversely, if someone has been exercising regularly, discuss strategies to avoid pitfalls.
5. When implementing an educational program, pay close attention to the way you deliver the information. Recognize the advantages and disadvantages of all delivery styles, as well as the relevance to the target population. For example, you would not want to use the Internet for older adults, who may not be technically savvy and who are looking for social companionship through exercise.
6. Use behavioural strategies that motivate the individual to be involved in his or her own exercise program, such as goal setting or monitoring progress.
7. Be sensitive to the age of the individual you are trying to help become more physically active.

Have you worked with children in a physical activity capacity as a coach or camp counsellor? Have you found it difficult to get kids to be active? What techniques did you use to motivate them to be active?
Photograph © Brand X/Jupiter Images.

Table 13.3 Interventions that Work Best for Children and Older Adults

Children	Older Adults
Target self-efficacy, enjoyment, social support from family and friends, and time spent outdoors (Sallis & Owen, 2002).	The health benefits associated with physical activity should be highlighted.
Environments to complete interventions are physical education classes, sport teams, and physical activities (Sallis & Owen, 2002).	Individual differences in health status must be included (e.g., the focus of an activity program for individuals with osteoarthritis will be different than for a healthy individual).
Use tangible behavioural and environmental strategies such as providing more parks, increasing lighting, and adding more physical education class time in the curriculum.	Exercise programs should be conveniently located in safe environments (Humpel, Owen, & Leslie, 2002).
Target the entire family in the behavioural change.	Older adults prefer lower-intensity and less-structured activities such as walking (King, 2001).
	Provide lots of social support from peers and health professionals (Wilcox, Tudor-Locke, & Ainsworth, 2002).
	Educational programs should target attitudes toward exercise while increasing self-efficacy.
	Group exercise programs should be older-adult specific.
	Activities in exercise programs should be geared toward keeping individuals more functionally well and independent.

Most exercise studies that we have reviewed in this section were based on adult participants (ages 20–55). Youth and older adults require special consideration since their needs may change as a function of their age (see Table 13.3). Children's physical activity is largely determined by outside sources such as parents, schools, communities, and sport organizations. They may require interventions that are based on behavioural and environmental manipulations.

Do your grandparents exercise? How do you think you could get them to exercise more?

Photograph © Brand X/Jupiter Images.

Canadian researcher Larry Brawley and colleagues identified physical activity as both a solution and a challenge for older adults (Brawley, Rejeski, & King, 2003). Physical training programs can be a solution for the functional decline associated with aging (Rejeski & Brawley, 2006). Overcoming the considerable barriers to exercise faced by older adults is a continuous challenge (see Chapter 10).

PHYSICAL ACTIVITY AS A TREATMENT IN INTERVENTION RESEARCH

In the previous section, we discussed interventions that may influence adherence to physical activity in healthy individuals. Chronic disease imposes many disruptions to people's lives and has a great impact on their psychological functioning. The role of physical activity changes when an individual becomes unhealthy for a long period of time. In these cases, researchers are no longer concerned with how specific interventions affect adherence rates, but rather the question becomes much more practical and applied: What can physical activity do to help individuals manage the many changes that occur with a long-term illness?

We turn our attention now to considering physical activity as the intervention that may affect many of the psychological and physiological consequences of coping with chronic illness. We cannot review all chronic illnesses, so we highlight three areas where significant advances have been made by Canadians: cancer, spinal cord injury, and Parkinson's disease.

Cancer

> "Why did I ride when I had cancer? Cycling is so hard, the suffering is so intense, that it's absolutely cleansing. At least for a while you have a kind of hall pass, and don't have to brood about your problems: you can shut everything else out, because the effort and subsequent fatigue are absolute" (Armstrong & Jenkins, 2001, p. 88).

When he was diagnosed in 1996 with stage IV testicular cancer, Lance Armstrong demonstrated how powerful exercise can be in the fight to cope with cancer. Dr. Kerry Courneya, from the University of Alberta, is an international research leader who has advanced our understanding of the effects of physical activity on breast cancer survivorship. Courneya and colleagues (Courneya, McKenzie, et al., 2008; Courneya, Segal, et al., 2008) have also advanced our knowledge of the factors that impede exercise adherence during breast cancer treatment (see Table 13.4). Over half of the barriers to physical activity that individuals experienced during treatment were attributed

Table 13.4 Outcome Cancer Factors Affected by Physical Activity, Found by Courneya and Colleagues
Quality of life
Improved self-esteem
Improved physical fitness
Improved body composition

Cancer survivors can gain many psychological, social, and physical benefits from regular physical activity. However, they may face unique challenges.

Photograph © Paula Lerner/Aurora Photos/Getstock.com.

to the disease and its treatments (e.g., feeling sick, fatigue). Similarly, a key predictor of exercise adherence during therapy was found to be the location of the exercise program. A recent review by Courneya and Friedenreich (2007) concluded that there have been major scientific advances in physical activity research in the control of cancer. Most of this work is coming from Canada. Clearly, exercise is beneficial for coping with cancer treatments. The next step will be to design successful interventions that help alleviate many of the barriers to exercise that individuals face as they navigate cancer treatments.

Spinal Cord Injury

Spinal cord injury (SCI) refers to damage to the spinal cord that results in a loss of motor, sensory, or autonomic function (i.e., paraplegia or quadriplegia). Nearly 50,000 Canadians are currently living with a disability associated with SCI, and these men and women are considered to be the most physically inactive segment of all society. Although inactivity has negative effects on the health and quality of life of all able-bodied Canadians, it is profoundly detrimental to the SCI community. It is associated with secondary health complications and severe reductions in independence, social participation, and psychological

Case Study 13.8

Spinal Cord Injury

Using the theory of planned behaviour, Latimer, Martin Ginis, and Arbour (2006) randomly allocated 54 men and women with SCI to an intervention or control condition. Participants in both conditions received basic education on how to start an exercise program and established the goal of exercising three times per week for at least 30 minutes each time.

Participants in the intervention condition also formulated implementation intentions, specifying where and when they planned to perform each exercise bout, as well as the type, duration, and intensity of each bout. At the end of the eight-week study, it was found that participants in the intervention condition were more likely to follow through with their exercise goals and reported more minutes per day of physical activity than participants in the control condition.

well-being (see Rick Hansen Foundation, www.rickhansen.com). Importantly, exercise has been shown to be an effective intervention for improving aerobic fitness, muscle strength, psychological well-being, and overall quality of life in people living with SCI (Martin Ginis & Hicks, 2007).

Only a handful of studies have tested the effectiveness of interventions for increasing physical activity in the SCI population. These interventions have been couched in various theoretical frameworks that we discussed previously and have utilized various intervention techniques, such as education, goal setting, problem solving, and the formulation of implementation intentions.

Although these results are very encouraging, there is still much work to be done to help Canadians with SCI become more physically active. Indeed, physical activity programs and information are two of the resources most desired, but least available to Canadians with SCI (Boyd & Bardak, 2004). In response to this need, a team of Canadian university researchers and community organizations have come together to form SCI Action Canada (www.sciactioncanada.ca). We are lucky to have the head of this initiative, Kathleen Martin-Ginis, as a contributor to this chapter. The team's mission is to advance physical activity knowledge and participation among Canadians living with SCI, through cutting-edge research and the dissemination of theory- and evidence-based interventions. Although SCI Action Canada is still in its infancy, it has already launched initiatives such as a telephone-based physical activity counselling service for people with SCI and a strategy for monitoring activity levels among Canadians with SCI. These national initiatives are important first steps toward increasing physical activity and ultimately improving the health and well-being among individuals in the SCI community.

Parkinson's Disease

One new line of research evaluating the potential of physical activity to affect symptoms associated with Parkinson's disease (PD) is being completed by Dr. Quincy Almeida at Wilfrid Laurier University. According to the Parkinson's Disease Foundation (www.pdf.org), PD is a movement disorder that is chronic and progressive. The cause is unknown, and there is currently no known cure. PD occurs when brain cells malfunction and die. Symptoms include tremors, rigidity, and impaired balance and coordination.

While still in its infancy, exercise interventions for individuals with PD are very promising. Researchers have found that the compliance rates for physical activity are

Case Study 13.9

Parkinson's Disease

Sage and Almeida (2009) compared aerobic training and sensory attention focused exercise (SAFE) to no exercise to determine which strategy would have a greater benefit for symptoms and gait in people with PD. The SAFE program involves 20–30 minutes of non-aerobic gait exercises focusing on body coordination, followed by 20–30 minutes of sensory attention exercises utilizing Thera-Bands.

While standard aerobic exercise improved gait, it did not affect disease severity. The SAFE program led to improvements in symptoms and functional movement control.

high, which is typical of populations with health conditions who find results through exercise. Future research directions include designing intervention strategies to help individuals incorporate exercise in their daily home routine as well as to maintain a regular exercise program.

REFLECTIONS 13.7

What barriers to exercise might an individual with spinal cord injuries experience that an individual with Parkinson's disease would not?

Conclusions about Interventions Used as Treatment

We have identified interventions targeting some unique populations and illnesses. While each group is unique, one thing is shared by all—physical activity is beneficial! An integrated approach to physical activity promotion that recognizes similar social cognitive factors crucial to all activity-enhancing interventions (e.g., attitudes, self-efficacy) across all populations while addressing the unique concerns or barriers that different populations might experience will lead to the most successful exercise behaviour interventions.

CHAPTER SUMMARY

Facilitating physical activity behaviour change is a complex process that will require a number of considerations. We began this chapter by introducing the idea of intervention research. Intervention research differs from determinant research in that interventions manipulate determinants believed to influence physical activity behaviour. In intervention research, physical activity can either be an outcome of the intervention or the intervention itself to attain another health outcome. Interventions where physical activity is an outcome can be theoretically based (e.g., theory of planned behaviour, social cognitive theory, and transtheoretical model) or concerned with understanding the effectiveness of non-theory-based constructs (e.g., technology, mass media, monitoring). In order for interventions to be effective, they need to be specifically designed to target adults, youth, and older adults. Multilevel interventions based on the recommendations that we provided are likely needed in order to optimize physical activity behaviour change.

As an intervention itself, physical activity has been used to help individuals deal with chronic conditions such as cancer, spinal cord injury, and Parkinson's disease. Some areas of research are more developed than others. Continued work is needed to find optimal strategies for physical activity among such populations.

From the public health perspective, it is necessary to continue to develop and evaluate the long-term effects of interventions geared toward increasing the activity levels and quality of life of all Canadians. We, who work in this area, believe that doing something to try and change physical inactivity is better than doing nothing at all. Remember, all interventions are successful if they help just one person exercise more regularly.

Common Myths about Physical Activity Interventions Revisited

MYTH: It's easy to get people to become or stay physically active.
The Canada Fitness and Lifestyle Research Institute documented that only 40% to 57% of the Canadian adult population is physically active, and that activity level is dependent on geographic location. Overall, 51% of Canadians are inactive.

MYTH: Exercise interventions offer long-term effects.
Most exercise intervention studies evaluate behaviour within a three-month to one-year period following the intervention. While interventions can be successful in the short term, most lose their effectiveness with long-term evaluation because lifelong activity is difficult for most individuals to maintain. Of those who do begin an exercise program, 50% will drop out within the first six months (Dishman, 1988). Physical activity also tends to decrease with increasing age (Cameron et al., 2007).

MYTH: If you have a positive attitude toward physical activity, you will always exercise.
Symons Downs and Hausenblas' (2005) review of exercise research based on the theory of planned behaviour concluded that successful exercise behaviour is most strongly associated with intention and perceived behavioural control. Attitudes, however, also affect our intentions. That is why having a positive attitude toward exercise may not always translate into successful behavioural change. A positive attitude will generate a favourable intention, but only intentions that are specific in terms of context, time, and action will evoke actual activity change.

MYTH: Individuals with chronic illnesses do not want to exercise because they have other things to worry about.
Individuals with chronic conditions such as cancer, cardiovascular disease, diabetes, spinal cord injury, or Parkinson's disease are strongly motivated to utilize physical activity to help improve survival rates, physiological functioning, and psychological and emotional health.

MYTH: An individual's physical activity level is determined by his or her motivation. It is not dependent on other key factors such as public health policies, incentives, or environmental barriers.
Physical activity patterns are determined by a number of items, including individual factors such as motivation or confidence; demographic factors such as ethnicity, geography, or culture; community factors such as the availability of resources or neighbourhood safety; political factors such as tax incentives or health strategies; and environmental issues such as climate and seasonal changes.

Review Questions

1. What is the difference between determinant and intervention research?
2. Explain how physical activity can be an intervention outcome and an intervention itself.
3. What is the best way to change attitudes?

4. What are four types of self-efficacy that are important in exercise settings?
5. Why should you consider the exercise stage that an individual is currently in when designing an intervention?
6. What physical activity interventions are most successful for youth and older adults?
7. Are findings based on research undertaken in other countries applicable to Canada? Why or why not?
8. Design an intervention to help a busy working mom become more physically active.
9. Identify the barriers to regular exercise that typical university students face. Develop a mass media campaign to target these barriers.

Suggested Reading

Blue, C. L., & Black, D. R. (2005). Synthesis of intervention research to modify physical activity and dietary behaviours. *Research and Theory for Nursing Practice: An International Journal*, 19, 25–61.

Kahn, E. B., Ramsey, T. L., Brownson, R. C., Heath, G. W., Howze, E. H., Powell, K. E., et al., and the Task Force on Community Preventive Services. (2002). The effectiveness of interventions to increase physical activity: A systematic review. *American Journal of Preventive Medicine*, 22, 73–107.

Lox, C. L., Martin Ginis, K. A., & Petruzello, S. J. (2006). *The psychology of exercise: Integrating theory and practice* (2nd ed.). Scottsdale, AZ: Holcomb Hathaway Publishers.

References

Ajzen, I. (1985). From intentions to actions: A theory of planned behaviour. In J. Kuhl, & J. Beckman (Eds.), *Action control: From cognition to behaviour* (pp. 11–30). New York: Springer-Verlag.

Ajzen, I., & Manstead, A. S. R. (2007). Changing health-related behaviours: An approach based on the theory of planned behaviour. In M. Hewstone, H. A. W. Schut, J. B. F. De Wit, K. VanDenBos, & M. S. Stroebe (Eds.), *The scope of social psychology: Theory and applications* (pp. 43–63). New York: Psychology Press.

Arbour, K. P., & Martin Ginis, K. A. (2008). A randomised controlled trial of the effects of implementation intentions on women's walking behaviour. *Psychology and Health*. Epub ahead of print.

Armstrong, L., & Jenkins, S. (2001). *It's not about the bike: My journey back to life*. (New ed.). London, UK: Yellow Jersey Press.

Bandura, A. (1986). Social foundations of thought and actions: A social cognitive theory. Englewood Cliffs, NJ: Prentice-Hall.

Bandura, A. (1997). *Self-efficacy: The exercise of control*. New York: W. H. Freeman.

Bauman, A., Madill, J., Craig, C. L., & Salmon, A. (2004). ParticipACTION: This mouse roared but did it get the cheese? *Canadian Journal of Public Health*, 95, S14–S24.

Baumeister, R. F., & Heatherton, T. F. (1996). Self-regulation failure: An overview. *Psychological Inquiry*, 7, 1–15.

Baumeister, R. F., Heatherton, T. F., & Tice, D. M. (1994). *Losing control: How and why people fail at self-regulation*. San Diego, CA: Academic Press.

Berger, B. G., Pargman, D., & Weinberg, R. S. (2002). *Foundations of exercise psychology*. Morgantown, WV: Fitness Information Technology.

Blanchard, C. M., Fortier, M., Sweet, S., O'Sullivan, T., Hogg, W., Reid, R. D., & Sigal, R. J. (2007). Explaining physical activity levels from a self-efficacy perspective: The physical activity counselling trial. *Annals of Behavioral Medicine*, 34, 323–328.

Boyd, E., & Bardak, L. (2004). Cross Canada Checkup. Interim report of the national consultations on SCI services in Canada–a qualitative overview. Vancouver, BC: Rick Hansen SCI Network.

Bravata, D. M., Smith-Spangler, C., Sundaram, V., Gienger, A. L., Lin, N., Lewis, R., et al. (2007). Using pedometers to increase physical activity and improve health: A systematic review. *Journal of the American Medical Association*, *298*, 2296–2304.

Brawley, L. R., Rejeski, W. J., & King, A. C. (2003). Promoting physical activity for older adults: The challenges for changing behaviour. *American Journal of Preventive Medicine*, *25*, 172–183.

Bright, A., Manfredo, M., Fishbein, M., & Bath, A. (1993). Application of the theory of reasoned action to the National Park Services controlled burn policy. *Leisure Research*, *25*, 263–280.

Brown, S., & Rhodes, R. (2006). Relationships among dog ownership and leisure-time walking in Western Canadian adults. *American Journal of Preventive Medicine*, *30*,121–136.

Brug, J., & Kremers, S. (2005). The transtheoretical model and stages of change: A critique. *Health Education Research*, *20*, 244–258.

Buckworth, J., & Dishman, R. K. (2002). *Exercise psychology*. Champaign, IL: Human Kinetics.

Cameron, C., Craig, C. L., & Paolin, S. (2004). *Increasing physical activity: Trends for planning effective communication*.Ottawa, ON: Canadian Fitness and Lifestyle Research Institute. Retrieved July 23, 2008, from http://www.cflri.ca/eng/statistics/surveys/pam2003.php

Cameron, C., Wolfe, R., & Craig, C. L. (2007). *Physical activity and sport: Encouraging children to be active*.Ottawa, ON: Canadian Fitness and Lifestyle Research Institute. Retrieved July 21, 2008, from http://www.cflri.ca/eng/provincial_data/pam2005/Canada.php

Chatzisarantis, N. L. D., & Hagger, M. S. (2005). Effects of a brief intervention based on the Theory of Planned Behavior on leisure-time physical activity participation. *Journal of Sport & Exercise Psychology*, *27*, 470–487.

Courneya, K. S., & Friedenreich, C. M. (2007). Physical activity and cancer control. *Seminars in Oncology Nursing*, *23*,242–252.

Courneya, K. S., McKenzie, D. C., Reid, R. D., Mackey, J. R., Gelmon, K., Friedenreich, C. M., et al. (2008). Barriers to supervised exercise training in a randomized controlled trial of breast cancer patients receiving chemotherapy. *Annals of Behavioral Medicine*, *35*, 116–122.

Courneya, K. S., Segal, R. J., Gelmon, K., Reid, R. D., Mackey, J. R., Friedenreich, C. M., et al. (2008). Predictors of supervised exercise adherence during breast cancer chemotherapy. *Medicine & Science in Sports & Exercise*, *40*,1180–1187.

Cramp, A. G., & Brawley, L. R. (2006). Moms in motion: A group-mediated cognitive-behavioral physical activity intervention. *International Journal of Behavioral Nutrition and Physical Activity*, *3*, 1–9.

Cress, M. E., Buchner, D. M., Prochaska, T., Rimmer, J., Brown, M., Macera, C., et al. (2005). Best practices for physical activity programs and behavior counseling in older adult populations. *Journal of Aging and Physical Activity*, *13*, 61–74.

Culos-Reed, S. N., Gyurcsik, N. C., & Brawley, L. R. (2001). Using theories of motivated behaviour to understand physical activity: Perspectives on their influences. In R. N. Singer, H. A. Hausenblas, & C. M. Janelle (Eds.), *Handbook of sport psychology*(2nd ed., pp. 695–717). New York: John Wiley & Sons.

Dawson, K. A., Tracey, J., & Berry, T. (2008). Evaluation of work place group and internet based physical activity interventions on psychological variables associated with exercise behaviour change. *Journal of Sports Science and Medicine*, *7*,537–543.

Dishman, R. K. (1988). *Exercise adherence: Its impact on public health*. Champaign, IL: Human Kinetics.

Eakin, E. G., Lawler, S. P., Vandelanotte, C., & Owens, N. (2007). Telephone interventions for physical activity and dietary behaviour change. *American Journal of Preventive Health*, *32*, 419–434.

Eng, T. R. (2001). The eHealth landscape: A terrain map of emerging information and communication technologies in health and health care. Princeton, NJ: Robert Wood Johnson Foundation.

Fitness Ontario. (1983). *Physical activity patterns in Ontario-II*. Toronto, ON: Ministry of Tourism and Recreation.

Glasgow, R. E., Davidson, K. W., Dobkin, P. L., Ockene, J., & Spring, B. (2006). Practical behavioural trials to advance evidence-based behavioural medicine. *Annals of Behavioral Medicine*, *31*, 5–13.

Gollwitzer, P. M. (1999). Implementation intentions: Strong effects of simple plans. *American Psychologist, 54*, 493–503.

Goodrick, G. K., Hartung, G. H., Warren, D. R., & Hoepfel, J. A. (1984). Helping adults to stay physically fit: Preventing relapse following aerobic exercise training. *Journal of Physical Education, Recreation, and Dance, 55*, 48–49.

Haber, D., & Looney, C. (2000). Health contract calendars: A tool for health professionals with older adults. *Gerontologist, 40*, 235–239.

Heinzelmann, F., & Bagley, R. W. (1970). Response to physical activity programs and their effects on health behaviour. *Public Health Reports, 85*, 905–911.

Humpel, N., Owen, N., & Leslie, E. (2002). Environmental factors associated with adults' participation in physical activity. *American Journal of Preventive Medicine, 2*, 188–199.

Katzmarzyk, P. T., Gledhill, N., & Shepard, R. J. (2000). The economic burden of physical inactivity in Canada. *Canadian Medical Association Journal, 163*, 1435–1440.

King, A.C. (2001). Interventions to promote physical activity by older adults. *Journal of Gerontology: Biological Sciences and Medical Sciences, 56A (Special Issue II)*, 36–46.

King, A. C., Ahn, D. K., Oliveria, B. M., Atienza, A. A., Castro, C. M., & Gardner, C. D. (2008). Promoting physical activity through hand-held computer technology. *American Journal of Preventive Medicine, 34*, 138–142.

King, A. C., Friedman, R., Marcus, B., Castro, C., Napolitano, M., Ahn, D., & Baker, L. (2007). Ongoing physical activity advice by humans versus computers: The Community Health Advice by Telephone (CHAT) trial. *Health Psychology*, 26, 718–727.

Klesges, L. M., Dzewaltowski, D. A., & Christensen, A. J. (2006). Are we creating relevant behavioural medicine research? Show me the evidence! *Annals of Behavioral Medicine, 31*, 3–4.

Latimer, A. E., Martin Ginis, K. A., & Arbour, K. P. (2006). The efficacy of an implementation intervention for promoting physical activity among individuals with spinal cord injury: A randomized controlled trial. *Rehabilitation Psychology, 51*, 273–280.

Lombard, D. N., Lombard, T. N., & Winett, R. A. (1995). Walking to meet health guidelines: The effect of prompting frequency and prompt structure. *Health Psychology, 14*,164–170.

Lox, C. L., Martin Ginis, K. A., & Petruzello, S. J. (2006). *The psychology of exercise: Integrating theory and practice* (2nd ed.). Scottsdale, AZ: Holcomb Hathaway Publishers.

Marcus, B. H., Nigg, C. R., Riebe, D., & Forsyth, L. D. (2000). Interactive communication strategies: Implications for population-based physical activity promotion. *American Journal of Preventive Medicine, 19*, 121–126.

Marcus, B. H., Owen, N., Forsyth, L. H., Cavill, N. A., & Fridinger, F. (1998). Physical activity interventions using mass media, print media, and information technology. *American Journal of Preventive Medicine, 15*,362–368.

Marcus, B. H., Rossi, J. S., Selby, V. C., Niaura, R. S., & Rossi, J. S. (1992). The stages and processes of exercise adoption and maintenance in a worksite sample. *Health Psychology, 11*, 286–395.

Martin Ginis, K. A., & Hicks, A. L. (2007). Considerations for the development of a physical activity guide for Canadians with physical disabilities. *Applied Physiology, Nutrition and Metabolism, 32*, S135–S147.

McAuley, E., & Blissmer, B. (2002). Self-efficacy and attributional processes in physical activity. In T. Horn (Ed.), *Advances in sport psychology* (2nd ed., pp. 185–205). Champaign, IL: Human Kinetics Publishers.

Prochaska, J. O., & DiClemente, C. C. (1983). Stages and process of self-change in smoking: Towards an integrative model of change. *Journal of Consulting and Clinical Psychology, 51*, 390–395.

Prochaska, J. O., DiClemente, C. C., & Norcross, J. C. (1992). In search of how people change: Applications to addictive behaviours. *American Psychologist, 47*, 1102–1114.

Rejeski, W. J., & Brawley, L. R. (2006). Functional health: Innovations in research on physical activity with older adults. *Medicine & Science in Sports & Exercise, 38*, 93–100.

Sage, M. D., & Almeida, Q. J. (2009). Symptom and gait changes after sensory attention focused exercise vs aerobic training in Parkinson's. *Movement Disorders*, *24*, 1132–1138.

Sallis, J. F., & Owen, N. (1999). *Physical activity and behavioural medicine*. Thousand Oaks, CA: Sage Publications.

Sallis, J. F., & Owen, N. (2002). Ecological models of health behavior. In K. Glanz, F. M. Lewis, & B. K. Rimer (Eds.), *Health behavior and health education: Theory, research and practice*(3rd ed., pp. 462–484). San Francisco: Jossey-Bass.

Statistics Canada. (2006). *Deaths*. Catalogue No. 84F0211X. Ottawa, ON: Ministry of Industry. Retrieved July 28, 2008, from http://www.statcan.ca/Daily/English/061220/d061220b.htm

Symons Downs, D., & Hausenblas, H. A. (2005). The theories of reasoned action and planned behaviour applied to exercise: A meta-analytic update. *Journal of Physical Activity and Health*, *2*, 76–97.

Tracey, J., Dawson, K., & Berry, T. (2009). Participant experiences in a group or internet-based physical activity intervention. *Malaysian Journal of Sport Science and Recreation*, *4*, 11–30.

Trost, S. G., Owen, N., Bauman, A. E., Sallis, J. F., & Brown, W. (2002). Correlates of adults' participation in physical activity: Review and update. *Medicine and Science in Sports and Exercise*, *34*, 1996–2001.

Vandelanotte, C., Spathonis, K. M., Eakin, E. G., & Owen, N. (2007). Website-delivered physical activity interventions: A review of the literature. *American Journal of Preventive Medicine*, *33*, 54–64.

Verthoef, M., Love, E., & Rose, M. (1992). Women's social roles and their exercise participation. *Women's Health*, *19*, 15–29.

Wilcox, S., Tudor-Locke, C.E., & Ainsworth, B.E. (2002). Physical activity patterns, assessment, and motivation in older adults. In R.J. Shephard (Ed.), *Gender, Physical Activity, and Aging*. (pp. 13–39). Boca Raton, FL: CRC Press.

Willis, J. D., & Campbell, L. F. (1992). *Exercise psychology*. Champaign, IL: Human Kinetics.

Young, R. J., & Ismail, A. H. (1977). Comparison of selected personality variables in regular and nonregular adult male exercisers. *Research Quarterly*, *48*, 617–622.

Chapter 14

Sport Psychology Interventions

Krista Munroe-Chandler
Craig Hall

Chapter Objectives

After reading this chapter, you should be able to do the following:

1. Define and describe each of the five psychological skills most often used in a psychological skills training program.
2. Explain why these psychological skills work.
3. Describe the measurement and implementation of the skills.
4. Describe the components of a psychological skills training program.

Christopher is a 15-year-old high-school volleyball player. He is consistent with his serve and has been working for the past season on his spike. He and his coach, John, have decided that for him to become a starter he needs to work not only on his physical skills but also on his mental skills. Christopher does not have a specific problem (e.g., extreme nervousness before competition); however, both he and John recognize the importance of enhancing mental skills. To help him improve his mental skills, they have asked for the help of an applied sport psychology consultant. The consultant meets with them, and together they develop a psychological skills training program.

After meeting with Christopher and John, the applied sport psychology consultant first conducted performance profiling. Based on the results, the consultant determined that Christopher needed to get psyched up for practices because he tended to be sluggish when he first stepped onto the court. He also needed to improve his focus during practice since he was spending time watching other players rather than focusing on what he needed to do. Finally, he needed to enhance his confidence at the net.

To accomplish these objectives, Christopher began to do exercises and listen to upbeat music just before a practice. He developed and followed a practice plan that outlined in detail what he had to accomplish during a practice. In addition, he started to regularly do imagery and developed and used a set of confidence-building self-statements at the net. This initial intervention proved very effective, and Christopher continues to work with the applied sport psychology consultant on improving the mental side of his game.

Athletes approach applied sport psychology consultants for two general reasons: (1) to seek help with specific problems, such as performance anxiety and lack of self-confidence, and (2) to work to improve the mental side of sport, such as imagery and attention control. In the above scenario, Christopher decided to work with a sport psychology consultant for the second reason. Rather than dealing with a specific problem, the consultant was faced with generating a psychological skills training program for Christopher. The challenge for the consultant was to determine what techniques should be incorporated into the psychological skills training program (or intervention) and what emphasis should be placed on each. In this chapter we will address these and other issues.

Common Myths about Sport Psychology Interventions

MYTH: Psychological skills training is a Band-Aid solution.

MYTH: Only elite athletes can benefit from psychological skills training.

MYTH: Athletes need a sport psychology consultant only when they are performing poorly.

INTRODUCTION

For decades, sport psychology consultants have been studying and developing psychological skills interventions to help athletes enhance their performance and psychological well-being. A **psychological skills training program**, or intervention, entails the structured and consistent practice of psychological skills and generally has three distinct phases: education, acquisition, and practice. In the education phase, athletes recognize the importance of mental skills in sport and how the skills affect performance. There are various approaches to accomplishing this; however, one of the simplest ways is to ask athletes about the importance of mental skills in sport. Although most athletes realize the importance of the mental side of sport, very few actually spend time developing these skills in comparison with the time spent on physical skills.

Athletes often have some understanding of a psychological skill, but they do not fully comprehend its complexity and its optimal use. Therefore, in the acquisition phase, the focus is placed on helping athletes acquire the various psychological skills and learn how to most effectively employ them. In the practice phase, the goals are to have the athletes automate the various psychological skills through overlearning and to implement these skills in practice and competition.

The psychological skills that have been researched most extensively and incorporated into psychological skills training programs are the following: goal setting, imagery, self-talk, arousal regulation, and attention control. Each of these five skills will be discussed in turn. We will define each skill and discuss why it works, how it can be measured, and how it can be integrated into a psychological skills training program. Measurement tools are discussed in some detail since without proper assessment there cannot be a successful psychological skills training program.

Athletes approach an applied sport psychologist to seek help with specific problems and to work to improve the mental side of sport.

Photograph © Joe Patronite/Image Bank/Getty Images.

GOAL SETTING

Goal setting is the most commonly used performance enhancement strategy in sport psychology. Leading sport psychology consultants working with Olympic athletes have reported that goal setting is the psychological intervention most often used (Gould, Tammen, Murphy, & May, 1989); however, most athletes rate their goals as being only moderately effective in enhancing sport performance (Burton, Naylor, & Holliday, 2001).

Types of Goals

A **goal** is a target or objective that people strive to attain. There are three types of goals that athletes can set. **Performance goals** focus on improving and attaining personal performance standards, such as learning an out-turn draw in curling or giving 100% effort at all times during a lacrosse match. **Process goals** focus on specific behaviours that an athlete must engage in throughout a performance, such as snapping the wrist when stroking a squash ball or pulling the arms in tight while executing a spin in figure skating. In contrast to the first two types of goals, **outcome goals** focus on social comparison and competitive results, such as winning a race or outscoring an opponent. Thus, outcome goals are dependent on the ability and performance of one's opponents. **Goal setting**, therefore, is the practice of establishing desirable objectives for one's actions. Research suggests incorporating all three types of goals when developing a goal-setting program (Filby, Maynard, & Graydon, 1999).

There are three types of goals that athletes can set: performance (to give 100% effort), process (to make an accurate pass to the winger), and outcome (to score a goal).

Photograph © Michael Kevin Daly/Corbis.

Effectiveness of Goal Setting

Research suggests that goal setting works in various ways. According to Locke and Latham (1985), goals direct attention, mobilize effort, foster persistence, and promote the development of new learning strategies. In addition, goals may influence athletes' performance by enhancing their self-confidence and their sense of satisfaction (Moran, 2004). Research has consistently demonstrated the positive effects of goal setting. Burton et al. (2001) noted that 78% of sport and exercise studies have shown moderate to strong effects on behaviour. For example, Wanlin, Hrycaiko, Martin, and Mahon (1997) conducted a multiple baseline design in which youth speed skaters received training in goal setting. Over the course of the intervention, the skaters made improvements in their skating as a result of their goal setting. Senécal, Loughead, and Bloom (2008) examined the effects of a season-long team goal-setting intervention on cohesion. Eight teams were randomly assigned to the team goal-setting group or control group. The team goal-setting group held higher perceptions of cohesion than the control group, indicating that team goal setting was an effective team-building tool for enhancing levels of cohesion.

Most athletes rate goals as being only moderately effective (Burton et al., 2001) even though goal setting is one of the most extensively employed interventions in sport psychology. This is likely due to the fact that athletes are not certain about how to effectively set goals, and as a result they do not think that goal setting works. Additionally, a number of barriers, such as lack of time and everyday distractions, hinder the practice of goal setting among athletes (Weinberg, 2002). Later in this chapter, we shall examine some ways of setting effective goals.

Assessing Goals

Performance profiling is a flexible assessment tool that allows for the identification of athletes' performance-related strengths and weaknesses. It is often used as a first step in developing an intervention program. In addition to its utility as a general assessment procedure, it can be used as an aid to goal setting (Butler & Hardy, 1992; Jones, 1993). There are five steps in performance profiling:

1. Identify key performance characteristics of an elite athlete in your sport. Think of the best person in your sport and identify the characteristics of that athlete. These can include physical, technical, tactical, and mental characteristics.
2. Identify the ideal rating for each of your characteristics. On a scale from 1 to 10, with 1 being "not at all important" and 10 being "extremely important," indicate your ideal scores. This rating is also your target.
3. Rate your current ability for each characteristic on a scale of 1 to 10, with 1 being "not at all like me" and 10 being "completely like me." Be as honest as possible.
4. Find your discrepancy score by subtracting your current rating from your ideal rating. The higher the discrepancy score, the weaker you perceive your ability for that characteristic.
5. Prioritize your targets. After identifying your performance weaknesses (highest discrepancy scores), pick out the two or three that are most in need of correction.

Having identified performance characteristics most in need of urgent attention, you can now implement strategies (set goals) to improve these characteristics. Take the example of a field hockey player who, through performance profiling, has identified her penalty stroke as a weakness. Accordingly, she sets two goals: (1) to improve her shot speed by 10%, and (2) to improve the height of her shot by 30 cm over the course of four weeks. How to set effective goals, such as those established by the field hockey player, is discussed next.

Recommendations for Goal Setting

The acronym SMART has been recommended to help athletes remember five important guidelines for effective goal setting (Weinberg & Gould, 2003). Goals should be specific, measurable, adjustable, realistic, and timely (see Table 14.1).

There are other important goal-setting guidelines that athletes should follow (see Table 14.2). First, athletes should set goals for both practice and competition. Often athletes

Table 14.1 Goal Setting Using SMART Guidelines

Specific	*Is the goal specific?*	Yes ☐ No ☐
	Set a goal that is specific (e.g., "increase speed by 10%") rather than vague (e.g., "to improve").	
Measurable	*Is the goal measurable?*	Yes ☐ No ☐
	Be sure you can measure the goal in order to assess progress.	
Adjustable	*Is the goal adjustable?*	Yes ☐ No ☐
	Don't be afraid to adjust the goals if necessary (e.g., due to less playing time or an injury).	
Realistic	*Is the goal realistic?*	Yes ☐ No ☐
	Goals should be moderately difficult. If goals are too easy, they are of little value. If they are too difficult, they may lead to a decrease in confidence.	
Timely	*Is the goal timely?*	Yes ☐ No ☐
	You need to identify a point in time in which the goal is to be achieved, thereby increasing motivation.	

Table 14.2 Goal-setting Guidelines

Goal-setting Guidelines
Set SMART goals.
Set goals for practice and competition.
Make goals public.
State goals positively rather than negatively.
Consider the four types of team goals.
Review goals regularly.

Source: Adapted from Holmes, P. S., & Collins, D. J. (2001). The PETTLER approach to motor imagery: A functional equivalence model for sport psychologists. *Journal of Applied Sport Psychology,* 13, 60 -83. Copyright 2001 by Taylor and Francis, Philadelphia.

focus only on competition goals; however, setting practice goals is important when one considers the time spent in practice compared with the time spent in competition. Second, it is important to write down the goals and make them public. In doing so, it is more likely that athletes will attempt to achieve their goals, given that people around them are aware of their objectives and can be helpful in motivating them to accomplish them. Third, goals should be stated positively rather than negatively: "I want to run the best 100 m time possible" rather than "I don't want to come in last in the 100 m." Fourth, for teams to maximize potential, Dawson, Bray, and Widmeyer (2002) suggested four types of goals to be considered: (1) individual athlete's goals for self, (2) individual athlete's goal for the team, (3) the team's overall goal, and (4) the team's goal for individual members. Finally, the progress toward goal achievement should be reviewed on a regular basis. Conducting this regular review allows the athlete to identify if the goals are appropriate.

An example of an intervention using SMART goals is the Wanlin et al. (1997) study previously mentioned (under "Effectiveness of Goal Setting"). All skaters in this study receiving the goal-setting intervention were first shown a videotape of the instructions to be followed throughout the duration of the study. Athletes were asked to develop a mission, set long-term goals, set subgoals and practice goals, and employ self-talk and visualization to help them achieve the goals. Moreover, athletes were asked to keep a logbook in which their daily practice goals were reported and measured. Athletes were told that the goals must be flexible as well as challenging. The skaters made improvements in their skating performance over the course of the goal-setting intervention.

REFLECTIONS 14.1

Consider a goal that you have set (personal, athletic, or academic). Does it follow the SMART guidelines? If so, congratulations; if not, revise your goal so that it does follow the SMART guidelines. If you are having difficulties, use Table 14.1 as an example. Now, set another goal using the SMART guidelines.

Common Goal-setting Problems

There are some common problems in implementing a goal-setting program (see Table 14.3). One of the most common mistakes made by athletes in implementing a program is setting

Table 14.3 Common Goal-setting Problems

Common Goal-setting Problems
Setting too many goals
Failing to recognize individual differences in goal-setting interest
Underestimating the time required to set goals
Failure to provide follow-up and evaluation

too many goals. Athletes end up setting so many goals that they cannot properly monitor them, and they find the evaluation to be overwhelming and lose interest. Those who are just beginning a goal-setting program should work on achieving a small number of goals. Performance profiling will assist the athlete in determining those few goals in need of immediate attention.

Another common problem occurs when athletes do not willingly participate in the goal-setting program. Some individuals will not be excited about goal setting and may even have a negative attitude toward it. Forcing athletes to set goals is not very effective because individual commitment is required. One solution for recognizing individual differences is to expose all athletes to goal setting and work more with those who show the most interest.

Underestimating the time it takes to implement a goal-setting program is another common problem. Often a coach will implement a program with athletes early in the season. As the season progresses, however, less and less time is spent on goal setting, and toward the end of the season the goal-setting program is completely forgotten. Coaches and athletes need to recognize the time required to undertake a goal-setting program. It is better to devote 15 minutes a week throughout the season to goal setting than to attempt to devote 15 minutes a day and not be able to follow through on it.

Finally, failure to provide follow-up is one of the major problems with goal-setting programs. Evaluation of goals is imperative, and the continued use of performance profiling throughout the season is one effective way to achieve this. Without follow-up and evaluation, goal setting is simply a waste of time and effort.

Conclusions about Goal Setting

It is almost impossible to conceive of a psychological skills training program that does not include goal setting. For athletes to enhance their performance, weaknesses must be identified and corrected. In overcoming weaknesses, it is almost inevitable that goals will be set (see Case Study 14.1). What becomes important is ensuring that athletes set SMART goals that are supported and evaluated. Although goal setting is a complex process that requires hard work and discipline, it can be extremely effective in helping athletes achieve excellence in sport (Burton et al., 2001). Thus, it is highly recommended that athletes of all competitive levels engage in goal setting.

IMAGERY

Canadian golfer Mike Weir stated prior to the 2008 PGA Championship,

> I'm working on visualization [imagery]. It's a drill to help me trust my feel. I remember Nick Price saying that he saw the hole with a third eye once he looked back from the hole and hit his putt. I'm trying to do that (Rubenstein, 2008).

Case Study 14.1

Correcting Weaknesses through Goal Setting

Dr. Carter meets with Janice, a competitive figure skater. In their first session, Dr. Carter has Janice complete a performance profile in order to assess her strengths and weaknesses in skating. From the results, it is evident that Janice currently rates herself a 6/10 on her lutz jump (the lowest characteristic). When Dr. Carter asked her what goals she would like to set with respect to lutz, her answer was to simply improve.

Based on the SMART goal-setting guidelines, Dr. Carter knows this goal is too vague. In order to be more specific, Dr. Carter asks Janice how she can improve her lutz jump. They determine that increasing the amount of practice on that specific jump by 20 minutes a week for the next six weeks will help her increase her landing of the jump by 20%. This goal will be evaluated at week three to determine if Janice is on track and if any adjustments are necessary.

Researchers and athletes alike have long been interested in imagery and its effect on sport performance. Some have gone so far as to hail it as the "central pillar of applied sport psychology" (Perry & Morris, 1995, p. 339). In addition, coaches view imagery as one of the most important psychological skills to teach their athletes (Rodgers, Hall, & Buckolz, 1991).

The Nature of Imagery

In the above quotation, Mike Weir refers to visualization. Visualization suggests that only one sense is being used, that of sight. It has been documented, however, that athletes try to incorporate as many senses as possible, including, sight, sound, smell, touch, and kinesthetic sense. The latter sense is particularly important for athletes since it involves the feel or sensation of bodily movements. The more polysensory the image, the more real it becomes, and the more effective it will be on sport performance. Given the multidimensional nature of imagery, White and Hardy (1998) have defined imagery as follows:

> [It is] an experience that mimics real experience. We can be aware of "seeing" an image, feeling movements as an image, or experiencing an image of smell, tastes, or sounds without actually experiencing the real thing. Sometimes people find that it helps to close their eyes. It differs from dreams in that we are awake and conscious when we form an image (p. 389).

Analytic Model of Imagery

Most of the recent imagery research has stemmed from Paivio's (1985) analytic model, which suggests that imagery has cognitive and motivational functions that operate on either a specific or a general level. Thus, **cognitive general imagery** includes images of strategies, game plans, or routines, for example, imaging a floor routine in gymnastics; **cognitive specific imagery** includes images of specific sport skills, for example, imaging a free throw in basketball. **Motivational general imagery** includes images relating to physiological arousal levels and emotions, for example, imaging feeling calm and relaxed in front of a crowd; **motivational specific imagery** includes images related to an individual's goals, for example, imaging receiving a gold medal. More recently, Hall, Mack, Paivio, and Hausenblas (1998) divided the motivational general function into a **motivational general-arousal** function, encompassing imagery associated with arousal and stress, and a **motivational general-mastery** function, representing imagery associated with being mentally tough, in control, and self-confident (see Table 14.4).

Based on the five functions, Martin, Moritz, and Hall (1999) developed an applied model for depicting how imagery works in sport (see Figure 14.1). Although the model shows that athletes use imagery in three different situations, athletes report using imagery most in competition and, more specifically, just prior to competition (Munroe, Giacobbi, Hall, & Weinberg, 2000). According to the model, the desired sport outcome should be matched to the correct function of imagery. For example, if an athlete wanted to reduce anxiety prior to a competition, the type of imagery used should be motivational general-arousal. Athletes of all ages have been found to use all five functions of imagery; however, they report using motivational general-mastery the most (Munroe, Hall, Simms, & Weinberg, 1998; Munroe-Chandler, Hall, Fishburne, & Strachan, 2007).

When you use imagery, try to make it polysensory: see the ball, feel the ball, smell the fresh-cut grass, hear the crowd cheer, taste the sweat on your lips.

Photograph by Richard Lam, courtesy of University of British Columbia Athletics.

The model also illustrates that the effect of imagery function on outcome is moderated by imagery ability, which includes both visual and kinesthetic imagery. Although minimal research has been conducted on imagery use by injured athletes, Driediger, Hall, and Callow (2006) found that such athletes use imagery for four main reasons: cognition, motivation, healing, and pain management.

There is considerable support for the main proposal of the model that the function of imagery should match the desired outcome. With respect to the cognitive functions of imagery, numerous studies conducted in a wide variety of contexts have shown that the use of cognitive-specific imagery is conducive to enhancing the learning and performance of motor skills (see Driskell, Copper, & Moran, 1994 for a review). Case studies and anecdotal evidence suggest that cognitive general imagery can be beneficial when used for the learning and performance of play strategies. For example, the performance benefits of using cognitive general imagery have been reported for rehearsing football plays (Fenker & Lambiotte, 1987), wrestling strategies (Rushall, 1988), soccer strategies (Munroe-Chandler, Hall, Fishburne, & Shannon, 2005), and entire canoe slalom races (MacIntyre & Moran, 1996).

Table 14.4 The Five Functions of Imagery

Level	Motivational Function	Cognitive Function
General	Mastery	Strategies
	Arousal	
Specific	Goals	Skills

Note: Adapted from Hall, C. R., Mack, D., Paivio, A., & Hausenblas, H. A. (1998). Imagery use by athletes: Development of the Sport Imagery Questionnaire. *International Journal of Sport Psychology, 29*, 73–89. Edizioni Luigi Pozzi; and Paivio, A. (1985). Cognitive and motivational functions of imagery in human performance. *Canadian Journal of Applied Sport Sciences, 10*, 22S–28S. Canadian Association of Sports Sciences.

Figure 14.1 Applied model of imagery use in sport

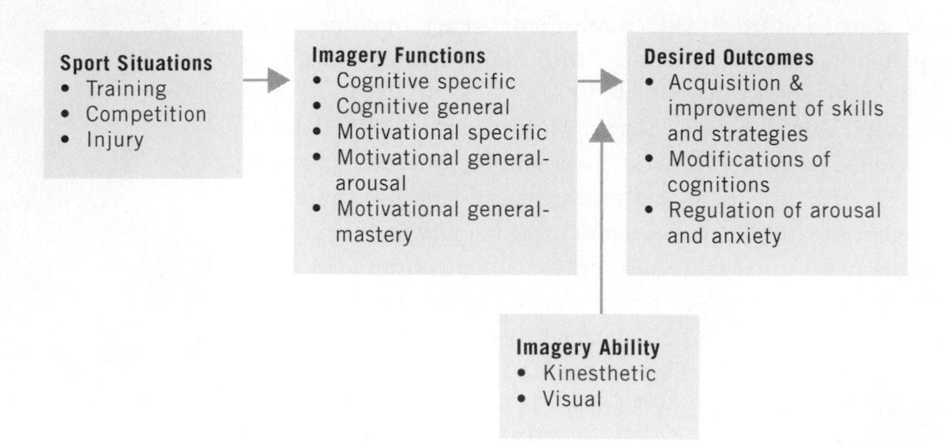

Note: From Martin, K. A., Moritz, S. E., & Hall, C. R. (1999). Imagery use in sport: A literature review and applied model. *The Sport Psychologist, 13,* 248, Figure 1. © 1999 by Human Kinetics Publishers, Inc. Adapted with permission from Human Kinetics (Champaign, IL).

With respect to motivational imagery, Munroe et al. (2000) reported that athletes use motivational-specific imagery to develop goals, and Callow and Hardy (2001) argued that a benefit to using motivational-specific imagery would be an increase in athletes' motivation to attain their goals. In another study, Callow, Hardy, and Hall (2001) investigated the effects of a motivational general-mastery intervention on the sport confidence of three elite badminton players. The researchers employed a single-subject multiple-baseline design. The two-week, six-session intervention was made up of motivational general-mastery imagery, consisting of images associated with control, confidence, and mental toughness in difficult situations. A significant increase in sport confidence was demonstrated for two of the players, and a stabilized confidence level was demonstrated for the third, thus indicating that a motivational general-mastery imagery intervention can improve sport confidence.

Lastly, research examining motivational general-arousal imagery has indicated that it can be used by athletes to regulate arousal and anxiety. More specifically, images of the emotions and arousal associated with competitive performance (e.g., anger, anxiety, excitement, fear, pressure, psyched up) are related to increased levels of state anxiety (Strachan & Munroe-Chandler, 2006; Vadocz, Hall, & Moritz, 1997). In contrast, images of performing in a relaxed and calm state are related to decreased levels of state anxiety (Murphy, Woolfolk, & Budney, 1988; Ryska, 1998).

While most of the motivational imagery research has been conducted with adult athletes, Munroe-Chandler, Hall, and Fishburne (2008) have recently examined the relationship between imagery use and confidence in young athletes. In their study with 122 soccer players aged 11–14 years, they found that motivational general-mastery was a significant predictor of self-confidence and self-efficacy in both recreational and competitive soccer athletes. These findings suggest that if a youth athlete, regardless of competitive level, wants to increase his or her confidence or self-efficacy through the use of imagery, the motivational general-mastery function should be emphasized.

Imagery Assessment Tools

Two types of imagery assessment tools have typically been used in sport psychology. One tool measures imagery ability, and the other assesses the frequency of imagery use. One of the most important factors influencing imagery effectiveness is imagery ability. Some athletes are better imagers than others, even though most athletes report using imagery. In addition, Rodgers et al. (1991) in their intervention study with figure skaters found that the imagery ability of the skaters improved with imagery practice. This suggests that imagery is not only an ability, but also a skill that can be improved through regular practice.

Instruments have been developed to measure imagery ability. The Movement Imagery Questionnaire-Revised (MIQ-R; Hall & Martin, 1997) is an eight-item questionnaire that assesses an individual's visual and kinesthetic imagery ability. Participants are asked to first physically perform four different movements, then visually or kinesthetically image the four movements. Each movement involves an arm, leg, or whole-body movement. Participants then rate how well they felt they were able to visually or kinesthetically image the movement, and imagery scores are calculated separately for both subscales.

A second instrument is the Vividness of Movement Imagery Questionnaire-2 (VMIQ-2; Roberts, Callow, Hardy, Markland, & Bringer, 2008), which assesses the internal visual, external visual, and kinesthetic imagery ability. Briefly, a 12-item scale is used by participants to rate different imagined actions or movements in three ways: by watching someone else do them, by doing it themselves, and by feeling themselves do the movements. Participants then rate the vividness of each image on a 1–5 Likert scale (1 = "perfectly clear and vivid," 5 = "no image at all").

Different tools assess the frequency of imagery use. There are questionnaires that provide information on imagery frequency (and other mental skills); examples are the Test of Psychological Skills (TOPS; Thomas, Murphy, & Hardy, 1999), the Ottawa Mental Skills Assessment Tool (Durand-Bush, Salmela, & Green, 2001), and the Mental Skills Assessment Questionnaire (MSAQ; Patrick & Hrycaicko, 1998). These types of questionnaires provide considerable information about a number of psychological skills, but they do not provide detailed information about any one skill, such as imagery.

In comparison, other instruments have been designed to assess only imagery. The Sport Imagery Questionnaire (SIQ; Hall et al., 1998) is a 30-item, self-report measure that asks athletes to rate how frequently they use the five functions of imagery as described in Table 14.4. See Table 14.5 for a list of sample items from the SIQ. A number of studies have employed the SIQ to examine and provide support for the applied model of imagery proposed by Martin et al. (1999). The Sport Imagery Questionnaire for Children (SIQ-C;

Table 14.5 Sport Imagery Questionnaire Sample Items

I imagine my skills improving. (cognitive specific)
I imagine alternative strategies in case my event/game plan fails. (cognitive general)
I imagine winning a medal. (motivational specific)
I imagine appearing self-confident in front of my opponents. (motivational general-mastery)
I get psyched up when imagining performing. (motivational general-arousal)

Hall, Munroe-Chandler, Fishburne, & Hall, 2009) is a 21-item questionnaire with statements measuring the frequency of imagery use in children 7–14 years of age. Statements are scored from 1 ("not at all") to 5 ("very often"), and participants are asked to circle the number that most applies to that particular statement. Each of the five functions of imagery is assessed throughout the 21 items.

Recommendations for Using Imagery

Holmes and Collins (2001) have provided some guidelines in their PETTLEP model that are useful when conducting imagery interventions (see Table 14.6).

For imagery use to be effective, it must be incorporated into a daily routine. Bull, Albinson, and Shambrook (1996) suggest brief sessions (five minutes) once or twice a day for athletes who are beginning imagery. As athletes become more comfortable with, and better at, using imagery, they should systematically increase the amount of imagery employed. Cumming and Hall (2002) argue that imagery requires deliberate practice and, just as for physical practice, more is better. Because imagery is a skill and improves with practice, athletes will become better imagers over the course of an imagery intervention. The better imagers they become, the more effective their imagery will be.

Table 14.6 The PETTLEP Model of Imagery

P	Physical	The physical nature of the imagery is dependent upon the task. You must determine whether relaxation or increased arousal is helpful prior to imaging.
E	Environment	The image should be as real or as close to the actual environment as possible. If you are unfamiliar with the competition venue, perhaps video footage or pictures will enhance your image.
T	Task	Depending on the task, your imagery perspective may vary. Skills that rely heavily on form have been found to benefit most from an external imagery perspective.
T	Timing	The temporal characteristics or timing of the image should be equal to that of your physical performance (e.g., if a skating routine takes three minutes to physically execute, so too should the imagery).
L	Learning	The content of the image should change based on the learning of the skill. For example, the content of your image when you are first learning a camel spin should be different from when you have mastered the skill.
E	Emotion	Images will be more effective if you attach meaning or emotion to them. If imaging winning a gold medal, feel the excitement and the joy that is part of it.
P	Perspective	Consider both perspectives, internal and external, when imaging.

Note: Adapted from Holmes, P. S., & Collins, D. J. (2001). The PETTLEP approach to motor imagery: A functional equivalence model for sport psychologists. *Journal of Applied Sport Psychology, 13,* 60–83, reprinted by permission of the publisher (Taylor & Francis, http://www.informaworld.com)

Here are other recommendations for using imagery:

- Images should be positive rather than negative (Hall, 2001).
- Athletes should be in a good mood when using imagery (Gregg, Hall, & Hanton, 2007).
- Athletes need to be encouraged to use imagery during those times when imagery use is typically less frequent, such as in the off-season and early competitive season (Munroe et al., 1998).
- Less-skilled athletes need to be encouraged to use imagery (Hall, 2001).
- Athletes of all ages can benefit from imagery interventions (Munroe-Chandler et al., 2007).

Conclusions about Imagery

Imagery is an integral part of many psychological skills training programs because of its wide-range applicability and the fact that imagery can be implemented virtually anywhere and anytime. Coaches, athletes, and sport psychology consultants have all recognized imagery as an effective intervention for influencing a number of factors, as evidenced in Martin et al.'s (1999) applied model. Moreover, every athlete (novice to elite) can benefit from the use of imagery, providing the imagery is built into a daily routine and fits the needs of the athlete.

SELF-TALK

One of the skills most highly promoted by applied sport psychology consultants and frequently included in psychological skills intervention training programs is self-talk (e.g., Bull et al., 1996; Hanton & Jones, 1999). Although many different definitions have been forwarded, Hardy (2006) recently proposed a strong definition of self-talk, following his extensive research on athletes' self-talk at the University of Western Ontario. He argued that **self-talk** should be defined as verbalizations or statements that are addressed to the self, are multidimensional in nature and somewhat dynamic, have interpretive elements associated with the content of the self-statements employed, and serve at least two functions, instructional and motivational.

Functions of Self-talk

Self-talk serves two basic functions in sport: instructional and motivational. **Instructional self-talk** is used by athletes for skill development, skill execution, strategy development, and general performance improvement (Hardy, Gammage, & Hall, 2001). For example, Landin and Hebert (1999) investigated the effectiveness of instructional self-talk by having varsity tennis players use the cue words *split* and *turn* in order to improve their volleying technique at the net. These two cue words were constructed to represent the two phases of the volleying: splitting the legs shoulder-width apart for a balanced position, and then turning the shoulders in order to reduce excessive racquet-head movement. Improvements in the players' volleying performance were observed, indicating that sport performance can be improved by self-talk.

According to Hardy, Gammage, and Hall (2001), athletes employ motivational self-talk for three purposes: (1) for mastery, for example, building self-confidence, staying focused, being mentally ready, coping in difficult circumstances; (2) for arousal, for example, psyching up, relaxing; and (3) for drive, for example, increasing effort, increasing drive, reaching their potential. To date, there has been little research investigating motivational self-talk in sport. An exception is the study by Hamilton, Scott, and MacDougall (2007), who found positive motivational self-talk to have a beneficial impact on endurance performance in a cycle ergometer task. One of the most consistent findings in sport psychology research is the direct relationship between positive thinking and successful performance. Undoubtedly, positive thinking entails considerable positive self-talk. Applied sport psychology books often stress that athletes need to change "I can't" to "I can" and "It's difficult for me" to "It's a challenge for me" if they want to be more successful (see Bull et al., 1996).

Assessment of Self-talk

Various approaches and measures have been employed by researchers to assess athletes' use of self-talk. The Self-Talk Grid (Hardy, Hall, & Alexander, 2001) measures two dimensions of self-talk: valence (positive versus negative) and directional interpretation (motivating versus de-motivating). Athletes simultaneously report on both dimensions by placing a checkmark on a 9 × 3 × 9 grid: they indicate the valence of their self-talk, from "extremely positive" to "extremely negative," as well as how they interpret their self-statements, from "extremely motivating" to "extremely de-motivating." A weakness of the Self-Talk Grid is that it does not provide a detailed account of athletes'

Table 14.7 Example Items of the Self-talk Use Questionnaire

Section on the STUQ	Example
When	How often do you use self-talk in relation to your sport before a practice?
What	In your opinion, generally what percentage of your self-talk is positive in nature? ________% generally what percentage of your self-talk is neutral in nature? ________% generally what percentage of your self-talk is negative in nature? ________% (Percentages given should total to 100%)
Why	How often do you say things to yourself in practice to refine an already learned skill?
How	How often do you combine self-talk with mental imagery when using self-talk to help learn/fine-tune a skill?

self-talk. As noted in Hardy's (2006) definition, self-talk is multidimensional, and the Self-Talk Grid assesses only two of the six dimensions of self-talk, valence and directional interpretation.

A more comprehensive questionnaire for assessing athletes' self-talk was developed by Hardy, Hall, and Hardy (2005). The Self-Talk Use Questionnaire (STUQ) is a 59-item, self-report instrument that assesses the frequency of athletes' use of self-talk. The STUQ has four sections: section 1 examines *when* athletes use self-talk; section 2, *what* athletes say to themselves; section 3, *why* athletes talk to themselves in both practice and competition; and section 4, *how* athletes use self-talk (see Table 14.7). The instrument appears to be both reliable and valid.

REFLECTIONS 14.2

You have just received a poor score on your tumbling routine. What could you say to yourself in order to build confidence and stay positive?

An alternative approach to using questionnaires, developed by Van Raalte, Brewer, Rivera, and Petitpas (1994), is a tennis-specific observational method called Self-Talk and Gestures Rating Scale (STAGRS). Independent judges rate athletes' usage of overt self-talk during a competitive tennis match. The STAGRS measures the use of positive, negative, and instructional self-talk (and gestures). Positive self-talk and gestures are the summed occurrences of complimenting opponents, fist pumps, and positive self-talk. Negative self-talk and gestures are the summed occurrences of ball abuse, frustration, hitting oneself, laughing in frustration, negative self-talk, opponent abuse, and racquet abuse. Finally, instructional self-talk is the summed occurrences of giving instructions to oneself (e.g., "Keep racquet head up") and practice motions without the ball. There are some limitations with the STAGRS. It assesses self-talk only in tennis, and it measures only overt self-talk; however, most of athletes' self-talk is covert.

Recommendations for Using Self-talk

Hardy (2006) identified six self-talk dimensions that should be used as a guide when developing a self-talk intervention for athletes. The first dimension, valence, refers to self-talk being positive or negative. Most of the self-talk research has compared positive versus negative self-talk and has consistently shown that positive self-talk is better. For example, Dagrou, Gauvin, and Halliwell (1992) found that a positive self-talk group significantly outperformed a negative self-talk and control group on a dart-throwing task. It is recommended that interventions focus on the use of positive self-talk.

The second dimension is concerned with how athletes' self-statements are verbalized, whether overtly or covertly. To date, there has been no direct comparison between the effectiveness of overt and covert self-talk in the sport domain. Nevertheless, it is known that both coping statements and goals are more effective if they are publicly known. It is recommended, therefore, that some of the self-talk in an intervention be overt.

Self-talk can facilitate skilled performance.

Photograph by Richard Lam, courtesy of University of British Columbia Athletics.

The third dimension involves the self-determination of the statements used by athletes. Statements can be conceptualized as assigned or freely chosen. Research, such as the tennis study conducted by Landin and Hebert (1999), demonstrates that assigned self-talk can be very effective. However, Hardy (2006) has argued that self-talk freely chosen by the athlete might have a greater motivational influence. Given that there is no research comparing the effectiveness of assigned versus freely chosen self-talk in sport, it is recommended that the coach, the sport psychology practitioner, and the athlete collaborate in the development of the athlete's self-talk statements.

The fourth and fifth dimensions of self-talk are closely related and entail the motivational interpretation of self-talk. The fourth dimension, directional interpretation, is concerned with whether athletes view their self-talk as motivating or de-motivating. The fifth dimension is intensity and is concerned with the extent to which athletes interpret their self-talk to be motivating—not at all or very much so. Different from the directional interpretation dimension, intensity is achieved regardless of whether athletes view self-talk as motivating or de-motivating. For interventions, we recommend that athletes use self-talk that they perceive as very motivating.

The final dimension of self-talk is frequency (i.e., how often athletes employ self-talk). Research has found that successful athletes use more self-talk than unsuccessful athletes. For example, Mahoney and Avener (1977) found that male gymnasts who qualified for the US Olympic team reported a greater use of self-talk in competition and practice than those gymnasts who did not qualify for the Olympics. Based on such findings, it is recommended that athletes be encouraged to use self-talk frequently (see Table 14.8).

Landin (1994) provided some additional guidelines for the use of verbal cues in sport. Verbal cues should be brief, phonetically simple, logically associated with the particular elements of the respective task, and compatible with the rhythm and timing of the task.

Table 14.8 The Six Dimensions of Self-talk

1. Valence—positive or negative
2. Verbalization—overt or covert
3. Self-determination—assigned or freely chosen
4. Directional interpretation—motivating or de-motivating
5. Directional intensity—not at all or very much so
6. Frequency—often or never

Case Study 14.2

Tips for Using Self-talk: An Application

Tom is a varsity basketball player who has doubted his abilities as a starter. His coach is aware of this because some of Tom's negative self-talk has been overt. The coach has suggested that Tom see a sport psychology consultant in the kinesiology department. Dr. Singh meets with Tom and provides him with some tips on how to use self-talk more effectively.

Dr. Singh recommends that his self-talk be brief, positive, motivating, easy to remember, and phonetically simple. Dr. Singh suggests that Tom use his self-talk in both practices and competitions as frequently as possible. Tom takes Dr. Singh's advice and over the next month implements these recommendations. The coach notices a considerable improvement in Tom's play and attitude and congratulates Tom on his improvements.

Conclusions about Self-talk

It is important that athletes practise positive self-talk. We encourage athletes to analyze the content of their self-talk and be on the lookout for negatively framed statements. When negative statements enter the mind, they should be immediately replaced with positive ones. Furthermore, athletes need to ensure that their self-talk incorporates both instructional and motivational statements. Athletes who invest in improving their self-talk will find their efforts well rewarded.

AROUSAL REGULATION

The relationship between arousal and anxiety is complex (see Chapter 5). Given that athletes may require different levels of arousal for peak performance, it is important that athletes learn to identify which mental and emotional states are necessary for success. The following two quotations from Canadian athletes represent the diversity in arousal levels needed for peak performance. Tania Vincent, national level speed skater, said, "I need to be nervous before a race because it gives me that extra boost. I transfer my nervousness to adrenaline and it helps me keep going" (Wilson, 1998, ¶6). Steve Podborski, one of Canada's greatest downhill skiers, stated, "I discovered that after a certain point of nervousness, I would start to deteriorate pretty rapidly. There was a real drop off point in my ability to perform if I got too nervous . . . so it was just being able to find that little narrow comfort zone" (Orlick & Partington, 1986, p. 69).

Once athletes can identify their optimal level of arousal, they can learn to voluntarily program these responses. Because the theories and research pertaining to the arousal–performance relationship are covered elsewhere in the text, this section will focus on techniques to reduce and increase levels of arousal.

Arousal was discussed in more detail in Chapter 5. For the purposes of our discussion, we will adopt the definition proposed by Zaichkowsky and Baltzell (2001). **Arousal** is a multidimensional construct containing physiological, cognitive appraisal, and affective components. Coaches and athletes would concur that performance fluctuations in sport are often the result of being overaroused or underaroused. Given the strong relationship between arousal and performance, it is not surprising that athletes use techniques to regulate their arousal level.

Techniques to Reduce Arousal

Many performance problems arise because of overarousal. In order to avoid any detrimental effects on performance, learning to relax is vital. Below we discuss various techniques that have been shown to effectively reduce arousal level.

Breathing If done properly, breathing is a simple technique used to relax. Diaphragmatic breathing, as opposed to quick shallow breathing, increases the amount of oxygen being delivered through the body and facilitates the removal of waste. When athletes feel overaroused prior to a competition, their breathing rate usually increases and breathing becomes very shallow. By learning to breathe better, athletes can achieve deep relaxation or momentary relaxation.

Breathing Exercise Take a deep breath (dig down into the belly) and imagine your lungs are divided into three levels. Begin by filling the lower level of the lungs with air. You will notice the diaphragm moving down slightly and forcing the abdomen out. Next, fill the middle level of the lungs by expanding the chest cavity and raising the ribcage. Finally, fill the upper level of the lungs. Notice a slight rise in the chest and shoulders. Hold the breath for several seconds; then exhale slowly. Repeat this exercise until you feel comfortable with this breathing technique. To help enhance this technique, you may want to consider rhythmic breathing, in which you inhale for a count of four and exhale for a count of eight (a 1:2 ratio). This helps to slow the breathing and allows you to focus on the exhalation (Williams & Harris, 1998).

Progressive Relaxation Jacobson (1938) first introduced this technique as a means to relax. Progressive relaxation was based on the notion that tension and relaxation are mutually exclusive. This means that one cannot be relaxed and tense at the same time. Although the initial training program devised by Jacobson was lengthy and required a substantial amount of training, abbreviated exercises that are just as effective have evolved (Carlson & Hoyle, 1993). Once the technique has been mastered, athletes can achieve a relaxed state in a matter of minutes, thereby making it useful just prior to competition or during breaks in competition.

Progressive relaxation involves systematically tensing and relaxing specific muscles in a predetermined order: left arm, right arm, left leg, right leg, abdomen, back, chest, shoulders, neck, and face muscles. The tensing (or contraction phase) teaches awareness and sensitivity, while the letting go (or relaxing phase) teaches awareness of the absence of tension. Bernstein and Carlson (1993) propose that once the athlete can achieve the abbreviated version (which normally takes several weeks of practice), an even shorter version can be attained. This includes tensing the entire body, holding for 5–10 seconds, and then releasing the tension to achieve a relaxed state.

Progressive Relaxation In the following abbreviated version of progressive relaxation, tense each group of muscles and hold for 5–10 seconds, and then relax for 30–40 seconds.

1. Make tight fists with both hands, tighten the biceps and the forearms. Hold the tension, and then relax.
2. Tighten the muscles of both thighs; at the same time, curl your toes and tighten the calves. Hold. Relax.

In order to avoid any detrimental effects on performance, learning to relax is vital; proper diaphragmatic breathing is a simple relaxation technique.
Photograph © Tongro Image Stock/Maxx Images.

3. Take a deep breath, hold it, and raise the shoulders while making the stomach hard and tightening the buttocks. Hold. Relax.
4. Tense all the facial muscles while also tensing the neck. Hold. Relax.

Meditation Meditation allows for deep relaxation of the mind, which, in turn, relaxes the body. Meditation has been found to facilitate athletic performance (Schaffer, 1992); however, the positive effects seem most prominent in activities involving gross motor movements, such as running. **Meditation** involves the uncritical focus of attention on a single thought, sound, or object (usually called the mental device). Although meditation is normally associated with Eastern and Western religious practice, Herbert Benson (1975) devised the relaxation response, which is a generalized version of meditation and one that is employed by athletes as a means to relax.

Meditation Exercise Before you begin, find a quiet place where you can get comfortable and where distractions are minimal. Choose a mental device (mantra), such as the word "calm" or "warm." Adopt a passive attitude in which thoughts and images enter the mind but are not attended to. Close your eyes, and relax all your muscles, beginning at your feet and progressing up to your face. Focus on your breathing. With each exhalation, repeat your mantra. Breathe easily and naturally. Continue this for 10–20 minutes. Once finished, remain seated with your eyes closed. After a few minutes, you may open your eyes. Practise the technique once or twice daily. Remember to remain passive by just letting the relaxation happen.

Autogenic Training **Autogenic training** focuses on feelings associated with limbs and muscles of the body. More specifically, the training consists of three components: (1) warmth and heaviness of the limbs, (2) visualizing relaxing scenes at the same time as imagining the first component, and (3) specific relaxing themes in self-statements. Spigolon and Annalisa (1985) provide some anecdotal evidence that autogenic training works to improve athletic performance. Just as progressive relaxation takes time and training to master, so does autogenic training. Several months of regular training are needed to become skilled at this technique.

Table 14.9 Autogenic Training Exercise

Stage	Sensation	Suggestion
1	Heaviness in the extremities	"My right (left) arm is heavy."
2	Warmth in the extremities	"My right (left) arm is very warm."
3	Regulation of cardiac activity	"My heartbeat is regular and strong."
4	Regulation of breathing	"My breathing rate is slow, calm, and relaxed: it breathes me."
5	Abdominal warmth	"My solar plexus is warm." (Place hand on upper abdominal area while saying this phrase.)
6	Cooling of the forehead	"My forehead is cool."

Autogenic Training Exercise Autogenic training consists of six sequential stages. As described in progressive relaxation, allow the feelings to happen without interference. Allow yourself to learn each stage before progressing to the next. Repeat the suggestion in each stage six times followed by the word "quiet" once (see Table 14.9). Once you have learned all the stages, the entire sequence can be practised.

Techniques to Increase Arousal

Although the techniques mentioned thus far have dealt with relaxation, there are times when athletes need to psych themselves up and become energized. While relaxation training is used to lower arousal to optimal levels, psyching up strategies are used to increase arousal levels. When underaroused, athletes cannot perform effectively. Their reactions will be slowed down and their coordination reduced. Many attempts by athletes to energize themselves or their teams have been done at the wrong time, thereby causing overarousal (Cox, 2002). Athletes and coaches must first identify the signs and symptoms of low energy, and then decide which of the following techniques is best suited to their needs. Below we discuss various techniques that have been shown to effectively increase arousal level.

Pep Talks The pep talk is one of the most widely used and recognized energizing strategies. It is important, however, that the pep talk be meaningful and be applied at the correct time. If your player or team is already energized prior to a competition, you may want to think twice before giving the "win one for the gipper" speech.

Bulletin Boards Catchy phrases or quotes displayed in a location that is visually prominent (e.g., locker room door, above athlete's stall) are an easy way to increase arousal (activation). Athletes seeing these on a daily basis will remember them and use them as reinforcement when needed.

Pre-competitive Workouts A pre-competitive workout can enhance activation. It is not uncommon for athletes to feel fatigued on the day of competition. Therefore, a light workout several hours prior to competition can combat this fatigue.

Verbal Cues Using energizing words such as *explode*, *quick*, or *go* can help a player or team to quickly become activated. There are situations where athletes do not have enough time to generate energy with a pre-competitive workout. In instances such as these, energizing words can be employed.

Breathing Although breathing is a technique that can be used to relax, it can also be used as an energizer. By increasing the rhythm of breathing and imagining activation and energy with each inhalation, an athlete can increase arousal.

Imagery Energizing images work in much the same way as energizing verbal cues. Be sure to formulate an image that is personally energizing. For instance, 2004 Olympic gymnastics floor champion Kyle Shewfelt stated, "The night before, I was trying to sleep, but I was going through my routine in my head. I wasn't too nervous, but I was trying to make it perfect . . . . [On competition day], I think I went through it about 5000 more times" (Senior men, 2004, ¶3). As a result, he was full of energy when arriving at the competition venue.

Music Many athletes use music to get psyched up. For many, music is part of their pre-competitive routine to help them achieve their optimal arousal level. Recently, the NBA decided that athletes could no longer wear headphones and listen to music in the warm-up. Vince Carter, formerly of the NBA Toronto Raptors, noted that his pre-competitive routine would suffer as a result of this decision (Carter told, 2004).

Measurement of Arousal Levels

Arousal can be measured in a number of ways, including physiological recordings, self-reports, and behavioural observations. A recent trend has been the construction of multidimensional self-report instruments, such as the Competitive State Anxiety Inventory-2 (CSAI-2; Martens, Burton, Vealey, Bump, & Smith, 1990).

Conclusions about Arousal Levels

Athletes' ability to effectively regulate arousal is one of the most important techniques in ensuring athletic success. Athletes need to know how and when to relax or become energized in both training and competition. Using the techniques and exercises outlined above will aid athletes in achieving optimal arousal levels.

REFLECTIONS 14.3

In previous chapters, we discussed the concepts of stress, anxiety, and coping, whereas this chapter has focused on specific psychological strategies. How would you develop a coping skills program for an athlete who reports experiencing high, debilitating levels of cognitive anxiety during critical parts of a competition? Think carefully about what information you would need and the potential psychological or mental skills a trained and competent helper could teach the athlete.

Research has shown that dual-task performance (e.g., dribbling a basketball while looking to make a pass) gets better with training.

Photograph © Jim Arbogast/Digital Vision/Getty Images.

ATTENTION CONTROL

Attention is fundamental to skilled motor performance (Abernethy, 2001). Players often attribute performing poorly to a loss of concentration or becoming distracted. Even a very temporary loss of focus can mar performance and spell the difference between winning and losing. For example, missing a short, easy putt in golf as a result of simply not exerting enough concentration has cost numerous professionals tournament wins. Given the importance of attention to successful sport performance, it comes as little surprise that many psychological skills training programs include attention control training (e.g., Bull et al., 1996).

Research has shown **attention** as a multidimensional construct having at least two components (Abernethy, 2001). First, it is considered to be a limited resource. This refers to the known limitations people have in performing two or more tasks at the same time. A basketball player, as an example, must dribble the ball and at the same time monitor the position of teammates and opponents. The second component of attention concerns the selective processing of specific information while ignoring other information. Alternatively, it can be considered as focusing on relevant cues while disregarding irrelevant ones. For example, a goalie in hockey must determine from where a shot is being taken while disregarding the jostling players in front of the net.

Research has shown that performing multiple tasks, such as dribbling a basketball while looking to make a pass, gets better with training (Abernethy, 2001). In addition, performers become better with practice at selecting pertinent information or cues (e.g., the goalie determining from where the shot is taken) and are less likely to be distracted by irrelevant ones.

Assessing Attention as a Limited Resource

Probably the most common approach to measuring attention as a limited resource in experimental psychology has been the use of dual-task procedures. These procedures determine the attention demands and characteristics of two different tasks that are performed simultaneously. The **primary task** is the task for which attention demand is assessed. The **secondary task** provides the principal performance measure from which the implications concerning primary task demand are obtained. The following is an example of a dual task. An ice hokey player is required to carry the puck down the ice; this is the primary task. While skating with the puck, the player is required to change direction when a coach blows the whistle, and this reaction-time task (e.g., turn around and go back) would be the secondary task. This signal could be given by the coach at various phases of the puck-handling task, such as at the start, when a defender is encountered, or when the player is carrying the puck with no defenders nearby. Tasks similar to this one have shown that all phases of performing a skill do not require the same amount of attention. This dual-task procedure, unfortunately, has rarely been used to measure attention in sport because of the difficulty in determining an appropriate secondary task, as well as in achieving baseline measures of performance for both the primary and secondary tasks.

An alternative method of assessing attention demands has been to use physiological measures of information processing load. Researchers have used such measures as pupil diameter, cardiac acceleration or deceleration, cardiac variability, and electroencephalogram event–related potentials as indicators of information processing load. For example, researchers have proposed that when a task is performed that requires an external attentional focus, heart rate slows down immediately before the task is executed. This proposal has received some support. Boutcher (2002) found evidence of cardiac deceleration among elite rifle shooters just before they pull the trigger, which suggests they seem to be able to switch on their attention on demand. The limitations of using these physiological measures are that they can be quite costly and are only indirect measures of attention demands (i.e., they may not always be good measures of attentional resource limitations).

Assessing Selective Attention

There are multiple means to assess attention (see Table 14.10). One approach to assessing the selection of relevant information is the use of visual occlusion techniques. **Temporal occlusion** examines the amount of time people take to select the information they need in order to respond. Researchers show people a videotape of a skill. At various points during the action, the videotape is stopped and the observers are required to make a response.

Event occlusion examines which characteristics of the performance people use to make a correct response. In this case, parts of the video are masked so that the observers cannot see selected parts of the action. The logic of this approach is that if people make poorer decisions when they cannot see a specific cue (e.g., the hitting arm of a badminton player making a shot), then that cue is important for successful performance.

Another approach to investigating the selection of relevant information is the use of eye movement recordings. Sophisticated equipment tracks the movement of the eyes and records where they are looking at a particular time. The assumption is that what a person is looking at should provide insight into what information in the environment a person is attending to. The question is, can we relate eye movements to visual attention? The answer seems to be yes, but with considerable caution. Although it is not possible to make an eye movement without a corresponding shift in attention, attention can be moved around the visual field without making eye movements. Therefore, visual fixation (periods when the eye remains relatively stationary) and attention are not one and the same. This means that eye movement recordings may underestimate what people are visually attending to.

A third approach to assessing selective attention is the use of self-report measures. These measures typically address how well people are able to focus their attention. Attentional focus is sometimes considered in terms of width (i.e., a broad or narrow focus) and direction (i.e., an external or internal focus). Taking a doubles tennis player as an example, the player would need a narrow external focus when volleying a ball at the net, but a broad internal focus when analyzing how to move at the net (e.g., to poach or not on a partner's upcoming serve). One of the most common measures of attentional focus is the Test of Attentional and Interpersonal Style (TAIS; Nideffer, 1976), and a number of

Table 14.10 Summary of Selective Attention Assessment Tools
Visual occlusion techniques: temporal and event
Eye movement recordings
Self-report measures
Test of Attentional and Interpersonal Style (TAIS)
Thought Occurrence Questionnaire for Sport (TOQS)

sport-specific versions of this instrument have also been developed (e.g., baseball version [B-TAIS], Albrecht & Feltz, 1987). Research has indicated, however, that the TAIS has some inadequacies and should be employed with caution (Ford & Summers, 1992).

Although researchers have questioned the use of the TAIS, there is a promising new instrument for the assessment of concentration skills. The Thought Occurrence Questionnaire for Sport (TOQS; Hatzigeorgiadis & Biddle, 2000) is a 17-item test that measures the degree to which athletes experience cognitive interference from distracting thoughts during competition. The three subscales measure (1) task-related worries, such as, "During the competition, I had thoughts that other competitors are better than I am"; (2) task-irrelevant thoughts, such as, "During the competition, I had thoughts about what I'm going to do when I go home"; and (3) thoughts of escape, such as, "During the competition, I had thoughts that I cannot stand it anymore."

Attentional focus has also been considered using two other broad categories, namely, association and dissociation. Association is defined as turning focus inward and toward bodily sensation (e.g., breathing, muscle soreness), while dissociation is focusing outward and away from the body (e.g., a favorite song, a relaxing setting). Research has shown that elite marathon runners utilized an associative strategy during races and a dissociative strategy during training runs (Morgan & Pollock, 1977). To explain these findings, Tenenbaum (2001) has put forth an effort-related model in which he contends that during exercise of high intensity and long duration, dissociative strategies are not effective or utilized because attention is compelled to remain internal and narrow. Recent research with rowers supports this model (Tenenbaum & Connolly, 2008). It was found that attention shifted from dissociation to association as workload increased on a rowing ergometer task. From an applied perspective, athletes working at a low or moderate workload can voluntarily shift between associative and dissociative modes and thus can choose the one they find most beneficial.

Using Attention-control Strategies

There are different techniques for controlling attention (see Table 14.11). The most commonly used technique for learning to control attention is **attention simulation training**, in which athletes replicate the kinds of attention-demanding situations they find themselves in during competition. Players should practise simultaneously working on two tasks that typically must be performed together to produce optimal performance. Players should also practise focusing on relevant cues and disregarding irrelevant ones. The practice, however, is only likely to be effective if it is sport specific. In other words, the training situations must allow the performer to practise the specific attention-sharing and cue-selection strategies required in the sport skill. A defender in soccer should practise dribbling the ball while looking to pass to one of the forwards, and a goalkeeper should practise stopping shots with other players in front of the net.

Table 14.11 Summary of Attention-control Strategies
Simulation training
Performance routines
Attentional cues
Imagery

Other attention-control strategies include performance routines, attentional cues, and imagery (Bull et al., 1996). **Performance routines** are a set sequence of thoughts and actions that are done before the performance of key skills. For example, professional golfer Mike Weir has a famous "waggle," which is part of a distinct pre-shot routine. What began as a physical move to counteract his hockey actions, the waggle has become part of his pre-shot routine (Wilson, 2003). It is now identical from one swing to the next. In order for performance routines to be effective in competition, they must be carefully planned and then extensively practised in training.

There are two types of routines used by athletes. Pre-event routines are the fixed thoughts and actions athletes undertake in the time leading up to competition (e.g., night before or morning of competition); pre-performance routines are the fixed thoughts and actions athletes undertake immediately before executing a skill (e.g., bouncing the ball three times before taking a foul shot). These routines work because they encourage athletes to focus on task-relevant information. They also remind athletes to remain in the present rather than dwell on past events or possible future outcomes. Finally, performance routines prevent the athlete from attending too much to skill technique instead of letting skills happen automatically.

Attentional cues are words and actions that direct the athlete's attention. These cues help athletes to focus their concentration on the task at hand and to refocus their concentration if lost. Three types of concentration cues are verbal, visual, and physical. A verbal cue is typically a single word, which is repeated at the appropriate moment. Some examples of verbal cues are *smooth*, *high*, *speed*, *ready*, and *power*. A visual cue entails focusing keenly on something in the athlete's surroundings. For example, looking at the strings of a squash racquet, staring at the logo on the shaft of a field hockey stick, and fixating on the button in curling are all visual cues an athlete may use. A physical cue involves doing an action, such as taking a deep breath, banging the stick on the ice, or slapping the thigh. Some athletes use a single cue while others prefer to use a combination. Just like performance routines, attentional cues need to be practised regularly and employed consistently before implementing them in competition.

Imagery as a means of controlling attention can be used in two ways. It can be used to prepare for various scenarios to ensure athletes will not be distracted by unexpected events. For example, a skater could imagine how to react if the music stops during the middle of her program. Moreover, imagery can be used as a means of "parking" errors in order to prevent dwelling on mistakes. For example, a volleyball player may image placing errors in the garbage can at the side of the court, or a soccer player may image placing errors in the tree at the end of the pitch. Just as with the other techniques discussed above, parking errors requires considerable practice. In doing so, the athlete creates a link between parking the image and focusing attention on relevant performance cues.

Conclusions about Attention Control

It is difficult to conceive of anything more important in sport than paying attention to the task at hand. Attention-control strategies are often perceived as inherent in elite athletes; however, the old adage "practice makes perfect" is apt when it comes to developing effective strategies. An athlete's control over attentional focus is learned through practice just like any other difficult physical skill. Using the techniques discussed above, athletes can improve their attention control and perform successfully during the critical moments in their sport.

CHAPTER SUMMARY

A variety of psychological intervention strategies to enhance sport performance have been discussed in this chapter. These strategies involve the following five key psychological skills. Athletes should set SMART goals that are supported and evaluated. Imagery should be part of every psychological skills training program because of its wide application and the fact that it can be implemented virtually anywhere and anytime. Athletes should analyze the content of their self-talk and modify negatively framed statements. Athletes need to know how and when to relax or become energized during both training and competition. Athletes should improve their attention control so that they can perform successfully during the critical moments in their sport.

The benefits of these strategies have been supported by research as well as by anecdotal reports from athletes, coaches, and applied sport psychologists. It is important to remember that these psychological strategies can be learned, practised, and applied in a variety of settings, such as during training, competition, and injury rehabilitation. These strategies will be beneficial, however, only if athletes are committed to putting the time and effort into mastering them. Consider the results for Christopher, the volleyball player, in the opening vignette.

Common Myths about Sport Psychology Interventions Revisited

MYTH: Psychological skills training is a Band-Aid solution.
Some athletes and coaches believe that the effective use of self-talk or imagery can be learned in one or two sessions to quickly fix a problem such as lack of confidence. Just as physical skills take time and effort to develop, so too do psychological skills. There are no quick fixes to problems, and dedicating time to psychological skills training over an extended period will enhance athletes' performance and help them reach their full potential.

MYTH: Only elite athletes can benefit from psychological skills training.
Successful performance at any level of sport involves technical, tactical, physical, and mental components. Although elite athletes can benefit from highly developed psychological skills, even young athletes will experience the gains garnered from improved psychological skills. Therefore, psychological skills training can be implemented at any stage of an athlete's career, but ideally it should be initiated at the grassroots level in order to ensure the most effective development of the mental side of sport.

MYTH: Athletes need a sport psychologist only when they are performing poorly.
Most successful athletes realize that achieving peak performance requires a detailed plan that includes an understanding of physiology and nutrition, implementation of cutting-edge technology, and employment of psychological skills training. It is harder to fix a problem once it has started than to keep a problem from occurring.

Review Questions

1. What are the five psychological skills discussed in this chapter?
2. Why are the five psychological skills effective?

3. Describe one way to measure each of these five psychological skills.
4. Describe the SMART guidelines for goal setting.
5. What are the guidelines for using imagery?
6. What are the six self-talk dimensions?
7. What are the techniques that effectively reduce arousal level?
8. What are the techniques that effectively increase arousal level?
9. Describe each of the four attentional control strategies and provide an example of each.

Suggested Reading

Abernethy, B. (2001). Attention. In R. N. Singer, H. A. Hausenblas, & C. M. Janelle (Eds.), *Handbook of sport psychology*(2nd ed., pp. 53–85). New York: Wiley.

Burton, D. (1989). Winning isn't everything: Examining the impact of performance goals on collegiate swimmers' cognitions and performance. *The Sport Psychologist*, *3*, 105–132.

Butler, R. J., & Hardy, L. (1992). The performance profile: Theory and application. *The Sport Psychologist*, *6*, 253–264.

Hall, C. R. (2001). Imagery in sport and exercise. In R. N. Singer, H. A. Hausenblas, & C. M. Janelle (Eds.), *Handbook of sport psychology*(2nd ed., pp. 529–549). New York: Wiley.

Williams, H. M., & Harris, D. V. (2006). Relaxation and energizing techniques for regulation of arousal. In J. M. Williams (Ed.), *Applied sport psychology: Personal growth to peak performance*(5th ed., pp. 285–305). Mountain View, CA: Mayfield.

References

Abernethy, B. (2001). Attention. In R. N. Singer, H. A., Hausenblas, & C. M. Janelle (Eds.), *Handbook of sport psychology*(2nd ed., pp. 53–85). New York: Wiley.

Albrecht, R. R., & Feltz, D. L. (1987). Generality and specificity of attention related to competitive anxiety and sport performance. *Journal of Sport Psychology*, *9*, 231–248.

Benson, H. (1975). *The relaxation response*. New York: William Morrow.

Bernstein, D. A., & Carlson, C. R. (1993). Progressive relaxation: Abbreviated methods. In P. M. Lehrer, & R. L. Woolfolk (Eds.), *Principles and practices of stress management*(2nd ed., pp. 58–87). New York: Guilford Press.

Boutcher, S. H. (2002). Attentional processes and sport performance. In T. Horn (Ed.), *Advances in sport psychology*(2nd ed., pp. 441–457). Morgantown, WV: Fitness Information Technology.

Bull, S. J., Albinson, J. G., & Shambrook, J. (1996). *The mental game plan: Getting psyched for sport*. Brighton, UK: Sports Dynamic.

Burton, D., Naylor, S., & Holliday, B. (2001). Goal setting in sport: Investigating the goal effectiveness paradigm. In R. N. Singer, H. A. Hausenblas, & C. M. Janelle (Eds.), *Handbook of sport psychology* (2nd ed., pp. 497–528). New York: Wiley.

Butler, R. J., & Hardy, L. (1992). The performance profile: Theory and application. *The Sport Psychologist*, *6*, 253–264.

Callow, N., & Hardy, L. (2001). Types of imagery associated with sport confidence in netball players of varying skill levels. *Journal of Applied Sport Psychology*, *13*, 1–17.

Callow, N., Hardy, L., & Hall, C. (2001). The effect of a motivational general-mastery imagery intervention on the sport confidence of high-level badminton players. *Research Quarterly for Exercise and Sport*, *72*, 389–400.

Carlson, C. R., & Hoyle, R. H. (1993). Efficacy of abbreviated progressive muscle relaxation training: A quantitative review of behavioral medicine research. *Journal of Consulting and Clinical Psychology*, *61*, 1059–1067.

Carter told to tune out. (2004, November 17). *The Windsor Star*, p. E2.

Cox, R. H. (2002). *Sport psychology: Concepts and applications*(5th ed.). New York: McGraw-Hill.

Cumming, J., & Hall, C. (2002). Deliberate imagery practice: The development of imagery skills in competitive athletes. *Journal of Sport Sciences*, *20*, 137–145.

Dagrou, E., Gauvin, L., & Halliwell, W. (1992). Effets du langage positif, négatif, et neuter sur la performance motrice [Effects of positive, negative, and neutral self-talk on motor performance]. *Canadian Journal of Sports Sciences*, *17*, 145–147.

Dawson, K. A., Bray, S. R., & Widmeyer, W. N. (2002). Goal setting by intercollegiate sport teams and athletes. *Avante*, *8*, 14–23.

Driediger, M., Hall, C., & Callow, N. (2006). Imagery use by injured athletes: A qualitative analysis. *Journal of Sport Sciences*, *24*, 261–271.

Driskell, J. E., Copper, C., & Moran, A. (1994). Does mental practice enhance performance? *Journal of Applied Psychology*, *79*, 481–492.

Durand-Bush, N., Salmela, J. H., & Green, D. I. (2001). The Ottawa Mental Skills Assessment Tool (OMSAT-3). *The Sport Psychologist*, *15*, 1–19.

Fenker, R. M., & Lambiotte, J. G. (1987). A performance enhancement program for a college football team: One incredible season. *The Sport Psychologist*, *1*, 224–236.

Filby, W., Maynard, I., & Graydon, J. (1999). The effect of multiple-goal strategies on performance outcomes in training and competition. *Journal of Applied Sport Psychology*, *11*, 230–246.

Ford, S. K., & Summers, J. J. (1992). The factorial validity of the TAIS attentional style subscales. *Journal of Sport & Exercise Psychology*, *14*, 283–297.

Gould, D., Tammen, V., Murphy, S., & May, J. (1989). An examination of US Olympic sport psychology consultants and the services they provide. *The Sport Psychologist*, *3*, 300–312.

Gregg, M., Hall, C., & Hanton, S. (2007). Perceived effectiveness of mental imagery. *Journal of Sport Behavior*, *30*, 398–414.

Hall, C. R. (2001). Imagery in sport and exercise. In R. N. Singer, H. A. Hausenblas, & C. M. Janelle (Eds.), *Handbook of sport psychology*(2nd ed., pp. 529–549). New York: Wiley.

Hall, C. R., Mack, D., Paivio, A., & Hausenblas, H. A. (1998). Imagery use by athletes: Development of the sport imagery questionnaire. *International Journal of Sport Psychology*, *29*, 73–89.

Hall, C. R., & Martin, K. A. (1997). Measuring movement imagery abilities: A revision of the movement imagery questionnaire. *Journal of Mental Imagery*, *21*, 143–154.

Hall, C. R., Munroe-Chandler, K. J., Fishburne, G., & Hall, N. (2009). The Sport Imagery Questionnaire for Children (SIQ-C). *Measurement in Physical Education and Exercise Science*, *13*, 93–107.

Hamilton, R., Scott, D., & MacDougall, M. P. (2007). Assessing the effectiveness of self-talk interventions on endurance performance. *Journal of Applied Sport Psychology*, *19*, 226–239.

Hanton, S., & Jones, G. (1999). The effects of a multimodal intervention program on performers: II. Training the butterflies to fly in formation. *The Sport Psychologist*, *13*, 22–41.

Hardy, J. (2006). Speaking clearly: A critical review of the self-talk literature. *Psychology of Sport and Exercise*, *7*, 81–97.

Hardy, J., Gammage, K., & Hall, C. R. (2001). A description of athlete self-talk. *The Sport Psychologist*, *15*, 306–318.

Hardy, J., Hall, C. R., & Alexander, M. R. (2001). Exploring self-talk and affective states in sport. *Journal of Sport Sciences*, *19*, 469–475.

Hardy, J., Hall, C. R., & Hardy, L. (2005). Quantifying athlete self-talk. *Journal of Sport Sciences*, *23*, 905–917.

Hatzigeorgiadis, A., & Biddle, S. J. H. (2000). Assessing cognitive interference in sport: Development of the thought occurrence questionnaire for sport. *Anxiety, Stress and Coping*, *13*, 65–86.

Holmes, P. S., & Collins, D. J. (2001). The PETTLEP approach to motor imagery: A functional equivalence model for sport psychologists. *Journal of Applied Sport Psychology*, *13*, 60–83.

Jacobson, E. (1938). *Progressive relaxation*. Chicago, IL: University of Chicago Press.

Jones, G. (1993). The role of performance profiling in cognitive behavioral interventions in sport. *The Sport Psychologist, 7*, 160–172.

Landin, D. (1994). The role of verbal cues in skill learning. *Quest, 46*, 299–313.

Landin, D., & Hebert, E. P. (1999). The influence of self-talk on the performance of skilled female tennis players. *Journal of Applied Sport Psychology, 11*, 263–282.

Locke, E. A., & Latham, G. P. (1985). The application of goal setting to sports. *Journal of Sport Psychology, 7*, 205–222.

MacIntyre, T., & Moran, A. (1996). Imagery use among canoeists: A worldwide survey of novice, intermediate, and elite slalomists. *Journal of Applied Sport Psychology, 8*, S132.

Mahoney, M. J., & Avener, M. (1977). Psychology of the elite athlete: An exploratory study. *Cognitive Therapy and Research, 6*,225–342.

Martens, R., Burton, D., Vealey, R. S., Bump, L. A., & Smith, D. E. (1990). Development and validation of the competitive state anxiety inventory-2. In R. Martens, R. S. Vealey, & D. Burton (Eds.), *Competitive anxiety in sports*(pp. 117–190). Champaign, IL: Human Kinetics

Martin, K. A., Moritz, S. E., & Hall, C. R. (1999). Imagery use in sport: A literature review and applied model. *The Sport Psychologist, 13*, 245–268.

Moran, A. P. (2004). *Sport and exercise psychology*. New York: Taylor & Francis Group.

Morgan, W. P., & Pollock, M. L. (1977). Psychological characterization of the elite distance runner. *Annals of the New York Academy of Sciences, 301*, 382–403.

Munroe, K. J., Giacobbi, P. R., Hall, C., & Weinberg, R. (2000). The four Ws of imagery use: Where, when, why, and what. *The Sport Psychologist, 14*, 119–137.

Munroe-Chandler, K. J., Hall, C., & Fishburne, G. (2008). Playing with confidence: The relationship between imagery use and self-confidence in youth soccer players. *Journal of Sport Sciences, 26*, 1539–1546.

Munroe, K. J., Hall, C. R., Simms, S., & Weinberg, R. (1998). The influence of type of sport and time of season on athletes' use of imagery. *The Sport Psychologist, 12*, 440–449.

Munroe-Chandler, K. J., Hall, C. R., Fishburne, G., & Shannon, V. (2005). Using cognitive general imagery to improve soccer strategies. *European Journal of Sport Sciences, 5*, 41–49.

Munroe-Chandler, K. J., Hall, C., Fishburne, G., & Strachan, L. (2007). Where, when and why athletes use imagery: An examination of developmental differences. *Research Quarterly for Sport and Exercise, 78*, 103–116.

Murphy, S. M., & Woolfolk, R. L. (1987). The effects of cognitive interventions on competitive anxiety and performance on a fine motor skill accuracy task. *International Journal of Sport Psychology, 18*, 152–166.

Murphy, S. M., Woolfolk, R. L., & Budney, A. J. (1988). The effects of emotive imagery on strength performance. *Journal of Sport & Exercise Psychology, 10*, 334–345.

Nideffer, R. M. (1976). The test of attentional and interpersonal style. *Journal of Personality and Social Psychology, 34*, 394–404.

Orlick, T., & Partington, J. (1986). *Psyched: Inner views of winning*. Gloucester, ON: Coaching Association of Canada.

Paivio, A. (1985). Cognitive and motivational functions of imagery in human performance. Canadian *Journal of Applied Sport Science, 10*, 22S–28S.

Patrick, T. D., & Hrycaicko, D. W. (1998). Effects of mental training package on an endurance performance. *The Sport Psychologist, 12*, 283–299.

Perry, C., & Morris, T. (1995). Mental imagery in sport. In T. Morris, & J. Summers (Eds.), *Sport psychology: Theory, applications and issues* (pp. 339–385). Brisbane, Australia: Wiley.

Roberts, R., Callow, N., Hardy, L., Markland, D., & Bringer, J. (2008). Movement imagery ability: Development and assessment of a revised version of the Vividness of Movement Imagery Questionnaire. *Journal of Sport & Exercise Psychology, 30*, 200–221.

Rodgers, W. M., Hall, C. R., & Buckolz, E. (1991). The effect of an imagery training program on imagery ability, imagery use, and figure skating performance. *Journal of Applied Sport Psychology, 3*, 109–125.

Rubenstein, L. (2008, August 6). Weir keeping a third eye on the Wanamaker prize. *The Globe and Mail*. Retrieved October 16, 2008, from www.globesports.com/servlet/story/RTGAM.20080806.wsptrube6/GSStory/GlobeSportsGolf/home

Rushall, B. S. (1988). Covert modeling as a procedure for altering an elite athlete's psychological state. *The Sport Psychologist, 2*, 131–140.

Ryska, T. A. (1998). Cognitive-behavioral strategies and precompetitive anxiety among recreational athletes. *Psychological Record, 48*, 697–708.

Schaffer, W. (1992). *Stress management for wellness* (2nd ed.). New York: Harcourt Brace Jovanovich.

Senécal, J., Loughead, T., & Bloom, G. (2008). A season-long team-building intervention: Examining the effect of team goal setting on cohesion. *Journal of Sport & Exercise Psychology, 30*, 186–199.

Senior men: Kyle Shewfelt. (n.d.). Gymn.ca. Retrieved December 23, 2004, from http://gymn.ca/athletes/interviews/shewfelt_04.shtml

Spigolon, L., & Annalisa, D. (1985). Autogenic training in frogmen. *International Journal of Sport Psychology, 16*, 312–320.

Strachan, L., & Munroe-Chandler, K. J. (2006). Using imagery to predict self confidence and anxiety in young elite athletes. *Journal of Imagery Research in Sport and Physical Activity, 1*, Article 3.

Tenenbaum, G. (2001). A social-cognitive perspective of perceived exertion and exertion tolerance. In R. N. Singer, H. Hausenblas, & C. Janelle (Eds.), *Handbook of sport psychology*(pp. 810–820). New York: Wiley.

Tenenbaum, G., & Connolly, C. T. (2008). Attention allocation under varied workload and effort perception in rowers. *Psychology of Sport and Exercise, 9*, 704–717.

Thomas, P. R., Murphy, S. M., & Hardy, L. (1999). Test of performance strategies: Development and preliminary validation of a comprehensive measure of athletes' psychological skills. *Journal of Sport Sciences, 17*, 697–711.

Vadocz, E. A., Hall, C. R., & Moritz, S. E. (1997). The relationship between competitive anxiety and imagery use. *Journal of Applied Sport Psychology, 9*, 241–253.

Van Raalte, J. L., Brewer, B. W., Rivera, P. M., Petitpas, A. J. (1994). The relationship between observable self-talk and competitive junior tennis players' match performance. *Journal of Sport & Exercise Psychology, 16*, 400–415.

Wanlin, C. M., Hrycaiko, D. W., Martin, G. L., & Mahon, M. (1997). The effects of a goal-setting package on the performance of speed skaters. *Journal of Applied Sport Psychology, 9*, 212–228.

Weinberg, R. S. (2002). Goal setting in sport and exercise: Research to practice. In J. Van Raalte, & B. Brewer (Eds.), *Exploring sport and exercise psychology*(2nd ed., pp. 25–48). New York: American Psychological Association.

Weinberg, R. S., & Gould, D. (2003). *Foundations of sport and exercise psychology* (3rd ed.). Champaign, IL: Human Kinetics.

White, A., & Hardy, L. (1998). An in-depth analysis of the uses of imagery by high level slalom canoeists and artistic gymnasts. *The Sport Psychologist, 12*, 387–403.

Williams, J. M., & Harris, D. V. (1998). Relaxation and energizing techniques for regulation of arousal. In J. M. Williams (Ed.), *Personal growth to peak performance*(3rd ed., pp. 219–236). Mountain View, CA: Mayfield.

Wilson, L. (1998, January 31). Eyes on the prize. *The Calgary Sun*. Retrieved December 20, 2004, from www.canoe.ca/ SlamNaganoShortTrackSkatingArchive/jan31_nstss.html

Wilson, M. (2003). A master champion. *GolfMag*. Retrieved December 23, 2004, from www.thegolfermag.com/the_golfer/archive/style03/story_style03_swingseq.htm

Zaichkowsky, L. D., & Baltzell, A. (2001). Arousal and performance. In R. N. Singer, H. A. Hausenblas, & C. M. Janelle (Eds.), *Handbook of sport psychology*(2nd ed., pp. 319–339). New York: Wiley.

Glossary

Chapter 2: Research Perspectives in Sport and Exercise Psychology

Alternative (research) hypothesis: A researcher's educated guess about what he or she expects to find in the study.

Anonymity: The inability to identify a participant involved in a research project.

Applied research: A category of research that focuses on generating solutions to immediate problems, irrespective of mechanistic minutia.

Authorities: Experts whose opinions are considered the final world in knowledge acquisition.

Basic interpretive qualitative study: A study that looks at perspectives and perceptions through interviews, observation, and document analysis.

Basic research: Category of research that tests the fundamental mechanisms producing conditions or events, without undue concern for practical utility.

Beneficence: The degree to which the proposed research will maximize the potential benefits while minimizing the possible harm to the research participants.

Case study: Intensive description and analyses of a single person, program, event, and so on.

Causal: This implies a relationship between the independent and dependent variables. It refers to agents that, when manipulated, bring about changes in the dependent variable of interest.

Confidentiality: Retention of participant data in confidence, whereby participants are not identifiable to others.

Consequential validity: A source of validity evidence that appraises the actual and potential consequences of test score use.

Content validity: A source of validity evidence that assesses the degree to which test items are relevant to, and fully representative of, the focal variable of interest.

Criterion validity: A source of validity evidence that assesses the degree to which test scores from one instrument (often called the predictor) are associated with scores from another instrument measuring a criterion of interest.

Dependent variable: Variable not under the control of the researcher and expected to change as a result of manipulating the independent variable.

Descriptive research: Method of research used to generate in-depth portrayals of a phenomenon of interest, usually answering questions of how much, when, and where.

Error of measurement: An error that is inadvertently introduced by the act of measuring the variable of interest.

Ethnography: The study of the culture operating within or around a group or team.

Extraneous variable: Any variable other than the independent variable that could influence the dependent variable in a research study; also called a confounding variable.

Grounded theory: A theory derived from participants' data.

Hypothesis: An educated guess regarding the outcome of a research study.

Idiographic: A concept that is used to describe research concerning a special or unique case that does not apply to most individuals on the majority of occasions.

Independent variable: The manipulated variable or cause, under the researcher's control, that explains the study outcomes.

Informed consent: An ethical process informing the research participants what their participation will entail and how their data provided will be treated during the research project and obtaining their consent to participate.

Internal validity threat: Another plausible explanation for the study findings.

Internal validity: The extent to which the results of a study can be attributed to a treatment of intervention rather than to a design flaw.

Interval: A level of measurement that consists of assignment of numbers to variables so that the distances between consecutive numbers are equal; equal differences in magnitude are reflected by equal distances between the numbers.

Intuition: The development of an implicit understanding of the phenomena of interest in the absence of formal training.

Justice: The notion that participants in a study should be the ones who will derive the benefits from the results.

Levels of measurement: Different ways of assigning numbers to variables.

Logic: Knowledge generated through the application of formal rules of reasoning to a problem.

Measurement: The process of assigning numbers to variables according to specific rules.

Narrative analysis: An approach to qualitative inquiry that collects data to present a story told in the first person.

Nominal: The most rudimentary level of measurement in which numbers have no quantitative values and are assigned as labels.

Nomothetic: A research method that concerns attempts to isolate rules or observations that pertain to most cases on most occasions or in most contexts; relates to or involves the search for abstract universal principles.

Non-experimental design: A study that establishes patterns of relationships between the variable(s) of interest in absence of group assignment or variable manipulation.

Null hypothesis: Indicates that there is no relationship between the variables or no difference between groups in a study.

Observed score: Actual numerical value derived from a test that is composed of an individual's true score plus some error of measurement.

Ordinal: A level of measurement that reflects the assignment and categorization of numbers that are ranked in terms of magnitude.

Phenomenology: A philosophical tradition that concerns the structure or essence of an experience for a group or an individual.

Population: The entire group under study.

Predictive research: Method of research used to establish directional relationships between phenomena of interest.

Psychometrics: A field of study concerned with the measurement of psychological variables.

Qualitative inquiry: An approach to knowledge acquisition that is used to understand the phenomenon of interest from the participant's point of view.

Quantitative inquiry: An approach to knowledge acquisition that focuses on quantifying or counting the amount of a particular variable or set of variables.

Quasi-experimental design: A study in which participants are not randomly assigned to different conditions.

Randomized experimental design: A study that randomly assigns participants to different conditions and manipulates the independent variable(s).

Ratio: A level of measurement wherein numbers are assigned in such a way that a true zero exists, representing a complete absence of the variable under study.

Reliability: The consistency or stability of scores derived from a test or measurement procedure applied on one or multiple occasions.

Research design: A plan to follow when executing a study.

Research ethics board (REB): An administrative body that ensures research is conducted in a manner that protects the integrity and safety of participants and researchers.

Sample: A selection of observations from a larger population.

Sampling: The process of selecting observations for the purposes of study.

Science: A dynamic yet imperfect process of knowledge accumulation through the process of research.

Scientific method: A series of steps that are organized sequentially to generate knowledge.

Study population: All of the accessible elements of a population.

Substantive theory: A theory that deals with a particular real-life situation.

Theoretical population: All of the possible elements of a population.

Theory: An interconnected set of concepts that explains how and why phenomena work together.

Tradition: Knowledge that is historically rooted, with no emphasis on current information.

True score: An individual's actual score (ability) on the variable of interest.

Validity: The meaningfulness of the inferences that can be drawn from the numbers once they have been generated; the extent to which test scores serve their intended function.

Variable: Any attribute or characteristic that can change or vary.

Chapter 3: Personality in Sport and Exercise

Adaptive (healthy) perfectionism: A subtype of perfectionism that is characterized by realistic goal setting, judging success through personal improvement and effort (task orientation), self-discipline, and achievement striving.

Agreeableness: One of the Big Five personality factors involving general compliance and positive approach toward others.

Competitiveness: A disposition for motivation toward achievement.

Conscientiousness: One of the Big Five personality factors that involves striving for achievement and self-discipline.

Disposition: A broad, natural or acquired habit or characteristic tendency in a person. In sport research, the term is often applied to constructs that are relatively stable, such as competitiveness, optimism, and motivational orientation.

Ego: The reality principle (of Freud) that mediates the individual's relationship with the environment.

Ethical principles: Guidelines that shape professional judgment and behaviour.

Extroversion: One of the Big Five personality factors involving level of assertiveness and energetic approach to the world.

Humanistic psychology: An approach to studying personality that focuses on personal responsibility, human growth, personal striving, and individual dignity.

Interactionist approach: Situational interplay between person and the environment that determines specific behaviours of the individual.

Id: The instinctual and driving force of personality.

Maladaptive (unhealthy) perfectionism: A subtype of perfectionism that is characterized by excessive, unrealistic standards of performance, high doubt, high self-criticism, fear of failure, and high distress.

Mental toughness: A combination of personal characteristics and psychological skills that allow individuals to cope with stress and anxiety while remaining focused on competition demands.

Meta-analysis: A research technique in which the results of many studies that meet criteria specified by the researcher are combined.

Neuroticism: One of the Big Five personality factors involving feelings of tension and nervousness.

Objective test: A highly standardized instrument that does not require the tester to integrate the meaning of the participant's responses.

Observational learning (modelling): Learning that occurs through observing, retaining, and at times replicating others' behaviours.

Openness to experience: One of the Big Five personality factors involving level of curiosity; the opposite of being closed-minded.

Perfectionism: A relatively stable multidimensional personality construct that involves unrealistic and high standards, inappropriate levels of expectation, and high self-criticism.

Personality: A relatively stable construct of the distinct characteristics that make an individual unique, including patterns of behaviour, thoughts, and feelings.

Projective test: A subjective instrument with open-ended questions.

Psychodynamic approach: An approach to studying personality suggesting that all behaviour is interconnected and driven by unconscious forces.

Risk taking: Narrowing of the margin of safety, both physically and psychologically.

Self-actualization: An individual's attempt to be the best that he or she can be, or a desire to fulfill one's potential.

Self-efficacy: The belief in one's capacities to achieve a goal or outcome.

Social learning theory: A theory suggesting that individuals learn by being reinforced or punished for behaviours, as well as by being exposed to, or observing, the behaviours of others.

State: A momentary feeling or thought that changes depending on the situation and time.

Sensation (stimulus) seeking: A trait defined as the seeking of varied, novel, complex, and intense sensations and experiences, and the willingness to take multiple risks for the sake of such experiences.

Superego: The voice of the conscience and morality.

Trait: A relatively stable characteristic or quality that may represent a portion of one's personality; a quality used to explain an individual's behaviour across time and situation.

Trait anxiety: A general disposition to respond to a variety of situations with feelings of concern or worry along with heightened physiological arousal.

Chapter 4: Motivation and Behavioural Change

Achievement goal orientation: A theory of motivation that focuses on differences in how individuals evaluate competence and define success and failure.

Action: A stage of change in which individuals have begun exercising in the past six months.

Amotivation: The absence of motivation.

Attitude: Positive or negative evaluations of engaging in a behaviour.

Autonomy: The feeling that one has choice and is in control of one's behaviour.

Autonomy support: An interactional style that is associated with the provision of choices and reduction of pressure.

Basic needs theory: Specifies that the fulfillment of psychological needs is associated with motivation and well-being.

Behavioural approach: One approach to understanding motivated behaviour that focuses on conditioning, or learning from the environment.

Behavioural belief: Consideration of the consequences of engaging in a behaviour and an evaluation of these consequences.

Behavioural outcomes: Behaviour is dependent on individual's knowledge and skills.

Causality orientations theory: Specifies how differences in personality characteristics influence the degree to which individuals are self-determined as opposed to controlled.

Cognitive approach: One approach to understanding motivated behaviour that emphasizes the role of thought patterns and cognitive habits.

Cognitive-behavioural approach: One approach to understanding motivated behaviour that outlines the reciprocal influence between cognitions and behaviour.

Cognitive evaluation theory: Specifies how various conditions that shape the development of intrinsic motivation.

Competence: Feeling effective and capable when undertaking challenging tasks.

Contemplation: A stage of change in which individuals are considering exercising in the next six months.

Control belief: Perception of the barriers and facilitators of engaging in a behaviour.

Decisional balance: Advantages and disadvantages of behavioural change.

Effectance motivation: An intrinsic need to deal effectively with the environment.

Ego goal orientation: Performance evaluations are based on comparisons with others as the determinant of competence.

External regulation: Activities are performed to fulfill an external demand, achieve a reward, or avoid punishment.

Goal: A desired outcome that directs behaviour.

Identified regulation: Physical activity participation is linked to important and valued goals.

Integrated regulation: Participating in physical activity because it is consistent with a person's identity.

Intention: A person's readiness to perform a behaviour.

Intrinsic regulation: Activity is engaged in because it is enjoyable, interesting, stimulating, or self-rewarding.

Introjected regulation: Activity is engaged in to avoid negative emotions.

Involvement: An interactional style whereby individuals feel others are invested in their health and well-being.

Involvement alternatives: Alternative activities that are more, or less, desirable in relation to participating in a current sport or exercise program.

Involvement opportunities: Opportunities that arise through sport or exercise participation.

Maintenance: A stage of change in which individuals exercise and have done so for more than six months.

Mastery experience: Past performance success and failure for similar behaviours.

Motivation: The reasons why we do the things we do.

Motivational climate: Athletes' perceptions of achievement goals promoted by significant others (e.g., coaches).

Normative belief: Perception of the values and importance that significant others place on behaviours and consequences.

Observational learning: Learning and acquiring behaviour by watching the actions and outcomes of others' behaviours.

Organismic integration theory: Describes the extent to which behaviour is motivated for different extrinsic reasons that represent varying degrees of internalization.

Outcome expectations: The expected positive and negative consequences associated with a behaviour.

Outcome expectancies: The expectations that a valuable outcome will follow a given behaviour.

Perceived behavioural control: The extent to which behaviour is volitional.

Personal investments: Personal resources devoted to sport or exercise participation.

Physiological and affective states: Physical and emotional cues associated with performance and behaviour.

Pre-contemplation: A stage of change in which individuals do not consider exercising in the next six months.

Preparation: A stage of change in which individuals have made small changes toward becoming more physically active.

Process of change: A strategy that individuals use to progress through the stages of change.

Relatedness: Feeling meaningful connections with others in environments such as exercise.

Self-determination theory: A global theory of human motivation and development that concerns the extent to which behaviours are undertaken volitionally as opposed to being controlled by some external agent.

Self-efficacy: Belief in one's capabilities to organize and execute the course of action required to produce specific outcomes.

Self-regulation: Self-directing behaviour by initiating, monitoring, and evaluating behaviour in a way that is consistent with accomplishing goals.

Social cognitive theory: A theory in which personal, behavioural, and environmental factors affect and determine behaviour.

Social constraints: The pressures and expectations from others or norms that make one feel obligated to participate.

Social persuasion: Verbal and non-verbal feedback from significant, knowledgeable others.

Sport commitment: The psychological state representing the desire or resolve to continue sport participation.

Sport enjoyment: The positive feelings related to the sport experience.

Structure: An interactional style associated with the provision of feedback and the clarification of expectations.

Subjective norm: Perceived social pressure to perform a behaviour that comes from personal and/or environmental sources.

Task goal orientation: Focuses on past performance or knowledge as the origin of perceptions of competence.

Theory of planned behaviour: A theory in which personal and social factors influence intention to engage in a behaviour.

Vicarious experience: Modelled behaviours associated with the development of and change in self-efficacy.

Chapter 5: Anxiety in Sport and Exercise

Anxiety: A negative emotional state caused by worry and apprehension that has two components—cognitive anxiety and somatic anxiety.

Arousal: Physiological and psychological activation that varies in intensity on a continuum ranging from deep sleep to peak activation or frenzy.

Attentional focus and selectivity hypothesis: The idea that an elevation in competitive state anxiety reduces the ability to attend to and process information.

Choking: Performing poorly under pressure.

Cognitive anxiety: The mental component of anxiety that reflects the athlete's concerns or worries and the reduced ability to focus or concentrate.

Competitive anxiety: Anxiety that is experienced in relation to sport competition.

Competitive trait anxiety: The specific trait anxiety associated with sport competition. (See trait anxiety.)

Self-handicapping: Using actions or strategies that externalize (excuse) failure and internalize (reasonably accept credit for) success (e.g., displaying diminishing efforts during training, exaggerating the pain associated with an injury, or complaining illegitimately about the unfairness of the referee).

Self-presentation: The process by which individuals attempt to monitor and control the impressions that others hold of them.

Self-presentation beliefs: Thoughts, attitudes, and cognitions related to how an individual is perceived by others; these could be related to motivation to be seen in a particular way, the specific images an individual wants to portray to others, the value placed on those images, and the way in which the individual decides to portray those images.

Self-presentational self-efficacy: The confidence that one can create a specific impression or perform a specific behaviour.

Social anxiety: The type of anxiety that occurs during social situations when individuals experience, or think that they will experience, evaluations from others.

Social physique anxiety: The anxiety resulting from the perceived evaluation of one's physique in social settings.

Somatic anxiety: The physiological and affective elements of anxiety.

State anxiety: The type of anxiety associated with worries and apprehension that change from moment to moment.

Trait anxiety: The stable part of an individual's personality that predisposes the individual to perceive situations as physically or psychologically threatening.

Chapter 6: Stress and Coping in Sport and Exercise

Acute stress: Stress occurring over a short period of time, with a sudden onset.

Avoidance coping: The attempt to get out of a stressful situation.

Bad news coping: Rigid, disorganized, and destructive responses to unmanageable levels of stress.

Challenge: The stress resulting from the interpretation of potential benefits from succeeding in a situation that presents difficult demands.

Chronic stress: Stress that presents over a long period of time.

Cognitive appraisal: Someone's interpretation of a situation.

Competitive stressors: Those stressors experienced prior to, during, or immediately following competition, such as injury, poor officiating, and expectations from others.

COPE training: A coping intervention in which individuals learn coping strategies in a planned sequence while recognizing that different strategies are going to be more or less effective, depending on the specific situation.

Coping: Cognitive and behavioural efforts to manage specific external or internal demands that are appraised as taxing or exceeding the resources of the person.

Coping style: Consistent ways of managing stress over different situations.

Dispositional anger: The tendency to experience anger across a variety of situations.

Dispositional perfectionism: The tendency to pursue perfectionistic standards.

Distress: Bad stress, which debilitates performance and well-being.

Emotion-focused coping: Attempting to change the way a situation is attended to or interpreted.

Eustress: Good stress, which facilitates performance and well-being.

Expected stressor: A stressor that an individual plans or prepares for.

Gender socialization hypothesis: The idea that males and females learn to use different coping strategies to manage the same kinds of situations.

Goodness-of-fit model: The effectiveness of coping depends on two fits: (1) the match between what is actually going on and how someone views it, and (2) the match between the perceived controllability of a situation and the actual control someone has.

Good news coping: Ways of coping that are organized, flexible, and constructive.

Harm/loss: A type of stress arising from an appraisal of a situation in which psychological damage has already been done and the loss is irrevocable.

Induced affect: A procedure in which an individual learns to turn off a high level of stress via the implementation of his or her integrated coping response.

Integrated coping response: A coping intervention that can be used across a wide variety of stressful situations in sport and generally consists of muscular relaxation and self-talk statements.

Macro-analytic: An approach to coping that considers the goals or functions of coping strategies that are used to deal with stress.

Management skills: Routine behaviours that help prevent stress from happening.

Micro-analytic: An approach to coping that involves specific coping strategies, or families of such coping strategies, to deal with stress.

Non-competitive stressors: Stressors that are related to sport but not directly part of an actual competition performance, such as having to deal with the media, travel, rehabilitation, and team meetings.

Optimism: The tendency to believe that good things will happen in the future.

Outcome of coping: The result (good or bad) of coping efforts.

Primary appraisal: An evaluation of what is at stake for an individual in a situation.

Problem-focused coping: Efforts that help to change the actual situation in some way.

Role constraint theory: Differences in stress between men and women are primarily the result of the different roles they play in society rather than any inherent gender differences.

Secondary appraisal: An evaluation of what can be done in a situation, which will depend on available resources, level of perceived control, and expectations regarding what is likely to occur in the future.

Self-presentation: The process by which individuals attempt to control the impressions others form of them.

Stress: An experience that is produced through a person–situation relationship that is perceived as taxing or exceeding the person's resources.

Stress inoculation training: A coping intervention that starts with small manageable doses of stress and gradually progresses to more stress-inducing situations.

Stress management training: A coping intervention in which athletes learn to turn off a high level of stress via the implementation of an integrated coping response.

Stress response: Physiological, cognitive, affective, and behavioural reactions when faced with heavy demands.

Stressors: The external events, forces, or situations that have the potential to be interpreted as stressful.

Threat: The anticipation of harm that might occur or is likely to occur.

Unexpected stressor: A stressor that is not anticipated.

Chapter 7: Group Cohesion in Sport and Exercise

Assembly effect: Variations in group behaviour that are a result of the particular combinations of individuals in the group.

Autocratic style: A decision style that involves independent decision making and stresses personal authority on the part of the leader.

Behaviour: An action relevant to achieving the outcome.

Collective efficacy: A group's shared perception of the group's capabilities to succeed at a given task.

Compliance: Responding positively to the request of others.

Decision style: The degree to which a leader allows participation by subordinates in decision making.

Democratic style: A decision style that allows participation by team members in joint decision making with the leader.

Group dynamics: The study of the nature of groups and their development and of the interrelationships of groups with individuals, other groups, and larger institutions.

Groupthink: A mode of thinking that individuals engage in when the desire of members of a cohesive group for a unanimous decision overrides their motivation to realistically evaluate other possible options.

Hazing: Using harassment, abuse, or humiliation as a way of initiating new members to a group.

Majority rule: A rule of decision making in groups based on the principles of equal participation and equal power for all members.

Mediators: Mechanisms that account for the effect of one variable on another variable.

Meta-analysis: A technique of literature review wherein a number of studies in an area that meet criteria specified by the researcher are quantified to allow the use of statistical techniques as a means of analysis.

Outcome: A result of a behaviour.

Positive feedback: Leader behaviours that reinforce an athlete by recognizing and rewarding strong performance.

Psychological momentum: A perception on the part of team members that the team is progressing toward its goal.

Self-handicapping: Using strategies that protect one's self-esteem by providing excuses for forthcoming events.

Social loafing: The reduction in individual effort when individuals work collectively compared to when they work alone.

Social support: Leader behaviours that are characterized by a concern for the welfare of the individual athletes, the fostering of a positive group atmosphere, and warm relationships with team members.

Team building: Programs promoting an increased sense of unity and cohesiveness within a team.

Training and instruction: Leader behaviours that are geared to improving team members' performance.

Chapter 8: Aggression and Moral Behaviour in Sport

Aggression: Any overt verbal or physical act that is intended to either psychologically or physically injure another living organism.

Antisocial behaviour: A behaviour that is intended to harm or disadvantage another individual or team.

Assertive behaviour: An action that is forceful, vigorous, and legitimate, but the individual performing this behaviour does not intend to harm another living being.

Catharsis: The purging, or cleansing, of aggressive feelings, typically, the venting of aggressive tendencies through socially acceptable means.

Collective efficacy for aggression: A team's perception of its ability to use aggressive behaviour as a tactic or strategy.

Deindividuation: The process occurring when an individual feels less identifiable by others.

False consensus effect: The false belief among individuals instigating aggression about the willingness of other fans to join in acts of aggression.

Hostile (reactive) aggression: Aggressive acts undertaken for the purpose of harming or injuring the victim.

Instrumental aggression: Aggression that serves as the means to a particular goal and causes an injury to the opponent that is impersonal and designed to limit the effectiveness of the opponent.

Moral behaviour: The carrying out of an action that is deemed right or wrong.

Moral development: The process of changing reasoning patterns that are related to an individual's cognitive growth and development and the capacity to reason morally.

Prosocial behaviour: A behaviour that is intended to assist or benefit another individual or team.

Revised frustration-aggression theory: The theory that aggression can have causes other than frustration and that frustration can lead to behaviours other than aggression.

Self-presentation: The way individuals present themselves (i.e., behave, dress) in social situations.

Team norms: Standards or expectations for the behaviour of members of the team.

Violent behaviour: An extreme act of physical aggression that bears no direct relationship to the competitive goals of sport; an incident of uncontrolled aggression outside the rules of sport.

Chapter 9: Youth Involvement and Positive Development in Sport

Companionship: Casual relationships that enable an individual to engage in various forms of social and recreational activities.

Constructive leisure activities: Activities (e.g., sport, music, art) that require sustained effort toward the achievement of a clear goal.

Deliberate play: Sport activities designed to maximize inherent enjoyment and regulated by flexible rules.

Deliberate practice: Sport activities that are highly structured, require effort, generate no immediate rewards, and are motivated by the goal of improving performance rather than by inherent enjoyment.

Developmental assets: Social and psychological "building blocks" for human development.

Early specialization: Limiting participation to one sport that is practised on a year-round basis.

Emotional support: Comforting gestures during times of stress and anxiety.

External assets: Developmental assets in the areas of support, empowerment, boundaries and expectations, and constructive use of time.

Informational support: Provision of advice or guidance in problematic situations.

Initiative: The ability to be motivated from within and to direct attention and effort toward a challenging goal over time.

Internal assets: Developmental assets in the areas of commitment to learning, positive values, social competencies, and positive identity.

Moderately involved parents: Parents characterized by firm parental direction but with enough flexibility so that their children are allowed significant involvement in decision making.

Over-involved parents: Parents who have an excessive amount of involvement in the athletic success of their children.

Relaxed leisure activities: Activities (e.g., watching television, hanging out) that are enjoyable but not demanding in terms of effort.

Tangible support: Concrete assistance given in stressful situations.

Under-involved parents: Parents who show a relative lack of emotional, financial, or functional investment in their children's sport participation.

Chapter 10: Aging and Involvement in Sport and Physical Activity

Compensation theory: A theory of aging based on the notion that age-related losses in one area can be offset by improvements in another area.

Disidentification: Reconceptualizing one's self-image to remove the value associated with a domain, thereby reducing the impact of negative performance.

Dose-response relationship: A change in an organism (e.g., change in fitness) caused by differing levels (i.e., doses) of a stressor (e.g., physical activity).

Implicit priming: A technique used to activate or reinforce a belief without conscious awareness (i.e., subliminal).

Master athletes: Athletes who are 30 years or older competing at the Master level of competition.

Morbidity: The quality or state of being unhealthy.

Mortality: The number of deaths in proportion to a population; death.

Quality of life: A multidimensional construct referring to an overall sense of well-being with a strong relation to a person's health perceptions and ability to function; includes aspects of physical and mental health and functioning, and social support.

Sarcopenia: A loss of skeletal muscle mass and strength, usually related to aging.

Selective maintenance model: A model of aging emphasizing the role of high-quality training and practice in acquiring and maintaining the domain-specific characteristics required for high levels of skill.

Self-efficacy: An individual's belief about his or her capacity to produce a designated level of performance.

Socioeconomic status: The relative position of an individual on a societal hierarchy based on access to, or control over, wealth, prestige, and power.

Stereotype: A popularly held belief about a type of person or group of people that does not take into account individual differences.

Chapter 11: Coaching Psychology

Coaching Association of Canada (CAC): An organization that aims to provide the foundations of skills, knowledge, and attitudes needed to ensure effective coaching leadership for Canadian athletes.

Coaching efficacy: The extent to which coaches believe that they have the capacity to affect the learning and performance of their athletes.

Coaching model: A model that helps explain how and why coaches perform as they do.

Coaching science: Research on the coaching, learning, and instructional processes as directed by coaches.

Coaching vision: Involves both the long-term goal of program growth and development and the short-term goal of what the coach believes each athlete or the entire team can achieve in any given season.

International Council for Coach Education (ICCE): An organization that strives to improve the quality and exposure of coaching at all levels around the world.

Mastery Approach to Coaching (MAC): A program to improve coaching behaviours through structured coach training and education programs; formally known as Coach Effectiveness Training.

Mission statement: A written statement that gives a team direction for the upcoming year.

Multidimensional model of leadership: A linear model comprising antecedents, leader behaviours, and consequences that conceptualizes leadership as an interactional process.

National Coaching Certification Program (NCCP): A knowledge- and course-based program run by the Coaching Association of Canada (CAC) that trains and certifies all coaches in Canada.

National Coaching Institutes (NCIs): Located across Canada, these institutes offer high-performance coaches an opportunity to learn from a variety of experts in different fields and to share experiences with coaches at a similar level of career development.

Transformational leadership: A theory of leadership that has been shown to influence followers' values, needs, awareness, and performance.

Chapter 12: Exercise and Mental Health

Anxiety: In its simplest form, anxiety may be defined as a subjective feeling of apprehension and heightened physiological arousal; it has been viewed as a negative emotional state characterized by nervousness, worry, and apprehension, and is associated with activation or arousal of the body.

Depression: A major depressive episode is categorized by either a depressed mood or a loss of interest or pleasure in all or most activities, and the presence of other symptoms for at least a two-week period.

Distraction hypothesis: A possible explanation for the exercise and mental health relationship that maintains that being distracted from stressful stimuli, or taking time out from daily routine activities, is responsible for the improvements in mental health associated with exercise.

Dose-response gradient: As it pertains to exercise psychology, increasing levels of physical activity should correspond with decreasing levels of negative psychological states and/or increased levels of positive psychological states.

Endorphin: A body chemical (peptide) that mimics the chemical structure of morphine and is particularly important in regulating emotion and perceiving pain.

Endorphin hypothesis: A possible explanation for the exercise and mental health relationship that suggests overall euphoria produced by the endorphins is responsible for reducing levels of anxiety, depression, confusion, and other negative mood states.

Monoamines: The neurotransmitters dopamine, norepinephrine, and serotonin.

Monoamine hypothesis: A possible explanation for the exercise and mental health relationship that suggests the improved affect associated with exercise can be explained by changes in one or more of the brain monoamines.

Mood: A conscious state of mind or predominant emotion; a host of transient, fluctuating affective states that can be positive or negative.

Negative affect: Reflects the person's general level of subjective distress, as witnessed by anger, guilt, fear, tension, sadness, scorn, and distrust.

Positive affect: Reflects the individual's level of pleasurable engagement with the environment and is characterized by mental alertness, enthusiasm, energy, and determination.

Self-concept: The multitude of attributes and roles through which individuals evaluate themselves to establish self-esteem judgments.

Self-efficacy: The strength of belief that one can successfully execute a behaviour.

Self-esteem: The degree to which individuals feel positive about themselves.

State anxiety: The ever-changing mood component of anxiety; it is a "right now" kind of feeling and is very situation specific.

Stress: A stimulus, a response, or an interaction between the person and the environment; it has also been defined as the non-specific response of the body to any demand placed upon it, whether the demand is pleasure or pain.

Thermogenic hypothesis: A possible explanation for the exercise and mental health relationship that suggests exercise releases pyrogens, which elevate the body temperature, causing a relaxation effect.

Trait anxiety: A part of the personality, an acquired disposition that influences behaviour on a long-term basis; trait anxiety predisposes an individual to view a wide range of events as threatening, even if that feeling is not objectively warranted by the circumstances.

Chapter 13: Physical Activity Interventions

Barrier self-efficacy: Confidence in one's ability to overcome barriers that may arise when participating in exercise.

Behaviour monitoring: Keeping track of exercise behaviour by keeping a physical activity diary, chart, or calendar that records physical activity each day or each week and any details related to the physical activity.

Behavioural approaches: Intervention approaches that teach individuals specific management skills necessary for successful maintenance of physical activity.

Delivery approaches: Intervention approaches based on how information is delivered to an individual (e.g., email, telephone, in person).

Determinant: A factor that predicts exercise behaviour.

Determinant research: Examines the factors that affect exercise behaviour.

Exercise self-efficacy: Confidence in one's ability to engage in physical activity.

Goal setting: The practice of identifying what an individual would like to work toward in terms of his or her physical activity participation.

Implementation intention: A mental association between a situational cue and a specific behaviour.

Individual factors: Exercise determinants that reside within the individual (e.g., sex, age).

Intervention: Modification of the specific factors that affect physical activity, based on an understanding of the commonalities among human behaviour and with an appreciation of the differences that exist between individuals.

Intervention research: Manipulates the factors that are known to influence exercise behaviour.

Mass media campaigns: Interventions that attempt to reach large numbers of individuals simultaneously through public forums.

Non-theory-based research: Evaluates interventions that are not based on theoretically proposed relationships.

Outcome research: Evaluates physical activity as an outcome variable; the focus is to develop interventions and test whether or not they positively affect exercise behaviour.

Persuasive communication: A strategy of behavioural change that provides specific belief-targeted messages.

Physical activity contract: A written document specifying the physical activity behaviour to be achieved that is developed by the individual and another person (e.g., physical activity counsellor, physician, personal trainer, significant other), who both sign the document.

Physical activity counsellor: A primary health team member who has skills to assist patients in making sustainable physical activity changes.

Program factors: Exercise determinants that are based on the program context (e.g., location to gym, structured or unstructured activity).

Psychological factors: Exercise determinants that are based on what the individual thinks or traits that he or she may possess (e.g., attitudes, confidence).

Scheduling self-efficacy: Confidence in one's ability to plan and organize exercise in one's life.

Self-efficacy: An individual's belief in his or her ability to produce desired outcomes.

Social factors: Exercise determinants that include aspects within the social setting or human interaction (e.g., social support, individual versus group exercise).

Stage matched: Specific intervention strategies that are sensitive to the specific needs of the individuals within different stages of change according to the transtheoretical model.

Task self-efficacy: Confidence in one's ability to complete the exercise task.

Theory-based research: Evaluates interventions that are based on theoretically proposed relationships among constructs.

Treatment research: Evaluates physical activity as the treatment variable; the focus is to modify an individual's life experience through the use of physical activity.

Chapter 14: Sport Psychology Interventions

Arousal: A multidimensional construct containing physiological, cognitive appraisal, and affective components.

Association: Turning focus inward and toward bodily sensation (e.g., breathing, muscle soreness).

Attention: A multidimensional construct having at least two components (limited resources and selectivity).

Attentional cues: Words and actions that direct an athlete's attention.

Attention simulation training: Training in which athletes replicate the kinds of attention-demanding situations they find themselves in during competition.

Autogenic training: Training that focuses on feelings associated with limbs and muscles of the body.

Cognitive general imagery: Images of strategies, game plans, or routines.

Cognitive specific imagery: Images of specific sport skills.

Dissociation: Focusing outward and away from the body (e.g., a favorite song, a relaxing setting).

Event occlusion: The process of examining which characteristics of a performance individuals use to make a correct response.

Goal: A target or objective that individuals strive to attain.

Goal setting: The practice of establishing desirable objectives for one's actions.

Imagery: An experience that mimics real experience. It differs from dreams in that we are awake and conscious when we form an image.

Instructional self-talk: The overt or covert speech that individuals use for skill development, skill execution, strategy development, and general performance improvement.

Meditation: A relaxation technique that involves the uncritical focus of attention on a single thought, sound, or object, allowing for deep relaxation of the mind, which in turn, relaxes the body.

Motivation specific imagery: Images related to an individual's goals.

Motivational general imagery: Images relating to physiological arousal and emotions.

Motivational general-arousal: Imagery associated with arousal and stress.

Motivational general-mastery: Imagery associated with the notion of being mentally tough, in control, and self-confident.

Motivational self-talk: The overt or covert speech that individuals use for mastery, arousal control, and drive.

Outcome goals: Goals that focus on social comparison and competitive results.

Performance goals: Goals that focus on improvement and attainment of personal performance standards.

Performance profiling: A flexible assessment tool that allows for the identification of an athlete's performance-related strengths and weaknesses.

Performance routine: A set sequence of thoughts and actions that are done before the performance of key skills.

Primary task: Typically the task of main interest; the task for which an assessment of attention demand is sought.

Process goals: Goals that focus on specific behaviours in which athletes must engage throughout a performance.

Progressive relaxation: The systematic tensing and relaxing of specific muscles in a predetermined order (left arm, right arm, left leg, right leg, abdomen, back, chest, shoulders, neck, and face muscles). The tensing teaches awareness and sensitivity while the letting go (or relaxing phase) teaches awareness of the absence of tension.

Psyching-up strategies: Strategies used to increase arousal levels.

Psychological skill training: A program or intervention that entails a structured and consistent practice of psychological skills and generally has three distinct phases (education, acquisition, and practice).

Secondary task: The task that provides the principal performance measure from which the implications concerning primary task demand are obtained.

Self-talk: Verbalizations or statements that are addressed to the self, are multidimensional in nature and somewhat dynamic, have interpretive elements associated with the content of the self-statements employed, and serve at least two functions, instructional and motivational.

Temporal occlusion: The process of examining the amount of time individuals take to select the information they need in order to respond.

Index

A

achievement goal orientation, 96
achievement goal theory, 96
 applications, 98
 motivation in youth sport and, 244
 research, 96
Act Now BC, 340
active lifestyle,
 benefits of, 339–340
 Canadian, 340
ACTIVE2010, 340
Adler, P., 186
age and aging,
 aggression and, 210–212
 barriers to exercise, 263, 263*t*
 benefits of exercise and, 259*t*
 cognitive performance and, 259–260
 enjoyment as factor in exercise, 268
 environment as barrier to exercise, 267–268
 maintenance skills and, 260, 261
 misidentification and, 265
 motor skills and, 260
 myths, 257, 273
 negative stereotypes and, 264–266
 perceived health as factor in exercise, 268
 performance decline and, 262, 262*f*
 performance theory of, 260, 260*f*
 physical activity and, 258, 258*t*
 see also master athletes
 selective maintenance model of, 261
 self-efficacy and, 268–269
 social and cultural barriers to exercise and, 267
 socioeconomic status as barrier to physical activity, 266
 successful, 270
aggression, 58
 age as factor in, 210–392
 annoyances as a factor in, 212
 behaviour modification to prevent, 219
 changing environment to prevent, 219
 collective efficacy for, 214–215
 competition frequency as factor in, 213
 consequences of, 215–216
 definitions of, 202
 education to prevent, 218–219
 fan violence, 216–217
 frustration-aggression theory and, 205
 gender as factor in, 209–210
 group cohesion as factor in, 215
 home advantage as factor in, 213–214
 hostile (reactive), 202
 in media, 219–220
 individual's role in, 214
 injuries as a result of, 215
 instrumental, 202
 moral disengagement and, 207–208
 myths, 198, 220–221
 perceptions of, 203, 204
 physical size as factor in, 212
 point differentials as factor in, 214
 psychodynamics and, 205
 psychological explanations for, 206
 punishment of, 218
 reducing, 217
 retaliation as factor in, 212
 self-presentation as a factor in, 213
 social learning theory and, 206–207
 team norms as factor in, 214
 testosterone and, 206
 theories, 205, 208–209, 209*t*
aggressive behaviours, 202
 definitions of, 202
aggressiveness, 39
agreeableness, 57
Albinson, J., 15, 374
Alderman, Dr. Rikk, 14, 15
Allsworth, J. E., 84
Almeida, Dr. Quincy J., 356
Altchiler, L., 313
Altman, J., 153
Alvolio, B. J., 291
American Academy of Kinesiology and Physical Education, 16
American Coaching Effectiveness Program, 283
American Psychological Association (APA), 4
 Division 47: Exercise and Sport Psychology, 7
 training guidance, 9
American Sport Education Program (ASEP), 283
Ames, C., 98
Amiot, C. E., 154
amotivation, 92
analytic model of imagery, 370
anger-hostility (ANG), 63
Angove, J., 125
annoyances,
 aggression and, 212
Anshel, Mark, 145, 158
Ansorge, C. J., 199
anterior cruciate ligament (ACL), 198
Anti, S., 70
antisocial behaviour, 200
anxiety disorder, 308
anxiety, 32, 37, 113, 312–313
 age as source of, 117
 competitive, 115, 129
 components, 114
 definitions of, 114
 exercise clothing as source of, 123
 exercise leader as source of, 124
 experience as source of, 117
 gender as source of, 118
 influence on behaviours, 125
 mental toughness and, 72
 mirrors as source of, 122
 myths, 113, 132
 other exercisers as source of, 123–124
 performance relationship, 129
 personal sources of, 117
 responses, 116–117
 see also state anxiety
 self-confidence belief as source of, 118–119
 self-presentational belief as source of, 119
 self-regulation strategies for, 120
 skill as source of, 117
 social physique, 115
 social, 115
 state, 116
 temporal patterning as source of, 121–122, 122*f*
 trait, 116, 118, 156
appetite loss, 309
Arbour, K. P., 355
Arms, R. L., 216
Armstrong, Lance, 354
arousal, 32, 37, 114, 379
 measurement, 383
 see also overarousal
 techniques to increase, 382–383
Artest, Ron, 197
Asci, F. H., 323
Asia,
 sport psychology in, 18–19
assembly effect, 168
Association for Applied Sport Psychology (AASP), 7, 16
 Ethical Principles and Standards, 13
 graduate program directory, 9
 standards, 11
Association for the Advancement of Applied Sport Psychology (AAASP), 16
Athletic Insight: The Online Journal of Sport Psychology, 7
Athletic Motivation Inventory (AMI), 63
 validity of, 63
attention simulation training, 386
attention, 384
 assessment as limited resource, 384–385
 assessment of selective, 385–386, 385*t*
 components, 384
 imagery controlling strategy, 387
 primary task, 384
 secondary task, 384
 strategies for controlling, 386–387, 386*t*
attentional cues, 387
attentional focus and selectivity hypothesis, 129
attitude, 86
Augaitis, L., 102
Australia,
 coaching education in, 282
 sport psychology in, 18–19
Australian Applied Sport Psychology Association, 19
Australian Football League, 146
Australian Institute of Sport, 18–19
Australian Psychological Society,
 College of Sport Psychologists, 7
Australian Sports Commission (ASC), 282
authorities, 29–30
autobiography, 47
autoethnography, 47
autogenic training, 381–382, 382*t*
autonomy support, 94
autonomy, 93
Avener, M., 378
avoidance coping, 150

B

Babcock, Mike, 279, 283
baby boomers, 257
bad news coping, 153
Bagley, R. W., 341
Bahrke, M. S., 327

Baker, J., 237, 262, 270
ballistic exercises, 31
Baltzell, A., 379
Banaji, M. R., 265
Bandura, Albert, 60, 186, 205, 206, 207, 208–209, 269
Bane, S. M., 313
Baricacute, R., 67
basic interpretive qualitative studies, 46
basic needs theory (BNT), 92, 94
Bass, B. M., 291
Bauman, Alex, 30, 350
Beal, D. J., 185
Beck, Aaron, 82
Behavior Modification and Coaching: Principles, Procedures, and Research, 15
behaviour monitoring, 351
behavioural approaches, 348
    physical activity, 351
behavioural beliefs, 86
    aging and barrier to physical activity, 267
behavioural outcomes, 89
behaviourism, 59–60
    motivation and, 81–82
behaviours, 57
    interconnected, 58
Bell, Gordon J., 42
Beller, J. M., 199
Benson, Herbert, 381
Benson, P. L., 231, 232, 233
Berglas, S., 184
Berkowitz, L., 168, 205
Bernstein, D. A., 380
Berry, T., 84, 345, 347, 349
Bertuzzi, Todd, 197, 200, 202
Bessette, N., 215
Biddle, S., 47, 96, 97
biography, 47
biological mechanism, 58
bipolar disorder, 308
Blake, Toe, 279, 285
blame attribution, 208
Blanchard, Chris M., 42, 315
Blinde, E. M., 240
Blondin, J. P., 150, 157
Bloom, Gordon A., 43, 176, 210, 284, 285, 291, 298, 299, 366
body mass index (BMI), 118
Botterill, Cal, 15
Bouffard, M., 150–151
Boutcher, S. H., 385
Bowman, Scotty, 279, 285
Bravata, D. M., 351
Brawley, Dr. Larry, 16, 170, 171, 178, 215, 341, 343, 345, 354
Bray, S. R., 212, 214, 368
breathing,
    to increase arousal, 383
    to reduce overarousal, 380
Bredemeier, B. L., 200
Brewer, B. W., 377
Brice, J. G., 212
British Association of Sport and Exercise Sciences (BASES), 18, 19
Brown, Paul, 286
Brown, S., 348
Brunelle, J. P., 219
Bryant, J., 219
Buckworth, J., 152
Bull, S., 15, 374
bulletin boards, 382
Burke, M. J., 185
Burnik, S., 67
burnout, 155
Burton, D., 366
Butt, S., 15

C

Cahoon, M. A., 215
Callow, N., 371, 372
Camacho, T. C., 329
Campbell, E., 146
Canada's Physical Activity Guide to Healthy Active Living, 91
Canada,
    coaching education in, 282
    history of sport psychology in, 14–16, 17
    sport psychology consultants in, 8–9
    trends in sport psychology in, 19, 20, 21, 22
Canadian Community Health Survey (CCHS), 258
Canadian Fitness and Lifestyle Research Institute (CFLRI), 87, 340, 358
Canadian Institutes of Health Research (CIHR), 20
Canadian Interuniversity Sports (CIS), 286
Canadian Psychological Association (CPA), 4
    Canadian Code of Ethics for Psychologists, 12, 13, 13*t*
    standards, 11
Canadian Society for Psychomotor Learning and Sport Psychology/Société Canadienne D'Apprentissage Psychomoteur et de Psychologie du Sport (SCAPPS), 7, 15–16
Canadian Sport for Life (CS4L) programs, 158
Canadian Sport Psychology Association (CSPA), 7
    Code of ethics, 13
    criteria for membership of, 11*t*
    standards, 11
cancer, 340
    physical activity and, 354–355, 354*t*
    prostate, 33
Cannon, J. G., 327
cardiovascular disease, 340
Carlesimo, P. J., 197
Carless, D., 47
Carlson, C. R., 380
Carpenter, B. N., 141
Carpenter, P. J., 101
Carroll, T., 199
Carron, Dr. Albert, 14, 15, 16, 104, 170, 171, 172, 173, 177, 180, 182, 183, 184, 185, 187, 188, 213, 215, 267
Carson, S., 240
Carter, A. D., 284
Carter, Vince, 383
Cartwright, D., 168
case studies, 47
catharsis, 205
Cattell's 16 Personality Factors (16PF) test, 62
Cattell's trait personality model, 57
Cattell, R. B., 57
causal (inference), 33
    conditions for, 33, 34
causality orientation theory (COT), 92, 94
Causgrove Dunn, J. L., 69, 97
Chantal, Y., 297
Charness, N., 260
Chatzisarantis, N. L. D., 344
Chelladurai, P., 175, 289, 290
child constructive leisure activities, 234
child relaxed leisure activities, 234
choking, 130
circuit resistance exercise (CRE), 313
Civil War in America (1760), 280
clinical and counselling psychologists,
    training, 10
clinical psychology, 10
coach effectiveness training (CET), 239, 287
coaches' roles, 239
    children's motor skills, 241
    children's psychological growth, 239
    children's social skills, 239–240
Coaching Association of Canada (CAC), 281
coaching behaviour assessment systems (CBAS), 287
coaching efficacy, 291–292
    dimensions, 291
    models of, 292*f*
coaching model, 293–293*f*
    athlete's personality component, 300
    coach's personality component, 299–300
    competition component, 298–299
    components, 295
    contextual factors, 300–301
coaching science, 280
coaching vision, 295
coaching,
    development, 284–285
    goals, 294–295
    holistic approach to, 294
    mentoring, 285
    myths, 280, 302
    pyramid of success model, 294
    training component, 296–297
    women in, 286
    youth, 286
Coaching: An International Journal of Theory, Research, and Practice, 283
cognition,
    aging and, 259–260
    motivation and, 82
cognitive anxiety, 114
cognitive appraisal, 141
cognitive evaluation theory (CET), 92, 94
cognitive evaluation, 82
cognitive intrusion frequency, 116
cognitive mechanisms,
    competitive anxiety and, 129–130
cognitive-behavioural approach,
    to motivation, 82
    to personality, 60
Cohen, R., 185
Cohen-Mansfield, J., 263
Colavecchio, P. G., 186
collective efficacy, 186
    for aggression, 214–215
Collins, D. J., 374
companionship (by parents), 242
compensation theory of maintenance skills, 260, 260*f*
competence, 93
competition frequency,
    aggression and, 213
Competitive State Anxiety Inventory-2 (CSAI-2), 383
competitive trait anxiety, 118
competitiveness, 67–68
    cultural diversity and, 68
    gender and, 68
compliance, 181
computer technology, 348
    physical activity and, 349

conceptual model of group cohesion, 171–172*f*
confidence, 32, 37
confusion-bewilderment (CON), 63
Connaughton, D., 71
Conroy, D. E., 97
conscientiousness, 57
consultant career, 8–9
roles of, 9
control beliefs, 87
COPE training, 158
coping (with stress), 148
avoidance-oriented, 153
culture and, 156
definitions of, 148–149
distraction-oriented, 154
effectiveness of strategies for, 152–153
emotion-focused, 150
gender and, 155–156
goodness-of-fit model of, 152–153
importance of in sport injuries, 154
individual factors in, 156–157
interventions, 158–159
levels of, 149
macro-analytic approach to, 149–150
micro-analytic approach to, 149, 150
news coping, 153
outcomes, 151–152
problem-focused, 149, 154
research, 153–154
state-like approach, 150–151
styles, 150–151
trait approach, 150
Copper, C., 173, 185
Cornelius, A., 154
Côté, J., 236, 237–238, 239, 241, 245, 293, 295, 299, 300
counselling psychology, 10
Courneya, K. S., 72, 213, 354, 354*t*, 355
Cox, R. H., 219
Craig, C. L., 350
Cramp, A. G., 341, 345
Cress, M. E., 351
Crocker, P. R. E., 15, 31, 94, 102, 104, 139, 149, 150–151, 152
Csikszentmihalyi, Mihaly, 5
Culos-Reed, S. N., 343
cultural diversity,
competitiveness and, 68
coping with stress and, 156
Cumming, J., 98, 374
Cumming, S. P., 288
Cunningham, D. A., 73
cusp catastrophe theory, 127–128, 128*f*
predictions, 128

D

d'Arrippe-Longueville, F., 297
Dagrou, E., 377
Davis, Hap, 63
Dawson, K. A., 345, 347, 349, 368
de Lima, Vanderlei, 197
Deakin, J., 262
Deci, Edward L., 91, 92, 93, 94
decisional balance, 84
Deeter, T. E., 68
deindividuation, 213
deliberate practice (in youth sport), 236
considerations, 236–238, 238*t*
delivery approaches (of interventions), 348
demographics, 84
depression, 308
clinical, 309
exercise and, 309–310
exercise as treatment for, 310–311
depression-dejection (DEP), 63
Desjardins, G. Jr., 295
determinants, 340
developmental assets, 231
external, 231
five C's of positive, 235
internal, 231
positive, 233–234, 233*t*
developmental model of sport participation (DMSP), 245, 246*f*
development stage, 248
elite performance, 248
recreational participation, 245–247
specializing years, 247
diabetes, 339–340
Diagnostic and Statistical Manual of Mental Disorders, 309
Dieffenbach, K., 68
Digman's five factor model, 57
Digman, J. M., 57
directional interpretation of symptoms, 116
Directory of Psychological Tests in the Sport & Exercise Sciences, 63
disabilities, 21
Dishman, R. K., 152
disidentification, 265
disposition, 56
dispositional anger, 157
dispositional perfectionism, 157
distraction hypothesis, 327–328
distress, 142
diversification, 19–20
Doan, Catriona LeMay, 68, 150
Dobreva-Martinova, T., 297
Dollard, J. C., 205
Donohue, Jack, 279
Doob, N., 205
Dorsch, K. D., 212, 215
dose-response gradient, 309
Douglas, K., 47
Driediger, M., 371
Dryden, Ken, 285
Dubois, A., 297
Dugdale, J. R., 145–146
Dunham, J. M., 70
Dunn, Dr. John, 69, 97
Durand-Bush, N., 68, 71, 285, 297
Dzewaltowski, D. A., 68

E

Eakin, E. G., 349, 350
early specialization (in youth sport), 236
considerations, 236–238, 238*t*
skill acquisition and, 237
Ebbeck, V., 200
Eccles, J. S., 242
Edge, K., 153
effectance motivation, 98
efficacy,
coaching, 291–292
ego goal orientation, 96
characteristics, 97*t*
ego motivation, 69
eHealth, 348
Elliot, A. J., 97
Elston, T., 32
emotion,
core themes, 144*t*
stress and, 143
emotional support (by parents), 241
Endler, N. S., 61
endorphin hypothesis, 325
Erickson, K., 284
Ericsson, K. A., 236, 261
Eriksson, Peter, 279
Erlick, D., 168
Estabrooks, P., 15, 172, 267
ethical principles, 65
ethical review requirements, 35*t*
ethics, 12
personality measurement and, 64–65
professional, 13
research issues, 35–36
research, 34–35
testing, 62
vigilance in, 21
ethnography, 47
team cohesion and, 47
Etnier, J. L., 64
Europe,
sport psychology in, 18
European Federation of Sport Psychology/Fédération Européenne de Psychologie des Sports et des Activités Corporelles (FEPSAC), 7, 18, 19
eustress, 142
evaluative concerns perfectionism (ECP), 70
event occlusion, 385
evidence-based knowledge, 30
exercise psychology research, 31
Exercising Your Way to Better Mental Health, 15
expectancy theory, 84
external regulation, 92
extrinsic motivation, 92
extroversion, 57
sport activities and, 73
Eys, M. A., 173

F

Fallon, E. A., 125
false consensus effect, 216
fan violence, 216–217
fatigue (FAT), 63
Faulkner, G., 47
Felicien, Perdita, 127, 146
Feltz, D. L., 168
Fenz, Walter, 117
Festinger, L., 170
Fishburne, G., 372
fitness magazines, 41
Fitzpatrick, D. A., 46
Focht, B., 122, 123
Folkesson, P., 212
Folkman, Susan, 152
Fournier, J. F., 297
Fox, L. D., 124
Fox, Terry, 59
Freud, Sigmund, 58, 205
Friedenreich, C. M., 355
frustration-aggression theory, 205

G

Gainey, Bob, 285
Gallimore, R., 297
Gammage, K., 98, 119, 123, 375
Garber, C. E., 84
García Bengoechea, E., 48
Gaudrea, P., 70, 150, 157
Gauvin, L., 377
gender socialization hypothesis, 156

gender,
aggression and, 209–210
anxiety and, 118
competitiveness and, 68
coping with stress and, 155–156
theory of planned behaviour (TPB) and, 87
geriatrics, 270
German Association for Sport Psychology, 19
gerontology, 270
Gifford, S. M., 146
Gilbert, W. D., 280, 284, 286
Gill, D. L., 4, 68
Glaser, Barney G., 47
Globe and Mail, 56
goal orientation, 201
goal setting, 351, 365
assessment, 366–367
effectiveness, 366
guidelines, 367–368*t*
problems, 368–369, 369*t*
specificity, measurability, adjustability, realism, and timeliness (SMART) principles and, 367, 367*t*, 368, 369, 370
weakness correction using, 370
goals, 88
outcome, 365
performance, 365
process, 365
types of, 365
Godin, G., 87
Golding, J. M., 272
Gollwitzer, 344
Gould, D., 68, 239–240, 313
Gould, Daniel, 143
Graf, Steffi, 197
Graham, T. R., 149
Granito, V. J., 174, 186
Great Britain,
coaching education in, 282–283
sport psychology in, 18
Green, Dennis, 286
Gretzky, Wayne, 291
Griffith, Dr. Coleman, 14
grounded theory, 47
group cohesion,
affective relationships in, 171
aggression and, 215
as mediator, 187
athlete's starting status as correlate for, 186
characteristics of, 170
coach as a correlate of, 175
collective efficacy for, 186
conceptual model of, 171–172*f*, 187–188
correlates of, 172–173
definitions of, 170
factors in, 169, 170
individual adherence to, 181
individual effort, 182
individual sacrifice, 183, 184
instrumental nature of, 171
intention to return, 181–182
leader's behaviour as a correlate of, 175
leader's decision style as correlate of, 175–176
leadership strategies for, 179
measuring, 171
myths, 167, 189–190
psychological momentum as correlate for, 186
see also team building
self-handicapping, 184
setting as a correlate of, 174
size as a correlate of, 173
social loafing, 182–183
team effectiveness and, 168
team success as correlate of, 185
group communication, 168
strategies for improved, 169
Group Dynamics in Sport, 15
group dynamics, 168
Group Environment Questionnaire (GEQ), 16, 171
Group Integration subscale, 43
in sport setting, 172
group leadership,
autocratic, 175
decision style, 175
democratic, 176
positive feedback, 175
social support, 175
training and instruction, 175
groupthink, 169
Guay, F., 297
Guralnik, J. M., 263
Gushue, Brad, 168, 185
Gyurcsik, N. C., 343

H

Hagger, M. S., 344
Hall, C., 98, 371, 372, 374, 375, 377
Halliwell, W., 377
Hamilton, R., 376
Haney, C. J., 120
Hanin, Yuri, 126, 127
Hansen, Rick, 59, 356
Hanton, S., 71
Hardy, J., 372, 375, 377, 378
Hardy, L., 370, 377
Harold, R. D., 242
Harrell, W. A., 212
Harter, Susan, 98, 99, 100
Hartley, Blythe, 66, 114, 116
Harwood, C., 98
Hausenblas, H. A., 15, 102, 123, 125, 173, 184, 343, 358, 371
Hay, J., 241
hazing, 180
health promotion, 29
Healthy U (Alberta), 340
Heart and Stroke Foundation of Canada, 20
Heinzelmann, F., 341
Hellison, D., 239
Hellstedt, J. C., 241
Hellsten, L. A., 72
Henry, Dr. Franklin, 14
Herbert, E. P., 378
Hesser, J., 84
Heymans, Emilie, 66
hierarchy of needs, 59, 59*f*
high-performance sport, 28
Hogg, J. M., 70, 145
Hollweg, Ryan, 57
Holmes, P. S., 348, 374
Holmgren, Mike, 286
Holt, N., 47, 145, 183
Holtman, Mallory, 198
home advantage,
aggression and, 213–214
Horne, J. A., 327
Horton, S., 262
Howard, J. H., 73
Howe, Gordie, 261
Hrycaiko, D., 15, 366
Hughes, Clara, 291
human development,
assets for, 231–233, 232*t*
humanistic psychology, 58–59
Huynh, Carol, 55, 67
hypothesis, 32–33
alternative, 33
example, 33
null, 33

I

iceberg profile, 64, 64*f*
id, 58
identified regulation, 92
ideograph, 32
Iditasport (Alaskan ultra-marathon), 67
imagery, 369–370
applied model for sport use, 371–372, 372*f*
as strategy to control attention, 387
as technique to increase arousal, 383
assessment tools, 373
cognitive general, 370
cognitive specific, 370, 371
functions, 371, 371*t*
motivational general, 370, 372
motivational specific, 370
see also visualization
usage guidelines, 374–375
implementation intentions, 344
implicit priming, 264
in motion (Saskatchewan), 340
In Pursuit of Excellence, 15
individual factors (in physical activity), 341
induced affect, 158
informational support (by parents), 242
initiative, 234
Inomata, K., 313
Institute for the Study of Sport and Physical Culture, St. Petersburg, 18, 19
Institute of Medicine (IOM), 233, 234
instructional self-talk, 375
integrated coping response, 158
integrated regulation, 92
intention, 85
intention-behaviour continuum, 83
interactionist perspective, 61–62
Interagency Advisory Panel on Research Ethics, 35, 36
interdisciplinary, 9
internal validity threat, 41, 42*t*
International Council for Coach Education (ICCE), 283
membership, 283
International Journal of Coaching Science, 283
International Journal of Sport and Exercise Psychology, 7, 19
International Journal of Sport Psychology, 7, 18, 19
International Journal of Sports Science & Coaching, 283
International Society of Sport Psychology (ISSP), 7, 18, 19
aggression and, 219
intervention research, 341
physical activity and, 341, 342
intervention strategies, 90
intrinsic regulation, 92
introjected regulation, 92
introversion, 73
intuition, 29
involvement, 94
alternatives, 101
opportunities, 101

J

Jackson, Phil, 300
Jacobson, E., 380
Janelle, C. M., 219
Janssen, Ian, 32
Japanese Society of Sport Psychology, 19
Jenkins, Colin, 80
Johnsgard, K., 327
Jones, E. E., 184
Jones, G., 70, 71, 117, 146
Jones, M. V., 130, 214
Jordan, Michael, 168, 169, 185, 300
Joseph, Kerry, 141
Journal of Applied Sport Psychology, 7, 16, 64, 70
Journal of Coaching Education, 283
Journal of Sport & Exercise Psychology, 7
Journal of Sport Psychology, 16
Jowett, S., 239

K

Kahn, R. L., 270
Kane, Lori, 55
Karau, S. J., 182
Katjna, T., 67
Katorji, J. K., 215
Katzmarzyk, P. T., 340
Kavanagh, B., 200
Kavussanu, M., 96, 97, 200, 201
Kerrigan, Nancy, 197
killer instinct, 67
kinesiology, 4
    programs, 20
King, A. C., 349, 350
Kirker, B., 212
Klavora, Peter, 15
Kleiber, D. A., 234
Kluger, M. J., 327
knowledge acquisition, 27
knowledge translation, 22
Kohlberg, Lawrence, 198
Kok, G., 87
Kowalski, K. C., 152
Kozub, S. A., 186
Kraemer, R. R., 325
Krampe, R. T., 236, 261
Kreek, Adam, 112
Kungl, A. M., 270
Kyllo, L. B., 64

L

Landers, D. M., 64, 152, 313
Landin, D., 375, 378
Lang, Kara, 37
Lapane, K. L., 84
Larouche, Michel, 279
Larson, R. W., 234
Latham, G. P., 366
Latimer, A. E., 355
Laumann, Silken, 70
LaVoi, N. M., 200
Lazarus, Richard, 141, 143, 144, 149, 151
Leadership Scale for Sports (LSS), 175
leadership, 289
    models of, 289–290
    research, 291
    transformational, 291
Leary, M. R., 125
Leatherdale, S. T., 103
Leavitt, Dr. Jack, 16
Leith, L. M., 15, 210–211, 311, 313
Lemaire, Jacques, 285
Lemieux, P., 212
Lemyre, F., 287
Levy, Becca, 264, 265, 266
licensing, 11
Lidor,
    Ronnie, 18
life expectancy, 257
life narrative, 47
life satisfaction, 5, 6
Lilli, W., 213
Llewellyn, D. J., 67
Locke, E. A., 366
Logan, J., 270
Lotysz, Greg J., 32
Loughead, T. M., 215, 366
Loughead, Todd, 210
Louvet, B., 151
Luxbacher, J., 207

M

MacDougall, M. P., 376
Mack, D. E., 118, 371
Madill, J., 350
Magnusson, D., 61
Mahon, M., 366
Mahoney, M. J., 378
majority rule, 169
Malone, C., 67
management skills, 149
Marcus, B. H., 84
Martens, R., 63, 121, 126
Martin G. L., 15, 102, 366
Martin-Ginis, K. A., 32, 355
Martin K. A., 124, 125, 371
Martinsen, E. W., 310
Marx, M. S., 263
Maslow, Abraham, 59
master athletes, 262–271
    as contrasted to non-masters, 272
    as role models, 271
    early sport participation and, 272
    effect on peer group, 271
    experience of, 272
    motives, 271
    personality and, 272
    psychological needs of, 272
    see also age and aging
    stereotypes of, 272
Masters, K. S., 271
Mastery Approach to Coaching (MAC), 288
mastery experience, 89, 97, 98*t*
Mattson, J., 212
McAuley, E., 313
McCallister, S. G., 240
McDonnell, J. F., 186
McDonough, M. H., 94
McGill University, 142, 283
McGowan, E., 119
McGuire, E. J., 212, 213
McKay, J., 146
McKelvie, S. J., 212
McLendon, C. L., 185
McMaster University, 344
McNeill, Allison, 279
McSorley, Marty, 203, 214
Meakin, D. C., 199
measurement (research), 37
    concepts, 38
    interval, 37
    levels, 37
    nominal, 37
    ordinal, 37
    ratio, 37
    reliability, 38–39
    validity, 39
Medhus, A., 310
mediational model of global self-worth, 243
mediator, 187, 188
Medic, N., 94
meditation, 381
Meichenbaum, Donald, 82, 158
Meisner, B., 270
Mellalieu, S. D., 117
Mental Game Plan, The: A Training Program for All Sports, 15
mental health,
    exercise and, 331*t*
    exercise to help, 325
    exercise to prevent problems of, 328–330
    myths, 308, 331
    problems, 308–309
Mental Skills Assessment Questionnaire (MSAQ), 373
mental toughness, 70–72
    characteristics, 71–72
mentoring, 285
Merriam, S. B., 44
meta-analysis, 64, 72, 173
    exercise and anxiety, 313
    self-esteem, 322
Mihalko, S. L., 313
Miller, N., 205
mission statement, 296
moderately-involved parents, 241
Moffett, A., 68
monoamine hypothesis, 325–326
Montepare, J. M., 265
mood disturbance,
    exercise and, 317*f*
mood, 315
    exercise and, 315–317
    Positive Affect and Negative Affect Schedule (PANAS), 315–316
    Profile of Mood States (POMS) and, 315–316
Moore, Steve, 197, 200, 202
Moraes, L. C., 293
moral behaviour,
    goal orientation, 201
    motivational climate and, 200
    myths, 198, 220–221
    social learning theory of, 199
    sport environment and, 199–200
    structural development theory of, 198–199
    team norms and, 200–201
moral development, 198–199
moral disengagement, 207–208
Moran, A., 129
Morgan, W. P., 63, 328
Moritz, S. E., 371
mortality, 263
Mothers in Motion, 341
motivation and behavioural change,
    myths, 80, 105
motivation theory, 31
motivation, 32, 37, 60
    achievement goal theory, 96
    applications of social influences, 104
    behavioural approach, 81–82
    cognitive approach, 82
    definitions of, 80
    ego, 69

in youth sport, 243
models, 83
research on social influences, 103–104
social cognitive theory (SCT), 88
social influences, 103
sport commitment model (SCM), 101
task achievement, 69
theory of competence motivation, 98–100
theory of planned behaviour (TPB), 85–86
transtheoretical model (TM), 83
understanding, 81*t*
motivational general-arousal function, 370–371
motivational general-mastery function, 371
motor learning, 15
aging and, 259–260
Motta, R., 313
Movement Imagery Questionnaire-Revised (MIQ-R), 373
Mowrer, O. H., 205
Mudrack, P. E., 170
Muenzer, Lori-Ann, 66
Mullen, B., 173, 185
multidimensional anxiety theory (MAT), 126
multidimensional model of leadership (MML), 289–290, 290*f*
multiple set resistance exercise (MSRE), 313
Munroe, K. J., 372
Munroe-Chandler, K. J., 372
music (to increase arousal), 383
Myers, L. M., 266
myths,
aggression, 198, 220–221
aging, 257, 273
anxiety, 113, 132
coaching, 280, 302
group cohesion, 167, 189–190
mental health, 308, 331
moral behaviour, 198, 220–221
motivation and behavioural change, 80, 105
personality, 55, 74
physical activity, 338–339, 358
research, 28, 49
sport psychology, 3, 23, 364, 388
stress, 140, 160–161
youth sport involvement, 228, 250–251

N

narrative analysis, 47
Nash, Steve, 291
National Association for Sport & Physical Education, 283
National Coaching Accreditation Scheme (NCAS), 282, 283
National Coaching Certification Program (NCCP), 16, 281, 283
Community Sport Stream, 281
Competition Stream, 282
Instruction Stream, 282
structure of, 281
National Coaching Foundation, 282
National Coaching Institutes (NCIs), 282
National Council for the Accreditation of Coach education in the united States, 283
National Population Health Study (NPHS), 329
National Research Council (NRC), 233, 234
negative affect, 315
negative reinforcement, 82, 264–266
Neuroticism Extroversion Openness Five Factor Inventory (NEO-FFI), 62
neuroticism, 57
Newman, B., 176
Nicholls, J. G., 96, 201
Noblet, A. J., 146
nomothetic, 32
non-experimental designs (research), 43–44
non-theory-based research, 343, 348
normative beliefs, 86–87
North American Society for the Psychology of Sport and Physical Activity (NASPSPA), 7, 15
Northeastern University,
Center for the Study of Sport in Society, 218
Notebook, J. T., 130

O

O'Brien Cousins, Sandra, 264
O'Neill, K., 267–268
obesity, 32, 340
observational learning (modelling), 60, 88
Ogilvie, Bruce, 15
Ogles, B. M., 271
Ohio Longitudinal Study of Aging and Retirement, 266
Okada, A., 313
Olivier, S., 214
online consulting, 21
Ontario Ministry of Health Promotion, 340
openness to experience, 57
operant conditioning, 82
operant strategies, 82
optimism, 157
organismic integration theory (OIT), 92, 94
Orlick, Terry, 15, 59, 71–72
osteoporosis, 340
Ostrow, A. C., 63
Ottawa Mental Skills Assessment Tool, 373
outcome expectancies, 88
outcome expectations, 88
outcome of coping, 151–152
outcome research, 342
physical activity, 342*f*
over-involved parents, 241
overarousal, 380
reducing, 380–381
see also arousal
Owen, N., 346, 349, 350

P

Paivio, A., 370
Paralympic Games, 21
Parente, D., 313
Parkinson's disease (PD), 20
physical activity and, 356
sensory attention focused exercise (SAFE) and, 356
Parkinson's Disease Foundation, 356
ParticipACTION (Ontario), 350
Partington, J., 71–72
Paskevich, D. M., 179, 215
Pearce, W., 262
pedometer, 351
peer groups, 103
Pelletier, L. G., 186
Penn State University, 176
pep talks, 382
perceived behavioural control, 86
Perceived Stress Scale (PSS), 319
perceptions of competence, 98–99
perfectionism, 68–70
adaptive (healthy), 69
dispositional, 70
maladaptive (unhealthy), 69
performance enhancement, 5–6, 21
anabolic steroids, 28
performance profiling,
steps, 366–367
performance, 32
anxiety relationship, 129
approach, 97
avoidance, 97
behaviour, 185
outcome, 185
Profile of Mood States (POMS) and, 64
profiling, 366
routines, 386–387
person-situation debate, 61
personal digital assistant (PDA), 349
personal investment, 101
personal standards perfectionism (PSP), 70
personality, 37
definitions, 55–56
development of, 58
ethics and measurement of, 65
exercise, 72
master athletes and, 272
measurement considerations, 62
measurement, 62
myths, 55, 74
objective tests, 62
projective tests, 62
research, 65–66
sport-specific measures, 62–63
states, 57
tests, 62
traits, 56–57
persuasive communication, 343, 344
Peterson, C., 239
Petitclerc, Chantal, 129, 291
Petitpas, A. J., 377
Petruzzello, S. J., 313
PETTLEP model of imagery, 374, 374*t*
phenomenology, 46
Phillips, D. R., 200
physical activity contracts, 351
physical activity counsellor (PAC), 345, 346
Physical Activity Group Environment Questionnaire, 172
physical activity,
behavioural interventions, 351
cancer and, 354–355, 354*t*
computer technology and, 348, 349
group-based interventions, 349
individual factors, 341
Internet-based interventions, 349
intervention components, 352, 353
intervention research, 342
interventions, 339, 339*t*
mass media interventions, 350
myths, 338–339, 358
older adults interventions, 353, 353*t*, 354
Parkinson's disease (PD) and, 356
pedometers, 351
program factors, 341
psychological actors, 341
self-efficacy and, 345
social cognitive theory (SCT), 345
social factors, 341
spinal cord injuries (SCI) and, 355–356
telephone interventions, 350
theory of planned behaviour (TPB), 343
transtheoretical model (TM), 346
physical education, 4
physical self-perceptions, 31
physical self-worth, 31

physical size,
aggression and, 212
physiological and affective states, 89
physiological mechanisms,
competitive anxiety and, 130
Pippen, Scottie, 300
placebo, 29
Plotnikoff, R. C., 84, 90
Podborski, Steve, 116, 127, 379
point differentials,
aggression and, 214
polling, 40
Pollock, M. L., 64
population (sampling), 40
Porcher, B. J., 213
Porter, K., 272
Positive Affect and Negative Affect Schedule (PANAS), 315–316
positive affect, 315
Positive Coaching Alliance (PCA), 283
positive reinforcement, 82
Power, F. C., 200, 242
Power, T. G., 241
Prapavessis, H., 119, 182, 183
pre-competitive workouts, 382
Prémont, Marie-Hélène, 67
Price, Nick, 369
primary appraisal (of stress), 141
Problem Athletes and How to Handle Them, 15
processes of change, 84
Profile of Mood States (POMS), 63, 64
assessments, 63
mood and, 315–316
sport performance and, 64
program factors (in physical activity), 341
progressive relaxation, 380
prosocial behaviour, 200
Psyching for Sport: Mental Training for Athletes, 15
psychodynamics, 58, 205
Psychological Behaviour in Sport, 15
psychological factors (in physical activity), 341
psychological momentum, 186
psychological needs, 92–94
psychological skills training intervention (PSTI), 29, 364–365
psychologist,
rules for use of term, 11
Psychology and Athletics, 14
Psychology of Coaching, The, 14
Psychology of Physical Activity, The, 15
Psychology of Sport and Exercise, 19
Psychology of Sport: The Behavior, Motivation, Personality and Performance of Athletes, 15
psychology, 4
exercise, 4
positive, 5–6
psychometrics, 38
psychomotor agitation, 309
psychotherapy, 308
psychotropic medication, 308
exercise as adjunct to, 310–311
Public Health Agency of Canada, 91

Q

qualitative research, 44
approaches, 46
assessing, 48
basic interpretive, 46
characteristics of, 45, 45*t*
exercise and stress, 320
grounded theory, 47
narrative analysis, 47
phenomenology, 46
substantive theory, 47
quality of life, 258
quantitative research, 44, 45*t*
quasi-experimental designs (research), 43

R

Raedeke, T. D., 122, 155
Rainey, D. W., 174, 186
randomized experimental designs (research), 42–43
Rechnitzer, P. A., 73
Rehm, J., 213
Reid, G., 267
relatedness, 93
reliability (research measurement), 38–39
assessing, 48
observed-score model, 38
true-score model, 38, 38*f*
Remember the Titans (movie), 171
reps, 31
research career, 7–8
research design, 41
research ethics board (REB), 34–35
research,
achievement goal theory, 96, 98
anonymity, 35–36
applied, 29
basic, 29
beneficence, 36
causal, 33, 34
confidentiality, 35–36
coping, 153–154
descriptive, 31
determinant, 340
ethical issues, 35–36
ethics and, 34–35
exercise psychology, 31
hypothesis, 32–33
idiographic, 32
informed consent, 36
intervention, 341, 342
justice, 36
leadership, 291
measurements, 37
myths, 28, 49
negative stereotypes of aging, 264–266
nomothetic, 32
non-theory-based research, 343, 348
outcome, 342
personality, 65–66
predictive, 31
qualitative, 44
quantitative, 44
sampling, 40, 40*f*
self-determination theory (SDT), 94
social cognitive theory (SCT), 90
social influences on motivation, 103–104
sport commitment model (SCM), 101–102
sport psychology, 28–29
sport-personality, 55
terminology, 31–32
theory of competence motivation, 100
theory of planned behaviour (TPB), 87
theory-based, 343
transtheoretical model (TM) of motivation, 84
treatment, 342
types, 35*t*
variable, 32, 37
resistance training, 31
retaliation,
aggression and, 212
Rethorst, C. D., 152
revised frustration-aggression theory, 205
Rhodes, R. E., 72, 84, 348
risk taking, 67
Rivera, P. M., 377
Roberts, G. C., 201
Rodgers, Wendy M., 42, 90, 373
Rodman, Dennis "The Worm", 300
Rogers, Carl, 59
role constraint theory, 156
Rosenberg, S., 168
Rotter, J. B., 60
Rowe, J. W., 270
Rowley, A. J., 64
Rubinstein, Lorne, 56
Russell, G. W., 197, 216
Ryan, Richard M., 91, 92–93, 94

S

Sabiston, C. M., 47, 104, 119
Sage, M. D., 356
Saleh, S. D., 175
Sallis, J. F., 346
Salmela, J. H., 68, 71, 285, 295, 299, 300–301
Salmela, John, 15
Salmon, A., 350
sample, 40
Sanchez, X., 67
Sanszole, M., 212
Sauvageau, Danielle, 279
Scale for Effective Communication in Team Sports (SECTS), 168
Scales, B., 122
Scanlan, T. K., 101
Schinke, R. J., 285
schizophrenia, 308
SCI Action Canada, 356
science,
definition of, 29
high-performance sport and, 28
theory, 31
scientific method (of research), 30
steps, 31
Scott, D., 376
Seal, A. R., 200
Sears, R. R., 205
secondary appraisal (of stress), 141
Seifert, George, 286
selective maintenance model of skill maintenance, 261
self-actualization, 58
self-concept, 321
exercise and, 324
structure of, 321*f*
self-confidence, 118–119
self-determination theory (SDT), 31, 91–92, 91*f*
applications, 94
characteristics, 92
concepts, 92–93
motivation in youth sport and, 244
motivational continuum, 93*t*
research, 94
self-efficacy, 32, 60, 84, 89, 90, 328, 345
aging and, 268–269
barrier, 345
exercise, 345
physical activity and, 345

self-presentational, 119
sources, 89t
task, 345
variables, 32
self-esteem, 321
exercise and, 322–324
meta-analysis of, 322
self-handicapping, 120
group cohesion and, 184
self-monitoring, 82
self-oriented perfectionism, 157
self-presentation, 119
aggression and, 213
beliefs, 119
self-presentational self-efficacy, 119
self-regulation, 89
strategies for anxiety, 120
Self-Talk and Gestures Rating Scale (STAGRS), 377
Self-Talk Grid, 376–377
Self-Talk Use Questionnaire (STUQ), 376t, 377
self-talk, 375
assessment, 376–377
dimensions, 378t
functions, 375–376
guidelines for using, 377–378
instructional, 375
Seligman, Martin E. P., 5
Selye, Hans, 142
Senécal, J., 366
sensation seeking, 67
sensory attention focused exercise (SAFE), 356
sets, 31
Shambrook, J., 374
Shapcott, K. M., 210
Sherwood, H., 153
Shewfelt, Kyle, 121
Shields, C. A., 104
Shields, D. L., 200
Shields, Kathy, 279, 286
Short, Sandra E., 32
Silva, J. M., 9, 202
Simard, Helen, 68
Simon, Chris, 57
Skinner, B. F., 59, 81
Skinner, E. A., 153
sleep disturbances, 309
Smith, Michael, 206, 207
Smith, N. E. I., 72, 155
Smith, R. E., 158, 287, 288
Smith, Ronald, 239
Smoll, F. L., 287, 288
Smoll, Frank, 239
Soberlak, P., 237
social anxiety, 115
social cognitive theory (SCT), 88, 88f, 344–345
applications, 90–91
constructs, 88–89
physical activity and, 345
research, 90
self-efficacy, 89
social constraints, 101
social factors (in physical activity), 341
social learning theory, 60
aggression and, 206–207
influences, 60
moral behaviour, 199
social loafing, 182–183
social persuasion, 89
Social Psychology of Sport, 15
Social Sciences and Humanities Research Council (SSHRC), 20
socioeconomic status,
aging and barrier to physical activity, 266
somatic anxiety, 114
Soviet Union, former,
sport psychology in, 18
Sparkes, A., 47, 183
Spathonis, K. M., 349, 350
specialization, 19–20
early, 236, 238
specificity, measurability, adjustability, realism, and timeliness (SMART) principles, 351
goal setting and, 367, 367t, 368, 369, 370
spinal cord injuries (SCI), 20
physical activity and, 355–356
Spink, K. S., 177, 180, 187, 188
Sport Cohesiveness Questionnaire, 171
sport commitment model (SCM), 101, 101f
applications, 102–103
research, 102
Sport Competition Anxiety Test (SCAT), 63
sport enjoyment, 101
Sport Imagery Questionnaire (SIQ), 373, 373t
Sport Imagery Questionnaire for Children (SIQ-C), 373
Sport Medicine Council, 2
Sport Orientation Questionnaire, 68
Sport Psychologist, The, 7, 16
sport psychology,
careers, 6, 7–9
consultant, 2, 8–9
definitions of, 4
graduate courses in, 10t
licensing, 11
myths, 3, 23, 364, 388
perspectives on, 4–5
preparing for a course in, 10
research, 7–28–29
teaching, 6
training for, 9
universities and, 14–15
worldview of, 18–19
Sport Psychology: A Canadian Perspective, 15
Sport Psychology: Practical Guidelines from Behavior Analysis, 15
sport sciences, 4
education, 9
Spray, C., 96, 97
Sprewell, Latrell, 197
Staff, C. H., 327
stage matched (physical activity interventions), 346, 347
Stanford University, 283
state anxiety, 312
exercise and, 313
Statistics Canada, 228
Steele, C. M., 265
Steinleitner, M., 213
Stephens, D. E., 201, 214
stereotyping, 264–266
master athletes and, 272
Stevens, D. E., 43, 176
Stoll, S. K., 199
Storr, A., 201
Stout, D., 212
Strathopoulou, G., 311
Strauss, Anselm L., 47
Strean, W. B., 48
stress inoculation training, 158
stress management training, 158
stress response, 141
stress, 37, 139, 318
challenge, 142
chronic, 145
cognitive appraisal process of, 141–142
definitions of, 141
emotion and, 143
exercise and, 318–320
heat/loss, 141
kinds of, 141–142
mental toughness and, 72
myths, 140, 160–161
Perceived Stress Scale (PSS) and, 319
potentials of, 142
sources, 143–145
specific sports effect, 146–147
threat, 142
stressors, 141
competitive, 146
expected, 145–146
non-competitive, 146
types of, 145–147
unexpected, 146
structural-development theory, 198–199
structure, 94
Stuart, M. E., 200
study population, 40
subjective norms, 86
substance abuse, 308
substantive theory, 47
suicides, 308, 309
Sullivan, P., 168
Summitt, Pat, 294
superego, 58
Sydor, Alison, 67
Symons-Downs, D., 343, 358
Sytotuik, D., 97

T

Takeshima, N., 313
tangible support (by parents), 242
task achievement motivation, 69
task goal orientation, 96
characteristics, 97t
teaching career, 6
team building, 176
approaches to, 176
conceptual framework for, 177f, 179
definition of, 176
distinctiveness as factor in, 178
four-stage model for, 177–178, 179–180
principles of, 178t
see also group cohesion
team cohesion, 47
team effectiveness,
decision making for, 169
group cohesion and, 168
team norms, 200–201
temporal occlusion, 385
Tenebaum, G., 212, 219
Tennant, L. K., 219
tension-anxiety (TEN), 63
Tesch-Römer, C., 236
Test of Attentional and Interpersonal Style (TAIS), 385–386
Test of Psychological Skills (TOPS), 373
testosterone, 206
Tharp, R. G., 297
theoretical population, 40

theory of competence motivation, 98
applications, 100–101
aspects of, 98–99
components of, 99*f*, 99–100
principle, 100
research, 100
theory of planned behaviour (TPB), 85–86, 86*f*, 343
applications, 88
factors, 86–87
physical exercise and, 343
research, 87
theory, 31
testing, 31
theory-based research, 343
thermogenic hypothesis, 327
Third International Conference of Ministers and Senior Officials Responsible for Physical Education and Sport (MINEPS III), 228
Thought Occurrence Questionnaire for Sport (TOQS), 386
Tracey, J., 345, 347, 349
tradition, 29–30
trait anxiety, 312
traits (personality), 56–57
models, 57
transformational leadership, 291
transtheoretical model (TM) of motivation, 83, 346
action stage, 83
applications, 85
concepts, 85*t*
contemplation stage, 83
factors influencing stage progression, 84
maintenance stage, 83
physical activity and, 346
pre-contemplation stage, 83
preparation stage, 83
research, 84
stages, 83–84
successful interventions using, 347*t*
Treasure, D., 199
treatment research, 342
physical activity, 342*f*
Tri-Council Policy Statement: Ethical Conduct for Research Involving Humans, 35
triangulation, 48
triathlon, 80
Trudel, P., 280, 286, 295, 299, 300
Tucholsky, Sara, 198
Turko, Thomas, 15
Tuscaronak, M., 67

U

UK Coaching Certificate (UKCC), 282
UK Coaching Framework, 282
under-involved parents, 241
Ungerleider, S., 272
United Nations Educational, Scientific and Cultural Organization (UNESCO), 228
United States Olympic Committee, 283
United States,
coaching education in, 283
history of sport psychology in, 14–16, 17
Université de Montréal, 15, 142
universities,
growth in sport psychology, 14–20
interdepartmental collaboration, 20
post-World War II, 14
pre-World War II, 14
see also individual universities
sport psychology and, 14–15
training demands, 20
University of Alberta, 15, 16, 69, 264, 354
University of California, Berkeley, 14, 16
University of Florida, 14
University of Illinois, 14
University of Lethbridge, 216
University of Ottawa, 15, 59, 68, 70, 287
University of Saskatchewan, 16
University of Tennessee, 294
University of Toronto, 15
University of Washington, 239
University of Waterloo, 16, 82, 117
University of Western Ontario, 16, 375
School of Kinesiology, 16
University of Windsor, 16
University of Winnipeg, 15
Uphill, M., 130

V

valence (of self-talk), 377
validity (research measurement), 39–39*f*
assessing, 48
Athletic Motivation Inventory (AMI) and, 63
consequential, 40
criterion, 39
internal, 41
Vallée, C. N., 291
Vallence, J. K. H., 69
Vallerand, R. J., 186, 297
Van Raalte, J. L., 377
Vandelanotte, C., 349, 350
variable (research), 32
dependent, 32
extraneous, 32
independent, 32
Vealey, Robin, 4
verbal cues, 383
Verma, S., 234
vicarious conditioning, 82
vicarious experience, 89
Vickers, J. N., 241
Vierling, Leigh, 67
vigour (VIG), 63
Vincent, Tania, 379
Visek, A., 211
visualization, 369, 370
see also imagery
Vividness of Movement Imagery Questionnaire-2 (VMIQ-2), 373

W

Wadey, R., 71
Wallace, Liz, 198
Walsh, Bill, 285
Walton, Gary, 294, 295
Wandzilak, T., 199
Wang, J., 96, 97
Wankel, Len, 15
Wanlin, C. M., 366, 368
Wann, D. L., 64, 213
Watanabe, E., 313
Watkinson, E. J., 46
Watson, Brad, 216
Watson, J., 211
Watson, John, 81
Weinberg, R. S., 313
Weir, Mike, 56, 112, 369, 370, 387
Weir, P., 270
Weiss, M. R., 244, 245
Weiss, W. M., 240
Wesch, N., 119
White, A., 370
Whitfield, Simon, 80, 149, 247
Whitlock, Ed, 269
Widmeyer, Dr. Neil, 16, 170, 171, 212, 213, 215, 368
Wilberg. Dr. Robert, 15
Wilfrid Laurier University, 356
Williams, K. D., 182
Williams, L., 244, 245
Wilson, Philip M., 31, 42, 94, 102
Wingate Institute for Physical Education and Sport in Israel, 283
Wipfli, B. M., 152
Wong, S. L., 103
Wooden, John, 294, 295
Woolger, C., 241, 242
World Congress of Sport Psychology (Ottawa, 1981), 19
World Congress of Sport Psychology (Rome, 1965), 18, 19
World Health Organization, 308
World Sport Psychology Sourcebook, 18

Y

Yale University, 264
youth coaching, 286
characteristics, 286–287
coach effectiveness training and, 287
developmental patterns, 289
effectiveness of, 287–288, 288*t*
leadership and, 289–290
Mastery Approach to Coaching (MAC), 288
multidimensional model of leadership (MML), 289–290, 290*f*
principles, 287–288
youth sport involvement,
coaching, 286
myths, 228, 250–251
youth sport,
best practices, 248–249
deliberate play, 236
deliberate practice, 236
early specialization, 236
motivational theories, 245
motivations for, 243
objectives, 229
parental expectations, 242
parental modelling, 242
parental role, 241
parental support, 241–242
participation outcomes, 230–230*t*, 231
programs, 235
successful interventions, 353, 353*t*
Yukelson, D., 176

Z

Zaichkowsky, L. D., 379
Zander, A., 168
Zebrowitz, L. A., 265
Zillman, D., 219
zones of optimal functioning (ZOF) theory, 126–127